The Essential Steps for Installing Linux

1. Create boot and root disks for Linux.
2. Partition the hard disk.
3. Boot Linux from a floppy disk.
4. Create a swap file.
5. Create a Linux filesystem.
6. Install the Linux software.
7. Configure the kernel.
8. Set the boot process.
9. Reboot into Linux from your hard disk.

Manual Installation of XFree86

1. Log in as root. You must install XFree86 as the superuser.
2. Create the directory /usr/X386. This directory may already exist on your system as it is created by some Linux installation scripts.
3. Change to the /usr/X386 directory.
4. For each file in the distribution set, use the `gzip` utility to extract and install the contents. The general format of the command is as follows:

```
qzip -dc tarfile ¦ tar xvof -
```

5. Repeat the process for each file in the XFree86 product set. You will have to change to each distribution directory manually (on a CD-ROM or different floppy disk, for example) and use `gzip` on each archive file in that directory.

D1415884

rdev Options

- -h   Displays help
- -r   Makes rdev act like the command ramsize (see below)
- -R   Makes rdev act like the rootflags command (see below)
- -s   Makes rdev act like the swapdev command (see below)
- -v   Makes rdev act like the vidmode command (see below)

rdev Companion Utilities

ramsize	Specifies the size of the RAM disk in kilobytes
rootflags	Lets you mount the root directory as read-only
swapdev	Identifies the swap device
vidmode	Specifies the video mode

fdisk Commands

- d   Deletes an existing partition
- l   Lists all known partition types
- n   Creates a new partition
- p   Displays the current partition table
- q   Quits fdisk without saving changes
- t   Changes a partition's type code
- v   Verifies the partition table
- w   Writes current partition table to disk and exits

edquota Options

- -g   Edits a group's quota
- -p   Duplicates quotas of one user for others
- -t   Edits soft time limits (before a hard limit is imposed)
- -u   Edits a user's quota (default action)

quota Options

- -g   Displays group quotas for the group of which the user is a member
- -q   Displays only filesystems where usage is over quota
- -u   Displays quotas for users (the default action)
- -v   Displays quotas on a filesystem where no storage is allocated

quotacheck Options

- -a   Checks all filesystems (not all versions of Linux quota support this option)
- -d   Displays debug information displayed during checking (slows down the check considerably)
- -g   Checks only the group you specify when followed by a group ID
- -u   Checks only the user you specify when followed by a user ID (or all users if none are specified, which is the default)
- -v   Shows what quotacheck is doing in verbose output

LINUX SYSTEM ADMINISTRATOR'S
SURVIVAL GUIDE

Tim Parker, Ph.D.

SAMS
PUBLISHING

201 West 103rd Street
Indianapolis, Indiana 46290

For Yvonne. She knows why.

Quis fallere possit amantem?

COPYRIGHT © 1996 BY SAMS PUBLISHING

International Standard Book Number: 0-672-30850-9

Library of Congress Catalog Card Number: 95-70084

99 98 97 96   4 3 2 1

Interpretation of the printing code: the rightmost double-digit number is the year of the book's printing; the rightmost single-digit, the number of the book's printing. For example, a printing code of 96-1 shows that the first printing of the book occurred in 1996.

Composed in New Century Schoolbook and MCPdigital by Macmillan Computer Publishing

Printed in the United States of America

PUBLISHER AND PRESIDENT	*Richard K. Swadley*
ACQUISITIONS MANAGER	*Greg Wiegand*
DEVELOPMENT MANAGER	*Dean Miller*
MANAGING EDITOR	*Cindy Morrow*
MARKETING MANAGER	*Gregg Bushyeager*

ACQUISITIONS EDITOR
Rosemarie Graham

DEVELOPMENT EDITORS
L. Angelique Brittingham
Todd Bumbalough

SOFTWARE DEVELOPMENT SPECIALIST
Wayne Blankenbeckler

PRODUCTION EDITOR
Heather Stith

COPY EDITORS
Margaret Berson
Michelle Shaw

TECHNICAL REVIEWERS
Mike Coulombe
Eric Garrison

RESOURCE COORDINATOR
Deborah Frisby

TECHNICAL EDIT COORDINATOR
Lynette Quinn

Formatter
Frank Sinclair

Editorial Assistants
Sharon Cox
Andi Richter
Rhonda Tinch-Mize

COVER DESIGNER
Tim Amrhein

BOOK DESIGNER
Alyssa Yesh

PRODUCTION TEAM SUPERVISOR
Brad Chinn

PRODUCTION
Georgiana Briggs, Mona Brown, Mike Dietsch, Jason Hand, Mike Henry, Donna Martin, Casey Price, Bobbi Satterfield, SA Springer, Andrew Stone, Suzanne Whitmer, Colleen Williams

INDEXER
Mary Jane Frisby

Overview

Introduction   xxii

PART I   INSTALLATION AND CONFIGURATION

1   Introduction to Linux   3
2   Linux Hardware and Software   17
3   Installing and Updating Linux   35
4   LILO   69
5   Installing and Configuring XFree86   97

PART II   EXPANDING YOUR SYSTEM

6   Devices and Device Drivers   135
7   SCSI Devices   143
8   Hard Disks   155
9   CD-ROM Drives   161
10   Sound Cards   183
11   Terminals and term   197
12   Tape Drives   221
13   Modems   229
14   Other Devices   237

PART III   MANAGING YOUR LINUX SYSTEM

15   Booting, init, and Shutdown   245
16   Users and Logins   259
17   System Names and Access Permissions   275
18   Filesystems and Disks   289
19   Printers and Print Spoolers   307
20   Managing Processes   321
21   Managing Resources   331
22   Backup, Backup, Backup!   337
23   The cron and at Programs   349
24   Security   359
25   Modifying the Kernel   367
26   Shell Programming   377

PART IV NETWORKING

27	UUCP	401
28	TCP/IP and Networks	419
29	Configuring Hardware and the Kernel for Networking	437
30	Configuring TCP/IP	447
31	Configuring SLIP and PPP	471
32	TCP/IP Utilities	487
33	NFS and NIS	507

PART V E-MAIL AND NEWS

34	E-Mail and Linux	525
35	Configuring sendmail	531
36	Using smail	543
37	Configuring Elm and Pine	555
38	USENET and Netnews	561
39	NNTP and INN	567
40	C News	575
41	Configuring trn and tin	587

PART VI THE INTERNET

42	Setting Up an Internet Site	593
43	Setting Up an FTP Site	599
44	Configuring a WAIS Site	615
45	Setting Up a Gopher Service	631
46	Configuring a WWW Site	651

PART VII APPENDIXES

A	Linux FTP Sites and Newsgroups	671
B	Commercial Vendors for Linux	685
C	The Linux Documentation Project	689
D	The GNU General Public License	691
E	Copyright Information	701
F	Hardware Compatibility	707
G	Glossary	719
H	What's on the CD-ROM	729
	Index	733

Contents

Introduction   xxii

PART I INSTALLATION AND CONFIGURATION

1 **Introduction to Linux**   3

What Is Linux? 4
    Linux's Kernel 5
    GNU Software 6
    X 6
    DOS Interface 7
    TCP/IP 7
Linux's History 8
Copyrights 9
Sources of Help 10
    Documentation 10
    USENET Newsgroups 11
    World Wide Web Sites 13
    Linux Journal 15
Recent Linux Distributions 16
Summary 16

2 **Linux Hardware and Software**   17

Minimum System Requirements 18
    Motherboard Requirements 18
    Hard Disks 20
    Video Systems 21
    Mouses 22
    Tape Drives 22
    CD-ROMs 22
    Removable Media 23
    Printers 23
    Modems 23
    Terminals 24
    Multiport Cards 24
    Network Cards 24
Where to Get Linux 24
    CD-ROMs 25
    FTP Sites 26
    World Wide Web Sites 29
    E-Mail 30
    Bulletin Board Systems 31

Linux Releases and Disk Sets 32
Summary 33

3 Installing and Updating Linux   35

Creating Boot and Root Disks 36
Selecting a Boot Kernel and Root Image 37
Creating the Boot and Root Floppy Disks 40
Partitioning the Hard Disk 42
Determining the Size of the Linux Swap Space Partition 43
Setting Up Partitions 44
Using UMSDOS 46
Installing the Linux Partitions 46
Linux's *fdisk* 47
Setting Up Linux Partitions 48
Enabling the Swap Space for Installation 51
Creating the Linux Filesystem Partition 53
Installing the Linux Software 54
Selecting the Source and Disk Sets 55
Creating a Boot Disk 58
Configuration Details 59
Setting the Boot Process 62
Viewing Installed Software Files 63
Troubleshooting 64
Software Installation Problems 64
Hard Disk and Disk Controller Problems 65
Device Conflicts 65
SCSI Problems 67
Problems Booting Linux 68
Summary 68

4 LILO   69

Installing LILO 70
Handling Disk Problems 71
Using the LILO Makefile 72
Updating LILO 72
Linux and Hard Disk Layouts 72
The Boot Sector 74
The Boot Process 76
Installing a Dedicated Linux Hard Disk 76
Using *BOOTACTV* 77
Installing DOS and Linux 78
Using *BOOTLIN* 79
Automated LILO Creation 80
Setting Boot Parameters 85

The Map Installer 86
   Map Installer Command-Line Options 87
   Map Installer Configuration File Options 89
Boot Images 91
The Disk Parameter Table 92
Removing or Disabling LILO 93
Troubleshooting LILO 94
Summary 95

5   Installing and Configuring XFree86   97

Understanding XFree86 98
Installing XFree86 Software 100
   Choosing an X Server 101
   Installing XFree86 Manually 102
   Installing XFree86 Using a Script 103
   Using the PATH Environment Variable 103
Configuring XFree86 104
   Deciding Where to Put Xconfig or XF86Config 106
   Using SuperProbe 107
   Using ConfigXF86 and XF86Config 109
Examining the Xconfig and XF86Config Files in Detail 119
   Pathnames 120
   Keyboard Settings 121
   Mouse Definition 122
   Monitor Model 124
   Video Cards.. 126
   The XFree86 Server 127
   Testing XFree86 Configurations 129
Using the .xinitrc File 129
Summary 131

PART II   EXPANDING YOUR SYSTEM

6   Devices and Device Drivers   135

Device Drivers 136
Character and Block Mode Devices 138
   Major and Minor Device Numbers 139
   The *mknod* Command 140
Device Permissions and Links 141
Summary 142

7   SCSI Devices   143

SCSI Chains and Devices 144
Supported SCSI Devices 146
SCSI Device Drivers 146

Hard Drives 146
CD-ROM Devices 147
Tape Drives 149
Other Devices 150
Troubleshooting SCSI Devices 150
Summary 153

8   Hard Disks   155

Buying a New Drive 156
Formatting and Partitioning the New Drive 157
Summary 159

9   CD-ROM Drives   161

Understanding the Different Types of CD-ROMs 162
Internal, External, and Changer CD-ROM Drives 162
ISO 9660 and CD-ROM Disk Formats 164
CD-ROM Speeds and Interfaces 164
Recordable CD-ROMs 167
Installing a CD-ROM Drive 167
Physically Install the Drive 168
Configure and Rebuild the Kernel 168
Create the Device Files 171
Mount and Test the CD-ROM Drive 174
Using /etc/fstab 177
Playing Audio CD-ROMs 178
Using PhotoCDs with Linux 179
Troubleshooting the CD-ROM Drive 179
Check the Kernel 179
Check the Device 180
Check the Drive Settings 181
Device Busy Errors 181
Summary 181

10   Sound Cards   183

Checking for Sound Card Support 185
Configuring Your Sound Card 186
Understanding Sound Card Device Files 187
Linking the Sound Card Files 187
Providing Configuration Information 189
Testing the Sound Card Drivers 189
Using the PC Speaker 191
Sampling Linux Sound Applications 191
Troubleshooting the Sound Card 192
Configuration Information 192
Check the File /dev/sndstat 193

No Such File or Device Errors 193
Incomplete Playing of Sound Files 194
Sounds Stop and Start When Playing 194
Summary 195

11   Terminals and term   197

Connecting Terminals 198
Using Multiport Cards 198
Connecting Serial Port Terminals 200
Wiring Serial Cables 200
Understanding the Login Process 202
init and inittab... 202
/etc/ttys and /etc/inittab 203
/etc/getty and /etc/gettydefs 204
The /etc/termcap File 206
Adding a Terminal 207
Setting Terminal Behavior with *stty* and *tset* 208
Resetting a Screwy Terminal 210
Using *term* 210
Installing *term* 211
Testing *term* 213
Running *term* 215
Using *term* with X 216
Using *term* Utilities 218
Summary 220

12   Tape Drives   221

SCSI Tape Drives 222
The *ftape* Program 223
Using the Tape Drive 227
Summary 228

13   Modems   229

Choosing a Modem 230
Installing a Modem 232
Configuring a Modem 233
Setting Fast Modem Speeds 235
Summary 235

14   Other Devices   237

Uninterruptible Power Supplies 238
Removable Cartridge Drives 240
Scanners, Optical Readers, and Similar Devices 241
Porting Files.. 241
Summary 241

PART III   MANAGING YOUR LINUX SYSTEM

15   Booting, init, and Shutdown   245

Starting Linux 246
    Using LILO to Boot 246
    Using a Boot Floppy Disk 247
Creating and Using a Maintenance Disk 249
Shutting Down Linux 250
Understanding the *init* Daemon 252
    Run Levels 252
    The /etc/inittab File 253
Using the *rdev* Family 256
Summary 258

16   Users and Logins   259

Understanding the Superuser Account 260
Establishing User Accounts 261
    Usernames 262
    Passwords 263
    User ID..264
    Group ID 264
    Comments 265
    Home Directory 265
    Login Command 266
Understanding Default System Usernames 266
Adding Users 267
Deleting Users 269
Using Groups 270
    Understanding Default System Groups 272
    Adding a Group 272
    Adding a User to New Groups 273
    Deleting a Group 273
Using the *su* Command 274
Summary 274

17   System Names and Access Permissions   275

Setting a System Name 276
    Creating Network System Names 277
    Storing the Hostname 278
Using File and Directory Permissions 279
    Understanding File Types...279
    Understanding Access Permissions 281
    Using Default Permissions 282
    Changing Permissions..283

Changing the Owner and Group 286
Summary 287

18 Filesystems and Disks   289

Mounting and Unmounting Filesystems 290
Mounting Filesystems Automatically with the /etc/fstab File 293
Filesystem Types 295
Options Values 296
Managing Disk Space 296
Checking Filesystems 297
Displaying Filesystem Statistics 299
Making the Most of Your Disk Space 302
Understanding Links 304
Summary 305

19 Printers and Print Spoolers   307

Adding Printers 308
Understanding the *lpd* Printing Daemon 310
Print Spoolers 311
The Printing Process 312
The /etc/printcap File 313
Managing Printers with *lpc* 315
Managing the Printer Queue with *lpq* and *lprm* 318
Summary 319

20 Managing Processes   321

Understanding Processes 322
Using the *ps* Command 322
Using *kill* 326
Using the *top* Command 328
Summary 330

21 Managing Resources   331

Understanding Quotas 332
Hard and Soft Limits 332
When to Use Quotas 333
Setting User Quotas 333
Using the *quota* Command 334
Using the *quotacheck* Command 335
Summary 335

22 Backup, Backup, Backup!   337

Why Make Backups? 338
Choosing Backup Media 339
Setting a Backup Schedule 340
Keeping Backup Logs 343

Using *tar* for Backups 344
Summary 346

23   The cron and at Programs   349

The *cron* Program 350
    Creating a *crontab* File 351
    Submitting and Managing *crontab* Files 353
    Using Complex *cron* Commands 354
The *at* Program 355
Summary 357

24   Security   359

Improving Passwords 360
Securing Your Files 361
Controlling Modem Access 361
    Callback Modems 362
    Modem-Line Problems 362
    How a Modem Handles a Call 363
Using UUCP 363
Controlling Local Area Network Access 364
Tracking Intruders 365
Preparing for the Worst 365
Summary 366

25   Modifying the Kernel   367

Upgrading and Installing New Kernel Software 368
Compiling the Kernel from Source Code 369
    Where to Find Kernel Sources 369
    Using New Kernel Sources 370
Adding Drivers to the Kernel 372
Upgrading Libraries 372
Using Linux's C Compiler 373
    Compiler Options 374
    Debugging and Profiling Options 375
    Debugging *gcc* Programs with *gdb* 375
Summary 376

26   Shell Programming   377

Creating and Running Shell Programs 378
Using Variables 380
    Assigning a Value to a Variable 380
    Understanding Positional Parameters and Other
        Built-In Shell Variables 381
Using Quotation Marks 382
Using the *test* Command 384

Using Conditional Statements 387
   The *if* Statement 387
   The *case* Statement 389
Using Iteration Statements 390
   The *for* Statement 390
   The *while* Statement 392
   The *until* Statement 392
   The *shift* Command 393
   The *select* Statement 394
   The *repeat* Statement 395
Using Functions 396
Summary 397

Part IV   Networking

27   UUCP   401

Configuring UUCP 402
Configuring Taylor UUCP 403
   Specifying Your System's Name 403
   Setting Up Remote Systems 404
   Ports and Modems 405
   Access Permissions 406
Configuring HDB UUCP 408
   Specifying Remote Systems 408
   Setting the Modem Device 408
   Setting Access Permissions 409
Understanding UUCP Connections 410
   Direct Connections 411
   Login Scripts 411
   Access Times 412
UUCP Security 413
Using UUCP 414
   Sending E-Mail with UUCP 416
   Transferring Files with UUCP 416
   Checking Transfers 418
Summary 418

28   TCP/IP and Networks   419

Network Terminology 420
   Servers 420
   Clients 421
   Nodes 421
   Local and Remote Resources 421
   Network Operating System 421

Network Protocols 422
Network Interface Card 422
Bridges, Routers, and Brouters 423
Gateways 423
What Is TCP/IP? 423
TCP/IP, the Internet, and Layered Architecture 425
IP Addresses 426
The Domain Name System 428
Network Basics 430
Network Topologies 430
Network Media 432
Networking Hardware 433
Summary 435

29 **Configuring Hardware and the Kernel for Networking**   **437**
Configuring the Kernel 438
Understanding Network Drivers 440
Adding Network Support to the Kernel 440
Forcing a Network Card Recognition 442
Setting Up PLIP 443
Setting Up SLIP and PPP Serial Ports 444
Summary 445

30 **Configuring TCP/IP**   **447**
Getting Ready to Configure TCP/IP 448
Setting Up the Basics 450
Setting Up the Loopback Interface 451
Setting Up an Ethernet Interface 453
Configuring PLIP 454
Gateways 455
Name Service and Name Resolver 457
The named Daemon and Name Servers 458
The hosts.conf File and Resolver Variables 460
Name Server Lookups: The resolv.conf File 461
The /etc/named.boot File 462
Resource Records 463
Resource Record Files 466
IN-ADDR-ARPA 468
Summary 469

31 **Configuring SLIP and PPP**   **471**
Setting Up the Dummy Interface 472
Setting Up SLIP 473

Configuring SLIP 474

Using dip 475

Setting Up PPP 476

Setting Up a PPP Account 476

Dialing Out: chat 477

Running pppd 479

Checking Problems 480

PPP Authentication 481

Using DNS for SLIP and PPP 484

Summary 485

32   TCP/IP Utilities   487

Configuration Files 488

Symbolic Machine Names: /etc/hosts 488

Network Names: /etc/networks 489

Network Protocols: /etc/protocols 489

Network Services: /etc/services 490

The Loopback Driver 491

The *ifconfig* Command 491

The *inetd* Daemon 493

The *netstat* Command 494

Communications End Points 495

Network Interface Statistics 497

Data Buffers 498

Routing Table Information 499

Protocol Statistics 500

The *ping* Command 502

The *arp* Command 503

The *traceroute* Command 504

The *rpcinfo* Command 505

Summary 505

33   NFS and NIS   507

What Is NFS? 508

Installing NFS 510

Mounting NFS Directories 513

NFS Administration 515

rpcinfo 515

nfsstat 516

What Are NIS and YP? 517

Installing NIS 519

Summary 521

PART V   E-MAIL NEWS

34   E-Mail and Linux   **525**

Linux Mail Software 526
E-Mail Structure 528
Summary 530

35   Configuring sendmail   **531**

Configuring *sendmail* 532
   The sendmail.cf File 533
   UUCP-Specific Modifications 535
   Configuration Table Locations 535
   Configuring decnetxtable 536
   Configuring domaintable 536
   Configuring genericfrom 536
   Configuring mailertable 536
   Configuring pathtable 537
   Configuring uucprelays 538
   Configuring uucpxtable 538
   Building sendmail.cf from sendmail.m4 538
Using *sendmail* Version 8 538
   Configuring sendmail 539
   Using the sendmail Templates 541
Summary 542

36   Using smail   **543**

How *smail* Handles Mail 544
Setting Up *smail* 545
   Configuring smail for UUCP 546
   Configuring smail for TCP Use 549
   Using Other Options 550
   Debugging smail 552
Modifying *smail*'s Behavior 552
Summary 554

37   Configuring Elm and Pine   **555**

Configuring Elm 556
Configuring Pine 557
Summary 560

38   USENET and Netnews   **561**

What Is USENET? 562
A Brief History of USENET 563
How USENET News Is Handled 564
Summary 566

39   NNTP and INN   **567**

How NNTP Handles News 568

Installing the NNTP Server Program 569

Configuring *nntpd* 570

Using INN 571

Installing the INN Software 572

Configuring INN 573

Summary 574

40   C News   **575**

How C News Handles News 576

Configuring C News...577

C News Configuration Files 577

C News Directories 579

The sys File 580

Implementing Batching 583

Final Steps 584

C News Utilities 585

Summary 586

41   Configuring trn and tin   **586**

Configuring *trn* 588

Configuring *tin* 589

Summary 590

PART VI   THE INTERNET

42   Setting Up an Internet Site   **593**

Choosing a Connection Method 594

Deciding What Services You Need 595

Directly Connecting through a Gateway 596

Connecting through Another Gateway 596

Using a Service Provider 597

Summary 597

43   Setting Up an FTP Site   **599**

What Is FTP? 600

Using FTP 600

Transferring Files...602

Quitting FTP 604

How FTP Uses TCP 605

Configuring FTP 606

Setting Up ftpd 607

FTP Logins...608

Setting Up the Directories 609

Setting Permissions 610

Testing the System 611

Securing FTP 612

Summary 612

44   Configuring a WAIS Site   615

Compiling and Installing freeWAIS 618

Setting Up freeWAIS 620

Starting freeWAIS 623

Building Your WAIS Indexes 624

WAIS Index Files 625

The waisindex Command 626

Getting Fancy 628

Summary 629

45   Setting Up a Gopher Service   631

Gopher and Linux 632

Configuring Gopher 634

The gopherd.conf File 635

The gopherdlocal.conf File 636

Setting Up the Makefile 639

WAIS and Gopher 643

Setting Up Your Gopher Directories 644

Setting Gopher Filenames 644

Using a Master File 645

Using Links 646

Starting Gopher 647

Letting the World Know 648

Summary 649

46   Configuring a WWW Site   651

Web Server Software 652

Unpacking the Web Files 653

Compiling the Web Software 653

Configuring the Web Software 655

Starting the Web Software 659

Setting Up Your Web Site 661

HTML Authoring Tools 662

Maintaining HTML 665

Summary 667

PART VII   APPENDIXES

A   Linux FTP Sites and Newsgroups   **671**

    FTP Sites 672
        What Is FTP? 672
        Connecting and Downloading Files with FTP 673
        Using ftpmail 675
        Linux FTP Archive Sites 676
    Bulletin Boards 676
        LINUX-related BBSs 677
    USENET Newsgroups 682

B   Commercial Vendors for Linux   **685**

C   The Linux Documentation Project   **689**

D   The GNU General Public License   **691**

E   Copyright Information   **701**

F   Hardware Compatibility   **707**

    System Architectures 708
    Computers/Motherboards/BIOS 708
    CPUs and FPUs 708
    Video Cards 709
    Hard Disk Controllers 709
    Hard Drives 711
    Removable Drives 711
    Mouses 711
    I/O Controllers 712
    Multiport Cards 712
    Sound Cards 713
    CD-ROM Drives 714
    Tape Drives 714
    Modems 715
    Network Adapters 715
    ISDN Cards 716
    Printers/Plotters 716
    Scanners 717
    Video Capture Boards 718
    UPS 718

G   **Glossary**   **719**

H   **What's on the CD-ROM**   **729**

  Sams Publishing Support 731
    Visit Us On-line 731
  InfoMagic Support 731
    By E-Mail 731
    By Phone 732
  Index   **733**

Acknowledgments

This book, unlike our popular *Linux Unleashed*, was conceived as a solo effort and as such meant an awful lot of my time was taken away from others. This book took a while to write because it contains a lot of technical information. To my parents and close friends, thanks for understanding why I couldn't visit. In particular, thanks to Yvonne, who understood why I had to spend evenings and weekends at the computer, muttering veiled curses about deadlines, Linux, and applications that crashed at the most inopportune times. Of course, I never said anything bad about my editors!

At Sams, those editors were Rosemarie Graham, who drove deadlines, tolerated changes, and generally tried to bear with me as I struggled to submit this material on time. Thanks also to Todd Bumbalough, who rode shotgun over the technical completeness of the material. To the production editors and technical reviewers, thanks are also due. Also at Sams, Grace Buechlein gracefully bore changes to her own schedules in order to fit this book in.

Finally, thanks to Rick McMullin, who graciously allowed me to steal some of his material for the shell programming chapter and some details of the gcc C compiler.

About the Author

Tim Parker is a well-known author with over 800 feature articles and reviews published in many different magazines. In addition, Dr. Parker has written or contributed to two dozen books. He is currently Technical Editor of SCO World Magazine, Contributing Editor of Canadian Computer Reseller, and a frequent contributor to UNIX Review Magazine. Dr. Parker is president of TPCI, based in Kanata, Ontario. TPCI provides technical writing, training, investigative, and consulting services to many large corporations, military installations, and law enforcement organizations.

When not busy writing books or articles, Dr. Parker can be found outdoors. He is a semi-professional photographer, white-water kayaker, and hiker. He is also a scuba diving instructor and licensed pilot.

Introduction

UNIX system administration used to be a skill learned by watching others, trying many things on spec, and scouring obscure magazine articles, obtuse man pages, and e-mail from others. In short, system administration was a skill that was learned over the years with no single reference to the role and functions a system administrator plays. UNIX, especially, was a tough system to administer properly because there were many versions of the software, a disparate support base, and few solid working applications. Luckily, time has changed these conditions.

With the popularity of computers in general, system administrators started writing down the details of their tasks. Publishers realized that there was a distinct and eager, albeit small, market for system administration books. The market grew as the number of systems and LANs expanded. The stabilization of the UNIX operating system in two, and now one, major version helped enormously as well.

Linux became a dominant UNIX product about two years ago when it started receiving worldwide acclaim as a reasonably stable PC version of UNIX. As more and more programmers got involved and started producing software for Linux, the attraction of the operating system continued to grow. Soon, PC users who didn't know anything about UNIX at all were running Linux and starting to deal with shells, filesystems, and devices.

After helping to write *Linux Unleashed* (a great book, definitely worth buying if you haven't already got a copy!), I realized that many users used that book and CD-ROM to get started with Linux, but they needed more advanced material on managing their systems and setting up network systems. That's when the *Linux System Administrator's Survival Guide* was born. This book expands on the *Linux Unleashed* material, providing more detail on many aspects of the operating system. Although some overlap exists between *Linux Unleashed* and this book, it has been minimized as much as possible.

Many Linux books are available, but to date there are no complete books on administering a Linux system. A few books do cover specific aspects of the task, such as networking or device drivers, but none cover the entire gamut. That's the task I set for myself when this book was born: give readers enough information to help them get their Linux systems running smoothly. The next problem was how to condense 20 years of UNIX system administration experience into a single book. It took a while, but I hope I've managed to include enough information on every aspect of system administration to keep you going.

Bear in mind that this book was written for the system administrator, although the material will certainly be applicable (and hopefully interesting) to any user who has mastered the basics of Linux. I cover practically every aspect of system administration in this book. When dealing with subjects, like security, that have entire books written on them, I cover only the basics. Also, I don't include all the details about the more obscure topics that aren't relevant to most readers.

This book should provide you with everything you need, from setting up filesystems to installing servers for popular Internet utilities. The book was not written for the advanced user; it was written for those just starting in system administration. I hope you find a lot of useful information in this book.

A note about the CD-ROM accompanying this book. You probably already have a Linux system up and running. Just in case you don't, or you want the latest versions of some of the Linux software, this book comes with the latest Slackware Linux CD-ROM distribution. You don't have to use this version of Linux to use the material covered in these pages. I've tried to make the material in each chapter relevant to as many versions as possible, and I usually give several possible pathnames and (in some cases) filenames when they may differ across versions or distributions. If your Linux system doesn't have a file or package in the location mentioned in this book, search your directory structure for the filenames given and substitute the pathname as necessary.

- Introduction to Linux

- Linux Hardware and Software

- Installing and Updating Linux

- LILO

- Installing and Configuring XFree86

P A R T   I

Installation and Configuration

- What Is Linux?

- Linux's History

- Copyrights

- Sources of Help

- Recent Linux
  Distributions

CHAPTER 1

Introduction to Linux

The Linux operating system has become immensely popular. USENET newsgroups dedicated to the Linux operating system have hundreds of messages a day, CD-ROMs of Linux archives are sold by the thousands, and even more DOS users are wandering around trying to figure out UNIX syntax and Linux installation problems. In many ways, the interest in Linux brings back the heady hacker days and the excitement of CP/M and early DOS machines.

Linux does have its problems though. One problem is the wide variety of Linux versions available, some of which are not very stable. The quality of the installation and configuration utilities also varies widely from Linux version to Linux version. Another problem is supporting documentation. Although this problem is decreasing as more people get involved, most available Linux documentation can be intimidating for first-time users (and some veterans). Commercial books dedicated to beginning Linux users are helping by offering a smoother explanation, but most books are simply rehashed Linux documents.

Although this book also uses the Linux documentation as a basis, it also uses almost two decades of UNIX system administration experience, years of working with Linux, and a lot of advice from other users. This book is not designed for new Linux users who can't find their way around a filesystem, although readers with any knowledge of UNIX will feel quite at home. Instead, this book is for Linux users who want to expand their systems, optimize them, and learn more about system administration.

Note

Two schools of thought exist on pronouncing *Linux*. Because Linux is similar to UNIX and was originally developed by a programmer with the first name Linus, many assume the long *i*, as in *line-ucks*, is correct. On the other hand, Linux was developed to replace a UNIX workalike called Minix (with a short *i*), so the rest of the Linux community calls the operating system *lih-nicks*. Which is correct? The original developers used the latter pronunciation, while most North Americans prefer the former. Choose whichever you wish.

WHAT IS LINUX?

Linux is a freely distributed, multitasking, multiuser operating system that behaves like UNIX. Designed specifically for the PC, Linux takes advantage of the PC's architecture to give you performance similar to UNIX workstations of a couple of years ago. Linux isn't a small, simple operating system like DOS (even in its latest incarnations). The development of UNIX has resulted in a mish-mash of files and directories, all of which are carried over to Linux for compatibility and programming reasons.

Linux includes a bunch of files for the operating system itself (called the kernel), a ton of utility programs, documentation files, add-on emulators for other operating systems, and much more. The following sections explain what you get when you install Linux on your system. Future chapters expand on these topics.

LINUX'S KERNEL

Linux is a complete multitasking, multiuser operating system that behaves like the UNIX operating system in terms of kernel behavior and peripheral support. Linux has all the features of UNIX, plus several recent extensions that add new versatility to Linux. All source code for Linux and its utilities is freely available.

The Linux kernel was originally developed for the Intel 80386 CPU's protected mode. The 80386 was designed with multitasking in mind (despite the fact that most of the Intel CPUs are used with single-tasking DOS), and Linux makes good use of the advanced features built into the CPU's instruction set. Memory management is especially strong with the 80386 (compared to earlier CPUs). A floating-point emulation routine allows Linux to function on machines that do not have math coprocessors (such as the SX series of Intel CPUs).

Linux allows shared executables so that if more than one copy of a particular application is loaded (either by one user running several identical tasks, or several users running the same task), all the tasks can share the same memory. This process, called copy-on-write pages, makes for much more efficient use of RAM.

The Linux kernel also supports demand paging, which means that only sections of a program that are necessary are read into RAM. To further optimize memory usage, Linux uses a unified memory pool. This pool enables all free memory on the system to be used as disk cache, effectively speeding up access to frequently used programs and data. As memory usage increases, the amount of cache is automatically adjusted.

To support large memory requirements when only small amounts of physical RAM are available, Linux supports swap space. Swap space enables pages of memory to be written to a reserved area of a disk and treated as an extension of physical memory. By moving pages back and forth between the swap space and RAM, Linux can effectively behave as if it had more physical RAM than it does, albeit at the cost of some speed due to the hard drive's slower access.

Linux uses dynamically shared libraries extensively. Dynamically shared libraries use a common library section for many different applications, effectively reducing the size of each application. Linux does allow full library linking (called statically linked libraries) for portability to machines that may not have the dynamic libraries.

To make Linux widely acceptable, it supports a number of different filesystems, including those compatible with DOS and OS/2. Linux's own primary filesystem, called ext2fs, is designed for optimal use of the disk.

Linux is ideally suited for application development and experimentation with new languages. Several different compilers, including C, C++, Fortran, Pascal, Modula-2, LISP, Ada, Basic, and Smalltalk, come with the distribution software. Many of the Linux compilers, tools, debuggers, and editors are from the Free Software Foundation's GNU project.

GNU SOFTWARE

GNU (a recursive acronym for Gnu's Not UN-IX) was developed by the Free Software Foundation (FSF) to provide royalty-free software to programmers and developers. Since it was created, many programmer packages and toolkits have been developed and assigned to FSF for distribution. Most of the GNU software mirrors (and often improves upon) commercially available software.

Linux includes many GNU utilities, including the languages mentioned earlier, debuggers, and compiler tools. Text processors, print utilities, and other GNU tools are also included with most Linux distributions. As more software becomes available from FSF, it can be ported and compiled under Linux because Linux behaves as a standard UNIX operating system.

X

X (sometimes improperly called X Windows) is a graphical user interface (GUI) designed at MIT to provide portable GUI applications across different platforms. The version of X supplied with Linux is called XFree86 and is a direct port of the standard X11R5 system to 80386-based architectures. (Updates to the latest version of X, called X11R6, are beginning to appear, too.) XFree86 has been extended to provide compatibility with some other GUIs, including Open Look.

XFree86 supports several different video cards at a number of resolutions, offering a high-resolution graphical interface. Any X application can be recompiled to run properly under Linux, and a number of games, utilities, and add-ons have been developed and supplied as part of the X system. The XFree86 system also includes application development libraries, tools, and utilities. With these features, programmers can write applications specifically for X without having to invest in expensive software development kits or libraries.

DOS INTERFACE

Because Linux is designed for PCs, some compatibility with Microsoft MS-DOS is naturally part of the operating system. Linux provides a DOS emulator, which allows many DOS applications to be executed directly from within Linux, as part of the distribution system. Don't expect complete portability of DOS applications, though, as some applications are written to access peripherals or disk drives in a manner that Linux can't handle. The WINE (WINdows Emulator) project has developed a Microsoft Windows emulator for Linux, which enables Windows applications to be run from within Linux.

Although Linux can emulate DOS and Windows, the emulation feature is not intended to support full DOS usage. Instead, it provides the occasional DOS user with the ability to run an application under Linux. For heavy DOS use, your system should be set up with both DOS and Linux in separate partitions, enabling you to enter either one at boot time. Chapter 2 explains how to set this up.

Linux does allow you to transfer files seamlessly between the Linux filesystem and DOS by accessing the DOS partitions on a hard disk directly, if so configured. This capability makes it easy to move files and applications back and forth between the two operating systems.

TCP/IP

TCP/IP (Transmission Control Protocol/Internet Protocol) is the primary networking system used by UNIX and Linux. TCP/IP is a full family of protocols that were developed for the Internet, and you must use TCP/IP when you venture out onto the Internet. If you want to connect with other UNIX machines, you will probably have to use TCP/IP as well. The Linux TCP/IP implementation provides all the networking software and drivers usually associated with a commercial UNIX TCP/IP package. With this implementation, you can create your own local area network (LAN), attach to existing Ethernet LANs, or connect to the Internet.

Networking is a strong feature of Linux, and will be dealt with in considerable detail later in this book. You don't have to network your Linux system, of course, but a network is cheap and simple to install and is a fantastic method for transferring files between systems. You can network over modems, too, so you can have your friends' Linux machines on a network.

LINUX'S HISTORY

Linux was developed as a freely distributable version of UNIX. UNIX is the most widely used operating system in the world and has long been the standard for high-performance workstations and larger servers. UNIX, first developed in 1969, has a strong programmer-oriented user group that supports the operating system.

Note

How did UNIX get its name? It was based on an operating system called MULTICS (MULTiplexed Information and Computing System). Ken Thompson, Dennis Ritchie, and Brian Kernighan were involved in the design of a new operating system based on MULTICS that would be much simpler. They called the new operating system UNICS (Uniplexed Information and Computing System), which was quickly changed to UNIX.

Because UNIX is a commercial product, it must be bought for each platform it runs on. Licensing fees for UNIX versions for PC machines range from a few hundred dollars to several thousand. In an attempt to make UNIX widely available for no cost to those who want to experiment with it, a number of public domain UNIX systems have been developed over the years.

One of the early UNIX workalikes was Minix, written by Andy Tanenbaum. Although Minix didn't have a full range of features, it provided a small operating system that could be used on PC machines. To expand on Minix, a number of users started developing an enhanced operating system that would take advantage of the 80386 CPU's architecture. One of the primary developers of this system, which became known as Linux, was Linus Torvalds of the University of Helsinki. He released an early version of Linux in 1991. A first commercial, almost bug-free release was unleashed to the programming community in March 1992.

Soon, many programmers were working on Linux, and as the challenge and excitement of producing a growing UNIX workalike caught on, Linux grew at a remarkable rate. As the number of developers working on Linux grew, the entire UNIX workalike operating system was eventually completed and now includes all the tools you will find in a commercial UNIX product. Linux continues to grow as programmers adapt features and programs that were originally written as commercial UNIX products to Linux. New versions of Linux and its utilities are appearing at an astounding rate. New releases often appear weekly.

To avoid any charges for Linux, the Linux developers do not use any code from other UNIX systems. There are no licensing fees involved with the Linux operating system, and part of its mandate is to be freely available. Some companies have undertaken the task of assembling and testing versions of Linux, which they package on a CD-ROM for a (usually) minimal price.

Linux is not based on a single version of UNIX; it is a consolidation of the best features of BSD UNIX and System V. BSD UNIX was developed at the University of California at Berkeley, starting in 1977. Several major releases increased the power of BSD UNIX. Several standard UNIX programs originated at BSD, although BSD stopped its UNIX development in the early 1990s. AT&T, which developed the first version of UNIX, continued their UNIX development by producing a series of UNIX versions called System III, System IV, and System V. Linux uses the last primary release of BSD UNIX called 4.4BSD as its base and takes some other features from the latest release of System V, called System V Release 4 (SVR4).

COPYRIGHTS

Just because Linux is distributed for free, it doesn't mean the software is not copyrighted. Linux has been registered as copyrighted under the GNU General Public License (GPL), which is known in the programming community as a copyleft instead of copyright because of its nature. The GPL allows you to redistribute the Linux software, along with the complete source code, to anyone who wants it. However, the original owner of the components retains the copyrights to the software.

Linux doesn't have any kind of warranty. Even if you buy the Linux software from someone and pay them for maintenance, you cannot ever pursue the Linux programmers. They make no statement of functionality. If Linux destroys all your accounting or database data, it's tough luck. You assume the risk. That having been said, Linux has proven itself very stable and no incidents of serious data damage have occurred as a result of its programming. However, if the chance that something may go wrong is too great a risk for your business, you may be better off buying a commercial UNIX system that does have a warranty.

According to the GNU GPL, you can even sell Linux. You can modify any of the code, and repackage it as you want. You do not own the software and cannot claim copyright, however, even if you have modified the source code. The GNU GPL also imposes one condition on the sale of Linux—you must provide all source code with the system if you sell it for profit so that others can further modify and sell it, too.

The authors and developers of Linux don't receive any royalties or shareware fees. For the most part, they provide the software to end users for the true love of programming and sharing their code with other programmers who appreciate it.

SOURCES OF HELP

Linux does not have a telephone support line. In one sense, you are on your own when you install Linux. On the other hand, many thousands of Linux users are willing to help everyone from neophyte to experienced programmer. All you have to know is where to look for help. The two sources of help are written documentation and the user community.

DOCUMENTATION

The first exposure most people get to Linux is the Linux INFO-SHEET, a relatively short ASCII document that is available from USENET, BBSs (bulletin board systems), and many user groups. The INFO-SHEET is a quick summary of Linux. It is posted at regular intervals to the Linux newsgroups on USENET.

As Linux was developed, several programmers started writing brief guides to their contributions as well as wider areas of the operating system. Although these documents were usually terse and awkward to read, they did provide others with enough information to continue using Linux. Over a short span of time, the documentation for Linux grew rapidly and a central organizing body was needed to help keep it on track and avoid duplication.

The Linux Documentation Project was created to provide a complete set of public domain documentation for Linux. From a few rough installation notes a couple of years ago, the documentation has expanded to include almost a thousand pages, some very good, some not. The following primary documents are currently available or soon to be released:

◆ *Linux Installation* explains how to install and configure Linux.
◆ The *Linux User's Guide* is a guide for first-time users.
◆ The *Linux System Administrator's Guide* is a guide to various aspects of system administration.
◆ The *Linux Network Administration Guide* explains how to set up and use networks.
◆ The *Linux Kernel Hacker's Guide* is a guide to modifying the Linux kernel.

In addition to these primary documents, there are about a dozen smaller guides to specific or esoteric aspects of Linux. These smaller guides are called How To documents. Together they form a growing document suite that covers practically every aspect of Linux. These documents are available with most distributions of the software. Not all the documents are up to date, as changes to the operating system have occurred since they were first written. Several different people wrote the Linux documents, so the styles and layout are not consistent. A perfect-bound printed copy of the Linux Documentation Project is available from Linux Systems Labs and some bookstores.

Note

You can contact Linux Systems Labs at 49884 Miller Ct., Chesterfield, MI 48047. Their telephone number is (810) 716-1700, and their fax machine number is (810) 716-1703. You can get information about LSL from their e-mail address info@lsl.com.

A number of Frequently Asked Questions (FAQ) files are available through the Linux newsgroups on USENET and as part of the distribution set. The FAQs tend to be quick problem-solving items, designed to save you from thumbing through many pages of on-line documentation. One FAQ called the META-FAQ provides basic information about Linux, where to get it, and the documentation that goes with it. It too is regularly posted to newsgroups.

A file called the Linux Software Map (LSM) contains a list of many of the components in Linux. Unfortunately, the LSM is incomplete and lacks considerable chunks of data. However, it is a good starting point if you want to see what is included with Linux. The LSM is updated at intervals and can be obtained from USENET, a Linux FTP site, or with a distribution set.

Finally, Linux mailing lists are available to anyone with e-mail access to the Internet. Information on the Linux mailing lists (there are quite a few) is available from USENET newsgroups or BBSs. See Appendix A for more information about the newsgroups, BBSs, and FTP sites.

USENET NEWSGROUPS

USENET is a collection of discussion groups (called newsgroups) available to Internet users. The over 13,000 newsgroups generate over 100M of traffic every day. Of all these newsgroups (which cover every conceivable topic), several are dedicated to Linux. These newsgroups are a useful forum for information and answers to questions about Linux.

You can read USENET newsgroups through newsreader software that accesses either the Internet or a local site that offers USENET service (called a newsfeed). Many on-line services, such as CompuServe and Delphi, provide access to the newsgroups (sometimes at an additional cost), and some have their own forums for Linux users. BBSs dedicated to Linux in whole or in part are also appearing, and many excerpt the USENET conversations for the BBS users who do not have access to USENET.

USENET newsgroups are divided into three categories: primary newsgroups that are readily available to all users, local newsgroups with a limited distribution (usually based on geography), and alternate newsgroups that may not be handled by all news servers due to the relaxed rules of etiquette on them. The primary newsgroups of interest to Linux users when this book was written are the following:

◆ The comp.os.linux.admin newsgroup deals with administering Linux systems.

◆ Proponents of the Linux system sound off in comp.os.linux.advocacy.

◆ The comp.os.linux.announce newsgroup contains announcements important to the Linux community. This is a moderated newsgroup, which means someone approves the postings before you get to see them.

◆ The comp.os.linux.answers newsgroup contains questions and answers to problems about Linux.

◆ Ongoing work on Linux in general is discussed in comp.os.linux.development.

◆ Ongoing work on Linux applications is discussed in comp.os.linux.development.apps.

◆ Ongoing work on the Linux operating system is discussed in comp.os.linux.development.system.

◆ The comp.os.linux.hardware newsgroup deals with issues concerning Linux and hardware support.

◆ The comp.os.linux.help newsgroup contains questions and advice about Linux.

◆ Linux-specific topics not covered by other groups are covered in comp.os.linux.misc.

◆ Linux networking issues are discussed in comp.os.linux.networking.

◆ The comp.os.linux.setup newsgroup deals with Linux setup and installation problems.

These primary newsgroups should be available at all USENET sites unless the system administrator filters them out for some reason. The other Linux newsgroups tend to change frequently, primarily because they are either regional or populated with highly opinionated users. The alt (alternate) newsgroups are the ones most likely to contain such users. One alt newsgroup in operation when this book was written is

```
alt.uu.comp.os.linux.questions
```

To find the several different newsgroups about Linux, use your newsreader software to search for all newsgroups with the word *linux* in the title. If you have access to USENET, regularly scan the newsgroup additions and deletions to check for new

Linux newsgroups or existing groups that have folded. Notices about newsgroup changes are usually posted to all existing groups, but every now and again one gets through without fanfare. On-line services that provide access to USENET usually maintain lists of all active newsgroups that can be searched quickly.

The traffic on most of these Linux newsgroups deal with problems and issues people have when installing, configuring, administering, or using the operating system. A lot of valuable information passes through the newsgroups quickly, so check them regularly. The most interesting messages that deal with a specific subject (called a thread) are often collected and stored as an archive for access through an FTP site.

WORLD WIDE WEB SITES

Not surprisingly, Linux has a good presence on the World Wide Web. Several sites offer Linux information, and a few home pages are specifically dedicated to Linux business. One of the most popular Linux Web sites is accessible as http://www.ssc.com/linux/linux.html. This site has a wealth of information and hyperlinks to other Linux sources. Figure 1.1 shows the home page for this site. From the home page, you can select the type of information you want by clicking the appropriate icon.

Figure 1.1.
The Linux home page
at www.ssc.com offers
access to many of the
most requested pieces of
information about
Linux.

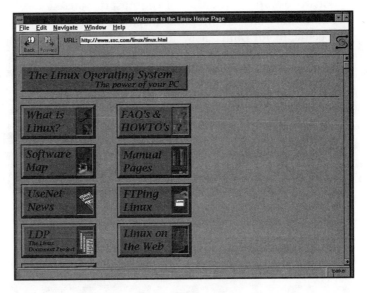

From the Linux home page at www.ssc.com, you can also link to other Linux sites, including those of commercial vendors of Linux products. Figure 1.2 shows the screen that appears when you click the Linux on the Web icon. These links are updated frequently, so they are a good place to start when navigating through the Web.

Figure 1.2.
The hyperlinks on the Linux home page at www.ssc.com point you to the latest Linux information.

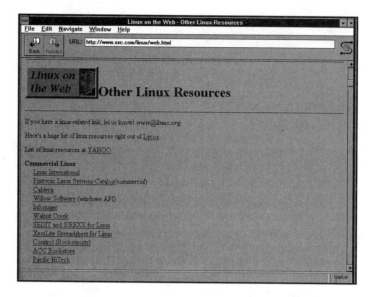

One of the key utilities the www.ssc.com home page offers is access to the Linux Software Map (LSM), which is the most complete index to Linux software available. The Linux Software Map includes all the software packages that were developed specifically for Linux, as well as utilities and applications that have been ported to Linux. Figure 1.3 shows the LSM home page. The Linux Software Map window lets you search for keywords in on-line documents and indexes, and then displays the results to provide a fast, easy method of finding software and documents. Searching the LSM page first can save you hours of digging through FTP and BBS archives.

Figure 1.3.
The Linux Software Map provides an almost complete list of available Linux software, applications, documents, and associated information.

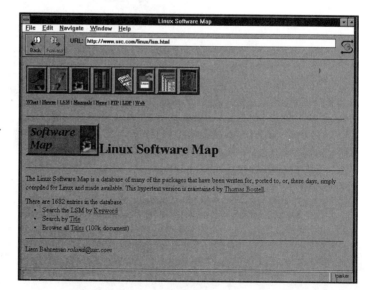

This section previously mentioned the Linux Documentation Project. Figure 1.4 shows the home page for the Linux Documentation Project. When accessing information from this page, keep in mind that the Project is an ongoing task, so don't expect to find a lot of information in finished form.

Figure 1.4.
The Linux Documentation Project's home page provides access to new Linux documentation.

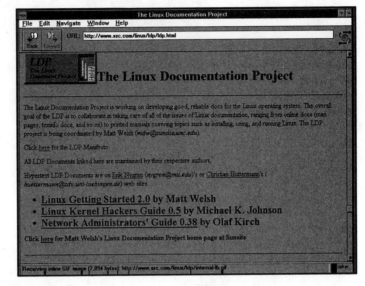

LINUX JOURNAL

The *Linux Journal* is a commercial publication dedicated to Linux. It covers the entire gamut of Linux topics, ranging from material suitable for newcomers to the operating system to very complex programming information. Figure 1.5 shows the home page for the *Linux Journal*, which is accessible through www.ssc.com. The magazine is not on-line, but its Web page can give you a sample table of contents, issue information, and subscription details.

Note

If you want more information about the *Linux Journal*, send e-mail to subs@ssc.com. Alternatively, you can write to the publisher at P.O. Box 85867, Seattle, WA 98145, or call the publisher at (206) 782-7733. Subscriptions are $22 per year in the U.S.

Figure 1.5.
The Linux Journal *is a magazine for Linux users, developers, and all other interested parties.*

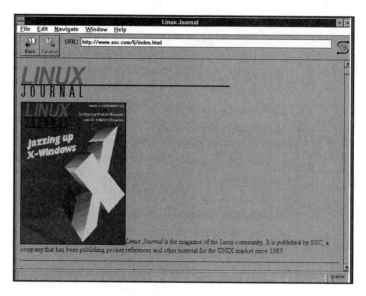

RECENT LINUX DISTRIBUTIONS

Several versions of Linux are available, depending on which CD-ROM or FTP site you visit. This book applies to practically every version written. As of this writing, the latest Linux kernel versions were 1.2.13 and 1.3.18. The CD-ROM included with this book provides Slackware release 3.0, which includes the Linux kernel version 1.3.18 (the last really stable version the author tested). You can change kernel versions by obtaining the source code for a new release, compiling it, and replacing your existing kernel. This procedure is covered in more detail later in the book.

You may find several CD-ROM distributions available at your local reseller. InfoMagic has a four CD-ROM set that bears the name Linux Developer's Resource. In addition to the complete Linux system, it includes source code, FTP archives, full documentation, several extension products, and demonstration software of commercial applications (including WordPerfect). Some of this material is included on the CD-ROM at the back of this book.

SUMMARY

Now that you understand what Linux is all about, you're ready to tackle the basics of Linux installation and the misunderstood LILO utility. The next three chapters complete the introductory material of this book. Then you'll be ready to dive into the true system administration material.

- Minimum System Requirements

- Where to Get Linux

- Linux Releases and Disk Sets

CHAPTER 2

Linux Hardware and Software

The Linux system is attractive because it offers a UNIX workstation environment that works even on old PCs. The hardware requirements are not very demanding, unless you want to get into application development and extensive GUI use. This chapter looks at the basic hardware necessary for Linux installation. The minimum requirements are discussed, as is support for most peripherals. Expanding your system with new hardware is covered later in this book.

MINIMUM SYSTEM REQUIREMENTS

Because Linux was mostly developed by PC users, the hardware support built into the operating system is fairly typical for a PC. Few esoteric devices have Linux drivers, unless a programmer took the time to write one for himself and then release it to the Linux community. Few third-party vendors offer hardware accessories (such as multiport boards) for Linux either, although this situation is slowly changing as Linux becomes widespread.

The minimum realistic system requirements for Linux are a motherboard with an 80386SX processor or better, 2M of RAM or more, a floppy disk drive, a hard drive with 40M or more, and a video card and monitor. Most users' systems exceed these requirements. The following sections examine the hardware requirements for a Linux system in a little more detail.

MOTHERBOARD REQUIREMENTS

The hardware required to set up a Linux system mirrors a typical PC installation. It starts with the motherboard, which should be an Intel 80386 or better (or use one of the Intel workalikes like AMD or Cyrix). Remarkably, Linux will even run on a slow 80386SX, although slow is the operative word. For application development work, though, an 80486DX or better is recommended due to the high CPU usage of the compiler and linker. The same recommendation applies to X users because X is a notorious CPU hog. You can compile applications on an 80386, just as you can run X on one, but the performance can sometimes deteriorate to the point of annoyance. For a realistic system running X and application developments, consider a fast 80486DX (50MHz at least) or a Pentium.

Linux uses a floating-point unit or FPU (also called a math co-processor, although the two terms do not refer to exactly the same thing) if you have one. FPUs are built into the 80486DX and Pentium series chips. If an FPU is not installed, Linux will provide a memory-based emulator that has reasonable performance. Either Intel or workalike add-on FPUs are supported, although some problems have been reported with Weitek FPUs.

Linux supports both ISA (Industry Standard Architecture) and EISA (Extended Industry Standard Architecture) motherboards, but doesn't support MCA (IBM's

MicroChannel Architecture) at the present time. Linux also supports VESA local bus motherboards, which give peripheral cards direct access to the motherboard components.

RAM requirements vary depending on the size of the Linux system you want to run. A minimum Linux system runs quite well with 2M, although a great deal of swapping is involved. Consider 4M of RAM an effective minimum, with more memory resulting in faster performance. For development work and X users, 8M is a good working minimum (although X can function with 4M, albeit with a lot of swapping).

Linux systems that have more than one user should increase the amount of RAM. The usage dictates the amount of RAM required. For example, 8M easily supports two users, even if both are running X. With a third-party multiport board supporting eight users, 16M RAM is a good choice, although the users cannot run X with this configuration. For X users, a good rule of thumb is 4M per user minimum, unless the Linux machine can offload the X processing to the user's machine in a client-server layout. (Linux doesn't have this capability at the moment, but it is being developed).

Linux uses all the available RAM in your machine. It does not impose any architectural limitations on memory as DOS and some other operating systems do. Any available memory is completely used. To extend the amount of physical RAM on the system, a Linux swap partition, called a swap space, is recommended. The swap space is used as a slower extension of actual memory, where data can be exchanged with physical RAM. Even RAM-heavy systems should have a swap space. The size of the swap space depends on the amount of RAM on the system, the number of users, and the typical usage.

Table 2.1 shows a general guideline for determining the amount of RAM your system should have. Begin by using the first column to determine which conditions are likely to exist on your system (such as running X, running larger applications, or adding users), and then move across to the minimum, recommended, and best performance columns. Consider any program that uses a lot of RAM, such as a word processor (not a line editor like vi), a database, a spreadsheet program, or a desktop publishing system, to be a large application. Large applications also include video players, some sound editors, and similar multimedia applications. The Development System entry is if you plan to do a lot of programming, including X application development.

When you have identified all the conditions you will encounter, add the RAM requirements for each condition down the column. For example, if you are going to run a system, with frequent use of a compiler (large application), X, and run an Internet WWW and FTP server for a minimum system, you would need 6M RAM. A minimum system runs slowly with lots of disk swapping. A system with the recommended amount of RAM is a balance between RAM usage and performance, and the best performance column minimizes swapping as much as possible. Remember that these numbers are only guidelines. You can never have too much RAM.

TABLE 2.1. DETERMINING YOUR RAM NEEDS.

Condition	Minimum	Recommended	Best Performance
Kernel and basic operation	2M	4M	4M
Large applications and compilers	1M	2M	2M
X	2M	4M	4M
Additional character-based users (per user)	.5M	.5M	1M
Additional X users	2M	4M	4M
Development system	2M	2M	4M
Internet Server (FTP, WWW, WAIS, or Gopher server)	1M	2M	4M

HARD DISKS

Although Linux can run completely from a floppy disk with no hard disk, running it this way doesn't offer a useful environment. Linux is designed primarily for hard disk use, and supports all the common hard disk controller systems including IDE (Integrated Drive Electronics), EIDE (Extended Integrated Drive Electronics), ESDI (Enhanced Small Device Interface), RLL (Run Length Limited), and SCSI (Small Computer System Interface). Linux supports the older 8-bit original PC controllers, although most controllers are 16-bit AT designs.

Linux is not choosy about the manufacturer and type of hard disk. As a rule, if DOS can handle the drive, so can Linux. This rule applies to all drives except SCSI drives, which require special handling. Linux still is restricted by most PC BIOS versions that impose limitations on the number of sectors, heads, and cylinders, however. There is an effective 1,024M size limit on drives with some older versions of Linux, and even some smaller drives can't be handled properly by Linux or DOS because of the BIOS. More recent versions of the operating system can overcome some of these limitations. The version of Linux on the CD-ROM accompanying this book, for example, can use disk space over the 1G limit.

Linux supports most standard SCSI devices, but not all of the many different SCSI controllers and protocols on the market work well with Linux. Linux does support the most common SCSI controllers, though. Some other controllers are supported with enhanced BIOS chips on the PC motherboard. A size limitation on the SCSI drives is still imposed by the BIOS of many early versions of Linux, so a 2G drive will have only 1G available to Linux and DOS. Other UNIX systems, like SCO UNIX, can use the rest of the drive. Later versions of Linux (mostly any kernel from version 1.1 and on) can use more than 1G of disk space on SCSI drives.

The size of disk space required by Linux depends on the parts of the operating system that are installed. A minimum effective system is 20M, which gives enough room for the basic utilities but not X. To load the entire basic Linux system, including development tools and X, provide at least 150M just for the files. Then add whatever space is required for your personal files and temporary storage for Linux. A good rule of thumb is to double the space requirements. In addition to the user space, remember to leave room for the swap space. Although the swap space size depends on what the system is used for, a good number to use is 16M.

You can use more than one drive, although you should place a bootable root Linux partition on the first drive. You also must load DOS on the first drive, although you can place partitions on other drives. The number of drives supported depend on the drive controller and BIOS. IDE systems are usually limited to two drives, but EIDE systems can handle four drives (two drives off two controllers). ESDI and RLL controllers are usually limited to two drives. SCSI controllers can handle up to seven drives per controller, and a single system can contain several controllers. SCSI is the most versatile (and also the most expensive) system.

Because hard disks are now inexpensive, obtaining large-capacity drives is relatively easy. Linux can share a disk with up to three other operating systems (more with a few tricks), so if you plan to load DOS and Linux, for example, allocate enough drive space for both operating systems.

VIDEO SYSTEMS

Linux can use almost any video card that works without special drivers under DOS, including CGA, EGA, VGA, Super VGA, and Hercules video cards. Linux also supports some enhanced resolution cards, such as the Cirrus Logic, Diamond, ATI, and Trident cards. Because hundreds of video cards are available for DOS, though, not all of the available cards have drivers for Linux. Because most cards support default VGA and SVGA modes, you can use these modes in almost every case.

X can use the bitmap capabilities of a high-resolution card, although X can run on a VGA or SVGA system as well. If you are using a specialty card designed for Windows, for example, make sure that a video driver is available for Linux.

MOUSES

Linux doesn't use the mouse for character-based sessions, but it is necessary for X. Linux handles practically every type of mouse and trackball that has DOS drivers, including Microsoft, Logitech, and Mouse Systems. Linux supports both bus and serial mouses.

Linux also supports some other pointing devices, including joysticks and pen systems used for cursor movement. Some systems use a pointer pad that you can drag either your finger or a stylus across; these systems work with Linux as long as they have drivers that emulate a mouse (which most do). Finally, some touch-screens also work with Linux.

TAPE DRIVES

Your Linux system can use any SCSI tape drive that has a controller recognized by Linux. Other tape drives use a proprietary interface that requires a dedicated hardware card. In most cases, if the IRQ, DMA, and memory address can be configured into Linux, the tape drive should be accessible. For example, you can use some older UNIX-style tape drives, such as those made by Wangtek and Archive, under Linux even though they have a proprietary board controlling them.

Some smaller QIC (Quarter Inch Cartridge) drives are becoming popular in DOS, driven by either the floppy controller card or the parallel port. Drivers for some of these tape drives are available for Linux, although not all of these tape drives are supported. Because many of these small QIC drives rely on proprietary compression schemes to boost data density on tapes, you may not be able to write more than the raw cartridge capacity to these drives. In general, if the QIC driver runs off the floppy disk controller card and is compatible with QIC-40 or QIC-80, it will work with Linux. QIC drives that run off the parallel port do not have a driver for Linux at this time.

CD-ROMs

Because most CD-ROMs use a SCSI interface, you need either a SCSI controller card or an interface on another card, such as a sound board. Linux recognizes and supports SCSI-based CD-ROMs as long as their SCSI controller cards are recognized. If the SCSI port is on a sound board, a special driver may be required. Some IDE CD-ROMs are also available; a driver is needed for them (some drivers are included with Linux). In addition, some proprietary CD-ROM drivers, such as those found on Sound Blaster sound boards, are supported with later versions of Linux. Check the supported hardware list available with each kernel release for a complete catalog of all supported CD-ROM drives. In general, the higher the kernel release number, the more likely a CD-ROM will be supported.

Linux can't read every format of CD-ROMs. At the present it handles only ISO-9660 format filesystems. Although ISO-9660 is widely used, not all CD-ROMs are written using it, so don't be surprised if a DOS or Macintosh CD-ROM can't be mounted properly. Some UNIX CD-ROMs are written with proprietary formats or with Rock Ridge extensions (which allow long filenames). These CD-ROMs are usually incompatible with Linux's requirements.

REMOVABLE MEDIA

Removable media support in Linux depends on the type of interface the media uses. Most SCSI-based systems can be used, although the changing of media while a filesystem is loaded is seldom properly supported. Iomega's Bernoulli systems and LaserSafe Pro magneto-optical cartridge systems can all be used with Linux without special drivers, as long as the cartridges can be formatted under DOS. Some other magneto-optical and removable magnetic media systems will also function properly.

Some removable media, especially those which do not use SCSI but rely on a dedicated hardware card, require special drivers. The very limited support in Linux for these devices is mostly provided by programmers who have written a driver for their own use and then made it public domain. No commercial removable media vendors are offering Linux-specific drivers at the moment, although this situation should change as Linux becomes widespread.

PRINTERS

Parallel and serial port printers are widely supported as dumb lineprinter devices. Although some drivers are available for specific popular printers, such as the Hewlett Packard LaserJets and DeskJets, many printers do not have dedicated drivers yet. If no driver exists for your printer, it will behave as an ASCII-only device.

There is no support at present for color printers, either laser, inkjet, or bubble-jet. A driver should be available for the most popular color printer models in the near future. Check the FTP and BBS sites (or the Linux WWW home pages) for more information.

MODEMS

Linux supports most serial asynchronous modems, as well as some synchronous modems. Support for ISDN modems is being developed as well. As a general rule, Linux can use any modem that DOS can use. Linux supports all baud rates, including the newer compression schemes, with some driver installation. More than one modem is supported on the system. Indeed, you can hang as many modems off a Linux system as you have serial ports.

TERMINALS

Linux supports character-based terminals connected through a serial port or a multiport card. You can use most existing character-based terminals, and you can add any terminal for which you have the control codes. Graphics terminals, in the UNIX sense, use simple ASCII graphic characters and are not X-capable.

Some versions of Linux support X terminals, although not all X terminals work properly. X terminals typically need a very high-speed connection to properly display graphics (either through a serial port or from a network). A PC running X client software can function as an X terminal as well.

MULTIPORT CARDS

Some UNIX-based multiport cards will work with Linux, as the vendor or users have released drivers. Before purchasing a multiport card, check the availability of drivers. Some multiport cards offer expansion parallel ports as well as serial ports, and these will also need drivers.

You can connect some multiport cards through a SCSI controller card instead of building them as dedicated cards that plug into expansion slots. Even SCSI-based expansion cards will need a driver for Linux to use them properly.

NETWORK CARDS

Because Linux is a UNIX system, its primary network protocol is TCP/IP. Other protocols can be used with Linux, but TCP/IP is the most widely used because it is included with each Linux software package and is the default network protocol. TCP/IP's role as the protocol of the Internet also makes it popular.

TCP/IP is usually used over Ethernet networks, so most of Linux's networking systems are designed around Ethernet. Many Ethernet network interface cards (NICs, also called network adapters) are available. The most popular Ethernet cards from 3Com, Novell, Western Digital, Hewlett Packard, and Intel all work cleanly with Linux. Many compatible Ethernet NICs from other vendors also function properly.

WHERE TO GET LINUX

Linux is freely available if you know where to look. Because Linux is distributed without a central organization controlling it (as with commercial UNIX versions), no single party is responsible for keeping Linux readily and easily available. You have to find a source and make sure the version you receive has all the components, is recent, and is relatively stable. Most distribution sources have the same releases available.

You can obtain a copy of Linux in several ways; use whichever method is most convenient or economical, depending on your priorities. The most common method of obtaining a complete set of Linux binaries and utilities is through a CD-ROM. Alternatives include FTP sites and BBSs (bulletin board systems). You can also get a copy mailed to you.

The method by which you obtain Linux also dictates to some extent how complete the distribution will be. CD-ROM versions, for example, usually have every piece of Linux software available included on the disk; in contrast, some BBSs and FTP sites offer only a small distribution that is enough to install and use as a basic system. The small systems, for example, may not include the language compilers and X software.

CD-ROMs

Almost a dozen CD-ROM based distributions of Linux are available. They differ in the version that is included on the disk, their organization, and the value-added features they have, such as new installation documents and utilities as well as supporting printed manuals. Of course, you also need a CD-ROM drive on your machine that will work with Linux. Don't assume that any non-SCSI CD-ROM drive will work—many of them won't!

The version you obtain should have a recent release of the Linux software (compare version numbers among CD-ROMs) as well as a complete set of accompanying utilities. It can be hard to identify the contents from the sparse identification on the cover of some CD-ROM collections, so you may find yourself unwittingly purchasing outdated material. Luckily, the CD-ROMs tend to be inexpensive. The CD-ROM included at the back of this book provides one of the most recent versions of Linux, along with many of the utilities and source libraries. With this CD-ROM, you won't need to buy another version until you want to upgrade to a later kernel.

A few vendors have dressed up their Linux collections with added utilities or boot disks that make installation much easier. The addition of precompiled games, applications, and user utilities makes these CD-ROMs a little more attractive. Some CD-ROMs also include an accompanying manual. For the most part, these manuals are simply printed versions of files on the CD-ROM, although some vendors have taken the time to write very readable instructions for Linux. If you are a newcomer to Linux, this type of document can be very useful.

FTP SITES

File Transfer Protocol (FTP) is a widely used Internet protocol (part of the TCP/IP family) that lets you transfer files from remote machines. Several anonymous FTP sites distribute Linux software. (Anonymous means you don't need an account on the remote machine to access the files; you log in as guest or anonymous and use your name or login as a password.) If you have access to the Internet, either directly or through an on-line service provider such as CompuServe, Delphi, or America Online, you can access the Linux distribution sites.

To use FTP, you must be on a machine that supports TCP/IP. This can be your existing PC running a DOS or Windows package that gives you FTP capabilities or a UNIX or Linux workstation that is connected to an Internet service. Both ends of an FTP connection must be running a program that provides FTP services. To download a file from a remote system, you must start your FTP software and instruct it to connect to the FTP software running on the remote machine.

The Internet has many FTP archive sites. These machines are designed to allow anyone to connect to them and download software. In many cases, FTP archive sites mirror each other so that they have exactly the same software. You connect to the site that is easiest to get to. See the section in this chapter called "Locating Linux FTP Archive Sites" for more information.

DOWNLOADING FILES FROM A LINUX FTP SITE

Using FTP to connect to a Linux FTP site is quite easy (assuming you have access to the Internet, of course). You must start FTP with the name of the remote system to which you want to connect. If you are directly connected to the Internet, enter the `ftp` command with the name of the remote site as shown in the following example:

```
ftp sunsite.unc.edu
```

If you are using an on-line service such as CompuServe or Delphi, you must access their Internet service and invoke FTP from there. Most on-line services let you to enter the name of the FTP site at a prompt.

When you issue the `ftp` command, your system attempts to connect to the remote machine. When it completes the connection successfully, the remote machine prompts you for a user ID. You must have a valid user ID and password for that system unless it supports anonymous FTP (which all Linux FTP sites do). If anonymous FTP is supported on the remote system, a message usually tells you that when you first connect.

The following login is for the Linux FTP archive site sunsite.unc.edu, one of the most popular sites:

```
ftp sunsite.unc.edu
331 Guest login ok, send your complete e-mail address as password.
Enter username (default: anonymous): anonymous
Enter password [tparker@tpci.com]:
¦FTP¦ Open
230-                WELCOME to UNC and SUN's anonymous ftp server
230-                        University of North Carolina
230-                       Office FOR Information Technology
230-                            SunSITE.unc.edu
230 Guest login ok, access restrictions apply.
FTP>
```

The login for an anonymous FTP site is usually guest or anonymous. The login message usually tells you which is used, or you can try both. The remote machine will prompt you for a password in most cases. You don't have to supply one with some systems, and others ask for your username or ID. This information is used for tracking purposes only and has no security problems associated with it (unless you don't have a password on your account!).

After the login process is finished, you see the prompt FTP>. This prompt indicates that the system is ready to accept FTP commands. Some systems display a short message when you log in that may contain instructions for downloading files as well as any restrictions that are placed on you as an anonymous FTP user. Other information may be displayed about the location of useful files. For example, you may see messages like this one from the FTP site sunsite.unc.edu:

```
To get a binary file, type:  BINARY and then: GET "File.Name" newfilename
To get a text file, type:    ASCII  and then: GET "File.Name" newfilename
Names MUST match upper, lower case exactly. Use the "quotes" as shown.
To get a directory, type: DIR. To change directory, type: CD "Dir.Name"
To read a short text file, type: GET "File.Name" TT
For more, type HELP or see FAQ in gopher.
To quit, type EXIT or Control-Z.

230- If you email to info@sunsite.unc.edu you will be sent help information
230- about how to use the different services sunsite provides.
230- We use the Wuarchive experimental ftpd. If you "get" <directory>.tar.Z
230- or <file>.Z it will compress and/or tar it on the fly. Using ".gz"  instead
230- of ".Z" will use the GNU zip (/pub/gnu/gzip*) instead, a superior
230- compression method.
```

Once you are on the remote system, you can use Linux (UNIX) commands to display file contents and move around directories. To display the contents of a directory, use the command ls or the DOS equivalent DIR. To change to a subdirectory, use the cd <dir> command. To return to the parent directory (the one above the current directory), use the command cd ... Unlike Linux, no keyboard shortcuts are available with FTP so you will have to type in the name of files or directories in their entirety (and correctly).

When you have moved through the directories and found a file you want to move back to your system, use the FTP get command, as shown in the following code:

```
get "file1.txt"
```

Tip

Although quotation marks around filenames are optional for most versions of FTP, they do provide specific characters to the remote version, thereby preventing shell expansion. Using quotation marks can prevent accidental transfers of many files instead of just one or error messages from FTP.

The commands get (download) and put (upload) are relative to your home machine, not to the remote. When you issue a get command, you are telling your system's FTP software to get a file from the remote machine. A put command tells FTP to put a file from your local machine onto the remote machine. Remember which command moves in which direction, or you could overwrite files accidentally.

When you issue a get command, the remote system transfers data to your local machine and displays a status message when it is completed. There is no indication of progress during transmission of a large file, so be patient. The following is a sample transcript of a get command:

```
FTP> get "file1.txt"
200 PORT command successful.
150 BINARY data connection for FILE1.TXT (27534 bytes)
226 BINARY Transfer complete.
27534 bytes received in 2.35 seconds (12 Kbytes/s).
```

FTP provides two modes of file transfer: ASCII (seven-bit characters) and Binary (eight-bit characters). Some systems automatically switch between the two, although it is a good idea to manually set the mode to ensure that you don't waste time. You must download all Linux distribution files in Binary mode. To set FTP in Binary transfer mode (for any executable file), type the command binary. You can toggle back to ASCII mode with the command ASCII. If you transfer a binary file in ASCII mode, it will not be executable. Transferring an ASCII file in Binary mode does not affect the contents of the file, so Binary is a good default transfer mode.

Bear in mind that the Linux archives are quite sizable, and transferring even a small distribution can take a while with asynchronous modems. If you use a slow modem (9,600 baud or less), you may want to consider an alternate method as you will have to stay connected for many hours. Some remote sites limit the amount of time you can stay connected. To quit FTP, type the command quit or exit. Both commands will close your session on the remote machine. Then terminate FTP on your local machine.

LOCATING LINUX FTP ARCHIVE SITES

The list of Linux FTP archive sites changes slowly, but the sites listed in this section were all valid and reachable when this book was written. Many of these sites are mirror sites, providing exactly the same contents. You can find the site nearest you by looking at the country identifier at the end of the site name (uk=United Kingdom, fr=France, and so on). If no country identifier is used, the site is probably in the U.S. With most versions of FTP, you can use either the site name or the IP address, although the IP address is the best addressing method if the local Internet gateway cannot resolve the site name. Make sure you enter the four components of the IP address correctly.

The primary sites (also called home sites) for the Linux FTP archives are tsx-11.mit.edu, sunsite.unc.edu, and nic.funet.fi. Home sites are where most of the new software loads begin. The majority of sites in the following list mirror one of these three sites. If you encounter difficulties connecting to a site, try another. If difficulties persist, there may be a problem with your access to the Internet.

Site name	IP Address	Directory
tsx-11.mit.edu	18.172.1.2	/pub/linux
sunsite.unc.edu	152.2.22.81	/pub/Linux
nic.funet.fi	128.214.6.100	/pub/OS/Linux
ftp.mcc.ac.uk	130.88.200.7	/pub/linux
fgbl.fgb.mw.tu-muenchen.de	129.187.200.1	/pub/linux
ftp.infdrrnatik.twmuenchen.de	131.159.0.110	/pub/Linux
ftp.dfv.rwth-aachen.de	137.226.4.105	/pub/linux
ftp.informatik.rwth-aachen.de	137.226.112.172	/pub/Linux
ftp.ibp.fr	132.227.60.2	/pub/linux
kirk.bu.oz.au	131.244.1.1	/pub/OS/Linux
ftp.uu.net	137.39.1.9	/systems/unix/ linux
wuarchive.wustl.edu	128.252.135.4	/systems/linux
ftp.win.tue.nl	131.155.70.100	/pub/linux
ftp.stack.urc.tue.nl	131.155.2.71	/pub/linux
ftp.ibr.cs.tu-bs.de	134.169.34.15	/pub/os/linux
ftp.denet.dk	129.142.6.74	/pub/OS/linux

WORLD WIDE WEB SITES

If you know how to use the World Wide Web (WWW) and have access to a Web server, you can obtain a copy of Linux from several Web sites, including those shown in Chapter 1. The primary FTP site offers Web access through the following URL:

```
http://sunsite.unc.edu/mdw/linux.html
```

Figure 2.1 shows the page on sunsite.unc.edu that enables you to download software through the World Wide Web browser. From this page, you can download new Linux source code and binaries. You can use any Web client software, such as Mosaic or Netscape, to access the Web site and use the menu-driven system to download a copy of the Linux files. The Web site also offers a documentation page.

Figure 2.1.
The sunsite.unc.edu
site is the primary
source for Linux
software.

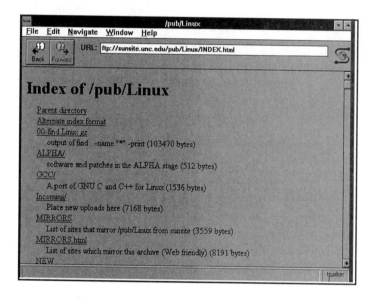

E-MAIL

If you don't have access to a Linux distribution site to FTP the software, you can still get the files transferred to you if you have a e-mail system that can reach a Linux site. This method is an alternative for those using on-line systems that allow Internet mail but do not allow direct access to FTP and those using some corporate systems that do not allow you to dial out directly to reach FTP sites but can transfer e-mail.

To get Linux by e-mail from an FTP site, use the site's ftpmail utility. All of the sites mentioned in the previous Linux FTP site list support ftpmail. To get complete instructions on using ftpmail, send an e-mail message to ftpmail login at one of the sites (for example, address your e-mail to ftpmail@sunsite.unc.edu). The body of the e-mail message should have only the word help in it. Any other comments may cause the ftpmail utility to incorrectly process your request. For this reason, you may want to suppress any signature files that are appended to your e-mail automatically.

Upon receiving your request, ftpmail sends you instructions for using the service. In most cases, you embed the FTP commands you want executed at the remote site as the body of your mail message. For example, to get a directory listing of the Linux directory, send a mail message with the following body:

```
open sunsite.unc.edu
cd /pub/Linux
ls
quit
```

The ftpmail utility at the remote site processes the commands as if they were typed directly into FTP. To transfer a file to yourself through e-mail, you could send the following mail message:

```
open sunsite.unc.edu
cd /pub/Linux
binary
get README
quit
```

This message sends you the file README back through e-mail. The ftpmail system is slower than FTP because you must wait for the e-mail to make its way to the target machine, be processed by the remote system's ftpmail utility, format a reply, and send the return message back to you. Still, ftpmail does provide a useful access method for those without FTP connections and an easy way to check the contents of the Linux directories on several machines without having to log in to them, which can be useful when you want to occasionally check for updates to the software.

Note The files you want to transfer may exceed your mail system's maximum file size limits. Some mail systems will break the files into smaller chunks and allow you to reassemble them when you receive them, but other e-mail systems impose a small size limit on e-mail, making it impractical to use ftpmail to get large files like the complete Linux software distribution.

BULLETIN BOARD SYSTEMS

Hundreds of BBSs around the world now provide access to the Linux distribution software and support Linux discussion groups. Some BBSs download new Linux releases regularly from the FTP home sites, while others rely on their users to update the software.

Any list of BBSs with Linux software would be lengthy and out of date quickly. The best method of obtaining this information is to request it from Zane Healy, who maintains a complete list of BBSs offering Linux material. Send e-mail requesting the Linux list to healyzh@holonet.net. If you don't have access to e-mail, try a few local bulletin board systems and post messages asking for local sites that offer Linux software, or ask someone with Internet access to post e-mail for you. Many BBSs will also have the list, although the accuracy of the list will vary.

LINUX RELEASES AND DISK SETS

A release is a collection of Linux software sufficient to install and run the entire operating system. The release is made up of a number of collections of software called a disk set (even though they may not come on disks). Most Linux systems have a number of disk sets included when you obtain the distribution set.

Although most of the CD-ROMs and FTP sites have the same software, a few label the disk sets differently. To illustrate the disk sets available with Linux, the following list details the current group of disk sets available with the Slackware distribution (one of the more popular CD-ROM versions of Linux and the one included with this book):

- Disk Set A is the base system. This set contains the kernel and a set of basic utilities including shell, editor, and user utilities. Disk Set A is the only disk set that fits on a single high-density floppy disk, which means you can use it to install and run Linux from a floppy disk.
- Disk Set AP contains Linux applications, including many different editors, all the standard UNIX command utilities, man pages, and GNU add-ons like GhostScript.
- Disk Set D contains software for program development. This disk set includes the GNU languages, development utilities, libraries, and compiler tools. There is also a lot of source code for libraries used to customize the Linux kernel.
- Disk Set E is the GNU emacs editor.
- Disk Set F contains FAQ (Frequently Asked Questions) files and other Linux help files.
- Disk Set N is networking software. This disk set includes the TCP/IP protocol set, UUCP, mail and other kinds of utilities, and a news system.
- Disk Set Q contains source files for the Linux kernel and boot images.
- Disk Set T contains the TeX and LaTeX2 test formatting systems. TeX is widely used for typesetting.
- Disk Set TCL1 is the Tcl language set, including Tcl, Tk, TclX, and utilities.
- Disk Set Y is a collection of games.
- Disk Set X is XFree86, which includes the X system and several window managers.
- Disk Set XAP contains applications for X, including file managers,

GhostView, libraries, games, and utilities.

- Disk Set XD is the X development kit, including X libraries, a server link kit, and PEX support. You must have this disk set if you are going to develop X-based applications.
- Disk Set XV is the window manager for X. This disk set includes the XView libraries and the Open Look window managers. You can use these window managers instead of the window manager included in Disk Set X.

Although Disk Set A will let you install a Linux system from a floppy disk, you should have Disk Sets A, AP, D, and F for a full installation (hard disk based with standard utilities). This collection gives you a character-based Linux system. If you want to run X, you also need Disk Sets X and XAP. Programmers need to load the development disk sets (D and XD, for X applications).

SUMMARY

This chapter examined the software and hardware that make up a Linux system. You should have hardware sufficient to run Linux before you start installing; otherwise, you will see all manner of error messages (if the system installs at all). Once you have the hardware ready and you know what software from the distribution set you are going to install, it's time to get Linux on a hard disk. The next chapter looks at the physical installation process. Chapter 4 covers LILO, the boot loader.

2

LINUX HARDWARE AND SOFTWARE

- Creating Boot and Root Disks

- Partitioning the Hard Disk

- Installing the Linux Partitions

- Installing the Linux Software

- Setting the Boot Process

- Viewing Installed Software Files

- Troubleshooting

CHAPTER 3

Installing and Updating Linux

You probably already have installed Linux. Even so, you may not be happy with the installation, either because of poor organization or because you were experimenting with it and would like to try again with a better configuration. This chapter discusses the issues you should address when you install Linux for the first time (or reinstall it, as the case may be) and how to update your existing Linux installation with new software releases.

The process for installing Linux is straightforward, although lots of little potential problems are scattered throughout the process. Don't believe the easy installation claims on many packages of the distribution software! Several steps require patience, experimentation, and a knowledge of what is going on before Linux will install painlessly. The essential steps for installing Linux are as follows:

1. Create boot and root disks for Linux.
2. Partition the hard disk.
3. Boot Linux from a floppy disk.
4. Create a swap file partition.
5. Create a Linux filesystem.
6. Install the Linux software.
7. Configure the kernel.
8. Set the boot process.
9. Reboot into Linux from your hard disk.

This chapter covers each of these steps in more detail. The process is very similar for installing from a CD-ROM and from a floppy disk (which may have come from an FTP site, for example). Because CD-ROM is the most common form of installation, this chapter uses that process as an example.

If you are installing from floppy disks and have downloaded the distribution files (or copied them from a CD-ROM), you will need a DOS-formatted floppy disk for each file in the distribution disk set. You can use standard DOS COPY commands to copy the disk set files to the floppy disks, using one floppy for each file in the distribution set. The files are all numbered so you know which floppy disk is in which set, and what their order should be.

CREATING BOOT AND ROOT DISKS

Even if you are installing from a CD-ROM, you need two high-capacity floppy disks (either 1.2M or 1.44M). These disks are the boot and root floppy disks. The boot floppy disk holds the kernel that is used to start Linux the first time, leading to your installation. The root floppy disk holds a small filesystem that includes utilities needed for the installation. The two disks together form a complete and very small implementation of Linux. Enough of a system is on the two floppy disks to play with Linux, although many of the utilities are missing.

In most cases, the boot and root floppy disks are copied from existing files called images. The image is a precompiled version of the system that you duplicate on the floppy disks, eliminating the need to start from scratch. CD-ROM and FTP distributions have directories for several boot and root images, depending on the hardware on your system. You must select the images that match your hardware as much as possible, copy them to the floppy disks, and start your system with the floppy disks. You can do most of these steps from DOS, although you can't use the DOS COPY command to create the boot and root floppy disks. You must create the floppy disks with a utility that ignores the DOS formatting. This utility, commonly called RAWRITE.EXE, is included with most Linux software distributions.

SELECTING A BOOT KERNEL AND ROOT IMAGE

CD-ROMs usually have directories under the root directory called bootdsks.144 and rootdsks.144 (for 3.5-inch 1.44M floppy disks) and bootdsks.12 and rootdsks.12 (for 5.25-inch 1.2M floppy disks), which contain the boot and root images, respectively. To find these directories, run DOS either from a floppy disk or a partition on your hard disk to examine the CD-ROM. The boot and root directories for 1.44M floppy disks from a typical CD-ROM Linux distribution are shown in Figure 3.1. If you are copying your files from an FTP site, you can select the boot and root images you need while connected to the remote FTP machine and transfer only the images you need to your local machine.

Figure 3.1.
The boot and root
directory entries for
1.44M floppy disk
images, which are used
to create the boot and
root floppy disks needed
to install Linux.

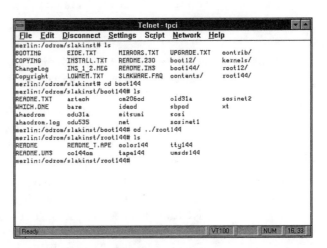

The types of boot kernels usually available are described in a file in the kernel image directories (usually called README, READ.ME, or WHICH.ONE). The boot kernel images are named to reflect the hardware for which they have drivers installed into the kernel. For example, the scsi kernel image has drivers in the kernel for SCSI-based systems; if you are on a PC that has a SCSI controller, hard disk, and CD-ROM, this is the image you want to copy to your boot floppy disk. The number of boot images available is quite large. These are the primary images available from most CD-ROMs and FTP sites and the hardware they are designed to handle:

aztech	IDE and SCSI hard disk drivers, and Aztech non-IDE CD-ROM support, including Aztech, Okana, Orchid, and Wearnes non-IDE CD-ROM drives
bare	IDE hard disk drivers only (no CD-ROM support)
cdu31a	IDE and SCSI hard disk drivers, with a Sony CDU31 or Sony CDU33a CD-ROM drive
cdu535	IDE and SCSI hard disk drivers, with a Sony 535 or Sony 531 CD-ROM drive
idecd	IDE and SCSI hard disk drivers, with IDE or ATAPI CD-ROM drive
mitsumi	IDE and SCSI hard disk drivers, with a Mitsumi CD-ROM drive
net	IDE hard disk drivers and Ethernet network card drivers
sbpcd	IDE and SCSI hard disk drivers with Sound Blaster Pro or Panasonic CD-ROM drivers. This image is for CD-ROM drives run off a Sound Blaster card (as supplied in many Sound Blaster multimedia kits).
scsi	IDE and SCSI hard drivers with SCSI peripherals (CD-ROM drives)
scsinet1	IDE and SCSI hard disk drivers, SCSI CD-ROM driver, and Ethernet drivers for networking. The SCSI drivers support Adaptec 152X, 1542, 1740, 274x, and 284x adapters, Buslogic adapters, EATA-DMA adapters (such as DPT, NEC, and AT&T cards), Seagate ST-02 adapters, and Future Domain TCC-8xx and 16xx adapters. SCSI adapters compatible with any of these cards will also work.
scsinet2	IDE and SCSI hard disk drivers, SCSI CD-ROM driver, and Ethernet drivers for networking. The SCSI drivers support NCR5380-based adapters, NCR 53C7 and 8xx adapters, Always IN2000 adapter, Pro Audio Spectrum 16 adapter, Qlogic adapter, Trantor T128, T128F, and T228 adapters, Ultrastor adapters, and the 7000 FASST adapters. Compatibles of any of these cards should also work.
xt	IDE and IBM PC-XT-compatible hard disk drivers

With some distributions, an extension is added to the kernel image name to indicate the floppy disk type. For example, if the kernel image is for a 1.44M floppy disk, it will have the filetype .144 as part of the name. Similarly, a filetype of .12 indicates a 1.2M image. You cannot interchange these images, or the diskette will be useless (in other words you cannot load a .12 image onto a 1.44M diskette). Most distributions don't bother with this convention, since the files are in the appropriate directories for the floppy disk size.

You have fewer choices for the root floppy image. Most distributions include four basic images, although a few more esoteric images also appear from time to time. Each of the root images has the disk size as part of its name (color144 and color12, for example). The basic root floppy images are the following:

◆ The color image offers a full-screen color-based installation script for installing Linux.

◆ The tape image is designed to support Linux installation from a cartridge tape. This kernel has limited functionality and depends on the type of tape drive used. Typically, QIC drives are supported, but users of some models have reported problems.

◆ The tty image is a dumb terminal installation version with no color or graphics.

◆ The umsdos image is used to install UMSDOS, which allows you to install Linux into an existing MS-DOS partition. The installation script creates the subdirectories it needs. UMSDOS is not as efficient or fast as a dedicated Linux partition, but you can retain your current disk partitions.

Tip

> The color root image is a lot more attractive than the tty image and can make the Linux installation a bit friendlier. The color image is intolerant of typing errors and doesn't always proceed smoothly, however. It's worth a try, in most cases, unless you know exactly how you want to install Linux. The color process tends to require much more user interaction, including clicking OK buttons at many stages.

Once you have determined which of the boot and root images you will use (if you are not sure, pick the boot image that most closely matches your hardware configuration and the color or tty root image), you can create the boot and root floppy disks. If you choose the boot and root images incorrectly, don't worry. All that will happen is that you won't be able to install Linux, and you'll have to start the process again.

CREATING THE BOOT AND ROOT FLOPPY DISKS

You can create the boot and root floppy disks either from DOS or from UNIX (or Linux). If you don't run DOS yet, and don't have a DOS boot disk, you will have to use another machine to create the two floppy disks. Because creating the floppy disk from DOS is the most common method, this section deals with this method first.

To create the boot and root floppy disks, you must use a utility program to write the image to floppy disk. If you obtained your boot and root images from an FTP or BBS site, the files may be compressed and archived. If they are, they will end with the filetype .gz. Before you can install the images to a floppy disk, you must decompress them with the gzip utility. If you are working from a CD-ROM, you will have to copy the files to a DOS hard disk because you can't write the decompressed image to the CD-ROM. Even if you start with decompressed files, it may be easier to copy the images to a temporary DOS directory as it will save you the hassle of worrying about directory pathnames.

To decompress a .gz file, issue the command

```
gzip -d <filename>
```

where filename is the name of the compressed file (including the .gz extension). The -d option tells gzip to decompress the file. After the file is decompressed, the .gz file is erased and only the decompressed file remains (with the same filename, without the .gz extension). To decompress the scsi.144 and color144 images, for example, you would issue the following commands:

```
gzip -d scsi.gz
gzip -d color144.gz
```

To write the images to the two floppy disks, you need two high-density floppy disks and the RAWRITE utility. The two floppy disks don't have to be blank, as the RAWRITE utility doesn't respect DOS file formats (although the disk must be formatted). The two floppy disks must be high density, though. You can mix disk types (in other words, you can use a 1.2M boot floppy disk and 1.44M root floppy disk) with some distributions of Linux, although it's not recommended for most systems. Keeping everything the same disk size is a lot easier. The disks must be formatted using DOS' FORMAT program. The boot floppy disk must be the correct size for your system's boot floppy disk drive (A: in DOS terms).

RAWRITE is a DOS program that writes the images, block-by-block, to the floppy disk. To use the RAWRITE program, just enter its name. RAWRITE prompts you for the name of the file to copy and the destination drive letter. RAWRITE will then copy the images. Once the process is completed, DOS cannot read the floppy disk. Label the disks as the boot and root floppy disks for convenience.

If you have access to a UNIX or Linux system, you can create the boot disks from within that operating system. You will need to put the two image files on the UNIX or Linux system, and use the dd utility to copy them to the floppy disks. This is also the procedure to follow if you are upgrading your existing Linux system to a newer release. First, make sure the images are decompressed (no .gz extension). If they are not, decompress them with the UNIX gunzip utility (a GNU utility that you may have to obtain from another source, if it's not included with your distribution). To decompress files in UNIX or Linux, issue the command

```
gunzip <filename>
```

where filename is the name of the image file with a .gz extension. The gunzip utility erases the compressed file and leaves a decompressed version in its place.

To copy the images to a floppy disk, you need to know the device name of the floppy drive within the operating system. For most systems, the first floppy drive is /dev/fd0, and the second floppy drive is /dev/fd1. (Some systems treat the floppy drives as raw devices, which have the names /dev/rfd0 and /dev/rfd1.) Copy the image files to the floppy disks with the command

```
dd if=<filename> of=/dev/fd0 obs=18k
```

where filename is the name of the decompressed image. The dd command converts file formats. The if and of parts of the command indicate the input and output filenames of devices. The obs portion of the command indicates the output block size (in this case, 18K).

For example, to copy the scsi and color144 images to the first floppy drive (3.5-inch 1.44M), issue the following two commands:

```
dd if=scsi of=/dev/fd0 obs=18k
dd if=color144 of=/dev/fd0 obs=18k
```

Linux is particularly stubborn about telling you your progress, so you won't see many messages. When dd starts the copy, it tells you how many blocks it will move. When it finishes, it returns the shell prompt to you without any message (unless the procedure failed). Figure 3.2 shows the command for copying the root kernel scsi to a floppy disk. After you copy both the root and boot kernels, you have completed this stage of the installation. The two floppy disks are now ready to boot a minimum Linux system for you.

3

Installing and Updating Linux

Figure 3.2.
You can use the dd
command to copy the
boot and root images to
floppy disk from any
Linux or UNIX system.

Partitioning the Hard Disk

Hard disks are divided into partitions, which are areas dedicated to an operating system. A hard disk can have up to four primary partitions, with some partitions being divided into more logical drives by the operating system software. A more complete discussion of partitions is in Chapter 4, "LILO."

If you are running Linux from a DOS partition using the UMSDOS root image, you don't have to worry about repartitioning your drives. Your existing drive's partitions will be used. However, because UMSDOS is a poor filesystem compared to Linux's, you will probably want to create your own Linux partitions. Check the later section "Using UMSDOS" for information on setting up UMSDOS.

Linux prefers two partitions: one for the Linux swap space and one for the Linux software filesystem itself. The swap space is used as an extension of your machine's physical RAM and can be quite small. Technically, you don't need a swap partition, especially if you have lots of RAM, but it is a very good idea to create one anyway as your system can grind to a halt suddenly if RAM is exhausted. The Linux filesystem partition tends to be quite large, as it must hold all the Linux software. You can have several Linux filesystem partitions to hold utilities, applications, and user files, although one partition must be designated as the boot partition (where the kernel and primary utilities are located).

If you are using a hard disk that has an operating system already installed on it, you will have to repartition your hard disk to make room for Linux. This process will destroy anything already on your hard disk, so make backups of any existing data you want to keep!

You use the `fdisk` utility to partition a hard disk. The Linux version of `fdisk` does the same task as FDISK in DOS, although the menus are completely different (and much more complicated). Many PC-based UNIX systems also use `fdisk` to partition hard drives.

Note

> A DOS utility called FIPS sometimes allows non-destructive changes to your partitions, assuming no data is on the areas that will be repartitioned. FIPS is available from many sources, including most of the Linux FTP sites and on some Linux CD-ROMs. However, you should make backups, just in case.

You must decide how much space to allocate to the different partitions before you start, as changing your mind later will mean destroying all the data you have saved to disk. The Linux swap space partition size depends on the amount of RAM in your system, the number of users you expect, and the type of development you will do.

If you are going to maintain a DOS partition on the same disk, you will have to balance the disk space requirements of both operating systems against your total disk capacity. A minimum Linux filesystem partition will be about 20M, although closer to 100M is needed for a full X-based installation.

Determining the Size of the Linux Swap Space Partition

How big should the swap space partition be? No single number works for all installations, unfortunately. Generally, because the swap space is used as an extension of physical RAM, the more RAM you have, the less swap space is required. Add the amount of swap space and the amount of RAM together to get the amount of RAM Linux will use. For example, if you have 8M of RAM on your machine's motherboard and a 16M swap space partition, Linux will behave as though you had 24M RAM.

Linux uses the swap space by moving pages of physical RAM to the swap space when it doesn't need them, and moving them back again when it needs the memory pages. Why not make a very large swap space and let Linux think it's in heaven? The swap space is much slower in access time than RAM, and there is a point at which the size of the swap space starts to act against your Linux system's efficiency instead of for it. In addition, most versions of Linux have an upper limit of 16M for each swap partition. Those versions of Linux will, however, let you partition more than 16M to a swap space, but it will only use the first 16M. If needed, though, you can create multiple swap partitions. Up to eight swap partitions can exist, each up to 16M in size. The latest versions of Linux allow swap partitions larger than 16M, but it is wise to keep that size as a guide.

You may not even need swap space if you have lots of RAM. For example, if you have 16M of physical RAM and don't intend to do any application development or run X, you probably won't make much use of the swap space because Linux can fit everything it needs in the 16M. (You still should have a small swap space, just in case.) If you are running X, developing applications, or running memory-hog applications like databases, swap space is crucial even if you have lots of physical RAM. Even 16M RAM is not enough for X, so you need swap space.

A good rule is to create a swap space with the maximum size limit of 16M. Unless you have a very small capacity hard disk, a swap space of this size won't be a major drain on your resources, and it gives Linux plenty of space with which to work. If you don't want to allocate this much space, a good rule is to have a total of 16M RAM (swap space plus physical RAM). Don't eliminate the swap space completely, though, even if you have a lot of RAM. At a minimum, set up a 4M swap space. Running out of RAM can cause Linux to lock up or crash.

Once a swap space partition has been created, it is just like any other partition on the hard drive. If you want to change its size, you have to remove the existing partition and create a new one, although the space must be contiguous on the hard drive (which can be difficult to do if you have used all the space the drive offers for other partitions).

SETTING UP PARTITIONS

You use the fdisk utility to set up the partitions on your hard disk. Remember that fdisk will destroy existing data on your disk! You can set up your Linux disk partitions either from DOS or from within Linux. It really doesn't matter which approach you use, although the DOS FDISK program is a little easier to use than Linux's. If you are using DOS FDISK to repartition a DOS area on your drives, use it to set up the Linux swap space and filesystem partitions, too.

To set up partitions for Linux, remove any existing partitions first (unless you want to keep them as they are). If you intend to use DOS on the same system as Linux, DOS should be the first partition on the disk so it can boot. (You can use LILO to get by this restriction, but it is still a good rule to leave DOS as the first partition.) If you are keeping an existing DOS partition on your hard drive, leave the first partition as DOS if you can.

Create a DOS boot disk that can reformat and transfer the DOS kernel to the hard drive, regardless of whether you are leaving an existing DOS partition or creating a new one. To create the boot disk, use the DOS

```
format a: /s
```

command (assuming A: is the drive the disk is in). The /s option transfers the operating system kernel. Next, copy the utilities FDISK, FORMAT, SYS, and CHKDSK to the boot disk. You should also copy an editor such as EDIT (which requires the QBASIC files as well), and your existing CONFIG.SYS and AUTOEXEC.BAT files (although you could rename them). This disk will let you format any new DOS partitions. Alternatively, if you are starting from scratch with a new DOS partition, you can reload DOS from the original floppy disks when ready to format the DOS partition.

If you are removing an existing DOS partition and recreating a smaller one (as you would if your entire disk was DOS before Linux came into your life), follow these steps (after making a backup of your DOS data):

1. Remove the existing DOS partition.
2. Create a new primary DOS partition as the first partition.
3. Make the DOS partition active.
4. Reboot the system from your boot disk (or DOS disks).
5. Format the DOS partition and transfer the DOS kernel (COMMAND.COM).
6. Restore your backup files to the DOS partition. (You can do this step at anytime).

Next, set up the Linux swap space partition by creating a partition of the proper size. You can do this step either from DOS or when you have booted Linux from the boot and root floppy disks. The rest of this section assumes that you are setting up the partitions from DOS, although the process is the same either way.

Most versions of FDISK allow you to enter the size of the partition in megabytes, with the utility calculating the sector numbers that apply to it. Set the size of the Linux swap space to whatever size you decided, up to a maximum of 16M. Don't make the partition active or format it! You can set up the swap space partition in an extended disk partition, but a primary partition is a better choice if your disk can support it.

Finally, create the Linux filesystem partition to be whatever size you want; you can even make it the size of the rest of the disk if that's the only partition missing. Again, don't activate or format the partition. When you are running the Linux installation routine, you will identify and format the swap space and filesystem partitions properly.

USING UMSDOS

UMSDOS allows you to use an existing DOS partition to house your Linux system. However, since you will be forcing Linux to use the DOS disk layout, you will suffer some performance limitations compared to creating a dedicated Linux partition. On the other hand, using UMSDOS lets you keep your disk drive the way it is, preventing the hassle of repartitioning and reformatting your drive. It is also a fast and easy way to install Linux if you only want to experiment for a while before installing a full system.

Note that UMSDOS does not let you run DOS and Linux at the same time. UMSDOS (UNIX in MS-DOS) only creates the Linux filesystem under the DOS formatted partition, although the partition is modified to allow long filenames, Linux file permissions, and more. When you start the system, you still have to choose between booting Linux or DOS as the operating system. If you start DOS, you can't use the extended Linux filenames, although you will be able to snoop around the directories. Filenames may not make much sense because of the contraction from long Linux filenames to DOS-compatible filenames, though.

The only limitation about UMSDOS is that the DOS filesystem is not designed as well as the Linux filesystem, so you get some performance degradation. This problem isn't major because most people don't notice the difference unless they are running a file-intensive application like X or compiling programs. You can always start with UMSDOS; then if you decide you like Linux enough, back up the Linux data and repartition the drive to create a true Linux filesystem.

If you want to use UMSDOS, you have to perform a few extra steps when setting up the disk. You must still create the boot and root disks, although you will need a root image that supports UMSDOS. (Most distributions have the root images umsds144 and umsds12 for this purpose.) When you boot Linux and it asks which partition to use for the filesystem, you specify the DOS partition. UMSDOS then initializes the filesystem for you. After that, the procedure for installing the rest of Linux is the same as it is for a dedicated Linux partition.

INSTALLING THE LINUX PARTITIONS

The Linux installation process starts when you boot your system from the boot floppy disk. After the kernel has loaded, you will be prompted to remove the boot floppy disk and insert your root floppy disk. When the root filesystem has been read, you either will be sent directly to an installation script or presented with the login prompt. Log in as root. No password is required, because you haven't yet added one to the system.

The first step is to set up the disk partitions, if you haven't already done so, using fdisk. If you have more than one hard drive, you can place your Linux partitions on either drive. If you are planning on keeping a DOS partition, though, make sure that partition is the first partition on the first drive. Linux isn't so picky. If you want to boot Linux cleanly, place a Linux filesystem on the first drive. You can also create Linux filesystems on the second drive. A Linux swap partition can be on either drive, although keeping it on the first drive with the first filesystem is a good idea.

LINUX'S *FDISK*

Linux's fdisk program is different than the one in DOS, so check the menus frequently to determine the proper commands. You invoke Linux's fdisk in the same manner as DOS'. If you don't specify a drive, fdisk assumes the first one in the system. Otherwise, you can specifically indicate which disk drive to partition by giving the device name on the command line, as in

```
fdisk /dev/hdb
```

which invokes fdisk for the second drive. If your system has IDE, ESDI, or RLL drives, the first drive is /dev/hda and the second is /dev/hdb. SCSI drives are /dev/sda, /dev/sdb, and so on. Because a single controller can support seven SCSI drives, you could have up to /dev/hdg. (You can go even higher with another controller card, but few Linux systems will require that many drives!)

Warning

You should not use Linux's fdisk utility to create partitions for operating systems other than Linux. If, for example, you want a DOS partition on your disk, create it with DOS' FDISK. Linux does not write the partition table properly for other operating systems.

As mentioned earlier, Linux's fdisk commands are different than the FDISK commands for DOS. The following list explains the commands you need to run Linux's fdisk utility:

Command	Action
d	Deletes an existing partition
l	Lists all known partition types
n	Creates a new partition
p	Displays the current partition table
q	Quits fdisk without saving changes
t	Changes a partition's type code
v	Verifies the partition table
w	Writes the current partition table to disk and exits

Linux's fdisk utility offers quite a few more commands, as Figure 3.3 shows. This screen is the output from the Linux fdisk help (m) command. Note the warning at the top of the screen. This warning is issued whenever your hard drive has more than 1,024 cylinders, which early versions of Linux (pre 1.0 kernels mostly) couldn't support. Later versions of Linux, including the version provided on this book's CD-ROM, all support much larger hard drives. The warning is a holdover from the earlier system and should really be taken out.

Figure 3.3.
Linux's fdisk *utility*
offers these commands.

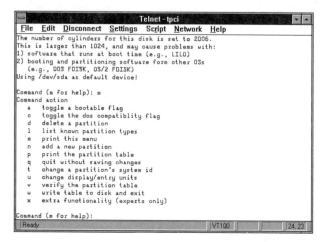

The process for setting up a partition is to first examine the partition table to make sure any existing partitions are correct. If you have a DOS partition on your drive, it should show in the partition table. If you created Linux swap and filesystem partitions when you were in DOS' FDISK, they should appear in the partition table too, although the partitions' types will be incorrect.

SETTING UP LINUX PARTITIONS

To create the Linux swap space partition, use the n command and give the starting sector number. Usually, this number will be immediately after any existing DOS partition (or other operating systems you have installed). Linux's fdisk lets you specify the size of the partition either by supplying an end sector number or by giving a size in megabytes (remember the swap space size has a practical maximum of 16M). If you give the size in megabytes, the format is usually +XXM, where XX is the number of megabytes (such as +16M). You can also specify kilobytes, but you don't want to create a swap partition that is less than 1M.

Note

Most PC BIOSs cannot handle more than 1,024 cylinders on a disk drive. You may not be able to create DOS or Linux partitions or filesystems that go beyond the 1,023th cylinder (numbering starts at zero). Some other operating systems, such as SCO UNIX, allow you to use anything beyond the 1,024 limit. Linux can use partitions beyond the 1,024 limit, but it can't boot from them. If you have a disk drive that has more than 1,023 cylinders, make sure your primary Linux partition ends before 1,023. You can create extra partitions following that cylinder and mount them as second filesystems. Alternatively, you can create a single large Linux filesystem that extends or starts beyond the 1,023rd cylinder and use a LILO boot floppy disk.

The `fdisk` program asks you whether you want to create a primary or an extended partition. If you are creating a primary partition, the program wants the number (one to four—remember a DOS partition has to be number one to boot). In most cases, you should create only primary partitions, unless you have a large disk drive. You can use extended partitions to add logical drives inside primary partitions, which is similar to the way DOS creates logical drives. In Linux, extended partitions are not the same as extended filesystems!

Note

Some distributions of Linux issue the message `Warning: Linux can't currently use X sectors of this partition`. This warning was in early versions of Linux that couldn't handle filesystems larger than 64K and can be ignored.

After you have created the Linux partition, assign it a type. Some versions of `fdisk` prompt for this information right away, and others let you select the option to assign filesystem types from the `fdisk` menu. In either case, pressing the letter l will display all known filesystem types. Choose the one that designates a Linux swap space (number 82), and check the partition table. Figure 3.4 shows the filesystem types supported by the version of Linux included with this book. As you can see, many filesystem types are allowed, although most users will only use the DOS, Linux swap, and Linux data types. The other filesystem types were included in earlier versions of Linux for compatibility with other operating systems.

Figure 3.4.
The filesystem types
supported by Linux,
identified by type
number and descrip-
tion.

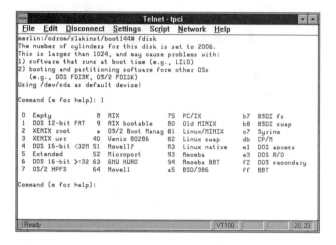

Your Linux swap space partition should have the correct size and partition type when you display the partition table with the p command. Although Linux doesn't care about the partition type numbers, some other operating systems do note them, so it's a good practice to label them correctly in order to prevent future problems. This practice also helps you keep the partition table organized.

Next, create your primary Linux filesystem partition in the same manner. If you want to use the rest of the disk drive for that partition, you can enter the end sector number of your drive (Linux's fdisk will tell you the range you can use). This number would be the usual default if your hard drive has a DOS, Linux swap space, and Linux filesystem partition on it. After you have created the Linux filesystem partition, identify its filetype as 82, which is a Linux native type. You can display the partition table at any time with the p command (inside fdisk only). Figure 3.5 shows a partition table set up on a 2.4G SCSI hard drive (/dev/sda), which has 500M for DOS (/dev/sda1), a 16M Linux swap space partition (/dev/sda2), and the rest of the drive for Linux data (/dev/sda3).

Make a note of the size of the swap space and filesystem partitions, in blocks, as you will need this information later. You can read this information straight from the partition table. After you create the Linux partitions and are satisfied with the partition table layout, save and exit fdisk. Make sure you write the table to disk with the w command. If you don't save the information, you will have to repeat the process again.

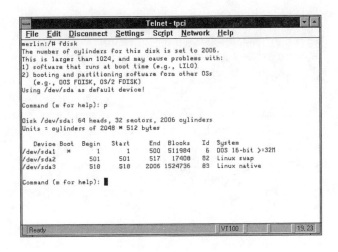

*Figure 3.5.
A completed partition
table with DOS and
Linux sharing a large
(2.4G) drive.*

ENABLING THE SWAP SPACE FOR INSTALLATION

Linux's installation routine requires a good chunk of RAM to proceed. If you have 4M of RAM or less, you will have problems installing Linux unless you have the kernel use the swap space partition. (If you have only 4M or less of RAM in your system, you should have a swap space of at least 8M, preferably 16M.) If you try to install Linux and get memory error messages, your system doesn't have enough RAM and the kernel needs to use the swap space. Even if you have lots of RAM, there's no reason not to enable the swap space now. To enable the swap space, issue the command

```
mkswap -c partition size
```

where `partition` is the name of the partition and `size` is the size of the partition in blocks. If you didn't make a note of this number earlier when setting up the partition table, you can start `fdisk` again and read the size in blocks from the partition table display.

For example, if you have set up the Linux swap space on partition /dev/hda2 (the second primary partition on the first non-SCSI drive) and it has a size of 13,565 blocks you would issue the command

```
mkswap -c /dev/hda2 13565
```

The `-c` option in the command line tells the `mkswap` utility to format the partition and check it for bad blocks. This option slows down the creation of the swap partition a little, but a bad block in the swap partition can cause your entire system to crash. If `mkswap` finds any errors in the swap space, it will generate an error message and mark the block as unusable by the operating system (the block is removed from the total available for swap space). Because mkswap flags bad blocks to be left alone, you can ignore the bad block messages unless there is a considerable number of them (ten or more is a good limit in a 16M partition), in which case your hard drive has too many bad blocks and you should consider either low-level formatting it or replacing it with a new drive.

After you set up the swap partition, you enable the Linux swap space partition with the swapon command. Usually, you have to specify the partition, although some versions use the partition table to figure out the partition automatically. It never hurts to be explicit, though. To enable the swap partition in the preceding example, you would enter the command

```
swapon /dev/hda2
```

You have to repeat the mkswap and swapon commands for each swap partition, if you created more than one. As soon as you execute the swapon command, the Linux kernel starts to use the new swap space as an extension of the physical RAM. Figure 3.6 shows a swap partition called /dev/sda2 (second partition on the first SCSI drive) being set up and activated. Note that you need to know the size of the partition in blocks. You get this number from the fdisk utility.

Figure 3.6.
Setting up and activat-
ing a swap partition on
/dev/sda2.

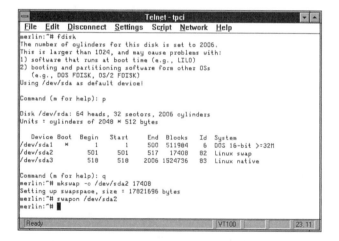

> ## Note
>
> If you've turned on the swap space and still get error messages when you try to install Linux, you need either more physical RAM or a larger swap space. Increasing the swap space now and then installing Linux is better than having to redo it later. To increase the size of a swap space partition, you may have to remove the existing Linux partitions and recreate them with fdisk.

CREATING THE LINUX FILESYSTEM PARTITION

Once you have a swap space configured and working, you can set up the Linux filesystem. Some Linux installation scripts automate this step, or you may have to execute it yourself. Either way, this section explains what is going on.

You have already allocated the partition table to support a Linux filesystem. Now you can create the filesystem with the mkfs (make filesystem) command. The exact format of the command depends on the type of filesystem you are setting up. The most popular filesystem (for reasons of speed and flexibility) is called the Second Extended filesystem (which has nothing to do with extended partitions on a hard disk). To create a Second Extended filesystem, issue the command

```
mke2fs -c <partition> <size>
```

where partition is the device name and size is the size of the partition in blocks (taken from the partition display in fdisk). For example, to create a filesystem in /dev/hda3 that is 162,344 blocks in size, the command would be

```
mke2fs -c /dev/hda3 162344
```

Note

When specifying the size of a partition, make sure you use blocks and not sectors or cylinders. Using the wrong value will result in errors or only a fraction of your partition being used.

The mke2fs utility checks the partition for bad blocks (the -c option), and then sets the filesystem up properly in that partition. If you are setting up a large partition, the disk check can take a few minutes, but you should not skip it unless you know your disk is good.

The other filesystems available to Linux are the Xia filesystem, the Extended filesystem, and the Minix filesystem. The Xia filesystem is good, but not as popular as the Second Extended filesystem. The Extended filesystem is an older version of Second Extended, and the Minix filesystem is compatible with the old Minix operating system (which Linux was written to replace). You can create these filesystems with the following commands:

Extended	mkefs
Minix	mkfs
Xia	mkxfs

All three commands take the same arguments as the Second Extended filesystem command. The Minix filesystem is limited to 64M. None of the mkfs commands format the filesystem; they just set it up. You are prompted for a filesystem format during the installation process.

INSTALLING THE LINUX SOFTWARE

After you create and format the partitions and create the filesystems, you can install the Linux software. This step may be automated, depending on the installation procedure included with your Linux distribution. Most versions of Linux include a utility called setup that installs the software for you. From the Linux prompt, type the command

```
setup
```

If you are running the color root image, you get graphic, full-screen windows for the installation process. Other root images use character-based installation messages instead. Many users who install Linux frequently avoid the color root image because it can take a little longer to answer all the questions the script poses and some typing errors are difficult to correct. Whichever root image you choose, carefully read each screen.

The setup utility supplied with the Linux system on this book's CD-ROM is shown in Figure 3.7. Some minor variations in menu choices exist between versions of Linux, but the primary options are much the same.

Figure 3.7.
The most common
setup utility menu.

Linux presents you with many choices during the installation. Although the default choices are correct for most people, check that the default is what you want. You have the option of letting Linux install everything without your prompting, except when disk sets change, but you should use this option only if you know exactly what is going on your disk. If you are installing Linux for the first time or want to choose the software to be installed by examining descriptions of each package, use the verbose options to show all messages and let you control the process.

SELECTING THE SOURCE AND DISK SETS

The `setup` installation script either asks you or lets you set several pieces of information. First, you need to specify the source of the software. You can usually accomplish this step by by selecting Source from the `setup` menu when `setup` starts its automatic installation process. If you have a CD-ROM, it should have been activated during the boot process if the drivers were correct for your hardware. Select the CD-ROM option. You may be asked to further narrow down the type of CD-ROM you have on your system. Choose the exact type(or the one closest to it) and hope for the best. If you are installing from another disk drive partition (such as another Linux partition or a DOS partition), provide the full device and pathnames. Figure 3.8 shows the Source option choices presented from the `setup` menu. From here, you can select CD-ROM. If Linux didn't identify your CD-ROM drive when it booted, you may be presented with another screen and asked to choose the type of CD-ROM drive your system has.

Figure 3.8.
The Source option on
the setup menu lets you
select where the Linux
software will be read
from.

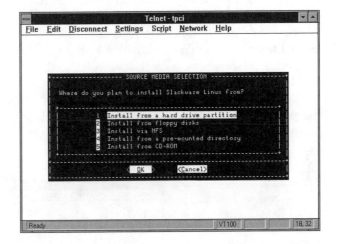

The installation program then asks for the target of the installation. The target is where you want the software to be installed. The newly created Linux partition is probably the location you want, so enter the partition's name. You will probably be asked whether you want to format that partition; answer `yes`. (Running `mkfs` or its variants does not format the partition for you.)

Next, Linux displays a list of the disk sets you can install. You may get to this screen through the normal installation process, or you can select Disk Sets from the `setup` menu. Choose the ones you want. The list of disk sets is usually a scrolling window, as shown in Figure 3.9. Make sure you scroll through the entire list and mark the disk sets you want to install.

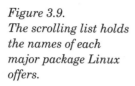

Figure 3.9.
The scrolling list holds
the names of each
major package Linux
offers.

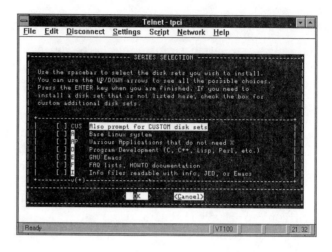

Some setup versions let you further refine the list of utilities when the disk set is installed. As a last step, verify the information, and then let Linux install itself. If this process doesn't start automatically, choose the Install option from the setup menu. Linux may double-check with you that you want to install the disk sets you've selected. This screen message looks similar to the one shown in Figure 3.10. This is your last chance to change your mind before Linux starts copying files to your hard drive. After you tell Linux to go ahead and install the software, watch for messages and prompts, and follow any on-screen instructions. If you are installing from a floppy disk, you will be prompted at intervals to change to the next disk in the disk set.

Figure 3.10.
The Linux installation
routine usually stops
and prompts you before
it starts installing
software.

As Linux installs software, it displays status screens like the one shown in Figure 3.11 whenever the disk set is changed. As each piece of software in a disk set is installed, its name, size, and a brief description is often displayed, as shown in Figure 3.12. Occasionally, you will be asked to choose whether to install a particular component, as shown in Figure 3.13. Choosing yes installs the package described on the screen; choosing no (use the scroll key to display the no option) skips that package and moves to the next.

Figure 3.11.
As Linux installs each selected disk set, setup displays the letter of the set. The e set being installed here is the GNU Emacs editor.

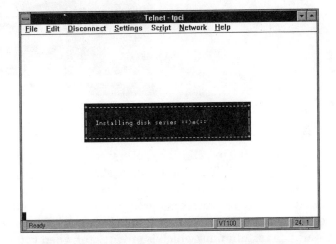

Figure 3.12.
Each package in a disk set that is installed by default is displayed in a status message, along with the size and brief description of the package.

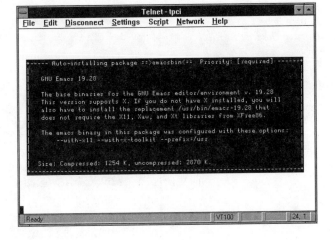

Figure 3.13.
Some disk sets contain
optional components.
When one is encoun-
tered, you are presented
with a screen like this
one that describes the
package and asks
whether you want to
install it.

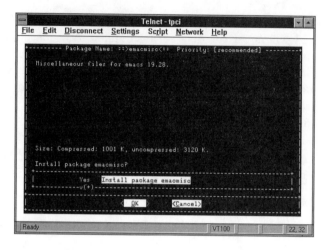

CREATING A BOOT DISK

At the end of the installation routine, you may be prompted as to whether you want to create a boot disk. Figure 3.14 shows this screen from the Linux CD-ROM included with this book. The boot disk enables you to access the system at any time, especially if the normal boot process fails. You should always make a boot disk for emergency purposes. This disk is not the same as the boot floppy disk you made to start the installation (which is only useful when you reinstall from scratch).

Figure 3.14.
During the installation
process, setup may ask
you whether you want
to create a boot disk.

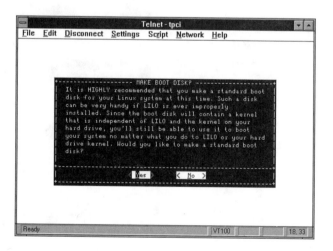

When you choose to create a boot disk, Linux prompts you for a floppy disk, as shown in Figure 3.15. Insert a floppy disk in the drive and choose Yes. (Choosing No abandons the creation of the boot disk.) Linux then proceeds to copy the kernel image and some extra information to the floppy disk. While Linux is creating the boot disk, it shows you a message like the one in Figure 3.16.

Figure 3.15.
When you choose to
create a boot disk,
Linux prompts you to
insert a floppy disk in
the drive and choose
Yes.

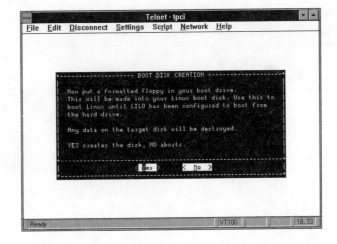

Figure 3.16.
This screen shows the
progress of the creation
of the boot disk.

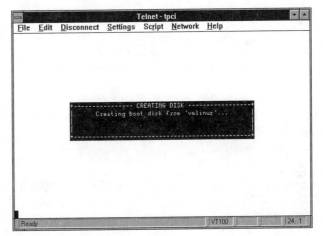

CONFIGURATION DETAILS

After installing disk sets and creating a boot disk, the setup routine may give you a choice to continue with the installation process by configuring your system or to leave the configuration until later. It's a good idea to continue with the process because back-tracking can be difficult sometimes. Although the order of prompts and the options presented to you are different depending on the version of the Linux system you are installing, usually you are asked to set up your modem first, as shown in Figure 3.17.

Figure 3.17.
The first configuration
information you are
asked about is your
modem.

If you have a modem installed on your system already, choose the Yes option to configure the port and modem speed now. Alternatively, if you are not sure which port you want to use or want to add the modem later, choose No. If you choose Yes to install a modem, you are asked for the device it is attached to, as shown in Figure 3.18. The devices are named in Linux format, with /dev/cua0 equivalent to COM1, /dev/cua1 equivalent to COM2, and so on. Choose the proper device. If your modem is used by DOS' COM2 port, for example, scroll to /dev/cua1 and choose OK. If you are not sure which port to use, try /dev/cua1, as most mouse ports are COM1 (/dev/cua0). You can always reconfigure the system later.

Figure 3.18.
Choose the device your
modem is attached to
by using the Linux
/dev/cua conventions.

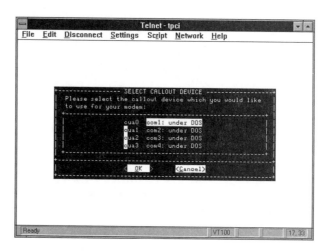

Next you will be asked whether you want to set up your mouse, as shown in Figure 3.19. You can set the mouse up later, but it's easier to do it when you first load the Linux software. If you choose to configure the mouse at this time, you have to choose the type of mouse you are using. Figure 3.20 shows the list of currently supported mouse types. Most mouse peripherals are serial, so select the serial mouse that matches your unit. If in doubt, choose Microsoft compatible serial mouse.

Figure 3.19.
Linux asks you whether
you want to set up your
mouse.

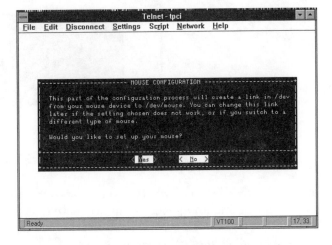

Figure 3.20.
Choose the type of
mouse your system
uses.

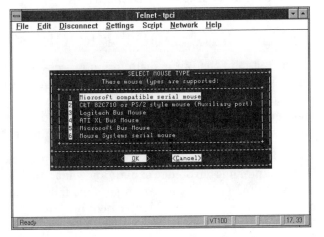

After you choose the mouse, you may be asked for more information about it. If the mouse is a serial mouse, you must choose the port it is attached to, as shown in Figure 3.21. The port numbering is similar to the modem port (although the device name is different), with /dev/S0 corresponding to COM1, /dev/S1 to COM2, and so on. Don't select the same port as the modem! If you are installing a bus mouse, you may be asked for the DMA the mouse uses.

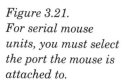

Figure 3.21.
For serial mouse
units, you must select
the port the mouse is
attached to.

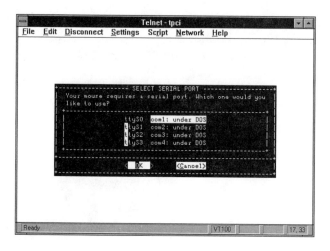

Finally, you may be asked whether you want to try out some screen fonts. This step is time-consuming and generally unproductive. It is much better to go with the default fonts for now and modify them later if you really don't like them. These fonts are used for all character-based messages.

SETTING THE BOOT PROCESS

The last step in the Linux installation process is setting the boot device. A utility called LILO (Linux Loader) usually boots Linux. LILO can boot your system in several different ways, depending on whether you want to use your system with another operating system. Most of the time, you will want LILO to boot your system into Linux with the option to load DOS (if you have it on your system).

The LILO screens explain most of the choices quite well, but LILO has a few quirks to it. Chapter 4 is devoted to explaining what LILO does and how to make it behave properly. For now, if you are impatient, follow the defaults, but don't let LILO overwrite your hard disk's Master Boot Record. Doing so can cause a bit of a hassle when you want to boot DOS. You can, though, let LILO write a boot sector to your Linux partition, and then use fdisk to make either DOS or Linux active. If you're not too sure about what to do with LILO, ignore it for now. You have a boot floppy disk that lets you start your machine. When you better understand LILO, you can set it up the way you want.

As a last step in the installation process, reboot your machine and let Linux boot from the boot floppy disk or from LILO, if you installed it. If everything boots properly, you can use Linux as you normally would. If you experienced problems booting, watch error messages and check the installation process to see which part went screwy. As long as you have your boot disk, you should be able to get into Linux without a problem.

VIEWING INSTALLED SOFTWARE FILES

When Linux is up and running, you may want to install or remove disk sets and other software. You can also check that components of a disk set have been properly installed. A few different utilities are available for this task, but the most common is called pkgtool. When you enter the pkgtool command name at the shell prompt, a menu that enables you to install new software, remove existing software, or view installed files in a package appears on-screen. Figure 3.22 shows the pkgtool menu. You can also use the setup utility for these tasks.

Figure 3.22.
The pkgtool *utility is one way to install, remove, or examine software on your Linux system.*

To view the contents of a package, select View from the main pkgtool menu, and then choose the name of the package from the list presented. Figure 3.23 shows the list of packages. The list should include all the disk set tools you have installed, as well as any additional software installed after the first installation. Selecting a tool name sends pkgtool to check all the files that should be in the software and report its success. Sometimes the list of software in a package can take a while to appear. Be patient! The list pkgtool presents usually has a brief description of the tool and a list of all the files in the installation. Figure 3.24 shows the entry for the base software package.

When the list of files is displayed, you can move through them with the space bar. To leave the list of files, select the Exit option at the bottom of the screen.

Figure 3.23.
When you select View
from the pkgtool *utility,*
you must choose which
package to view.

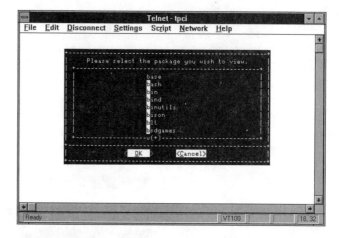

Figure 3.24.
The pkgtool *utility*
shows the components
installed for each
package on your
system.

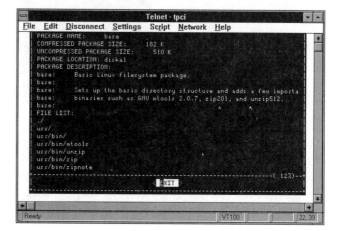

TROUBLESHOOTING

Many different problems can occur while setting up and installing a Linux system, although most of them are self-explanatory from error messages. The following sections look at a few of the most commonly encountered problems.

SOFTWARE INSTALLATION PROBLEMS

You may encounter a few errors when installing Linux. If you get the message device full, you have run out of disk space and need to either break up the installation into several partitions or install fewer components. If you haven't yet installed the basic system, you need more disk space. You have to delete your partitions and start the installation process again, allocating more space to Linux.

Errors such as `read error`, `file not found` and `tar: read error` are indicative of a problem with either the disk medium you are installing from, or an incomplete disk set. These problems usually occur with floppy disks and may indicate that you have a bad floppy disk. All you can do in most cases is replace the floppy disk with a new one.

HARD DISK AND DISK CONTROLLER PROBLEMS

When Linux boots, it displays a few messages, one of the most important being a partition check. You see messages like the following:

```
Partition check:
hda: hda1 hda2 hda3
hdb: hdb1 hdb2
```

In this example, the first non-SCSI disk has three partitions and the second disk has two. Your system's output is probably different, of course. If you don't see any partition information, either the hard disk controller is not recognized properly or the disk drives are not accessible. Check the following potential causes for these problems:

◆ Check the cables inside the computer. The hard disk cable should run from the adapter card to each drive's connector. Make sure the cables are connected in the proper manner (the red strip on the cable is at pin 1 on the connector).

◆ Check that the power connector is attached to each disk drive. Without power, your drive doesn't spin up and Linux can't touch it.

◆ Check the partition table to make sure you created a Linux partition properly.

If the drive is still not working properly with Linux but works OK when you boot DOS, a kernel driver for the hard disk is likely at fault. Some IDE drives, for example, are not as well-behaved (not conforming to the IDE standards) as others, and your IDE kernel driver may not be able to talk to your drives. Try using a different kernel image and see if the problem solves itself. If you are using a SCSI kernel and adapter and the drives are not recognized, use the utilities that came with the SCSI adapter card to force a check of the hard drives. They may have a SCSI ID set incorrectly.

DEVICE CONFLICTS

One of the most commonly encountered problems is hardware that is not recognized properly. This problem can happen to a CD-ROM, a network card, and even a hard disk. Most of the time, a conflict in the IRQ (interrupt), DMA (Direct Memory Address), or I/O address settings causes this problem. When two devices have the same settings on any one of these three characteristics, Linux and the BIOS may not be able to communicate with the device properly.

A symptom of this problem may be Linux hanging when it tries to find a specific device, as explained in the boot messages. When Linux boots up, it generates messages that explain what it is doing. If you see a message that it is trying to connect to the network card, for example, and it never gets past that point, chances are that the network card has a conflict with another device. (Totally failed cards are very rare and don't usually stop the boot process, as Linux ignores devices it can't access. The problem with a working card with conflicting settings is that Linux is getting messages from two devices that don't act the same.)

To check for conflicts, run a diagnostic utility under DOS, such as MSD or Norton Info. These utilities can show you the current IRQ, DMA, and I/O addresses and pinpoint any conflicts. You can also use them to find available settings. Alternatively, you can check the settings of every device in your system for conflicts. Usually, network cards conflict with sound boards, non-SCSI tape driver cards, video cards, and similar add-on cards. Most cards use DIPs or jumpers to set these parameters, so check them against the documentation. To help isolate the problem, remove cards that are not necessary, such as a sound card, and see whether the boot process moves past the device that caused the hangup.

Another problem that can occur is with SCSI devices (and a few others, although much rarer) that must have specific settings in the kernel image. Some kernels, especially special-purpose kernels that have been developed for non-mainstream adapters, were compiled with settings that are default values for adapters or disk drives, and if the settings have been changed, the kernel hangs up. To check for this type of problem, investigate any documentation that came with the kernel image.

The most common devices in a PC (COM ports, parallel ports, and floppy disks) and their IRQ, DMA, and I/O addresses are shown in in the following list. These are the default values for a PC, but they may be changed by users. Because only two COM ports (serial ports) are usually supported by DOS, they share IRQ values. The I/O addresses are different, though. Both floppy disks share the same I/O addresses, IRQ, and DMA.

Device	IRQ	DMA	I/O Address (Hex)
COM 1 (/dev/ttyS0)	4	N/A	3F8
COM 2 (/dev/ttyS1)	3	N/A	2F8
COM 3 (/dev/ttyS2)	4	N/A	3E8
COM 4 (/dev/ttys3)	3	N/A	2E8
LPT 1 (/dev/lp0)	7	N/A	378-37F
LPT 2 (/dev/lp1)	5	N/A	278-27F
Floppy A (/dev/fd0)	6	2	3F0-3F7
Floppy B (/dev/fd1)	6	2	3F0-3F7

Note

> You may have noticed that the serial ports are called /dev/ttyS0, /dev
> /ttyS1, and so on in the list of devices. Yet they were called /dev/cua0,
> /dev/cua1, and so on when you configured the modem. The ports are
> the same (/dev/ttyS0 is the same as /dev/cua0); Linux just handles the
> devices differently. Don't get too confused about these device driver
> names yet. Just remember that /dev/cua refers to a modem port.

Network cards, SCSI adapters, sound boards, video cards, and other peripherals all
must have unique IRQ, DMA, and I/O addresses, which can be difficult to arrange
with a fully loaded system. For more information on available values, check your
device or card installation manual for recommended values and potential conflicts.

SCSI PROBLEMS

SCSI is one of the most versatile interfaces, and it pays for that versatility in
potential problems. Linux is usually good about reporting problems with SCSI
devices, although the error messages may leave you wondering about the real cause
of the problem.

The following list explains many of the common SCSI errors and their probable
causes. Find the message that closely matches the error message Linux displays to
determine your corrective steps.

`SCSI device at all possible IDs`	One or more devices is at the same SCSI ID as the controller. Check and change device IDs. Controllers should be ID 7.
Sense errors	This error is probably caused by bad termination. Check that both ends of the SCSI chain are terminated. If that is not the problem, the cable is likely at fault.
Timeout errors	This error is usually caused by a DMA, IRQ, or I/O address conflict. See the preceding section for more information.
`SCSI adapter not detected`	The BIOS is disabled or the kernel doesn't recognize the SCSI adapter. Check the drivers.

`Cylinders Beyond 1024`	Your disk has more than 1,024 cylinders, which the PC BIOS can't handle. Linux can use more than 1,024 cylinders, but it can't boot from a partition that extends across that cylinder boundary.
`CD-ROM drive not recognized`	Some CD-ROM drives require a CD in the drive to be recognized properly. Insert a CD and reboot.

PROBLEMS BOOTING LINUX

If you have installed Linux and the system doesn't boot properly from your hard disk, it may be a problem with LILO or with the partitions. If you created a boot floppy disk, boot from that. If that boots without a problem, check the partition table by executing `fdisk`. Make sure the Linux partition is active. If it is and you still can't boot from the hard disk, boot from the floppy disk and run LILO again to configure the boot sector. See Chapter 4 for more information on LILO.

A problem will sometimes occur when Linux can't find the main Linux partition. Boot from the floppy disk and hold down the Shift or Ctrl key. This will produce a menu that enables you to specify the boot device explicitly. This problem can usually be corrected with LILO.

SUMMARY

Much of this chapter may have been familiar to you if you have installed Linux before, although some users really don't know what goes on during the automated installation script. Knowing the process, and staying on top of it, helps prevent problems with the Linux installation. The next step is using LILO to configure the boot system properly, a commonly misunderstood process. The next chapter looks at LILO.

- Installing LILO

- Linux and Hard Disk Layouts

- The Boot Sector

- The Boot Process

- The Map Installer

- Boot Images

- The Disk Parameter Table

- Removing or Disabling LILO

- Troubleshooting LILO

CHAPTER 4

LILO

Whenever you hear about Linux, you also hear about LILO. LILO is the boot loader Linux uses to load the operating system kernel. Whenever you change or move the Linux kernel, you must invoke LILO to rebuild a map of the kernel locations. LILO is versatile—it can boot Linux kernels from any type of filesystem, including a floppy disk, as well as from other operating systems. This chapter looks at LILO, the way hard disks are laid out with Linux, the most common boot processes, and LILO's interactions with each. This information should help you install and use LILO effectively.

Several versions of LILO are available. Most current versions support one of two different directory structures. The more traditional (and older) structure resides in the /etc/lilo directory. The newer structure has files scattered in several directories, including /etc, /sbin, and /boot. Because the older /etc/lilo structure is the most common, it is used for examples in this chapter. If you are using the new structure (check for the existence of /etc/lilo), substitute the new pathnames as necessary.

INSTALLING LILO

Most systems will have LILO already installed and configured. If your system already has LILO installed, you can skip this section unless you want to update your version. A quick installation procedure is available with most versions of Linux to install a minimum set of LILO. This procedure is described in the file QuickInst.old or QuickInst.new, depending on the version of Linux. You can only use the QuickInst routines for a first-time LILO installation or to replace an existing LILO set. You cannot use them for updates as any existing configuration information is overwritten.

A full installation of LILO requires that all the files in the LILO distribution archive (usually called lilo.*xxx*.tar.gz where *xxx* is the version number) are extracted into a directory other than /etc/lilo. (Otherwise, installation will fail if the final destination is the same as the source directory.) After the distribution files are located in a temporary directory, follow these steps:

1. Check the Makefile for valid configuration information (see the following LILO Makefile section).

2. Compile LILO. If you want to use the older /etc/lilo directory structure, issue the first command that follows. If you want to use the new directory structure, issue the second command.

   ```
   make -f Makefile.old
   make -f Makefile.new
   ```

3. Copy all the LILO files to the target directory with one of the following commands, depending on whether you selected the new or old directory structure:

```
make -f Makefile.old install
make -f Makefile.new install
```

4. Check the directories. You should see the following files: any_d.b, boot.b, chain.b, disktab, lilo, os2_d.b. If the files do not exist or errors are generated in the process, restart the installation. Check the Makefile for accurate information. Once LILO has been installed properly, you can use it to install a boot process.

Note

Before you can compile LILO for use, you have to configure the kernel by running make config. All kernel header files must be in the directory /usr/include/linux for LILO to compile properly. The LILO installation and compilation process should be run from a Bourne shell (or complete compatible). Problems have been reported with versions of the Korn shell when LILO is compiled, so use /bin/sh or /bin/bash.

HANDLING DISK PROBLEMS

Some systems may have difficulty with hard disks that do not allow the disk parameters (heads, sectors per track, and cylinders) to be read. If you get error messages about bad geometry or the LILO installation fails with disk errors, the disk parameters are a likely source of trouble, especially if you're dealing with SCSI disks and hard disks with a capacity of 1G or more.

In this case, you must manually enter the disk parameters into the disktab file. The section "The Disk Parameter Table" later in this chapter discusses this step in more detail. Edit the disktab file as explained to include the disk parameters. Then test the new LILO configuration by copying it to a floppy disk and booting from it. Follow these steps:

1. Change to the LILO directory (usually /etc/lilo).
2. Execute the following command to copy the LILO configuration to the floppydisk. Substitute the kernel image name after the image parameter.

   ```
   echo image=kernel_name | ./lilo -C - -b /dev/fd0 -v -v -v
   ```

3. Reboot your system from the floppy disk.

If the configuration is correct, LILO reads the floppy disk for the boot loader, and then loads the kernel from the hard disk. If everything boots properly and you can move around the filesystem, the disk parameters are correct. If you can't access the hard disk filesystem, the parameters are incorrect and should be entered again.

4

LILO

USING THE LILO MAKEFILE

The LILO Makefile supplied with the LILO installation files is valid for most installations, although you should carefully check all the entries. LILO uses either the Makefile, which contains all the instructions for a C compiler to compile a binary from the source code, or another file called /etc/lilo/config.defines. If the config.defines file exists, Makefile is ignored. For most purposes, editing the Makefile is sufficient, although if you plan to use LILO a lot, the config.defines file is a better alternative because it isn't overwritten with new versions of LILO.

The Makefile has several parameters that control the compilation process. You may need to change some of the values, depending on your system requirements. Check the following parameters in the Makefile and ensure that the values they have set are what you want:

◆ IGNORECASE makes image names case insensitive. This parameter is active by default and should be left alone.

◆ NO1STDIAG does not generate diagnostic messages when read errors are encountered in the boot loader. This parameter is disabled by default. It's best to leave it disabled unless you don't care about the error messages.

◆ The NOINSTDEF parameter tells you that if the install option is omitted from the command line, don't install a new boot sector. Instead, modify the old one. This parameter is disabled by default.

◆ ONE_SHOT disables the command-line timeout if any key is pressed. This parameter is disabled by default.

◆ READONLY prevents overwriting of the default command-line sector of the map file. This parameter is disabled by default.

UPDATING LILO

If you want to update an existing version of LILO with a newer one, the process is the same as a first-time installation except that existing configuration files are renamed to .old. For example, chain.b is renamed to chain.old. If the new version of LILO behaves properly, you can delete the .old files. Whenever you update the version of LILO, you must update the boot sector to add the new locations and map file format. To update the boot sector, run LILO.

LINUX AND HARD DISK LAYOUTS

To understand how LILO works, you must understand how a hard disk is laid out. You probably already know that a hard disk is essentially a set of concentric tracks, radiating out from the center of the disk platter. Each track is divided into a number of sectors.

Hard disks are identified by the number of platters (or more accurately, the number of heads; the number of platters can be greater than the number of heads because one or more surfaces, typically the top and bottom, might not be used for data storage), the number of tracks per inch of disk platter (measured radially), and the number of sectors per track. The capacity of each sector leads to the total capacity of the disk by multiplying by the number of sectors per track, the number of tracks, and the number of platters with heads.

Linux is usually integrally tied with DOS, so it is useful to look at the way DOS uses a hard disk. A single-purpose (single DOS operating system, for example) hard disk (and most floppy disks) has a boot sector, followed by a data area that includes an administrative block. The boot sector is the first sector on the hard disk and is read when the system starts to load the operating system. The boot sector contains a bootstrap to direct the machine to the startup routines. The data area stores files, including the operating system startup code. (A bootstrap is a short piece of code that tells the BIOS how to load the operating system. It essentially starts the operating system load process by providing the bare bones instructions necessary to read the operating system files from disk.)

Although the administrative block is usually part of the data area, users commonly cannot access it directly. Each file on the hard disk has an entry in the administrative block's tables that indicates the file's location in terms of the head, track, and sector and the file name. Other information, such as owner, permissions, date, and time, is usually stored in the administrative block as well. In DOS, this information makes up the File Allocation Table (FAT); UNIX and Linux use the superblock or i-node tables. The administrative table is not usually read until the boot process has been started.

When the hard disk has lots of space, you will probably want to install more than one partition. Multiple partitions are especially useful if you want to support more than one operating system (DOS and Linux, for example) on the same hard disk. You can create up to four primary partitions on a DOS disk.

Warning

With some operating systems, you can have more than four partitions, but if you are using DOS on the hard disk, don't create more than four primary partitions. Doing so may cause DOS to improperly read any data in the DOS partition because DOS has a built-in limitation of four partitions per disk. DOS' FDISK can't handle more than that amount. If you need to provide more than four logical disk drives, you can use extended partitions. An extended partition is a primary partition that has been subdivided.

4

LILO

A partition table that contains the details of the partitions on the disk is written to the first sector (boot sector) of each hard disk (not each platter). This sector is sometimes called the Master Boot Record or MBR. Although the terms boot sector and MBR are often used interchangeably, MBRs differ from boot sectors in that MBRs contain partition information. In other words, you can call a hard drive's boot sectors MBRs, but floppy disks' boot sectors are never MBRs. Extended partitions also have partition tables written to their beginning sectors. A program called the map installer creates Linux boot sectors.

When a hard disk has several partitions, Linux refers to them by device numbers after the primary disk name, such as /dev/hda1, /dev/hda2, and so on. In this case, /dev/hda is the first hard drive (/dev/hdb would be the second, /dev/hdc the third, and so on). Within the first hard drive, the partitions are named /dev/hda1, /dev/hda2, and so on. A second hard disk called /dev/hdb has partitions called /dev/hdb1, /dev/hdb2, and so on. The disk names may have other letters, depending on the type of hard disk and its adapter. For example, a hard disk may be called /dev/sd1 instead of /dev/hda. Extended partitions would be numbered /dev/hda5, /dev/hda6, and so on because only four primary partitions, or /dev/hda4, are allowed.

THE BOOT SECTOR

To understand the Linux boot process, a look at the DOS boot sector is necessary. Figure 4.1 shows the DOS boot sector layout. The program code is the bootstrap to the operating system. The disk parameters include the File Allocation Table (FAT).

Figure 4.1.
The DOS boot sector
layout.

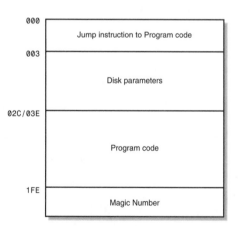

Linux's LILO boot sector is similar to the DOS boot sector, except that the disk parameter section is not used and the boundaries between code sections are different. The differences between the two boot sectors can cause a problem for DOS if the Linux LILO boot sector is written to a DOS disk's Master Boot Record, because

DOS won't be able to load properly. Figure 4.2 shows the Linux boot sector layout. The magic number referred to in this and the previous boot sector layout is a two-byte number used by some operating systems to verify that the sector read is the boot sector.

Figure 4.2.
The Linux LILO boot
sector layout.

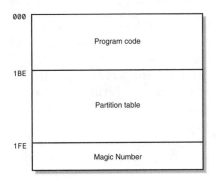

You could, in theory, use the Linux LILO boot sector to boot DOS, as the partition table area of the boot record could contain DOS' FAT, but in practice, the boot process usually fails. It is much better to use a boot sector written to the DOS partition.

Warning

Because the DOS and Linux LILO boot sectors differ, you should install DOS before Linux. Doing so ensures that the DOS boot sector is written to the hard disk. If you install Linux first and the Linux LILO boot sector is written to the hard disk, DOS cannot boot.

You can save the LILO boot sector on a boot floppy disk, in the Master Boot Record of the hard disk, on the boot sector of the Linux partition, or in the boot sector of an extended partition. You cannot store it in any non-Linux partition or on any hard disk other than the first. Note that although DOS cannot handle a boot sector in an extended partition, Linux can through extensions to `fdisk` or a utility program called `activate`.

Warning

A common problem with LILO is that it will write a LILO boot sector anywhere, even into locations that the operating system cannot access. Make sure you are writing your LILO boot sector to a valid location. If you have already installed Linux and are making changes, keep a boot floppy disk at hand.

THE BOOT PROCESS

During the boot process, the boot sector is read to obtain the bootstrap for the operating system. In the case of DOS, the Master Boot record or boot sector is read, and then COMMAND.COM is loaded. COMMAND.COM is DOS' kernel.

Although usually the boot system is set up when the Linux installation process is followed, you may want to alter Linux's boot system. Depending on your requirements and machine hard drive configuration, you can take one of several approaches. The following sections look at a few of the typical configuration examples to show how you can modify the boot process. These sections begin by explaining the process to follow to install LILO manually, although you can often perform these processes automatically when installing the Linux software. This section looks at the automated installation process and its options later on. For now, though, the details of each alternative should help you decide how to install LILO on your system.

INSTALLING A DEDICATED LINUX HARD DISK

With a dedicated Linux installation, or a Linux boot by default despite other operating systems on the hard disk, the Linux LILO boot sector can replace the Master Boot Record. LILO will then boot straight into Linux from the Master Boot Record without touching partition boot sectors. In some cases, though, you may have to explicitly specify the boot sector. In other words, you may have to specify `boot=/dev/hda` (or whichever device holds the modified master boot record) at the `boot` prompt if the default values do not work.

Warning

> If you replace the Master Boot Record with LILO for a dedicated Linux system then later remove Linux, you will have to low-level format the hard drive or restore the old MBR before another operating system, such as DOS, can use the drive.

To install LILO as a dedicated Linux boot, follow these steps:

1. Boot Linux as usual. Make sure you have a boot floppy disk in case of problems.
2. Copy your existing Master Boot Record to a floppy disk in case of problems. The command to copy the MBR from the main drive (/dev/hda) to a floppy disk using 512 character blocks (the default) is

```
dd if=/dev/hda of=/fd/MBR bs=512 count=1
```

3. Use the setup or LILO installation program to copy LILO into the boot sector, setting LILO in the Master Boot Record.

4. Reboot the machine to boot from the Master Boot Record.

Your machine should load Linux automatically. If Linux does not boot, use your boot floppy to start Linux and either repeat the process or restore the original Master Boot Record from the floppy disk using the command

```
dd if=/fd/MBR of=/dev/hda bs=446 count=1
```

USING *BOOTACTV*

A slight modification of the last boot process is replacing the normal MBR with a utility called BOOTACTV, which prompts for the partition to boot from. This utility requires that a non-DOS-compatible copy of the boot sector be written, so you should use it only when Linux will be the dominant operating system and LILO is not booting the other operating systems properly.

When in place, the Master Boot Record holds a copy of BOOTACTV. When booted, BOOTACTV enables you to choose which operating system to boot. BOOTACTV can then read a boot sector from a partition to load that operating system. When the MBR holds BOOTACTV, you can't use the MBR as you normally would with other operating systems, such as DOS or OS/2. You can, though, replace BOOTACTV with a normal MBR.

To install BOOTACTV, follow these steps:

1. Boot Linux as usual. Make sure you have a boot floppy disk in case of problems.

2. Copy your existing Master Boot Record to a floppy disk in case of problems. The command to copy the MBR from the main drive (/dev/hda) to a floppy disk using 512 character blocks (the default) is

    ```
    dd if=/dev/hda of=/fd/MBR bs=512 count=1
    ```

3. Use the setup or LILO installation program to copy LILO into the boot sector of the Linux partition (not the Master Boot Record).

4. Install BOOTACTV into the Master Boot Record. The BOOTACTV utility is usually called bootactv.bin and should be in the current directory when you install it into the MBR with the command

    ```
    dd if=bootactv.bin of=/dev/hda bs=446 count=1
    ```

5. Reboot the machine to boot BOOTACTV from the Master Boot Record.

Your machine should load BOOTACTV and allow you to boot any other operating system on a partition. If Linux or another operating system does not boot, use your boot floppy disk to start Linux. If only Linux doesn't boot, the boot sector LILO for the

4

LILO

Linux partition is not working and can be rewritten using the setup or LILO configuration utilities. If none of the partitions boot, remove BOOTACTV by replacing the old Master Boot Record with the command

```
dd if=/fd/MBR of=/dev/hda bs=446 count=1
```

You can also reinstall the Master Boot Record from within DOS, if you have a DOS boot floppy disk. When in DOS, issue the command

```
fdisk /mbr
```

Tip

If you don't want to alter your Master Boot Record but have more than one partition dedicated to Linux, you can install BOOTACTV on one of the partition's boot sectors and use the fdisk utility to toggle the active partition. However, if the hard disk is repartitioned or the filesystems are altered in size, the boot sector will have to be rewritten. To write BOOTACTV to the fourth primary hard disk partition, for example, copy the existing MBR to the partition's boot sector, and then install BOOTACTV with the following commands:

```
dd if=/dev/hda of=/dev/hda4 bs=512 count=1
dd if=bootactv.bin of=/dev/hda4 bs=446 count=1
```

INSTALLING DOS AND LINUX

Most Linux installations coexist with DOS and use the DOS Master Boot Record. In this case, the MBR is read and the active partition (set by fdisk) is booted automatically. This installation method is one of the safest because no changes to the DOS-installed Master Boot Record are performed, and it is easy to remove or reconfigure partitions at any time without worrying about compatibility with the MBR.

Note

Later versions of DOS (6.00 or higher) will overwrite an existing MBR if they are installed after Linux. If this happens, you won't be able to boot Linux from the MBR, although DOS will boot. You can fix the problem by running LILO again or by making the Linux partition active.

You can change the active partition at any time using the fdisk utility or the Linux utility activate. The setup program within Linux can usually change the boot partition, too. Only one partition on a hard disk can be active at a time. Some operating systems, including Linux, let you change your mind about which operating system to boot after the active partition has been read, assuming a delay was built into the boot process. Linux, for example, can display the boot prompt and wait for a reply or a timeout to occur before starting to boot Linux.

To use this type of approach for Linux, install LILO into the boot sector of the Linux partition. To make it bootable, run fdisk and set that partition number as the active partition. Rebooting the machine will boot into the active partition. When Linux is replaced or removed, the boot sector of the new operating system will overwrite the Linux partition's boot sector, requiring no changes to the MBR.

USING *BOOTLIN*

With the Linux BOOTLIN configuration, which is also a common method of installation, the Master Boot Record does not change. During the boot process, the Master Boot Record is read, and then a decision about which operating system to load is made. This decision is usually based on a user prompt. Essentially, this boot process is the same as a normal DOS boot except the program BOOTLIN is invoked in either the CONFIG.SYS or AUTOEXEC.BAT files. This program can then execute a program that lets you choose the operating system to load. BOOT.SYS, for example, may be used to present a menu that enables you to choose between a Linux and DOS boot.

To install BOOTLIN in your DOS partition, follow these steps:

1. Boot Linux. Make sure you have a boot floppy disk in case of problems.
2. Place a copy of the Linux kernel in your DOS partition either through DOS or with one of the Linux Mtools. You only have to copy the kernel file into the home directory (or any subdirectory) of the DOS partition. You can even do this step from the floppy disk.
3. Copy BOOT.SYS and BOOTLIN.SYS to the DOS partition, using the same process you used to copy the Linux kernel.
4. Add both the BOOT.SYS and BOOTLIN.SYS files to your CONFIG.SYS file.
5. Make sure DOS is the active partition, and reboot the machine.

When DOS starts, the BOOT device driver should give you the option of booting DOS or Linux. If you have problems, remove the BOOT.SYS and BOOTLIN.SYS files from the CONFIG.SYS file and you are back to normal.

Using BOOT.SYS has a useful advantage in that no boot sectors are altered to support several operating systems. As a result, loading and removing operating systems from a hard disk is easier. You can use both the Master Boot Record with active partition and BOOT.SYS approaches so that the hard disk starts to boot whichever operating system has the active flag, and then pauses and waits for confirmation from the user (or a timeout to occur). In this case, no changes to the Master Boot Record need to be made.

AUTOMATED LILO CREATION

Most recent versions of Linux, including the one supplied on this book's CD-ROM, let you manage LILO through a menu-driven routine usually started through setup. Typically, when you have made any changes to the installation (such as adding new software), the last component of the setup program asks you whether you want to work with LILO. Figure 4.3 shows this screen.

Figure 4.3.
Whenever you make
changes to Linux
through the setup
utility, it asks whether
you want to use LILO.

From the menu-driven system shown in Figure 4.3, select the Begin option. Usually, the first thing the program asks for is any boot-time instructions that need to be specified when Linux starts, as shown in Figure 4.4. Normally, there are no boot-time instructions, but if you had to enter any parameters to start the Linux installation process, specify the same options here.

The next prompt, shown in Figure 4.5, asks where you want your LILO instructions written. The primary options were discussed earlier in the chapter. This version of LILO lets you select the Master Boot Record (MBR), the master sector of the primary Linux partition (called a superblock on this screen), or a floppy disk. The method you select depends on how you want Linux to start and whether it coexists with another operating system. For a minimal impact on your system, select the floppy disk boot option. This option requires you to place the boot floppy disk in the floppy disk drive when starting the machine, but then it boots cleanly into Linux. If the boot floppy disk is left out of the floppy disk drive, any other active partition (such as DOS or OS/2) is booted. Because the LILO instructions are only written to floppy disk with this approach, existing MBRs or partition boot sectors don't change at all. This approach makes it very easy to remove Linux and prevent problems with other operating systems that exist on your drives.

Figure 4.4.
The LILO installation process starts by asking whether you need any special boot-time instructions.

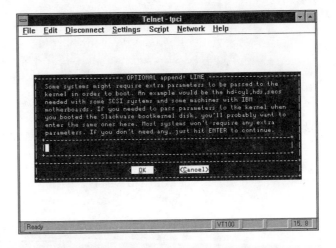

Figure 4.5.
You are asked where you want to install LILO.

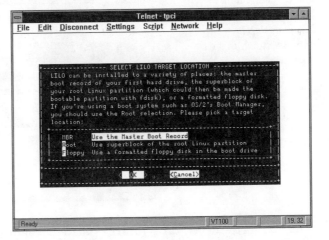

If you are installing only Linux, or plan to have very rare use of existing DOS or OS/2 partitions, use the Master Boot Record or partition boot sector. The only drawback to this approach is that you must low-level format your hard drive if you want to remove Linux in the future. The Linux MBR is not compatible with DOS'.

A compromise is to use the partition boot sector (superblock). This approach lets you boot straight into Linux when the partition is active or use fdisk to activate any other partition. Although this option has more impact than the floppy disk boot option, you can easily remove it by reformatting the partition and installing a new operating system.

Note

If you are installing Linux to experiment with it and you are not sure whether you will leave it on your hard drive, use the boot floppy disk. This option provides the most hassle-free approach for backing out of Linux in the future. You can always rerun LILO and write the boot instructions to the MBR or superblock later.

The LILO system asks you whether you want a delay before Linux starts to boot, as shown in Figure 4.6. You can decide to not pause, to wait either 5 or 30 seconds, or to wait until LILO is told explicitly to boot. This last option is useful if you have two operating systems on your hard drive because it saves you from fooling around with fdisk to alter the active partition. A good compromise is either 5 or 30 seconds.

Figure 4.6.
You can set a delay
before booting into
Linux with one of the
options shown in this
menu.

After you set the delay, LILO returns you to the main LILO menu (shown in Figure 4.3). The next step is to identify the partitions that LILO will know about. The menu lists three operating systems: DOS, OS/2, and Linux. If you have either DOS or OS/2, you can give the partition information to LILO to allow it to boot this operating system instead of Linux (assuming you have a delay in the boot process). Begin with the Linux operating system, though. Select Linux on the menu (the menu choices are in order of most common use from top to bottom, generally) to display the Linux partition information screen shown in Figure 4.7.

Figure 4.7.
Use this screen to
identify the boot Linux
partition. In this
example, only a single
Linux data partition
exists.

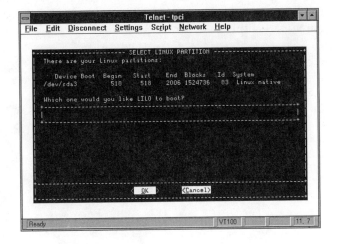

The example shown in Figure 4.7 shows a single Linux data partition on the hard drive, called /dev/sda3. The Linux swap partitions never show up on these lists (unless they were misidentified when they were installed). Enter the name of the Linux partition that is to be used for the boot partition (in the example, /dev/sda3 would be typed in the entry field). The next screen, shown in Figure 4.8, asks for a name for this partition. This name is used to identify the partition at boot time. For Linux partitions, just enter the word Linux to provide an unambiguous name for the partition.

Figure 4.8.
You need to assign a
name to the Linux
partition.

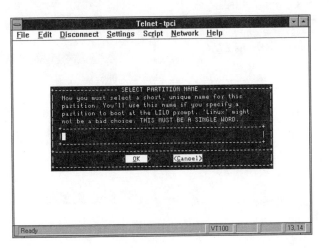

4

LILO

After entering the partition name, you are back to the main LILO menu. Now, add any other operating systems, such as DOS or OS/2. To install a DOS partition, for example, select DOS from the menu. A screen very similar to the one for selecting the Linux partition appears, as shown in Figure 4.9. Enter the name of the DOS partition (in this case, /dev/sda1).

Figure 4.9.
When you add another operating system to LILO, the partitions that apply are displayed. You can add this partition to the LILO boot table.

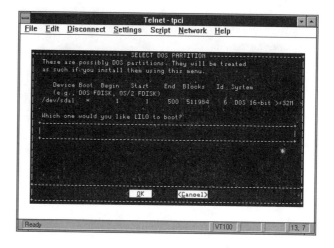

After the partition has been identified, name the partition as shown in Figure 4.10. Again, a simple name is best, so enter DOS or OS/2 as applicable. Don't bother with fancy names; they are more trouble than they are worth!

Figure 4.10.
As with the Linux partition, you need to assign a name to the other partitions LILO will know about.

After you name all the partitions, you are brought back yet again to the LILO menu. The next step is to install the LILO information. Select the Install option from the menu. The system writes all the partition details you've supplied, and then you can exit LILO. The other options on the LILO menu allow you to modify an existing LILO table. In most cases, it's easier to just start again. You can use this automated LILO installation any time you want. Take care that you enter the proper information, though, as an error can make it impossible to access a partition. Keep an emergency boot disk handy!

Setting Boot Parameters

Regardless of which boot process you use, LILO pauses momentarily when Linux is booting to check that the Shift, Ctrl, and Alt keys are not pressed and that Caps Lock and Scroll Lock are set. If none of the keys are pressed and the locks are on, LILO displays the boot prompt. At this point, LILO is waiting for the name of the boot image to use to be entered. If a timeout occurs or Enter is pressed, the default boot image is loaded. The boot image is the kernel of whichever operating system is to be loaded, including DOS.

If you want to boot an image other than the default, you can enter its name at the boot prompt. To obtain a list of all known boot images, enter a question mark or hit the Tab key (depending on the image and keyboard setting). Recent versions of Linux set the boot image name in a LILO file, as described in the next section. With some earlier versions of Linux, the name of the default boot image is located in the file /etc/rc (or in a file in the subdirectory /etc/rc.d) on a line with the keyword

```
BOOT_IMAGE=
```

You also can specify parameters for the kernel by entering them at the boot prompt. Unless overridden, the parameters will be used by the default image when it boots. Valid parameters differ a little depending on the version of Linux, but most versions support the following:

- The no387 parameter disables any on-board floating-point unit (FPU).
- The root parameter boots from a device specified after the root parameter, such as root=/dev/sda1. The root command takes either a hexadecimal device number or the full pathname of the device.
- The ro parameter mounts the root filesystem as read-only.
- The rw parameter mounts the root filesystem as read-write.
- The single parameter boots the Linux system into single-user (system administrator) mode.

4

LILO

As mentioned in the preceding list, you can use a hexadecimal device number in the root parameter. The device numbers are assigned depending on the type of device. For floppy disk drives, the numbers are assigned starting with 200: /dev/fd0 is 200, /dev/fd1 is 201, /dev/fd2 is 202, and so on. Hard disks have numbers assigned depending on the type of device. For most hard disks, the numbers start at 301 (not 300 because there is no /dev/hd0): /dev/hda1 is 301, /dev/hda2 is 302, and so on. When a second hard drive is used, the numbers jump to 340: /dev/hdb1 is 341, /dev/hdb2 is 342, and so on. For /dev/sda devices, numbering starts at 801: /dev/sda1 is 801, /dev/sda2 is 802, and so on. The second hard drive starts at 811: /dev/sdb1 is 811, /dev/sdb2 is 812, and so on. Because floppy disk and hard disk drives are usually the only devices that can act as boot devices, these numbers should suffice for all occurrences except removable media.

You can combine parameters if you separate them with a space. At the boot prompt, the line

```
image5 root=/dev/hda2 single ro
```

will boot the kernel called image5 located on the device /dev/hda2, for example. The filesystem will be mounted as a read-only device, and single-user mode will be invoked.

THE MAP INSTALLER

The map installer is the program that updates the boot sector and creates the map file. The map installer is usually the file /etc/lilo/lilo. Whenever the map installer is running, it checks for errors in the boot sector. If an error is detected, no changes to the boot sector are written, and the installer terminates.

When a boot sector is successfully updated by the map installer, the old boot sector contents are copied into the directory /etc/lilo with the name boot.hex_num where hex_num is the hexadecimal device number of the partition that was rewritten. The hexadecimal device numbers were mentioned in the previous section. When the map installer writes to a partition's boot sector, the old copy of the boot sector is stored in a file with the name part.hex_num. Again, hex_num is the number of the device.

You can modify the map installer's behavior by supplying command line parameters when the installer is invoked or by making entries in the configuration file /etc/lilo /config. On later versions of Linux, including the version supplied on the CD-ROM with this book, the file is /etc/lilo.conf. A sample /etc/lilo.conf looks like the following:

```
# LILO configuration file
# generated by 'liloconfig'
#
# Start LILO global section
boot = /dev/fd0
```

```
#compact          # faster, but won't work on all systems.
delay = 50
vga = normal      # force sane state
ramdisk = 0       # paranoia setting
# End LILO global section
# Linux bootable partition config begins
image = /vmlinuz
  root = /dev/sda3
  label = Linux
  read-only # Non-UMSDOS filesystems should be mounted read-only for checking
# Linux bootable partition config ends
# DOS bootable partition config begins
other = /dev/sda1
  label = DOS
  table = /dev/sda
# DOS bootable partition config ends
```

As you can see, this lilo.conf file uses a boot floppy disk to hold the LILO image (/dev /fd0) and avoids overwriting the MBR or superblock of a partition. The Linux partition is /dev/sda3 and is called Linux. A DOS partition, /dev/sda1, called DOS also exists on the hard drive. You can use many of the available options from either the LILO command line or the configuration file. The following sections discuss the configuration options.

MAP INSTALLER COMMAND-LINE OPTIONS

The LILO map installer utility accepts a number of options on the command line. Many of the command-line options are mirrored by configuration variables, discussed in the next section. The following list describes the command-line options:

◆ The -b dev option uses dev as the boot device. If no value is specified, the default device given by the boot configuration variable is used.

◆ The -c option turns on compact, which merges read requests for adjacent sectors into one request to reduce load time. This option is often used for boot floppy disks. You also can use the compact configuration variable to specify this option.

◆ The -C file option uses file as the configuration file. If no file is specified, /etc/lilo/config is used as the default.

◆ The -d secs option specifies the number of tenths of a second to wait before booting the first image. You also can specify this number in the configuration variable delay.

◆ The -f file option uses file as the name of the disk parameter table (called disktab). If a filename is omitted, the file /etc/lilo/disktab is used.

◆ The -i sector option installs the kernel as the new boot sector. The argument to be used with this option can be read from the install configuration variable.

4

◆ The -I *name* option displays the path of the named kernel image file. If no matching name is found, an error is generated. You can add the v option after the name to verify the existence of the image file. This option uses the BOOT_IMAGE environment variable.

◆ The -l option generates linear sector addresses instead of the default sector/head/cylinder addresses. You also can specify this option with the configuration variable linear.

◆ The -m *file* option uses *file* as the location of the map file. If no filename is given, /etc/lilo/map is used.

◆ The -P fix option allows LILO to adjust sector/head/cylinder addresses using the table file. You also can specify this option with the fix-table configuration variable.

◆ The -P ignore option overrides correction of sector/head/cylinder addresses. You also can specify this option with the ignore-table configuration variable.

◆ The -q option displays the currently mapped files.

◆ The -r *dir* option performs a chroot command on *dir* before continuing. This option is necessary if the root filesystem is mounted in a different location from the map installer command. Because the current directory is changed with this command, use absolute pathnames for all files.

◆ The -R *words* option stores words in the map file for use by the boot loader. The *words* are parameters that the boot process uses as part of the default command line. The first word must be the name of the boot image.

◆ The -s *file* option copies the original boot sector to *file* instead of /etc/lilo /boot.hex_num.

◆ The -S *file* option is the same as -s, but it overwrites the old file if one exists.

◆ The -t option performs a test by executing the entire installation process except writing the map file and boot sector. Ideally, you use this option with the -v option to verify accurate behavior of the map installer.

◆ The -u *dev* option restores the backup copy of the boot sector for *dev*. If no device is specified, the default value is used. If the default is not a valid value, the current root device is used. The backup copy is checked for a time stamp before the write is completed.

◆ The -U *dev* option is the same as -u except that it doesn't check for the time stamp.

◆ The -v *level* option uses the verbose output level specified to display messages.

◆ The -V option displays the version number of the map installer, and then exits.

MAP INSTALLER CONFIGURATION FILE OPTIONS

You can store configuration options for the map installer in the file /etc/lilo/config or /etc/lilo.conf (depending on the version of Linux). The file consists of sets of parameter-value pairs, although some options do not need a value. You can use whitespace between the parameter and the equal sign and between the equal sign and the value. You can include comments by starting the line with a pound sign. A newline character terminates the comment. As a rule, variable names are case insensitive, and values are usually case sensitive. It is good practice, though, to keep all entries lowercase (as is UNIX convention).

You can put the following options into the map installer configuration file /etc/lilo /config or /etc/lilo.conf:

- The `alias=name` option allows an image to be called by the string *name* as well as its normal filename.

- The `append=string` option appends *string* to the command line passed to the kernel. This option is mostly used to pass boot parameters for hardware devices that are not automatically detected by the kernel.

- The `backup=file` option copies the original boot sector to *file* instead of /etc /lilo/boot.hex_num. You also can specify a device (like /dev/null) instead of a file.

- The `boot=dev` option specifies the device that contains the boot sector. If no name is specified, the currently mounted root partition is used.

- The `compact` option merges read requests for adjacent sectors into a single read request, reducing the load time and file size. This option is commonly used with floppy disks.

- The `delay=secs` option gives the time in tenths of a second that the system should wait before booting the image. If no delay is provided, the boot is immediate.

- The `disktab=file` option gives the name of the disk parameter table. If no filename is given, /etc/lilo/disktab is used.

- The `fix-table` option lets LILO adjust sector/head/cylinder addresses. This option is usually used with operating systems that may change these addresses. LILO readjusts incorrect entries if `fix-table` is specified.

- The `force-backup=file` option is similar to `backup`, but it overwrites any existing file. If `force-backup` is used in the configuration options, any other backup option is ignored.

- The `install=sector` option installs the image in the specified boot sector. If no value is given, /etc/lilo/boot.b is used.

- The `label=name` option renames an image to the alternate string name.

4

LILO

◆ The linear option generates linear sector addresses instead of sector/head /cylinder addresses. Linear addresses are independent of disk geometry and are translated in real time. Linear boot disks may not be portable.

◆ The literal=string option is similar to the append variable but it removes any other options, using only those specified in string.

◆ In the map=file option, file is the map file location. If no value is given, /etc /lilo/map is used.

◆ The message=file option uses the contents of file as a message displayed before the boot prompt. The message cannot be larger than 64K. If the message is changed or moved, the map file must be rebuilt.

◆ The optional option makes an image optional. If the image's file can't be located, it is not booted. This option is useful for testing new kernels.

◆ The password=password option sets a password for all images. If the restricted option exists, a password is required only to boot the image to which the configuration file refers.

◆ The prompt option forces the boot prompt without checking for any keypresses. This option is usually combined with the timeout option to force unattended reboots.

◆ The ramdisk=size option sets the optional RAM disk to size. A setting equal to zero suppresses the RAM disk.

◆ The read-only option mounts the root filesystem as read-only.

◆ The read-write option mounts the root filesystem as read-write.

◆ The restricted option relaxes password protection.

◆ The root=dev option specifies the device to be mounted as the root filesystem. If the value current is used, the root device is the device on which the root filesystem is currently mounted (unless changed with the -r command-line option).

◆ The serial=parms option sets a serial line for control, initializing the line and accepting input from it (as well as the console). The format of the parameters is port, baud_rate, parity, bits. When serial is set, the delay value is set to 20 automatically, unless this value is overridden.

◆ The timeout=secs option sets the number of tenths of a second that the system waits for keyboard input before loading the image. This option is also used to specify password input timeouts. The default value is infinite.

◆ The verbose=level option displays progress messages. The higher the level, the more messages are displayed. If the -v command-line option is also included, the highest level specified in either variable is used.

◆ The vga=*mode* option sets the VGA text mode for use during booting. Valid values include normal (80×25 text mode), extended or ext (80×50 text mode), and ask (prompt for the mode during boot). To obtain a list of available modes, boot with the parameter vga=ask and press Enter when asked for a value. Case is not important in the values of the vga option.

If any parameter is not specified either on the command line or in the configuration file, default values are used. Some values are also maintained within the kernel image (such as ramdisk, root, and vga).

BOOT IMAGES

LILO can boot a kernel image from several locations, such as a regular file on the root filesystem or any other mounted filesystem, a block device such as a floppy disk, or the boot sector of another partition or disk. The type of boot is dictated by entries in a configuration file. Boot image configuration files can have several variables defined, all of which have been mentioned in the preceding sections. Valid configuration file variables include alias, label, optional, password, ramdisk, read-only, read-write, restricted, root, and vga.

To boot a kernel image from a file, all that is necessary in the configuration file is the name of the image. For example, the line

```
image=/linux_main
```

boots the image called linux_main.

To boot an image from another device, the sectors that must be read on that device have to be specified. Several methods of providing the sector information exist. The starting sector must be provided, but you can then either specify a number of sectors to be read (start+length) or the end sector number (start-finish). If only one number is provided (the start sector), only that sector is read.

For example, the contents of this configuration file

```
image=/dev/fd0
    range=1+512
```

will boot the kernel from the floppy disk, starting at sector 1 and reading the next 512 sectors.

You can specify more than one configuration for an image because LILO stores values in an image descriptor file and not in the image itself. For example, a configuration file can contain the following entries:

```
image=/linux_main
    label=linux-hda1
    root=/dev/hda1
```

4

LILO

```
image=/linux_main
     label=linux-hda3
     root=/dev/hda3
image=/linux_main
     label=linux-flop
     root=/dev/fd0
```

This code has three configurations for the same Linux kernel (linux_main), but it also has different root devices with three different alternate names. The boot devices for the image are /dev/hda1, /dev/hda3, and /dev/fd0, respectively. Whitespace in the configuration file is ignored, so the indentations are for ease of reading only.

THE DISK PARAMETER TABLE

LILO is usually able to obtain information about the hard disks and floppy disks on the system by reading the kernel. On some systems (especially some SCSI adapters and adapters that do not behave as IDE or SCSI normal devices), though, this isn't possible. When LILO can't obtain the disk parameter information, it generates an error message about "bad geometry."

The disk parameters can be physically read by LILO from the file /etc/lilo/disktab, which exists only with some versions of Linux. When the disktab file exists, it takes precedence over any auto-detected values. The disktab file contains the device number (hexadecimal), its BIOS code, and the disk geometry. A sample disktab file could have the following entries:

```
# /etc/lilo/disktab - LILO disk paramter table
#
# Dev. num   BIOS code   Secs/track   Heads/cyl   Cyls   Part. Offset
#
   0x800       0x80         32           64        1714      0
   0x801       0x80         32           64        1714     1001
```

This example shows a SCSI disk with two partitions. The first partition, /dev/sda1, has a device number 800, and the second partition, /dev/sda2, has the device number 801. Both partitions have the BIOS code 80. Both the device number and BIOS code have to be given in hex format, which accounts for the leading 0x. The disk has 32 sectors per track, 64 heads per cylinder, and 1,714 cylinders. Because both partitions are on the same disk, these parameters will be the same.

The partition offset is an optional field. The first partition starts at offset 0, and the second starts at offset 1,001 (the number of sectors from the start of the disk). The partition offsets need only be explicitly given when the kernel cannot obtain that information. Most hard disks (including removable and optical disks) don't need the partition offsets, but CD-ROMs sometimes do.

4

Tip

> When filling in the /etc/lilo/disktab file you don't have to have the details exactly right. Most systems will remap the drive parameters to 32 sectors per track and 64 heads, whether those numbers are correct or not. (This is a BIOS action.) The number of cylinders must be at least equal to or higher than the number of actual cylinders to avoid truncation of the disk space the operating system recognizes.

Some BIOS versions will not allow disks exceeding certain values. This problem usually occurs with IDE and SCSI controller cards that are designed for DOS systems with relatively small (<1G) disk drives and older BIOSs. Device drivers allow some high-capacity drives to be used, although some systems will have a problem accessing files beyond the 1G limit.

REMOVING OR DISABLING LILO

To prevent LILO from booting the system, you must disable the boot sector (by using fdisk to change the active partition) or remove it completely. Most versions of LILO can be quickly disabled with the command

```
/etc/lilo/lilo -u
```

If you are using the newer directory structure, substitute the pathname as necessary. Some later versions of LILO use the menu-driven setup utility instead of a lilo binary. In most cases, there is a file called /etc/lilo/install that can accomplish the same procedures.

When removing a LILO boot sector in the Master Boot Record of the disk, you must replace the MBR with another record. If you want to replace the MBR with a DOS MBR, from a booted DOS floppy disk, enter the command

```
fdisk /mbr
```

Because backup copies of the boot sector are created whenever LILO creates a new version, you can copy the older versions of the boot sector back in place (assuming they are still available). For example, to restore the Master Boot Record saved in a file called boot.0800 (800 is the device number of a SCSI drive), issue the command

```
dd if=/etc/lilo/boot.0800 of=/dev/sda bs=446 count=1
```

If you are using another device, substitute the name of the saved boot file and the device name.

LILO

TROUBLESHOOTING LILO

LILO displays error messages when it can't function properly. These error messages should be sufficient to identify the problem. The most common error messages and their solutions are shown in Table 4.1.

TABLE 4.1 COMMON LILO ERROR MESSAGES.

Message	Solution
Can't put the boot sector on logical partition X	LILO attempted to put the boot sector on the correct root filesystem on a logical partition. MBRs can only boot primary partitions by default. Override with the `-b` option and an explicit boot partition value, or use the configuration variable `boot=device`.
Got bad geometry	The disk controller (mostly SCSI) doesn't support automatic geometry detection. Use the file /etc/lilo/disktab to provide the disk parameters.
Invalid partition table, entry X	The sector/head/cylinder and linear addresses of the first sector of the partition don't match. This error usually occurs when an operating system creates partitions not aligned to tracks. Try the `fix-table` option.
First sector doesn't have a valid boot signature	The first sector of the device doesn't seem to be a valid boot sector. Check the device name or rerun LILO to install the boot sector.
Cylinder number is too big	A file is located beyond the 1,024th cylinder, which LILO can't access because of BIOS limitations. In most cases, the extra disk space is lost.
XXX doesn't have a valid LILO signature	XXX was located but it isn't a valid LILO entry. If XXX is the boot sector, use the `-i` option or the `install` option to install the LILO boot sector.

Message	Solution
XXX has an invalid stage code	The entry at *XXX* is corrupted. Rerun LILO.
Kernel *XXX* is too big	The kernel is larger than 512K, which LILO can't handle. Remove some unused drivers and recompile the kernel.
Partition entry not found	The partition is not in the partition table. Use `fdisk` to enter the partition number in the partition table.
Sorry, don't know how to handle device *XXX*	LILO can't determine the disk parameters. Use the file /etc/lilo/disktab to specify them.

SUMMARY

This chapter should include all the information you need to install and use LILO to create your boot sectors for Linux. LILO is quite versatile and can handle several different configurations with ease. It allows you to tailor your installation to boot the best way for your use.

Although LILO is only used when first setting up your Linux system and after kernel changes, you should know the basics of its operation so you know what is happening to your hard disks and their boot sectors. Knowing about LILO is especially important when you use other operating systems in addition to Linux on the same system.

4

LILO

- Understanding
  XFree86

- Installing XFree86
  Software

- Configuring XFree86

- Examining the
  Xconfig and
  XF86Config Files in
  Detail

- Using the .xinitrc File

CHAPTER 5

Installing and Configuring XFree86

X is a graphical user interface (GUI). The version of X supplied with most Linux software packages is XFree86, which is an implementation of the X Window system developed at MIT. XFree86 is available for several different PC UNIX versions, including Linux, and has been expanded over the more traditional X system to include the wide variety of hardware that is used in PC machines.

Note

The official name of the GUI is X. It is often also called X Window system or X Windows, although these uses are greatly discouraged. (The latter version smacks of Microsoft's Windows product.) For the most part, you can use the terms X, X11 (from X version 11), XFree86, and X Window system interchangeably, but avoid X Windows! It's a sure method of annoying veteran UNIX users!

At least two major releases of XFree86 are available with Linux. Most distributions have version 2.X, although a few now offer the latest release (version 3.1.1 at the time of this writing). This chapter discusses installation and preliminary configuration of both XFree86 versions, although most of the examples use the more recent XFree86 3.x version.

Warning

It is important to understand the complete XFree86 installation process before you install your software. In some cases, you can cause damage to hardware and the already installed Linux software if you select inappropriate drivers.

UNDERSTANDING XFREE86

XFree86 is a public domain version of the X11 windowing system developed by MIT and now copyrighted to the MIT Consortium. In keeping with the Linux developers' desire to have no copyright code that requires licensing as part of the operating system, XFree86 was developed specifically for the PC architecture. XFree86 works with many PC-based UNIX systems including Linux.

Several versions of XFree86 are available, and they are all based on different releases of X. The most commonly used Linux version of XFree86 is release 2.X, which is based on X11 release 5 (abbreviated as X11R5). The latest versions of XFree86 are releases 3.X, which are based on X11 release 6 (X11R6), the most current version of the X Window system. Bug fixes and minor changes in utilities are often available as incremental version numbers. You can load these incremental versions over a release of the same number. For example, if you have loaded XFree86 version 2.1 and obtain the fix release 2.1.1, you must load it over 2.1 and not by itself. The bug fix releases do not contain the complete system, only the updates.

Warning

Do not use XFree86 version 2.0! It has several critical bugs. Instead, use at least version 2.1 or 2.1.1.

A few problems arose in the early days of the XFree86 development, primarily because of a lack of information from the official X Consortium (which controls the standards of X). To solve the problem, The XFree86 Project Inc. was founded. It became a member of the X Consortium and was thereby granted access to information about new releases well before they were available to the general public. XFree86 is now a trademark of The XFree86 Project Inc.

Many Linux versions of XFree86 contain directories and references to a product called X386. X386 was an earlier version of X11R5 for the PC architecture, and XFree86 retained many of the X386 naming conventions for directories and files. However, X386 and XFree86 are different products and have no connection (other than naming conventions).

The latest versions of XFree86 require a practical minimum of at least 8M of RAM in your machine to run, and a virtual memory of at least 16M. In other words, you would need a swap space of at least 8M with an 8M RAM machine, although more is highly recommended. (XFree86 can run with 4MB, but it runs slowly enough to be annoying.) If you have 16M of RAM, you don't need the swap space although it should be used for safety's sake, especially if you plan on running memory-hogging applications. If you plan on using X a lot, set up your system to have 32M of virtual RAM for the best performance (preferably at least 16M RAM and the rest swap space).

Note

Tweaking version 2.X of XFree86 to run in 4M of RAM is possible, although it is a slow process (both tweaking and running) and is therefore not recommended. XFree86 version 3.X will not run properly in 4M (although it can, with a lot of effort, be shoehorned in, but it then runs so slow as to be useless). XFree86 v 3.x will run in 8M RAM, although 16M is preferable. Again, a total of at least 16M virtual memory is recommended, with 32M preferable.

INSTALLING XFREE86 SOFTWARE

Most XFree86 distributions are provided as part of the software on a Linux CD-ROM or floppy disk set. This chapter uses a CD-ROM distribution (from the CD-ROM included with this book) as the example because it is the most common form of distribution. The instructions, however, apply equally for floppy disk distributions and software packages obtained from an FTP or BBS site.

Typically, the XFree86 software is located in a set of directories called x1, x2, x3, and so on. The Slackware distribution has directories running up to x14. Other distributions may differ in the number of directories. XFree86 applications are also stored in a set of directories called xap1, xap2, and so on. The software is usually supplied in gzipped format. The contents of each directory are usually summarized in a text file, which gives the filenames and their purposes.

Before you install the XFree86 software, verify that it will work with your existing Linux software. XFree86 releases depend on certain versions of the Linux kernel, the C library (libc), and the ld.so file version. A file in the distribution directories should explain the lowest version number of each of these three items that is necessary to run XFree86. If you obtained the XFree86 software packaged with a Linux release, it is likely to be compatible, and you can skip the verification stage.

If your X software wasn't installed by a setup program, you can install the XFree86 software manually by unzipping each file and then extracting the files in the archive. You must then properly load the files into the final directories. This process can be tedious and lengthy and should be avoided unless you want to know exactly what is going on. Instead, use the installation routines that the Linux vendor supplies, such as setup.

XFree86 version 2.X uses directories that mirror those used by the X386 software product. For most Linux systems, the primary directory is /usr/X386. To maintain consistency with software packages and utilities that expect a more common X11R5, X11R6, or X11 directory, Linux generally uses links between the X386 directory and the other directories as necessary. The Linux installation routine often creates these links.

XFree86 version 3.X abandons the /usr/X386 directory convention in favor of the more common X location /usr/X11R6. When upgrading an installation of XFree86 version 2.x to version 3.x, bear in mind the change of directory names and either change links or remove the old /usr/X386 versions completely. Make sure your search path variable is changed, too.

Note

To simplify the directory structure for XFree86, links to a directory called /usr/X11 usually are created. This directory can then be linked to /usr/X386 and /usr/X11R6. Check your directory structure to determine which links are in place on your system. Also check your PATH environment variable to see which directory is in the search path (if one has been added at all).

CHOOSING AN X SERVER

Before installing XFree86, you must decide which type of server you will use. The XFree86 servers are drivers for the video system. As a GUI, X uses the video card in your system extensively. Several drivers are available in most XFree86 distribution sets, and the names of the files tend to indicate the video card for which they are designed. For example, you may encounter the following server files in most XFree86 versions:

XF86_Mono	Monochrome video card (generic)
XF86_VGA16	16-color VGA video card (generic)
XF86_SVGA	Color SVGA video card (generic)
XF86_S3	Accelerated server for S3-based video cards
XF86_Mach8	Accelerated server for Mach8 video cards
XF86_Mach32	Accelerated server for Mach32 video cards
XF86_8514	Accelerated server for 8514/A video cards

The generic indications in the preceding list mean that the server has no card-specific instructions; the other servers have card-specific video card requirements. For example, you can use the XF86_S3 server only with video cards using the S3 chipset. Check with your video card documentation (or use a diagnostic utility program) to determine your video card's chipset. Your distribution version of XFree86 will probably have other specific server versions, so check the documentation for compatibility details.

The generic server drivers work with most cards that provide VGA and SVGA support. However, because the generic driver provides only the basic VGA and SVGA video instructions, any fancy features or extra power your video card may have will not be used. Card-specific servers, on the other hand, enable you to use the full capabilities of fancy video cards.

Warning

Installing an X server with the wrong specific video card driver can cause damage to your system. If you are not sure of the video card chipset, use a generic driver. Most video cards can handle VGA and SVGA generic drivers without a problem. If you're not sure, use generic.

Most distributions of XFree86 have a default of a standard VGA system prewritten into the configuration files. You can use this default setting without worrying about other configuration items in some cases, but it is better to check the configuration files manually before running XFree86 for the first time.

To change the server name that XFree86 uses, modify the symbolic link to the file called X under the XFree86 bin directory (such as /usr/X386/bin/X or /usr/X11R6 /bin/X). You can change the server at any time by creating a new link to the required server file. For example, if you want to use the SVGA server when your system is currently configured for the VGA server, issue the following commands:

```
rm /usr/X11R6/bin/X
ln -s /usr/X11R6/bin/XF86_SVA /usr/X11R6/bin/X
```

The first line removes the current link and the second adds the link between XF86_SVGA and X. The directory names for the XFree86 base directory may change, depending on the version of XFree86 you are running (although if they are linked together, it won't matter which you change).

INSTALLING XFREE86 MANUALLY

As mentioned earlier in this section, you can install XFree86 without using the installation scripts. You may want to install XFree86 this way if you have to perform installation across directories or place the files in directories other than their default values. Some users like to manually install XFree86 so that they know what is happening at each step. Manually installing XFree86 is a great way to learn the intricacies of the X operating system (although it can be a long operation).

To manually install the XFree86 distribution software, you must extract the files into the proper directories using the gzip command. The general process is quite simple:

1. Log in as root. You must install XFree86 as the superuser.
2. Create the directory /usr/X386. This directory may already exist on your system as some Linux installation scripts create it.
3. Change to the /usr/X386 directory.

4. For each file in the distribution set, use the `gzip` utility to extract and install the contents. The general format of the command is

```
gzip -dc tarfile | tar xvof -
```

5. Repeat the process for each file in the XFree86 product set. You must change to each distribution directory manually (on a CD-ROM or different floppy disk, for example) and use `gzip` on each archive file in that directory.

The `tar` utility flags shown in the preceding command line ensure that the original ownership of the files is preserved and that the output is displayed on-screen for you. Once all the XFree86 files have been installed into the correct directories, you can continue with the configuration process.

INSTALLING XFREE86 USING A SCRIPT

Most users want to automate the installation process. This installation method is faster, requires less interaction from the user, and is much less prone to errors. For this reason, most XFree86 distribution releases either include an installation script or use the Linux `setup` program.

When installing using the `setup` script (or similar utility) supplied with Linux distributions, you are usually prompted as to whether you want to install XFree86 during the initial Linux installation. If you answered affirmatively to this question, the binaries for XFree86 are already installed. If you didn't get prompted for XFree86 installation, it may have been installed automatically. Check the directories /usr/X386/bin or /usr/X11R6/bin for files. If a large number of files exist in either directory, XFree86 was installed for you.

Just because XFree86 was installed from the distribution media automatically doesn't usually mean you can use it immediately. You should still go through the configuration process using the `ConfigXF86` or `xf86config` utilities, or manually editing the Xconfig or XF86Config file (depending on the version of XFree86). Most automated installations will include default VGA or SVGA preconfigured files, but it's still a good idea to check the contents of the Xconfig or XF86Config file before you try to run XFree86.

USING THE PATH ENVIRONMENT VARIABLE

Put the XFree86 binary directory in your path by using the environment variable `PATH` or `path` (depending on the shell). The location of the variable's definition depends on the type of shell you are using and the login you use to run XFree86. In general, you should add either /usr/X386/bin (XFree86 version 2.x) or /usr/X11R6/bin (XFree86 version 3.x) to the path definition statement.

For example, if you use bash (Bourne Again Shell) for most purposes, a .profile file is read when you log in to set environment variables. If you log in as a user other than root, the .profile file is kept in your home directory. If you use the root login, the .profile may be kept in the root directory or you may be using the default system .profile kept in the file /etc/profile (note the lack of a period when the file is in /etc. This convention is used to show that it is a globally available .profile).

If the XFree86 bin directory isn't already in the path, add it to the path or PATH variable definition. A .profile file for bash may have the following line after adding the XFree86 directory:

```
PATH="/sbin:/usr/bin:/bin:/usr/X11/bin:/usr/openwin/bin"
```

For C shell users (including tcsh) other than root, the syntax is a little different. The startup file .login or csh.login contains a line defining the path. Adding the XFree86 directory is a matter of tacking it to the definition:

```
set path = ( /sbin /usr/bin /bin /usr/X11/bin /usr/openwin/bin . )
```

Of course, your exact path definition lines will probably differ. As long as you add the XFree86 bin directory to the path and then log out and back in, the shell should find the proper binary files.

CONFIGURING XFREE86

Before you can run XFree86, you should specify some configuration information. This part tends to frustrate newcomers to XFree86 because getting your configuration files exactly right so that XFree86 runs properly can be a convoluted process. The step-by-step instructions in this section should streamline the process.

A utility called either ConfigXF86 or xf86config that is provided with many distributions of Linux and XFree86 simplifies the entire XFree86 installation process, but only if you have one of the supported graphics cards. A list of cards supported by ConfigXF86 and xf86config is usually included in the Hardware HOWTO file provided with the Linux distribution software. If you can't find the HOWTO file, you can obtain it from most FTP and BBS locations (see Chapter 2, "Linux Hardware and Software"). Make sure the version of the file corresponds to the Linux version you are running. The section "Using ConfigXF86 and xf86config" provides more details about ConfigXF86 and xf86config. (You can, in some cases, provide enough information for ConfigXF86 and xf86config to use your unlisted video card for the installation. This procedure is discussed in the "Using ConfigXF86 and xf86config" section.) If you don't have the Hardware HOWTO file or your video card is not listed and you don't want to use a generic driver, you must manually configure XFree86. Even if you use the ConfigXF86 or xf86config script to install XFree86, you may still have to make manual modifications to your installation.

Most of the configuration details for XFree86 version 2.x are contained in a file called Xconfig; XFree86 version 3.x uses a file called XF86Config or Xconfig, depending on the version. The bare-bones instructions for setting up an Xconfig or XF86Config file are spread out over several text files included with the XFree86 distribution set. Check the README, VideoModes.doc, README.Config, and README.Linux files. Also, read the man pages for Xconfig, XF86Config, XFree86, and Xfree86kbd. Finally, check the man pages for the server version you are running, if some are provided. It's a good idea to print out the man pages for easier reference.

You need a few items of information to properly complete the Xconfig or XF86Config file. Before you start configuring XFree86, take a moment to note the following details:

◆ XFree86 server to be used

◆ Type of mouse on your system and the port to which it is connected

◆ Your video card's brand name and chipset. If you're not sure of the chipset, either consult your documentation or use a utility program like SuperProbe (Linux) or MSD (DOS).

◆ Your video monitor brand name and model number, as well as the size of the monitor. It also helps to know the maximum horizontal and vertical scan frequencies; this information is usually available from the monitor's documentation.

◆ Type of keyboard you will be using if not the U.S. generic type. Most users have the U.S. type, although some countries have customized keyboards that require different key mappings.

If you don't know some of the information and don't have an easy way (such as a utility program) to find out, check the documentation that comes with XFree86. Many distributions contain a directory such as /usr/X11/lib/X11/doc (usually linked to /usr/X386/lib/X11/doc or /usr/X11R6/lib/X11/doc) that contains a number of files describing many cards and monitors supported by XFree86 and the essential configuration information (such as monitor scan rates, which are always difficult to determine because you invariably don't remember where you placed the manual). Figure 5.1 shows an extract from the /usr/X11R6/lib/X11/doc/Monitors file. This entry shows the parameters that a Gateway 2000 system with a CrystalScan monitor requires. The Monitors file has entries for most popular monitor models. Another file included with most CD-ROM distributions is AccelCards, which lists popular video cards and their parameters. Figure 5.2 shows an extract from this file, which shows the S3 card series. Use these files, and any others in the doc directory, to identify the hardware you will be using.

Figure 5.1.
The Monitors file in the X11/doc directory offers configuration information for many popular monitor models.

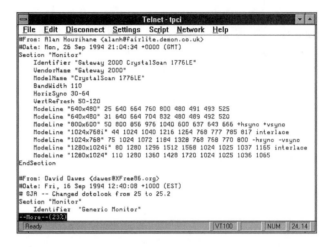

Figure 5.2.
The AccelCards file lists many popular video cards and the configuration information they require.

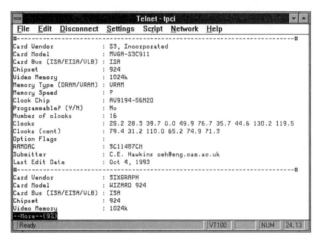

When you've noted all this configuration information, you are ready to start. Configuring XFree86 begins with the Xconfig or XF86Config file.

DECIDING WHERE TO PUT XCONFIG OR XF86CONFIG

You can put the Xconfig or XF86Config file in several places on the Linux filesystem. Usually, it resides in the /usr/X386/lib/X11 directory, which is also where a sample Xconfig or XF86Config file is often found. If you have easy access to the /usr/X386 /lib/X11 directory, it's the best place for the Xconfig or XF86Config file. (Formally, the file is referenced in /usr/X11R6/lib/X11 or /etc, but because /usr/X386 is linked to /usr/X11R6, the two directories point to the same place. The documentation may reference the X11R6 directory, but you can use either /usr/X386 or /usr/X11R6 as long as the link to the X386 directory is in place.)

Note

Unless you are manually installing configuration information, don't worry about whether you should use Xconfig or XF86Config. Automated installation scripts will use the proper file. If you are performing a manual configuration, use Xconfig for XFree86 version 2.X and XF86Config for XFree86 version 3.x.

If you can't use the /usr/X386/lib/X11 directory (maybe it's read-only or on a remote server) or don't want to because you need a customized version of the Xconfig file, you can also place the file in the /etc directory or in your home directory. If the Xconfig file is in your home directory, it applies to your sessions only; any configuration information will not be valid for other users. The /etc directory location for the XFree86 Xconfig file means the configuration information is applicable to all users.

You can also put the Xconfig file in the directory /usr/X386/lib/X11 specific to a particular host machine. To do this, append the name of the host machine to Xconfig filename. For example, the file Xconfig.merlin applies the configuration information only to users logging in from the machine called merlin.

The Linux convention for the Xconfig file is to place it in the /etc directory. Because this location is not the usual one for XFree86 installations, you must create a link to the /etc/Xconfig file from /usr/X386/lib/X11 or your home directory. This link enables XFree86 to find the Xconfig file. To create the link just mentioned, issue the following command:

```
ln -s /usr/X386/lib/X11 /etc/Xconfig
```

The -s option creates a symbolic link (compared to a hard link), which is explained in Chapter 18, "Filesystems and Disks."

USING SUPERPROBE

SuperProbe is a utility that attempts to determine the type of video card (and the amount of video RAM installed on that card) in a PC system. It works on ISA, EISA, and VLB (local bus) architectures, but not on MCA or PCI architectures (although SuperProbe versions for these systems may be available by the time you read this book). If you already know which video card you have, SuperProbe is of little use to you.

SuperProbe attempts to identify video cards by probing for certain known unique registers on each video card it knows about. This process has one drawback—some instructions executed by SuperProbe can cause your machine to lock up. Although it is unlikely damage will occur because of SuperProbe, the filesystem will have to be cleaned if the machine must be reset. For this reason, make sure you are the only user on the machine. Making a backup of your system is also advisable.

Warning

> Running SuperProbe by itself is almost guaranteed to lock up any machine. Use it with care and follow the instructions in this section for giving SuperProbe a basic idea of the testing it should do.

SuperProbe is usually included as part of the XFree86 distribution set on CD-ROMs; you also can get it from FTP and BBS sites that offer Linux software. SuperProbe is not exclusive to Linux; it can run under several other PC UNIX systems as well. A man page is available for SuperProbe.

SuperProbe uses a number of command-line options to specify its behavior. Although the exact options change with each new release of the software, the basic options of interest to you are limited to a few:

-bios	Specifies the video card BIOS' address, normally set to C0000. If you had to set your BIOS address to some other value, it should be specified with this option.
-info	Displays a list of all video cards SuperProbe knows about and the card's names as recognized by SuperProbe.
-no_16	Disables 16-bit testing. This option is used only for old, 8-bit video cards.
-no_bios	Disables testing of the video card BIOS and assumes the card is an EGA, VGA, SVGA, or later type. If your video card is new, this option is useful for preventing many BIOS-caused system freezes.
-no_dac	Disables testing for a RAMDAC type. You can use this option with VGA and SVGA cards to prevent potential freezes.
-no_mem	Skips the testing for the amount of video RAM installed on the video card.
-order	Specifies the order in which chipsets should be tested. This option is useful if you think you know the types of chipsets, but want confirmation. Alternatively, if you suspect the video card has one of a few chipsets, you can list just those.

-verbose   Displays information on-screen as to SuperProbe's actions and results. You should use this option in all cases to show progress and potential problems.

One of the first steps to take is to display a list of all the video cards SuperProbe knows about. Issue the command

SuperProbe -info

and you will see a list that shows the cards, chipsets, and RAMDACs that SuperProbe can recognize. Note that the utility name SuperProbe is mixed case, with uppercase S and P. This format is unusual for a Linux system and may take experienced UNIX and Linux users a moment to get used to.

If you have an older 8-bit card, you can determine the chipset with the command

SuperProbe -no16 -verbose

If you have a 16-bit (or higher) card that you suspect to be an S3, Cirrus Logic, or Tseng chipset, for example, you can use the -order option to simplify testing (and prevent potential problems), as in

SuperProbe -order S3,Cirrus,Tseng -verbose

There are no spaces between chipsets specified after the -order option. The -verbose option lets you see what is going on. Narrowing the search for a chipset in this way prevents lockups. Even if you know exactly what video card is in your system, don't assume SuperProbe will function properly. SuperProbe has an annoying habit of hanging up a system because of conflicts with other cards or devices. Use it with care.

USING CONFIGXF86 AND XF86CONFIG

ConfigXF86 and XF86Config use simple interfaces from which you select supported video cards and video monitors. (ConfigXF86 was written by Stephen Zwaska, by the way.) If the ConfigXF86 or XF86Config utility supports your video card (check the Hardware HOWTO and XFree86 README files), you can use the ConfigXF86 and XF86Config installation routine to simplify the configuration process enormously. If ConfigXF86 or XF86Config is provided with your XFree86 distribution, it is in the directory /usr/X386/bin.

Documentation for ConfigXF86 and XF86Config is usually placed in /usr/X386/bin with the executable file. Some versions of Linux and XFree86 don't supply the documents, though. The documentation is often supplied in multiple formats. An ASCII version is called ConfigXF86.txt, and a PostScript version (or the XF86Config version) is called ConfigXF86.ps.

When you run either ConfigXF86 or XF86Config, some general information appears on-screen. Figure 5.3 shows the introductory screen of XF86Config, which is used as an example for the screen shots throughout this section. After this screen, you may receive a status message telling you about existing files and distributions of X. In most CD-ROM based installations, you are told that you already have an earlier version of X, as shown in Figure 5.4. This version was installed by setup, in most cases.You can ignore these messages and continue on with the configuration, although you should read the messages about paths.

Figure 5.3.
The introductory screen
of XF86Config explains
what the program is
going to do and what
information you need to
provide.

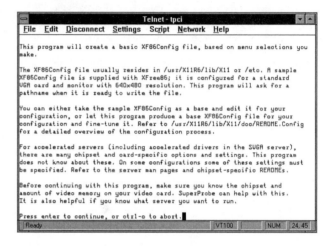

Figure 5.4.
Most versions of
XF86Config warn you
that you have an earlier
version of X already on
your drive.

You are then prompted for the information you gathered earlier about your system. In most cases, you are shown a list of supported values and asked to choose one. Following through these choices in order provides the utility with the proper information to build your Xconfig file. The XF86Config utility, for example, asks you for your mouse type, as shown in Figure 5.5. Choose the mouse model you are using from this list. Don't assume that because you configured a mouse when you installed Linux that X will pick up the correct type.

Figure 5.5.
Because X is mouse-
dependent, XF86Config
asks you for the type of
mouse you will be
using.

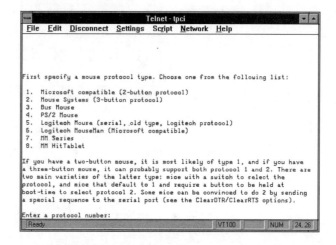

Depending on the type of mouse you choose, you may be asked about special mouse button functionality. Figure 5.6, for example, shows the prompt after selecting a Logitech MouseMan mouse, which has three buttons (as do most UNIX workstation mouse models). This screen enables you to use the three buttons for their proper functions. After this screen, you are asked for the port of the mouse, as shown in Figure 5.7. If you installed a mouse when you installed Linux (such as with setup), you may have already supplied the port the mouse will use. This port was linked to the special device driver /dev/mouse. If you have installed a mouse already, press Enter. Otherwise, give the mouse port name.

Some versions of the configuration routine ask whether you want to enable special character bindings on the keyboard, as shown in Figure 5.8. This option is used most often for non-English characters. For most users, the answer is no.

Figure 5.6.
If the type of mouse you selected in the previous screen supports special options, you are asked whether you want them to be enabled.

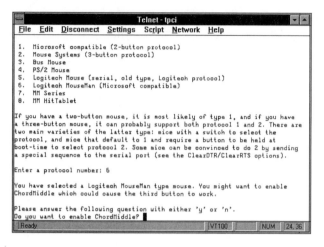

Figure 5.7.
X must know the port your mouse is attached to. If you have already configured a mouse, press Return.

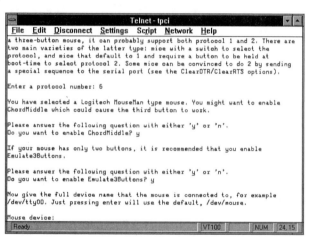

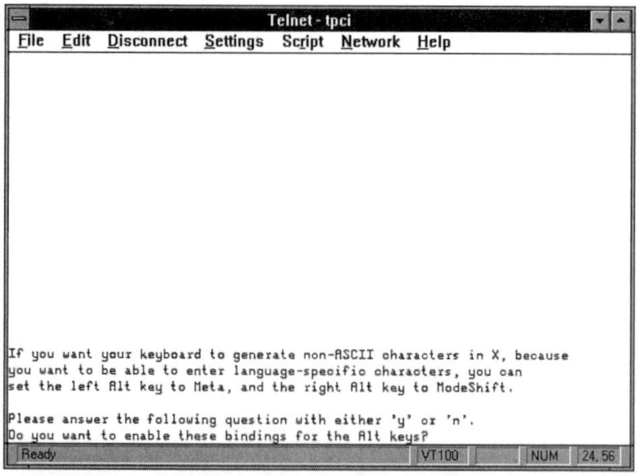

Figure 5.8.
X provides support for non-English characters through extended keyboard bindings.

Now comes the trickier parts. You must supply the information about your monitor and video card that you determined earlier. The screen shown in Figure 5.9 asks about the horizontal sync frequencies your monitor uses. If you are not sure, use a generic (VGA or SVGA) setting. Choosing the wrong setting may cause damage to your monitor!

Figure 5.9.
Select the proper
horizontal sync fre-
quency for your monitor
from this screen.

Next, you must set the vertical sync rate. Again, err on the side of the more common rates. This screen is shown in Figure 5.10. If you are not sure, choose the lowest number. The horizontal and vertical sync frequencies for most popular monitors are given in the Monitors file in the doc directory, mentioned earlier. You are then asked to enter a name for the monitor, which is used to identify it in the configuration files. Figure 5.11 shows this screen. You can enter the actual model name or any string you want; it doesn't have to match your actual monitor name because the string is not used for anything except identification.

Figure 5.10.
You need to set the
vertical sync frequen-
cies, too.

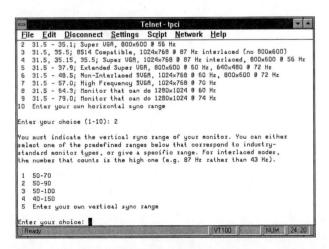

Figure 5.11.
After setting the
frequencies your
monitor uses, you
get to name it.

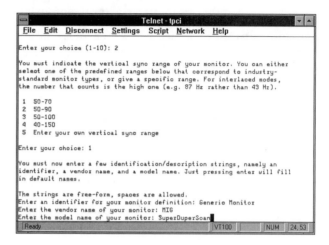

After configuring the monitor, you must configure your video card. The configuration program may ask you whether you want to look at the video card database (see Figure 5.12). If you do not have the parameters your card supports already at hand, take advantage of this option. You can page through a list of video cards, as shown in Figure 5.13, until you find a card that matches your card. Choose the number in the left-hand column to display the card's information, as shown in Figure 5.14. Sometimes the information is very brief. You may want to copy down some of this information for later reference.

Figure 5.12.
The configuration
program may give you
the option of looking up
your video card in the
video database.

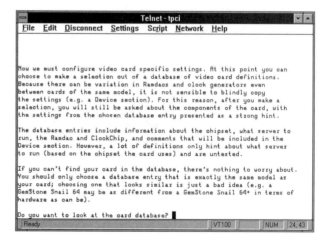

5

Figure 5.13.
The video card data-
base has several pages
of cards listed.

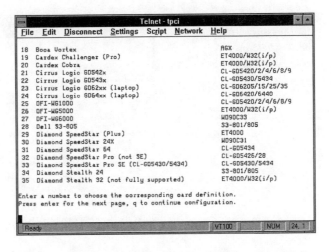

Figure 5.14.
The video card data-
base shows the X
configuration informa-
tion about your card
when you select the
proper number from the
list.

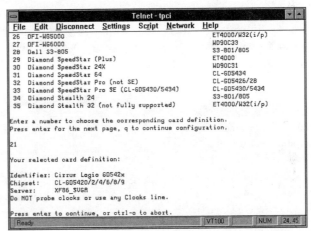

After choosing the video card, you select a server as shown in Figure 5.15. The servers available under X were discussed earlier in this chapter. Enter the number that corresponds to the server you want to use. If you don't want to experiment with video card-specific servers, choose the VGA or SVGA server (the VGA entry is a safe bet for a first-time installation). You can change the server later, so don't worry about getting the best performance you can out of your video card at this time—it's more important to get X running properly!

Figure 5.15.
Use this screen to
specify the type of X
server you want to run.

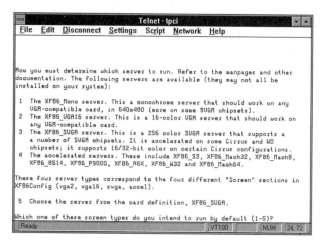

Depending on your installation configuration, you may be asked whether you want the configuration routine to set up some links for you, as shown in Figure 5.16. It doesn't hurt to have these links set unless they will cause a conflict with directory naming.

Figure 5.16.
On some systems, the
configuration routine
offers to set links to
different X directories
for you.

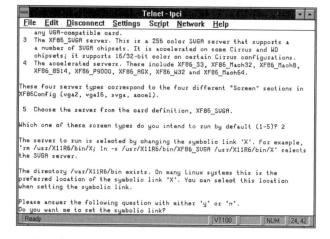

The next step is to tell X how much memory your video card has, as shown in Figure 5.17. The more RAM your video card has, the faster X can run. If you are not sure how much RAM your card has, choose a low number. Most video cards sold in the last year or two have at least 1M video RAM, but you should verify your card's RAM complement in your documentation.

Figure 5.17.
Choose the amount of
video RAM on your
card.

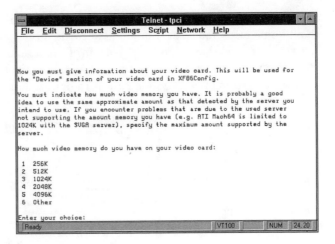

As a final step in the video card configuration, you are asked to name the card. As with the monitor names, these strings are used for identification only and can be set to anything you want.

Some video cards can handle special processing. A screen like the one shown in Figure 5.18 asks you which options you want to enable. Make sure you know what you are doing if you select some of these options; some of them can hang your system if used incorrectly. If you are not sure or you are configuring a generic system, don't enable any options. Just press Enter to ignore them.

Figure 5.18.
Some cards have
special features that
you can enable through
this screen.

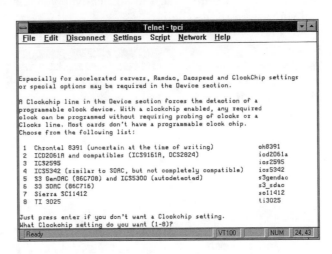

The screen shown in Figure 5.19 follows the special processing screen and asks about some clock features. Some video cards do not support this feature and will hang if it is tried. As you see at the bottom of the screen, the configuration utility has identified the video card in this configuration as not supporting this feature, so the SuperProbe system should not be run. If in doubt, don't use it!

Figure 5.19.
Many high-speed video cards can be optimized with the use of a Clocks option, although some cards (including the one in this example) do not support the option.

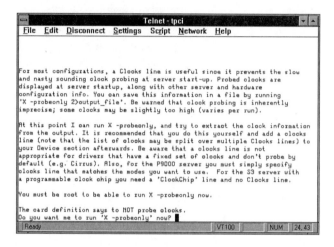

Finally, the configuration script asks whether you want it to write the information to the X configuration file, as shown in Figure 5.20. If you answer yes, the configuration file is updated automatically. If you answer no, all your entries are lost and you return to the shell.

Figure 5.20.
The final step in the configuration process is writing the configuration file. This prompt verifies that you want to generate the file.

After the XF86Config or Xconfig file has been created using the script, resist the temptation to start up X immediately. Instead, take the time to examine the file manually to prevent any chance of damage to your hardware from an incorrect setting. The following section on manually configuring the Xconfig or XF86Config file explains all the settings. Once you're sure all is fine, launch X with the command startx. If the X server fails to start, run the configuration utility again and check all your answers carefully. In case of problems, always choose generic settings just to get X working.

EXAMINING THE XCONFIG AND XF86CONFIG FILES IN DETAIL

If you are manually entering your configuration information into the Xconfig or XF86Config files, you need to know how the files are laid out and how to enter your specific details. All versions of XFree86 have at least one sample configuration file, usually called Xconfig.eg or XF86Config.eg and located in the lib directory. Use this file as a template for creating your own configuration file. Copy the example file to a new file without the .eg extension, and make the changes described in the following paragraphs.

The Xconfig and XF86Config files are not short, but lots of comments are scattered throughout. The format of the configuration files is a set of sections for each aspect of the XFree86 configuration. The general order of sections is as follows:

> Pathnames to binaries and screen fonts
>
> Keyboard information
>
> Mouse information
>
> Server file
>
> Video information

If you have run the automated configuration file generator utilities like XF86config or XF86Config, check the entries in the generated file. If you are manually editing the file, proceed slowly and methodically to prevent errors.

Note

The code excerpts shown in the rest of this section are from the XF86Config file created by XFree86 version 3.x because it is the latest version and is usually included with new software distributions. The Xconfig file for XFree86 version 2.x is similar, and you should have no problem following the same procedures by examining the Xconfig file.

You will notice that each section in the Xconfig or XF86Config file starts with the keyword section followed by the name of the section. The section is terminated with the keyword EndSection. This keyword makes it easier to find the sections you want to work with. Comments in the file all start with a pound sign.

PATHNAMES

In most cases, the pathnames provided in the configuration files don't need changing unless you installed XFree86 in a directory other than the default value. The paths used by XFree86 for screen fonts and other files are given in a section of the configuration file that looks like the following:

```
Section "Files"

# The location of the RGB database.  Note, this is the name of the
# file minus the extension (like ".txt" or ".db").  There is normally
# no need to change the default.

RgbPath  "/usr/X11R6/lib/X11/rgb"

# Multiple FontPath entries are allowed (which are concatenated together),
# as well as specifying multiple comma-separated entries in one FontPath
# command (or a combination of both methods)

FontPath  "/usr/X11R6/lib/X11/fonts/misc/"
FontPath  "/usr/X11R6/lib/X11/fonts/Type1/"
FontPath  "/usr/X11R6/lib/X11/fonts/Speedo/"
FontPath  "/usr/X11R6/lib/X11/fonts/75dpi/"
FontPath  "/usr/X11R6/lib/X11/fonts/100dpi/"

EndSection
```

The preceding code defines the search paths for the screen fonts and RGB database. If you installed XFree86 into the default directories or let the installation routines proceed with default values, you should not have to change anything here.

Note that the directories referenced in this XF86Config file follow the formal naming conventions for X, using /usr/X11R6. Because this directory is linked to /usr /X11, /usr/X386, and potentially other directories in most installations, the link can be followed to the target file. Verify that the directories point to the screen fonts by changing into each directory in turn and examining the files it contains. If the directory doesn't exist or is empty, XFree86 won't be able to load the fonts properly and will crash or generate error messages. If you add new fonts to your XFree86 installation, they should go in one of the font directories specified in the XF86Config file.

KEYBOARD SETTINGS

In most installations, the keyboard setting defaults to a U.S. 101-key keyboard with standard key mappings. This setting is valid for most computer systems. Tweaking this file will help simplify your life, though, so don't completely ignore the keyboard section. The following code shows the keyboard section from the XF86Config file:

```
Section "Keyboard"

    Protocol  "Standard"

# when using XQUEUE, comment out the above line, and uncomment the
# following line

#    Protocol  "Xqueue"

    AutoRepeat  500 5

# Let the server do the NumLock processing.  This should only be required
# when using pre-R6 clients
#    ServerNumLock

# Specify which keyboard LEDs can be user-controlled (eg, with xset(1))
#    Xleds       1 2 3

# To set the LeftAlt to Meta, RightAlt key to ModeShift,
# RightCtl key to Compose, and ScrollLock key to ModeLock:

#    LeftAlt     Meta
#    RightAlt    ModeShift
#    RightCtl    Compose
#    ScrollLock  ModeLock

EndSection
```

Leave the Protocol set as standard. The Xqueue line is commented out and should remain that way unless you implement an Xqueue for XFree86. The AutoRepeat setting tells XFree86 how long to wait for a key to be pressed before generating multiple keystrokes (for example, if you hold the x key down for more than a certain number of milliseconds, multiple x's start to appear).

ServerNumLock controls whether the NumLock key is on or off when XFree86 starts up. The ServerNumLock option is commented out by default in most sample configuration files. If you are running XFree86 version 2.x (or earlier), it is a good idea to uncomment the line. This helps tailor your keyboard for better operation under XFree86. With XFree86 version 3.x, you can leave it commented out as the server will handle the NumLock behavior.

In theory, you can use the Xleds setting to permit programming of the LED buttons on most keyboards (for Num Lock, Caps Lock, and Scroll Lock). Leave it commented because the LEDs are not used for much user feedback.

The rest of the section controls how the Alt, Ctrl, and Shift key behave. Some UNIX applications expect special keystrokes called meta keys, composed of a special key held down and another key pressed (like Ctrl+C in DOS or UNIX). These entries let you control which keys are interpreted as Alt, Meta, Control, and ModeLock. Most installations will have no problem with all these lines commented out because the number of Linux applications that need special keystrokes is very small (and those are in limited distribution).

You can use XFree86 to translate keystrokes to international characters automatically. In most cases, the keyboard layout is read by XFree86 from the kernel, although you can override this setting. The X11 standards only allow four key tables to be modified, much fewer than Linux.

MOUSE DEFINITION

XFree86 uses the mouse heavily, so you must specify the type of mouse on the system and how it is connected. XFree86 supports most popular mouse types, and any types not directly supported can usually be used in emulation of one of the more popular types like Microsoft or Logitech. The mouse section of the XF86Config file is labeled as Pointer (from pointing device) and looks like the following:

```
Section "Pointer"

    Protocol  "Microsoft"
    Device  "/dev/mouse"

# When using XQUEUE, comment out the above two lines, and uncomment
# the following line.

#    Protocol  "Xqueue"

# Baudrate and SampleRate are only for some Logitech mice

#    BaudRate  9600
#    SampleRate  150

# Emulate3Buttons is an option for 2-button Microsoft mice

#    Emulate3Buttons

# ChordMiddle is an option for some 3-button Logitech mice

#    ChordMiddle

EndSection
```

The Protocol section is the name of the mouse or the emulation to use. The names of supported mouse types are listed in the Xconfig or XF86Config man page, so if you use a mouse from a vendor other than Microsoft or Logitech, check the man page or other supplied documentation to find the name of the protocol to specify. Another method of identifying the type of mouse is to watch the startup messages when Linux boots—it will often identify the type of mouse. Microsoft mice inevitably use the Microsoft protocol. Many Logitech mice are Microsoft compatible, but newer versions use the MouseMan protocol. Because Dexxa and many other mice vendors emulate the Microsoft mouse, you can use the Microsoft protocol with them as well.

The Device entry specifies the port the mouse is attached to, using Linux device terminology. In most cases, the entry /dev/mouse is sufficient, as the Linux installation procedure will have configured the mouse already. If you are using a mouse configured on the PS/2 port of IBM PS/2 models, use the PS/2 device driver and not a serial port device driver. Valid device drivers are listed in the man page or the documentation files accompanying XFree86, but most versions support the following devices:

/dev/mouse	Linux default mouse driver
/dev/inportbm	Microsoft bus mouse only
/dev/logibm	Logitech bus mouse only
/dev/psaux	PS/2 port mouse

A bus mouse requires a specific IRQ to be set in both XFree86 and the kernel. Make sure the IRQ is the same in both places.

As with the keyboard, there is an option for Xqueue users. Because most XFree86 installations don't use Xqueue, leave this line commented out. The baud rate and sampling rate lines, as the comment indicates, are for some older Logitech mice. Most mice will not need these lines, so keep them commented out. If your mouse does not work without these settings, try 9600 baud, followed by 1200 baud if that doesn't work. Some earlier versions of XFree86 liked to have a baud rate specified, but try it without an entry first.

The Emulate3Buttons option is useful if you have a two-button mouse. When active, Emulate3Buttons allows you to simulate the press of a middle button by pressing both the left and right mouse buttons simultaneously. Many Linux (and UNIX) applications make use of three buttons on the mouse, so this option is useful for Microsoft and compatible mice owners.

Finally, the ChordMiddle option is used with some Logitech mouse models. If you use the Logitech driver, try the mouse under XFree86 without this option turned on. If the mouse doesn't behave properly, try uncommenting this line. Most Logitech mice don't need ChordMiddle turned on, although some models won't recognize the middle button properly without it.

MONITOR MODEL

Setting the monitor properly is an important step in configuring XFree86, and one that is easy to mess up. If some of the settings are incorrect, damage can occur to the monitor, so take care! Patience and common sense will help, although the monitor's operations manual is a much better source of information. If you are unsure about any settings, select the most basic level until you can get more information. For example, if you're not sure whether your monitor supports high resolutions, stick with VGA or SVGA until you can get confirmation.

The monitor section in the XF86Config file is broken into smaller subsections for convenience. The first section asks for information about the monitor type and model number, as shown in the following code:

```
Section "Monitor"

    Identifier  "Generic Monitor"
    VendorName  "Unknown"
    ModelName   "Unknown"
```

The entries in this section are text strings only and have no real configuration value for XFree86. The only time they are used is when the text strings are echoed back to you when XFree86 starts up, or a utility displays configuration information. You can enter the proper values for these items to make XFree86 a little more friendly to work with.

The next subsection deals with the horizontal bandwidth of the monitor. This section is important, and you should try to find the actual values for your monitor. Some settings for specific brands are listed in the documentation accompanying XFree86, especially in the documents Monitors and VideoModes.doc. Check your distribution directories for any specification document files. If you can't find specific values for these settings, use the lowest setting as a default, unless you know your monitor is capable of higher values. The bandwidth section looks like the following:

```
# Bandwidth is in MHz unless units are specified

    Bandwidth  25.2

# HorizSync is in kHz unless units are specified.
# HorizSync may be a comma separated list of discrete values, or a
# comma separated list of ranges of values.
# NOTE: THE VALUES HERE ARE EXAMPLES ONLY.  REFER TO YOUR MONITOR'S
# USER MANUAL FOR THE CORRECT NUMBERS.

    HorizSync   31.5  # typical for a single frequency fixed-sync monitor

#    HorizSync  30-64         # multisync
#    HorizSync  31.5, 35.2    # multiple fixed sync frequencies
#    HorizSync  15-25, 30-50  # multiple ranges of sync frequencies
```

The bandwidth settings have good comments next to them. If you were installing a multisync monitor, for example, you could comment out the 31.5KHz line and uncomment the 30-64KHz line.

The vertical refresh rate is set in another subsection and is as critical to your monitor's good health as the bandwidth section. Again, check the documentation for more information. The vertical refresh subsection code looks like the following:

```
# VertRefresh is in Hz unless units are specified.
# VertRefresh may be a comma separated list of discrete values, or a
# comma separated list of ranges of values.
# NOTE: THE VALUES HERE ARE EXAMPLES ONLY.  REFER TO YOUR MONITOR'S
# USER MANUAL FOR THE CORRECT NUMBERS.

    VertRefresh 60  # typical for a single frequency fixed-sync monitor

#    VertRefresh  50-100       # multisync
#    VertRefresh  60, 65       # multiple fixed sync frequencies
#    VertRefresh  40-50, 80-100 # multiple ranges of sync frequencies
```

The comments in the file help out again, showing you the most common settings. You can use these settings as a guide, but check your documentation for specifics.

Setting the video modes correctly is very important, as too high a video resolution may cause snow, a blank screen, or a system crash. The SuperProbe utility discussed earlier can help determine supported video modes, although most monitors have a good list of supported modes in their documentation. The XFree86 Monitors file also lists many popular monitors and their modes. The subsection for setting the video modes is as follows:

```
# Modes can be specified in two formats.  A compact one-line format, or
# a multi-line format.

# A generic VGA 640x480 mode (hsync = 31.5kHz, refresh = 60Hz)
# These two are equivalent

#    ModeLine "640x480" 25.175 640 664 760 800 480 491 493 525

    Mode "640x480"
        DotClock  25.175
        Htimings  640 664 760 800
        Vtimings  480 491 493 525
    EndMode

# These two are equivalent

#    ModeLine "1024x768i" 45 1024 1048 1208 1264 768 776 784 817 Interlace

    Mode "1024x768i"
        DotClock  45
        Htimings  1024 1048 1208 1264
        Vtimings  768 776 784 817
        Flags  "Interlace"
    EndMode
```

The preceding examples show a standard VGA (640×480) resolution and a high 1024×768 resolution. You can modify these entries to match your specific resolution requirements. As you can see from the preceding code, you need to know the dot clock and horizontal and vertical timings for your monitor and video card. Note that you can specify all the details for the modes on a single line, but the more verbose listing is easier to read and work with.

VIDEO CARDS

The next subsection of the XF86Config file deals with the video card your system uses. You can have several cards defined with different resolutions, or you can enter just the one that you will use the most. For example, the following subsection has a VGA and SVGA generic driver defined:

```
Section "Device"
    Identifier  "Generic VGA"
    VendorName  "Unknown"
    BoardName   "Unknown"
    Chipset  "generic"
    VideoRam  256
    Clocks  25.2 28.3
EndSection

Section "Device"
    # SVGA server auto-detected chipset
    Identifier  "Generic SVGA"
    VendorName  "Unknown"
    BoardName   "Unknown"
EndSection
```

The Identifier, VendorName, BoardName, and optional Chipset entries are strings and are used only for identification purposes. The VideoRam (the amount of RAM on the video board) and Clocks entries are used to specify any particular behavior for your card. Carefully check these entries to verify the information, as illegal entries can cause damage to some video boards.

If you have a particular video board that has special features, you can create a Device entry for that board. For example, the following entry is used for a Trident TVGA board:

```
Section "Device"
    Identifier  "Any Trident TVGA 9000"
    VendorName  "Trident"
    BoardName  "TVGA 9000"
    Chipset  "tvga9000"
    VideoRam  512
    Clocks  25 28 45 36 57 65 50 40 25 28 0 45 72 77 80 75
EndSection
```

The information in the VideoRam and Clocks lines was taken from the documentation file that accompanies XFree86, although it could have been entered manually from the video card's documentation.

Some video boards require more detail, provided by additional entries in the Devices subsection. For example, the following is the code for an Actix GE32+ video card with 2M of RAM on board:

```
Section "Device"
    Identifier  "Actix GE32+ 2MB"
    VendorName  "Actix"
    BoardName  "GE32+"
    Ramdac  "ATT20C490"
    Dacspeed  110
    Option "dac_8_bit"
    Clocks   25.0  28.0  40.0   0.0  50.0  77.0  36.0  45.0
    Clocks  130.0 120.0  80.0  31.0 110.0  65.0  75.0  94.0
 EndSection
```

The Ramdac and Dacspeed options, as well as an Options line, have been added to the entry. The entries that are allowed in this subsection change with each release of XFree86, so check the man pages or documentation files for more details if you want to get the most out of your video card.

THE XFREE86 SERVER

Earlier, this chapter showed how to choose an XFree86 server for your X server. The server section of the Xconfig or XF86Config file is where the server specification is located. The server subsection from an XF86Config file looks like the following:

```
Section "Screen"
    Driver  "svga"
    Device  "Generic SVGA"
    Monitor  "Generic Monitor"
    Subsection "Display"
        Depth  8
        Modes  "640x480"
        ViewPort  0 0
        Virtual  800 600
    EndSubsection
EndSection
```

The preceding section shows a generic SVGA driver. The card supports the VGA 640×480 and SVGA 800×600 resolutions. If you have a more powerful video card and monitor combination, you can use a specific server file, if it exists, such as the driver for the Actix GE32+ card with 2M RAM. The following code is set to use the special accelerated server file for the Actix card, supporting up to 1280×1024 resolutions:

```
Section "Screen"
    Driver  "accel"
    Device  "Actix GE32+ 2MB"
    Monitor  "Generic Monitor"
    Subsection  "Display"
        Depth  8
        Modes  "640x480"
        ViewPort  0 0
        Virtual  1280 1024
    EndSubsection
    SubSection "Display"
        Depth  16
        Weight  565
        Modes  "640x480"
        ViewPort   0 0
        Virtual  1024 768
    EndSubsection
 EndSection
```

The options in this subsection will not apply to all cards, but you can set their values
if you know them. The most important (and most often used) options are:

◆ The Depth option sets the number of color planes (the number of bits per
pixel). Usually the depth is 8, although VGA16 servers have a depth of 4
and monochrome displays have a depth of 1. Accelerated video cards can
have depths of 16, 24, 32, or even 64 bits per pixel, usually indicated as
part of the model name (for example, the Diamond Stealth 24 card has a
pixel depth of 24). You should, however, check before you assume the card's
model name really is the depth.

◆ The Modes option displays a list of the video mode names defined in the
ModeLine option in the Monitor section. This option shows all the modes the
card supports and you want to use. The first mode on the list is the default
value when XFree86 starts. You can then switch between the other modes
when XFree86 is running.

◆ The Virtual option specifies the virtual desktop size. With extra RAM on the
video card, you can have a virtual desktop larger than the screen display,
and then you can scroll around the virtual desktop with the mouse. You
could, for example, have a virtual desktop of 1,024×768, but only display
800×600 (SVGA). The support for different virtual desktop sizes depends on
the amount of RAM your video card has and the depth you use. For example, 1M of RAM on the video card can support 1,024×768 with a depth of
8. Two megabytes of RAM will support the same size with a depth of 16, or
it can support a 1,280×1,024 desktop at a depth of 8. To use a virtual
desktop, use the fvwm window manager (usually used by default).

◆ The ViewPort option is used with the virtual desktop to define the coordi-
nates of the upper left corner of the virtual desktop when XFree86 starts.

Check the list of servers to see whether there is one specifically designed for your video card. If you are not sure what kind of video card you have, use a generic driver.

TESTING XFREE86 CONFIGURATIONS

After you complete the Xconfig or XF86Config file, it's time to take the plunge and start XFree86. Use the command

```
startx
```

and the X startup script should load all the requisite drivers and daemons, clear the screen, and then show the basic X Window session. If XFree86 can't load, it usually displays error messages as part of the termination process. Check these messages to see whether there's any hint as to the problem. Usually, XFree86 runs into supported video mode problems. (For those used to using X on other UNIX systems, startx is a front-end utility to xinit, which is usually used to start X.)

If you can't get XFree86 running, the easiest debugging method is to set all the configuration information to the lowest denominator, such as a simple VGA system. If that works, you can individually adjust settings to more complex resolutions and configurations. This process usually helps isolate the cause of the problems. If the generic VGA drivers don't work, a configuration problem is usually the cause. Check the configuration files carefully.

USING THE .XINITRC FILE

The .xinitrc file is a startup file (similar to the .profile or .cshrc startup files for the shells) for X. It usually includes any local modifications to the configuration defined in the Xconfig or XF86Config files, as well as instructions for starting specific applications or window managers when XFree86 starts. If you use either the startx or runx commands to start XFree86, the .xinitrc is renamed without the period.

The system's .xinitrc file is usually kept as /usr/lib/X11/xinit/xinitrc or in /etc/X11 /xinit/xinitrc. The latter path is more common with XFree86 and Linux, and the former is the path for X. (Linux places the file in the /etc/X11 directory structure instead of /usr/lib as some Linux installations prefer to mount the /usr directories as read-only, sometimes because they reside on a CD-ROM.)

If you want to customize the behavior of the XFree86 session, copy the the system's default .xinitrc file to your home directory and edit it with any editor. When XFree86 starts, it first checks your home directory for the .xinitrc file, and then reads the default startup file if one isn't found. There are man pages for startx and xinit that explain some of the details of the startup file.

The following code is an example of a .xinitrc file from a straightforward XFree86 installation. The file has been cut into smaller sections so each subsection can be examined in a little more detail. The first subsection deals with setting paths:

```
userresources=$HOME/.Xresources
usermodmap=$HOME/.Xmodmap
sysresources=/usr/X11R6/lib/X11/xinit/.Xresources
sysmodmap=/usr/X11R6/lib/X11/xinit/.Xmodmap
```

These paths are usually set up by the XFree86 software, but you should check them to make sure they are valid. Remember to follow links to other directories. These variables are all that is required for XFree86.

The next subsection checks for the existence of some system resources and performs actions based on the check. Most, if not all, of these checks don't need to be modified unless you have very special requirements for your X session.

```
# merge in defaults and keymaps

if [ -f $sysresources ]; then
    xrdb -merge $sysresources
fi

if [ -f $sysmodmap ]; then
    xmodmap $sysmodmap
fi

if [ -f $userresources ]; then
    xrdb -merge $userresources
fi

if [ -f $usermodmap ]; then
    xmodmap $usermodmap
fi
```

The final subsection in the .xinitrc file runs the setroot program, if present, to set the background color (to Steel Blue in this case). Finally, the fvwm window manager is executed and starts your session:

```
# start some nice programs
xsetroot -solid SteelBlue
fvwm
```

If you want to use another window manager, such as Motif's mwm manager, change the last line in this subsection. Make sure that the window manager file is in the search path, so the startup routines can find it.

If you want to create an xterm session from within the .xinitrc file (you will need xterm or other utility to start other tasks within XFree86), add the line:

```
xterm -e /bin/bash
```

In this case, the bash shell is invoked within the xterm session. You can, of course, use any shell you want.

If you create .xinitrc files for your own use, place them in your home directory. You could, for example, use a .xinitrc file like the following:

```
#!/bin/sh

xterm -fn 7x13bold -geometry 80x32+10+10 &
xterm -fn 7x13bold -geometry 80x32+30+50 &
oclock -geometry 70x70-7+7 &
xsetroot -solid SteelBlue &
exec fvwm
```

This file starts two xterm sessions and the clock and places them on the desktop, sets the background color to Steel Blue, and finally, starts the desktop manager. Note that the last command in the script is preceded by the exec command, and the last command is not sent to background. If you send the last command to background or forget the exec command, X will start up and then immediately shut down.

SUMMARY

If you followed the steps outlined in this chapter, your X system should now be functional and you can start working with the X system as your primary interface to Linux. The specifics of working with X are beyond the scope of this book. If you are not sure how to use X, check the documentation files that came with the release, or consult a user-oriented book. Once you've worked in X, it's hard to go back to character-based terminals!

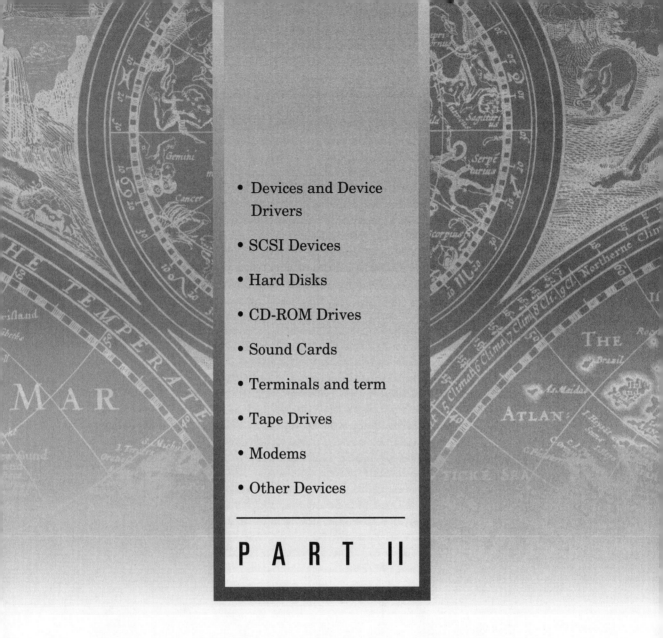

- Devices and Device Drivers

- SCSI Devices

- Hard Disks

- CD-ROM Drives

- Sound Cards

- Terminals and term

- Tape Drives

- Modems

- Other Devices

PART II

Expanding Your System

- Device Drivers

- Character and Block Mode Devices

- Device Permissions and Links

CHAPTER 6

Devices and Device Drivers

One of the primary concepts of Linux that you must understand to administer a Linux system properly is that of devices. Without a basic knowledge of devices and device drivers, you can't add new hardware, manage existing hardware, or change your Linux hardware configuration. Luckily, devices and device drivers are very easy to understand.

This short chapter is devoted to devices and device drivers. In this chapter, you learn what a device driver is, how to handle the two different types of devices (character and block mode), what the major and minor device numbers are, and how to use the `mknod` command. Once you understand these concepts, you can change, add to, and manage your Linux hardware easily. Devices are referred to throughout this section of the book, so you should understand these concepts before going on.

DEVICE DRIVERS

The Linux operating system has no built-in instructions for handling hard drives, floppy disk drives, keyboards, monitors, or any other peripheral or piece of hardware attached to the system. All the instructions for communicating with the peripheral are contained in a file called a device driver. Device drivers are usually small pieces of assembler or C code that have a set of instructions for sending and receiving data with the device.

You make the device driver a part of the Linux kernel by linking it. Linking means that the code becomes part of the operating system kernel and is loaded automatically when Linux boots, which allows Linux to communicate with the device much faster than if it had to read the instructions from the device driver every time a request to communicate with the device was issued. Linux can have many different device drivers linked to it; the number is limited only by the amount of RAM in your system. Practically, though, the number of device drivers is kept to a few dozen because most systems don't have too many devices attached.

When an application instructs a device to perform some action, the Linux kernel doesn't have to worry about the mechanism to perform the act. It simply passes the request to the device driver and lets it handle the communications. Similarly, when you are typing at the keyboard, your terminal's device driver accepts the keystrokes and passes them to the shell, filtering out any special codes that the kernel doesn't know how to handle by translating them into something the kernel can perform.

You can use a single device driver to instruct Linux about communicating with many different devices, as long as they use the same basic instructions. For example, if you have four terminals attached to your Linux system but they all use the same serial communications method, a single device driver linked into the kernel can handle all four terminals. Linking new device drivers into the kernel is dealt with later in this book in Chapter 25, "Modifying the Kernel."

The use of device drivers is one of the real strengths of the UNIX operating system (and therefore Linux too) because it provides a continual method for expanding the system using the same kernel and adapting existing systems to new devices as they are developed. When a new hardware device is developed, it can be used with Linux by programming a device driver, which is usually not a difficult task for an experienced programmer.

Linux also uses a special file called a device file, which contains information about the permissions of the device, the type of device it is, and some numbers that identify the device to the kernel. Linux keeps all device files in the /dev directory by default and convention. Figure 6.1 shows part of a typical Linux /dev directory listing. You can't see all the device files on a single screen because there are so many of them. Over 500 device drivers and their files are included with the Slackware Linux system on the CD-ROM supplied with this book. Many are simply duplicates of a basic device driver with a different device number, but each file has to be separate.

Figure 6.1.
A partial listing of the
/dev directory.

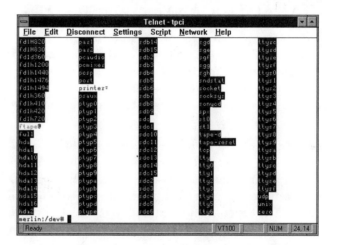

You can keep device files anywhere on the Linux filesystem, but keeping them all in /dev makes it obvious that they are device files. If you check the /dev directory, you see that many of the files are actually links to other files. These links enable you to name devices more clearly. You can access the CD-ROM drive as /dev/cdrom instead of /dev/sbpcd2, for example. Likewise, the mouse device can be linked to /dev/mouse. These links are a convenience for the user and are not necessarily important for Linux. Figure 6.2. shows a long listing of some of the device files. You can see that the file cdrom is linked to the file /dev/scd0. Chapter 18, "Filesystems and Disks," discusses links and what they mean.

Figure 6.2.
A long directory listing
of the /dev directory
shows that some of the
files are links to other
files, as both cdrom and
core are here.

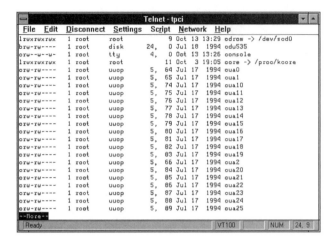

CHARACTER AND BLOCK MODE DEVICES

Everything attached to the computer that Linux communicates with is treated as a device. Terminals, printers, and asynchronous modems are character mode devices; they communicate by using characters sent one at a time and echoed back by the other end. Hard drives and most tape drives, on the other hand, use blocks of data, which is the fastest way to send large chunks of information. They are called block mode devices.

Some devices can be both character and block mode devices, although not at the same time. Some tape drives, for example, can handle both character and block modes, which means that such drives will have two different device drivers. The device driver that is used depends on how the user wants to read or write data with the device. For the fastest throughput, a block mode device is used. For retrieval of a single file or backing up just a single directory, for example, a character mode device driver is preferable.

Note

Another way to differentiate between character and block mode devices is by how the buffering to the device is handled. Character mode devices want to do their own buffering. Block mode devices, which usually communicate in chunks of 512 or 1,024 bytes, have the kernel perform the buffering. This buffering is usually transparent to users.

The device driver file has all the details about whether the device is a character mode or block mode device. To figure out which type of device a peripheral is, look at the permission block of the device driver file. If the first character of the permission block is a b, the device is a block mode device. A c as the first character in the permission block indicates a character mode device. In the following extract from a /dev directory listing, you can see the device's type from the first character in the permission blocks:

```
crw-rw----   1 root     uucp       5,  74 Jul 17  1994 cua10
crw-rw----   1 root     uucp       5,  75 Jul 17  1994 cua11
brw-rw----   1 root     floppy     2,   0 Jul 17  1994 fd0
brw-rw----   1 root     floppy     2,   1 Jul 17  1994 fd1
brw-rw----   1 root     disk       3,   0 Jul 17  1994 hda
brw-rw----   1 root     disk       3,   1 Jul 17  1994 hda1
brw-rw----   1 root     disk       8,   1 Jul 17  1994 sda1
brw-rw----   1 root     disk       8,  10 Jul 17  1994 sda10
brw-rw----   1 root     disk       8,  11 Jul 17  1994 sda11
crw--w--w-   1 root     root       4,   0 Jul 17  1994 tty0
crw--w--w-   1 root     root       4,   1 Jul  7 18:16 tty1
crw--w--w-   1 root     root       4,   2 Jul  7 17:58 tty2
crw-rw-rw-   1 root     tty        4,  64 Jul 17  1994 ttyS0
crw-rw-rw-   1 root     tty        4,  65 Jul  7 18:00 ttyS1
```

You may notice that this listing has two numbers where the file size usually belongs. These numbers are the major and minor device numbers. The next section explains these numbers.

Device drivers are usually named to indicate the type of device they are. Most terminals, for example, have a device driver name tty followed by two or more letters or numbers, such as tty1, tty1A, or tty04. The letters *tty* identify the file as a terminal (*tty* stands for teletype), and the numbers or letters identify the specific terminal. When coupled with the directory /dev, the full device driver name becomes /dev /tty01. Hard drives, as you saw in earlier chapters, have names like /dev/hda and /dev/sda (for IDE and SCSI drives respectively).

MAJOR AND MINOR DEVICE NUMBERS

A system may have more than one device of the same type. For example, your Linux system may have a multiport card (multiple serial ports) with ten Qume terminals hanging off it. Linux can use the same device driver for each one of the terminals, as they are all the same type of device. The same concept applies to multiple printers, so you can use the same device driver for two Hewlett Packard LaserJet printers attached to two parallel ports, for example.

The operating system must have a method of differentiating the ten terminals or two printers, however. Device numbers are that method. Each device is identified by a major number that identifies the device driver to be used and a minor number that identifies the device number. For example, the ten Qume terminals may all use a device driver with the same major number (which really points to the device driver file in the /dev directory), but each has a different minor number that uniquely identifies the Qume terminal to the operating system. In the following listing, you can see that all the device drivers for the ttyX device (which is the console and associated screens) have the same major device number of 4, but the minor device number changes from 0 to 9:

```
crw--w--w-  1 root     tty       4,   0 Jul 17  1994 tty0
crw--w--w-  1 root     root      4,   1 Oct 13 13:48 tty1
crw--w--w-  1 root     root      4,   2 Oct 13 13:26 tty2
crw--w--w-  1 root     root      4,   3 Oct 13 13:26 tty3
crw--w--w-  1 root     root      4,   4 Oct 13 13:26 tty4
crw--w--w-  1 root     root      4,   5 Oct 13 13:26 tty5
crw--w--w-  1 root     root      4,   6 Oct 13 13:26 tty6
crw-rw-rw-  1 root     tty       4,   7 Jul 17  1994 tty7
crw-rw-rw-  1 root     tty       4,   8 Jul 17  1994 tty8
crw-rw-rw-  1 root     tty       4,   9 Jul 18  1994 tty9
```

In directory listings, the major device number is always shown first, followed by the minor device number. Every device on the system has both major and minor device numbers assigned in such a way as to ensure that they are unique. If two devices are assigned the same number, Linux can't properly communicate with them. You can't create a device number within the device driver or by numbering the files. You create device numbers with the command mknod (make node) and remove them with the rm command. You must use mknod every time you want to configure a new device on your system.

Note

Some devices use the major and minor device numbers in a strange way. Some tape drives, for example, use the minor number to identify the density of the tape in order to adjust their output. These types of exceptions are rare, luckily, and don't occur on most Linux systems. You do not have to create these types of device numbers because an installation script usually handles the setup of the device drivers and their numbers.

THE *MKNOD* COMMAND

The mknod (make node) command is used for several different purposes. Its most common usages are to create a FIFO (first in first out) device file, which is a form of queue for the device, or a character or block mode device file. The format of the mknod command is

```
mknod [options] device b¦c¦p¦u major minor
```

You can use the following options with this command:

- The `--help` option displays help information and exits.
- The `-m` (or `--mode`) option sets the mode of the file to `mode` instead of the default `0666` (symbolic notation only).
- The `-p` option lets you set file permissions.
- The `--version` option displays version information, and then exits.

The argument after the device or path name specifies whether the file is a block mode device (`b`), character mode device (`c`), FIFO device (`p`), or unbuffered character mode device(`u`). One of these arguments must be present on the command line for the device number to be properly assigned.

Following the type of file argument are two numbers for the major and minor device numbers assigned to the new file. You must supply these numbers; `mknod` does not generate them for you. Every device on a UNIX system has a unique number that identifies the type of device (the major number) and the specific device itself (the minor number). You must specify both a major and minor number for any new block, character, or unbuffered mode devices. You don't need to specify device numbers for a type `p` device. You can pull the major and minor device numbers out of thin air as long as they don't conflict with any other device, but there is a general numbering convention for all devices. These numbering systems are discussed in more detail in the chapters on specific devices later in this part.

DEVICE PERMISSIONS AND LINKS

When you create a new device with the `mknod` command, it is given the permissions associated with the symbolic value `666`. You can override this value either on the `mknod` command line (with the `-p` option) or by using `chmod` afterwards to change the permissions.

Device file permissions are important as they can control access to the device. For example, a CD-ROM drive is a read-only device, and changing the permissions to prevent write access can help forestall many error messages when a user tries to write to the CD-ROM. Permissions are also useful for creating read-only partitions on a disk, such as a directory of databases or utilities that you don't want anyone modifying. Chapter 17, "System Names and Access Permissions," looks at the `chmod` command and file permissions in more detail.

As a general rule, the default permissions are valid for most devices unless you want to lock out access. When Linux installs the device files, it sets all the system devices (such as /dev/mem, the physical RAM) with the proper permissions and you shouldn't change them.

SUMMARY

This chapter introduced device drivers and device numbers, both of which are important when you add new hardware to your system. The next few chapters look at the different hardware that you can add to expand your Linux system and how they are configured. This chapter's information will be important as you configure Linux to accept new devices.

- SCSI Chains and Devices

- Supported SCSI Devices

- SCSI Device Drivers

- Troubleshooting SCSI Devices

CHAPTER 7

SCSI Devices

SCSI (Small Computer Systems Interface) is the most widely used method for connecting devices in UNIX systems. It is also used in higher-end PC machines because it has more intelligent device handling and faster transfer speeds than the less expensive IDE. SCSI devices and adapter cards are usually more expensive than IDE drives and cards, which has discouraged many PC buyers from using SCSI.

Adding SCSI devices to a Linux system is relatively easy compared to the same process with IDE and other interfaces. The next few chapters look at adding CD-ROM drives, tape drives, and other devices using other interfaces, but this chapter deals specifically with SCSI. In this chapter, you learn how to attach SCSI devices to Linux, how to configure them, and how to solve common SCSI problems.

SCSI CHAINS AND DEVICES

SCSI uses a dedicated controller card (often called a SCSI adapter card) to which you can connect a chain of devices. SCSI devices are connected to each other by a flat-ribbon cable (internally) or a shielded cable (externally). The SCSI cables run from one device to the next, forming a long, connecting chain. A SCSI chain will have the SCSI adapter at one end of the chain when all devices are internal. Alternatively, the adapter can be in the middle of the chain when both internal and external devices are used. Each SCSI chain can support seven different devices (apart from the adapter card). If more than seven SCSI devices need to be added to a system, up to seven SCSI adapter cards can be used (although most PC systems would not have enough slots for such a configuration). A new SCSI standard has recently been adopted that allows up to 14 devices per chain, but this kind of system is still expensive and relatively rare.

Each SCSI device on a chain has a SCSI ID number, from zero to seven. By convention, the controller card is set to use number seven, and a bootable SCSI hard drive (if one is to be used) is set to use SCSI ID zero (although some UNIX workstation systems insist that the primary drive not be ID zero, just to be different). The other numbers between zero and seven are available for any other SCSI devices, although each ID can be used by only one device on each chain. If two devices have the same SCSI ID number, problems will occur when the operating system tries to communicate with the device. In most cases, the system will still boot, but parallel streams of information or a complete failure of the SCSI chain can occur when the identical SCSI IDs are accessed. Each SCSI chain has a number from zero through seven as well, so if you have two SCSI adapter cards, each device will have a chain number and a SCSI ID number that uniquely identifies the device to the operating system.

Most SCSI devices have all the electronics needed to control themselves attached to the device, making it easier for devices to talk to each other without having fancy drivers in the operating system. These built-in electronics are also why SCSI devices tend to cost more than IDE systems, which rely on the operating system or controller card to provide drivers for communicating with the devices.

One of the major advantages of a SCSI system, especially in the context of a Linux or UNIX operating system, is that you don't have to do anything special to configure the system when you add a new SCSI device. Once you add a new SCSI device to the system and ensure it has a unique SCSI ID on its chain, the SCSI controller card recognizes the device automatically (the device's on-board electronics identify the type of device to the card when the card starts up). The operating system may still need a special driver to talk to some devices, but Linux has built-in drivers for most typical SCSI devices (like hard drives, tape backup units, CD-ROMs, and printers). You just need to turn on the appropriate driver by adding it to the operating system kernel.

SCSI devices must be terminated at each end of the chain to ensure that any electrical signals along the chain are properly handled. SCSI terminators are usually passive, consisting of a set of resistors that provide an electrical indication that the chain ends at that point. Some SCSI chains use an active terminating resistor, which is an electrically powered resistor that ensures the termination is properly performed. Active termination is seldom encountered in PC systems—it is usually required only on large, industrial installations that have very long SCSI chains. Without proper termination, electrical signals along the SCSI chain may not be properly transmitted, resulting in lost data.

Each SCSI chain should only have two terminators, one at each end. Most SCSI controller cards have a set of switches or a block of removable resistors that act to terminate one end. Most SCSI devices also have a switch or a bank of resistors that allow that device to terminate the chain. Some devices are clever enough to sense that they are the last SCSI device in a chain and terminate without any intervention from you. Only the device at the end of the chain must be terminated. If a device in the middle of the chain is terminated, the controller card won't recognize devices further along the chain.

SCSI devices can communicate with each other quickly over the chain, removing the need for the operating system to intervene in some cases. For example, a tape drive can dump information straight to another SCSI device without involving the operating system too much. This capability helps increase the effective speed of the SCSI system, and makes SCSI devices particularly flexible under Linux.

7

SCSI DEVICES

SUPPORTED SCSI DEVICES

There are a lot of SCSI devices available, ranging from the traditional devices (hard disks, tape drives, scanners, plotters, printers) to some more esoteric devices (telescope motor drive controllers, video cameras, light and sound systems). You can't assume that because Linux supports SCSI any SCSI device will work. All the traditional SCSI devices are supported, however, and the rest can have a driver written for them.

Most versions of the Linux operating system have a hardware compatibility file in the distribution set that lists all devices that have been tested and are known to work properly with the SCSI system. Before you purchase a new SCSI device, check this compatibility file carefully. Some SCSI controller cards are not supported by Linux, although all the major brands are. Again, the compatibility file can help you determine the adapter cards that are supported. If you are converting an existing PC-based SCSI system to Linux, check each device with the compatibility list before you begin installation to prevent frustration later.

Some SCSI devices (like plotters) that aren't very common are shipped with their own kernel patches for DOS, OS/2, and UNIX. A few even provide Linux drivers now. When a Linux driver is provided, make sure the patches correspond to the version of the Linux kernel you are using. If they will work with your version of Linux, link the driver into the kernel, and then rebuild the kernel before making the device available. If a SCSI device doesn't have a Linux kernel patch and isn't supported as part of the basic distribution driver set, check with the manufacturer of the device or Linux distribution sites and user groups for a suitable driver or alternative.

SCSI DEVICE DRIVERS

All devices on a Linux system must have a device driver so the kernel can communicate with the device. SCSI devices are no different. Linux is usually distributed with a complete set of SCSI device drivers that only need to be configured properly and linked to the kernel to make the device accessible.

HARD DRIVES

SCSI disk drives are always block devices and should always use major device number eight because this number is the convention the kernel expects this device number). Linux doesn't support any raw SCSI devices (despite its similarity to BSD UNIX, which does support raw SCSI devices). A raw device is accessed in a different manner than a normal device; data can be sent to it without any special handling. The standard naming convention for SCSI hard drives is /dev/sd*letter* for the entire disk device (such as /dev/sda and /dev/sdb) and /dev/sd*letter partition* for the partitions on that device (such as /dev/sda1 and /dev/sda2).

Linux allocated 16 minor device numbers to each SCSI disk device, with minor device number 0 representing the whole disk drive, minor numbers between 1 and 4 representing the four primary partitions, and minor numbers 5 through 15 representing any extended partitions. With Linux, SCSI disk minor device numbers are assigned dynamically starting with the lowest SCSI ID numbers. Figure 7.1 shows a listing extract from the /dev directory of an installed Linux system. As you can see, all the SCSI hard drives have the major device number set to 8 and the minor device numbers vary from 0 to 15. The entire hard disk /dev/sda has major number 8 and minor number 0. The four primary partitions have minor numbers 1 through 4 (/dev/sda1 through /dev/sda4). Any extended partitions are numbered from 5 through 15 (/dev/sda5, /dev/sda6, and so on).

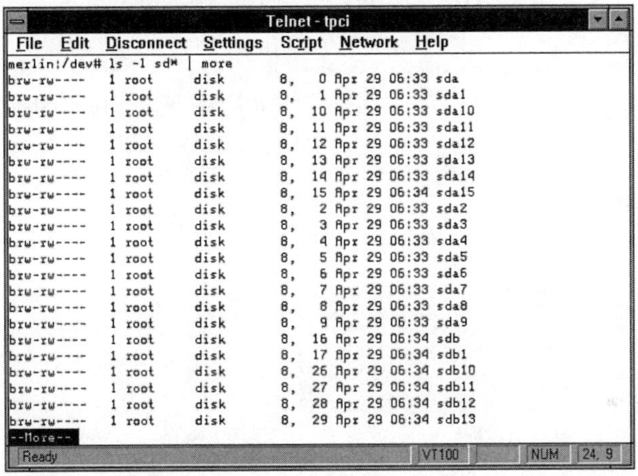

Figure 7.1.
The SCSI hard disk device drivers have major number 8 and minor numbers 0 through 15 for each drive.

Because Linux talks directly to the SCSI interface, Linux presents a few problems when partitioning SCSI disks. Each disk drive is viewed as the SCSI host sees it, with block numbers from zero up to the highest block number. All blocks are assumed to be free of errors. As a result, there is no easy way to get at the disk geometry. For comparison, DOS requires a head-cylinder-sector mapping, which is not as efficient but does allow direct manipulation. To partition the drive, you will have to either use the entire disk for Linux (in which case the installation takes care of the partitioning) or use DOS or Linux's fdisk program to create partitions for other operating systems first. For systems that support both SCSI and IDE hard drives, you may have to reconfigure the system's BIOS to recognize the SCSI drive as the primary (boot) device.

CD-ROM DEVICES

SCSI CD-ROM drives with a block size of 512 or 2,048 bytes (which covers practically every consumer model that works with a PC) will work with Linux, but any other block size will not. Most CD-ROM drives and CD-ROM discs have either 512 or 2,048 byte blocks, so this limitation shouldn't cause a problem. Linux CD-ROM drives must also support the ISO 9660 format for disk layout, although again practically every name-brand PC CD-ROM drive supports this format.

SCSI CD-ROMs use the major device number 11 and minor device numbers are allocated dynamically, with the first CD-ROM drive found being minor zero, the second minor one, and so on. The naming convention used with Linux is /dev/sr(*digit*), such as /dev/sr0 and /dev/sr1 for the first and second CD-ROM drive installed. Figure 7.2 shows the device drivers for a CD-ROM supplied with most Linux systems. Because a PC rarely has more than two CD-ROM drives attached, only two device drivers are usually included. As you can see from the figure, the /dev/cdrom device driver has been linked to /dev/sr0 (which is the first SCSI CD-ROM drive).

Figure 7.2.
Usually only two device drivers are supplied for SCSI CD-ROM drives, as few systems will have more than two CD-ROM drives.

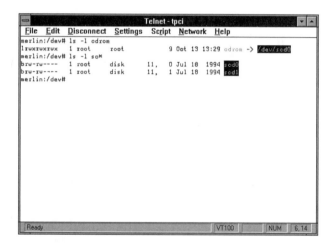

After setting the CD-ROM SCSI address properly (the system should recognize the device when the SCSI card boots), you must mount the CD-ROM device. Chapter 18, "Filesystems and Disks," discusses mounting in more detail. You can perform the mount manually, or embed the proper command in the startup sequence so the drive is always available. The general command to mount a CD-ROM device is

```
mount /dev/sr0 /mount_point
```

where `mount_point` is a directory that can be used. You must create the directory beforehand for the mount to work, and the directory must be empty. For convenience, you should create a directory called /cdrom that is always the mount point. (Most versions of Linux create this directory automatically if a CD-ROM was used to install the software.)

If your CD-ROM doesn't mount properly with this command, it may be because of the disk type. The correct syntax to mount an ISO 9660 (also called High-Sierra) CD-ROM is

```
mount -t iso9660 /dev/sr0 /mount_point
```

For this command to work correctly, you must have the kernel set to support the ISO 9660 filesystem. If you haven't done this, rebuild the kernel with this option added. (See Chapter 25, "Modifying the Kernel.")

Linux attempts to lock the CD-ROM drive door when a disk is mounted in order to prevent filesystem corruption due to a media change. Not all CD-ROM drives support door locking, but if you find yourself unable to eject a CD-ROM, it is probably because the disk is mounted (it doesn't have to be in use). Chapter 9, "CD-ROM Drives," discusses CD-ROM drives in more detail.

TAPE DRIVES

Linux supports several SCSI tape drives. Check the hardware configuration guide before purchasing one, though, to ensure compatibility. The most popular SCSI tape models, including the Archive Viper QIC drives, Exabyte 8mm drives, and Wangtek 5150S and DAT tape drives, are all known to work well.

SCSI tape drives use character device major number nine and the minor numbers are assigned dynamically. Usually, rewinding tape devices are numbered from zero, so the first tape drive is /dev/rst0 (character mode, major number nine, minor number zero), the second device is /dev/rst1 (character mode, major number nine, minor number one), and so on. Non-rewinding devices have the high bit set in the minor number so that the first non-rewinding tape device is /dev/nrst0 (character mode, major device nine, minor device 128).

The standard naming convention for SCSI tape drives is /dev/nrst*digit* for non-rewinding devices (such as /dev/nrst0, /dev/nrst1, etc) and /dev/rst*digit* for rewinding devices (such as /dev/rst0 and /dev/rst1).

Generally, Linux supports tape devices that use either fixed or variable length blocks, as long as the block length is smaller than the driver buffer length (which is set to 32K in most Linux distribution sources, but can be changed by reconfiguring the kernel). Tape drive parameters like block size, buffering process, and tape density are set by the mt program where needed.

7

SCSI DEVICES

A common problem with SCSI tape drives occurs when you are trying to read tapes from other systems (or another system can't read a tape made in Linux). This problem occurs because of different block sizes used by the tape system. On a SCSI tape device using a fixed block size, you must set the block size of the tape driver to match the hardware block size used when the tape was written (or to variable). You change this setting with the `mt` command:

```
mt setblk <size>
```

Replace `size` with the block size, such as 20. If you want a variable block length, set `size` to zero. Some Linux versions don't have a version of `mt` that lets you change block sizes (usually the GNU version). If that's the case, get the BSD version of `mt`, which does support this feature.

OTHER DEVICES

There are many more SCSI devices available, such as scanners, printers, removable cartridge drives, and so on. The Linux generic SCSI device driver handles these devices. The generic SCSI driver provides an interface for sending commands to all SCSI devices.

SCSI generic devices use character mode and major number 21. The minor numbers are assigned dynamically from zero for the first device. Generic devices have the names /dev/sg0, /dev/sg1, /dev/sg2, and so on.

TROUBLESHOOTING SCSI DEVICES

Many common problems with SCSI devices are quite easy to solve. Finding the cause of the problem is often the most difficult step, and reading the diagnostic message displayed by the operating system when it boots or attempts to use a SCSI device can usually help with this step. Table 7.1 lists the most common problems with SCSI devices, their probable causes, and possible solutions.

TABLE 7.1 COMMON SCSI PROBLEMS.

Problem	Cause	Solution
SCSI devices show up at all possible SCSI IDs.	You have configured the device with the same SCSI address as the controller (which is typically set at SCSI ID seven).	Change the jumper settings to another SCSI ID.

Problem	Cause	Solution
A SCSI device reports using all possible LUNs.	The device probably has bad firmware.	The file drivers/scsi/scsi.c contains a list of bad devices under the variable blacklist. Try adding the device to this list and see whether it affects the behavior. If not, contact the device manufacturer.
Your SCSI system times out.	Delay in sending signals to the device.	Make sure the interrupts of the controller card are enabled correctly and there are no IRQ, DMA, or address conflicts with other boards in your system.
You get sense errors from error-free devices.	You have bad cables or improper termination on the chain.	Make sure the SCSI chain is terminated at both ends using external or on-board terminators. Don't terminate in the middle of the chain, as this can cause problems, too. You can probably use passive termination. For long chains with several devices, try active termination for better behavior.
The tape drive is not recognized at boot time.	Either the SCSI chain didn't recognize the tape drive or the device driver is not installed.	Try booting with a tape in the drive.
A networking kernel does not work with new SCSI devices.	The autoprobe routines for many network drivers are not passive and can interfere with some SCSI drivers.	Try to disable the network portions to identify the guilty program, and then reconfigure it.

7

SCSI DEVICES

continues

TABLE 7.1 CONTINUED

Problem	Cause	Solution
A SCSI device is detected but the system is unable to access it.	You probably don't have a device driver file for the device.	Device drivers should be /dev directory and configured with the proper type (block or character) and unique major and minor device numbers. Run mkdev for the device.
The SCSI controller card fails when it uses memory mapped I/O.	This problem is common with Trantor T128 and Seagate boards) and is caused when the memory mapped I/O ports are incorrectly cached.	You should have the board's address space marked as uncachable in the XCMOS settings. If you can't mark them as uncachable, disable the the cache and see whether board functions properly.
Your system fails to find the SCSI devices and you get messages like scsi : 0 hosts or scsi%d : type: when the system boots.	The autoprobe routines on the controller cards rely on the system BIOS autoprobe and can't boot properly. This problem is particularly prevalent with SCSI adapters in the following list: Adaptec 152x, Adaptec 151x, Adaptec AIC-6260, Adaptec AIC-6360, Future Domain 1680, Future Domain TMC-950, Future Domain TMC-8xx, Trantor T128, Trantor T128F, Trantor T228F, Seagate ST01, Seagate ST02, or Western Digital 7000.	Check that your BIOS is enabled and not conflicting with any other peripheral BIOSs (such as on some adapter cards). If the BIOS is properly enabled, find the board's signature by running DOS' DEBUG command to check whether the board is responding. For eample, use the DEBUG command d=c800:0 to see whether the board replies with an acknowledgment (assuming you have set the controller card to use address 0xc8000; if not, replace the DEBUG command with the proper address). If the card doesn't respond, check the address settings.

Problem	Cause	Solution
Sometimes the SCSI system locks up completely.	Many possible causes, including a problem with the host adapter.	Check the host adapter with any diagnostics that came with the board. Try a different SCSI cable to see whether that is the problem. If the lockups seem to occur when multiple devices are in use at the same time, you probably have a firmware problem. Contact the manufacturer to see whether upgrades are available that could correct the problem. Finally, check the disk drives to ensure that there are no bad blocks that could affect the device driver files, buffers, or swap space.

SUMMARY

More information about some specific SCSI devices is in the following chapters, but SCSI on the whole is a convenient and reliable interface that is well worth the investment. Adding SCSI devices is much simpler than adding any other kind of devices. For this reason, SCSI is popular among UNIX users, and now, among Linux PC users, despite its extra costs. The next few chapters look at some general hardware devices in more detail. This information is necessary when you expand your system by adding new peripherals.

7

SCSI DEVICES

- Buying a New Drive

- Formatting and Parti-
  tioning the New Drive

CHAPTER 8

Hard Disks

Adding an additional hard disk to your Linux system is not difficult. Linux is extremely cooperative with this task, allowing great flexibility in the type, speed, capacity, and partitioning of new drives. This short chapter shows you how to add a new hard disk and get it running properly with Linux. If you are adding a hard disk to your Linux system, you will also want to read Chapter 18, "Filesystems and Disks," which explains in more detail how to access the Linux areas of your new drive. Note that some versions of Linux only allow partitions from one drive (the primary boot drive) to be used.

BUYING A NEW DRIVE

When you bought your PC, you had a hard drive installed in it. Depending on when you bought it, the drive could have a capacity of as little as 40M or as much as 550M of disk space. Prices of hard drives have dropped dramatically over the past couple of years and show no signs of slowing, offering higher capacities for less money every year. Current trends toward newer electronics and manufacturing efficiencies have pushed the disk drive market to the point where drives under 500M are expected to be unavailable in the very near future.

Adding a new high-capacity or an older lower capacity drive is a simple solution to the perennial problem of disk space shortages. One important (and often over-looked) criterion to consider when buying a hard drive is to purchase a drive that is compatible with your existing hard disk controller card (unless you plan to replace your existing drive and controller type). PC users have to worry about several different interfaces. Most commercial systems bought for home and small office use IDE (Integrated Drive Electronics) interfaces and drives. IDE controllers can only support two peripherals, such as two IDE drives or one IDE drive and one IDE CD-ROM drive. If you are using IDE, make sure you can add a new device. IDE has recently been upgraded to EIDE (Enhanced IDE), which allows up to four devices to be attached, two devices each on up to two controllers.

An older interface is ESDI (Enhanced Small Device Interface), which also could handle only two drives. ESDI drives are no longer manufactured, and ESDI controller users should seriously consider scrapping their controller card and using a newer EIDE or SCSI controller. SCSI controllers are the most powerful and flexible system you can add to a PC, although they tend to cost considerably more than IDE, for example. SCSI interface busses are faster than IDE, and you can add up to seven devices to a SCSI chain. Chapter 7, "SCSI Devices," covered SCSI in much more detail.

None of these interface types are interchangeable. If you are not sure which interface you have, either check your documentation or ask your dealer. You can always change interfaces, but this change requires a new controller card and replacement of any existing devices.

Before you buy a new drive, check whether your machine has space for it; not all machines have available expansion slots. Small-footprint desktop PCs usually only have a single drive bay, for example. With these types of machines, your only option is to replace the existing drive with a new one of higher capacity, discarding (or selling) the old drive.

Assuming you have room for a new drive, installing it is not difficult, but it can be unnerving the first time. Many dealers will install new drives for you, often free of charge. Most hard drives come with good instruction sheets and all the parts you need, so if you feel adventurous, go ahead and try installing the drive yourself. Usually, the process involves fastening the new drive into an available drive bay with a few small screws, attaching a power connector, and then finally attaching a cable from the interface card that also routes through your other drives (and sometimes the CD-ROM or tape drive, as well). Depending on the type of system you currently have, you might use the existing drive cable if there is a spare connector, or you may need to buy a new cable.

Once the drive is installed, you need to make the PC aware of its existence. SCSI drives are an exception, as the SCSI controller handles all the device information. In the BIOS, you set all the hard drives to None if you are using SCSI, and leave the SCSI controller to inform the BIOS of all peripherals attached to it. For any other drive type, you need to add the drive information to the BIOS table. You can usually access this table by pressing Del or Ctrl+Alt+Esc during the boot sequence (an on-screen message usually tells you the key sequence to use). When you enter the disk drive setup screen, you need to specify the number of cylinders, heads, and sectors per track of the new drive. For most drives, the other information requested in the BIOS drive configuration screen can be ignored. If you have any problems with the BIOS installation, check the documentation that came with the drive, or call your dealer.

FORMATTING AND PARTITIONING THE NEW DRIVE

To set up your new hard drive's partitions, you use fdisk just as you did when you set up the first hard drive (covered in the Chapter 3 of this book). If you are going to create a DOS partition on the new drive, most system administrators prefer to boot from a DOS floppy disk or a DOS partition of the first hard drive, and then use the DOS version of fdisk to set up the new drive. (The DOS fdisk program is easier to use than Linux's.)

When in fdisk, switch to the second drive. If you don't see an option on the fdisk menu to change drives, the new drive has not been recognized by the BIOS or SCSI controller card, in which case you should check the configuration again. Once on the

8

second drive, you can partition any DOS areas that you want before you set up the Linux partitions. After setting up DOS partitions, you can format them using DOS' FORMAT command.

Note

With some newer high-capacity drives, the DOS FDISK program can't access all the area on the disk. Many manufacturers now supply a utility disk with a replacement for FDISK that enables you to access the whole drive, format it, and update the partition tables. Use this utility over the standard FDISK if you have a choice. Most new high-capacity IDE disks also include a device driver used by some versions of DOS to access the whole disk area. Recent versions of Linux shouldn't have a problem with these drives.

When you are ready to set up the Linux partitions, boot your machine into Linux and enter the fdisk program. You should be able to access the second hard disk from the menu now. If you have created a DOS partition, it should show up in the partition table. Add any Linux partitions you want following the same process you used with the first drive. You can add more swap partitions to complement those on your first hard disk, or set up the drive with one or more Linux filesystems. Remember to specify the filesystem types within fdisk.

To format any new swap space partitions, use the command

```
mkswap -c partition size
```

where partition is the name of the partition and size is the size of the partition in blocks (displayed in the partition table). The -c option tells mkswap to check for bad blocks in the partition. For example, to format a /dev/hdb2 partition for Linux, issue the command

```
mkswap -c /dev/hdb2 15404
```

where 15404 is the disk size in blocks, taken from the partition table shown in Linux's fdisk.

After you format the swap partition, you can enable the Linux swap space partition with the swapon command followed by the partition name, such as:

```
swapon /dev/hdb2
```

Once the swapon command is executed, Linux will use the new swap space.

To set up the Linux filesystem partitions, create the filesystems with the `mkfs` (make filesystem) command. The format of the `mkfs` command depends on the type of filesystem you are setting up, but most users will want to use the Second Extended (ext2) filesystem. To create a Second Extended filesystem, issue the command

```
mke2fs -c <partition> <size>
```

where `partition` is the partition name and `size` is the size of the partition in blocks (taken from the partition display in `fdisk`).

Note

> Some versions of Linux don't require you to specify the partition size because the `mke2fs` utility determines the number automatically. In general, any release later than 0.5 can do this calculation for you.

The `mke2fs` command checks the partition for bad blocks (started by the `-c` option), and then sets a filesystem up in that partition. You can use other filesystems supported by Linux, although most are slower than the Second Extended filesystem. After you create the partitions, you can mount them for use. See Chapter 18, "Filesystems and Disks" for information about the process of adding the new filesystems to your existing Linux configuration.

SUMMARY

Adding a second (or third, or fourth) hard drive is a handy and fast way to expand the amount of disk space available to Linux, as well as increasing your swap space if you are having memory problems. The process is simple and Linux is tolerant of errors. If you run into major problems, simply start the process again. There is no real limit to the number of partitions and drives you can mount on Linux, as your hard disk controller card's limits are usually reached first.

8

HARD DISKS

- Understanding the Different Types of CD-ROMs

- Installing a CD-ROM Drive

- Using /etc/fstab

- Playing Audio CD-ROMs

- Using PhotoCDs with Linux

- Troubleshooting the CD-ROM Drive

CHAPTER 9

CD-ROM Drives

The CD-ROM drive has changed from an expensive peripheral to almost a mandatory drive for most PC users. As prices of CD-ROM drives have dropped and the amount of software distributed by CD-ROM has increased, the CD-ROM drive has become a necessary system component, especially for users of large software packages like Linux. Because of its device driver architecture, Linux supports CD-ROM drives easily. This chapter looks at the support built into Linux for a CD-ROM and gives general instructions for installing and configuring a CD-ROM drive.

UNDERSTANDING THE DIFFERENT TYPES OF CD-ROMs

A CD-ROM holds a large amount of material (approximately 650M) in a convenient size. CD-ROMs are non-volatile—they don't lose data when exposed to magnetic fields, and they are difficult to damage. As with any new technology, though, CD-ROMs took a while to become a common item, and several different, competing formats were developed while the technology was evolving. Most formats were incompatible with each other or were specific to a type of hardware or CD-ROM software driver. The adoption of a single CD-ROM standard format has helped spread CD-ROM usage throughout the UNIX and Linux communities.

Several different types of CD-ROM drives are available. Choosing the right drive for your Linux system is often a matter of balancing features against costs. Although it's tempting to purchase the state-of-the-art drive, you may be wasting your money if you do so.

INTERNAL, EXTERNAL, AND CHANGER CD-ROM DRIVES

You can buy CD-ROM drives in both internal and external models. You must attach an internal CD-ROM drive to a drive bay and a controller card (which you may already have) within your computer. An internal CD-ROM drive draws its power from a connector to the PC power supply. Before you purchase an internal CD-ROM drive, make sure you have a drive bay available for it and a spare power connector.

Don't assume that drive bays are available inside your machine for a CD-ROM drive just because you see featureless plastic panels on the front. There may be hard drives mounted behind these panels. Take off the cover of your machine and check for a full-width (5.25-inch wide) slot that can hold your CD-ROM drive. If you don't have any power connectors available inside the machine, you can attach a Y-connector to expand a single connector to two.

Warning

Before you add an internal CD-ROM drive, check that your power supply has adequate reserve to power it and all the other devices within your machine. Newer machines usually have enough power, but some older PC units are underpowered and have power supplies capable of powering only floppy and hard drives. If you have any doubts, check the ratings on the power supply, or consult your dealer. CD-ROM drives do not require a lot of power, but a surge from the CD-ROM drive may adversely affect other devices in your system.

External CD-ROM drives are easier to connect, in most cases, because they have an external power supply and attach to the outside edge of a board in one of your machine's expansion slots. Some interface types (such as IDE) do not support external drives easily because the IDE controller card has no external connector. Check the interface and cabling before you purchase an external CD-ROM drive. External CD-ROM drives tend to be more expensive then internal drives because of the additional case and power supply.

Most CD-ROM drives hold a single CD, either in a slide-out tray like many audio CD players or in a CD caddy, which is a holder that you open and into which you insert the CD. You then place the caddy inside the CD-ROM drive. Caddy and caddyless systems work equally well, with some users preferring no caddy and others liking the caddies. Most current high-end CD-ROM drives use caddies.

CD-ROM changers are also available. These CD-ROM drives hold four or more CDs at the same time. Most CD-ROM changers use a cartridge that holds six CDs, a system similar to the one used in audio CD changers. A few changers hold 18 or more CDs. These changers allow you to load up the unit with your favorite discs, and then select the one you want using software. Only one disc is loaded in the CD-ROM drive mechanism at a time, with the others just held internally for convenience. In other words, you can't access two CDs in a multi-CD changer at the same time because there is only one read mechansim into which the stored CD-ROMs are shuffled. Not all operating systems support changers because the commands to alter and remount CDs can be cumbersome to implement, especially in a real-time operating system like Linux. Linux handles some CD-ROM changers that behave as regular CD-ROM drives, although you may have to change CD-ROM discs manually by unmounting a currently loaded disc, changing to another disc, and then remounting. Newer drivers are beginning to appear for popular changers that automatically perform this process, although none are supplied with Linux distributions at this time.

ISO 9660 AND CD-ROM DISK FORMATS

CDs can be formatted in several different ways, depending on the type of machine the information is designed for. A CD-ROM designed for a PC, for example, is not necessarily readable on a Macintosh. For this reason, a standardized format was developed for CD-ROMs called ISO 9660. The ISO 9660 format was called the High Sierra format before being adopted by ISO, and both terms are still in common usage.

The ISO 9660 format dictates filenames in a strict DOS format (eight-character filename and three-character filetype). This format is fine for DOS-based machines and operating systems, but it is very restrictive for UNIX, which allows long filenames and doesn't force a convention for filetyping. To get around the DOS format limitations, a system called the Rock Ridge Extensions was developed. The Rock Ridge Extensions allow unused fields in the ISO 9660 data format to be used to provide much longer filenames, as well as UNIX-based information such as links, permissions, and so on. The Rock Ridge Extensions are in wide use for most UNIX and Linux ISO 9660 disks, although all these disks can be used in the basic ISO 9660 format too.

A few years ago, Kodak developed a graphics file storage format called PhotoCD. PhotoCD allows photographic and other visual images to be stored on a CD-ROM as digital data. The CD-ROM drive can then quickly recall this digital data and assemble it into the image it represents. Linux supports PhotoCD formats through utilities that allow PhotoCD files to be displayed.

Most CD-ROM device drivers also enable the user to play standard music CD discs by providing an on-screen control that steps through tracks and handles pauses, fast forwards, and so on. Audio-only CD-ROMs have no picture information and can't be decoded by Linux, other than as a sound source. Linux includes utilities that support the playing of audio-only CD discs, such as Workman (available in both character and X versions).

CD-ROM SPEEDS AND INTERFACES

CD-ROM drives are available in a number of different speeds, which dictate the transfer rate of data between the CD-ROM and the computer. The first generation of drives was called single speed and could transfer information at approximately 150K per second. Double-speed CD-ROM drives, as the name suggests, effectively double the transfer rate to over 300K per second. Quad-speed and six-speed drives increase the transfer rates even more. Of course, as the speed increases, so does the price.

9

Pure CD-ROM speed is not as important as your system's capability to receive the information. If your CD-ROM drive is capable of reading data at 750K per second, for example, but your interface card to the CD-ROM drive is capable of handling only 300K per second, the extra speed is useless. Also, if your device driver or application talking to the CD-ROM can't keep up, extra speed is again wasted.

The speed issue depends to a large degree on the type of interface you are using between the CD-ROM player and your system. The best interface is SCSI (see Chapter 7, "SCSI Devices," for more information) because it supports the highest transfer speeds and widest variety of supported CD-ROM players. Linux using a SCSI interface can provide full support for the fast CD-ROM drives, and a quad-speed drive is noticeably faster at retrieving a large file than a double-speed drive, for example. Because SCSI costs considerably more than other interfaces, most Linux systems use either an IDE (Integrated Drive Electronics) or sound card–based (proprietary) CD-ROM connector. These interfaces have a limited throughput and the newer six-speed CD-ROM drives can be much faster than the interface can handle in a heavily loaded system. For these interfaces, a quad-speed or even a double-speed CD-ROM drive is usually sufficient.

SCSI is a standard bus interface that connects all peripherals in a long chain. You can plug a CD-ROM drive into the chain at any location. Each SCSI device has all the device electronics and basic communications drivers built into the drive's electronics (which accounts for the drive's higher price). These built-in components mean that any SCSI CD-ROM drive can be plugged into a SCSI system. As long as it's SCSI, it will work with Linux. (Linux also requires the CD-ROM drive to have block sizes of 512 or 2,048 bytes, but most CD-ROM drives support these sizes. A few proprietary CD-ROM drives used by workstation and minicomputer manufacturers do not conform to these block sizes, but it is unlikely you could purchase such a CD-ROM drive easily.)

SCSI also allows more than one CD-ROM drive on a system at a time. You can easily have two, three, four, or more CD-ROM drives connected and available simultaneously. In contrast, a CD-ROM changer houses several CD-ROM discs at a time in cartridges, but only one CD disc is loaded and active at a time.

Some available SCSI-based CD-ROM interface cards are not fully SCSI interfaces, but a reduced set designed to support the CD-ROM drive only. These cards work with Linux as they conform to the SCSI standards, but you cannot add hard drives and other SCSI devices to them. Check the CD-ROM drive's documentation to determine whether the interface card supplied with the CD-ROM (if there is one) offers full or partial support.

True IDE CD-ROM drives plug into the IDE controller card that handles the hard drive in most PC systems. Older IDE systems can only handle two devices, which means that you can only have one hard drive and your CD-ROM drive. Newer EIDE (Extended IDE) cards can handle four devices. The IDE CD-ROM drives use a modified version of the hard disk standard called ATAPI. IDE CD-ROM drives are still fairly new, and they are generally inexpensive (as the IDE interface card has all the electronics, not the drive). A few IDE CD-ROM drivers are compatible with Linux, and more are being added as CD-ROM drives are released.

Warning

Don't confuse IDE CD-ROM drives with proprietary CD-ROM drives. Proprietary CD-ROM drives use the PC Bus, as does IDE, and can be misleadingly labeled. Check the descriptions carefully. IDE CD-ROM drives attach to an IDE controller card; they never attach to a sound card.

Proprietary CD-ROM drives are another problem, as the many different models of CD-ROM drive all have different communication methods. Proprietary drives are usually packaged either as a stand-alone CD-ROM or combined with a sound card as a multimedia system. In all these proprietary systems, the CD-ROM plugs into a special connector on the interface card. Most proprietary CD-ROM drives are internal models. These proprietary CD-ROM drives are not interchangeable and generally require different device drivers for each model. Some proprietary CD-ROM interface cards allow up to four CD-ROM drives to be connected to one controller and up to four controllers to be present at a time. The newer Matsushita/ Kotobuki drives all support this expansion, for example.

The most commonly used proprietary CD-ROM drive is one manufactured by Matsushita and partners, which is sold under many trade names (including Creative Labs, Panasonic, and others). Linux also supports several Sony CD-ROM drives and some Philips drives. A list of all supported CD-ROM drives is supplied with the Linux distribution set and is updated with each new release. Check the list supplied with your version of Linux and the manufacturer of the drive you're considering before you purchase a CD-ROM drive, if possible. Note that many companies relabel these drives with their own brand names, so it may be a little difficult to determine who manufactured the drive and its model number just by looking at the box. If you can't tell who made the CD-ROM drive, and it's not a major brand name (such as Creative Labs), postpone purchasing the unit until you can get more information about it. Most boxes have a telephone number for the vendor, so copy it down and give the vendor a call. (Beware of salespeople who give you the "of course it will work" line; most of them have no idea!) If your distribution software does not have support for your proprietary CD-ROM, you can check the FTP and BBS sites for new drivers. The primary proprietary models are supported, though.

Another differentiating factor with CD-ROM drives is the amount of RAM provided on the drive unit. This difference is common among SCSI drives. Most drives have 256K RAM, and others sport 1M or more. Plextor drives (such as the Plextor 4Plex and 6Plex) are usually available with 1M and are some of the fastest CD-ROM drives available for Linux and DOS/Windows. In theory, the more RAM there is on board, the more buffering and caching the drive can perform. Because Linux has a cache system of its own, the on-board RAM is generally not as important a factor as access speed, although more RAM does provide a small increase in speed.

RECORDABLE CD-ROMS

A slight variation on the CD-ROM drive is the newer CD-R (Compact Disk - Recordable) drive, which is essentially a CD-ROM drive that can write to a CD. CD discs are only capable of being written to once, so these devices are usually limited to special applications. Most CD-R drives are designed for DOS/Windows, although a few have generic UNIX drivers designed for high-end multimedia workstations.

You can add a CD-R drive to a Linux system, although few drivers are available for actually writing data to the CD-R. If you have a CD-R drive that you want to use with Linux, you can install it as a CD-ROM drive for read-only purposes. If you want to write data to the CD, you will have to find an application that is compatible with Linux or find a CD-ROM device driver that treats the CD-R as a normal filesystem. Such applications and drivers are currently rare and difficult to find, although the dropping prices of CD-R units will result in more interest in this type of device. Check an FTP site for recent developments along this line.

INSTALLING A CD-ROM DRIVE

If you have just bought a CD-ROM drive or want to add an existing drive to your Linux system, you must follow a series of steps to install and configure the drive properly. This section assumes that you have checked to ensure that Linux supports the drive and that a device driver is available (either in the Linux distribution software or on a separate disk or file).

Although adding a CD-ROM drive to your Linux system may seem to be a daunting task, it is quite simple. Doing the following process will result in a working CD-ROM with a minimum of effort, even if you are not very familiar with Linux:

1. Physically install the drive.
2. Configure and rebuild the Linux kernel.

3. Create the device files.

4. Mount and test the CD-ROM.

The following sections describe each of these steps in a little more detail.

PHYSICALLY INSTALL THE DRIVE

Linux doesn't impose any special requirements on the physical installation of a CD-ROM drive. Follow the manufacturer's directions. The instructions for installing your CD-ROM drive should be supplied with the drive itself.

For an internal drive the basic steps are as follows:

1. Place the drive in an unused drive bay.

2. Screw the drive into place.

3. Plug in the power connector and run the interface cable to the CD-ROM drive. (If you have a SCSI CD-ROM drive, plug the CD-ROM drive into an unused SCSI cable plug.)

4. Plug the interface board into a PC slot, and attach the cable from the CD-ROM drive.

5. Some CD-ROM drives have a special cable for digital sound which connects between the CD-ROM and a sound card. If your drive has such a connector, attach it.

External drives are easier to install because you need only add the interface board to an empty slot on the motherboard (assuming you need a new interface board) and attach the cable from the CD-ROM drive to the port on the back of the board. You add SCSI drives to the external SCSI chain. Make sure you have the proper connectors to add the CD-ROM drive to the chain. Also, when adding a SCSI CD-ROM, make sure that you set the SCSI ID to an unused value (see Chapter 7, "SCSI Devices," for more information on SCSI IDs). The SCSI ID is usually set with jumpers on internal CD-ROM drives, although some drives use DIP switches. External SCSI CD-ROM drives use a variety of methods to change SCSI ID numbers. The most popular method is a dial that shows the proper ID.

CONFIGURE AND REBUILD THE KERNEL

You must add ISO 9660 filesystem support and the CD-ROM device driver to the Linux kernel to provide support for a CD-ROM drive. Linux requires CD-ROMs to have the ISO 9660 (High Sierra) format, so your Linux system must have ISO 9660 filesystem support built in before the you can use the CD-ROM drive. The Linux ISO 9660 drivers include support for the Rock Ridge Extensions. The ISO 9660 driver is provided as part of the distribution set. Most Linux kernels have the ISO 9660 drivers included automatically when you install Linux from a CD-ROM. You can verify that the drivers are loaded by displaying the boot messages with the following command:

```
dmesg ¦ more
```

Examine the lines at the bottom of the output. As shown in Figure 9.1, you will see a line similar to the following

```
ISO9660 Extensions: RRIP_1991A
```

if the ISO 9660 drivers are included in your kernel. If you don't see any message about ISO 9660 drivers, add them manually.

Figure 9.1.
If your Linux kernel
has the ISO 9660
drivers already linked,
you will see a message
during startup that
shows the extension
name.

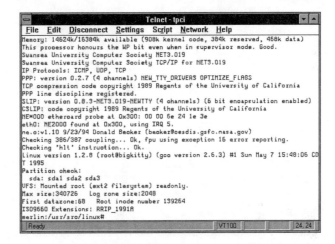

To add the ISO 9660 driver on most systems, you select a `configure` option from the Linux `setup` program or install script. Alternatively, on some Linux systems, you can change to the Linux source directory (usually /usr/src/linux) and perform a

```
make config
```

command and select the proper driver from the list presented. After adding ISO 9660 filesystem support, you must relink and rebuild the kernel. See Chapter 25, "Modifying the Kernel," for more information on rebuilding the kernel.

As with all physical devices on a Linux system, a CD-ROM drive requires a device driver. This device driver must be available before you start the installation process. Most popular IDE and proprietary CD-ROM drives have a device driver provided as part of the Linux distribution software. For some CD-ROM drives, you may have to obtain a driver from an FTP or BBS site, or even write it yourself. Whichever method you use, have the device driver file readily available to Linux for this step. If your device driver is on floppy disk, copy it to the /dev directory.

SCSI CD-ROM drives are the easiest to add to a Linux system. If you are adding a SCSI CD-ROM drive, the kernel configuration routine may ask you whether you want to add SCSI support. Answer yes. This question may be followed by a question about SCSI CD-ROM support, depending on the version of Linux you are running. Again, answer yes to this question. Some later versions of Linux with setup scripts enable you to select the CD-ROM drive from a list, as shown in Figure 9.2. When you install Linux from a CD-ROM, the drivers are linked in automatically. Select the SCSI option and continue with the configuration process.

Figure 9.2.
The Linux setup
program lets you add
support for a CD-ROM.

For IDE and proprietary CD-ROM drives, use the setup or installation routine supplied with Linux. Linux asks you for the type of CD-ROM drive you want to add. Select the drive type that matches your drive, assuming it is on the list. For example, if you are using a Creative Labs CD-ROM drive connected to one of the Creative Labs sound cards, you would select the Matsushita/Panasonic or Mitsumi drive, depending on the type of CD-ROM drive supplied in your package.

If your CD-ROM drive is not on the list presented by the installation or setup script, as is sometimes the case with IDE and some Sony CD-ROM drives, you must manually apply the patch for the drive yourself. If you need to manually patch the kernel, you must rebuild it using the process explained in Chapter 25, "Modifying the Kernel."

If you are using a CD-ROM drive driven by a sound card, you can configure the sound card at the same time as the CD-ROM interface. Some sound cards are not supported by Linux, but their CD-ROM interface is. Check the on-line documentation and FTP or BBS sites for specific information about your sound card.

CREATE THE DEVICE FILES

For the most popular CD-ROM drives, the device files may already be installed in your /dev directory, especially if you used an installation or setup script to add your CD-ROM drive. For other CD-ROM drives, you will have to perform this step manually. Even if the device files were created for you, you should still check the directories manually to ensure that they were installed properly.

To create the device files, you run a command that differs based on the type of CD-ROM drive you are installing. The mknod command is used to create the proper major and minor device numbers (see Chapter 6, "Devices and Device Drivers," for more information on device numbers). For example, you can create a SCSI CD-ROM drive file with the command

```
mknod /dev/scd0 b 11 0
```

The device name /dev/scd0 refers to the first CD-ROM drive the kernel finds. A second drive would be /dev/scd1, the third would be /dev/scd2, and so on. Most Linux systems use this naming convention for SCSI CD-ROM drives. The command line indicates that the CD-ROM drive is a block mode device and has a major device number of 11 and a minor device number of 0. A second SCSI CD-ROM drive would have a minor device number of 1; you would add it with the following command:

```
mknod /dev/scb1 b 11 1
```

Figure 9.3 shows the /dev/scd device drivers used for a SCSI CD-ROM. Linux usually aliases the device /dev/cdrom to the primary CD device (in this case /dev/scd0), as you can see from the symbolic link.

Figure 9.3.
Two SCSI CD-ROM
device drivers are
present in most Linux
systems.

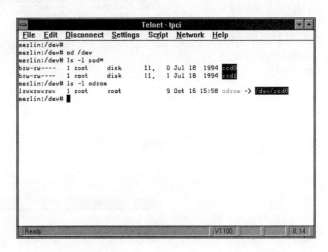

Proprietary and IDE CD-ROM drives require different device names, and the names vary considerably depending on the model. In most cases, the Linux documentation files that explain supported CD-ROM drives will include the name of the device file to use.

To create a CD-ROM device file for a Matsushita drive (common with Creative Labs and other multimedia add-on CD-ROM drives), use the command

```
mknod /dev/sbpcd b 25 0
```

or

```
mknod /dev/sbpcd0 b 25 0
```

This command uses the device driver /dev/sbpcd or /dev/sbpcd0 (the sb portion refers to the Sound Blaster drive card). The device major number is 25, and the minor number is 0. If you have a second drive of the same type, add it as /dev/sbpcd1 with the command

```
mknod /dev/sbpcd1 b 25 1
```

You can add more CD-ROM drives of the same type, incrementing the device driver number and the minor device number each time, up to the limit of four CD-ROM drives on the controller. Figure 9.4 shows the device drivers for four Sound Blaster–type CD-ROM drives created by a typical Linux installation. Whether they are used by the kernel depends on the kernel configuration. The device drivers /dev/sbpcd and /dev/sbpcd0 are the same.

Figure 9.4.
By default most Linux
versions include four
Sound Blaster–type
CD-ROM device
drivers.

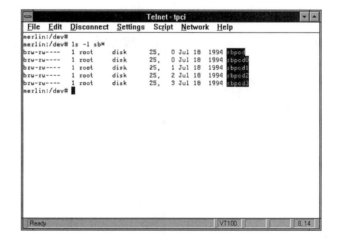

If you use more than one controller for these types of CD-ROM drives, you must create a new major device number (26, 27, and so on) for each controller. Few Linux installations will have more than one CD-ROM drive, let alone more than one controller for multiple CD-ROM drives. In case you're curious, the commands to create a second controller card with two CD-ROM drives of the same type attached are

```
mknod /dev/sbpcd0 b 26 0
mknod /dev/sbpcd1 b 26 1
```

A device file for a Sony CD-ROM drive is usually created with the command

```
mknod /dev/cdu31a b 15 0
```

which uses the device file /dev/cdu31a (based on the most common Sony CD-ROM drive model, the CDU31A or CDU33A) and has a major device number of 15. Additional CD-ROM drives of the same type would have incrementing minor device numbers. Sony CDU535 and CDU531 CD-ROM drives use a different device driver:

```
mknod /dev/cdu535 b 24 0
```

This driver corresponds to the features these models offer.

Mitsumi CD-ROM drives (also popular in multimedia packages) are supported with the command

```
mknod /dev/mcd b 23 0
```

which lists the device file /dev/mcd and a major device number of 23. Minor device numbers increment if more than one CD-ROM drive of the same type is used.

If you are supporting two different models of CD-ROM drives on the same system (off two different cards), you must create two device files, one for each drive. For example, if you were running both a Mitsumi and Sony drive, you would issue the commands shown previously for the two drives. Because the major and minor device numbers as well as the device files are different, having two drives poses no problems to Linux.

Once you have created the device files with the mknod command, link the new device driver to the file /dev/cdrom to make the CD-ROM drive easier to access (and the device driver file easier to remember). You can then call the file /dev/cdrom instead of the more complex device file. For example, to link a Mitsumi device file to /dev/cdrom, issue the command

```
ln -s /dev/mcd /dev/cdrom
```

Then all references to /dev/cdrom apply to /dev/mcd. Substitute the name of the device driver you have installed for /dev/mcd, of course. When you perform a directory listing of the /dev/cdrom device, you see an arrow after the name showing its link. For example, this entry

```
lrwxrwxrwx  1 root     root            9 Oct 16 15:58 cdrom -> /dev/scd0
```

shows that /dev/cdrom is symbolically linked to /dev/scd0.

As a last step, if you intend to play audio-only CD discs through the CD-ROM drive you installed, you must make sure the permissions on the device file allow read and write access. You can do this with the command:

```
chmod 666 /dev/cdrom
```

assuming you have the /dev/cdrom link set up. Substitute the name of your CD-ROM device driver if you don't use the links.

MOUNT AND TEST THE CD-ROM DRIVE

Now that the kernel has been rebuilt and the device files are properly set, the CD-ROM drive can be tested. Reboot the Linux system and watch the messages displayed when the machine boots. Depending on the type of CD-ROM drive you have added, you should see some status messages that indicate the CD-ROM drive is recognized and communicating properly.

For most IDE and proprietary CD-ROM drives, you see a message similar to Trying to detect a Panasonic CD-ROM drive at... followed by an address. This message tells you that the kernel is searching for what it believes will be a Panasonic CD-ROM device at a particular address. You provided the information about the type of CD-ROM drive and its address when the kernel was configured for the drive. If the CD-ROM is found properly, a message such as 1 Panasonic CD-ROM at... is displayed. Otherwise, you see an error message that tells you the drive couldn't be found.

SCSI CD-ROM device drivers sometimes display status messages, but not always. A typical SCSI CD-ROM message is the following:

```
Vendor: TOSHIBA    Model: CD-ROM XM-3401TA  Rev: 1094
  Type:   CD-ROM                      ANSI SCSI revision: 02
Detected scsi CD-ROM sr0 at scsi0, id 3, lun 0
```

This message shows that the CD-ROM was configured with SCSI ID 3. In this case, the kernel got the name and model number of the drive from the on-board SCSI electronics (a neat feature of SCSI devices).

If you can't read the messages about the CD-ROM drive when you boot Linux because the screen scrolls by too quickly, you can recover all the boot messages with the command

```
dmesg
```

The dmesg utility tells the kernel ring buffer to show the startup messages. This utility provides a handy way to get help with troublesome devices (not just CD-ROM drives) by sending the output to a file then e-mailing it to a technical support person. If you want, you can pipe the dmesg output to a paging utility like less or more:

```
dmesg ¦ less
```

This command lets you scroll backward and forward through the startup messages until you find what you are looking for.

If you installed your CD-ROM drive using a script or installation utility, the CD-ROM will probably be mounted automatically due to changes made in the startup commands. If the changes were not made or you installed your CD-ROM drivers manually, you will have to mount the CD-ROM onto your filesystem manually. (You can tell whether the mount was performed automatically by trying to read the CD-ROM directory.) You should mount and unmount CD-ROM drives while you are logged in as superuser (root).

When you mount a CD-ROM drive (or any other device), it is mounted into a subdirectory on the Linux filesystem tree. For convenience, it is useful to mount the CD-ROM drive in a subdirectory called /cdrom (which you must create before you try mounting the CD-ROM there). That way, you can change to the CD-ROM contents quickly. To mount an ISO 9660 CD-ROM on the /cdrom directory, issue the command

```
mount -t iso9660 -r /dev/cdrom /cdrom
```

The -t option of the mount command indicates the type of filesystem. The -r option mounts the CD-ROM as a read-only device because you cannot write to it. This option is not strictly necessary, but it prevents many error messages should you accidentally try to write to the CD-ROM disc. The device name /dev/cdrom refers to the device file; if you didn't link to this name earlier, use the actual device filename. Finally, /cdrom is the mount point. You can mount the CD-ROM disc anywhere.

If you receive an error message when you try the mount command, it is probably because the device file doesn't exist or the CD-ROM drive wasn't recognized during startup. Check all the installation information mentioned earlier and try rebooting the system. If you tried to mount the CD-ROM at a mount point that Linux couldn't reach (perhaps because the directory doesn't exist), check the mount point and create it if necessary. The directory you are mounting the CD-ROM onto must be empty.

To test the mount, try changing to the CD-ROM mount point and perform a directory listing. For example, if you mounted the CD-ROM at /cdrom, issue these commands:

```
cd /cdrom
ls
```

If you get error messages at this point, either there is no disc in the CD-ROM (or it is inserted improperly) or the filesystem is of the wrong type. The error message should give you a clue as to the problem. If you didn't see anything when you performed the ls command, the disc may be improperly spun up, inserted incorrectly, or of the wrong filesystem type. If you did get a directory listing, all is well, and you can move around the CD-ROM disc as if it were part of your normal filesystem (which it is as far as Linux is concerned).

Note

If you want to use the CD-ROM drive to play audio CD discs, the drive should not be mounted. If it is mounted by default, unmount it before playing an audio CD.

To remove a CD-ROM disc or remove the CD-ROM drive from access, you must unmount the CD-ROM drive. You cannot unmount a drive that is currently in use or is being accessed. Also, the CD-ROM drive cannot invoke any processes. To unmount the CD-ROM drive, use the umount command with the name of the mount point (not the name of the CD-ROM device):

```
umount /cdrom
```

This command will unmount the CD-ROM drive and make the directory it was mounted on empty.

Warning

Do not change CD discs without unmounting the drive first! When you want to change discs, unmount the CD-ROM drive, change discs, and then remount the drive. If you do not follow this process, the entire Linux filesystem may become corrupt!

Some CD-ROM drives require you to eject the disc caddy with the command

```
eject
```

This command helps clear the filesystem table from memory. Most versions of Linux (including the one provided with this book's CD-ROM) do not support the eject command by default, although some CD-ROM drivers can add it.

USING /ETC/FSTAB

The /etc/fstab file is used to control the mounting of devices when Linux boots. If you want to mount the CD-ROM automatically every time you start up Linux (if it isn't done already), modify the file /etc/fstab to include the mount. The format of the fstab command for a system mounting two filesystems and a SCSI CD-ROM is as follows:

```
/dev/sda3    /        ext2      defaults   1   1
/dev/sda1    /dos     msdos     defaults   1   1
/dev/scd0    /cdrom   iso9660   ro         1   1
```

Each line in the /etc/fstab file refers to a different filesystem. Fields on each line must be separated with whitespace (either tabs or spaces). The order of filesystems in the /etc/fstab file is important, as they are followed when the filesystems are mounted or unmounted. Therefore, the primary filesystem must be mounted first, followed by the subsidiary filesystems.

In previous example, the primary Linux filesystem /dev/sda3 is mounted first. It is an ext2 filesystem type. The DOS partition /dev/sda1 is then mounted in the directory /dos, followed by the SCSI CD-ROM drive mounted in /cdrom. If the /dev/sda3 filesystem were not mounted first, the other two commands would fail.

The different fields in the /etc/fstab file are as follows:

- The filesystem name of the block special device (usually the partition or device name)
- The mount point for the filesystem. Swap partitions that are mounted have the mount point specified as none.
- The type of filesystem the device uses. Currently, the following values are valid: mini, ext, ext2, xiafs, msdos, hpfs, iso9660 (CD-ROMs), nfs (network file systems), swap (for swap space), and ignore. If the filesystem type is ignore, the entry is ignored. This type is used to include disk partitions that are not currently in use.
- The mount options used with the filesystem. This command-separated list usually contains just the type of mount. You can display a complete list of options with the mount man page. Most disks have the default value, which is ro (read-only) for CD-ROMs.
- The frequency with which the filesystem needs to be dumped by the dump command. If no value is given, a zero is assumed, and dump doesn't dump the filesystem. Most versions of Linux do not support this option (including the version supplied with this book).

◆ A number indicating which order the filesystems should be checked at reboot time by fsck. A root filesystem should have a value of 1, and other filesystems can have higher values. If a filesystem is mounted within the root fileystem, it is checked in order. If a value of zero is present, fsck ignores the drive. Many versions of Linux do not support this option.

If you plan on using a single CD-ROM disc frequently (such as the Linux distribution CD or a disk of utilities), mounting the CD-ROM drive by using /etc/fstab is handy. Modify the fstab file as shown previously, substituting your device device name and mount points.

The mount and umount commands are usually executed only by root. To allow users to mount and unmount CD-ROM drives, you must modify the entry in the /etc/fstab file. Change the entry to read

```
/dev/scd0   /cdrom   iso9660   user,noauto,ro   1  1
```

The new options on the CD-ROM line allow any user to mount and unmount the drive. The noauto option tells Linux not to mount the filesystem when it first boots, which allows users to change and mount CD-ROMs without worrying about the initial filesystem state. Change the device driver name to match your device name. Alternatively, some utilities allow users to mount and unmount CD-ROM drives without requiring modification to the /etc/fstab file. One, called usermount, is popular and only allows access to CD-ROMs (not other devices), which is useful.

PLAYING AUDIO CD-ROMS

If you want to play an audio-only CD on your CD-ROM drive, you must unmount the filesystem (see the previous section) and have an application capable of playing the disc. Linux includes a number of CD applications, some command-line based and some for the X Window interface. You can get a lot more information about these applications from the documentation that came with your Linux distribution set or from the application's files.

The basic audio CD application supplied with Linux is Workman, which runs under X and lets you move through the audio disc with an on-screen control panel that looks just like a CD player's controls. A character-based version of the program is called WorkBone. Several other applications, such as cdtool, Xmcd, cdplayer, and xcdplayer are also available. More programs are released on FTP and BBS sites regularly, expanding the features supported. Some CD-ROM drives require special versions of the audio CD software, so check the documentation carefully.

9

USING PHOTOCDS WITH LINUX

If you want to use Kodak's PhotoCD format to view photographs and other images on your Linux system, you need to obtain a PhotoCD utility. Note that not all CD-ROM drives support PhotoCD formats.

The primary PhotoCD utility for Linux is called hpcdtoppm, which converts PhotoCD files to pixmap format. These files can then be displayed using any viewing tool or even saved as use for background for your X session. The photocd utility is similar and can also convert PhotoCD files to Targa and Windows bitmap formats. The utility xpcd, written by the same author as photocd, allows you to examine thumbnail views of pictures stored on a PhotoCD and load them at different resolutions. You can also select specific areas of an image to convert or examine.

TROUBLESHOOTING THE CD-ROM DRIVE

If you have installed a CD-ROM drive and configured it properly, yet you still cannot read from the disk, there are a number of potential solutions. Sometimes the problem is simple—you forgot to mount the drive or misspelled its name. Unless you specifically know the problem, try these solutions in the order that they are presented to isolate the problem's root cause.

CHECK THE KERNEL

Check that the kernel has been relinked and rebuilt with the new CD-ROM device drivers added. You can check the date of the kernel build with the command

```
uname -a
```

If the date doesn't correspond to the date of your linking and rebuilding, the build wasn't completed properly and the CD-ROM drivers are missing. Rebuild the kernel.

Alternatively, you can look at a list of the drivers that are compiled into the kernel by looking at the file /proc/devices. This file lists all the devices, as in the following example:

```
Character devices:
 1 mem
 4 ttyp
 5 cua
 6 lp
 7 vcs
10 mouse
```

```
Block devices:
 2 fd
 8 sd
11 sr
```

In this example, the device number 11 refers to the SCSI CD-ROM drive. If you linked in a kernel for a Matsushita CD-ROM, for example, there would be a line in the file that looks like the following:

```
25 sbpcd
```

The numbers in the first column are the major device numbers; the second column has the device driver initials. Check the device numbers you created and compare them to this file. If the major device number is not listed, the CD-ROM driver is not linked to the kernel. Rebuild the kernel.

CHECK THE DEVICE

If the device drivers are linked into the kernel and the CD-ROM device has been mounted but you can't see anything on the disc, try the following command and watch the light on the CD-ROM faceplate that indicates drive activity:

```
dd if=/dev/cdrom of=/dev/null bs=2048
^C
```

Substitute the name of the CD-ROM device if it is not linked to /dev/cdrom. This command tries to copy the contents of the CD-ROM to /dev/null. After issuing the command, issue a Ctrl+C to interrupt it, as the command doesn't really do anything useful. If the drive indicator light blinked or stayed on for a while, yet you still can't read anything on the disk, the disc in the drive is probably not an ISO 9660 filesystem format, or it is ISO 9660 format, but you forgot to link in the ISO 9660 drivers.

Verify that the ISO 9660 drivers are active by examining the contents of the /proc/ filesystems file. You should see this line under the nodev section:

```
iso9660
```

If this line doesn't show up in the file, the ISO 9660 device driver is not linked to the kernel. Relink the kernel with this option.

If the ISO 9660 driver is linked in and shows up in the /proc/filesystem file, check that when you mount the CD-ROM drive you specify the option

```
-t iso9660
```

on the command line.

If you are specifying the ISO 9660 driver and it is linked in to the kernel, chances are the CD is not ISO 9660 format. Try another disc and hope for better results.

CHECK THE DRIVE SETTINGS

If you are having problems with a proprietary CD-ROM drive, chances are the settings for the interface are not correct. The settings are usually defined in a file with the name of the device, such as sbpcd.h for a Matsushita drive. The location of the file varies, so use a wildcard find routine to locate it:

```
find / -name sbpcd* -print
```

When you find the file, which usually has a .h extension (such as sbpcd.h), check the contents to ensure that the I/O address, DMA, and IRQ (if applicable) match your card's settings. If you can't find a configuration file, check the settings of the card manually. There may be a conflict with the I/O address, DMA, or IRQ and another device on your system.

DEVICE BUSY ERRORS

If you get device busy errors, and you are running a SCSI system, you may have assigned the CD-ROM device a SCSI ID the same as another device. Check the SCSI IDs.

If you get the device busy message when you try to unmount a CD-ROM drive, then a process is using the drive and is preventing the CD-ROM drive from unmounting successfully. Make sure you are not currently in the CD-ROM directory structure when you try to unmount it. If you can't find the suspect process, use the command

```
fuser -v /cdrom
```

to display the processes currently using the device (change the name of the mount point if necessary to match your system).

SUMMARY

Despite the amount of information presented in this chapter, adding a CD-ROM drive to your system and properly configuring it can take less than 15 minutes. Unfortunately, the wide variety of proprietary CD-ROM drives means that there will always be a few that are not mentioned in the Linux documentation and will require varying degrees of extra work to properly configure. If you can, stick to one of the major brands that you know is supported. CD-ROMs make a Linux user's life much easier by offering large libraries of utilities and distribution software, and a CD-ROM drive is definitely worth adding to most systems.

- Checking for Sound Card Support

- Configuring Your Sound Card

- Using the PC Speaker

- Sampling Linux Sound Applications

- Troubleshooting the Sound Card

CHAPTER 10

Sound Cards

UNIX wasn't designed with sound cards in mind, and only a few applications make use of one (DOOM being the most popular). Linux also lets you load a special driver to make use of the PC speaker for more than the occasional beep, useful when you don't have a proper sound card. However, sound cards are a common accessory in PCs, especially those designed for multimedia applications. Making your sound card work under Linux is not difficult, as long as you know the manufacturer and model of your sound card. Software device drivers for the most common models are included with most Linux distribution software packages, and some other drivers are available from FTP and BBS sites. This chapter looks at how you can install the device drivers for your sound card and make sure they work properly under Linux.

Linux doesn't support many DOS sound file formats (such as .WAV and .MID), but relies instead on sound files and commands that are taken from the Sun workstation product line. Sun audio files are the general format for Linux, usually with the .au filetype appended. You can play other sound files, although some may need conversion to Sun format first. Sun workstation device drivers are used as the model for the sound card drivers in Linux, although the drivers are designed to work with standard PC sound cards.

A Linux system can support two sound cards, although most installations will involve only one card. The two cards must be different and cannot have any of the same configuration information (both must have different I/O addresses, IRQs, and DMAs). If you have a separate dedicated card for a MIDI interface, you may want to use two cards. For example, you may have a PC equipped with a Sound Blaster card for the usual game effects and a Roland MIDI card for professional-sounding audio. Linux can support both types of devices at the same time. You can't use two cards that both support Sound Blaster, even as emulations, as the drivers will conflict unless you disable one card.

Note

The drivers and software associated with the device drivers for sound cards changes frequently, so check for the latest versions and examine any documentation that accompanies them. It may supersede the information in this chapter. Many versions of Linux now include automated installation scripts for sound cards or support the `mkdev sound` command. Check for the installation scripts before installing the sound card manually.

Checking for Sound Card Support

The list of sound cards supported by Linux includes most of the popular models, and many others emulate one of these supported models and so can be run in emulation mode without a problem. The most popular supported models of sound cards are the following:

- ◆ Creative Lab's Sound Blaster, Sound Blaster Pro, Sound Blaster 16, Sound Blaster AWE (as well as most Sound Blaster–compatible systems, including ATI's Stereo F/X, Thunderboard, and others)
- ◆ Adlib's Adlib series and compatibles
- ◆ ProAudioSpectrum 16 and Logitech's SoundMan 16
- ◆ Gravis' Advanced Gravis UltraSound
- ◆ Microsoft's Microsoft Sound System
- ◆ Roland MPU 401 MIDI–based interfaces and sound boards

A complete list of supported sound boards is usually supplied with the Linux distribution software. Because the location of the files describing the sound support varies considerably, search for any files to do with sound using the `find` command. You can do this search easily with a CD-ROM distribution package. Mount the CD-ROM (see Chapter 9, "CD-ROM Drives," for more information) and issue a `find` command with the string `sound` as a starting point:

```
find / -name sound* -print
```

This search should at last point you to the directories that contain information about the sound boards, drivers, and C source code for the drivers. The sound drivers for the version of Linux included with this book, for example, are stored in /usr/src/linux/drivers/sound of your installed Linux system. Figure 10.1 shows the output from a `find` command run against this version of Linux. In this example, the `find` command reports matches in the DOS filesystem, too, because that is mounted as /dos. You may want to unmount your CD-ROM drive before issuing this command to save time. If you can't search your distribution media, or don't have a complete Linux distribution handy, check the README files that were supplied with your software for potential locations of drivers.

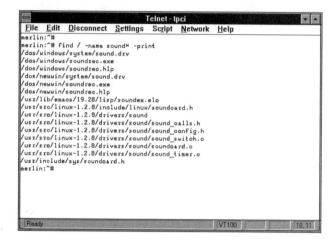

Figure 10.1.
You can search for
the sound card drivers
by issuing a find
command.

CONFIGURING YOUR SOUND CARD

Once you have determined that your model of sound card is supported, you can begin the process of making it available to Linux. Install the sound card, if necessary. This procedure usually involves nothing more complex than placing the card in an available slot on the motherboard. Because Linux uses its own device drivers, installing the DOS-based software has no effect on the card under Linux.

When you install the sound card, note the basic configuration information, such as the card's DMA, IRQ, and I/O address. Some cards have more configuration information, including 8-bit and 16-bit DMAs, MIDI addresses, and so on. Most sound cards use the default values without a problem, so you can check the card's documentation for these values. If you had to change some of the default settings to make the card work under DOS, have the changed values readily available for the Linux device configuration.

Later versions of Linux include sound card drivers for the most common cards as part of the basic driver package. In some cases, the setup or installation script includes a sound card configuration section. This script installs the proper drivers and relinks the kernel automatically. If your setup or install script handles the sound card setup for you, there is little else you need to do except reboot the system and test the sound card.

The sound card drivers are stored in different locations, depending on the Linux distribution. A good general location to look for drivers is the directory /usr/src/linux/drivers/sound, although the names tend to change somewhat. A quick method of finding the drivers is to search for the sound directory using the command

```
find / -name sound -print
```

If your Linux software is supplied on CD-ROM, you will want to search the CD-ROM as well as the hard disk filesystem because few installation routines copy all the drivers to the hard drive.

UNDERSTANDING SOUND CARD DEVICE FILES

Linux uses a number of device files in association with a sound card. Each device driver is in the /dev directory by convention (although it can, in theory, be anywhere). Linux supports up to two different sound cards, so two device driver files are possible for each type of driver.

The system administrator can change the device driver files and their purposes, but the administrator should retain the basic names for ease of integration with applications that require specific device names. The sound card device drivers are the following:

- /dev/audio is the first audio device (Sun compatible)
- /dev/audio2 is the second audio device (Sun compatible)
- /dev/dsp is the first digital sampling device
- /dev/dsp2 is the second digital sampling device
- /dev/midi is the MIDI device driver
- /dev/mixer is the sound mixer device
- /dev/pcaudio is the audio device driver for the PC speaker
- /dev/pcsp is the PC speaker's digital sampling device
- /dev/pcmixer is the PC speaker's mixer device
- /dev/sequencer is the sequencer device for MIDI, FM, and GUS files
- /dev/sndstat is a file that displays the sound card device driver's status

The PC speaker devices (/dev/pcaudio, /dev/pcsp, and /dev/pcmixer) are only used when the PC speaker device driver is loaded into the kernel.

LINKING THE SOUND CARD FILES

Before you link in the sound card drivers, you must isolate the proper files that the compiler uses to form the device driver that is linked into the kernel. These files are usually supplied as part of the distribution software, or you can obtain them from the FTP or BBS sites. You may be able to skip the compilation step if you can find a precompiled device driver.

Each sound card has several source code files, usually with the .c extension, that take care of various aspects of the sound card support. These files include the

10

device's initialization file and the drivers for the mixer, sequencer, MIDI interface, and so on. As a bare minimum, you need the file that initializes the card. This file is usually named after the sound card itself, such as sb_card.c for the Sound Blaster card or gus_card.c for the Gravis UltraSound card. In addition to the .c files, there are essential matching .h files for each component. You also need the files soundcard.c, soundcard.h, and audio.c (only for later versions of Linux), which are the driver skeletons to which the specific sound card details are linked.

An important component of the sound card device driver is the soundinstall script that constructs the drivers. This script may be supplied as a specific file, or it may be attached to the end of a documentation file. Slackware releases, for example, include a file called Readme.Linux in the sound directory that has the script appended to the end of the file. This script must be cut out and run by itself. The soundinstall script checks for the existence of a current device file, removes it if it exists, and then uses mknod to create a new device file. Of course, you also can perform these steps manually.

To compile the sound card drivers, follow a sequence of steps that places the required files in particular locations (as defined in the compilation script or Makefile), and then invoke the compilation process. The procedure is as follows:

1. Copy the file soundcard.h to /usr/include/linux from whatever directory it currently resides in.

2. Copy the sound card .h files (such as sb.h) to /usr/include/sys.

3. Create a symbolic link between the /usr/include/linux and /usr/include/sys versions of soundcard.h by using the command

   ```
   ln -s /usr/include/linux/soundcard.h /usr/include/sys/soundcard.h
   ```

4. Compile the device drivers using the Makefile for sound card devices. You can skip this step if you have the device driver already compiled, as with some distributions of Linux.

5. Run the soundinstall script to create the sound card devices, or create them manually.

The soundinstall script uses the mknod command to create the device drivers in the /dev directory. If you want to perform the steps manually, these basic mknod commands are required:

```
mknod -m 666 /dev/mixer c 14 0
mknod -m 666 /dev/sequencer c 14 1
mknod -m 666 /dev/patmgr0 c 14 17
mknod -m 666 /dev/midi00 c 14 2
mknod -m 666 /dev/dsp c 14 3
mknod -m 666 /dev/audio c 14 4
mknod -m 666 /dev/sndstat c 14 6
```

Some of these commands aren't needed if your sound card doesn't support the functions (such as a MIDI interface or sequencer). The preceding steps are for the first sound card. If you are installing two sound cards, you have to repeat the commands with the second device names. The `soundinstall` script handles this step automatically.

PROVIDING CONFIGURATION INFORMATION

When the installation process is running, either from an installation script like `setup` or `install` or from a compilation of the sound card drivers, you are asked for a number of configuration parameters. These parameters are used to generate a file called local.h that defines the sound card configuration information. You are prompted for the type of sound card, IRQ, DMA, and I/O address, as well as other information pertaining to each type of driver.

If you don't get asked for this kind of information, you must edit the local.h file (if it exists) manually. A file called sound_config.h contains generic configuration information. You can edit this file to complete any configuration parameters that are not prompted for by the configuration routine. Most of the sections of the sound_config.h file are clearly labeled as to their purpose.

The installation procedure should end with the Linux kernel rebuilding, relinking, and then setting the new kernel as the boot image so that the drivers are active when you start Linux. Without this step, none of the changes you made will be effective.

TESTING THE SOUND CARD DRIVERS

After the kernel has been rebuilt with the sound card drivers embedded, reboot the machine to test the sound card. Watch the startup messages carefully to see the initialization messages. If you miss the messages, you can recall them with the command

```
dmesg
```

which shows all the kernel's startup messages on-screen again.

If the sound card drivers were properly installed in the kernel, Linux tries to contact the sound card and initialize it. In the startup messages, you see a line similar to

```
snd1 <SoundBlaster Pro> at 0x220 irq 5 drq 1
```

which, in this case, shows that the driver for a Sound Blaster Pro card (or compatible) was loaded with the I/O address set to 220H, an IRQ of 5, and a DMA of 1. If the sound card had values for any of these parameters that were different from the ones shown, the card initialization would probably fail.

If you are booting Linux for the first time after installing new drivers, some diagnostic, warning, or extra error messages may be displayed. These messages may not be repeated every time you reboot, just the first time. For this reason, you should use the dmesg command to check for these messages after relinking and rebooting the kernel with the sound card driver.

Assuming the drivers are linked properly, the device drivers initialize the card and the Linux registers that use it. All you need to do now is test the sound card with an application that tries to access the card. Any sound file will do. A few samples are usually included with the sound card drivers, or you can obtain sound files from FTP or BBS sites or possibly the Linux distribution disks.

To test the sound card, use the cat command to send the test file to the sound device. For example, if you have a sound file called parrot_sketch.au (many sound files have .au as their extension, although this is far from a convention) and your sound card is called /dev/audio, you can send the file to the sound card with the command

```
cat parrot_sketch.au > /dev/audio
```

If you don't hear anything from the sound card (and you have headphones or speakers connected with the volume set properly), the drivers are not communicating with the card properly. (Or your sound file is not properly formatted, in which case a prudent test is to use another sound file to confirm that the problem is the configuration.) Try the steps outlined in the Troubleshooting section later in this chapter. If you hear your sound file played properly, all is well and you have completed your sound card's installation.

If your sound card is capable of recording, and you have linked in a driver that supports recording from the sound card's microphone (or other input), you can test the recording capability of the sound card by recording a few seconds of audio and storing it in a file. The easiest way to do this procedure is to use the command

```
dd bs=8k count=10 < /dev/audio > test_mic.au
```

This command records 10 seconds from the input of /dev/audio and stores it in the file test_mic.au. You can then play this sound file back to check the fidelity of the recording with the command

```
cat test_mic.au > /dev/audio
```

If you heard whatever sounds you recorded, the input sampling of the sound card is working properly. If you heard silence or got an error message, either the sound card driver doesn't support recording or the settings are incorrect.

USING THE PC SPEAKER

Don't have a sound card in your system, or you do have one but it is not supported and you don't want to hassle with drivers? Use the PC speaker instead. The quality of sound from a PC internal speaker is a lot more limited than a sound card, but it isbetter than no sound at all.

The Linux drivers for the PC speaker are usually located in an archive file with the name pcsndrv followed by the version number, such as pcsndrv-0.6.tar.z. You can search your filesystem or distribution media for a file with this name using the command

```
find / -name pcsndrv* -print
```

Many Linux software distributions do not include the PC speaker sound drivers, but they are available from almost all FTP and BBS sites. For example, the latest PC speaker sound drivers are located in the directory /pub/Linux/kernel/misc-patches at the sunsite.unc.edu FTP site. Check for the most recent release of the drivers.

Installing the PC speaker sound driver is a matter of linking the device driver into the kernel, and then rebuilding the kernel. The documentation that accompanies the device driver explains the process in detail.

SAMPLING LINUX SOUND APPLICATIONS

The number of Linux applications that use sound is increasing almost daily. This section describes sample applications for each type of sound card function. These applications are generally supplied with Linux distributions. For a complete list of all applications that support music, check the Linux documentation or local download sites. The USENET newsgroups also are helpful for finding the most useful applications for particular purposes.

♦ For playing simple audio files, a common application is called play. You call this application with the name of the audio file. Other applications, such as wavplay, do the same thing, some with better interfaces than others.

♦ For mixing, the utilities aumix and xmix are useful. They let you control the input and output of the sound card and combine sound files into another sound files in some cases.

♦ To play MIDI files, you need a special player like mp. MIDI files are stored in a different format than most Linux sound files, so they have to be interpreted differently. Linux's MIDI players can interface with a wide variety of MIDI equipment, including many commercial synthesizers and drum machines.

10

SOUND CARDS

- Several conversion utilities are available to help you convert audio files from one format to another. A good starting utility is Sox. You may need to convert audio files that were originally designed for another operating system or machine.
- Recording sound samples requires an application that can interface with the sound card inputs. One widely used application for this purpose is called vrec. It will work with many of the microphone-equipped sound cards used by DOS and Windows.

TROUBLESHOOTING THE SOUND CARD

If you have properly installed the sound card, yet don't hear anything when you try to test it (or get error messages during initialization), it's time to follow a few simple diagnostic and troubleshooting procedures. Follow these steps in the order they're presented to try and isolate the problem.

CONFIGURATION INFORMATION

Check the initialization messages from the kernel. When the machine reboots with the kernel that has the sound drivers linked in, you should see some initialization messages similar to

```
snd1 <Sound_Card_Name> at 0x330 irq 1 drq 1
```

where the sound card's name and configuration parameters are shown. Verify the sound card parameters! Incorrect prarmeters are the most common cause of sound card failure, as many users assume default values when the values have been changed. Sometimes the default values are used on the sound card but are incorrectly entered in the configuration information.

If no lines in the bootup messages refer to the sound card driver, then the driver is inactive or not linked to the current boot kernel. Make sure you linked the drivers to the current boot kernel. Some Linux systems don't display any boot messages if the configuration information is correct, and others generate a message telling you the information is correct.

Use the sound card's manual to determine the default settings and compare them to the board. Physically remove the sound board and examine the jumpers, DIPs, or whatever method is used for setting the configuration. Some boards use software configuration, so you should boot your machine in DOS and use the diagnostics supplied with the card to examine and set the board. Write down all the settings, and then check the device driver configuration file to ensure that they match.

A good method of checking settings is to run a DOS application that uses the sound board. If the settings work in DOS, they will work in Linux. However, if a DOS application can't access the sound card properly, that indicates a configuration problem (or the sound card is defective). If the settings are incorrect, re-enter them into the device driver configuration information, recompile and relink the kernel, and then reboot the machine and test the sound card again.

CHECK THE FILE /DEV/SNDSTAT

The file /dev/sndstat should contain some basic information about the sound card and its initialization. Not all versions of Linux provide this file, so don't be too surprised if it doesn't exist. In this case, skip this step. If the /dev/sndstat file does exist, the contents should show the name of the configured card and its parameters, as well as any additional installed devices. For example, a file may contain the following lines:

```
Sound Driver 3.1
HW config:
Type 1: SoundBlaster Pro at 0x220 irq 5 drq 1
PCM devices:
0: SoundBlaster Pro 3.2
Synth devices:
0: Yamaha OPL-3
Midi devices:
0: SoundBlaster
Mixer(s) installed
```

This sample file shows the drivers and components that are installed for a typical Sound Blaster Pro card. Additional messages may appear for other drivers or for error conditions. Check the file for anything of use, and verify the configuration parameters with your sound card documentation.

If you can't find the /dev/sndstat file or it is empty, either your Linux version doesn't support that file or the sound card was not recognized during boot. Usually the HW config section is filled in even if the sound card was not found.

NO SUCH FILE OR DEVICE ERRORS

If the sound card seems to load but then you can't test it, or you get the error message

```
No such file or directory
```

when the sound card tries to initialize or you run an application that uses the sound card, the problem is the device driver files. Typically, these problems mean that the device driver files do not exist or the files are not in the proper location.

Check to ensure the device driver files are linked into the kernel and are in the /dev directory. Check the section "Understanding Sound Card Device Files" earlier in this chapter for a list of the sound card device driver files you should have. If the device driver files exist, check that the major and minor device numbers do not conflict with any other active device.

10

SOUND CARDS

If you get the error message

```
No such device
```

when an application tries to use the sound card, it means the device driver wasn't loaded in the kernel boot process. Check to make sure you did relink the kernel and you have booted the system using the new image.

If you get the message

```
device busy
```

when an application is running and trying to communicate with the sound card, it means that more than one process is using the sound card at the same time. Linux allows only one process to access the sound card device at a time. You can determine which processes are using the sound card using the `fuser` command. For example, if the problem is with the /dev/audio device file, issue the command

```
fuser -v /dev/audio
```

and examine the output to see which processes are currently using the device. Repeat the command for the /dev/dsp device if the /dev/audio device has no conflict.

If the device busy error message persists, it is likely a DMA error. Make sure you are not using DMA 0 for the sound card. Some sound cards allow this DMA channel to be chosen, but Linux uses DMA 0 as a special refresh channel for DRAM. Change to DMA channel, reconfigure the kernel, relink, rebuild, reboot, and then test again.

INCOMPLETE PLAYING OF SOUND FILES

If you only hear a small section of a sound file and then the playing abruptly stops, or you get an error message after a file has started to play, the problem is probably an incorrect IRQ or DMA setting. You may see messages that tell you the IRQ or DMA has timed out.

To correct this problem, check the DMA and IRQ values on the sound card and in the configuration files. If the values match, check for a conflict with other devices in your PC. Odds are that the IRQ or DMA is shared with another device (network cards are a common culprit). Change the settings on whichever card is the easiest. (If you already have a network up and running, change the sound card if it will let you.)

SOUNDS STOP AND START WHEN PLAYING

Sounds stop and start when playing because the sound card, computer, or hard disk can't keep up with each other. The simplest method of solving this problem is to choose a lower sampling rate or switch to mono. Alternatively, if your system is running many processes (as it will with some games), try eliminating applications you don't need. X applications that run on the desktop are good at gobbling up huge chunks of processor time. Freeing up enough CPU time to support the sound card will help. For a longer-term solution, consider either upgrading your computer to a faster processor or getting a sound card with more capabilities, including on-board RAM.

Summary

The sound card is a useful peripheral when it's properly supported by a Linux application. It is also one of the most frustrating devices to get working properly. If you can use an automated installation utility instead of trying to manually build the drivers, do so. They will save you a lot of grief!

A growing number of applications support sound cards, especially games and X applications, so when you have your sound card properly configured and tested, keep your eye out for these types of applications. They make using Linux a lot more interesting.

10

SOUND CARDS

- Connecting
  Terminals

- Understanding the
  Login Process

- Adding a Terminal

- Setting Terminal
  Behavior with stty
  and tset

- Resetting a Screwy
  Terminal

- Using term

CHAPTER 11

Terminals and term

The most common Linux installation involves only a single screen, which is the system console that came with the PC that Linux is running on. If you are running your Linux system for yourself and don't want to add another terminal to your system, your Linux configuration is complete as far as terminals are concerned and you can skip this chapter.

If, on the other hand, you want to add another PC or a terminal to your system, either for yourself to access (from another room, for example) or to provide access to Linux for others in your home or office, you need to know how to add and configure terminals. This chapter explains how to add terminals (including PC and Macintosh devices running terminal emulation software) to Linux and how to configure them. It also explains how to use the `term` program, which allows you to multiplex your serial lines, essentially supporting more than one device on a line.

Connecting Terminals

For the purposes of this book, the word terminal doesn't necessarily mean the old, dumb, ASCII-based terminals that many feel are remnants of days gone by. Although those machines are definitely terminals (and fully usable with Linux), modern terminals can range from inexpensive graphics-based systems to complex X workstations that have more built-in computing power than most PC machines (at a suitably hefty price). A terminal can also be any other computer (PC, Macintosh, UNIX system, Commodore 64, Amiga, and so on) that runs a terminal emulation package, which makes the machine act like a terminal.

You may want to add terminals to your system to allow other users to work with Linux at the same time you do (it is a multiuser system) or to provide access to your database of videotape movies (not to mention games) by running a terminal into your living room. If you are a parent, you can run terminals into your children's rooms, letting them use the system for education and entertainment. You may want to let friends access your system when they visit, or call in over the modem.

For whatever reason you need new terminals, you can add them to your Linux system by connecting them through an existing serial port on the back of your PC or through a multiport card with many serial ports on it.

Using Multiport Cards

Because many PC machines have a maximum of four serial ports (and the majority of systems only have two), expanding your Linux system using serial ports can be limiting. If you use an external modem, a serial printer, or other serial port devices, you may not have any serial ports left for terminals. In this case, you must use a multiport card.

Multiport cards are an easy and effective method of adding serial ports to a Linux system. Multiport cards have a plug-in board that is placed in a slot on your PC system and an oversized connector on the outer board edge to which a cable is attached. The cable either leads directly to a number of serial ports (in which case the cable is called an octopus) or to a hardware device that has serial ports laid out on it.

Multiport cards come in two basic types. The first is essentially a fast, somewhat intelligent serial port server. These cards are inexpensive because they are simple to manufacture. However, they lack any on-board processing or memory, so every device connected to the multiport card takes its toll on the Linux system's CPU and RAM.

The other type of multiport card is the intelligent controller. These cards cost much more, but have an on-board CPU to offload the Linux system's CPU. The on-board CPU can handle all the communications requests and, in some cases, is smart enough to provide terminal commands. These cards usually have RAM mounted on the board too, which provides a cache system for speeding up access. In general, these intelligent boards are much better for supporting four or more terminals and other devices than their dumber brethren, but you may be spending money on features you don't need if you have less than that number of attached devices.

Multiport cards can provide from 2 to 32 additional serial ports per card, and you can add multiple boards to the increase capacity even further, although this situation is very rare for Linux installations. A couple of manufacturers even offer systems that can support 256 terminals spread out in a cluster arrangement. Some multiport boards include parallel ports for printers, and a few high-end boards are designed to use SCSI devices.

Each port on the multiport card is usually wired for use by any serial device, including terminals, modems, printers, scanners, and so on. However, a few cards designed for simple terminal use support only a few of the wires in a serial port. These cards cannot support modems, printers, and similar complex devices properly. Different card manufacturers have different supported systems, so if you decide to go with a multiport card for your system, check the specifications carefully.

The types of connectors on multiport cards differ, too. Most use either standard DB25 (25-pin) connectors or DB9 (9-pin) connectors, identical to the ones found as PC serial ports. Some cards use the RJ45 connector, which looks like a wide modular telephone-style jack. Adapters are used to connect the RJ11 connector to a standard serial cable. Again, if you decide to use a multiport card, check the types of connectors and make sure the wiring of the connector is consistent with your serial devices or that converters and adapters are readily available.

If you are going to use a multiport card on your Linux system, make sure you use one with software device drivers that are designed for Linux. You cannot use any multiport card device driver designed for other versions of UNIX without modification. Because the drivers are usually already compiled, you cannot modify the drivers yourself. Several multiport card drivers, specially modified or written by Linux users to suit the most popular multiport cards, are available from FTP and BBS sites. As Linux becomes more popular, more multiport card vendors are developing optimized drivers for their products to integrate with Linux.

Multiport cards come with complete instructions for installing the device drivers for the multiport card, as well as configuring the terminals and other devices. Because the details of the configurations change depending on the manufacturer of the multiport card, you should consult the documentation accompanying your card for further information.

CONNECTING SERIAL PORT TERMINALS

If you have a spare port, you can use your PC's serial ports to add terminals. In most cases, connecting the terminal is a matter of running a cable between the terminal and the serial port, and ensuring the proper connectors are used. You then update the Linux configuration files to tell the operating system to provide service for the terminal. The remote terminal should be active after this step.

You can choose any serial port for a terminal, although the port should not be shared with other devices (such as a modem) unless you are willing to disable other devices when the terminal is needed. If you need to run more than one device off a serial port, you can get switch boxes to connect the devices to. These boxes usually have a rotary switch on the front for routing the internal wiring to the proper port.

Serial port terminals are sometimes limited by the speed of the UARTs used in the PC, although most new PC machines have the faster 16550 UARTs capable of high-speed communications. Even older machines are very usable for all but graphics applications, as most character-based terminals don't need speeds above 38,400 baud. (In fact, 9,600 baud is fast enough for most character-based applications, although 19,200 is better.)

WIRING SERIAL CABLES

The wiring of cables between the terminal and the Linux PC depends on the type of connectors at both ends. The same problems usually occur whether you are using a serial port or a multiport card for your serial ports. In most cases, the cables you will use will be a DTE (Data Terminal Equipment) to DTE type. Some terminals and PC serial ports require DCE (Data Communications Equipment) cabling. As a general rule, terminals and remote computers use DTE, and modems use DCE. The difference between DTE and DCE cabling is in the way the wires run from each end connector; DTE crosses several of the wires between pins at either end.

Some store-bought cables are designed specifically for terminals and cross the internal wires as part of their connector design, and other cables are designed for modems and have wires that run straight through. If you find your terminal doesn't work even after following all the configuration instructions discussed in this chapter, chances are your cables are incorrectly wired. A null modem adapter (which forces a cross between wires) is the easiest solution, and you can add it anywhere in the chain from the terminal to the Linux PC.

A typical DCE cable (such as for a modem) uses straight through wiring, meaning that pin 1 on the PC end goes to pin 1 on the modem end, pin 2 through to pin 2, and so on. This cable is called a straight cable or modem cable.

DTE cables cross wires to allow sending and receiving ends accept signals on the same pins, so that pin 2 in a connector is always for transmit, for example, and pin 3 is always for receive. By crossing pins 2 and 3 between the two ends, one connector's transmit pin becomes the other connector's receive pin. When connecting a terminal, some of the pins must be crossed to permit signals to pass properly. The wiring of these cables (often called null modem cables) requires several such crosses or shorts to make the connection valid.

The sex of the connectors at each end of the cable is also important when buying or making a cable. Carefully note whether the connectors at each end are male (pins sticking out) or female (no pins). Usually, a PC has male serial port connectors (requiring a female end on the cable), and a terminal has female connectors (requiring a male connector on the cable), although if you are connecting a remote PC, you will need female connectors at both ends. Multiport cards differ widely in their sex and types of connectors, so check before buying cables!

Serial port connectors on a PC are either DB9 (9-pin) or DB25 (25-pin) D-shaped connectors. Not all the wires in either the 9-pin or 25-pin connector are required for a terminal. You can make a complete simple terminal cable with only three pins (send, receive, and ground), although Linux also likes to use the Carrier Detect wire to tell when a terminal is attached and active. Table 11.1 shows the important pins of 25-pin, DTE connector cables and their meanings. The pin numbers change with 9-pin connectors, but the crossings from one to another are the same.

TABLE 11.1. DTE CABLES FOR A 25-PIN CONNECTOR.

Terminal Pin	Computer Pin	Meaning
1	1	Ground
2	3	Transmit Data / Receive Data

continues

TABLE 11.1. CONTINUED

Terminal Pin	Computer Pin	Meaning
3	2	Receive Data / Transmit Data
4	4	Ready to Send
5	5	Clear to Send
6	20	Data Set Ready / Data Terminal Ready
7	7	Ground
8	20	Carrier Detect / Data Terminal Ready
20	6,8	Data Terminal Ready / Data Set Ready, Carrier Detect

Note

If the wiring of a cable is not clearly indicated and your terminal doesn't work at all, you may need to purchase a null modem device. A null modem device is a connector that has the pin crossings within it, effectively converting a straight through cable to a null modem cable, and vice versa.

UNDERSTANDING THE LOGIN PROCESS

Administering a Linux system requires that you know many of the small processes involved in the kernel and device communications. One of the most important processes for users is observing a login prompt on their screens and logging in to the system successfully. Many users have no idea of the steps Linux goes through to provide a login prompt, so this section examines that process. An understanding of the login process is also necessary to know how to configure new terminals on your system, as several files must be modified to support the new devices.

INIT AND INITTAB

The login process begins when the /etc/init daemon (sometimes stored in /sbin/init) is executed during the booting of the Linux system. The init process reads instructions from the file /etc/inittab and executes them in order. Usually, the init daemon is responsible for running a copy of the /etc/getty program for each terminal connected to the system. Without a getty process, the terminal and kernel can't communicate.

The init daemon knows whether a terminal is connected because of entries in the /etc/ttys and /etc/inittab files. The /etc/ttys file lists all ports on the system and the type of terminal that is connected to them. The /etc/inittab file holds a complete list of all terminals and their parameters. The section "/etc/ttys and /etc/inittab" examines these files in more detail.

When the /etc/ttys and /etc/inittab files indicate that a terminal is connected and active, the init daemon runs the /etc/getty program for that terminal. The getty program sets the communications parameters for the terminal and displays the login prompt on-screen. When a user logs in on a terminal, the getty process executes the login program to request a password. The login program validates the username and password against the entries in the /etc/passwd file.

If the login is validated properly, the login program displays the message of the day (stored in the file /etc/motd) and executes whatever the user is supposed to run as a startup program (usually a shell). As a final step, login sets the TERM environment variable, then exits.

/ETC/TTYS AND /ETC/INITTAB

Terminal configuration information is stored in the /etc/ttys and /etc/inittab files. The files are ASCII and can be modified by any editor, although you should be careful to keep the proper format and not disrupt existing entries. Before making any changes to the terminal configuration files, make a copy in case the changes you make are not effective and the file cannot be returned to its original state easily.

If you don't want to edit these files manually, some menu-driven programs are available that perform changes to the files for you based on a set of questions you answer. These administration utilities tend to be a little slower than editing the files manually, but they do ensure that the entries are in the proper format.

The /etc/ttys file is composed of two columns separated by any whitespace character. The first column shows the type of terminal assumed to be connected and is used to set the TERM environment variable. The second column holds the device name, less the /dev portion. A typical /etc/ttys file from a new installation of Linux looks like the following:

```
console tty1
console tty2
console tty3
console tty4
console tty5
console tty6
vt100 ttyp0
vt100 ttyp1
vt100 ttyp2
vt100 ttyp3
```

11

You use the /etc/inittab file to set the behavior of each terminal. The format of the /etc/inittab file follows this pattern:

```
ID:runlevel:action:process
```

The ID is a one or two character string that uniquely identifies the entry. For terminals, this string corresponds to the device name, such as 1 for tty1. The runlevel decides the capabilities of the terminal with the various states the Linux operating system can be in. Run levels vary from 0 to 6. If no entry is provided, the terminal supports all run levels. You can mention multiple run levels in the field.

The action indicates the behavior of the terminal device when the system starts and when a getty process is terminated on it. Several valid entries for the action field apply to terminals:

- ◆ once starts the process once
- ◆ ondemand always keeps the process running (the same as respawn)
- ◆ respawn always keeps the process running

A simple /etc/inittab file showing terminal startup commands (taken from an earlier version of Linux for clarity's sake, as the latest version complicates the lines a little) looks like the following:

```
# inittab for Linux
S1:1:respawn:/etc/getty 9600 ttyS0
S2:1:respawn:/etc/getty 9600 ttyS1
```

The lines indicate that a getty process should be started for ttyS0 (first COM port) and ttyS1 (second COM port) at 9600 baud and should be respawned (restarted) if the getty process terminates. You can use lines like these when you add terminals to serial ports. Multiport boards usually use commands in different files to start their getty processes.

/ETC/GETTY AND /ETC/GETTYDEFS

The /etc/getty program is referred to quite a lot when dealing with terminals. Basically, /etc/getty is a program that sets the communications parameters between Linux and a terminal, including the speed, protocol, and any special handling of the cable.

The /etc/getty program is called by /etc/init when the system boots or when the process terminates. When called, /etc/getty opens the serial port or other connection to the terminal and sets the communications parameters based on information in the file /etc/gettydefs (getty definitions). The getty process then generates the login prompt on the remote terminal. Many special handling and command options are available with the getty process, but most of them are of little interest to users and casual system administrators.

The /etc/gettydefs file supplies the settings getty uses for communications. The format of each line in the gettydefs file is as follows:

```
label:initial flags: final flags: login prompt: next label
```

you use the `label` to identify each line so that when /etc/getty is started with an argument (as it usually is, transparent to the user), the argument is used to match the label and provide the configuration information. You use `initial flags` and `final flags` to set any behavior for the connection before and after the login program has executed. The `login prompt` is the prompt to be displayed on the terminal. Usually it is just `login:`, but it can be any string unique to that terminal.

Finally, you use the `next label` to send getty to another line in case it can't use the current one. This parameter is typically used with modem lines that start at a high speed (such as 9,600 baud), and then go to 4,800, 2,400, and 1,200 in sequence, trying to connect at each step. For terminals, the next label is usually a pointer back to the line's first label.

An extract from a sample /etc/gettydefs file looks like the following:

```
console# B19200 OPOST ONLCR TAB3 BRKINT IGNPAR ISTRIP IXON IXANY
     PARENB ECHO ECHOE ECHOK ICANON ISIG CS8 CREAD
# B19200 OPOST ONLCR TAB3 BRKINT IGNPAR ISTRIP IXON IXANY PARENB
     ECHO ECHOE ECHOK ICANON ISIG CS8 CREAD #Console Login: #console

9600H# B9600 # B9600 SANE IXANY PARENB TAB3 HUPCL #login: #4800H

4800H# B4800 # B4800 SANE IXANY PARENB TAB3 HUPCL #login: #2400H

2400H# B2400 # B2400 SANE IXANY PARENB TAB3 HUPCL #login: #1200H

1200H# B1200 # B1200 SANE IXANY PARENB TAB3 HUPCL #login: #300H

300H# B300 # B300 SANE IXANY PARENB TAB3 HUPCL #login: #9600H
```

If you look at the file that accompanies your Linux system, you will see that there are many more lines, but they all have the same format as the preceding examples. The easier lines to look at are the shorter ones (the last five lines in the preceding extract).

These lines are for a modem starting at 9,600 baud. The initial flag is set to B9600, which sets the baud rate at 9,600 baud. The final flags, used when a connection has been established, set the characteristics of the line (such as a tab meaning three spaces). Finally, the field at the end points to the next lower speed to provide checks for slower modems or poor lines that prevent fast logins.

The first lines in the preceding extract are typical for the system console. They set many initial and final flags that control how the console behaves. The reference at the end of the line is back to the same definition, as the terminal is hard-wired to the system. Terminals are defined in much the same manner, although their entries

11

don't have to be as complex as the console's. A few simple terminal definitions are as follows:

```
# 38400 fixed baud Dumb Terminal entry
DT38400# B38400 CS8 CLOCAL CRTSCTS # B38400 SANE -ISTRIP CLOCAL CRTSCTS # login:
#DT38400

# 19200 fixed baud Dumb Terminal entry
DT19200# B19200 CS8 CLOCAL # B19200 SANE -ISTRIP CLOCAL # login: #DT19200

# 9600 baud Dumb Terminal entry
DT9600# B9600 CS8 CLOCAL # B9600 SANE -ISTRIP CLOCAL # login: #DT9600
```

In each definition line, the baud rate is set with 8 bits (CS8) used. The flags are used to set initial behavior. The login is a simple prompt, and the end of the definition points back to the same line. These simple definitions in an /etc/gettydefs file suffice for all dumb terminals, once you select the proper speed. If you are using a terminal with more advanced capabilities, you can add those to the gettydefs file, too.

Note

You may not have to change the entries in the default gettydefs file as it usually contains many different configurations. Examine the file carefully to find an entry that will work with the terminal you are using. If you do make changes to the gettydefs file, issue the command `getty -c gettydefs` to make the changes effective without rebooting.

THE /ETC/TERMCAP FILE

The /etc/termcap file holds the instruction codes for the Linux kernel and getty to communicate with different terminals. Most terminals that are supported by the Linux operating system have an entry inside this file, so the file can be quite large. If you are going to make changes, copy a version to a safe filename first.

Each entry in the termcap file has a name or label to identify the terminal it refers to, along with several variations on the name, and then a set of codes and values for different terminal characteristics. Because terminals use many different codes for different actions, some of the more talented terminals use many codes.

An extract from a termcap file shows the definitions for two fairly simple terminals, the Wyse 30 and Wyse 85:

```
w0¦wy30-vb¦wyse30-vb¦wyse 30 Visible bell:\
       :vb=\E'8\E'\072\E'9:\
       :tc=wy30:
wc¦wy85¦wyse85¦Wyse 85 in 80 column mode, vt100 emulation:\
       :is=\E[61"p\E[13l\E>\E[?1l\E[?3l\E[?7h\E[?16l\E[?5W:\
       :co#80:li#24:am:cl=\E[;H\E[2J:bs:cm=\E[%i%d;%dH:nd=2\E[C:up=2\E[A:\
       :ce=\E[0K:cd=\E[0J:so=2\E[7m:se=2\E[m:us=2\E[4m:ue=2\E[m:\
```

```
:ku=\E[A:kd=\E[B:kr=\E[C:kl=\E[D:\
:kh=\E[H:xn:\
:im=:CO=\E[?25h:CF=\E[?25l:ic=\E[1@:dc=\E[1P:\
:dl=\E[1M:al=\E[1L:GS=\EF:GE=\EG:pt:
```

The meaning of each set of codes is not really of interest to most users and system administrators. You only have to start changing or rewriting terminal entries if you are adding a terminal type that does not exist in the termcap file already.

Note

Most terminals offer multiple emulations. If you can't find the terminal type you need in the termcap file, look for an emulation that is supported (usually a Qume, VT, or Wyse type). It is easier to emulate a different terminal than write a termcap entry for a new type.

The /etc/ttys file uses the terminal characteristics in the /etc/termcap file. The first column of the ttys file gives the default terminal type used to set the TERM environment variable. The startup routine uses a pattern-matching utility to find a matching line in the termcap file, and then reads the codes that follow and uses those for all communications.

ADDING A TERMINAL

Terminals are added to Linux in much the same manner as other devices, though the mknod command. To add a terminal, you must know name of the port to which the terminal will be connected. Linux refers to the serial ports on a PC as /dev/ttyS0 (for COM1), /dev/ttyS1 (for COM2), and so on.

Most PC systems have one or two serial ports, although up to four can be accommodated on a PC (/dev/ttyS0 to /dev/ttyS3). Linux uses the serial ports based on their addresses in the BIOS. The usual addresses for the serial ports are as follows:

ttyS0 (COM1)	0x03f8
ttyS1 (COM2)	0x02f8
ttyS2 (COM3)	0x03e8
ttyS3 (COM4)	0x02e8

If you are not sure about which serial port is which, you may have to either use a DOS-based diagnostic utility (like MS-DOS' MSD.EXE or a commercial package like Norton Utilities or Central Point Tools) or start at the lowest address and work up, testing the terminal each time. If the PC has only one port, it is almost always configured as COM1 (/dev/ttyS0). The Linux installation script usually configures the two PC serial ports, so you may only need to set the speeds and parameters for a terminal attached to a serial port. If you are using a multiport board, you will probably have to install drivers.

To create a new terminal device, you must run the mknod (make node) command to create the new device driver file, and then change the permissions on the file to let root or a root-started daemon run it. A typical command for creating a new terminal device is

```
mknod -m 660 /dev/ttyS0 c 4 64
```

where the -m 660 sets the permissions on the file, /dev/ttyS0 specifies the first serial port on the machine (COM1), the c indicates that the terminal is a character mode device (almost all terminals, except very high-speed high-end models are character devices), and the major and minor device numbers are set to 4 and 64, respectively. For the other serial ports on the PC (COM2 through COM4), the commands would be

```
mknod -m 660 /dev/ttyS1 c 4 65
mknod -m 660 /dev/ttyS2 c 4 66
mknod -m 660 /dev/ttyS3 c 4 67
```

The changes in the minor device number with the different commands above are required, although you can use any number you wish. The only requirement is that there must be a unique combination of major and minor device numbers for each terminal.

After the mknod command has been executed, you must set the device driver to the proper ownership. Issue the command

```
chown root.tty /dev/ttyS0
```

to set the ownership of /dev/ttyS0 (or whichever port you are working with) to root.tty, a special Linux ownership for the device driver files that provides the startup daemons with access.

You also need to change the entry in the /etc/ttys file to include the terminal type and device you have added so that the startup of the terminal can be performed properly. Because the /etc/inittab file already contains entries for the standard serial ports, you can edit the entry for your new terminal's port, if necessary, to set the baud rate and other parameters that may be required.

SETTING TERMINAL BEHAVIOR WITH
STTY AND *TSET*

The stty command enables you to change and query a terminal option. The stty command is very complex, with dozens of options that modify the behavior of the terminal device driver. Luckily, only the most intense system administrators have to use the many options, so this section ignores most of the details. If you are curious, check the man page for more information.

To see the current settings of a terminal, use the stty command without any arguments or with just the device name, such as

```
stty /dev/ttyS1
```

The stty utility displays a set of parameters that indicate how the terminal is configured. You can use this information to verify that the terminal has read the configuration information properly from the /etc/inittab and /etc/gettydefs files. If the parameters don't match, check the configuration files to see whether there is a typographic error (very common) or an illegal command.

Like stty, the tset command has many options, most of which are seldom used (especially if you are not dealing with strange terminals and weird connectors). The tset command is used to initialize the terminal driver with a terminal's command set. If the tset command is given with a specific argument, it uses that. Otherwise, it uses the value defined in the TERM environment variable.

You can use tset within the startup files of a user who always logs in from a remote terminal (through a modem) to force a particular configuration, saving a few setup commands. If you put the command

```
tset -m dialup:vt100
```

in the shell startup file (.profile, .cshrc, and so on), the terminal type will be set to vt100 every time a connection is made through the modem. Of course, this command sets the terminal type even if someone isn't using a VT100 terminal. You can use the command

```
tset -m dialup:?vt100
```

to have the user connecting through the modem prompted for the terminal type. The prompt will look like the following:

```
TERM=(vt100)?
```

If the user presses Enter, the TERM variable is set to vt100. If the user doesn't want to use that value, the user can enter the correct string at the prompt.

In the examples shown so far, tset seems to be quite simple, but it has a very complex structure when dealing with hard-wired terminals. To properly configure a terminal connected through a serial port, you need a command like the following:

```
eval 'tset -s -Q -m dialup:?vt100 -m switch:z29'
```

The full details of this type of command are unimportant for most system administrators. If you want more information, check the man pages for tset and stty that came with your Linux system.

11

RESETTING A SCREWY TERMINAL

Every now and again a terminal connected through a serial port starts acting screwy, either not showing a prompt or generating garbage. There are two quick ways to try to reset the terminal. If they don't work, you should shut down the terminal and restart it. (You may have to kill the processes that were running on the terminal.)

The first approach is to issue a set of Ctrl+J characters on the screwy terminal, and then type stty sane followed by another Ctrl+J. The command stty sane should reset the terminal characteristics to normal (rereading the terminal characteristics from the configuration files). You probably won't see the letters you are typing, so enter them carefully. If you make a mistake, start the process again with a couple of Ctrl+Js. If the terminal isn't behaving at this point, type reset and press Enter or Ctrl+J. If this action doesn't work, you should reset the terminal manually.

Often, a problem with a terminal is not with the Linux software but the terminal itself. You can easily cure this type of problem by turning off the terminal, waiting a few seconds, and then turning it back on. If the problem was a terminal character code, the terminal should behave immediately. If it doesn't, check the processes running on the main Linux machine; there may be a hung process or runaway routine. You can kill the processes for that terminal and restart it.

USING *TERM*

The term program, which was developed by Michael O'Reilly, is included with many versions of Linux and is readily available on FTP and BBS sites. This program enables you to multiplex your serial lines so that you can support more than one device on a line. You can, for example, use the same serial port to control both a terminal (including an X terminal) and a modem simultaneously. The general process for working with term is to log into a remote machine normally, run the term program on the remote, and then run term locally. Once the two term processes are properly talking, you can use the same line for your terminal and modem sessions, transferring files while you continue to move around the remote filesystem.

Although term shares many of the features of more complex TCP/IP protocols such as PPP and SLIP, it is unique in that it requires no kernel drivers. The term program functions by essentially making your serial port into a service port, much as SLIP and PPP do. The program manages the connection requests coming into the serial port and can maintain multiple processes through that port. The machine on which the serial port is based, called the server, can talk to other machines or peripherals (the clients) through the serial port protocol term imposes.

Installing *TERM*

Most Linux distributions include a compiled version of the term utility, so you don't have to compile the program. If you have only source code, you must compile it using the make utility. Each distribution supplies instructions for compiling term. Several versions of term are currently available, and each version has slightly different compilation processes and requirements. Check the documentation carefully before you begin the compilation.

The term system requires you to set a number of environment variables. Because any system user can run term, these variables should be defined for each user in the user's startup files. If the root login wants to use term, the environment variables must be defined in the root startup files. The environment variables that are important to term are as follows:

◆ The TERMDIR variable defines the directory term uses as its home directory (usually your home directory).

◆ The TERMSHARE variable defines the directory to be used when term is in shared mode (usually the same directory as TERMDIR).

◆ The TERMMODE variable indicates whether term should run in private or shared mode.

Note

For versions of term prior to 1.16, only the TERMDIR environment variable is necessary because these versions do not support private and shared mode.

The commands needed to set the environment variables differ depending on the shell you use. The TERMDIR variable is usually set to your home directory, so it is defined in the following manner for the C shell or compatible (including tcsh) in the .cshrc or .login file:

```
setenv TERMDIR $HOME
```

In the Bourne and Korn shells (and their compatible shells), this variable is defined in the .profile file using the following lines:

```
TERMDIR=$HOME
export TERMDIR
```

You can explicitly define the directories if you want, as in the following example:

```
setenv TERMDIR /usr/tparker/termdir
```

Terminals and term

If you are running a version of term later than 1.15, term supports shared and private usage. Define the TERMMODE variable in the same startup location as the TERMDIR command. For the C shell and compatible shells, use the following line if you want to run in private mode:

```
setenv TERMMODE 0
```

For the Bourne and Korn shells (and compatibles), you can set term to run in private mode with the following lines:

```
TERMMODE=0
export TERMMODE
```

If you want to run in shared mode, set the TERMMODE variable to a value of 1, and define the TERMSHARE variable to show where the shared directory is, as in the following examples for the C shell:

```
senenv TERMDIR /usr/tparker/term
setenv TERMMODE 1
setenv TERMSHARE $TERMDIR
```

The following commands are examples for the Bourne and Korn shells:

```
TERMDIR=/usr/tparker/term
TERMMODE=1
TERMSHARE=$TERMDIR
export TERMDIR TERMMODE TERMSHARE
```

Versions of term later than 2.0.0 also have an environment variable called TERMSERVER that must be defined when there is more than one modem and the modems can be used simultaneously. This variable tells term which modem line to use for which connection name. The variable is defined with the name of the connection. Suppose you were setting up three modems and three connections (called conn1, conn2, and conn3) for the C shell. You would add the following line to the startup file to tell term to use Conn1 for its connection:

```
setenv TERMSERVER Conn1
```

For the Bourne and Korn shell, you would use the following commands:

```
TERMSERVER=Conn1
export TERMSERVER
```

When the term command is started in these cases, the connection name must be specified as well. For example, with the above configuration information, you would start term with the command:

```
nohup term -v /dev/modem1 Conn1 &
```

This command line applies only to those systems with multiple modem connections using term.

TESTING *TERM*

After you add the `term` environment variables to the startup files (and you have logged out and back in to make the changes effective), you can test the `term` daemon and its configuration. The `term` program uses a daemon running in the user's memory space to manage the simultaneous demands placed on a serial port.

A `test` program is included with most versions of `term`. If the test utility is not compiled and you have a C compiler present on your system, you can compile the program with the following command:

```
make term
```

In some distributions of Linux, the `test` program is already compiled. If you don't have a compiled version or a compiler, you can either search the BBSs and FTP sites for a compiled copy, or skip the testing step and start the `term` program (hoping for the best while you do so).

When the `test` program is available, run it at the command line by typing the utility's name (you should be in the directory `term` resides in to avoid confusion with the shell `test` command):

```
./test
```

When `test` starts, issue the following command to test the upload capability:

```
tupload ./test /tmp
```

This command places a copy of the `test` utility in the /tmp directory.

All local output from the `term` program is stored in the file local.log, and the remote output is stored in the file remote.log. You can examine these files if you run into problems or want to check the status of a session. You can force debugging information to these files by starting `term` with the following option:

```
-d255
```

This option is handy if you have been experiencing problems and want to see the log of all transactions.

Another utility supplied with the `term` package is `linecheck`, which is useful for testing the transparency of a connection. The `linecheck` utility sends each of the possible 256 ASCII characters (8-bit characters, of course) over the link and verifies that they are transferred properly.

To use `linecheck`, you should be connected to a remote terminal using any communications package you want, such as kermit (see the procedure for using `term` explained in the next section). Once you have established the connection between remote and local sites, switch to the remote machine and issue the following command:

```
linecheck linecheck.logfile
```

This command places all output of the `linecheck` utility in the file linecheck.logfile in the current directory on the remote system.

Then switch back to your local system and escape from the terminal mode. If you stay in terminal mode, the terminal software will misinterpret many of the characters `linecheck` generates. After you escape from terminal mode, issue the following command:

```
linecheck linecheck.logfile > /dev/modem < /dev/modem
```

This command tells `linecheck` to save results in the file linecheck.logfile (in your current directory on the local system) and take all input from the modem port and send all output to the modem port.

When the `linecheck` utility has terminated, examine the file linecheck.logfile on both the local and remote systems. There may be a set of numbers at the bottom of the file that `linecheck` has determined your system can't transfer. These numbers must be specified in the `term` startup file called termrc in order to prevent future problems.

For example, if the `linecheck` utility determines that it cannot send the character with ASCII value 200 from the local to remote system, but that this value transfers properly from the remote system to the local system, place the following line in your local system's termrc file:

```
escape 200
```

On the remote system, you must add the following line to tell the remote to ignore that ASCII value:

```
ignore 200
```

For each `escape` command on one system, there should be a matching `ignore` command on the other!

There will probably be several characters that can't be handled both ways, primarily because some of the valid ASCII characters are reserved by the communications software as escape characters to get you between modes.

If you can't get proper output from the `linecheck` utility, the XON/XOFF protocol is probably getting in the way. You can disable this command and rerun the `linecheck` utility with the following command:

```
linecheck linecheck.logfile 17 19 > /dev/modem < /dev/modem
```

RUNNING *TERM*

The `term` utility is started both on the remote system and on the local systems, which means you must have copies of it properly configured both locally and remotely. Because you will want to transfer files with `term`, it is best to run in 8-bit mode. Start up your communications software and make sure your serial ports are set for 8-bit characters.

To use `term`, log in to the remote system and start up `term`. A useful command syntax to start `term` is the following:

```
exec term -l $HOME/termlog -s 38400 -c off -w 10 -t 150
```

Although this command line may seem like a lot to type, it includes the most useful `term` options. You can place it in a script file or alias it (with shells that allow aliasing) to make starting the `term` process easier.

Use the `exec` command to replace the currently running shell version on the remote with `term`. If you don't use `exec`, you leave your shell running on the remote machine, which ties up memory and process time for nothing. If you are in the process of debugging a `term` connection or want to terminate `term` at some point during your session, don't use the `exec` command in front of `term`.

The `-l` option specifies a log file for errors. In this case, all error messages are saved in the home directory in the file termlog. You can leave off the entire option if your `term` session is behaving properly and switch it on only after you have encountered a problem.

The `-s` option specifies the speed at which to run the connection. This speed should match the speed of the modem with any on-the-fly compression systems active. For example, 38,400 baud is usually possible on most 14.4kbps modems that use compression. If the speed rate is set too fast, you may lose characters. Slow down the connection if necessary. Note that most PC machines require a 16550 UART for speeds higher than 9600 baud.

The `-c` option turns off data compression built into `term`. Because this command line represents a 14.4kpbs modem with inherent compression, the `term` compression is turned off to prevent double compression, which doesn't gain anything for performance. If your modem speed is 9600 baud or slower with no inherent compression, use the `-c on` option instead to active the `term` compression algorithm. Compression must match at both ends of the connection.

The `-w` and `-t` options are used to optimize a fast link over a 14.4kbps (or faster) modem. They set the transmission sliding window and timeout parameters. Usually, these settings are fine and need not be altered.

After establishing the remote `term` session, escape from your communications software to a local session and start `term` on your local machine with the following command:

```
term -r -l $HOME/logfile -c off -s 38400 -w 10 -t 150 < /dev/modem > /dev/modem &
```

The options mean the same thing as they did for the remote process. You must add the `-r` option on one end of the connection, or `term` will instantly die. This option sets one end of the connection as the server and the other as a client. As shown in the above example, you can run the entire command (which is best saved in a script or alias) in the background, which enables you to use the terminal window for other things. The `term` program executes without any problem in the background.

Now `term` should be functioning properly. If you experience problems, examine the log files or run the `test` and `linecheck` utilities to isolate the problem. If the connection works but is very slow, check the log files to see whether they contain timeout messages. If they do, double-check the configuration because that is the most likely source of problems.

The connection may seem a little jumpy (characters coming in bursts), but that is normal, especially when compression is active. For most purposes, the `term` session is much slower than a normal login to a remote. The real advantage to `term` is when you are transferring files at the same time you are moving about on the remote system.

To terminate `term`, you can force a fast destruction of the connection by killing the process on both ends. A better approach, which properly closes the connection, is to issue the following command:

```
echo '00000' > /dev/modem
```

As long as the string you send has five zeros, the connection will close properly. Some versions of `term` include the command `tshutdown`, which closes the `term` session for you. Check the distribution software. If your `term` version is 1.14 or higher, `tshutdown` should work.

USING *TERM* WITH X

You can use the `term` utility from within an X terminal window. X (or XFree86 with most versions of Linux) enables you to open a window specifically to run `term`. Most of the X connection handling is with a utility called `txconn`. You must execute the `txconn` program on the remote machine (connected over a network, as X doesn't work with any reasonable degree of speed over a modem) and place it in the background as a daemon. When `txconn` goes to the background, it returns a message containing a display number that identifies the process:

```
Xconn bound to screen 11
```

When you connect to the remote `txconn` daemon from an X window, you use this number to identify the screen. You identify the screen by using the DISPLAY environment variable. If the binding was to screen 11, as shown in the preceding message, you would set the variable to

```
setenv DISPLAY remotename:11
```

where `remotename` is the name of the remote machine (for the C shell). With the Bourne or Korn shell, you set the same environment variable with the following commands:

```
DISPLAY=remotename:11
export DISPLAY
```

When the `term` client is started in the local X window, it will connect to screen 11 on the remote machine. Because `txconn` knows about screen 11 on the remote, all X instructions will be transferred to the local machine's X window.

Note

If `txconn` doesn't allow you to connect or you get permission messages, you may have to issue the command `xhost +` on your local machine to allow the remote to open and control a window on your local session. This form of the `xhost` command allows any remote machine to access your windows. If you want to be sure only the remote server can open windows, use its machine name in place of the plus sign, such as `xhost merlin`. Alternatively, use the `xauth` command to control access. See the `xauth` man page for more information.

You can run the local machine with windows opening on the remote system's X session using `txconn`, but a better approach is to use the `tredir` command, which is covered in the "Using `term` Utilities" section.

Running X sessions over a modem using `txconn` is possible, although the high amount of traffic X involves can bring even the fastest modem to a crawl. A local area network connection has enough speed to sustain X window traffic. A low-overhead version of X called LBX is available for some platforms that may help solve the overhead problem for modems. Also useful is a utility called `sxpc`, which compresses X protocol packets for transmission over modems. You can get `sxpc` with some versions of `term`, and it has worked well with 14.4kbps and faster modems, although performance is predictably slow.

USING *TERM* UTILITIES

The `term` software comes with a number of utility commands for handling file transfers. The utilities vary depending on the version of `term`. All these utilities require a `term` link to be established and functioning before you can use them.

The utilities that generally accompany `term` are the following:

- The `fet` utility is a front end to term that automates many of the startup functions. This utility is not available with many older versions of term.

- The `tmon` utility is a monitoring utility that shows a time histogram for transmitted and received characters.

- The `trdate` utility sets the time on the local machine to match that of the remote machine. This utility must be executed as root.

- The `trdated` utility is a daemon version of `trdate` that can be started in rc.local to update the time every five minutes.

- The `tredir` utility allows networking services to be performed over `term`. See the description later in this section for more information.

- The `trsh` utility is a remote shell similar to Berkeley's `rsh`. When used without arguments, trsh spawns an interactive shell o the remote system. When an argument is given, the argument is executed on the remote system.

- The `tupload` utility transfers a file to the opposite end of the connection. By default, current directories at each end are assumed. The tupload file is given relative to the local system (sending a file from the local to remote system, for example). To transfer from the remote to the local machines, use the `trsh` command to go into the remote and issue a `tupload` command there. If you want to change the directory for an upload, you must give the destination as a second argument. For example, to transfer the file bigfile to /usr/tmp to the other end of the connections, issue the following command:

```
tupload bigfile /usr/tmp
```

The `tredir` utility is a powerful tool and can be used to good advantage with `term`. The `tredir` program runs as a daemon in background and provides port services (much like other networking daemons). The `tredir` daemon monitors ports and forwards requests from the `term` remote. The `tredir` daemon redirects network services over the `term` link. The `tredir` system works with modems and over networks.

To show how `tredir` works, suppose you want to redirect a local serial port to the Telnet port on a remote machine (ports are assigned for specific protocols and services). To redirect local port number 2024 to remote port 23 (the Telnet port on the remote machine), issue the following command:

```
tredir 2024 23
```

Now whenever you use port 2024 on the local machine, it is redirected to the Telnet port on the remote. To connect to the local port 2024, you could use the `telnet` command. The following output shows that you access the remote Telnet port when you issue the `telnet` command from the shell prompt (the remote machine's name in this example is brutus):

```
$telnet localhost 2024
Trying 147.92.142.1
Connecting to brutus...
login:
```

So you have redirected the Telnet session, but what good is this action in the normal course of events? It is quite useful when you want to redirect output to machines for reading e-mail, news, databases, accessing the Internet, and so on. Suppose you have a corporate e-mail server. You could use `tredir` to set up a direct link to the server's Telnet port, and then easily access that machine directly from your local machine without worrying about protocols, windows, and so on.

One sneaky way of using `tredir` is to open X windows on a remote machine from your local machine. This technique relies on the fact that X uses a set of ports for protocol communications. An X server software package waits for instructions on a port number given by the following formula

```
port=6000+display_number
```

where `displaynumber` is the number of the window on the X session. For example, X window number 8 listens for instructions on port 6008.

If you want to open a window from your local X session on a remote X server, you can use these port numbers and `tredir`. The process involves mapping a local window onto an unused window on the server. For example, the command

```
tredir 6008 brutus:6004
```

establishes a redirection between the local X window identified by port 6008 (which is on your local machine) to the remote X window given by port 6004 (the remote machine's name is brutus in this example). Do not use 6000 as a port number because it is the root console of all X sessions. Instead, pick a higher number.

After you issue the `tredir` command, establish your DISPLAY variable to point to the port that is being remapped on your local machine:

```
setenv DISPLAY localname:8
```

This C shell command sets your display default to the local machine's window number eight (which is remapped through `tredir`). Of course, you should put your machine's name in the command.

Finally, when you issue the `xterm` command on your local machine, it should open a window on the remote machine for you. If this command doesn't work, it's because of restrictions on the remote machine. Run the `xhost +` command when logged in as root to solve the problem, or use the `xauth` command to establish your machine as authorized to open windows.

Finally, some `term`-friendly utilities are available in Linux FTP sites, including versions of FTP, Telnet, and Mosaic. Check with the local distribution software sets, as well as FTP and BBS sites to find out which utilities have been modified to work with `term` if you plan to use `term` as a primary utility.

SUMMARY

Although few systems will have terminals hanging off them, running several terminals from a single PC is a great way to share the resources of your system. It makes it very handy when two or more people want access, especially for games!

This chapter has shown you the basics of handing terminals with the Linux system. The information presented applies to most versions of Linux, although there may be some slight changes in options and arguments as the different utilities are enhanced or streamlined. If you want more information about any of the commands mentioned in this chapter, refer to the man pages and other documentation that came with Linux.

The `term` package is a powerful, easy-to-use utility that lets you simplify many file transfer and remote session actions when you can access a remote Linux machine also running `term`. Once you have set the environment variables `term` requires, it operates quickly and easily. Check for new releases of the `term` package periodically; the authors and other programmers are always adding new features and software utilities.

- SCSI Tape Drives

- The `ftape` Program

- Using the Tape Drive

CHAPTER 12

Tape Drives

A tape drive is one of the most important devices you can own because it provides you with an easy way to back up your work. Tape drives have dropped in price to the point where anyone can afford them, especially the floppy tape-driven units that are becoming widespread.

Installing a tape drive is usually not difficult, but you will need a device driver for it. Many manufacturers of tape drives don't bother with Linux (or UNIX) when it comes to drivers, instead opting to concentrate on the lucrative DOS market. The DOS drivers cannot be used with Linux.

Instead, carefully check the tape unit before you purchase it, if you intend to use it for Linux. In general, SCSI tape devices are supported, as are most tape drives that use the floppy interface. When this chapter was written, no drivers were yet available (although they were being developed) for tape drives that use the parallel port. This chapter looks at the types of tape drives you can use with your Linux system. It also explains how to use ftape, the most popular QIC tape unit control software.

SCSI TAPE DRIVES

Except for the SCSI drives that use special tape encoding, practically all SCSI tape drives (of any size and capacity of tape) work with Linux. Installing a SCSI tape drive is the same as installing any other SCSI device; you must set a unique SCSI ID for the drive and plug the drive into the SCSI chain. Several SCSI tape device drivers are available for Linux, all of which have slightly different target machines or markets. Select a device driver from those provided on your distribution media or the FTP or BBS sites and link it into the kernel.

The SCSI tape driver usually has a major device number of nine and a minor number of zero. The devices are usually called /dev/nrst0 (for a non-rewind device) and /dev/rst0 (for a rewind device). Check the /dev directory to see whether entries for these devices already have been created. The command

```
ls /dev/*rst*
```

lists all the SCSI tape devices. If no devices are present, you must make them with the commands

```
mknod -m 666 /dev/nrst0 c 9 9
mknod -m 666 /dev/rst0 c 9 0
```

These commands create device files for the rewind (rst) and non-rewind (nrst) drivers with the major number nine and the minor number zero. The file permissions are set to 666 (see Chapter 17, "System Names and Access Permissions").

Once the device drivers have been created, you can begin using the tape drive. Specific tape parameters such as the length of blocks, buffers, tape density, and so on, are usually set with the `mt` program or through the `tar` command. There are two versions of the `mt` command generally distributed with versions of Linux, and the usage of these commands differs notably. Check your man pages or on-line help to find the proper syntax to set the block size and other parameters. For example, usually you can set the tape drives block size with the command

```
mt setblk 20
```

which sets the block size to 20. If you want to use variable length blocks on your tape drive (make sure the drive supports them), use the command

```
mt setblk 0
```

If you get error messages with the version of `mt` included with your Linux system, the version is probably the GNU version. This version does not allow you to set such parameters, so you should get the BSD-derived `mt` version instead.

Note

If your SCSI tape drive isn't recognized when Linux boots (and the tape device has been properly configured), reboot the machine with a tape in the tape drive. The activity of tensioning the tape usually lets Linux know that the tape device is on the SCSI chain.

You can verify that the Linux kernel has found your SCSI tape drive properly by examining the boot messages. (Use the `dmesg` command to replay the boot messages.) You see lines similar to the following if the SCSI tape drive is recognized:

```
aha274x: target 4 now synchronous at 4.4Mb/s
  Vendor: TANDBERG  Model:  TDC 3800        Rev: =05:
  Type:   Sequential-Access                 ANSI SCSI revision: 02
Detected scsi tape st0 at scsi0, id 4, lun 0
scsi : detected 1 SCSI tape 1 SCSI cdrom 1 SCSI disk total.
```

The tape drive's electronics provide Linux with the name and type of tape drive, as do most SCSI devices.

THE *FTAPE* PROGRAM

The `ftape` program is a tape device interface meant for QIC-117, QIC-40, and QIC-80 drives only. Both QIC-40 and QIC-80 tape drives connect through the floppy drive controller cable, so if your tape drive is not connected through the floppy drive cable, you probably cannot use `ftape`.(Sometimes the floppy cable is routed to another hardware board mounted in the PC expansion chassis and then to the tape drive. Some of these drives work with ftape and others do not.) In general, you cannot use ftape with tape drives that connect to the parallel port. You cannot use the ftape program with SCSI or QIC-02 tape drivers or some of the newer compression-based small cartridge drives either. If you're not sure whether the ftape program will work with your tape drive, experiment. All you will use up is time.

One caveat with current versions of ftape is that you cannot format a tape under Linux. Instead, you must either purchase preformatted tapes or boot into DOS (even if from a floppy disk) and run a utility program, usually supplied with the tape drive, to format the tape cartridges.

If you installed Linux from a setup routine on a CD-ROM, you probably were given the option of installing ftape at that time. The kernel may already be linked in for you. If you are using Linux version 0.99p114t or later, ftape is probably linked in. You can verify whether ftape is active on your system by examining the system boot messages (use dmesg to show the messages) for a line like the following:

```
ftape: allocated 3 buffers aligned at: 00220000
```

You see this message with later Linux kernels even if you have only a SCSI tape drive.

If the driver is not linked in, either extract the files from your distribution media or obtain the latest version of ftape from the FTP or BBS sites. If you can only get source code for the ftape program, you will also need a compiler. The software distribution package for ftape should include a complete installation file that you can follow. This section looks at the general process of installing ftape in a little detail.

The ftape device driver must be installed in the /dev directory and linked into the Linux kernel to be active. After you have obtained the full ftape distribution software, copy the files to a subdirectory for ftape. Check the /dev directory for an existing ftape device with the command

```
ls /dev/*rft*
```

which lists all raw floppy tape devices as shown in Figure 12.1. If several are listed, you may not need to make new devices. For a normal tape installation, there are four non-rewind floppy tape devices called /dev/nrft0, /dev/nrft1, /dev/nrft2, and /dev/nrft3, as well as four rewind devices called /dev/rft0, /dev/rft1, /dev/rft2, and /dev/rft3.

Figure 12.1.
QIC tape drives (and
several other non-SCSI
tape drives) have device
drivers starting with rft
and nrft.

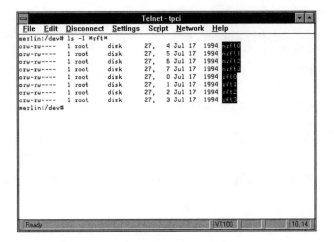

If no floppy tape devices are currently installed, you must make them using the following commands:

```
mknod -m 666 /dev/nrft0 c 27 4
mknod -m 666 /dev/nrft1 c 27 5
mknod -m 666 /dev/nrft2 c 27 6
mknod -m 666 /dev/nrft3 c 27 7
mknod -m 666 /dev/rft0 c 27 0
mknod -m 666 /dev/rft1 c 27 1
mknod -m 666 /dev/rft2 c 27 2
mknod -m 666 /dev/rft3 c 27 3
```

The mknod command makes the proper device driver files (see Chapter 6, "Devices and Device Drivers"). This command creates all eight character mode devices (four rewind and four non-rewind) with file permissions of 666 (see Chapter 17 "System Names and Access Permissions"), major device numbers of 27, and minor device numbers ranging from zero through three.

If you want to set up a symbolic link to the device /dev/ftape, issue the command

```
ln  /dev/rft0 /dev/ftape
```

The use of a symbolic link lets you use the device name /dev/ftape to access the tape drive instead of having to type the name of whichever tape driver is needed. In other words, you are aliasing ftape to the proper driver. You also can link the non-rewind device to /dev/nftape using the command

```
ln /dev/nrft0 /dev/nftape
```

12

To install the device driver into the kernel, you must change to the source directory for the Linux kernel files (usually /usr/src/Linux) and issue the `make` command to rebuild the kernel:

```
cd /usr/src/Linux
make config
```

At one point in the `make` routine, you are asked whether you want to include QIC-117 tape support. Answer `yes`, and when the `make` routine asks for the value of NR_FTAPE_BUFFERS, answer 3. You do not have to install the QIC-02 support to use `ftape`, so answer `no` to that question (if it gets asked).

Finally, to rebuild the kernel properly, issue the following three commands:

```
make dep
make clean
make
```

Once the kernel has been rebuilt, copy it to the startup directory that holds your boot kernel (make a copy of the old kernel for safety's sake) and reboot your machine.

If your copy of the `ftape` program is provided only as source code, you will have to compile the program. Use the makefile program included with the source to do the compiling. Most versions of the Linux distribution software include the compiled version of `ftape`, so you probably will not have to bother compiling the program.

To test the tape device, place a formatted tape in the drive and issue the command

```
mt -f /dev/rft0 rewind
```

If you get an error message about the device not being found, your device driver is not linked into the kernel or the device driver file is not properly set up. If you get a status message about the tape already being rewound or no message at all, the tape drive has been recognized.

Note

Some versions of `ftape` and the Linux kernel do not allow you to use the tape drive and floppy drive at the same time. If you try, the Linux kernel freezes. Reboot the machine and avoid using both devices at the same time.

USING THE TAPE DRIVE

You can use the tape drive to backup and restore files using the standard `tar` commands, as well as `cpio`. For more information on using these commands, see Chapter 22, "Backup, Backup, Backup!" As a quick guide, use the following instructions for making and restoring backups of your filesystems.

To create a backup of the complete filesystem on tape, use the command

```
tar cvf /dev/ftape /
```

for ftape tape devices, or

```
tar cvf /dev/rst0 /
```

for SCSI devices. These commands assume that the device exists in the /dev directory and is linked into the kernel. The c option creates the archive file; the v option tells `tar` to echo its actions to the screen for you to see, and the f option tells `tar` which device (/dev/ftape) to use for the file. The trailing slash shows the directory structure to backup (in this case, the entire filesystem). If you decide to back up the entire filesystem, you may want to unmount devices like CD-ROM drives first to prevent their contents from being saved, too. Figure 12.2 shows a `tar` command used to backup the ./mail directory to a tape device using the linked device driver /dev/tape. Each file that is placed on the tape is displayed on-screen because of the verbose (v) option.

Figure 12.2.
Using tar to back up a small directory to the tape device.

12

To restore an entire archive from tape (such as the entire filesystem created above), use the command

```
tar xvf /dev/ftape
```

or use /dev/rst0 for SCSI devices. In this case, the x option tells tar to extract the contents of the media; the v option tells tar to echo all messages to the screen, and the f option specifies the tar device (in this case /dev/ftape). Because no single files or directories are specified, tar extracts the entire contents of the tape and places them in the current directory position.

You can display the contents of a tar archive with the command

```
tar tvf /dev/ftape
```

(/dev/rst0 for SCSI tape drives), where t tells tar to show the contents, v is for a full display, and f is the device indicator. There are many more options and capabilities to tar, so see Chapter 22 for more information.

SUMMARY

More tape devices are being added to the Linux supported products list, including parallel-port and board-driven tape drives. If you already own one of these products, watch for a specific kernel driver for it. If you are planning to purchase a tape drive, check for Linux drivers first.

When you have a tape drive, you can be conscientious about making tape backups, and thus protecting your files and data. Losing an important file is very annoying, especially when a few minutes of your time could have saved the information for you. Tape drives are one of the easiest and most inexpensive methods of making reliable backups. Every system should have one!

- Choosing a Modem

- Installing a Modem

- Configuring a Modem

- Setting Fast Modem Speeds

CHAPTER 13

Modems

If you want to talk to the outside world (a friend's computer, another network, the Internet, or a BBS, for example), or you want to let others talk to your Linux system, you need a modem. Modems used to be expensive, complex pieces of equipment that required a considerable amount of UNIX expertise to install and configure properly. Now, using one of today's highest speed modems is as easy as plugging it in and modifying a file or two. This short chapter looks at the installation requirements for a modem.

CHOOSING A MODEM

Linux works with just about any modem as long as it plugs into the system somehow and has a device driver. Choosing the modem then becomes a matter of using an existing modem on your PC or buying one specifically for Linux.

Modems are a competitive market. The fight between companies for the flashiest advertisements, most features, and best included software is leading to lower prices and better bargains. Most of the software included with modems is for DOS or Windows, you don't need to worry about any type of software for Linux. If you intend to run the modem on your DOS partitions, consider the software for that aspect only.

Note

> As a general rule, if a modem works with DOS, it will work under Linux. When you install the modem, specify the serial port name, and Linux can work with the modem. A modem can work equally well with both operating systems.

A common problem in choosing from today's modems is the plethora of acronyms, speeds, and features that are touted for different modems. Modem standards have gone crazy in the last few years, as better telephone circuits (including fiberoptics) and more efficient data compression algorithms have been developed. Compression algorithms are the current fad in the market. They use sophisticated mathematical systems to pack as much as five times as many bits per second along a line. For this reason, everyone seems to want data compression in modems, but most users don't realize that the compression scheme must be identical on both ends of the line, or the default speed is the best a modem can achieve.

The current state-of-the-art modems use V.FC (V.Fast Class, also known as V.34), which has a speed of 28,800bps. V.FC modems are usually used with data compression schemes to boost the effective throughput to speeds as high as 115kbps. V.FC was developed as a project between Hayes Microcomputer Products and Rockwell. Over 100 modem manufacturers have agreed to accept it as a working standard. The

13

V.34 standard has now been officially adopted. The same situation does not apply to some of the compression algorithms—they are de facto, not actual standards. This point is probably moot as the sheer weight of the companies behind these modem standards should carry them through to adoption.

To help you keep up with the different modem speeds in use today, the following table lists the communications speeds (in bits per seconds) and their names.

Base communication speeds

V.FC (V.Fast Class)	28,800bps
V.34 (V.Fast)	28,800bps
V.32turbo	19,200bps
V.32bis	14,400bps
V.32	9,600bps
V.22bis	2,400bps
212A	1,200bps
V.21	300bps
103	300bps

Data compression systems

V.42bis	4:1 compression to 115,200bps on a 28,800bps line
MNP5	2:1 compression algorithm used in older modems

Fax standards

V.17	14,400bps, 12,000bps, 9,600bps, and 7,200bps
V.29	9,600bps and 7,200bps
V.27ter	4,800bps and 2,400bps
V.21 Channel 2	300bps

A current trend in DOS and Windows systems is to use enhanced serial port devices, which are necessary to sustain the high baud rates that the modern fast modems can reach. Most of these devices are addressed as standard serial ports by the operating system, so they will work with Linux. Any accelerator device that requires a special driver, though, will not work unless you port the driver to Linux (not an easy task). Your standard serial ports should be at least 16550 UARTs (instead of the older 16450 UARTs) if you intend to run your modem at speeds higher than 9,600 baud. If you have an older PC, check with your dealer about upgrading the serial ports. The upgrade is usually very inexpensive and makes a major difference in modem performance with fast speeds.

Note

The 16550 UART has a 16-byte buffer, but the 16450 has only a 1-byte buffer. In general, the 16450 UARTs can only be used to 9,600 baud. Any higher throughput speeds require 16550 UARTs.

Linux doesn't care whether your modem is an internal or external model, as long as it has a serial port designation that it can be addressed through. The choice between internal and external modem has become one-sided lately. Five years ago, the internal modem was the modem of choice. Most name-brand modems now are external, probably because of easier upgradability. Most manufacturers offer both types of modems. Note that internal modems save you a serial port on the back of the machine and almost always use a 16550 or faster UART.

One thing to consider with many new modem models is their software upgradability. Some modems allow you to load new versions of the controlling software through a DOS session. You obtain the new software through a bulletin board or on-line service. This capability reduces the obsolescence factor considerably. Most new modems adapt themselves automatically to any of the adopted modem standards (as well as fax standards, if you purchase a fax modem).

INSTALLING A MODEM

If the modem you purchase is an internal modem, you must open your machine and add it in an unused slot. Make sure you set the communication port parameters to an unused value. Most internal modems are set by default to use DOS COM3 or COM4. These values also work with Linux, as long as you can copy the serial port device driver to those values. The COM3 and COM4 settings can cause a problem with the PC architecture because COM3 shares the same IRQ with COM1 and COM4 shares the same IRQ with COM2. For this reason, try not to use both COM ports that share an IRQ at the same time. In other words, if you are using both COM2 and COM4 for modems at the same time, you are going to have problems.

External modems plug in to an unused serial port, either on the main PC backplane or on an expansion port board. Either way, the cabling has to be set for DCE (Data Communications Equipment) and use a modem cable (which has pins straight through it). For more information on cabling serial devices, see Chapter 11, "Terminals and term."

You can support more than one modem on a system because Linux treats them as devices and doesn't impose limits. If you have two serial ports, you can use two modems. If you have a 32-port multiport board attached to your system, you can use all of the ports for modems if you want. You set the limits. Bear in mind, however, that modems are usually dedicated as either call-in or call-out devices, not both (a holdover from a old UNIX convention), although Linux lets you switch modes easily.

CONFIGURING A MODEM

The easiest way to configure a modem to work with Linux is to use the setup or configuration utility that came with your Linux software system. In most cases, the setup utility asks you during the installation process whether you are using a modem, what port it is on, and what its maximum speed is to be set at. If you add a modem after installing Linux, you can access these routines by rerunning the setup or configuration program. Using one of these automated systems prevents you from having to modify files manually.

Note

When you are assigning modems to a serial port, remember that Linux starts numbering at 0. DOS' COM1 is Linux's /dev/cua0; COM2 is /dev/cua1, and so on.

During the automated installation process, you are asked for the maximum speed of your modem. If the speed isn't represented on the list you see, choose the next fastest speed. For example, if your modem claims to be able to run at 28,800 bps and that speed isn't on the configuration menu, choose the next fastest, which is probably 38,400. The modem adjusts itself independent of Linux.

If you must configure the modem manually (either because you have no automated routine or you simply want to), you need a device driver for one of the available serial ports on your machine. Usually there are two device drivers for each serial port, one for calling out and the other for calling in (Linux can't handle both functions at the same time). The device drivers are differentiated by their major device numbers (minor device numbers are the same, usually set to 64 and up for serial port devices). Modems used for dialing in have a major device number set to four, and dial-out modems have the major device number set to five. The device drivers have different names, too. Dial-in modems have device names like ttyS0, ttyS1, and so on. Dial-out modems have device names like cua0, cua1, and so on.

Check to see whether there are device drivers for your serial ports by listing the /dev/ttyS* files for dial-in drivers and /dev/cua* files for dial-out drivers. The listings should show the device numbers in the fifth and sixth columns. The numbers should correspond to those shown in the following list:

COM1 dial-in (/dev/ttyS0): major 4, minor 64

COM2 dial-in (/dev/ttyS1): major 4, minor 65

COM3 dial-in (/dev/ttyS2): major 4, minor 66

COM4 dial-in (/dev/ttyS3): major 4, minor 67

COM1 dial-out (/dev/cua0): major 5, minor 64

COM2 dial-out (/dev/cua1): major 5, minor 65

COM3 dial-out (/dev/cua2): major 5, minor 66

COM4 dial-out (/dev/cua3): major 5, minor 67

If the devices have different numbers, you can use whatever they are set at or delete them and recreate the devices. If the devices work as they are set, don't bother changing them unless conflicts arise with other devices. If you have to create (or re-create) a device driver for the serial ports, use the following command as a example:

```
mknod -m 666 /dev/cua1 c 55 65
```

This command creates the dial-out serial port device driver for COM2 (/dev/cua1) with major number 5 and minor number 65, sets it as a character mode device (which asynchronous modems have to be set as), and sets the file permissions to mode 666. (For more information on the mknod command, see Chapter 6, "Devices and Device Drivers." For more information on file permissions, see Chapter 17, "System Names and Access Permissions.")

Many Linux systems use a symbolic link from the active dial-out device driver to a new device called /dev/modem. Using this link makes configuration a little easier, especially if you change the active dial-out port regularly, because you simply have to relink the /dev/modem device file instead of modifying many applications. To set up the link, issue the command

```
ln /dev/cua1 /dev/modem
```

If you do use a link to /dev/modem, make sure that you use that device file in all the applications that will use the serial port; otherwise, the device locking process will not work correctly. The preceding examples use the COM2 port; change the device name as required (along with the major and minor numbers, as necessary).

Finally, invoke handshaking protocols for any port used by a modem. This task is easy to do, although most applications and user guides fail to mention it. To turn on handshaking, issue the command

```
stty crtscts < /dev/cua1
```

Replace the device name with the proper modem device (or use /dev/modem if you set up the link). You can check the status of the handshaking flag at any time with the command

```
stty -a /dev/cua1
```

13

which shows a list of all flags. If the crtscts flag has a minus sign in front of it, handshaking is turned off, and you should turn it on.

Once the modem is installed, you can use any communications program (kermit, UUCP, cu, and so on) to test it. Make sure you specify the dial-out modem line properly. These programs are usually not used for dial-in modems, which are mostly set to allow standard logins.

Setting Fast Modem Speeds

Serial ports are usually limited by Linux to 38,400 baud. (When you ran setup, you were asked for the maximum baud rate the modem port could support, and the largest number on the list was 38,400.) In order to run faster modems, you must use the setserial command. The setserial command enables you to set a 38,400 baud port to run at 57,600 baud with the following command:

```
setserial /dev/cua2 spd_hi
```

Replace /dev/cua2 with the name of the modem device you are configuring for high speed. (You can also use the /dev/modem device name if you linked it earlier to the modem device driver.)

To run your modem at 115,200 baud, use the spd_vhi option:

```
setserial /dev/modem spd_vhi
```

Both the spd_hi and spd_vhi options can be specified by a non-root user, so regular Linux system users can tailor a modem port when they want to change speeds. You can return the modem port to the normal 38,400 baud rate with the following command:

```
setserial /dev/modem spd_normal
```

The setserial commands work with Linux kernels of version 1.0 and higher. The command is enhanced considerably with each later version, so check the man page to see what options are available for customizing serial ports with your Linux release.

Summary

Installing a high-speed modem (or even an older, slower model) is easy with Linux, as long as you have a device driver properly set up. Dozens of applications work under Linux to offer everything from terminal emulation to complex communications protocols. Most modem use is for dialing out, although you may want to configure a modem for friends to log in to your system.

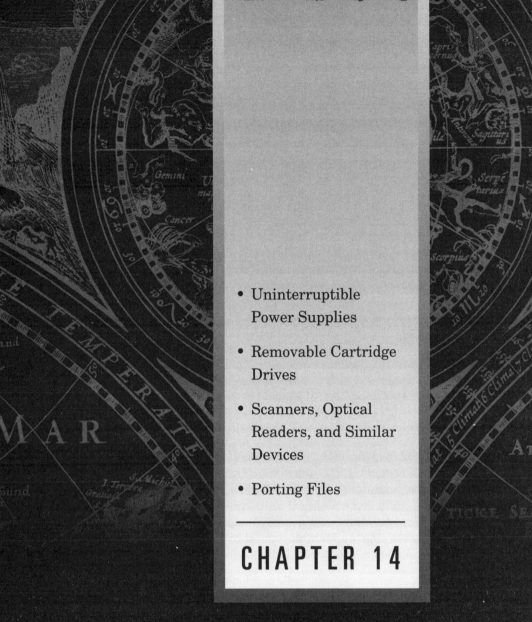

- Uninterruptible Power Supplies

- Removable Cartridge Drives

- Scanners, Optical Readers, and Similar Devices

- Porting Files

CHAPTER 14

Other Devices

The previous chapters covered the most common devices that Linux users add to their systems, but there are still a few more available peripherals you may want to add to your system. These include an Uninterruptible Power Supply (UPS), scanners, and devices that don't fall handily into any one category, such as high-capacity magneto-optical drives and DAT tape library machines. This short chapter looks at a few of the most common peripherals you may want to add.

Uninterruptible Power Supplies

A few years ago, only the large workstation or network server owner purchased a UPS (Uninterruptible Power Supply). Like tape drives, the UPS is now considered an important peripheral. If you run your Linux system unattended or all the time, you should include a UPS with your system, even at the expense of compromise on another component like an extra hard drive or high-speed modem; the UPS can save your entire system from problems.

Power bars with spike filters used to be considered adequate for many users' needs. Spike filters do serve a purpose; if it's a matter of a spike filter or nothing, most spike filters are a good idea. However, several spike filters on the market can cause more problems than they solve by burning out their circuitry when a spike of sufficient intensity hits. The surge is then passed on to all units plugged into the power supply.

As prices of UPSs have dropped and the power supply from the utility companies has seemingly gotten worse, UPSs are quickly becoming a necessary component. Besides protecting the computer equipment attached to the UPS, the UPS provides battery backup power to allow you to shut your Linux system down cleanly when the power fails, preventing corrupted filesystems. More recently, software that integrates with Linux is beginning to appear that can shut your system down completely by itself in case of problems.

UPSs are available in several different configurations, but a typical unit consists of a battery that is charged whenever the electrical supply is good. Some UPSs provide all power from the outputs of the UPS from the battery, thereby ensuring a flat, controlled electrical supply. This way a guaranteed 120 volts can be supplied with no fluctuation. Some UPSs use a regulating supply to tame incoming spikes and surges, complementing low voltages from the UPS battery. All UPSs have a fast-acting shunt that switches the output supply to the battery in case of main power failure.

Some UPS units lack the battery aspect and instead regulate the power directly. A battery backup may be further down the line, or one may not be used at all (which leaves the system exposed to blackouts). For sites with chronic problems (especially industrial buildings or remote locations), such regulation may be necessary to ensure long life from computer equipment.

More common, though, are the plug-in battery-based UPS units. Usually these units vary widely in price and features. The capacity of the battery and the amount of filtering the internal circuitry can perform also varies among the available models. Most manufacturers offer units based on voltage and wattage capacities. Choosing a unit with too much capacity can result in overspending, but an underpowered unit can cause problems by not providing all units plugged into it with enough power.

A typical home computer and monitor requires a small UPS. A 200V, 130W unit is common, although most people should consider 400V a minimum unless they have very few devices (such as just one floppy drive and one hard drive). Workstations and servers can require much more, typically in the 600V, 400W range. When choosing a UPS, total the power supply draws from all the equipment that will be plugged in to the system. For example, a typical, well-equipped PC has a 250W power supply, the monitor may draw 90W, and a modem and other external devices may add another 40W. Rounding up is the rule, so this type of system should have a 600V, 400W UPS.

The number of output jacks on the rear of a UPS tends to increase as capacity increases. A 200V unit may have four sockets, and a 600V UPS offers six, for example. Many users plug power bars into the rear jacks of a UPS, which makes more sockets available (often necessary with bulky connectors like modem power supplies), but can lead to unintentional overloading of the UPS capacity.

The amount of capacity of a UPS dictates the length of time it can be run off battery power. A typical system is designed to provide about 20 minutes of battery power when a power failure occurs. After that, the system must be powered off. Extra-long battery support is available either by purchasing a unit with a much higher capacity rating than you need or by adding external batteries. Practically all UPSs have an audible alarm when power failures occur, and some also let you know through a tone when surges, spikes, or sags are dealt with. These alarms can be useful but also annoying, so the capability to turn them off is important.

Other than capacities, UPSs differ in a couple of other important aspects: front-panel information and software support. The front panel of a UPS, while seemingly innocuous, can provide valuable information to a user. Small UPSs usually have a light or two to show that the unit is on, and a simple alarm when the power fails (and the user should start to shut down the system). Higher-end systems have multiple status lights or full displays. Some UPS software is now available for a variety of operating systems that can display this type of information in a window on your PC.

UPS software is an important point for many units today. The UPS software installs on an operating system and has capability to shut down the computer automatically and properly when power problems become serious. This capability is especially important with operating systems like Linux, which can experience data loss if the

14

system is not shut down in a specific sequence. In these cases, the UPS software sends a signal to a driver on the computer when power failures occur and can invoke timers to send users warning messages. Eventually, the software can start a complete, orderly shutdown of the computer and peripherals, which can then stay off until started by the administrator. Few software packages allow unattended restarts. Several companies are porting their UPS automated shutdown software to Linux (most have a generic UNIX version that may work, too). If software is not available for your UPS, you can develop the routines if you are a competent programmer. The UPS signals a problem through a serial port pin, and your software needs only to watch for that signal and then start a shutdown process.

REMOVABLE CARTRIDGE DRIVES

Several removable cartridge drive systems are currently available. Some use traditional disk platter technology, and others use magneto-optical techniques. For all these drives, the degree to which they will integrate with Linux depends on the drivers necessary to make them function.

SCSI systems are the easiest. The Linux SCSI interface recognizes most SCSI-based cartridge drives, and you can format the cartridge and mount it as a filesystem, just as you would with any other secondary disk drive. Whenever you change the cartridge, unmount the filesystem, insert the new cartridge, and mount the new filesystem. The entire process requires no special Linux interface at all. Usually, the only problem with removable cartridge drives is the formatting of the cartridge, which often must be done under DOS. Split partitions on the removable cartridges are also supported up to the normal Linux limit. (See Chapter 18, "Filesystems," for more information.)

Non-SCSI drive systems tend to not function with Linux unless a device driver has been developed specifically for that drive. The popularity of parallel port adapter drives has surged for Windows and DOS machines, but no driver for them is currently available for Linux. The same is true of the quasi-SCSI devices that require a special adapter card to function. Again, for these, a special device driver is necessary, and the kernel must be rebuilt to handle the devices.

If you are considering adding a new mass-storage device, check the Linux FTP and BBS sites carefully to ensure that a device driver is available. The popularity of many DOS and Windows-based devices means that a programmer is likely to port them to Linux eventually, so it's a matter of waiting for the driver to appear.

SCANNERS, OPTICAL READERS, AND SIMILAR DEVICES

Most scanners and similar devices don't have available device drivers for Linux. Again, SCSI devices are the easiest to work with under Linux as the SCSI interface handles all the device communications for the unit. The problem then is providing an application that can talk to the device. For a scanner, for example, you need a user application that can accept the data coming over the SCSI stream from the scanner head and massage it into a presentable image. There are a few scanner utilities available for Linux, with several more under development.

For non-SCSI devices, the device drivers have to be written. Few non-SCSI devices have any driver support at all, although some experimental device drivers and applications are appearing on the FTP and BBS sites. As with any new device, make sure you can find a device driver for the unit before you purchase it (unless you are going to use it under another operating system).

PORTING FILES

If you want to use a device that doesn't have a device driver under Linux, you can still use the device under some conditions. If you are using the DOS emulator, it may allow some DOS-based devices to function properly. The same applies for WINE, the Windows emulator. You can run some Windows-based devices and applications through the emulator, with the files saved to the Linux filesystem.

Failing that approach, you can use the devices in their native operating system by booting into DOS or Windows, and then save the files in an area that Linux can access. When you reboot to Linux, you can copy the files into whatever target directory you want and start manipulating them there. You can avoid a lot of file format problems by using a standard filetype, such as TIFF for graphics. Most Linux applications will handle file formats from DOS applications.

SUMMARY

The need to continually expand a Linux system's peripheral arsenal can be overwhelming at times, although you should be careful not to over tax the kernel's capabilities. At all times, remember that each physical device you add to the PC needs a Linux device driver and applications that can access the device. As this chapter mentioned several times, many new device drivers are appearing on BBS and FTP sites as more programmers get involved in the Linux project. Always check these sites for information on newly supported hardware and software.

14

OTHER DEVICES

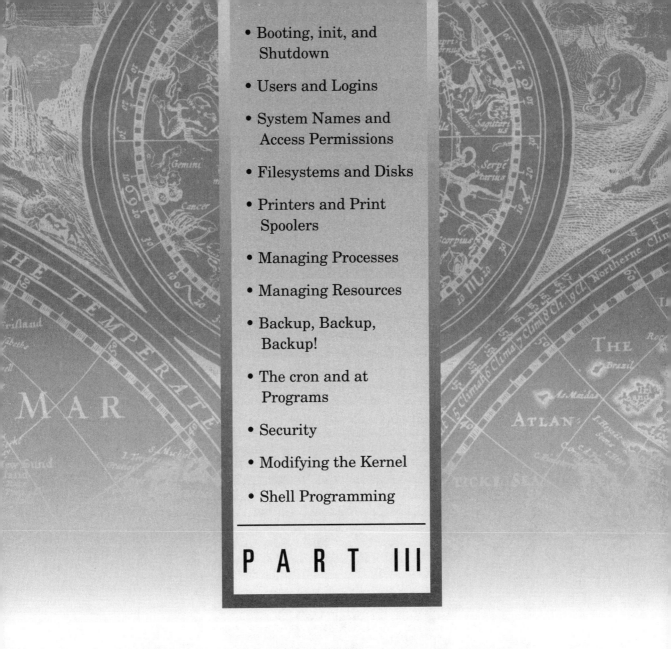

- Booting, init, and Shutdown
- Users and Logins
- System Names and Access Permissions
- Filesystems and Disks
- Printers and Print Spoolers
- Managing Processes
- Managing Resources
- Backup, Backup, Backup!
- The cron and at Programs
- Security
- Modifying the Kernel
- Shell Programming

PART III

Managing Your Linux System

- Starting Linux

- Creating and Using a
  Maintenance Disk

- Shutting Down Linux

- Understanding the
  init Daemon

- Using the rdev
  Family

CHAPTER 15

Booting, init, and
Shutdown

The most basic tasks you face with a Linux system are starting the machine properly and shutting it down when you are finished. Although the two processes sound simple, there are several ways of accomplishing each task and several hazards associated with performing the processes incorrectly. UNIX, as a whole, doesn't like shocks to the filesystem, such as fast power-offs, so you must carefully shut down the system to preserve your information.

This chapter looks at the startup and shutdown procedures used with Linux and the `init` daemon. The `init` daemon is probably the most important process running on any Linux system. Understanding what `init` does and how to use it properly can help you on the way to getting the best performance from your Linux system.

STARTING LINUX

Starting the Linux system can be as simple as turning on the power switch of your PC. If Linux is configured to autoload, Linux will be up and running after a few seconds. Few systems are set up to run only Linux though, and even fewer have it boot automatically when the power is turned on. Although automatic startup is convenient, many Linux users prefer to be able to choose which operating system to boot into (if other operating systems are loaded on the system) or to change the level of access to Linux.

You can start a Linux system by using a boot floppy disk or using LILO in one of several configurations. Each method has benefits and potential problems, which are discussed in the following sections.

USING LILO TO BOOT

LILO is the most common user method of booting a Linux system because it doesn't involve using a boot floppy disk. Chapter 4, "LILO," examined LILO in detail. LILO is a program that sits in the boot sector of a disk partition or the master boot record of the entire hard disk and points to the partition and location of the Linux kernel image.

If LILO is installed as a first-stage boot loader (meaning it boots Linux automatically), Linux starts to boot whenever the power is turned on. If you want to halt the boot process, you can use the Ctrl+Alt+Del sequence when the machine starts the boot sequence. (You must be careful when you hit Ctrl+Alt+Del, as you may reboot the machine by accident. Wait until you see the loader start its actions.) The Ctrl+Alt+Del sequence instructs LILO to pause and display the following prompt:

```
boot:
```

From this boot prompt, you can tell LILO which operating system to load (DOS, Linux, OS/2, and so on). If you press the Tab key when the boot prompt is displayed, LILO displays a list of all partitions and operating systems it knows about. The operating system partitions must have their configuration information included in the LILO information. Providing this information is simply a matter of identifying the partition device name and a name for the operating system when you are creating the LILO configuration file. Chapter 4, "LILO," covered these steps.

Because LILO writes data to the disk drive that other operating systems cannot read, it is not always the best solution if you install and remove operating systems frequently from your hard disks. Whenever you make changes to the configuration of your Linux system or other partitions on the hard disk, update the LILO information by rerunning LILO.

Using a Boot Floppy Disk

If you don't want to rely on LILO (which modifies disk sectors and may cause problems when you use several operating systems or change operating systems frequently), you can use a boot floppy disk to start up Linux. A boot floppy disk is a single floppy disk that contains a complete copy of the Linux kernel and instructions for accessing the root partition on your hard drive. The boot floppy disk must be of the proper format to run on the first disk drive on your system (drive A in DOS terms). Linux cannot boot from a second (drive B) floppy disk drive.

In many ways, a boot floppy disk is the easiest and most versatile method of starting Linux. If, for example, you have your hard disk partitioned to contain both DOS and Linux, with DOS the normal boot partition, simply turning on your PC boots DOS without a hitch. If you want Linux to boot, you insert the boot floppy disk and start the machine. Linux boots from the floppy disk, and then accesses the hard drives as if it had booted from them.

If you are using a boot floppy disk to start Linux, be sure to update the kernel image on the floppy disk every time you make a change to the system that involves rebuilding the kernel. Keep in mind that you must rebuild the kernel almost every time you add devices or device drivers. Use the procedure outlined in the following paragraphs to update your existing floppy disk, or, even better, create a new floppy disk and save your current floppy disk for emergencies. You are not prompted to create a new boot floppy disk when you make changes to the kernel, so you must remember to perform this step.

To create a boot floppy disk, you need a blank, formatted, high-density floppy disk (1.44M or 1.2M, depending on the A drive on your system). Format the floppy disk under DOS to lay down the sector and track information properly for Linux to read. Some small kernels can fit on low-density floppy disks, but high-density drives are most likely to be used on your system because they are the standard. The high-density floppy disk can have information on it as well as the Linux kernel, but make sure you have enough disk space for the kernel image.

Some versions of Linux (such as Slackware) can create the boot floppy disk as part of the normal setup routine. If you are using a distribution that has a setup routine, try choosing the Configure option on the menu, follow through the prompts, and see whether you are prompted to create a boot floppy disk at the end. Alternatively, some distributions have a separate menu option for creating the boot floppy disk.

If you want to create the boot floppy disk manually, locate the Linux kernel on your system. Usually it is in the root directory. The kernel name changes depending on the version of Linux, but it is often called Image or vmlinux. Some versions of Linux store the kernel image in the /etc directory.

Some versions of Linux also store the kernel in a compressed format. The names of compressed kernels end in z, as in vmlinuz or vmlinux.z. A compressed kernel takes up less space on the hard disk or floppy disk, and it is decompressed when the Linux kernel boots. A compressed kernel takes a little longer to load than a kernel that isn't compressed, but because it is decompressed only when the system boots, the trade-off is usually beneficial (unless you have tons of empty disk space).

You should be able to find the kernel quite easily by watching the startup messages when you boot the system and noting the kernel name, and then using `find` or `whereis` to locate it. Much easier is to change to the root directory and look for a large file called Image or vmlinux. The file is owned by root and has only read permission in many distributions of Linux. For example, when you do a listing command (such as `ls -l`), you see an entry like the following:

```
-r--------  1  root  root    457700  Aug 10 13:52 vmlinuz
```

This entry shows a kernel image file of almost half a megabyte that is compressed. The date and time of the kernel match the last time you rebuilt the kernel or the time and date you installed Linux.

Once you have identified the kernel file, instruct Linux that the file is the root device and indicate which partition it is on by using the `rdev` command. For example, to set the root device to the kernel vmlinuz in the root directory of the partition /dev/sda3, you would issue the command

```
rdev /vmlinuz /dev/sda3
```

Because you must specify the path to the kernel completely, the leading slash is included to show the root directory.

If you issue the rdev command by itself, it displays the current partition of the root filesystem:

```
$rdev
/dev/sda3 /
```

You can use this command to check the current settings if you are not sure which partition is your root filesystem. (This chapter looks at the rdev command in a little more detail in a later section.)

After you set the root device, you can copy the kernel to your formatted floppy disk. Use the cp command and the device name of the floppy disk:

```
cp /vmlinuz /dev/fd0
```

Once the image file has been transferred, the floppy disk should be able to boot Linux. If it doesn't, either the image didn't transfer properly due to a lack of disk space or a corrupted disk sector, or there is a problem with the kernel image.

CREATING AND USING A MAINTENANCE DISK

Every system should have a maintenance disk (also called an emergency boot disk) that you can use to boot the Linux system in case anything happens to the boot system (such as LILO). A maintenance disk is a combination boot and root disk that boots a complete Linux kernel independent of your hard disk installation. After you load the maintenance disk, you can use it to mount the hard disk and check for problems, or use one of the hard disk utilities to rebuild LILO or the kernel, depending on the problem with the drive.

To create a maintenance disk, you create a root filesystem on a floppy disk, copy essential tools to it, install LILO, and then make the disk bootable by copying the kernel. Perform this process every time you make a change to the Linux kernel so that your maintenance disk has the same kernel build. Keeping your maintenance disk up-to-date prevents hassles with utilities and devices.

You probably already have a set of maintenance disks in the pair of floppy disks you used to install Linux in the first place. Although these disks are not configured for your system, you can use them to load Linux and mount your hard drive. Many Linux setup procedures have a built-in routine to create boot floppy disks. You can use this routine to create the maintenance floppy disk.

If you have to boot off the maintenance floppy disk for any reason, mount the existing hard drive with the mount command. For example, if you are booting off your floppy disk and want to mount the partition /dev/sda2 (which wouldn't boot Linux for some reason), issue the command

```
mount -t ext2 /dev/sda2 /mnt
```

which mounts the hard drive partition under the directory /mnt. The directory must exist before you perform this operation, and it should be empty. The -t option specifies the file type. If your filesystem is not an extended filesystem, change the type.

SHUTTING DOWN LINUX

The temptation to treat Linux like DOS can be overwhelming when you are ready to finish with your session. Simply turning off the power should shut down everything, right? Well, it does, but it also can completely corrupt all the contents of your hard disk partition, as well as lose any information you were just working on. Granted, that's a very rare and extreme case, but arbitrarily turning off the power to a Linux session is still a bad idea.

Linux manages the hard disk and user spaces in RAM, using i-node tables to maintain the disk information and a memory manager for user information. Linux writes any changes to the i-node tables to the disk drive every so often, but it maintains the RAM copies as the most recent because of RAM's greater speed. If you shut down the power before Linux writes any changes to the disk, the disk contents and the i-node tables written on the disk may not match, causing lost files and an incorrect list of what disk space is available. Even worse, if Linux was in the process of writing the i-node table or any other information at the moment the power is turned off, the write process is interrupted, and disk head crashes or bad sector information can result. The same principle applies to any processes that are running. If, for example, you were running a database reindex when you killed the power, the indexes and databases may be corrupted. Shutting down the Linux system properly makes sure that all processes write and close all open files and terminate cleanly.

There are two easy ways to shut down the Linux system properly. The easiest is to use the Ctrl+Alt+Del sequence. On many Linux versions, this keyboard combination issues a shutdown command that closes all the processes properly, and then reboots the machine. Linux essentially traps the Ctrl+Alt+Del sequence and uses it to shut down the machine. Not all versions of Linux support this sequence, though, so check your documentation carefully.

Warning

If your system doesn't trap Ctrl+Alt+Del and reboots the machine when you issue it without shutting down Linux properly, it's the same effect as turning off the power. Make sure your Linux version supports this command before you use it!

The other method of shutting down Linux is with the UNIX command

```
shutdown
```

When you issue the `shutdown` command, Linux starts to terminate all processes and then shuts down the kernel. The `shutdown` command displays several different messages, depending on the version of Linux, but all inform you of the process or check that you really want to shut down the system.

The `shutdown` command allows you to specify a time until shutdown, as well as an optional warning message to be displayed to all users logged in. The format of the command is

```
shutdown time message
```

As an example, this command

```
shutdown 15 'Backup Time!'
```

shuts down the system after 15 minutes and display the message "Backup Time!" to all users on the system, prompting them to log off. This command is handy when you enforce a policy of shutting down at specific intervals, either for maintenance or backups.

In most versions of Linux, the `shutdown` command accepts the `-r` option. This option causes the PC to reboot after the shutdown has occurred. You can use this option to reboot to another operating system or to restart Linux after making changes to the kernel or devices. You can use the `-r` option with a time or message, if you want. The command

```
shutdown -r 5
```

reboots the system after five minutes.

In most cases, using Ctrl+Alt+Del or the `shutdown` command results in the display of a number of status messages on the main console. When Linux has finished shutting down the system, you see the message

```
The system is halted
```

When this message appears on-screen, it is safe to shut off the system power or reboot the machine. Although it may seem a little strange to have to follow these extra steps, you will find that many high-end operating systems such as UNIX (and even Windows NT and Windows 95) require you to follow a specific shutdown procedure to prevent loss of information. Get in the habit!

UNDERSTANDING THE *INIT* DAEMON

The init daemon is usually invoked as the last step in the booting of the Linux kernel. The init daemon is one of the most important Linux daemons because it creates processes for the rest of the system. The init daemon is executed when Linux starts and stays active until Linux is shut down. Understanding what init (and its linked utility telinit) does and how it controls the operating system is important to better administering the Linux system.

Both init and telinit use several configuration files to perform their tasks, so the following sections look at those files in detail, too. These files are closely involved in the starting and stopping of terminals and console sessions. The init program is usually kept in the /bin directory, although some versions of Linux keep it in /sbin. The same directories apply to the telinit utility. The configuration files are always kept in /etc, though.

RUN LEVELS

When the init daemon is executed, it reads instructions from the file /etc/inittab, which is primarily used to start getty processes for terminals and other processes required by Linux. While examining the /etc/inittab file, init searches for an entry labeled initdefault, which sets the default initial run level of the system. If no initdefault level is defined in the /etc/inittab file, the system prompts for the level.

A run level is a particular set of processes ranging from a bare minimum for system administration only to a full operation supporting all configured devices. Run levels are defined by a number from zero to six. An additional superuser level (often called single-user level as only root can log in) is defined as *s*. The init daemon knows which processes are associated with each run level from information in the /etc/inittab file.

When you use the s run level to display the system in single-user mode, the /etc/inittab file is not read. Instead, the utility /bin/su is invoked for the system console (defined by /dev/console). The init process can save the current state of a system when instructed to change to single-user mode from a higher run level. With some versions of init, the current state of the system is saved in a file called /etc/ioctl.save by the program ioctl. When the console is restarted to a higher run level, the states in this file are restored. If no ioctl.save file is found, the default states are used.

When starting up into multiuser mode (run levels higher than single-user mode), the init daemon performs any entries identified by the instructions boot and bootwait in the /etc/inittab file. Following these instructions usually allows filesystems to be mounted. After these instructions are processed, the rest of the entries that match the selected run level are executed.

The run level of the system can be changed by a user with access to the commands that affect the level. This access is usually restricted to the system administrator for security reasons. You change the run level by using the utility program /etc/telinit (which is linked to /etc/init). The `telinit` utility is responsible for sending messages to the `init` daemon to alter the current run level to the requested new level. To alter the run level, add the required level (zero through six or s) to the `telinit` command. For example, the command

```
telinit 2
```

changes the run level to level two and causes `init` to reread the /etc/inittab file and execute all processes for that level or terminate those for higher levels. To drop into superuser (single-user) mode, use the s option:

```
telinit s
```

Note

When switching to the superuser level, you can use either an upper-case or lowercase s. The `telinit` and `init` utilities can handle both cases.

You can specify a time delay for the change, in seconds, after the `-t` option. The command

```
telinit -t5 3
```

changes the run level to level three after five seconds. If no time is specified, Linux uses the default value of 20 seconds.

When you change the run level, `init` sends a SIGTERM warning signal to all processes that are not valid with the new run level. After sending the SIGTERM signal, `init` waits the specified number of seconds (or the default 20 seconds), and then terminates the process forcibly.

Note

If a process started by `init` has spawned new processes that are not in the same process group, `init` doesn't terminate them when you change the run level. You must terminate these processes manually.

THE /ETC/INITTAB FILE

As mentioned previously, the /etc/inittab file is tied closely to the `init` daemon. Look at the /etc/inittab file on your system to understand which processes are started and which run level is invoked when Linux starts. Extracts from a sample /etc/inittab file show the processes involved in starting the system with init. The first section in the sample /etc/inittab file identifies the default run level, in this case level five:

```
id:5:initdefault:
```

The next section in the /etc/inittab file handles the system startup through the files in the /etc/rc.d directories:

```
si:S:sysinit:/etc/rc.d/rc.S
```

Following this section is a pointer to the file /etc/rc.d/rc.K, which is used when the system enters the single-user run level:

```
su:S:wait:/etc/rc.d/rc.K
```

Next is a pointer to the file /etc/rc.d/rc.M for when the system is started in multiuser level (any one of the levels one through six):

```
rc:123456:wait:/etc/rc.d/rc.M
```

The most common run level is five, which is the normal operating level for Linux in multiuser mode. Most installations seldom use the other levels, although they can be used in some circumstances to control access to peripherals. Run levels are best left as the system wants them to prevent problems. This means using run level s for superuser mode and run level five for general use.

Because Linux runs on PC machines, it can support the "three-fingered salute" or Ctrl+Alt+Del sequence. This sequence is not usually supported on PC UNIX systems, so a special instruction is mapped to the sequence in the /etc/inittab file:

```
ca::ctrlaltdel:/sbin/shutdown -t3 -rf now
```

When the Ctrl+Alt+Del sequence is intercepted, the system begins a shutdown as shown by the command at the end of the preceding line.

The /etc/inittab file then holds an instruction to start a getty process for each terminal and virtual screen on the system. This sample /etc/inittab file starts six virtual screens (tty1 through tty6) and two serial lines (ttyS0 and ttyS1):

```
c1:12345:respawn:/sbin/agetty 38400 tty1
c2:12345:respawn:/sbin/agetty 38400 tty2
c3:45:respawn:/sbin/agetty 38400 tty3
c4:45:respawn:/sbin/agetty 38400 tty4
c5:45:respawn:/sbin/agetty 38400 tty5
c6:456:respawn:/sbin/agetty 38400 tty6

s1:45:respawn:/sbin/agetty 19200 ttyS0
s2:45:respawn:/sbin/agetty 19200 ttyS1
```

The terminal and serial line instructions are examined in more detail in Chapter 11, "Terminals and term."

The lines in the /etc/inittab file follow a specific format. The format follows this pattern:

```
ID:runlevel:action:process
```

The ID is a one- or two-character string that uniquely identifies the entry. In most cases, this string corresponds to the device name, such as 1 for tty1, 2 for tty2, and so on. The runlevel decides which of the run levels the line applies to (varying from zero to six). If no entry is provided, then all run levels are supported. Multiple run levels may be identified in the field.

The action indicates the command to execute when init reads the line. The following items are all valid entries for the action field:

♦ The boot action runs when inittab is first read.

♦ The bootwait action runs when inittab is first read.

♦ The initdefault action sets the initial run level.

♦ The off action terminates the process if it is running.

♦ The once action starts the process once.

♦ The ondemand action always keeps the process running (the same as respawn).

♦ The powerfail action executes when init gets a power fail signal.

♦ The powerwait action executes when init gets a power fail signal.

♦ The sysinit action executes before accessing the console.

♦ The respawn action always keeps the process running.

♦ The wait action starts the process once.

If init senses a powerfail condition (such as termination of power to the PC signaled by an Uninterruptible Power Supply) and the system was in multiuser mode, some special powerfail conditions are executed upon restart. These conditions usually check the filesystem for problems prior to bringing the system back up. The /etc/inittab file can contain specific instructions for these conditions, as shown in the following code:

```
# What to do when power fails (shutdown to single user).
pf::powerfail:/sbin/shutdown -f +5 "THE POWER IS FAILING"

# If power is back before shutdown, cancel the running shutdown.
pg:0123456:powerokwait:/sbin/shutdown -c "THE POWER IS BACK"

# If power comes back in single user mode, return to multi user mode.
ps:S:powerokwait:/sbin/init 5
```

All these powerfail conditions assume that some device manages to send the powerfail signals to the init process. Special device drivers that interface with UPSs usually do this.

The init daemon doesn't terminate when it has finished reading /etc/inittab. It stays active and monitors the system for specific instructions to change the run level (from a telinit command). It is also responsible for watching all the processes it started, including the getty processes for terminals. Whenever a process init started (called a child process, with init as the parent process) is terminated for any reason, init records the event and a reason for the termination (if possible to identify) in the files /etc/utmp and /etc/wtmp.

Whenever init senses the termination of a a child process, a power fail signal, or a run level change, it rereads the /etc/inittab to check for instructions. You can make changes to the inittab file (using any ASCII editor) while the system is running, but the changes will not be effective until the system reboots or one of the reread conditions occurs. An alternative is to use the q argument to force init to reexamine the /etc/inittab file. To force a reread of the /etc/inittab file, issue the command

```
init q
```

The init process checks how many times it has to restart (respawn) a process. If a process must be restarted more than 10 times in a two minute period, init assumes that there is an error in the command line of /etc/inittab for that process and generates an error message on the system console. The init process then refuses to respawn that process for five minutes or until it's forced to restart by the superuser. This step is useful because it prevents the system from wasting CPU cycles when a typographic error was made in the /etc/inittab file.

USING THE *RDEV* FAMILY

The rdev command is a utility not just for identifying the root device, as shown earlier in this chapter (it's used when creating a boot floppy disk), but for obtaining all kinds of information about your Linux system and making some configuration changes. The rdev utility can be cumbersome to use, and many administrators ignore it and its companion utilities completely.

Note

If you use LILO to boot Linux, you can ignore all the rdev commands as these parameters are set in the LILO configuration. The only times you will need rdev is when you change kernels and want to make a boot floppy disk for emergency use, or you want to change the RAM disk size. If you don't use LILO, you may occasionally need to use the rdev commands, although it is rare that they will be necessary as the Linux setup procedures define most of these parameters for you. The exception is changes in RAM disk size.

When run by itself, rdev displays the currently defined root partition and directory:

```
$dev
/dev/sda3 /
```

In this example, /dev/sda3 (third partition on the first SCSI hard disk) is the current root partition. You can use rdev to change the root partition and point to the kernel image to be used by Linux by providing both parameters as arguments:

```
rdev /vmlinuz /dev/sda3
```

This command changes the kernel image used to vmlinuz in the root directory of the third partition. You usually perform this command only when you create an emergency floppy disk.

The rdev command has several options for changing the way it acts, as shown in the following list:

-h   Displays help

-r   Makes rdev act like the command ramsize (see below)

-R   Makes rdev act like the rootflags command (see below)

-s   Makes rdev act like the swapdev command (see below)

-v   Makes rdev act like the vidmode command (see below)

Although you can use these options to alter rdev's behavior, you can also use the following commands directly:

◆ The ramsize command specifies the size of the RAM disk in kilobytes.

◆ The rootflags command enables you to mount the root directory as read-only.

◆ The swapdev command identifies the swap device.

◆ The vidmode command specifies the video mode.

In order to change many of the parameters, you must specify an offset that indicates the decimal value of the kernel location with the rdev command, which is why many administrators don't like the command. To use rdev or one of the utilities in its family, you must calculate the offsets according to the following rules:

Offset 498   Root flags

Offset 504   RAM disk size

Offset 506   VGA mode

Offset 508   Root device

The rootflags command has many options, only one of which really works to enable you to mount the root directory as read-only. Because this feature is seldom (if ever) necessary, most administrators can effectively ignore the `rootflags` command. (If you are running off a CD-ROM or from a small hard drive that contains only the binaries, you may want to consider using `rootflags`, but because you can accomplish the same task using file permissions, there's not much need to use `rootflags`.)

The `vidmode` command (or `rdev -v`) lets you change the video mode. If you issue the `vidmode` command by itself with some versions of Linux, it displays the current settings. More recent versions (including the one on this book's CD-ROM) show a help screen:

```
$ vidmode
usage: rdev [ -rsv ] [ -o OFFSET ] [ IMAGE [ VALUE [ OFFSET ] ] ]
  rdev /dev/fd0  (or rdev /linux, etc.) displays the current ROOT device
  rdev /dev/fd0 /dev/hda2      sets ROOT to /dev/hda2
  rdev -R /dev/fd0 1           set the ROOTFLAGS (readonly status)
  rdev -s /dev/fd0 /dev/hda2   set the SWAP device
  rdev -r /dev/fd0 627         set the RAMDISK size
  rdev -v /dev/fd0 1           set the bootup VIDEOMODE
  rdev -o N ...                use the byte offset N
  rootflags ...                same as rdev -R
  swapdev ...                  same as rdev -s
  ramsize ...                  same as rdev -r
  vidmode ...                  same as rdev -v
Note: video modes are: -3=Ask, -2=Extended, -1=NormalVga, 1=key1, 2=key2,...
      use -R 1 to mount root readonly, -R 0 for read/write.
```

The legal values for `vidmode` are as follows:

-3   Prompt

-2   Extended VGA

-1   Normal VGA

0   The same as pressing 0 at the prompt

1   The same as pressing 1 at the prompt

2   The same as pressing 2 at the prompt

n   The same as pressing n at the prompt

You can change the video mode using one of these values on the command line or using a number or letter to emulate pressing a value at the prompt.

SUMMARY

This chapter looked at the proper procedures for starting and stopping a Linux system. As you have seen, shutting down the system properly is vitally important. This chapter has also looked at the `init` process, an important aspect of the Linux system. Now that these basic procedures are out of the way, you are ready to look at some of the important aspects of system administration.

- Understanding the Superuser Account

- Establishing User Accounts

- Understanding Default System Usernames

- Adding Users

- Deleting Users

- Using Groups

- Using the su Command

CHAPTER 16

Users and Logins

All access to a Linux system is through a user account. Every user account must be set up by the system administrator, with the sole exception of the root account (and some system accounts that users seldom, if ever, use). Although many Linux systems only have one user, that user should not use the root account for daily access. Most systems allow several users to gain access, either through multiple users on the main console, through a modem or network, or over hard-wired terminals. Knowing how to set up and manage users' accounts and their associated directories and files is an important aspect of Linux system administration.

This chapter looks at the root login, which is the most powerful user account there is. From there, the chapter examines several aspects of setting up new user accounts on your Linux system. This chapter also looks at groups and how they are involved in the Linux system.

UNDERSTANDING THE SUPERUSER ACCOUNT

When you install the Linux software, one master login is created automatically. This login, called root, is known as the superuser because there is nothing the login can't access or do. Although most user accounts on a Linux system are set to prevent the user from accidentally destroying all the system files, for example, the root login can blow away the entire Linux operating system with one simple command. The root login has no limitations.

The sheer power of the root login can be addictive. When you log in as root you don't have to worry about file permissions, access rights, or software settings. You can do anything at anytime. This power is very attractive to newcomers to the operating system, who tend to do everything while logged in as root. It's only after the system has been damaged that the root login's problem becomes obvious—there are no safeguards! As a rule, you should only use the root login for system maintenance functions. Do not use the superuser account for daily usage!

The root login should be kept only for those purposes where you really need it. Change the login prompt of the root account to clearly show that you are logged in as root, and think twice about the commands you issue when you use that login. If you are on a stand-alone system and you destroy the entire filesystem, only you are inconvenienced. If you are on a multiuser system and insist on using root for common access, you will have several very mad users after you when you damage the operating system.

So after all those dire warnings, the first thing you should do on a new system is create a login for your normal daily usage. Set the root password to something other users of the system (if there are any) will not easily guess, and change the password frequently to prevent snooping.

You also can create special logins for system administration tasks that do not need wide-open access, such as tape backups. You can set a login to have root read-only access to the entire filesystem to decrease the potential for damage. This login lets you back up the system properly, but prevents you from erasing the kernel by accident. Similar special logins can be set up for e-mail access, gateways to the Internet, and so on. Think carefully about the permissions each task requires and create a special login for that task; your system will be much more secure and have less chance of accidental damage.

The most important thing to note is that the superuser account doesn't have to be called root, although this account is created automatically as root when Linux installs itself. In theory, this account can have any name, but the name root is almost always used. The superuser account is always defined as the account with a user ID number of zero. User ID numbers are defined in the /etc/passwd file.

ESTABLISHING USER ACCOUNTS

Even if you are the only user on your Linux system, you should know about user accounts and managing users. You need to know how to establish a user account because you should have your own account (other than root) for your daily tasks. If your system lets others access the operating system, either directly or through a modem, you should create user accounts for everyone who wants access. You may also want a more generic guest account for friends who just want occasional access.

Every person using your Linux system should have their own unique username and password. The only exception is a guest account or perhaps an account that accesses a specific application such as a read-only database. By keeping separate accounts for each user, your security is much tighter, and you have a better idea of who is accessing your system and what the user is doing. A one-to-one correspondence between users and accounts makes tracking activities much easier.

The file /etc/passwd contains all the information about user accounts. The /etc/passwd file should be owned only by root and should have its group ID set to zero (which usually indicates a root or system group, as defined in the /etc/group file). Set the permissions of the /etc/passwd file to allow write access by root only; all other accounts can have read access. (Groups and permissions are dealt with later in this section.) The lines in the /etc/passwd file are divided into a strict format:

```
username:password:user ID:group ID:comment:home directory:login command
```

To understand this format, look at a sample /etc/passwd file. The following /etc/passwd file is created when a Linux system is newly installed:

```
root::0:0:root:/root:/bin/bash
bin:*:1:1:bin:/bin:
```

```
daemon:*:2:2:daemon:/sbin:
adm:*:3:4:adm:/var/adm:
lp:*:4:7:lp:/var/spool/lpd:
sync:*:5:0:sync:/sbin:/bin/sync
shutdown:*:6:0:shutdown:/sbin:/sbin/shutdown
halt:*:7:0:halt:/sbin:/sbin/halt
mail:*:8:12:mail:/var/spool/mail:
news:*:9:13:news:/usr/lib/news:
uucp:*:10:14:uucp:/var/spool/uucppublic:
operator:*:11:0:operator:/root:/bin/bash
games:*:12:100:games:/usr/games:
man:*:13:15:man:/usr/man:
postmaster:*:14:12:postmaster:/var/spool/mail:/bin/bash
nobody:*:-1:100:nobody:/dev/null:
ftp:*:404:1:::/home/ftp:/bin/bash
```

Each line in the /etc/passwd file is composed of seven fields separated by a colon. If nothing is to be entered in a field, the field is left blank, but the colons are retained to make sure each line has seven fields (which also means each line will have six colons). The seven fields (from left to right on each line) are as follows:

The username is a unique identifier for the user.

The password is the user's password (encrypted).

The user ID (UID) is a unique number that identifies the user to the operating system.

The group ID (GID) is a unique number that identifies the user's group (for file permissions).

The comment is usually the user's real name, but sometimes it is a phone number, department, or other information.

The home directory is the directory in which the user is placed when he or she logs in.

The login command is the command executed when the user logs in; normally, this command starts a shell program.

You should know what each field does and how other programs on your Linux system use it. Note that this type of user file is used with almost every UNIX system in the world, so once you know it for Linux, you know it for most UNIX versions.

USERNAMES

The username is a single string, usually eight characters or less, that uniquely identifies each user. Because the username is the basis of most communications between users and other machines, the username you use (or assign to others) should be simple and obvious. Usually, this name is a permutation of the user's real name. A typical username may be a combination of the user's first and last names, such as tparker or timp. A username composed of the first initial and last name is fairly common in large networks.

Note that the characters in these examples are all lowercase. Case is important in Linux (as with all UNIX versions), so tparker and Tparker are two different logins. Because most Linux commands are lowercase, the convention is to also keep usernames lowercase. Underscores, periods, numbers, and some special characters are allowed, but they should be avoided because they make login names look strange and can also cause problems for some applications.

Small systems, such as one comprised of a single machine, may use more familiar names, such as the user's first name. A small system may have users with the names tim, bill, yvonne, and so on. If two users have the same name, there must be some method to differentiate between the two (such as bill and billy).

A few users like to create cryptic usernames that reflect their hobbies, nicknames, pets, lifestyle, or personality. You may find usernames like vader, grumpy, wizard, and hoops. This type of naming is fine on small systems that are used by one or two users, but it quickly becomes awkward on larger systems where other users may not know their coworkers' usernames. On the whole, if more than a couple of friends use your system, discourage this type of username.

PASSWORDS

The system stores the user's encrypted password in the password field. This field is very sensitive to changes, and any modification to it can render the login useless until the system administrator performs a password change. Only the system administrator or the user can change the password by using the passwd command.

Note

Some versions of UNIX do not keep the passwords in the /etc/passwd file because of potential security problems. If the password fields on your system are all set to x, then another file (called a shadow password file) is in use. However, all versions of Linux currently available do use this field by default.

Systems running either Yellow Pages or NIS (Network Information Service), both of which rely on a central file of usernames and passwords, do not use the password field. Few Linux systems use either YP or NIS, however, so you can ignore this distinction for the moment.

When a user logs in, the login program logically compares the password the user typed to a block of zeros, and then compares that result to the entry in the password field. If they match, the user is granted access. Any deviation causes login to refuse access.

16

You can use this field to restrict access to the system. If you want to prevent a login from ever being used for access, such as a system login like lp or sync, place an asterisk between the two colons for the password field. This asterisk restricts all access. In the sample /etc/passwd file shown previously, many system logins have an asterisk as their password, effectively blocking access.

You can also use this field to allow unrestricted access by leaving it blank. If no password entry exists (the field has nothing in it), anyone using the username is granted access immediately, with no password requested. Do not leave passwords open unless you are using your Linux system for your own pleasure and have nothing of value on the filesystem.

Don't attempt to put a password directly in the password field using an editor. You cannot recreate the encryption method, and you'll end up locking the user account out. Then only the system administrator will be able to change the password and allow access.

USER ID

Every username has an associated, unique user ID. Linux uses the user ID, also called the UID, to identify everything associated with the user. The user ID is preferable to the username because numbers are easier to work with than the characters in a name and take up less space. Linux tracks all processes started by a user, for example, by the user ID and not the username. Some utilities translate the user ID to display the username, but utilities generally examine the /etc/passwd file to match the UID to the name.

The user ID numbers are usually assigned in specific ranges. Most UNIX systems, for example, allocate the numbers from 0 to 99 for machine-specific logins and the user ID numbers from 100 and up for users. Using this model will make your system consistent with others. In the sample /etc/passwd file shown previously, you can see that root has a UID of 0, and the other system-created logins have larger numbers. The login nobody is a special login used for NFS (Network File System) and has a UID of -1, an invalid number. When you assign user ID numbers, assign them sequentially so that the first user is 100, the second 101, and so on.

GROUP ID

The group ID (GID) is used to track the user's startup group (in other words, the ID of the group the user belongs to when he or she logs in). A group is used for organizational purposes to set file permissions, although many organizations don't bother with groups. Group ID numbers range upwards from zero. Most UNIX systems have system groups numbered from 0 to 49 (some operating system versions use only the numbers 0 to 9 for the system) and user groups from 50 on up. The default group, called group, is assigned number 50.

The system uses the GID when tracking file permissions, access, and file creation and modification specifications. If your system has only a single-user group, you need not worry about the GID. If you work with several groups (as might be implemented on a large system), you need to examine the /etc/group file (discussed later in this chapter).

COMMENTS

The system administrator uses the comment field to add any information necessary to make the entry more explanatory. Typically, this area is used to enter the user's full name, although some system administrators like to add department or extension numbers for convenience. (This field is sometimes called the GECOS field, after the operating system that first used it.)

Some utilities use the comment field to display information about users, so make sure you don't place any sensitive information there. E-mail systems, for example, can access this field to show who is sending mail. Although you don't have to use the field, it can make things much easier for administrators and other users on larger systems when they can discover the real name behind the username.

HOME DIRECTORY

The home directory field indicates to the login process where to place the user when he or she logs in. This place is usually the user's home directory. Each user on the system should have a dedicated home directory, and the user's startup files initialize the environment variable HOME to this value. The directory indicated in this field is the user's initial working directory only and places no restrictions on the user (unless file permissions have been set to restrict movement).

For the most part, user home directories are located in a common area. Linux tends to use the /home directory, so you will find home directories like /home/tparker, /home/ychow, and so on. Other versions use /usr, /user, or /u as user home directories. In some cases where the system administrator has experience with another version of UNIX that uses an alternate directory structure, you may find the home directories changed to make life easier (and more familiar) for that administrator. Linux doesn't care what the name of the home directory is as long as it can be entered.

LOGIN COMMAND

The `login` command is the command to be executed when login terminates. In most cases, this command is a shell command that starts a program such as the C shell or Bourne shell to provide the user with a shell environment. In some cases, it may be a single application or front-end system that restricts what the user can do. For example, the uucp login (used for e-mail and other simple networking tasks) only executes the `uucp` command. If the login command field is left empty, the operating system usually defaults to the Bourne shell (although this default may change depending on the manner in which the operating system is set up).

Many versions of Linux allow users to change their login shell with the commands `chsh` or `passwd -s`. When you use these commands, Linux searches the file /etc/shells for a match. Only those commands in the /etc/shells file are allowed as valid entries when the user tries to change his or her startup shell, which helps you keep tighter security on the system. (You can add or remove lines in the /etc/shells file using any editor.) The superuser account has no restrictions on the entry in this field (or any other user's field). If your system uses the /etc/shells file, make sure this file has the same file permissions and ownership as the /etc/passwd file, or a user can sneak through the system security by modifying the startup command for his or her login.

UNDERSTANDING DEFAULT SYSTEM USERNAMES

The previous extract from the /etc/passwd file lists over a dozen system-dependent usernames. These names serve special purposes on the Linux system. A few of these logins are worth noting as they have specific uses for the operating system and system administrators:

> The root login is the superuser account (UID 0) and has unrestricted access. It owns many system files.
>
> The daemon login is used for system processes. This login is used only to own the processes and set their permissions properly.
>
> The bin login owns executables.
>
> The sys login owns executables.
>
> The adm login owns accounting and log files.
>
> The uucp login is used for UUCP communication access and files.

The other system logins are used for specific purposes (postmaster for mail, and so on) that are usually self-evident. You should not change any of the system logins. In most cases, they have an asterisk in the password field to prevent their use for entry purposes.

Adding Users

You can add users to your system by manually editing the /etc/passwd file or by using an automated script that prompts you for the new user's details and writes a new line to the /etc/passwd file for you. The automated approach is handy for new system administrators who are uneasy about editing as important a file as /etc/passwd or for those occasions when you have to add several users and the risk of error increases. You can modify the /etc/passwd file only when you are logged in as root.

Warning

Before making changes to your /etc/passwd file, make a copy of it! If you corrupt the /etc/passwd file and don't have a copy of it, you can't log in, even as root, and your system is effectively useless except in system administration mode. Keep a copy of the /etc/passwd file on your emergency floppy disk or boot floppy disk in case of problems.

To add an entry to the /etc/passwd file, use any editor that saves information in ASCII. Add the new users to the end of the file, using a new line for each user. Make sure you use a unique username and user ID (UID) for each user. For example, to add a new user called `bill` to the system with a UID of 103 (remember to keep UIDs sequential for convenience) and a GID of 50 (the default group), a home directory of /home/bill, and a startup shell of the Bourne shell, add the following line to the /etc/passwd file:

```
bill::103:50:Bill Smallwood:/home/bill:/bin/sh
```

Note that the the password is blank because you can't type in an encrypted password yourself. As soon as you have saved the changes to /etc/passwd, set a password for this account by running the command

```
passwd bill
```

This command prompts you for an initial password. Set the password to something that Bill can use, and ask him to change the password the first time he is on the system. Many system administrators set the initial password to a generic string (such as `password` or the login name), and then force the new user to change the password the first time he or she logs in. Using generic strings is usually acceptable if the user logs in quickly, but don't leave accounts with generic login strings sitting around too long; someone else may use the account.

After you have added the necessary line to the /etc/passwd file, create the user's home directory. Once created, you must set the ownership to have that user own the directory. For the above example, you would issue the following commands:

```
mkdir /home/bill
chown bill /home/bill
```

All users must belong to a group. If your system has only one group defined, add the user's username to the line in the /etc/group file that represents that group. If the new user is to belong to several groups, add the username to each group in the /etc/group file. The /etc/group file and groups in general are discussed in the following section.

Finally, copy the configuration files for the user's shells into the user's home directory and set the system to allow the user access for customization. For example, if you were to copy the Bourne shell's .profile file from another user called yvonne, you would issue the following commands:

```
cp /home/yvonne/.profile /home/bill/.profile
chown bill /home/.profile
```

Also, manually check the configuration file to ensure that no environment variables are incorrectly set when the user logs in. For example, there may be a line defining the HOME environment variable or the spool directories for printer and mail. Use any ASCII editor to check the configuration file. If you are using the Korn or C shell, there are other configuration files that need to be copied over and edited. Bourne shell compatibles need only a .profile, but the C shell and compatibles need .login and .cshrc. The Korn shell and compatibles need a .profile and usually another file with environment variables embedded in it.

In general, the process for manually adding a new user to your system is as follows:

1. Add an entry for the user in the /etc/passwd file.
2. Create the user's home directory and set its ownership.
3. Copy the shell startup files and edit their settings and ownerships.

The Linux system has a hold-over command from the Berkeley BSD UNIX version. The command vipw invokes the vi editor (or whatever the default system editor has been set to) and edits a temporary copy of the /etc/passwd file. The use of a temporary file and file lock acts as a lock mechanism to prevent two different users from editing the file at the same time. When the file is saved, vipw does a simple consistency check on the changed file, and if all appears proper, the /etc/passwd file is updated.

The automated scripts for Linux tend to have the names useradd or adduser. When run, they prompt you for all the information that is necessary in the /etc/passwd file. Both versions let you exit at any time to avoid changing the /etc/passwd file. The automated scripts also usually ask for an initial password, which you can set to anything you want or leave blank. One advantage of the automated scripts is that they copy all the configuration files for the supported shells automatically and, in some cases, make environment variable changes for you. These scripts can simplify the process of adding users enormously.

A quick note on passwords: they are vitally important to the security of your system. Unless you are on a stand-alone Linux machine with no dial-in modems, every account should have a secure password. You assign and change passwords with the passwd command. The superuser can change any password on the system, but a user can only change their own password. Chapter 24, "Security," deals with secure passwords.

DELETING USERS

Just like adding new users, you can delete users with an automated script or manually. The automated scripts deluser or userdel ask which user you want to delete, and then remove that user's entry from the /etc/passwd file. Some scripts also clean out the spool and home directory files, if you want. You must log in as root in order to make any deletions to the /etc/passwd file.

To delete the user manually, remove the user's entry from the /etc/passwd file. Then you can clean up the user's directories to clear disk space. You can completely delete all the user's files and his or her home directory with the command

```
rm -r /home/userdir
```

where /home/userdir is the full pathname of the user's home directory. Make sure there are no files you want to keep in that directory before you blow them all away!

Next, remove the user's mail spool file, which is usually kept in /usr/spool/mail/ username. For example, to remove the user walter's mail file, issue the command

```
rm /usr/spool/mail/walter
```

The spool file is a single file, so this command cleans up the entries properly. To finish off the mail cleanup, check that the user has no entries in the mail alias files (usually /usr/lib/aliases), or you can force all mail for that user to another login (such as root) with an entry in the aliases file. Finally, make sure that there are no entries in the user's cron and at files that the system will continue to execute. You can display the user's crontab file (explained in Chapter 23) using the crontab command.

If you need to retain the user for some reason (such as file ownerships, a general access account, or accounting purposes), you can disable the login completely by placing an asterisk in the password field of the /etc/passwd file. That login cannot be used when an asterisk is in the password field. To reactivate the account, run the passwd command.

The process for manually deleting a user (or using an automated script that doesn't clean up directories and files) is as follows:

1. Remove the user's entry from /etc/passwd and /etc/group files.
2. Remove the user's mail file and any mail aliases.
3. Remove any cron or at jobs.
4. Remove the home directory if you don't want any files it holds.

Occasionally, you may want to temporarily disable a user's account, such as when the user goes on extended leave or vacation. If you want to temporarily disable the login but be able to recover it at any time in the future, add an asterisk as the first character of the encrypted password. Don't alter any characters in the existing password, but add the asterisk to the beginning. When you want to reactivate the account, remove the asterisk and the password will be back to whatever it was set as before you made the changes.

USING GROUPS

Every user on a UNIX and Linux system belongs to a group. A group is a collection of individuals lumped together for some reason. The users in a group may all work in the same department, may need access to a particular programming utility, or they may all have access to use a special device such as a scanner or color laser printer. Groups can be set up for any reason, and users can belong to any number of groups. However, a user can only be a member of one group at a time, as groups are used for determining file permissions and Linux only allows one group ID per user at any point in time.

Groups can have their permissions set so that members of that group have access to devices, files, filesystems, or entire machines that other users who do not belong to that group may be restricted from. Group permissions can be useful when you have an accounting department, for example, whose members need access to the company's accounts. You don't want non-accounting people to go snooping through financial statements, however, so creating a special group that has access to the accounting system makes sense.

Many small Linux systems have only one group, the default group, because this is the simplest way to manage a system. In these cases, each user's access to devices and files is controlled by the devices' or files' permissions, not the group. When you start to get several different users in logical groupings, though, groups start to make more sense. You can even use groups to control your friend's or children's access to areas on your home Linux system.

Group information is maintained in the file /etc/group, which is similar in layout to the /etc/passwd file. The default /etc/group file from a newly installed Linux system looks like the following:

```
root::0:root
bin::1:root,bin,daemon
daemon::2:root,bin,daemon
sys::3:root,bin,adm
adm::4:root,adm,daemon
tty::5:
disk::6:root,adm
lp::7:lp
mem::8:
kmem::9:
wheel::10:root
floppy::11:root
mail::12:mail
news::13:news
uucp::14:uucp
man::15:man
users::100:games
nogroup::-1:
```

Each line in the file has four fields separated by colons. Two colons together mean that the field is empty and has no value specified. Each line in the file follows this format:

```
group name:group password:group ID:users
```

Each group has a line of its own in the file. The fields in the /etc/group file (from left to right) are as follows:

> The group name is a unique name, usually of eight characters or less.

> The password field is usually left as an asterisk or blank, but a password can be assigned that a user must enter to join the group. Not all versions of Linux or UNIX use this field, and it is left in the file for backwards compatibility reasons.

> The group ID (GID) is a unique number for each group, which is used by the operating system.

> The users field contains a list of all user IDs that belong to that group.

Every Linux system has a number of default groups that belong to the operating system; these groups are usually called bin, mail, uucp, sys, and so on. You can see the system-dependent groups in the default /etc/group file shown previously. In that file, all but the last two entries are system groups. Never allow a user to belong to one of these groups as it gives them access permissions that can be the same as root's. Only system logins should have access to these operating system groups.

16

UNDERSTANDING DEFAULT SYSTEM GROUPS

You may have noticed in the startup /etc/group file shown previously that a lot of groups are defined. These groups are used to set file permissions and access rights for many utilities. It's worth taking a quick look at some of the most important groups and their functions:

The root/wheel/system group is usually used to allow a user to employ the su command to gain root access. This group owns most system files.

The daemon group is used to own spooling directories (mail, printer, and so on).

The kmem group is used for programs that need to access kernel memory directly (including ps).

The sys group owns some system files. On some systems, this group behaves the same as kmem.

The tty group owns all special files dealing with terminals.

The default group for the SlackWare Linux version /etc/group file shown previously is called users and has a GID of 100. Many systems have the default group called group, as this is the standard convention on most UNIX systems.

ADDING A GROUP

To add a group, you can edit the information in the /etc/group file manually using any ASCII editor, or you can use a shell utility like addgroup or groupadd that does the process for you. Most system administrators find it easier to do the changes manually, as you can see the entire group file at the time you are editing it. Not all versions of Linux have an addgroup or groupadd utility.

To manually add a group to the /etc/group file, first make a backup copy of the file. Use any ASCII editor and add one line to the file for each new group you want to create. Make sure you follow the syntax of the file carefully, as incorrect entries prevent users from belonging to that group. In the following examples, two new groups have been created:

```
accounts::51:bill
scanner::52:yvonne
```

The two groups have GIDs of 51 and 52; like user IDs, the GIDs should be assigned sequentially for convenience. The users that are in the group are appended. In these cases, only one user is in each group. You see how to assign multiple users to a group in the next section. The groups do not have to be in order of GID or group name, although it's convenient to have the file ordered by GID. You can add new lines anywhere in the file.

Check the /etc/group file for file permissions and ownership after you have made changes to it. The file should be owned by root and have a group owner of root (or system, depending on the group with GID 0). The file permissions should prevent anyone but root from writing to the file.

Adding a User to New Groups

Users can belong to many groups, in which case their user IDs should be on each group line that they belong to in the file /etc/group. Each username on a line in the /etc/group file is separated by a comma. There is no limit to the number of users that can belong to a group in theory, but in practice the line length of the Linux system (255 characters) acts as an effective limiter. There are ways around this limit, but few systems require it.

The following excerpt from a /etc/group file shows several groups with multiple members:

```
accounts::52:bill,yvonne,tim,roy,root
prgming:53:bill,tim,walter,gita,phyliss,john,root
cad:54:john,doreen,root
scanner:55:john,root,tim
```

The usernames on each line do not have to be in any particular order. Linux will search along each line to find the usernames it wants.

A user can be a member of only one group at a time while logged in, so users must use the command newgrp to change between groups they are members of. The starting group a user belongs to when they log in is given by the GID field in the /etc/passwd file.

Deleting a Group

If you decide you don't want a particular group to exist anymore, remove the group name from the /etc/group file. Also, check the /etc/passwd file to see whether any users have that group ID as their startup GID, and change it to another group that they are members of. If you don't change the GIDs, the user won't be able to log in because they have no valid group membership. You should also scan the entire filesystem for files and directories that are owned by that group and change them to another group. Failure to make this change may prevent access to that file or directory. Some Linux versions have shell scripts that remove group lines from the /etc/group file for you. The utility is generally called delgroup or groupdel. Most versions of Linux don't bother with this utility.

USING THE *su* COMMAND

Sometimes you will want to execute a command as another user. If you are logged in as superuser and want to create files with bill's permissions and ownership set, it is easier to log in as bill than work as root and reset all the parameters. Similarly, if you are logged in as a user and need to be superuser for a little while, you would have to log out and back in to make the change. An alternative is the su command.

The su command changes your effective username and grants you the permissions that username has. The su command takes the username you want to change to as an argument. For example, if you are logged in as a typical user and want to be root, you can issue the command

```
su root
```

and the Linux system will prompt you for the root password. If you supply it correctly, you will be root until you press Ctrl+D to log out of that account and back to where you started. Similarly, if you are logged in as root and want to be a user, you can issue the command with the username, such as:

```
su tparker
```

You won't be prompted for a password when changing from root to another user as you have superuser powers. When you press Ctrl+D, you are root again. If you are logged in as a normal user and want to switch to another non-root login, you have to supply the password, though.

SUMMARY

This chapter looked at the basics of the /etc/passwd and /etc/group files, the two files connected with user access to Linux. As you have seen, a system administrator can easily modify these simple files to add users and groups at any time. Always bear in mind that these are vital files that should be edited carefully and have their permissions checked after each edit.

- Setting a System
  Name

- Using File and
  Directory Permissions

CHAPTER 17

System Names and Access
Permissions

Instead of referring to your Linux system as "it" or "that thing," you can give it a name that it recognizes to some extent. This name is especially important when you deal with e-mail or networks where others must have some method of identifying your machine from all the others on the network. This chapter starts by looking at how to give your machine a name and what rules you must follow to ensure other machines can work with your newly named machine.

The rest of this chapter looks at access permissions, a confusing subject for many system administrators. The permission block is often completely misunderstood, and the permissions attached to files and directories are often set incorrectly, preventing access to users who need it or worse, allowing wide-open access to sensitive information. After explaining how permissions work, this chapter explains how to change and set permissions and ownerships.

SETTING A SYSTEM NAME

Because Linux is designed with networking in mind, it enables you to identify each machine with a unique name. You can name your system anything you want. In some cases, the setup or installation script that installed Linux for you may have asked you for a system name. You can keep the name you entered then or enter a new one.

The name that identifies your Linux system is called a hostname. This name, as mentioned, facilitates networking and associated services like e-mail. It also lets you give your system a bit of a personality. You can display the current Linux system hostname with the `hostname` command:

```
$ hostname
artemis
```

This code shows that the system's hostname is `artemis`. If you have no system hostname defined, Linux defaults to either no name or a system default name. The name information is read from the Linux system startup files.

If your system isn't networked, you can call your system anything you like, but remember that you have to live with it! To set your system name, run the `hostname` command with the `-s` option as shown in this example:

```
hostname -S superduck
```

This sample code sets your system hostname to `superduck`. This name is tagged onto all your e-mail and some system utilities when generating output. Some versions of Linux limit the hostname to a number of characters (usually 14 characters), but try any name you want. If Linux doesn't allow it, you should get an error message or see a truncated version of the name.

CREATING NETWORK SYSTEM NAMES

If you are running on a network, the hostname is important. On a network, each machine must have a unique name, or the network can't identify which of the duplicate names the network information is for. If you are creating a local area network that is not connected to the Internet or has no formal network name, you can pick any network name you want. Your machine name and network name combined form the full machine name. For example, the command

```
hostname -S superduck.quackers
```

is composed of a machine name of superduck and a network name of quackers. As long as all the other machines on the network have the same network name, your machines can communicate properly. Your machine is uniquely identified by the combination of machine and network name.

If your system can access the Internet, your network probably has been assigned a network name by the Internet Network Information Center (NIC), which assigns network names, called domains, in accordance with strict naming conventions. Each domain has a unique name portion and an extension that identifies the type of organization to which the network belongs. For example, the company Quacks-R-Us may have a domain name quacks.com. The seven different extensions in use are as follows:

.arpa	A governmental network identifier
.com	Commercial company
.edu	Educational institution
.gov	Governmental body
.mil	Military
.net	An Internet-administered (usually) network
.org	Anything that isn't in one of the other categories

These identifiers are usually used only for networks based in the U.S. Other countries have unique identifiers based on the country's name. For example, if Quacks-R-Us were based in the United Kingdom, the domain name could be quacks.uk. Each country has a two-letter designation that identifies it to the Internet. (Some companies have a U.S.-style extension even though they are outside U.S. borders. These companies usually have been registered by a U.S. company or have been on the Internet a long time.)

The combination of domain name and extension, as assigned by the NIC, is unique to each network. When combined with a hostname on the network, the result is a unique name for your machine. For example, if your local network has the domain name of `quack.com` and you want to name your machine `superduck`, you set the name of your machine with this command, which combines the machine and network names:

```
hostname -S superduck.quack.com
```

The chapters in Part IV, "Networking," discuss machine names and network names in more detail. You may also want to check with a good TCP/IP book for more information. The author's *Teach Yourself TCP/IP in 14 Days* from Sams is a good place to start.

STORING THE HOSTNAME

Linux stores the hostname in the file /etc/hosts. If you have just installed Linux and haven't configured a machine name, the /etc/hosts file contains a bunch of comment lines and one line of code:

```
127.0.0.1     localhost
```

Note

Some Linux versions store the hostname in the /etc/rc or /etc/rc.local files or in the directory /etc/rc.d, although this convention is absent from most versions of Linux.

The /etc/hosts file consists of two columns, one for the IP address and the second for machine names. The four numbers (written in a format called dotted-quad as there are four groups of numbers with periods between them) are the IP address. IP stands for Internet Protocol and is an essential component of the TCP/IP network protocols used on the Internet and most local area networks involving UNIX. The IP address for machines connected to the Internet is assigned by the Network Information Center, just as the domain name is. (The IP address and domain name also are mapped to each other so the network can use numbers instead of names, a much more efficient system.) If you are not connected to the Internet, your IP address can be anything as long as each set of numbers is in the range 0 to 255.

The IP address is composed of the network identifier and the machine identifier. The four parts of the IP address are split over these two identifiers in special ways. If you are connecting to an existing TCP/IP network, your network administrator will give you the IP address you should use. The IP address 127.0.0.1 is a special address known as the loopback address. This address lets TCP/IP on your machine form a connection to itself. Every machine has a loopback driver, which is identified by the entry 127.0.0.1 in the /etc/hosts file and the name localhost.

If you have identified your machine by a hostname already, that name is in the /etc/ hosts file. For example, the stand-alone machine called superduck from earlier in this section is given on the same line as the localhost entry:

```
127.0.0.1      superduck localhost
```

This line tells the system that the localhost is called superduck and to use that name as the system identifier.

This naming process gets a little more complicated when you are on a network, as each machine on the network has an IP address that is unique. If your network is not connected to the Internet, you can make up any IP address for your network. If you are on the Internet, your network IP address is assigned, and the network administrator can give you your machine's IP address or you can choose an unused address.

Suppose you are connecting to the Internet and your IP address is 47.123.23.37 and your domain name is quacks.com. Your /etc/hosts file looks like the following:

```
127.0.0.1       localhost
47.123.23.37    superduck.quacks.com
```

The name superduck may appear on the localhost line as well, although it doesn't have to. The /etc/hosts file may have other lines when you are connected to a large network that you move around in frequently. At least these two lines should appear when you are connected to a network, though.

USING FILE AND DIRECTORY PERMISSIONS

Linux handles access to all files and directories on the filesystem through the permission block. The permission block is part of the i-node table's entries for each file and directory. You can display the permission block for a file or directory by doing a long directory listing.

The first column of the long directory listing is the permission block. It is always composed of 10 characters. Each file and directory, regardless of its type, on a Linux system has a permission block associated with it. The permission block is made up of two different types of information. The first character is a file type indicator, and the next nine characters are the access permissions themselves. The following sections look at these two types of information in a little more detail.

UNDERSTANDING FILE TYPES

Linux uses the first character in the permission block to indicate the type of entry the i-node table contains. Because Linux doesn't differentiate between files and directories in the i-node table, this character is the only way for the operating system to know whether the entry refers to a regular file or a directory. Directories are not physical entities on a Linux system; they are instead an organizational scheme used to make the user's life easier. The i-node table entries for a file and directory look very similar.

Linux supports a number of valid file types, each of which has a single character value that is used in the first character of the permission block. The most common file type characters that Linux uses are the following:

-    ordinary file
- b   block mode device
- c   character mode device
- d   directory
- l   link

Some versions of Linux and UNIX support other file types (such as s for special), but these types are seldom encountered and are of no real interest as far as permissions are concerned.

Most files on the Linux system are ordinary files. An ordinary file can be data, an application, a text file, or any file that contains information (whether directly readable by the user or not). The ordinary files are indicated by a hyphen in the file type block. Any file users create is an ordinary file.

Chapter 6, "Devices and Device Drivers," looked at the difference between block and character mode devices, which are indicated by a b or c file type. These files are composed of instructions that let Linux talk to peripherals. Most device file types are stored in the directory /dev by convention, although they can exist anywhere in the filesystem. When Linux encounters a file with either of these two file types, it knows how to read the file for input and output control.

The directory file type indicates that the entry in the i-node table refers to a directory and not a file. All directories on the system are really empty files as far as Linux is concerned, but they can be logically assembled into the usual directory structure based on the i-node table entries.

Links are sometimes identified in the file type character as an *l*, although not all operating system versions support this character. If your version of Linux doesn't use the l file type to indicate a link, you will have to rely on the second column of output from a long directory listing that shows the number of links the entry has.

UNDERSTANDING ACCESS PERMISSIONS

All UNIX systems (including Linux) control access to files and directories using permissions that are read from the permission block. Access to a file or directory can be one of three possible values. These values are given by a single character as shown in the following list:

r   read

w   write

x   execute

If you have read access to a file, you can display the contents of the file (using any utility like cat or more) or read the file into an application (such as a word processor or a database). If you have write permission to a file, you can modify the contents and save the changes over the old file. If you have execute permission, you can execute the file, assuming it is a binary file or shell script. If the file is ASCII and you execute it, nothing much will happen except a few error messages.

These three permission values are combined into a three-character block in the order given above (in other words, rwx for read, write, and execute). If a permission is not accessible, a hyphen is used in that permission's place to show that it is absent. In other words, the permission block r-x indicates that the file has read and execute permission, but not write permission. Similarly, the permission block --- indicates that the file has no access permissions and cannot be read, written to, or executed.

These permissions are used for directories, too, although their meanings are slightly different. Read permission for a directory means you can display the contents of the directory listing (using ls, for example). Write permission for a directory means you can add files to the directory. Execute permission means you can change into that directory (using cd). The permission block r-x on a directory, for example, means you can display the directory's contents and change into that directory, but you can't add a new file to the directory.

These three permissions are set for each of three different levels of access. There is a permission block for the owner of the file (called the user), another for anyone in the owner's group (called the group), and another for everyone else on the system (called other or world). The three-character blocks for read-write-execute permission are combined for the three groups (user, group, and other) to produce the nine-character permission block you see in the long directory listing.

Once you get used to thinking in terms of user, group, and other, you can easily read the file permissions blocks. For example, the file permission block

```
rw-r--r--
```

means that the user (owner of the file) has read and write permission, the group (second block of three characters) has read permission only, and everyone else on the system (other) has only read permission also. In the following example, the permission block

```
rwxr-xr--
```

means that the owner can read, write, and execute the file. Anyone in the same group as the owner can read and execute the file. Finally, anyone else on the system can read the file but can't make changes or execute it.

The same approach applies for directories. For example, if a directory has the following permission block

```
rwxr-xr-x
```

the owner of the directory can change into the directory, add files, and display the contents of the directory. Everyone else on the system (in the owner's group and everyone else) can display the contents of the directory (with an ls command, for example) and change into the directory (using cd), but they can't add files to the directory.

USING DEFAULT PERMISSIONS

When you save a file or create a new directory, it is assigned a default set of permissions. These permissions are set for each user according their file creation mask, called the umask (user's permission mask) by UNIX. Every user on the system has a umask setting, either one that's set for them in their startup files (.profile, .cshrc, and so on) or the system's default umask setting.

You can display the current value of your umask setting by entering the umask command at any shell prompt:

```
$ umask
022
```

The three-number block returned by the umask command is the current umask setting. (Some systems return a four-number block, the first number of which is always zero. In this case, only the last three numbers are of any importance for the umask.) The three numbers are octal representations of the read-write-execute permissions you see in a file's permission block. The numbers have the following meaning:

0	read and write (and execute for directories)
1	read and write (not execute for directories)
2	read (and execute for directories)
3	read
4	write (and execute for directories)
5	write
6	execute
7	no permissions

Using this list, you can see that the umask setting of 022 means that the user has read and write permission for his own files (0), the group has read permission (the first 2), and everyone else on the system has read permission (the second 2). Whenever a user creates a file with this umask setting, the permission block will look like the following:

```
rw-r--r--
```

As mentioned earlier, Linux uses a system default umask setting when a user logs in unless the user's setting is explicitly changed, either on the command line or in one of the startup files. If you want to change the umask value, use the umask command with the three-digit permission setting you want. For example, the command

```
umask 077
```

sets the permissions to give the owner read and write permission and to withold permissions from everyone else on the system. This umask value can be very useful for restricting access to files.

If you want to temporarily change your umask setting, enter the umask command and the new setting at the shell prompt. The new values will be in effect until you change them again. If you want to permanently change your umask setting, add a line like the preceding one to your shell's startup file (.profile, .cshrc, and so on).

Changing Permissions

You may want to change the permissions attached to a file or directory. You change permissions with the chmod command, which can operate in either symbolic or absolute mode. Symbolic mode is the easiest mode to learn and use, but absolute mode offers better control.

Using chmod in symbolic mode requires that you follow a strict syntax. Once you understand that syntax, the command is easy to use. Symbolic mode lets you instantly understand the changes that you are making to permissions. The general syntax of the chmod in symbolic mode is

```
chmod who-change-perms files
```

where who indicates who you want the changes to apply to. Valid values are u for user, g for group, and o for other, in any combination and order. The change indicates whether you want to take away permissions (-), add them (+), or explicitly set them (=). You can use only one symbol in each chmod command. The perms indicate whether you want to change read (r), write (w), or execute (x) permission. These three components (who, change, and perms) of the command are run together without a space. A few examples may help make this concept a little clearer. The command

```
chmod u+rwx bigfile
```

alters the permissions on bigfile to add read, write, and execute for the user. If any of these three permissions already existed on bigfile, they are left alone, but they are added if they didn't exist before the command. The permissions for the group and other users are not affected, as this command deals specifically with the user's permissions. On the other hand, the command

```
chmod go-x bigfile
```

takes away execute permission for the group and other, without changing the group's and other's read or write permissions (they stay the way they were) or the user's permissions (as a u was not included in the command). You can use wildcards in the chmod command, as well, so the command

```
chmod uo+w chapter*
```

adds write permission for the user and other for any file starting with chapter.

If you don't specify whether the command applies to user, group, or other, all three are affected, so the command

```
chmod +rwx
```

changes the permissions for user, group, and other to read, write, and execute.

You also can use the symbolic mode of chmod to set permissions explicitly. As you have seen, if you do not specify a parameter on the command line, it is not changed. In other words, if you issue the command

```
chmod u+r bigfile
```

only the read permission for the user is changed, and the write and execute permissions are left as they were.

You can do the same sort of command to set permissions for directories, remembering what they mean in the context of changing into, adding to, and listing directories. For example, the command

```
chmod go+rx mydir
```

allows users in group and other to list mydir's contents and change into mydir, but they cannot add files to this directory.

Sometimes you want to explicitly set the permissions to some value, for which you can use the equal sign. For example, the command

```
chmod u=rx bigfile
```

turns on read and execute permission for the user, but turns off write permission (whether it was on or off before the command, it will be off after). However, the group and other permission blocks are left unaffected. If you want to make changes to all three blocks (user, group, and other) at the same time, you must use chmod's absolute mode.

The chmod command's absolute mode uses numbers to specify permissions. There are three numbers, one for the user, one for the group, and one for the other permissions. All three must be specified on the command line. Each number is the sum of values that represent read, write, and execute permissions. The following list shows the values:

000	no permissions
001	other, execute
002	other, write
004	other, read
010	group, execute
020	group, write
040	group, read
100	user, execute
200	user, write
400	user, read

You can see that the numbers are in three columns. From left to right, they represent user, group, and other permissions. To use these numbers, add together the values of one (execute), two (write), and four (read) to form the combination you need. For example, if you want to set read and execute permissions, the number you specify is five. Setting all the permissions gives you seven, and a value of zero signifies no permissions. You then use these numbers on the `chmod` command line. For example, the command

```
chmod 644 bigfile
```

sets user permissions to read and write (six), group permissions to read (four), and other permissions to read (four). Permissions that aren't set are replaced with blanks, resulting in following file permission block:

```
rw-r--r--
```

You may recognize this block as the default permission block for users with a umask of 022. This example points out the fact that the umask and chmod absolute numbering schemes are not the same.

Absolute mode is useful for setting the entire permission block in one shot. Although the addition process may seem awkward at first, it becomes quite easy after a while. A couple of settings are used frequently. The 644 setting shown previously produces the usual permissions for files, and the command

```
chmod 755 mydir
```

sets mydir to allow only the owner to add files and let everyone list the contents and change into the directory. You can use wildcards with this mode of `chmod` to make blanket changes.

Which mode of chmod you use at any time depends on the type of permission change you want to make. If you just want to change a single permission (such as adding execute permission for yourself or read-write permission for the group), the symbolic format is easy. For setting complete permission block details, the absolute mode is fastest.

CHANGING THE OWNER AND GROUP

Every file and directory on a Linux system has an owner and a group, both of which can be seen in the long directory listing. The owner of the file is usually the username of the person who created the file, and the group of the file is the group the person was in when the file was created. You may want to change the owner and group when sharing files or moving them to another user. To do this, use the `chown` and `chgrp` commands.

To change the owner of a file or directory, use the `chown` command with the name of the new owner. For example, the command

```
chown bill datafile
```

changes the owner of `datafile` to `bill`. When the command is issued, it checks to make sure that the specified owner is valid (by searching /etc/passwd) and that you own the file. Only the file owner or the superuser can change file ownerships. You can use wildcards to change many files or directories at once. For example, the command

```
chown yvonne chapter*
```

changes the owner of all files starting with `chapter` to `yvonne`.

To change the group owner of a file or directory, use the `chgrp` command (not to be confused with `newgrp`, which changes your current group). For example, the command

```
chgrp accounts bigfile
```

changes the group to `accounts`. Again, Linux checks that the group name exists in /etc/group and that the person changing the group is in the group that currently owns the file. As with `chown`, you can use wildcards to change many files and directories at once.

If you know the UID or GID of the user or group, you can use it on the command line instead of the name. Linux searches the /etc/passwd and /etc/group files to make sure the UID or GID is valid, and you must have permission to change the owner for this procedure to work.

Warning

Use caution when changing ownerships. It's easy to change an owner or a group, and then realize you have locked yourself out of the file!

SUMMARY

This chapter explained how to give your system a name and assign access permissions. Naming a system is very important when you are connected to a network, but it is more of a personality issue when you are running a stand-alone system. Still, it is nice to refer to your machine as more than thing or the default darkstar name.

File permissions are one of the most misunderstood and misused concepts of UNIX, yet they are surprisingly easy to manage. Using the commands explained in this chapter should make it easy for you to alter file permissions and ownership to suit your needs.

- Mounting and Unmounting Filesystems

- Mounting Filesystems Automatically with the /etc/fstab File

- Managing Disk Space

- Understanding Links

CHAPTER 18

Filesystems and Disks

One of a system administrator's most important tasks is managing the Linux system's hard disks and filesystems. Keeping both in proper order helps the Linux operating system perform at its best. This task involves doing a set of actions regularly. This chapter describes the actions involved in keeping the Linux filesystems and the hard disks they reside on in peak condition. (This chapter does not look at the steps involved in adding new hard disks to your Linux system; this process was covered in Chapter 8, "Hard Disks.")

The general actions a system administrator must perform to keep filesystems running smoothly are the following:

◆ Check filesystems for corrupt sectors
◆ Check filesystems for integrity and correct i-node tables
◆ Check file permissions and ownerships to ensure proper access
◆ Make filesystems (local and remote) available to users as necessary
◆ Manage the Linux system's disk space
◆ Perform regular backups for data security

Although some of these actions are performed automatically every time Linux boots (such as checking the filesystem for corruption), you should know how to force these processes manually, as well as know what they do and how to correct problems that may arise. With the exception of performing backups for data security (covered in more detail in Chapter 22, "Backup, Backup, Backup!") and checking file permissions (covered in Chapter 17, "System Names and Access Permissions"), this chapter looks at all these actions.

MOUNTING AND UNMOUNTING FILESYSTEMS

To understand why filesystems must be mounted, you have to know how Linux organizes the disks and filesystems that make up the entire directory structure. Linux uses a single directory structure, regardless of how many disks and disk partitions are involved. Each partition's filesystem must be part of the larger directory structure. The entire directory tree has only one root directory, and other filesystems are attached at lower levels.

To visualize this concept, imagine a standard Linux filesystem with the root partition (/) at the top; all the other partitions branch off from the root partition. The root partition is on a partition of the first hard disk. Usually, that disk also has other directories on it, such as /dev, /lib, /etc, and so on. Essentially, all the directories needed to start a minimal Linux operating system have to be on the primary partition.

However, suppose you want to have a very large /usr filesystem because you intend to support a lot of users with very large database files. Your primary disk partition may not be able to contain all the files you want to save, so you can use another partition (on the same or a different hard disk) and format it as a Linux filesystem, and then attach it to the root filesystem at the /usr directory point. Whenever a user moves from the /bin directory (on the first partition) to /usr/tparker, for example, the user moves to another partition or disk. The move across partitions is completely unnoticeable to the user because the two partitions look like a single directory tree. The /usr directory is said to be mounted on the root directory.

More accurately, the partition that holds the /usr filesystem is mounted on the root filesystem in the /usr location. It could just as easily have been mounted at the /home location. Linux doesn't care where you mount a filesystem as long as you mount it as a directory that exists in the root filesystem (so /usr or /home, depending on where you mount the filesystem, would have to be an empty directory on the root filesystem) and no conflict exists between directory names. If the partition were mounted at /home, the user would access /home/tparker instead of /usr/tparker.

You can stretch this concept even further. Suppose one user, such as /usr/tparker, has to access a very large library of pictures stored on a CD-ROM drive. You can attach the filesystem on the CD-ROM to the existing filesystem as /usr/tparker/cd_rom, for example, with the operating system knowing to move to the CD-ROM whenever the user accesses that directory. Again, this transition is unnoticeable to the user. This example shows that you can mount a filesystem onto another mounted filesystem.

Linux lets you mount partitions anywhere from any source, as long as they fit into the overall filesystem structure. The only place you cannot mount a filesystem is at the root directory location, which must exist on the root filesystem. Linux also allows you to mount some other operating system filesystems, such as a DOS or OS/2 filesystem, onto your Linux filesystem. Essentially, you let Linux know where to access the filesystem (/dos, /usr/dos, or some other directory name) and tell Linux the type of filesystem, and it lets you move through that filesystem's directories and files as you would any Linux directory. You can mount a filesystem in only one location at a time; you cannot mount one filesystem (of any kind) as both /usr and /home, for example.

All these filesystem mounting options make Linux very versatile. If a friend has a hard drive full of data you want to access and the data is a filesystem Linux can understand, your friend can bring the hard drive to your machine and attach it to your controller, and then you can mount your friend's filesystem anywhere that is available on your existing filesystem. You can mount any device that can hold a filesystem, including CD-ROMs, floppy disks, magneto-optical drives, removable cartridges, and so on.

To mount a filesystem, you use the mount command. The general syntax of the mount command is

```
mount device_name mount_point
```

where *device_name* is the name of the device (partition, hard disk, CD-ROM, and so on) and *mount_point* is the name of the directory to which you want to mount the device. For example, to mount the partition /dev/sda4 (fourth partition on the first SCSI hard disk) to the /usr directory, issue the following command:

```
mount /dev/sda4 /usr
```

To mount a CD-ROM filesystem (such as /dev/cdrom) on the directory /cdrom (assuming the directory exists), use the following command:

```
mount /dev/cdrom /cdrom
```

Alternatively, you can use the following command to mount a CD-ROM filesystem, because you can mount a filesystem anywhere:

```
mount /dev/cdrom /usr/tparker/data/pictures/cd-rom
```

Note

Only the root mounts and unmounts filesystems. Although it's possible to enable users to mount filesystems, this practice can lead to security problems and is therefore generally discouraged. Log in as the superuser to mount or unmount filesystems.

You can mount a filesystem as read-only so that any attempt to write to the filesystem generates an error message. This feature is useful to prevent frustrated users of a mounted CD-ROM filesystem, for example, or if you want to make sure nobody writes to a mounted filesystem on another partition (which may contain data you don't want to be corrupted). To mount a filesystem as read-only, use the -r option:

```
mount -r /dev/cdrom /cdrom
```

Some older versions of UNIX and Linux allow the -r option to be at the end of the command line:

```
mount /dev/cdrom /cdrom -r
```

When one of the mounted filesystems is disconnected (so users cannot access the directories), the filesystem has been unmounted. Any mounted filesystem can be unmounted except for the root filesystem, which is always active. To unmount a filesystem, use the umount command. (One of the most common errors for system administrators is typing this command as unmount instead of umount). The umount command takes the name of either the device or the mount point. To unmount the CD-ROM mounted in the last example, you can use either of the following two commands:

```
umount /dev/cdrom
umount /cdrom
```

You don't have to unmount all filesystems before you shut down the system, as Linux can handle the unmounting as part of the shutdown process.

MOUNTING FILESYSTEMS AUTOMATICALLY WITH THE /ETC/FSTAB FILE

Any previously mounted filesystems are not necessarily mounted automatically when the system restarts(other than root, which is always mounted automatically when the system starts). When Linux boots, it must know where to find the filesystems to be mounted. Linux uses the /etc/rc initialization file (run when Linux boots) to execute the command:

```
mount -av
```

When Linux executes this command, it knows to read the file /etc/fstab to find out which filesystems have to be mounted and where they should be mounted.

Note

> You also can use the following command to mount all the filesystems in the /etc/fstab file:
>
> ```
> mountall
> ```
>
> Not all versions of Linux support the mountall command, but all should support the mount command line.

Each line in the /etc/fstab file follows this format:

```
device mount_location filesystem_type options dump_frequency pass_number
```

This section looks at a few of these parameters in more detail, as well as provide valid values. In practice, the /etc/fstab file is an ASCII file composed of several columns. The following is a sample /etc/fstab file:

```
/dev/sda1       /               ext2        defaults    1   1
/dev/sda2       /usr            ext2        defaults    1   1
/dev/sda3       /usr/data       ext2        defaults    1   1
/dev/cdrom      /cdrom          iso9660     ro          1   1
/dev/sda4       /dos            msdos       defaults    1   1
/dev/sdb1       /data           ext2        defaults    1   1
```

This rather complex-looking table is quite easy to understand. The first column gives the device name, followed by the mount point, the type of filesystem, and instructions about how to treat the filesystem. For example, the root filesystem in the above table is /dev/sda1 and is a typical ext2 Linux filesystem. The CD-ROM device is mounted as /cdrom; it is an ISO 9660 (CD-ROM) filesystem and is mounted as read-only. The DOS filesystem is mounted as /dos.

Linux mounts the filesystems in the order they are given in /etc/fstab. Note in the preceding sample file that the entry that mounts /usr/data follows the entry that mounts /usr. If the /usr/data entry came before the /usr entry, the mount wouldn't work because the /usr directory wouldn't yet exist. If one mount fails, Linux ignores it and executes the rest of the entries. If a mount of a directory that is used further down the file fails, the dependent mounts fail too. For example, if the mount of /usr fails for some reason, the mount of /usr/data fails too, as /usr doesn't exist.

The last two numbers on each line in /etc/fstab show the dump frequency and the pass number. These two numbers do not mean anything with some versions of Linux, so check the fstab man page for more information. The dump frequency tells Linux how often the filesystem should be backed up. One means the backup should occur daily, two means the backup should be every other day, and so on. This number is used for automated backup routines that can parse the /etc/fstab file for this information.

The pass number indicates the order in which the fsck utility should check the filesystem. One means the filesystem should be checked first, two means it should be checked second, and so on. If more than one filesystem has a pass number of one, the filesystems are checked in the order they occur in the /etc/fstab file. The root filesystem must have a value of one, and the convention is to set other partitions higher. However, because most Linux versions don't use the pass number, all filesystems usually have this number set to one. If your version of Linux does use this number and you have more than one disk drive on your Linux filesystem, set the numbers on each disk in order (1, 2, 3 and so on to match the mount order), and then use a parallel scheme for each additional disk drive. This way, fsck checks filesystems on each disk in parallel.

You can include swap partitions in the /etc/fstab file as well. List these partitions as type swap with the mount directory set to none and the dump frequency and pass number set to zero, as shown in the following example:

```
/dev/sda2              none                 swap             sw        0      0
```

When you include a swap partition in /etc/fstab, you can activate it using the swapon command. When you execute the command

```
swapon -a
```

Linux reads the /etc/fstab file and activates all swap partitions. This command is usually embedded in the /etc/rc file (so it is executed automatically when Linux boots), although it can be run from the command line just as easily.

FILESYSTEM TYPES

The types of filesystems that Linux supports vary depending on the version of Linux you are using. Most versions support the following filesystem types, though. You can use them in the /etc/fstab file:

ext2	This type is the second extended filesystem, which is the most common type of Linux partition.
ext	This type is the original Linux extended filesystem, which has been replaced by ext2.
minix	This type is the original Minix filesystem, which is rarely used but is still supported because it was the first Linux filesystem format.
xia	This type is the Xia filesystem, which is rarely used because it has been superseded by ext2.
umsdos	This type is the UMS-DOS filesystem, which is used to install Linux on a DOS partition (with no dedicated Linux partition).
proc	This type is the filesystem based on /proc, which is used for some processes that use system information.
iso9660	This type is the ISO 9660 filesystem, which is used on most CD-ROM disks.
xenix	This type is the SCO Xenix filesystem, which provides support for Xenix under Linux.
sysv	This type is the UNIX System V filesystem, which provides support for System V drives under Linux.
coherent	This type is Mark Williams' Coherent UNIX version, which provides support for Coherent filesystems under Linux.
msdos	This type is a DOS partition that Linux can access.
hpfs	This type is the High Performance filesystem, which provides support for HPFS under Linux.

18

FILESYSTEMS AND DISKS

Some versions of Linux do not include support for all filesystems included above, especially the lesser-used filesystems like coherent and minix. A filesystem called nfs, which supports the Network filesystem, is supported on recent Linux versions.

OPTIONS VALUES

The options field in the /etc/fstab file can have several different values, depending on the version of Linux. For most versions of Linux (which are based on BSD UNIX), you can use the following options to describe the filesystem characteristics:

default	Varies depending on version, but normally read-write, suid, and quota
rw	Read-write
ro	Read-only
suid	Access in SUID mode allowed
nosuid	Access in SUID mode not allowed
quota	Quotas may be in effect
noquota	Quotas may not be in effect

If the filesystem type is nfs, many more options are supported. The default option tends to be the best choice for typical filesystems mounted on a local hard drive.

Note

You may see the term SUID used often when dealing with system administration. SUID stands for Set User ID and is a permission bit associated with all files and directories. There is also a bit called SGID, for Set Group ID. Any file or directory with these bits set act as though they were owned by another user. For example, you could be logged in as a normal user and execute a binary file that has SUID set. The binary will execute as though it was run by root. Both SUID and SGID are dangerous bits to work with as they can cause security problems.

MANAGING DISK SPACE

UNIX system administrators have a saying: no matter how much disk space you have, it's not enough. This maxim is as true for Linux as it is for UNIX. Disk space has a way of being gobbled up, especially when several users are sharing a system. By the time you have loaded your operating system, favorite applications, compilers, and user files, your disk space is probably close to full. If it isn't, wait six months and it will be.

Disk drives are very inexpensive now, so many system administrators prefer to battle the disk space problem by adding larger hard disks or extra disk drives. This option is certainly valid and prevents a lot of hassle cleaning up files, but you still should force some kind of disk space usage policy on yourself and other users to make sure disk space is not wasted. To create such a policy, you have to know how to determine disk space usage, manage disk space effectively, and clean up disks.

CHECKING FILESYSTEMS

Part of Linux's startup routine (driven by an entry in /etc/rc) is to check all mounted filesystems to make sure that they are not damaged or corrupted. This check is performed with every reboot. However, if your machine is not rebooted often or you are experiencing disk errors, start a filesystem check manually.

In general, you use the utility fsck (filesystem check) to check filesystems. Linux uses some special versions of fsck to check Linux-dependent filesystems, though, so you may not have direct access to fsck. For example, many Linux versions have a dedicated fsck version called e2fsck to check the ext2 filesystem.

When fsck does exist on a Linux version, it is often just a front-end search engine that looks in the /bin, /sbin, /etc/fs, and /etc directories for one of the proper filesystem fsck versions, and then executes that version. The search and execution processes are transparent to you in most cases.

The fsck utility does several tasks. As part of its operation, it scans the entire filesystem for any of the following problems:

◆ A block shared by many files (cross-linked)

◆ Blocks in use but marked as free

◆ Inconsistent entries among files and i-node tables

◆ Incorrect link counts

◆ Illegal entries in the i-node tables

◆ Inconsistencies between i-node table size values and the disk space used by a file

◆ Illegal values in files

◆ Lost files that don't appear in the i-node table

The entire process occurs quickly, so there is no reason not to run fsck regularly. If fsck does report errors, shut down the system to superuser mode only and rerun fsck. The problem may have occurred because of a user application; this step identifies that type of problem. If the disk still has problems, you can correct them in superuser mode.

Note

In most cases, `fsck` runs only on unmounted filesystems (except root). If you want to check a filesystem, unmount it, and then run `fsck`. To check root, switch the system to single-user mode, and then run `fsck`. Although some versions of Linux don't require these steps, they are good safety precautions to prevent accidental changes to the disk or i-node tables.

The `fsck` command takes the name of either the device or the mount point of the filesystem you want to check. For example, both of these command lines invoke `fsck` properly:

```
fsck /dev/sda1
fsck /usr
```

If `fsck` is working on several disk drives (because of mounting), it tries to work in parallel whenever possible to reduce the amount of time required for the disk checking.

A number of options are useful with `fsck` or its filesystem-specific versions. The options supported by most Linux systems that are commonly used by system administrators are as follows:

`-a`	This option automatically repairs the filesystem without prompting you (use this option with care).
`-r`	This option interactively repairs the filesystem (the system asks for instructions). Use it only when checking a single filesystem.
`-t <type>`	This option specifies the type of filesystems to check. If `type` is preceded by `no`, only the other types of filesystems are checked. This option uses the filesystem types from the /etc/fstab file.
`-v`	This option provides verbose output.

Many other options are supported by `fsck` and its versions (like `e2fsck`), but a system administrator seldom (if ever) needs these other options. The `fsck` man page summarizes all the available options for you.

Get in the habit of running `fsck` occasionally, just to check the filesystem integrity. If you reboot often, the automated `fsck` checks the filesystem for you. But if you ever get disk error messages, `fsck` is the first place to turn.

DISPLAYING FILESYSTEM STATISTICS

Two commands are frequently used to check filesystem statistics (such as space used, space available, and so on). They are df (disk filesystem) and du (disk usage). Both commands are included with practically all versions of Linux.

The df command is the most widely used statistics generator for filesystems. It displays information about all the filesystems on the system, their total capacities, the amount of free space available on each, and the current mount locations. The following is an example of output from a df command:

```
merlin$ df
Filesystem        1024-blocks   Used Available Capacity Mounted on
/dev/sda3             478792    94598   359465     21%   /
/dev/sda1             511712    44288   467424      9%   /dos
/dev/scd0             663516   663516        0    100%   /cdrom
```

This system has a single SCSI hard disk with two partitions, one Linux and one DOS. The Linux partition /dev/sda3 has 478,792K total on the disk, of which 94,590K are used. The amount of disk space available is 359,465K. The Linux partition is 21 percent used. (Remember that a kilobyte is 1,024 bytes, so the numbers shown in the output are kilobytes.) Similarly, the DOS partition /dev/sda1 has only 9 percent of its 511,712K capacity used. The CD-ROM has 100 percent of its 663,516K used. It's mounted as /cdrom.

This command shows you a handy display of the capacity of all the Linux partitions on your system and their usage. If you are handy with utilities like awk, you can total the capacities and used space by adding the columns, which makes a handy single shell language utility. Some system administrators like to run this type of summary command in background every day and post the information to themselves through mail or a broadcast when they log in.

Note

You may occasionally see disk capacities in excess of 100 percent. This is caused by Linux holding back about 10 percent of the disk for the superuser's use exclusively, which means about 110 percent of the displayed capacity is available to root. Whenever the capacity approaches 100 percent, though, it's time to clear off the disk!

A handy option of the df command shows similar information about the i-node tables:

```
merlin$ df -i
Filesystem         Inodes   IUsed   IFree  %IUsed Mounted on
/dev/sda3          123952    8224  115728     7%   /
/dev/sda1               0       0       0     0%   /dos
/dev/scd0               0       0       0     0%   /cdrom
```

18

This display, from the same system as the previous df output above, shows the number of i-nodes available, how many are used, the number that remain free, and the percentage used. No correlation exists between disk space usage and i-node table usage, so you should display both sets of information. An i-node is used every time a file is used. If many small files are saved, the i-node table can fill up, but you may still have plenty of disk space for new files. Check both disk space usage and i-node table usage for maximum information.

The df command ignores any filesystems that have zero blocks in them unless you specify the -a or -all option. Filesystems with zero blocks are used occasionally for special purposes such as automounting particular devices. The df command also ignores any filesystems that have the filesystem options set to ignore in the /dev/fstab file (usually only swap files have this setting). By default, the df command displays all filesystems mounted on the system, unless you specify one particular filesystem, as in the following example:

```
merlin$ df
Filesystem          1024-blocks  Used Available Capacity Mounted on
/dev/sda3              478792    94598   359465     21%    /
```

Note

The df utility displays disk space in 1K blocks unless you set the environment variable POSIXLY_CORRECT in the system startup files. If this variable is set, 512-byte blocks are used to report information. This setting is helpful if you use an older filesystem type that uses disk sectors of 512 bytes.

The df command provides a number of command-line options, most of which are supported in all Linux versions. The available options for df are in the following list:

-a, -all	This option includes all filesystems with zero blocks (usually special filesystems).
-help	This option displays help information.
-i, -inode	This option displays i-node information.
-k, -kilobyte	This option displays disk space in 1K increments. (This option is used to override the environment variable set to 512 bytes blocks; see preceding note).
-p	This option uses POSIX format to display all information of a filesystem on one line with no wrapping. If a filesystem name is longer

	than 20 characters, this option forces the columns to be misaligned.
-T	This option displays the type of filesystem in addition to disk usage information.
-t\<type\>	This option displays only filesystems whose type matches the one you specify.
-v	This option displays the version number.
-x\<type\>	This option displays all filesystems not of the type you list.

18

You can use most of these options in combination as you need them. You can embed the most frequently run commands in a shell script to be run whenever you want.

The du command also displays useful disk usage statistics. When run by itself, the du command displays the amount of disk space used by all files and subdirectories under any specified directory or the current directory if none other is listed (these excerpts have been edited to reduce space):

```
merlin$ du
125                 /info/a_temp
4                   /info/data
265                 /info/data/book
726                 /info/data/book/chap_1
2                   /info/zookeeper
...
273263              /info
merlin$ du /usr/tparker
35                  /usr/tparker/bin
2736                /usr/tparker/book
3                   /usr/tparker/source
...
7326                /usr/tparker
```

The output from du shows each directory's disk usage in blocks in the first column and name of the directory in the second. You can usually convert the blocks in the first column directly to kilobytes used because most Linux filesystems use 1K blocks. (As with df, the du utility displays disk space in 1K blocks unless you set the environment variable POSIXLY_CORRECT in the system startup files.)

If you run du on a large directory tree, the output can be very long (and boring to read). You can summarize the information using the -s (summarize) option:

```
merlin$ du -s /usr/ychow
3315                /usr/ychow
```

The output with this option includes all subdirectories and the directory being reported. This output is useful for determining the amount disk space each user on the system uses.

Note

You can easily combine the du command with other commands to generate lists of disk usage by directory. For example, to show a complete list of all directories in order of size, issue the command

```
du / ¦ sort -rn
```

The du command has several useful options. Most Linux versions support the following options:

-a, -all	This option displays a total count for all files and directories.
-b, -bytes	This option displays size in bytes.
-c, -total	This option displays a grand total.
-k	This option displays the sizes in kilobytes, overriding any environment variable set to 512 bytes.
-l	This option displays the size of all files (including links).
-s	This option displays only totals.
-v	This option displays version information.
-x	This option ignores directories on another filesystem (mounted into the current filesystem, of course).

The du command may take a while to generate output if there are a lot of entries to process, especially when run, for example, from the root filesystem on a heavily loaded system. The best use for the du command is in scripts or cronjobs that are run when the system is not heavily loaded.

MAKING THE MOST OF YOUR DISK SPACE

When you're running out of disk space, the easiest solutions are to buy another disk, create another Linux partition, or add a remote disk to your system. Presumably, if you can do any of these solutions you will, but sometimes expanding the total amount of disk space is not practical or desirable. Instead, the solution is to manage what you have.

As a general rule, disk performance starts to degrade when the system hits 90 percent capacity or more. This system degradation is primarily due to fragmentation of the disk and the heads having move further to access and save files. Many system administrators use about 75 percent capacity as the first warning sign to do something about disk space. You'll develop your own guidelines, but try to avoid running out of disk space; you can find yourself in very awkward circumstances if you do.

A good first step to reducing disk space usage is to examine all the applications and software sets loaded on your system and remove the ones you don't use. For example, if you are not using the C compilers you loaded when you installed Linux, you can remove them and free up over 50M of disk space.

Another good practice is to scan user areas for users with large disk usage. Tell those users to clean up their areas by deleting or archiving material they don't want or need. In many cases, users keep multiple copies of files around, just in case. Remove the old ones! Get rid of automatic backup files, and clean out large log files. Just cleaning out the system logs can free up 30M on some systems. The primary log files you should look at are the following:

/usr/spool/lp/log	printing log
/usr/lib/cron.log	cron log file
/usr/spool/uucp/LOGFILE	UUCP log file

These three files can grow to amazing sizes. There are also log files for all the printers, many communications packages, the system, compilers, and other utilities. Check your filesystem for files that grow unreasonably large. Also check mailboxes, which can collect error messages (such as from a bad cron job) and grow to many megabytes in size.

If you want to keep some of the lines in the log files instead of just deleting them all, use the tail command with the number of lines you want to keep. For example, the following series of commands keeps the first 100 lines of the log file, but deletes the rest:

```
cd /usr/spool/lp
tail -100 log > tmp
mv tmp log
```

Next, get in the habit of routinely backing up material you don't need except as archive material. Use floppy disks, a tape drive, or other archive material and stick the data on the shelf instead of on your hard drive. You'll save lots of room by regularly going through your system and cleaning up files. If you really need to keep them on your hard disk, use compress or gzip to shrink the file size noticeably. To find all files that haven't been accessed (read or write) in a certain number of days, use the find command. This command searches for all files older than 120 days and displays them on-screen:

```
find / -atime +120 -print
```

When you have the list of old files, you can consider archiving them.

You can write a shell script that searches for and deletes unwanted files, such as core files, .bak (and similar backups for editors and word processors)files, .log files, .error files, and so on. You can create a list of the files you want to regularly remove from your system, embed them in a `find` command such as the following one, and execute the command to clean out disk space. The following command looks for all files called core and deletes them:

```
find / -name core -exec rm {} \;
```

The `find` command locates all core files and passes the path to the `rm` command. The trailing backslash and semicolon are necessary to execute the command properly. There are more elegant (and less CPU-intensive) methods of doing the same task, but this command is a solid, reliable method.

UNDERSTANDING LINKS

File links are an oft-misunderstood aspect of filesystems, despite their simplicity. A link, in its simplest form, creates a second filename for a file. For example, if you have the file /usr/bill/testfile and want to have the same file in the /usr/tim directory, you don't have to copy it. Just create a link with the following command:

```
ln /usr/bill/testfile /usr/tim/testfile
```

The format of the command is always the current filename followed by an additional filename, just as with the `cp` or `mv` commands.

The reason for links is basically twofold in this example. First, both the file /usr/bill/testfile and /usr/tim/testfile refer to the exact same file, so any changes made by bill or tim are reflected immediately in the other directory (removing the need to copy files every time). Both bill and tim can modify the file, as long as they don't make changes to the file at the same time.

The link also gets by file permission and ownership problems. If bill owns the file /usr/bill/testfile and is the only one who can write to it, he can create a link to /usr/tim/testfile and set the ownership of the new link to tim. In this way, both bill and tim can work on the same file despite ownerships and permissions, as each copy has its own ownerships. If set correctly, the ownerships and permissions can prevent anyone other than bill and tim from reading or writing to the file.

In the preceding example, the `ln` command is creating hard links. A hard link is a link in the same filesystem with two i-node table entries pointing to the same physical contents (with the same i-node number because they point to the same data). If you want to see the effect of a link on the i-node table, display the i-node entry for a file in a directory, for example:

```
$ ls -i testfile
14253 testfile
```

Then, create a link to another filename and display the i-node entries again:

```
$ ln testfile test2
$ ls -i testfile test2
14253    testfile    14253    test2
```

As you can see, both file i-node numbers are the same. A directory listing of the two files shows that they have their own permissions and ownerships. The only thing indicating a link is the second column of the ls output, which shows a two for the number of links. Deleting a linked filename doesn't delete the file until there are no more links to it.

A symbolic link is another type of link that doesn't use the i-node entry for the link. You used these links when you were creating device drivers, such as /dev/modem instead of /dev/cua1. The -s option to the ln command creates a symbolic link. For example, you can recreate the preceding example with a symbolic link:

```
$ ls -i bigfile
6253 bigfile
$ ln -s bigfile anotherfile
$ ls -i bigfile anotherfile
6253 bigfile    8358 anotherfile
```

As you can see, the i-node table entries are different. A directory listing shows the symbolic link as an arrow:

```
lrwxrwxrwx   1  root   root    6 Sep 16:35   anotherfile -> bigfile
-rw-rw-r--   1  root   root    2 Sep 17:23   bigfile
```

The file permissions for a symbolic link are always set to lrwxrwxrwx. Permissions for access to the symbolic link name are determined by the permissions and ownership of the file it is symbolically linked to (bigfile in this case).

The difference between hard links and symbolic links is more than just i-node table entries. You can create symbolic links to files that don't exist yet, which you can't do with hard links. You can also follow symbolic links to find out what they point to, which is an almost impossible task with hard links. The kernel processes the two types of links differently, too.

SUMMARY

This chapter examined the common disk and filesystem utilities you have available for checking the integrity of the filesystem. It also looked at the basic methods you should use to keep down disk space usage. This chapter also briefly examined links and how you can use both symbolic and hard links to help provide access to some files. Following these simple steps can make your life a lot easier.

18

FILESYSTEMS AND DISKS

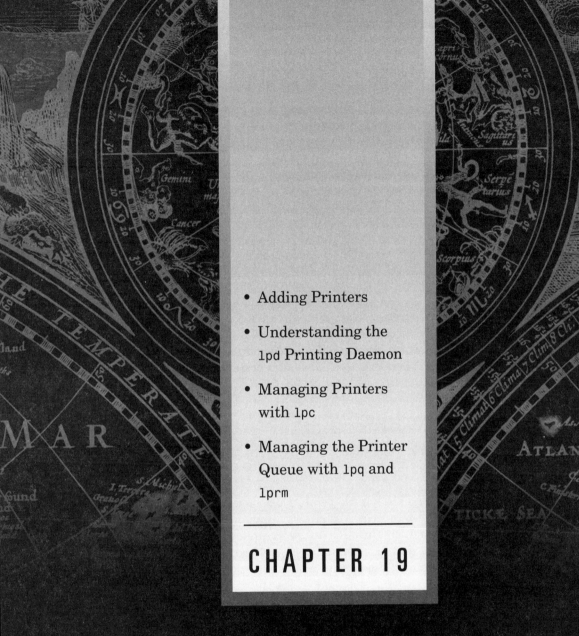

- Adding Printers

- Understanding the lpd Printing Daemon

- Managing Printers with lpc

- Managing the Printer Queue with lpq and lprm

CHAPTER 19

Printers and Print Spoolers

Printers can cause quite a few problems for system administrators because the configuration and handling of a printer under Linux is considerably different than under DOS or OS/2. The unintuitive nature of the printer commands also complicates the handling of printers and print systems. Despite these quibbles, printers are quite easy to configure as long as you know a little about Linux, device drivers, and the printers you are using. Managing the printer queues is also relatively easy, but like many things in Linux, you must know the tricks to make the system work for you.

The printing capabilities of Linux are not as powerful and easy-to-use as most commercial versions of UNIX. Linux is based on BSD UNIX, which is not the most talented version with respect to printer administration. Luckily, few users use more than one or two printers in a typical parallel-port or serial-port based installation, so administration requirements are simplified enormously. When you work with large, networked printer environments, however, Linux's limitations in this area are more apparent. A word of warning: Linux's printer administration routines have a reputation for quirky behavior, such as suddenly stopping the print spooler for no apparent reason!

ADDING PRINTERS

Linux supports both parallel and serial printers, as well as network printers (available from another machine on the local area network). Most parallel and serial printers are character mode devices, although a few high-speed printers are block mode devices (although block mode printers are usually much too expensive for a small Linux-based system). Unfortunately, Linux does not have a simple-to-use printer installation and configuration utility like many UNIX versions, so you must create printer devices and files manually. (A few printer installation and configuration scripts are beginning to appear, although they are not in general use yet.)

Parallel printers are referred to as devices /dev/lp0, /dev/lp1, or /dev/lp2, depending on the number of the parallel port with which they are used. Most printers attached to a PC parallel port are attached to /dev/lp0, the first parallel device.

Parallel port device	I/O address	DOS equivalent
/dev/lp0	0x03bc	LPT1
/dev/lp1	0x0378	LPT2
/dev/lp2	0x0278	LPT3

Linux uses the mknod (make node) command to create a parallel printer device. The command to make a parallel printer device on the first parallel port (/dev/lp0) is

```
mknod -m 620 /dev/lp0 c 6 0
```

In this example, the device /dev/lp0 is created as a character mode device with major device number six and minor device number zero. (See Chapter 6, "Devices and Device Drivers" for more information about device drivers and device numbers.) Usually, minor device numbers start at zero and are incremented upwards. Because this printer is the first one added, the minor device number is set to zero. The -m option sets the file permission mask (to 620 in this case).

After you create the printer device driver file, you must change the ownership of the device driver to root, daemon, or root.daemon. The owner root is a good default value, but root.daemon is better because it adds a little more security to the ownerships by setting the owner to root and the group to daemon with a single command:

```
chown root.daemon /dev/lp0
```

After changing the ownership of the file, check the file permissions. Set them to mode 620 by using the following command:

```
chmod 620 /dev/lp0
```

To configure a device other than the first parallel port (/dev/lp0), you must change the device name itself to the device number. For each possible parallel port, the mknod commands are as follows:

```
mknod -m 620 /dev/lp0 c 6 0
mknod -m 620 /dev/lp1 c 6 1
mknod -m 620 /dev/lp2 c 6 2
```

In these examples, the minor device numbers have been incremented to correspond to the port number. Although numbering the devices in this manner is not absolutely necessary, it can help with identification when you want to know which port the device is hanging off of.

After issuing the mknod and chown commands, check to ensure that the ownerships are set properly. You should also create a spool directory for the printer. The permissions and ownership requirements of the spool directory are important and are discussed in "The /etc/printcap File" section later in this chapter.

UNDERSTANDING THE *LPD* PRINTING DAEMON

Printing services are handled by a daemon called lpd (line printer daemon). The lpd daemon is usually started automatically in the /etc/rc boot process when the system moves to multiuser mode. The lpd daemon handles a number of tasks and keeps running as long as Linux is active (unless terminated by the superuser or a daemon crash). One of the important parts of the daemon's startup procedures is to read the printer configuration file, /etc/printcap.

The /etc/printcap file is used to identify instructions for communicating with all the printers that are configured and attached to the system (in the same manner that /etc/termcap contains terminal definitions). Once it has started itself, lpd starts up two other daemons called listen and accept that handle any incoming print request.

You probably won't ever have to modify the lpd daemon. Because the Linux daemon is a little unstable, though, you may have to restart or terminate it while you make some configuration changes. To start the lpd daemon, use this syntax:

```
lpd [-l] [port]
```

The -l option starts a logging process that copies a note to a log file every time a print request is handled. Although the -l option can be useful when you're debugging a printer installation or configuration, be careful about leaving it running for too long—the log files tend to become very large. If you do keep logging active, use a cron process to clean the log file at regular intervals.

The port option of the lpd command enables you to specify an Internet port number for the daemon if you want the system default information to be ignored. You will probably never have to use this option on a stand-alone or small network, but it can be useful with very large networked printing systems (which are unlikely to be based on Linux).

When a print request is received over the network (or locally), the lpd daemon performs a short validation routine to see whether the user who sent the request is allowed to use the printer. This routine uses the /etc/hosts.equiv and /etc/hosts.lpd files. If the machine name of the sending user is not in either file, the print request is refused. Your local machine is always in hosts.equiv (as localhost), so all users on your machine can have their print requests granted.

If you have to terminate the lpd daemon, obtain its process ID number using the ps command, and then issue a kill command with that process number. Chapter 20, "Managing Processes," explains these steps in more detail. When the lpd daemon is terminated, no print requests are accepted.

PRINT SPOOLERS

When a print request (often called a print job) is received by lpd (or its associated listen and accept processes), the pages to be printed are copied to another area, called the print spool area, of the filesystem. This action frees up your console when you issue a print request and enables you to continue to make changes to the files you want to print after they have been sent to the daemon.

In most cases, the print spool area is in the /usr/spool/lp directory. Under this spool directory, each installed printer has a dedicated directory, which is usually given the printer's name specified during the printer installation routine. For example, a printer called hplaser uses the spool directory /usr/spool/hplaser. All the print requests for each printer are stored in its directory. In this directory, each request is assigned a unique filename and a print request identification number. The daemon for this printer adds the print request number to a queue and notifies you of what the number is. You can then use the print request identification number to check the status of the print request or remove the request from the queue.

Some versions of Linux let you set the size of the print spool area though an entry in the minfree file in the spool directory. The minfree file gives the number of disk blocks (usually a block is 1K) set aside for spooling requests. You can change the minfree file with any ASCII editor. If you have lots of disk space, you needn't worry about this value because the spooler will use available space as necessary. If you are tight for disk space, though, you may want to reserve a little space for the spooler that can't be used for other reasons. The size of the disk space reserved for the spooler should be dependent on the number of users and the amount of printing they will do. A good rule of thumb is about 100K per user for normal use.

Each printer's spool directory may contain two special files called status and lock. Each file is one line long and can be modified with an ASCII editor. The files contain a description of the current state of the printer. The lpd daemon creates and manages these files, which several printer commands use display status information to the user.

THE PRINTING PROCESS

This section follows a typical print request through the print system so you can see how the printer daemons work and how Linux handles each stage of the request. When you issue a print request with a print command (such as lpr), the command generates output for the printer to print. The command then copies that output into the queue in the spool directory for the printer you have requested.

You can specify the printer destination on the print command line or set a default printer name as an environment variable so the system always knows which printer to use. After determining the destination printer name, lpr checks the file /etc/printcap for the printer's configuration information (including the spool directory name).

Note

The lpr program is the only one in the Linux system that can queue files for printing. Any other program that offers printing capabilities, including most editors and word processors, executes the print request by calling lpr.

As part of the spooling task, lpr checks for any special instructions on how to print the file. These instructions may refer to fonts, paper sizes, colors, processing languages, or any other printer configuration information. Printer instructions can come from the command line (in the form of arguments you provide with the print command), from environment variables (set up by the shell's startup files or you), or from the system's default values.

When the print request is copied into the spool directory, lpr creates two files. One file has the letters cf (control file) followed by the print ID number. This cf file contains information about the print job, including the owner's name and special printing instructions such as line spacing or paper selection. The other file starts with the letters df (data file) and holds the contents of the file to be printed. After lpr creates the df file, it sends a signal to the lpd daemon that indicates that a print job is waiting in the spool directory. The lpd daemon then starts a daemon to handle the printer's queue (if one isn't already running). A daemon is present for every printer queue as long as there is something to print. When the print queue is empty, the printer daemon terminates.

After lpd gets the print job signal from lpr, it checks the file /etc/printcap to see whether the printer is a local or remote printer. For remote printers (one attached to another machine on the network), lpd starts a network connection to the remote machine and transfers both the control and data files to the remote's spool directories and informs the remote machine's lpd daemon that a print request is queued. To end the process for a remote print request, lpd deletes the local copies of the cf and df files. For local printer requests, lpd checks to make sure the printer exists and is enabled, and then sends the print request to the daemon running that printer queue. Once the files have been printed, they are deleted from the spool directories.

THE /ETC/PRINTCAP FILE

As you have seen already in this section, the /etc/printcap file is used by both the print commands (such as lpr) and the lpd daemon. The /etc/printcap file contains information about every printer that is accessible from the Linux machine, including all remote printers that have been configured on the local machine. The following extract from the /etc/printcap file for the Hewlett Packard LaserJet 4M laser printer shows the straightforward format of this kind of file:

```
# HP Laserjet
lp|hplj|hplaserj-tparker|HP LaserJet 4M next to the water fountain:\
     :lp=/dev/lp0:\
     :sd=/usr/spool/lp/lp0:\
     :lf=/usr/spool/lp/errorlog:\
     :mx#0:\
     :of=/usr/spool/lp0/hpjlp:\
```

Comments anywhere in the information are identified by a pound sign (also called a hash mark) in the first column. The first field in each printer's entry is a list of all the names users can use to refer to the printer. These names can be used with environment variables and as options on the lpr command line. All the valid printer names are separated by a vertical bar. Usually each entry has at least three names: a short name that is four characters or less (such as hplj), a more complete name with an owner, if necessary (such as hplaser-tparker), and a full descriptive name with any other information necessary to identify the printer to a user (such as HP LaserJet 4M next to the water fountain).

19

*N*ote

If a print job is submitted without a destination name and one cannot be determined from environment variable values, the job is routed to the Linux system default printer name lp. Therefore, one of the printers (usually the system default printer) should also have the name lp as part of its identifying names in order to prevent error messages.

Following the printer name is a set of two-character parameters and values used to define configuration information about the printer. The format of these entries follows one of the following models:

NN	A Boolean value
NN=string	Set equal to string
NN#number	Set not equal to number

Most assignments in this area of the /etc/printcap file are shown with colons beginning and ending each definition to enhance readability (and make the file easier for the print utilities to parse for information). Null values are allowed; you can create them by putting two colons together with no space between them.

When you use a Boolean value (with no assignment following the two character identifier), the value is set to True by default. If you want the value to be False, don't include the two-character identifier in the description. You use Booleans to specify simple information, such as printer control language support.

As with terminal definitions in the /etc/termcap file, many codes are allowed in the /etc/printcap file. A few of the more important and prevalent parameters are worth mentioning as they are useful for administration purposes:

sd	The spool directory
lf	The log directory for error messages
af	Accounting log file
mx	What type of files can be printed
of	Output filter program to be used when printing

Not all these parameters need to be present in every printer definition in the /etc/printcap file, but they are likely to be present as they provide basic information.

The sd parameter specifies the spool directory for the printer. As mentioned earlier, all printers should have their own spool directories. The spool directories are usually composed by taking the printer name and creating a directory with that name under the /usr/spool directory, such as /usr/spool/lp/hplj and /usr/spool/lp/epson. Spool directories are necessary for both remote and local printers.

Note

When you add a new printer is added to the system, you may have to create a spool directory manually by using mkdir. Set the permissions for the spool directory to 775. The directory must be owned by root or daemon, and you should set the group ID to root or daemon as well. In both cases, daemon is arguably the better ID for user and group, although root works fine (but may pose a very slight security problem).

The lf parameter specifies the log directory for error messages. You can put the printer error log file anywhere on the system, although most Linux systems have it in the /usr/spool/lp directory for easy access. All printers can share the error log, as each log entry includes the name of the printer. Putting all the error messages in one directory makes it easier to clean up the log files on a regular basis.

A printer accounting log file, as specified by the parameter af, is used to record the number of printouts sent by a user on systems where users are charged for printing. When an accounting file is used, an entry is written to the accounting log file after a print job is finished. If the system doesn't use accounting records (most Linux systems don't), you can ignore the accounting log file entry in the /etc/printcap file, although you may want to have the accounting file active for statistical purposes. You can display account information with the Linux pac command. Use the man pac command to display the man pages for more information about pac.

The mx parameter enables you to identify the types of files to be printed. Usually this parameter is set to mx#0, meaning that there are no restrictions on the types of files. You may want to restrict the type of printing on some lasers or inkjets that have high per page costs, for example, or prevent pages with color instructions from being printed as grayscales on a monochrome laser printer.

You use output filters, specified by the parameter of, to modify the format of the outgoing print file to fit the printer. For example, a common output filter changes the number of lines per page. Many laser printers can't handle 66 lines per page, so the output filter repaginates output to 60 lines per page (or whatever the number of lines per page is set to). Sometimes special codes must be added to force line feeds, font changes, or paper bin selections. All these items are part of the output filter. Several other types of filters are available, but the output filter is the most common.

Managing Printers with *LPC*

Linux systems control printers through a utility called lpc. The lpc program enables you to do several important functions involving the printers on your Linux system:

- ◆ Display printer status information
- ◆ Enable or disable the printer
- ◆ Enable or disable the printer queue
- ◆ Remove all print requests from a printer's queue

19

PRINTERS AND PRINT SPOOLERS

◆ Promote a particular print request to the top of the queue

◆ Make changes to the lpd daemon

You cannot use the lpc program for remote printers. It only affects those printers directly attached and configured on the local machine. If you must manage a remote printer, log into the remote machine as root and make the changes through that login.

Warning

> The lpc utility is one of the most unpredictable and unreliable programs included with the Linux operating system. It can hang up for no obvious reason and can display faulty status messages.

When executed on the command line without any arguments, lpc prompts you for a command. The following list summarizes all the valid lpc commands and their arguments (a vertical bar indicates a choice of arguments):

◆ abort *printer_name* ¦ all   This command is similar to the stop command except that it doesn't allow a print job that is currently being printed to finish before stopping the printer. When you use it with the all argument, all printers are stopped. Any job that is terminated by the abort command is requeued when the printer is restarted.

◆ clean *printer_name* ¦ all   This command removes all print jobs that are queued, including any active print jobs. (In many cases, the currently printing job proceeds normally because it already has been passed to the printer daemon or the printer's RAM buffer and can't be stopped by lpc.) If you use the all argument, all printers have their print queues removed.

◆ disable *printer_name* ¦ all   This command disables the spooling of print requests to the printer (or all printers, depending on the argument). Any jobs that are already queued are unaffected. Any user trying to send a print job to a disabled printer receives a message indicating that the printer is disabled and the print job is refused. Printers are enabled and disabled through changes in the lock file in the spool directory.

◆ down *printer_name message*   This command is used to take a printer off-line (usually for extended periods). You can include a message of any length as well. This message is placed in the status file in the spool directory and is displayed to users trying to queue to the printer. Use the down command when a printer has serious problems and must be removed from the system.

◆ enable *printer_name* ¦ all   This command enables the spooling of print requests to the printer (or all printers) after a halt.

◆ exit   This command exits from lpc (the same as quit).

◆ help or ?   This command shows a short list of all lpc commands. If you type in an lpc command after the help command, the system displays a one-line description of the command you typed.

◆ quit   This command exits from lpc (the same as exit).

◆ restart *printer_name* ¦ all   This command restarts the printer daemon. This command is usually used after the daemon has died for an inexplicable reason. If you supply the all argument is supplied, all printer daemons are restarted.

◆ start *printer_name*   The command starts the printer queue daemon for the printer you specify, allowing it to print requests.

◆ status *printer_name*   This command displays the printer name, whether it has the spool queue enabled, whether printing is enabled, the number of entries in the print queue, and the status of the daemon for that printer. If no entries are in the queue, there will be no printer daemon active. However, if there are entries in the queue and the printer daemon shows as no daemon present, then the daemon has died and must be started again with the restart command.

◆ stop *printer_name*   This command stops the printer. Print requests can still be spooled, but they are not printed until the printer is started. If a job is being printed when you issue the stop command, the printer stops after it completes the job. The start and stop commands alter the contents of the lock file in the print spool directory. The stop command also kills the daemon for spooling to that printer.

◆ topq *printer_name* *print_ID*   This command moves the print request with *print_ID* to the top of the print queue.

◆ topq *printer_name* *username*   This command moves all print requests owned by *username* to the top of the queue.

◆ up *printer_name*   This command reactivates a printer that was taken down. See the down command for more information.

The lpc utility is not very user-friendly, but it is the only way to handle the printers and their queues in Linux. Several front-end menu-driven utilities are beginning to appear that simplify this task, but they are of variable quality and are not widely available.

19

PRINTERS AND PRINT SPOOLERS

MANAGING THE PRINTER QUEUE WITH *LPQ* AND *LPRM*

Instead of totally relying on the lpc command, you can use the several commands that help you administer the printer queue directly. These commands are designed to simplify the two tasks that are commonly required by a system administrator: displaying the current queue and removing print jobs in a queue.

To display the current print queue for any printer, use the lpq command. It has the following syntax:

```
lpq [-l] [-Pprinter_name] [job_ID ...] [username ...]
```

With no arguments, lpq displays information about the current printer queues. The lpq command normally displays information about who queued the print job, where it is in the queue, the files being printed, and the total size of the files. The -l option displays more information about each entry in the printer queue. Usually only one line of information is displayed.

You can display a specific printer with the -P option followed by the printer's name. If no name is supplied, the default system printer is displayed. If one or more job_IDs or usernames are provided, only information about the specified jobs or jobs queued by the specified user is shown.

To remove files from a printer queue, use the lprm command. This command is often mistyped as lpr, which does not remove the file from the queue. To use lprm, you must know the print job ID, or, if you are logged in as root, you can remove all jobs for a particular printer. The syntax of the lprm command is as follows:

```
lprm [-Pprinter_name] [-] [job_ID ...] [username ...]
```

If the single hyphen argument is used, lprm removes all jobs owned by the user who issues the command. If you are logged in as root and issue this command, all print jobs are removed.

You can remove a particular printer's jobs by using the -P option. For example, the command

```
lprm -Phplj -
```

removes all print jobs queued on the printer hplj by the user who issues the command or all print jobs for that printer if the command is issued by root. If a print job ID or a username is supplied as an argument, lprm removes the specified job or all jobs submitted by the specified user. If no arguments are supplied, the currently active job submitted by the user is deleted.

Warning

It is easy to accidentally remove all print jobs for a printer when you use the lprm command while logged in as root. Take care to use the proper syntax.

When lprm removes files from the queue, it echoes back a message to the display. If there are no files to remove, nothing is echoed back (and you will be left wondering what, if anything, happened).

Note

Because users cannot access the Linux printer spooling directories, they can only remove queued print jobs with the lprm command. If you are a system administrator, you may want to let all system users know how to use this command to save unwanted print jobs from printing.

If you try to use lprm on a job that is currently being printed, it may not be terminated properly as the file may already reside in the printer's buffer. In some cases, terminating a job that is currently printing can cause the printer to lock because some output format files cannot handle the termination instructions and freeze when the lock file in the spool directory changes. In cases like this, you must use the ps command to find the output filter process ID and then kill that filter.

Tip

When you have a printer lockup problem that doesn't solve itself when you use the lpc utility, try killing the lpd daemon and restarting it. If that doesn't work, you probably have to reboot the entire system.

SUMMARY

Handling printers on a Linux system is not onerous, as long as you know the commands and processes that perform the daily tasks you need. Installing the printer is quite easy, although you have to be careful to set the permissions and ownerships properly. Once installed, printers tend to be either troublefree or troublesome. All you can do is hope for the former!

- Understanding Processes

- Using the ps Command

- Using kill

- Using the top Command

CHAPTER 20

Managing Processes

Everything that runs on a Linux system is a process. Knowing how to manage the processes running on your Linux system is a critical aspect of system administration. This chapter tells you how to find out which processes are running on your system and what they are doing. You can then use this information to manage the processes as necessary.

In the course of discussing processes, this chapter doesn't bother explaining the mechanics behind how processes are allocated or how the Linux kernel manages to time slice all the processes to run a multitasking operating system. Instead, this chapter looks at the nitty-gritty aspects of process control you need to keep your system running smoothly.

UNDERSTANDING PROCESSES

You may hear the terms process and job used when talking about operating systems. A formal definition of a process is that it is a single program running in its own virtual address space. Using this definition, everything running under Linux is a process. A job, on the other hand, may involve several commands executing in series. Likewise, a single command line issued at a shell prompt may involve more than one process, especially when pipes or redirection are involved.

Several types of processes are involved with the Linux operating system. Each has its own special features and attributes:

An interactive process is a process initiated from (and controlled by) a shell. Interactive processes may be in the foreground or background.

A batch process is a process that is not associated with a terminal but is submitted to a queue to be executed sequentially.

A daemon process is a process that runs in the background until it's required. This kind of process is usually initiated when Linux boots.

USING THE *ps* COMMAND

The easiest method of finding out which processes are running on your system is to use the ps (process status) command. The ps command is available to all system users, as well as root, although the output changes a little depending on whether you are logged in as root when you issue the command. When you are logged in as a normal system user (not root) and issue the ps command by itself, it displays information about every process you are running. The following output is an example of what you might see:

```
$ ps
  PID TTY STAT   TIME COMMAND
   41 v01 S      0:00 -bash
  134 v01 R      0:00 ps
```

The output of the ps command is always organized in columns. The first column is labeled PID, which means process identification number. The PID is a number that Linux assigns to each process to help in handling all processes. PIDs start at zero and increment by one for each process being run, up to some system-determined number (such as 65,564). When Linux reaches the highest number, it starts numbering from the lowest number again, skipping the numbers used by active processes. Usually, the lowest number processes are the system kernel and daemons, which start when Linux boots and remain active as long as Linux is running. To manipulate processes (to terminate them, for example), you must use the PID.

The TTY column in the ps command output shows you which terminal the process was started from. If you are logged in as a user, this column usually lists your terminal or console window. If you are running on multiple console windows, you see all the processes you started in every displayed window.

The STAT column in the ps command output shows you the current status of the process. The two most common entries in the STAT column are S for sleeping and R for running. A sleeping process is one that isn't currently active. A running process is one that is currently executing on the CPU. Processes may switch between sleeping and running many times every second.

The TIME column shows the total amount of system (CPU) time used by the process so far. These numbers tend to be very small for most processes, as they require only a short time to complete. The numbers under the TIME column are a total of the CPU time, not the amount of time the process has been alive.

Finally, the NAME column contains the name of the process you are running. This name is usually the command you entered, although some commands start up other processes. These processes are called child processes, and they show up in the ps output as though you had entered them as commands.

As a general convention, login shells have a hyphen placed before their name (such as -bash in the preceding output) to help you distinguish the startup shell from any shells you may have started afterwards. Any other shells that appear in the output don't have the hyphen in front of the name, as the following example shows:

```
$ ps
  PID TTY STAT   TIME COMMAND
   46 v01 S      0:01 -bash
   75 v01 S      0:00 phksh
   96 v01 R      0:00 bash
  123 v01 R      0:00 ps
```

This example shows that the user's startup shell is bash (PID 46) and that the user started up the Korn shell (pdksh, PID 75) and another Bourne shell (bash, PID 96) afterwards. Notice also that the process status, ps, appears in this output (and the previous one) because it is running when you issued the command. The ps command always appears in the output.

20

When a user issues the ps command, that user sees only his own processes. If you issue the ps command when you are logged in as the superuser, you see all the processes on the system because the root login owns everything running. Because this command can produce very long outputs, especially on a system with several users, you may want to pipe the output from the ps command to a page filter (such as more or less) or save the output in a file for further examination. Both commands are shown in the following code:

```
ps | more
ps > /tmp/ps_file
```

The ps command has a number of options and arguments, although most system administrators use only a couple of common command line formats. A useful ps option for checking user processes is -u, which adds several columns to the output of the ps command. The following output is from a user (not root) command using this option:

```
$ ps -u
USER        PID %CPU %MEM SIZE  RSS TTY STAT START   TIME COMMAND
bill         41  0.1  6.8  364  472 v01 S    23:19   0:01 -bash
bill        138  0.0  3.3   72  228 v01 R    23:34   0:00 ps -u
```

The most important addition to the output is the USER column, which shows who started and owns the process. The name listed under the USER column is the user's login name, as found in the /etc/passwd file (ps does a lookup procedure in the /etc/passwd file to convert the user identification number to the proper username).

This option also adds the column labeled %CPU, which shows the percentage of CPU time that the process has used so far. The column %MEM shows the percentage of your system's memory currently used by the process. These numbers can be handy for finding processes that consume far too much CPU or memory. If you see a user process that has very high usage, check to make sure it is a valid process and not a runaway that will continue to drain your system's resources.

When you issue this command logged in as root, you see all the processes running on the system. As before, consider paginating the output to make it readable. You also can use the -u option to specify a user's processes by adding the appropriate username. For example, if you are logged in as root and want to see only yvonne's processes, issue the following command:

```
ps -u yvonne
```

Most users can issue this command to examine other user's processes, as well. This command lets them find out who is hogging all the CPU time! The -u option also enables the superuser see the processes users are running when they report problems without having to wade through all the system processes as well. Finally, the -u option with a username is handy to help terminate user processes when they are hung or start to run away.

Users can see all the processes running on the system (instead of just the processes they started) by using the -a option. Because the superuser sees all the processes on the system anyway, the root login doesn't have to use this option, although it is still legal to use it. This output doesn't change, though. When issued by a user (not root), the -a option produces the following output:

```
$ ps -a
  PID TTY STAT   TIME COMMAND
    1 psf S     0:00 init
    6 psf S     0:00 update (sync)
   23 psf S     0:00 /usr/sbin/crond -l10
   29 psf S     0:00 /usr/sbin/syslogd
   31 psf S     0:00 /usr/sbin/klogd
   33 psf S     0:00 /usr/sbin/lpd
   40 psf S     0:00 selection -t ms
   42 v02 S     0:01 -bash
   43 v03 S     0:00 /sbin/agetty 38400 tty3
   44 v04 S     0:00 /sbin/agetty 38400 tty4
   45 v05 S     0:00 /sbin/agetty 38400 tty5
   46 v06 S     0:00 /sbin/agetty 38400 tty6
   41 v01 S     0:01 -bash
  140 v01 R     0:00 ps -a
```

This relatively short output shows a very lightly loaded system. Most of the entries are the Linux operating system kernel and daemons, as well as serial port getty processes. Only the last two commands are started by the user who issued the ps command. Of course, you can't tell who started each process with this output. To see who started each process, you can combine the -u and -a options (note that you use only one hyphen, followed by the option letters):

```
$ ps -au
USER       PID %CPU %MEM SIZE  RSS TTY STAT START   TIME COMMAND
root         1  0.0  3.0   44  208 psf S   23:19  0:00 init
root         6  0.0  1.8   24  128 psf S   23:19  0:00 update (sync)
root        23  0.0  3.0   56  212 psf S   23:19  0:00 /usr/sbin/crond -l10
root        29  0.0  3.4   61  236 psf S   23:19  0:00 /usr/sbin/syslogd
root        31  0.0  2.8   36  200 psf S   23:19  0:00 /usr/sbin/klogd
root        33  0.0  2.9   64  204 psf S   23:19  0:00 /usr/sbin/lpd
root        40  0.0  2.0   32  140 psf S   23:19  0:00 selection -t ms
root        42  0.1  6.9  372  480 v02 S   23:19  0:01 -bash
root        43  0.0  2.3   37  164 v03 S   23:19  0:00 /sbin/agetty 38400 tt
root        44  0.0  2.3   37  164 v04 S   23:19  0:00 /sbin/agetty 38400 tt
root        45  0.0  2.3   37  164 v05 S   23:19  0:00 /sbin/agetty 38400 tt
root        46  0.0  2.3   37  164 v06 S   23:19  0:00 /sbin/agetty 38400 tt
yvonne      41  0.0  6.8  364  472 v01 S   23:19  0:01 -bash
yvonne    2519  0.0  3.4   80  236 v01 R   23:39  0:00 ps -ua
```

This command produces a list with all the same columns as the -u option, but it shows all the processes running on the system. The order in which you enter the options doesn't matter, so -au is functionally the same as -ua.

A few other `ps` command line options are occasionally useful. The `-1` option adds information about which processes started each process (useful when you want to identify child processes):

```
$ ps -1
  F   UID  PID PPID PRI NI SIZE  RSS WCHAN     STAT TTY   TIME COMMAND
  0   501   41    1  15  0  364  472 114d9c    S    v01  0:00 -bash
  0   501  121   41  29  0   64  208 0         R    v01  0:00 ps -1
```

The PPID (Parent Process ID) column shows which process started that particular process. The preceding extract shows that the `ps` command was started by the `bash` process, as the shell is the parent of all user commands. The PPID for the login Bourne shell is PID 1, which is the `init` process of the operating system. (Think about what this relationship means. If init ever terminates, all other processes die, too.)

Note

> The Linux version of the `ps` command has a few idiosyncrasies. The hyphen before an option is not strictly necessary, so `ps u` works as well as `ps -u`. However, because UNIX convention (and most UNIX versions) require a hyphen, you should use them.

Most system administrators get by with three versions of the `ps` command (when logged in as root). To display information about the system as a whole, the following two command lines show practically everything there is to know about processes:

```
ps -ef
ps -le
```

The meaning of the primary columns in the output from the two commands has been mentioned earlier in this section. The rest of the columns are either evident from their shortform or are not that important. For complete information, see the `ps` man page (which is not entirely accurate or complete, unfortunately).

USING *KILL*

A process that locks up a terminal or doesn't do anything is generally referred to as a hung process. Sometimes a user has a process that doesn't terminate properly (especially common with programmers). This kind of process is called a runaway process. In both cases, the only way to get rid of the process and restore some normalcy to the system is to terminate the process by issuing the `kill` command.

To use `kill`, you must have access to another window or console where you can issue commands. If your terminal is completely locked up, you will have to find another one from which to log in. As a user, you can only kill your own processes; you cannot affect any process another user or the system is running. As root, you can terminate any process with the `kill` command.

In order to use the `kill` command, you need the process identification number (PID) of the process to be terminated. Use the `ps` command, as explained in the preceding section, to find out this information. Next, use the `kill` command with the PID as an argument. For example, the following terminal session shows a user process called `bad_prog` started by walter that has hung up and needs to be killed. The PID is obtained by displaying all of walter's processes:

```
$ ps -u walter
USER       PID %CPU %MEM SIZE  RSS TTY STAT START   TIME COMMAND
walter     561  0.1  6.8  364  472 v01 S   13:19   0:01 -bash
walter     598  9.3  4.1 2736  472 v01 R   15:26   2:01 bad_prog
$ kill 598
```

When you issue the `kill` command, you don't get any return message if it works properly. The only way to verify that the process was properly terminated is to issue another `ps` command and look for the PID or process name.

Because some processes spawn child processes with different PIDs, you must be sure to check that all the child processes are terminated as well. The best way to do this is to watch the names of the executing processes for a few minutes to ensure that the child isn't dormant, only to return later. This problem usually happens while the child processes are being generated by a parent. Check the PPID column (use the `ps -l` option) to see which process is the parent and terminate that process as well.

Note

When you are killing processes and are logged in as root, make sure you type the correct PID or you may inadvertently terminate another process. Check the PID carefully! Also, don't kill any system processes unless you know what they do and why they need to be terminated.

If the process doesn't terminate properly with the `kill` command, you need to use sterner measures. The `kill` command has several levels of operation. When issued with no arguments other than the PID, the `kill` command tries to gracefully terminate the process (which means any open files are closed and `kill` is generally polite to the process). If this command doesn't work, use the `-9` option, which is a little more forceful in its attempt to terminate the process. Essentially, the command tries to terminate the process without regard to open files or child processes, although you seldom have to worry about problems with this type of termination because Linux handles it all. For example, to forcefully terminate the process with PID 726, issue the following command:

```
kill -9 726
```

If the process still doesn't terminate, it's time to get ruthless and use the -15 option, the most potent form of kill command. Only use this option when the other forms of the kill command are not working, as it doesn't try to be nice to the process or any open files at all. To use this option on the same sample process, issue the command:

```
kill -15 726
```

If that doesn't work, the process may be unkillable. This situation does happen quite often with Linux, and the only solution is to shut down and reboot the machine.

To help prevent a user from killing other user's processes, ps checks for the process owner when you issue a kill command. If a user tries to kill another user's process, a message like the following one is displayed:

```
kill:  - Not owner
```

The superuser doesn't get this message because the superuser login can kill anything except some system processes (such as init).

USING THE *TOP* COMMAND

Sometimes you may want to watch the system's behavior to spot problems, monitor system loading, or check for runaway processes. Instead of running the ps command at regular intervals, Linux offers the top command as an alternative. When you issue the top command, the screen shows a continual snapshot of the system, taken every five seconds (unless you specify a different time increment). By default, top shows the most CPU-intensive tasks on the system as a full-screen display.

The syntax of the top command allows you to alter much of the utility's behavior from the command line, although most changes are also available from within top:

```
top [-] [d delay] [q] [S] [s] [i]
```

The command line options supported by top are as follows:

d	Specifies the delay between screen updates (can be changed from within top using the s command)
q	Forces top to refresh without a delay
S	Uses cumulative mode (the CPU time each listed process shows includes any children the process spawned)
s	Runs top in secure mode (disables interactive commands)
i	Ignores idle or zombie processes

The top command can be very useful when you are tweaking a system's performance or want to see how heavily used the system is when a large number of users or processes are involved. Many system administrators run top with a slow delay (such as every 60 seconds) on a space terminal or console window throughout the day to get a fast assessment of the system's performance and load. If you do run top for a long period, use the s option to switch on secure mode. This option disables many of the interactive commands that can enable any user with access to the top screen to manipulate processes.

The output from the top command shows several summary lines at the top of the screen, followed by a list of the most CPU-intensive processes:

```
1:58pm  up 59 min,  2 users,  load average: 0.13, 0.34, 0.98
26 processes: 25 sleeping, 1 running, 0 zombie, 0 stopped
CPU states:  0.9% user,  6.4% system,  0.0% nice, 92.7% idle
Mem:   14620K av,  6408K used,  8212K free,  4632K shrd,  2328K buff
Swap:     0K av,     0K used,     0K free

  PID USER     PRI  NI SIZE  RES SHRD STAT %CPU %MEM  TIME COMMAND
  236 root      19   0   93  316  344 R     7.3  2.1  0:00 top
    1 root       1   0   48  232  308 S     0.0  1.5  0:00 init
   63 root       2   0  388  556  572 S     0.0  3.8  0:00 -bash
  209 root       1   0   98  320  356 S     0.0  2.1  0:00 in.telnetd
   24 root       1   0   60  228  296 S     0.0  1.5  0:00 /usr/sbin/crond -110
                                                                             K
    6 root       1   0   36  164  336 S     0.0  1.1  0:00 bdflush (daemon)
    7 root       1   0   36  168  340 S     0.0  1.1  0:00 update (bdflush)
   38 root       1   0   73  280  332 S     0.0  1.9  0:00 /usr/sbin/syslogd
   40 root       1   0   44  240  320 S     0.0  1.6  0:00 /usr/sbin/klogd
   42 bin        1   0   84  240  320 S     0.0  1.6  0:00 /usr/sbin/rpc.portmap
   44 root       1   0   76  292  320 S     0.0  1.9  0:00 /usr/sbin/inetd
   46 root       1   0   68  212  304 S     0.0  1.4  0:00 /usr/sbin/lpd
   51 root       1   0  116  280  376 S     0.0  1.9  0:00 /usr/sbin/rpc.nfsd
```

The top utility displays several useful pieces of information in the first few lines. The uptime display on the first line shows the total amount of time the system has been up since the last reset. Following the uptime are three load averages that are constantly updated. The load averages show the average number of processes run in the last one, five, and fifteen minutes.

The total number of processes that are running at the time of the snapshot are shown on the second line, broken down following the total into the number of processes currently running, sleeping (not executing), zombie (status unsure or defunct), and stopped.

The CPU states line (the third line of the header) shows the percentage of CPU time in user mode, system mode, nice tasks, and idle. (A nice process has a negative nice value, which sets the priority of the process. Note that a nice task is counted by Linux as both a user task and a system task, so the total of the process values may add up to more than 100 percent.)

The fourth header line of the top output shows memory usage, including the amount of available memory, free memory at the moment of the snapshot, currently used

20

MANAGING PROCESSES

memory, the amount of shared memory, and the amount of memory used for buffers. The last header line shows the swap statistics, which reflect the use of the system's swap space. The line shows the total swap space, available swap space, and used swap space. Following the header is the list of CPU-intensive processes, structured like the ps command's output.

While top is running, you can issue some commands to alter its behavior (unless you started top with the -s option to disable interactive commands). The following interactive commands are available:

^L	Redraws the screen
h/?	Displays help
k	Kills a process (you are prompted for the PID and the signal level such as 9 or 15, as discussed earlier under the kill command)
i	Ignores idle and zombie processes
n/#	Changes the number of processes displayed
q	Quits
r	Renices a process (you are prompted for the PID and the nice value)
S	Toggles cumulative mode
s	Changes the delay between updates

Note that some terminals cannot display the output of the top command properly. When run, top should clear the entire screen and display a full screen of information. If you see overlapping lines or the screen has large blank areas, the terminal is not properly supported for top output. This problem often occurs when you use telnet across a network or emulate a terminal like a VT100.

SUMMARY

This chapter has shown you how to obtain listings of the processes currently executing on your Linux system and how to terminate those processes when they require it. Although you may not have to use this knowledge often, every operating system has occasions when something gets out of hand and needs you to control it. The problems multiply as the number of users increases. Process commands enable you to correct the problem without terminating the operating system.

- Understanding Quotas

- Setting User Quotas

- Using the quota Command

- Using the quotacheck Command

CHAPTER 21

Managing Resources

Even with today's high-capacity hard disks at reasonable prices, disk space shortages are chronic (especially on multiuser systems). Even the largest hard drives can get reduced to small available space when multiple operating systems, the full Linux system, swap space, and several users are brought into play. To combat this space shortage, there are several ways to manage the disk space you have available more effectively.

For multiuser systems, the ideal solution is to restrict the amount of space each user can use. This concept was first implemented in BSD UNIX with the quota command; the command then carried over to most versions of the software. Linux, because it is based primarily on BSD UNIX, also includes the quota system. This chapter looks at the quota command and how you can use it.

UNDERSTANDING QUOTAS

One of the best tools for managing resources is quota and its attendant utilities. The quota tool is used to display users' disk usage and their limits. When invoked, quota scans the /etc/fstab file and checks disk usage in the order of filesystems in the /etc/fstab file.

Quotas are preassigned amounts of disk space that a user or group can occupy. Normally, the limits do not prevent users or groups from exceeding their allotment, but exceeding the limits can result in warning messages appearing on-screen and usage reports being sent to root.

HARD AND SOFT LIMITS

Even if a user is considerably over quota, restricting the user from saving information can be difficult and may be the wrong thing to do in many cases. To help enforce restrictions and minimize complications, though, limits come in two types: soft and hard. A hard limit cannot be exceeded regardless of circumstances. If the user is trying to save valuable information and is over the hard limit, something has to go first. Because a user receives no warning when they are approaching a hard limit, this step is rather drastic, but it can be necessary with some users. A soft limit allows users to exceed their quotas for a while, but they get warning messages. You can set the system to allow only so many warnings before imposing a hard limit. Ideally, you should set your system to have a soft limit somewhat smaller than a hard limit, so users get warnings before they are unable to save anything else. Just setting a hard limit with no warning mechanism can result in annoyed users!

When to Use Quotas

Not all filesystems need quotas. If you have several hard drives broken into filesystems, you may use some for unlimited storage, and others, which are near capacity, may need quotas. The decision as to which filesystems require quotas is up to you. Most versions of Linux that adhere closely to the BSD standards require a modification in the /etc/fstab file to indicate that the filesystem uses quotas. The word quota must go in the fourth column of the file, as in the following entry:

```
/dev/sda3    /usr    rw,quota    1    3
```

This entry indicates that quotas are in place on the /usr filesystem. If the entry has the keyword noquota, you can change it to quota.

Setting User Quotas

The system administrator sets user quotas in a file called quota.user in the root directory of the filesystem to which the quotas apply. Similarly, group quotas (if used) are set in the file quota.group also in the root directory of the filesystem. You need to manually create the quota files, either by using cat to save a blank file or by using touch. The following commands show how to set quotas on the /usr filesystem:

```
cd /usr
touch quota.user
chmod 600 quota.user
touch quota.group
chmod 600 quota.group
```

The chmod command makes the file writable by root only. You set the quota limits with the edquota command, which is usable only by root. Follow edquota with the name of the user (or multiple users) or group that you want to set quotas for, as in the following example:

```
/usr/etc/edquota tparker ychow bsmallwood
```

You may not need to specify the path if the edquota command is in the default system search path. This command starts an editor (the default is vi). If you provide a group name, a temporary file stores information about the users in the group, and then writes the information to the quota.group file afterwards.

You can control edquota's behavior with a number of options. These options are usually supported by Linux' version of edquota:

- -g   Edit a group's quota
- -p   Duplicate quotas of one user for others

-t Edit soft time limits (before a hard limit is imposed)

-u Edit a user's quota (default action)

If you want to use the same quota entries for several users, you need edit only one and then use the -p option to duplicate the entries. For example, the command

```
edquota -p tparker ychow bsmallwood
```

uses the tparker user entries for ychow and bsmallwood.

After you set the quotas you want to use on the filesystems, you must turn on the quota system with the quotaon command. You can turn on quotas for a single filesystem with the command

```
quotaon /dev/sda3
```

which turns on quota checking for the partition /dev/sda3. To turn on quota checking for all partitions, use the following command:

```
quotaon -a
```

The quotaoff command, not surprisingly, performs the reverse action with the same arguments.

USING THE *QUOTA* COMMAND

The syntax for the quota command is as follows:

```
quota [options] [user] [group]
```

These options for the quota command are valid:

-g Displays group quotas for the group of which the user is a member

-q Displays only filesystems where usage is over quota

-u Displays quotas for users (the default action)

-v Displays quotas on a filesystem where no storage is allocated

You can combine these options. For example, if you use both -g and -u, both the user and group quotas are displayed. The system administrator can display quotas for all users with the -u option followed by a username, as in the following:

```
quota -u tparker
```

You can only use the command with this option when logged in as root. If non-root users issue the quota command, they can display only their user quotas and their group's quota.

Using the *quotacheck* Command

When you have quotas in place and running, you can use the quotacheck command at any time to scan your filesystems for current disk usage. The results of the scan are written into the quota.user and quota.group files in the filesystem root directories.

Set the quotacheck command to run every time the system is booted so that the quota files are updated automatically. The best way to accomplish this task is to place the quotacheck command in the rc startup files. Because checking filesystems can take some time, use this command primarily with multiuser systems that see a lot of use. Otherwise, get in the habit of using quotacheck at intervals or when an error has occurred on a mounted filesystem.

The quotacheck command accepts a number of options to display different information:

-a   Checks all filesystems (not all versions of Linux quota support this option)

-d   Debugs information displayed during checking (slows down the check considerably)

-g   Followed by a group ID, checks only that group

-u   Followed by a user ID, checks only that user (or all users if no user is specified, which is the default)

-v   Verbose output showing what quotacheck is doing

Using quotacheck regularly helps make sure the filesystem quotas are being followed.

Summary

The quota system lets you set limits on the amount of disk space your users occupy in order to prevent potential problems when capacities are exceeded. Using quotas also makes sense when you are sharing your system with friends, but don't want them to take your system for granted as a storage depot!

- Why Make Backups?

- Choosing Backup Media

- Setting a Backup Schedule

- Keeping Backup Logs

- Using tar for Backups

CHAPTER 22

Backup, Backup, Backup!

The title of this chapter reflects the three rules of system administration: 1) Backup; 2) Backup; and 3) Backup! Although this advice may sound trite, the number of people who have lost important or valuable data, not to mention all the configuration information they spend days getting correct, is enormous. Even if you don't have a tape drive or other backup storage device, get in the habit of backing up the most important pieces of information. This chapter looks at how to properly back up information.

If you run a system that has many users, network access, e-mail, and so on, backups are a very important aspect of the daily routine. If your system is used for your own pleasure and is not used for any important files, backups are not as important except as a way to recover your configuration and setup information. You should make backups either way; the difference is the regularity with which you make them.

WHY MAKE BACKUPS?

A backup is a copy of the filesystem or files on part of a filesystem stored onto another medium that can be used later to recreate the original. In most UNIX systems, the medium used for backups is tape, but you can also use floppy disks or secondary and removable hard disks.

So many potential sources of damage to a modern computer system exist that they can be overwhelming. Damage to your hard disks and their filesystems and data can occur from hardware failures, power interruptions, or badly typed commands. Part of the potential for damage with Linux is the nature of an operating system itself. Because Linux is a multiuser and multitasking operating system, many system files are open at any moment. At most millisecond increments, data is being written to or read from a hard disk (even when the system has no users or user-started background processes on it). Also, Linux maintains a lot of information in memory about its current state and the state of the filesystems. This information must be written to disk frequently. When CPU processes are interrupted, system files and tables can be lost from memory. Disk files can be left in a temporary state that doesn't match the real filesystem status.

Although damage to a filesystem can occur from many sources, not all of which are under the control of the system administrator, it is the administrator's task to make sure the system can be restored to a working state as quickly as possible. Having a backup is sometimes your only chance of getting back lost information. Although the process of making backups can be tiresome and time-consuming, this inconvenience is often outweighed by the time required to recoup any lost information in case of problems. With utilities like cron available, the task of backing up is much easier, too.

One final aspect about backups you need to consider is where to keep the backup media after it has been used. For most home users, the only option is to store the tapes, drives, floppy disks, or other media in the same place as the Linux machine. Make sure the location is away from magnetic fields (including telephones, modems, televisions, speakers, and so on). For systems that are used for more than pleasure, consider keeping copies away from the main machine, preferably away from the same physical location. This type of off-site backup enables you to recover in case of a catastrophe, such as a fire, that destroys your system and backup media library.

CHOOSING BACKUP MEDIA

By far the most commonly used medium for backups is tape, especially tape cartridges. Tape is favored because it has a low cost, a relatively easy storage requirement, and reasonable speed. The process of writing and reading data from a tape is reliable, and tapes are portable from machine to machine. All you need, of course, is a tape drive. If you don't have one, you need to find another usable medium for backups.

Possible alternative media include removable hard disks of many different types, such as the Iomega Bernoulli or ZIP drives. These cartridges use magnetic head technology just like a normal hard drive. You can remove these disk-platter systems, which usually come in a protective cartridge, from the main system and store them elsewhere. You can then cycle through several of these disks as you would with tapes. In some cases, removable cartridges are available for a competitive price compared to tape cartridges, although some high-capacity removable cartridges cost more (but also offer more storage). The cost of the removable cartridge drive varies depending on the capacity, manufacturer, and technology, but it is also competitive with a tape drive in many cases.

Several new magneto-optical cartridge systems for DOS and Windows are usable under Linux, too. These systems tend to be small 3.5-inch cartridge systems that fit into a small drive unit. A 230M magneto-optical cartridge and drive can cost less than some tape drives, and they present a more secure backup medium because magneto-optical systems are not susceptible to magnetic fields. They have a potentially longer life, too. Large-capacity magneto-optical systems, now approaching 2.4G, are currently available, although they tend to cost as much as a new computer.

Another possibility is another hard disk. With the price of hard disks dropping all the time, you can add another hard disk just for backups to your system (or any other system connected by a network) and use it as a full backup.

The popularity of writable CD-ROM and WORM (write once, read many) drives makes them a possibility as well, although you must bear in mind that this type of media can only be written to once (the disks can't be reused). This type of media does have an advantage for archival purposes where you may need to prove certain file dates are accurate. CDs are also useful for permanent storage of important files like accounting records, personal letters, documents such as wills, and binaries. CD-ROM discs can hold 750M of data, although most consumer discs are designed for 650M.

Consider a floppy disk drive as a last resort backup device for large filesystems, although it is very good for backing up small files. High-capacity floppy disk drives are beginning to appear now, but the lack of Linux drivers makes them unusable for most backup situations.

SETTING A BACKUP SCHEDULE

One of the most important aspects of making backups is to make them regularly. Regularity is much more important for systems that support many users and have constantly changing filesystems. If your Linux machine is used only for your own purposes, you can make backups whenever you feel there is material that should be backed up.

For most systems with a few users, constant Internet access for e-mail or newsgroups, and similar daily changes to the filesystem, a daily backup schedule is important. You don't have to make a full backup of everything on your hard drives every day, but you should consider using incremental backups, which copy only those files that are new or have changed since the last backup.

Most UNIX system administrators prefer to perform backups during the night or early hours of the morning because few users are logged in, there is no real load on the CPU, and the system has the least number of open files at this time. Because backups are easily automated using cron (see Chapter 23, "The cron and at Programs"), you can set the exact backup time to minimize the impact on any other background processing tasks that the system may be running. Because you don't have to manually start the backup process, you can do it at any time. All the system administrator has to do in this kind of backup schedule is check that the backup was completed properly, change the backup media, and log the backup.

For those systems with a single user and a lightly loaded Linux system, backups can be done practically anytime, although it is a good idea to have the backups performed automatically if your system is on all the time. If your Linux system is only active when you want to use it, get in the habit of making a backup while you do other tasks on the system.

When DOS or Windows users move to UNIX, they sometimes have the bad habit of keeping a single tape (or other media) and continually recycling that one unit every time they make a backup. It is foolhardy to keep only one backup copy of a system as this prevents you from moving back to previous backups. For example, suppose you deleted a file a week ago and had it safely stored on a backup tape at that time. When you reuse the backup tape, the old contents are erased and you can never get the old file back.

Ideally, you should keep backup copies for days, or even weeks, before reusing them. On systems with several users, this habit is even more important because users only remember that they need a file they deleted two months ago after you have recycled the tape a few times. Some backup scheduling methods can help get around this problem, as you will see in a moment. The ideal backup routine varies depending on the system administrator's ideas about backups, but a comprehensive backup system requires at least two weeks of daily incremental backups and a full backup every week.

A full backup is a complete image of everything on the filesystem, including all files. The backup media required for full backups is usually close to the total size of your filesystem. For example, if you have 150M used in your filesystem, you need about 150M of tape or other media for a backup. With compression algorithms, some backup systems can get the requirements much lower, but compression is not always available. Also, you may need several volumes of media for a single full backup, depending on the capacity of the backup unit. If your tape drive can only store 80M on a cartridge and you have to backup 150M, you need two tapes in sequence for the one backup. Because the Linux system's cron utility can't change tapes automatically, full backups over several volumes require some operator interaction. Obviously, making a full system backup on low-capacity media (like floppy disks) is a long, tedious process because there are many volumes that must be switched.

Incremental backups (sometimes called differential backups) back up only the files that have been changed or created since the last backup. Unlike DOS, Linux doesn't have a file indicator that shows what files have been backed up. However, you can use the modification date to effectively act like a backup indicator.

Incremental backups are sometimes difficult to make with Linux unless you restrict yourself to particular areas of the filesystem that are likely to have changed. For example, if your users are all in the /usr directory, you can backup only that filesystem area instead of the entire filesystem. This kind of backup is often called a partial backup, as only a part of the filesystem is saved. (Incremental backups can be made under any operating system by using a background process that logs all changes of files to a master list, and then uses the master list to create backups. Creating such a scheme is seldom worth the effort, though.)

How often should you back up your system? The usual rule is to back up whenever you can't afford to lose information. For many people, this criteria means daily backups. Imagine that you have been writing a document or program, and you lose all the work since the last backup. How long will it take to rewrite (if at all possible)? If the rewriting of the loss is more trouble than the time required to perform a backup, make a backup!

So how can you effectively schedule backups for your system, assuming you want to save your contents regularly? Assuming that your system has several users (friends calling in by modem or family members who use it) and a reasonable volume of changes (e-mail, newsgroups, word processing files, databases, or applications you are writing, for example), consider daily backups. The most common backup schedule for a small, medium-volume system requires between 10 and 14 tapes, depending on whether backups are performed on weekends. (The rest of this section uses tapes as the backup medium, but you can substitute any other device that you want.)

Label all backup tapes with names that reflect their use. For example, label your tapes Daily 1, Daily 2, and so on up to the total number of daily use tapes, such as Daily 10. Cycle through these daily use tapes, restarting the cycle after you have used all the tapes (so that Daily 1 follows after Daily 10). With this many tapes, you have a two week supply of backups (ignoring weekend backups, in this case), enabling you to recover anything going back two weeks. If you have more tapes available, use them to extend the backup cycle.

The backups can be either full or partial, depending on your needs. A good practice is to make one full backup for every four or five partial. You can make a full backup of your entire filesystem on Mondays, for instance, but only back up the /usr directories the other days of the week. Make an exception to this process if you make changes to the Linux configuration so that you have the changes captured with a full backup. You can keep track of the backups using a backup log, which is covered in the next section.

An expansion of this daily backup scheme that many administrators (including the author) prefer is the daily and weekly backup cycle. This backup system breaks up the number of tapes into daily and weekly use. For example, if you have 14 tapes, use 10 for a daily cycle as already mentioned. You can still call these tapes Daily 1 through Daily 10. Use the other four tapes in a biweekly cycle and name them Week 1, Week 2, Week 3, and Week 4.

To use this backup system, perform your daily backups as already mentioned, but use the next weekly tape when you get to the end of the daily cycle. Then you cycle through the daily tapes again, followed by the next weekly tape. (Your backup cycle is Daily 1 through Daily 10, Week 1, Daily 1 through Daily 10, Week 2, and so on.)

This backup cycle has one major advantage over a simple daily cycle. When the entire cycle is underway, there are 10 daily backups, which cover a two-week period. The biweekly tapes extend back over four complete daily cycles, or eight weeks. You can then recover a file or group of files from the filesystem as it was two months ago, instead of just two weeks. This backup method gives you a lot more flexibility in recovering information that was not noticed as missing or corrupt right away. If even more tapes are available, you can extend either the daily or biweekly cycle, or add monthly backups.

Keeping Backup Logs

Many system administrators begin their careers by making regular backups, as they should. However, when they get to the point where they have to restore a file from a backup tape, they have no idea which tapes include the file or which tapes were used on what days. Some system administrators get by this problem by placing a piece of paper or stick note on each tape with the date and contents on it. This solution means you have to flip through the tapes to find the one you want, though, which can be awkward when you have lots of tapes. For this reason, you should keep a backup log. (A log is a good idea for backups on other operating systems as well.)

Whenever you make a backup, you should update the backup log. A backup log doesn't have to be anything complex or elaborate. You can use the back of a notebook with a couple of vertical columns drawn in, use a form on the computer itself (which you should print out regularly, of course), or keep a loose-leaf binder with a few printed forms in it. A typical backup log needs the following information:

- The date of the backup
- The name of the backup tape (Daily 1, for example)
- The filesystem being backed up
- Whether a full or partial backup was performed, and if partial, which directories were backed up

You can record these four bits of information in a few seconds. For larger systems, you can add a few other pieces of information to complete a full backup record:

- Who made the backup
- Whether the backup was automatic (cron) or manual
- Storage location of the tape

The dates of the backup help you keep track of when the last backup was performed and also act as an index for file recovery. If one of your system users knows they deleted a file by accident a week ago, you can determine the proper backup tape for the file restoration from the backup log dates.

For convenience, keep the backup log near the system. Some administrators prefer to keep the log in the same location as the backup media storage instead. Some system administrators also keep a duplicate copy of the backup log in another site, just in case of catastrophe. Do what is appropriate for your system.

USING *TAR* FOR BACKUPS

The tar (tape archiver) program is usually the command you use to save files and directories to an archive medium and recover them later. The tar command works by creating an archive file, which is a single large entity that holds many files within it (much like PKZIP does in DOS, for example). The tar command only works with archives it creates.

The format of the command is a little awkward and takes some getting used to, but fortunately most users only need a few variations of the command. The format of the tar command is as follows:

```
tar switch modifiers files
```

The files section of the command indicates which files or directories you want to archive or restore. You probably want to archive a full filesystem such as /usr. In the case of recovery, you may want a single file such as /usr/tparker/big_file.

The switch controls how tar reads or writes to the backup media. You can use only one switch with tar at a time. The valid switches are as follows:

c   Creates a new archive media

r   Writes to end of existing archive

t   Lists names of files in an archive

u   Adds files that are not already modified or archived

x   Extracts from the archive

You can add a number of modifiers to the tar command to control the archive and how tar uses it. Valid modifiers include the following:

A   Suppresses absolute filenames

b   Provides a blocking factor (1-20)

e   Prevents splitting files across volumes

f   Specifies the archive media device name

F   Specifies the name of a file for tar arguments

k   Gives size of archive volume (in kilobytes)

l   Displays error messages if links are unresolved

m   Does not restore modification times

n   Indicates the archive is not a tape

p   Extracts files with their original permissions

v   Provides verbose output (lists files on the console)

w   Displays archive action and waits for user confirmation

The `tar` command uses absolute pathnames for most actions, unless you specify the A modifier.

A few examples may help explain the `tar` command and how to use `tar` switches. If you are using a tape drive called /dev/tape and the entire filesystem to be archived totals less than the tape's capacity, you can create the tape archive with the following command:

```
tar cf /dev/tape /
```

The f option enables you to specify the device name, /dev/tape in this case. The entire root filesystem is archived in a new archive file (indicated by the c). Any existing contents on the tape are automatically overwritten when the new archive is created. (You are not asked whether you are sure you want to delete the existing contents of the tape, so make sure you are overwriting material you don't need.) If you include the v option in the command, `tar` would echo the filenames and their sizes to the console as they are archived.

If you need to restore the entire filesystem from the tape used in the preceding example, issue the command:

```
tar xf /dev/tape
```

This command restores all files on the tape because no specific directory has been indicated for recovery. The default, when no file or directory is specified, is the entire tape archive. If you want to restore a single file from the tape, use the command

```
tar xf /dev/tape /usr/tparker/big_file
```

which restores only the file /usr/tparker/big_file.

Sometimes you may want to obtain a list of all files on a tape archive. You can do this with the following command:

```
tar tvf /dev/tape
```

This command uses the v option to display the results from `tar`. If the list is long, you may want to redirect the command to a file.

Most tapes require a blocking factor when creating an archive, but you don't need to specify a blocking factor when reading a tape because `tar` can figure it out automatically. The blocking factor tells `tar` how much data to write in a chunk on the tape. When archiving to a tape, you specify the blocking factor with the b modifier.

For example, the command

```
tar cvfb /dev/tape 20 /usr
```

creates a new archive on /dev/tape that has a blocking factor of 20 and contains all the files in /usr. Most tapes can use a blocking factor of 20, and you can assume this factor as a default value unless your tape drive specifically won't work with this value. The only times blocking factors are changed are for floppy disks and other hard disk volumes. Note that the arguments following the modifiers are in the same order as the modifiers. The f precedes the b modifier so the arguments have the device before the blocking factor. The arguments must be in the same order as the modifiers, which can sometimes cause a little confusion.

Another common problem is that a tape may not be large enough to hold the entire archive, in which case more than one tape will be needed. To tell tar the size of each tape, you need the k option. This option uses an argument that is the capacity in kilobytes. For example, the command

```
tar cvbfk 20 /dev/tape 122880 /usr
```

tells tar to use a blocking factor of 20 for the device /dev/tape. The tape capacity is 122,880 kilobytes (approximately 120 M). Again, note that the order of arguments matches the order of the modifiers.

Floppy disks create another problem with tar, as the blocking factor is usually different. When you use floppy disks, archives usually require more than one disk. You use the k option to specify the archive volume's capacity. For example, to back up the /usr/tparker directory to 1.2M floppy disks, the command would be

```
tar cnfk /dev/fd0 1200 /usr/tparker
```

where /dev/fd0 is the device name of the floppy drive and 1200 is the size of the disk in kilobytes. The n modifier tells tar that this is not a tape. As a result, tar runs a little more efficiently than if the modifier had been left off.

SUMMARY

This chapter looked at the basics of backups. You should maintain a backup log and make regular backups to protect your work. Although tar is a little awkward to use at first, it soon becomes second nature. You can use the tar command in combination with compression utilities such as compress. Alternatively, you can use utilities like gzip and gunzip that combine both utilities into one program. Although this program may be more convenient, tar is still the most widely used archive utility and is therefore worth knowing.

A number of scripts are beginning to appear that automate the backup process or give you a menu-driven interface to the backup system. These scripts are not in general distribution, but you may want to check FTP and BBS sites for a utility that simplifies backups for you.

- The cron Program

- The at Program

CHAPTER 23

The cron and at Programs

Automating tasks is one of the best ways to keep a system running smoothly. If you take all the repetitive system administration commands you need to run regularly and have them run in background without your direct involvement, system administration becomes much less onerous and bothersome. The utilities cron and at were developed to help make your job easier. Both allow you to execute commands automatically at specified times, without bothering you.

THE *CRON* PROGRAM

The cron (short for chronograph) utility is designed to allow commands to execute at specific times without anyone directly initiating them. Linux loads cron as a clock daemon when the system starts up. (The cron utility is usually run from an rc file entry; you can disable it by commenting out the line that starts cron.) When operating, cron reads the days and times it is supposed to execute a task from a file called the crontab file.

Whenever one of the crontab file's day and time specification entries matches the system's date and time, the cron daemon executes the command. The cron utility doesn't just execute the task once; the task is run again whenever the specified day and time match the system day and time. The task continues to be run until you terminate the cron utility or modify the crontab file. The automatic execution of tasks means that cron is ideal for automating regular system administration tasks such as tape backups, database reorganization, and general file cleanups (such as emptying log files and queues).

On most systems, access to cron is limited to the system administrator, although you can easily activate it for some or all users on your system. System administrators control who can send processes to be executed by cron through one of two different files, often called /usr/lib/cron/cron.allow or /usr/lib/cron/cron.deny. Many Linux systems use the names /etc/cron.d/cron.allow and /etc/cron.d/cron.deny. Both files have one username (which matches the entry in /etc/passwd) per line.

The file /usr/lib/cron/cron.allow (or /etc/cron.d/cron.allow) can contain a list of all usernames that are allowed to use cron. For example, the file

```
tparker
yvonne
bill
```

allows only the logins tparker, yvonne, and bill (as well as the superuser) to submit anything to cron.

The file /usr/lib/cron/cron.deny can contain a list of usernames that are not allowed to use cron. For example, the file

```
walter
anne
```

allows everyone except the logins walter and anne to use cron.

By using one of these optional files, system administrators can control cron usage. If neither the cron.allow or cron.deny files exist, only the superuser (root) can submit processes to cron. To allow all users to use cron, create an empty cron.deny file.

CREATING A *CRONTAB* FILE

To instruct cron to process commands at particular days and times, you use a utility called crontab. The crontab program reads a file that contains the details of what you want cron to do and queues it. In addition, crontab performs several other administrative tasks, such as displaying your current cron task list, removing the list, and adding new tasks to the list.

The file that crontab reads to determine what you want to submit to cron is usually named crontab for convenience, although you can call it anything. The crontab utility has a command option that allows you to specify the filename you want it to use. If you don't use this option, the crontab utility reads the default filename, crontab.

The crontab instruction file has a simple structure. The file consists of one complete line for each process to be submitted that specifies when to run the process and what command to execute. The format of each line is as follows:

```
minute hour day-of-month month-of-year day-of-week command
```

An example two-line extract from a crontab file looks like the following:

```
20 1 * * *    /usr/bin/calendar -
0  2 * * *    /bin/organize_data
```

Each line in the crontab file has six columns separated by whitespace (spaces or tabs). The columns, from left to right are as follows:

- ◆ The minute of the hour (0-59)
- ◆ The hour of the day (0-23)
- ◆ The day of the month (1-31)
- ◆ The month (1-12)
- ◆ The day of the week (Sun=0, Mon=1, ... Sat=6)
- ◆ The program to be executed at the specified day and time

This rather strange (at first glance) format is necessary to enable you to completely specify when a process is to run. Without the five different categories for days and time, you couldn't uniquely specify any event that occurs one or more times a month. These columns are quite easy to complete.

The last column contains the command or script filename that is to be executed. A script that is to be executed can have many lines and call other scripts, or it can be only a single line. The first process is initiated when the crontab file matches the day and time. It is important to provide an absolute pathname to the command (even if it's in your PATH), as the cron jobs do not inherit your environment variables and thus don't know where to look for commands. Also, you must have execute permission for the utility or script. If you are submitting crontab files as a user (not superuser), you must have file permissions or ownership set to allow you normal access, as cron executes the processes as though you owned them.

Each time and day column in the crontab file can contain a single number anywhere in the range of valid numbers, two numbers separated by a minus sign to show an inclusive range (such as 1-5 to show one through five), a list of numbers separated by commas to mean all of the values explicitly specified, or an asterisk meaning all legal values.

Look at the following sample lines of a crontab file to see how this file works:

```
20  1  *  *  *   /usr/bin/calendar -
0   2  1  *  0   /bin/organize_data
10,30,50  9-18  *  *  *   /bin/setperms
```

This example specifies three different processes. The first command is /usr/bin/calendar - (the hyphen is an important part of the command). This process is executed at 20 minutes past one in the morning (cron uses a 24-hour clock) every day of the week and each day of the year. The asterisks mean all values (every day).

At 2:00AM, a script file called /bin/organize_data is executed on the first day of every month (the 1 in the third column) and every Sunday (the 0 in the fifth column). If the first day is a Sunday, it executes only once, of course. The third line shows that a script called /bin/setperms runs at 10, 30, and 50 minutes past the hour every hour between 9:00AM and 6:00PM (18:00), every day of the week.

The entries in a crontab file do not have to be in any special order. As long as each entry is on a line by itself and has all six fields specified properly, cron organizes the information for its own use. If you have an error in the crontab file, cron mails you a notice of the problem when it processes your file. (This notice can be annoying if you have the entry with the error set to execute often because cron mails you each time it tries to execute the entry and finds a problem. Your mailbox quickly gets filled with cron error messages.)

Keep the crontab files in your home directory and name them crontab, unless you want to have several versions of the files, in which case you can use any naming convention you want. Keeping the names simple helps you identify which file you want cron to execute.

SUBMITTING AND MANAGING *CRONTAB* FILES

After you write your crontab file, you can submit it for cron to execute. When you submit a crontab file, a copy of the file is made and kept in a cron directory, usually /usr/spool/cron/crontabs. The file has the name of the submitting user. A crontab file submitted by yvonne, for example, has the name /usr/spool/cron/crontabs/yvonne. Any crontab files submitted by the superuser usually have the name root.

To submit your crontab file to cron, use the crontab command followed by the name of the file with the cron commands in it. For example, the command

```
crontab crontab
```

submits the file called crontab in the current directory to cron. If you had previously submitted a cron file, it is removed and the new file is used instead.

Warning

> Always submit a change to cron using the crontab file and an edited ASCII file. Never make changes to the file in /usr/spool/cron/crontabs; the changes will not be read by cron and can potentially mess up any existing cron tasks.

You can see what you have submitted to cron by using the -1 (list) option. This option shows all the crontab entries the cron utility knows about (essentially displaying the contents of the file with your username from /usr/spool/cron/crontabs). For example, the command

```
crontab -1
```

shows all cron tasks for the user who submits the command.

To remove your crontab file and not replace it, use the -r (remove) option. This option erases the file with your filename from the /usr/spool/cron/crontabs directory. The syntax for this command is as follows:

```
crontab -r
```

Finally, you can call up your current cron file and start an editor (the default editor as defined by your environment variables or a system default variable) by using the -e (editor) option. When you issue the command

```
crontab -e
```

crontab reads your existing crontab file and loads it into the default editor (such as vi). When you save the edited file, it is submitted to cron automatically.

Changes to the crontab file are usually effective within five minutes at most, as cron reads the contents of the /usr/spool/cron/crontab file at least once every five minutes and often more frequently (most Linux systems have cron check the directories every minute). Because you have to wait for cron to check the contents of the crontab file, execution of a process you have submitted to cron can sometimes be delayed by a few minutes, so don't rely on cron to be exactly on time. The more heavily loaded a system is, the greater the delay in execution.

On some systems, system administrators can log all cron usage by modifying an entry in the file /etc/default/cron. One line in the file should contain the variable CRONLOG. If you set the value equal to YES, cron logs every action it takes to the file /usr/lib/cron/log. Not all versions of Linux allow cron logging. If you do enable cron logging, check the log file frequently as it can grow to a large size quite quickly.

USING COMPLEX *CRON* COMMANDS

The crontab file can contain any type of command or shell script, as long as the line is valid (in other words, it could be executed from the shell prompt). A common problem with many shell commands is the generation of output, especially error messages, which is mailed to you and can clog up your mailbox quickly. For this reason, if you anticipate error message output (from a compiler, for example), you can redirect the output to /dev/null. For example, the command

```
0 * * * * date > /tmp/test1 2>/dev/null
```

sends the output of the date command to a file called /tmp/test1 every hour and sends any error messages to /dev/null (which essentially discards such messages). You can do the same with the standard output, if you want, or you can redirect it elsewhere. For example, the cron command

```
30 1 * * * cat /usr/tparker/chapt* > /usr/tparker/archive/backup
```

concatenates all the files starting with chapt in /usr/tparker into one, large file called /usr/tparker/archive/backup. Again, you can redirect the standard output.

You can also do piping in the crontab file. For example, if you have a list of users who are logged in the system during the day in the file /tmp/userlist, you can have a crontab entry that looks like the following:

```
0 1 * * * sort -u /tmp/userlist ¦ mail -s"users for today" root
```

This line sorts the output of /tmp/userlist so that there is only one entry for each user (the -u or unique option) and mails it to root.

An important point to remember with cron is that all commands are executed, by default, in the Bourne shell (or bash, if it is the sh equivalent on your system). If you use C shell commands, the cron task will fail.

THE *AT* PROGRAM

The at program is very similar to cron, except that at executes a command only once at a prespecified time and cron keeps executing a command. The format of the at command is as follows:

```
at time date < file
```

You can specify most of the at command parameters in several different ways, which makes the at command versatile. you can specify the time, for example, as an absolute time (18:40 or 22:00) or as two digits that are taken as hours (so 10 means ten o'clock in the morning as a 24-hour clock is the default). You can add an am or pm to the time to make it clear which you mean, so 10pm is unambiguously in the evening.

The at command handles a few special words instead of time designations. The command recognizes the words noon, midnight, now, next, and zulu for GMT conversion. (Some at versions generate an error message if you try to execute a command with the time set to now.)

The date is an optional field that you use when the time is not specific enough. If you don't supply a date, at executes the command the next time the specified time occurs. If you specify a date, at waits until that date to execute the command. You can give the date as a month's name followed by a day number (May 10) or a day of the week (either spelled out in full or abbreviated to three characters). You also can specify a year, but this specification is seldom necessary. As with the time, the at command recognizes two special words that relate to dates: today and tomorrow (although the word today is redundant as the command executes today by default if the time is set properly).

The file to be read in as input to the at command can be any file with commands in it. Alternatively, you can type in the commands and press Ctrl+d when you're finished, although this method is not recommended due to the high potential for error.

Suppose you have a file called reorg.data with the following commands in it:

```
/usr/tparker/setperms
/usr/tparker/sort_database
/usr/tparker/index_database
/usr/tparker/clean_up
```

If you want to execute this file at 8:30PM, issue any one of the following commands:

```
at 20:30 < reorg.data
at 8:30 pm < reorg/data
at 20:30 today < reorg.data
```

23

THE CRON AND AT PROGRAMS

Even more variations are possible, but you can see the syntax. If you want to execute the command on Friday, issue the command in one of these formats:

```
at 8:30 pm Friday < reorg.data
at 20:30 Fri < reorg.data
```

Some versions of at are even more talented and handle special words. For example, this command

```
at 0900 Monday next week < reorg.data
```

executes the commands next week on a Monday. Not all versions of at can handle these complex formats, however. Check the man pages to see which formats your version supports, or just try these formats and see whether you get an error message.

When you submit a program to at for execution, you get back a job identification number. This number uniquely identifies the at command you just issued. For example, look at the output from this at command:

```
$ at 6 < do_it
job 827362.a at Wed Aug 31 06:00:00 EDT 1995
```

In this case, the job ID is 827362.a and the ID is needed to make any changes to the job.

You can list all the jobs you have queued with at using the -l (list) option. The output usually tells you when the command is set to execute, but not what the command is:

```
$ at -l
user = tparker job 827362.a at Wed Aug 31 06:00:00 EDT 1995
user = tparker job 829283.a at Wed Aug 31 09:30:00 EDT 1995
```

Some versions of Linux may support the shorter form of the command with atq (display the at queue). If you get an error message when you issue the atq command, you have to use the at -l format.

To remove an at job from the system, you need the job ID and the at -r (remove) command. For example, the command

```
at -r 2892732.a
```

removes the specified job. Linux doesn't return any message to indicate the job has been canceled, but you will see the job is gone if you list the queue. You can remove only your own jobs (root can remove any). Some Linux versions support the atrm command as well as the -r option.

All jobs that are queued to at are kept in the directory /usr/spool/cron/atjobs with the job ID number as the filename. As with cron, an at.allow and an at.deny file in either the /usr/lib/cron or /etc/cron.d directory controls who can and can't use at. As with cron, create an empty at.deny file if you want all users on your system to be able to use at.

When an at job executes, all output (standard output and error messages) is mailed back to the username who submitted the job unless it has been redirected. The at command retains all the environment variables and directory settings of the user. If you look at a queued job in /usr/spool/cron/atjobs, you see all the variables defined prior to the command to be executed.

SUMMARY

As you have seen, cron and at are quite easy to use. They are also a system administrator's best friends, as you can automate tiresome tasks like cleaning up databases, checking disk space, flushing log files, and making tape backups with cron or at. Although cron and at can't do everything for you, they can handle repetitive tasks with ease.

Most Linux systems have a number of sample cron files supplied with the operating system. Examine those files (or list the current crontab file while logged in as root) to see what the operating system wants to execute on a regular basis. Use those commands as the starting point and add your own commands. Probably the worst that can happen if you mess up a crontab file is that you will get a lot of mail!

23

THE CRON AND AT PROGRAMS

- Improving Passwords

- Securing Your Files

- Controlling Modem Access

- Using UUCP

- Controlling Local Area Network Access

- Tracking Intruders

- Preparing for the Worst

CHAPTER 24

Security

This chapter covers the basics of keeping your system secure. It takes a quick look at the primary defenses you need to protect yourself from unauthorized access through telephone lines (modems), as well as some aspects of network connections. In addition, it explains how to protect your user files and ensure password integrity.

This chapter doesn't bother with complex solutions that are difficult to implement because they require a considerable amount of knowledge and apply only to a specific configuration. Instead, it looks at basic security methods, most of which are downright simple and effective.

IMPROVING PASSWORDS

The most commonly used method for breaking into a system through a network, over a modem connection, or sitting in front of a terminal is through weak passwords. Weak (which means easily guessable) passwords are very common. When system users have such passwords, even the best security systems cannot protect against intrusion.

If you are managing a system that has several users, implement a policy requiring users to reset their passwords at regular intervals (usually six to eight weeks is a good idea) and to use non-English words. The best passwords are combinations of letters and numbers that are not in the dictionary. Sometimes, though, having a policy against weak passwords isn't enough. You may want to consider forcing stronger password usage by using public domain or commercial software that checks potential passwords for susceptibility. These packages are often available in source code, so you can compile them for Linux without a problem.

What makes a strong password (one that is difficult to break)? Here are a few general guidelines that many system administrators adhere to:

◆ Avoid using any part of a user's real name and any name from the user's family or pets (these passwords are the easiest to guess).

◆ Avoid using important dates (birthdates, wedding day, and so on) in any variation.

◆ Avoid numbers or combinations of numbers and letters with special meaning (license plate number, telephone number, special dates, and so on).

◆ Avoid any place names or items that may be readily identified with a user (television characters, hobby, and so on).

◆ Avoid any word that could be in the dictionary (don't use real words).

Producing a strong password isn't that difficult. Get your users into the habit of mixing letters, numbers, and characters at random. Suppose a user wants to use `lionking` as a password. Encourage modification to `lion!king!`, `l_ionk_ing`, `lion5king`, or some similar variation. Even a slight variation in a password's normal pattern can make life very difficult for someone trying to guess the password.

Note

Change the root password often and make it very difficult to guess. Once someone has the root password, your system is totally compromised.

Check the /etc/passwd file at regular intervals to see whether there are entries you don't recognize that may have been added as a route in to your system. Also make sure each account has a password. Remove any accounts that you don't need anymore.

SECURING YOUR FILES

Security begins at the file permission level. Whether you want to protect a file from the prying eyes of an unauthorized invader or another user, carefully set your umask (file creation mask) to set your files for maximum security. You should have to make a conscious effort to share files.

Of course, this precaution is really only important if you have more than one user on the system or have to consider hiding information from others. If you are on a system with several users, consider forcing umask settings for everyone that set read-and-write permissions for the user only and give no permissions to anyone else. This procedure is as good as you can get with file security.

Consider encrypting really sensitive files (such as accounting or employee information) with a simple utility. Many such programs are available. Most require only a password to trigger the encryption or decryption process.

CONTROLLING MODEM ACCESS

For most Linux users, protecting the system from access through an Internet gateway isn't important because few users have an Internet access machine directly connected to their Linux box. Instead, the main concern should be to protect yourself from break-in through the most accessible method open to system invaders: modems.

24

Modems are the most commonly used interface into every Linux system (unless you are running completely stand-alone or on a closed network). Modems are used for remote user access, as well as for network and Internet access. Securing your system's modem lines from intrusion is simple and effective enough to stop casual browsers.

CALLBACK MODEMS

The safest technique to prevent unauthorized access through modems is to employ a callback modem. A callback modem lets users connect to the system as usual, and then hangs up and consults a list of valid users and their telephone numbers and calls back the user to establish the call. Callback modems are quite expensive, so this solution is not practical for many systems. Callback modems have some problems, too, especially if users change locations frequently. Also, callback modems are vulnerable to abuse because of call-forwarding features of modern telephone switches.

MODEM-LINE PROBLEMS

The typical telephone modem can be a source of problems if it doesn't hang up the line properly after a user session has finished. Most often, this problem stems from the wiring of the modem or the configuration setup.

Wiring problems may sound trivial, but many systems with hand-wired modem cables don't properly control all the pins; the system can be left with a modem session not properly closed and a log-off not completed. Anyone calling that modem continues where the last user ended. To prevent this kind of problem, make sure the cables connecting the modem to the Linux machine are complete. Replace hand-wired cables that you are unsure of with properly constructed commercial ones. Also, watch the modem when a few sessions are completed to make sure the line hangs up properly.

Configuration problems can also prevent line hangups. Check the modem documentation to make sure your Linux script can hang up the telephone line when the connection is broken. This problem seldom occurs with the most commonly used modems, but off-brand modems that do not have true compatibility with a supported modem can cause problems. Again, watch the modem after a call to make sure that it is hanging up properly.

One way to prevent break-ins is to remove the modem from the circuit when it's not needed. Because unwanted intruders usually attempt to access systems through modems after normal business hours, you can control the serial ports the modems are connected to by using cron to change the status of the ports or disable the port completely after hours. If late-night access is required, one or two modem lines out of a pool can be kept active. Some larger systems keep a dedicated number for the after-hours modem line, usually different than the normal modem line numbers.

HOW A MODEM HANDLES A CALL

For a user to gain access to Linux through a modem line, the system must use the getty process. The getty process itself is spawned by the init process for each serial line. The getty program is responsible for getting usernames, setting communications parameters (baud rate and terminal mode, for example), and controlling timeouts. In Linux, the /etc/ttys file controls the serial and multiport board ports.

Some Linux systems allow a dialup password system to be implemented. This kind of system forces a user calling on a modem to enter a second password that validates access through the modem. If this feature is supported on your system, it is usually with a file called /etc/dialups. The Linux system uses the file /etc/dialups to supply a list of ports that offer dialup passwords; a second file (such as /etc/d_passwd) has the passwords for the modem lines. Access is determined by the type of shell used by the user. You can apply the same procedure to UUCP access.

USING UUCP

The UUCP (Unix to Unix CoPy) program allows two Linux systems to send files and e-mail back and forth (see Chapter 27, "UUCP"). Although this program was designed with good security in mind, it was designed many years ago and security requirements have changed a lot since then. A number of security problems have been found over the years with UUCP, many of which have been addressed with changes and patches to the system. Still, UUCP requires some system administration attention to ensure that it is working properly and securely.

UUCP has its own password entry in the system password file /etc/passwd. Remote systems dialing in using UUCP log in to the local system by supplying the uucp login name and password. If you don't put a password on the system for the uucp login, anyone can access the system. One of the first things you should do is log in as root and issue the command

```
passwd uucp
```

to set a UUCP password. If you want remote systems to connect through UUCP, you have to supply them with your password, so make sure it is different than other passwords (as well as difficult to guess). The slight hassle of having to supply passwords to a remote system administrator is much better than having a wide-open system.

24

Alternatively, if you don't plan to use UUCP, remove the uucp user entirely from the /etc/password file or provide a strong password that can't be guessed (putting an asterisk as the first character of the password field in /etc/passwd effectively disables the login). Removing uucp from the /etc/passwd file doesn't affect anything else on the Linux system.

Set permissions to be as restrictive as possible in all UUCP directories (usually /usr/lib/uucp, /usr/spool/uucp, and /usr/spool/uucppublic). Permissions for these directories tend to be lax with most systems, so use chown, chmod, and chgrp to restrict access only to the uucp login. Set the group and username for all files to uucp as well. Check the file permissions regularly.

UUCP uses several files to control who is allowed in. These files (/usr/lib/uucp/Systems and /usr/lib/uucp/Permissions, for example) should be owned and accessible only by the uucp login. This setup prevents modification by an intruder with another login name.

The /usr/spool/uucppublic directory can be a common target for break-ins because it requires read and write access by all systems accessing it. To safeguard this directory, create two subdirectories: one for receiving files and another for sending. You can create more subdirectories for each system that is on the valid user list, if you want to go that far.

A neat trick to protect UUCP is to change the UUCP program login name so that random accessing to the uucp login doesn't work at all. The new name can be anything, and because valid remote systems must have a configuration file at both ends of the connection, you can easily let the remote system's administrator know the new name of the login. Then no one can use the uucp login for access.

CONTROLLING LOCAL AREA NETWORK ACCESS

Most LANs are not thought of as a security problem, but they tend to be one of the easiest methods into a system. If any of the machines on the network has a weak access point, all the machines on the network can be accessed through that machine's network services. PCs and Macintoshes usually have little security, especially over call-in modems, so they can be used in a similar manner to access the network services. A basic rule about LANs is that it is impossible to have a secure machine on the same network as non-secure machines. Therefore, any solution for one machine must be implemented for all machines on the network.

The ideal LAN security system forces proper authentication of any connection, including the machine name and the username. A few software problems can contribute to authentication difficulties. The concept of a trusted host, which is implemented in Linux, allows a machine to connect without hassle assuming its name is in a file on the host (Linux) machine. A password isn't even required in most cases! All an intruder has to do is determine the name of a trusted host and then connect with that name. Carefully check the /etc/hosts.equiv, /etc/hosts, and .rhosts files for entries that may cause problems.

One network authentication solution that is now widely used is Kerberos, a method originally developed at MIT. Kerberos uses a very secure host that acts as an authentication server. Using encryption in the messages between machines to prevent intruders from examining headers, Kerberos authenticates all messages over the network.

Because of the nature of most networks, most Linux systems are vulnerable to a knowledgeable intruder. There are literally hundreds of known problems with utilities in the TCP/IP family. A good first step to securing a system is to disable the TCP/IP services you don't use at all, as others can use them to access your system.

Tracking Intruders

Many intruders are curious about your system but don't want to do any damage. They may get on your system with some regularity, snoop around, play a few games, and then leave without changing anything. This activity makes it hard to know you are being broken into and leaves you at the intruder's mercy should he decide he wants to cause damage or use your system to springboard to another.

You can track users of your system quite easily by invoking auditing, a process that logs every time a user connects and disconnects from your system. Auditing can also tell you what the user does while on your system, although this type of audit slows the system down a little and creates large log files. Not all Linux versions support auditing, so consult your man pages and system documentation for more information.

If you do rely on auditing, scan the logs often. It may be worthwhile writing a quick summary script program that totals the amount of time each user is on the system so that you can watch for anomalies and numbers that don't mesh with your personal knowledge of the user's connect times. You can write a simple shell script to analyze the log in gawk. You can also use one of the audit reporting systems available in the public domain.

Preparing for the Worst

If someone does break in to your system, what can you do? Obviously, backups of the system are a help, as they let you recover any damaged or deleted files. But beyond that, what should you do?

First, find out how the invader got in and secure that method of access so it can't be used again. If you are not sure of the access method, close down all modems and terminals and carefully check all the configuration and setup files for holes. Also check passwords and user lists for weak or outdated material.

If you are the victim of repeated attacks, consider enabling an audit system to keep track of how intruders get in and what they do. If you are concerned about damage, force off any intruders as soon as you see them log in.

Lastly, if the break-ins continue, call the local authorities. Breaking into computer systems (whether a large corporation or your own home system) is illegal in most countries, and the authorities will usually know how to trace the intruders back to their calling points. They're breaking into your system and shouldn't get away with it!

SUMMARY

For most Linux systems, security isn't an issue because you are the only one who is using the machine. If, however, you share your machine with others or make it available for on-line access to anyone on the network (or the Internet), don't underestimate the chances of someone trying to break in; they will. Make your system as secure as you can. Common sense helps a lot, but don't forget that hackers are a wily, industrious, and tenacious bunch.

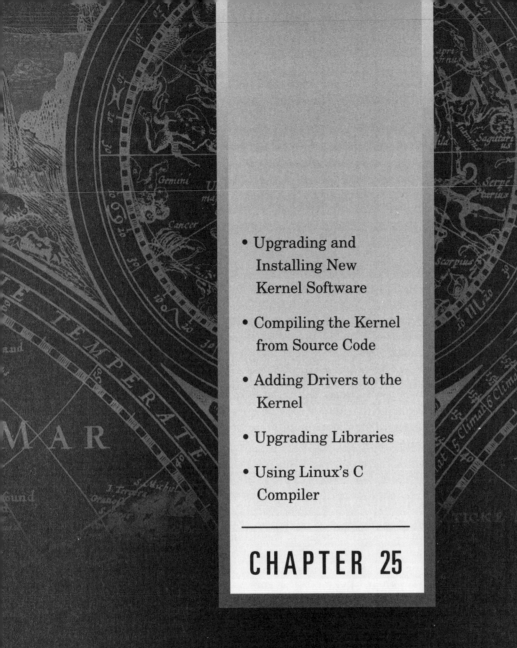

- Upgrading and Installing New Kernel Software

- Compiling the Kernel from Source Code

- Adding Drivers to the Kernel

- Upgrading Libraries

- Using Linux's C Compiler

CHAPTER 25

Modifying the Kernel

Usually you will want to leave the Linux kernel alone except when performing a major upgrade, installing a new networking component (such as NFS or NIS), or installing a new device driver that has special kernel requirements. The details of the process used to install the kernel drivers are usually supplied with the software. Because this isn't always the case, though, this chapter should give you a good idea of the general process for working with the kernel.

Warning

Don't modify the kernel without knowing what you are doing. If you damage the source code or configuration information, your kernel may be unusable, and in the worst cases, your filesystem may be affected. Take care and follow instructions carefully. Keep in mind that this chapter only covers the basics of kernel manipulation.

The several versions of Linux in common use have a few inconsistencies between them. For that reason, the exact instructions supplied in the following sections may not work with your version of Linux. The general approach is the same, however, and only the directory or utility names may be different. Most versions of Linux supply documentation that lists the recompilation process and the locations of the source code and compiled programs.

Note

Before doing anything with the kernel or utilities, make sure you have a good set of emergency boot disks and a complete backup on tape or floppy disk. Although the process of modifying the kernel is not difficult, it does cause problems every now and again that can leave you stranded without a working system. Boot disks are the best way to recover, so make at least one extra set.

Because the kernel is compiled with the C compiler supplied as part of Linux, the latter part of this chapter looks at the C compiler and its flags and how you can use it to your advantage. This information isn't meant to be a complete reference to the C system, of course, but it should be useful for some basic manipulations you may require when modifying the kernel (or any other source code compiled by C).

UPGRADING AND INSTALLING NEW KERNEL SOFTWARE

Linux is a dynamic operating system. New releases of the kernel or parts of the operating system that can be linked into the kernel are made available at regular intervals to users. Whether you want to upgrade to the new releases usually depends on the features or bug fixes that the new release offers. You will probably have to relink the kernel when you add new software, unless the software is loaded as a utility or device driver.

Avoid upgrading your system with every new release, for a couple of reasons. The most common problem with constant upgrades is that you may be stuck with a new software package that causes backward compatibility problems with your existing system or that has a major problem with it. Most new releases of software wipe out existing configuration information, so you will have to reconfigure the packages that are being installed from scratch. Also, the frequency with which new releases are made available is so high that you can probably spend more time loading and recompiling kernels and utilities than using the system. Read the release notes carefully to ensure that the release is worth the installation time and trouble. Remember that few installations proceed smoothly!

The best advice is to upgrade only once or twice a year, and only when there is a new feature or enhancement that will make a significant difference to the way you use Linux. It's tempting to always have the latest and newest versions of the operating system, but there is a lot to be said for having a stable, functioning operating system, too.

If you do upgrade to a new release, bear in mind that you don't have to upgrade everything. The last few Linux releases have changed only about five percent of the operating system with each new major package upgrade. Instead of replacing the entire system, just install those parts that will have a definite effect, such as the kernel, compilers and their libraries, and frequently used utilities. This method saves time and reconfiguration.

Compiling the Kernel from Source Code

Upgrading, replacing, or adding new code to the kernel is usually a simple process. You obtain the source for the kernel, make any configuration changes, compile it, and then place it in the proper location on the filesystem to run the system properly. The process is often automated for you by a shell script or installation program, and some upgrades are completely automated with no need to do anything more than start the upgrade utility.

Where to Find Kernel Sources

Kernel sources for new releases of Linux are available from CD-ROM distributions, FTP sites, user groups, and many other locations. Most kernel versions are numbered with a version and a patch level, so you see kernel names like 1.12.123

where 1 is the major release, 12 is the minor version release, and 123 is the patch number. Most kernel source sites maintain several versions simultaneously, so check through the source directories for the latest version of the kernel.

Patch releases are sometimes numbered differently, and do not require the entire source of the kernel to install. In most cases, the patch overlays a section of existing source code, and you only need to recompile the kernel to install the patch. Patches are released quite frequently.

Most kernel source programs are maintained as a gzipped tar file. Unpack the files into a subdirectory of /usr/src, which is where most of the source code is kept for Linux. Some versions of Linux keep other directories for the kernel source, so you may want to check any documentation supplied with the system or look for a README file in the /usr/src directory for more instructions.

USING NEW KERNEL SOURCES

Often, unpacking the gzipped tar file in /usr/src creates a subdirectory called /usr/src/linux, which can overwrite your last version of the kernel source. Before starting the unpacking process, rename or copy any existing /usr/src/linux (or whatever name is used with the new kernel) file so you have a backup version in case of problems.

After unpacking the kernel source, you need to create two symbolic links to the /usr/include directory (if they are not created already or set by the installation procedure). Usually, the link commands required are the following:

```
ln -sf /usr/src/linux/include/linux /usr/include/linux
ln -sf /usr/src/linux/include/asm /usr/include/asm
```

If the directory names are different with your version of Linux, substitute them for /usr/src/linux. Without these links, the upgrade or installation of a new kernel cannot proceed.

After ungzipping and untarring the source code and establishing the links, you can begin the compilation process. You must have a version of gcc or g++ (the GNU C and C++ compilers) or some other compatible compiler available for the compilation. You may have to check with the source code documentation to make sure you have the correct versions of the compilers; occasionally new kernel features are added that are not supported by older versions of gcc or g++.

Check the file /usr/src/linux/Makefile (or whatever path Makefile is in with your source distribution). This file has a line that defines the ROOT_DEV, the device that is used as the root filesystem when Linux boots. Usually the line looks like the following:

```
ROOT_DEV = CURRENT
```

If you have any other value, make sure it is correct for your filesystem configuration. If the Makefile has no value, set it as shown in the preceding line.

The compilation process begins with you changing to the /usr/src/linux directory and issuing the command

```
make config
```

which invokes the `make` utility for the C compiler. The process may be slightly different for some versions of Linux, so check any release or installation notes supplied with the source code.

The `config` program issues a series of questions and prompts you to answer to indicate any configuration issues that need to be completed before the compilation begins. These questions may be about the type of disk drive you are using, the CPU, any partitions, or other devices like CD-ROMs. Answer the questions as well as you can. If you are unsure, choose the default values or the one that makes the most sense. The worst case is that you will have to redo the process if the system doesn't run properly. (You do have an emergency boot disk ready, don't you?)

Next, you have to set all the source dependencies. This step is commonly skipped and can cause a lot of problems if is not performed for each software release. Issue the following command:

```
make dep
```

If the software you are installing does not have a `dep` file, check the release or installation notes to ensure that the dependencies are correctly handled by the other steps.

Now you can finally compile the new kernel. The command to start the process is

```
make Image
```

which compiles the source code and leaves the new kernel image file in the current directory (usually /usr/src/linux). If you want to create a compressed kernel image, you can use the following command:

```
make zImage
```

Not all releases or upgrades to the kernel support compressed image compilation.

The last step in the process is to copy the new kernel image file to the boot device or a boot floppy disk. To place the kernel on a floppy disk, use the following command:

```
cp Image /dev/fd0
```

Use a different device driver as necessary to place the kernel elsewhere on the hard drive filesystem. Alternatively, if you plan to use LILO to boot the operating system, you can install the new kernel by running a setup program or the utility /usr/lilo/lilo. Don't copy the new kernel over your old boot disk's kernel. If the new kernel doesn't boot, you may have to use the older boot disk to restart your system.

Now all that remains is to reboot the system and see whether the new kernel loads properly. If you have any problems, boot from a floppy disk, restore the old kernel, and start the process again. Check documentation supplied with the release source code for any information about problems you may encounter or steps that may have been added to the process.

ADDING DRIVERS TO THE KERNEL

You may want to link in new device drivers or special software to the kernel without going through the upgrade process of the kernel itself. This procedure is often necessary when you add a new device like a multiport board or an optical drive that should be loaded during the boot process. Alternatively, you may be adding special security software that must be linked into the kernel.

Add-in kernel software usually has installation instructions provided, but the general process is to locate the source in a directory that the kernel recompilation process can find (such as /usr/src). Instructing the `make` utility to add the new code to the kernel may require modifications to the Makefile. Either you or an installation script can make these modifications. Some software has its own Makefile supplied for this reason.

Then, begin the kernel recompilation with the new software added in to the load. The process is the same as shown in the preceding section, with the kernel installed in the boot location or set by LILO. Typically, the entire process takes about 10 minutes and is quite troublefree unless the vendor of the kernel modification did a sloppy job. Make sure that the source code provided for the modification works with your version of the Linux kernel.

UPGRADING LIBRARIES

Most of the software on a Linux system is set to use shared libraries (a set of subroutines used by many programs). When the message

```
Incompatible library version
```

appears on-screen after you upgrade the system and you try to execute a utility, it means that the libraries have been updated and need to be recompiled. Most libraries are backwards-compatible, so existing software should work properly even after a library upgrade.

Library upgrades are less frequent than kernel upgrades and can be found in the same places. There are usually documents that guide you to the latest version of a library, or there may be a file explaining which libraries are necessary with new versions of the operating system kernel. Most library upgrades are gzipped tar files, and the process for unpacking them is the same as for kernel source code except the target directories are usually /lib, /usr/lib, and /usr/include. Usually, any files that have the extension .a or .aa go in the /usr/lib directory. Shared library image files, which have the format libc.so.version, are installed into /lib.

You may have to change symbolic links within the filesystem to point to the latest version of the library. For example, if you were running library version libc.so.4.4.1 and upgraded to libc.so.4.4.2, you must alter the symbolic link set in /lib to this file. The command would be

```
ln -sf /lib/libc/so/4/4/1 /lib/libc.so.4
```

where the last name in the link command is the name of the current library file in /lib. Your library name may be different, so check the directory and release or installation notes first.

You will also have to change the symbolic link for the file libm.so.version in the same manner. Do not delete the symbolic links; if you do, all programs that depend on the shared library (including ls) will be unable to function.

USING LINUX'S C COMPILER

Linux uses a C compiler for every compilation of the kernel (and most utilities, too). The C compiler that is available for all versions of Linux is the GNU C compiler, abbreviated gcc. This compiler was created under the Free Software Foundation's programming license and is therefore freely distributable. The GNU C Compiler that is packaged with the Slackware Linux distribution is a fully functional ANSI C compatible compiler. If you are familiar with a C compiler on a different operating system or hardware platform, you will be able to learn gcc very quickly.

The GCC compiler is invoked by passing it a number of options and one or more filenames. The basic syntax for gcc is as follows:

```
gcc [options] [filenames]
```

The operations specified by the command line options are performed on each of the files that are on the command line. There are well over 100 compiler options that can be passed to gcc. You will probably never use most of these options, but you will use some of them on a regular basis.

COMPILER OPTIONS

Many of the gcc options consist of more than one character. For this reason, you must specify each option with its own hyphen. You cannot group options after a single hyphen as you can with most Linux commands. For example, the following two commands are not the same:

```
gcc -p -g test.c
gcc -pg test.c
```

The first command tells gcc to compile test.c with profile information (-p) and also to store debugging information with the executable (-g). The second command just tells gcc to compile test.c with profile information for the gprof command (-pg).

When you compile a program using gcc without any command line options, it creates an executable file (assuming that the compile was successful) and calls it a.out. To specify a name other than a.out for the executable file, you use the -o compiler option. For example, to compile a C program file named count.c into an executable file named count, use the following command:

```
gcc -o count count.c
```

As shown in the preceding example, the executable file name must occur directly after the -o on the command line.

Other compiler options enable you to specify how far you want the compile to proceed. The -c option tells gcc to compile the code into object code and to skip the assembly and linking stages of the compile. This option is used quite often because it makes the compilation of multifile C programs faster and easier to manage. Object code files that are created by gcc have a .o extension by default.

The -S compiler option tells gcc to stop the compile after it has generated the assembler files for the C code. Assembler files that are generated by gcc have a .s extension by default. The -E option instructs the compiler to only perform the preprocessing compiler stage on the input files. When this option is used, the output from the preprocessor is sent to the standard output rather than being stored in a file.

When you compile C code with gcc, it tries to compile the code in the least amount of time and also tries to create compiled code that is easy to debug. Making the code easy to debug means that the sequence of the compiled code is the same as the sequence of the source code and no code gets optimized out of the compile. There are many options that you can use to tell gcc to create smaller, faster executable programs at the cost of compile time and ease of debugging. Of these options, the two that you will use most are the -O and the -O2 options.

The -O option tells gcc to perform basic optimizations on the source code. These optimizations make the code run faster in most cases. The -O2 option tells gcc to make the code as fast and small as it can. The -O2 option causes the compilation speed to be slower than it is when using the -O option, but it typically results in code that executes more quickly.

In addition to the -O and -O2 optimization options, you can use a number of lower-level options to make the code faster. These options are very specific and should only be used if you fully understand the effect of these options on the compiled code. For a detailed description of these options, refer to the gcc man page.

Debugging and Profiling Options

The gcc compiler supports several debugging and profiling options. Of these options, the two that you are most likely to use are the -g option and the -pg option.

The -g option tells GCC to produce debugging information that the GNU debugger (gdb) can use to help you to debug your program. The gcc program provides a feature that many other C compilers do not have. With gcc, you can use the -g option in conjunction with the -O option (which generates optimized code). This feature can be very useful if you are trying to debug code that is as close as possible to what will exist in the final product. When you are using these two options together, be aware that gcc will probably change some of the code that you have written when gcc optimizes the code.

The -pg option tells gcc to add extra code to your program that, when executed, generates profile information that the gprof program uses to display timing information about your program.

Debugging *GCC* Programs with *GDB*

Linux includes the GNU debugging program called gdb. You can use gdb debugger to debug C and C++ programs. It enables you to see the internal structure or the memory that a program is using while it is executing. This debugging program enables you to perform the following functions:

- ◆ Monitor the value of variables that your program contains
- ◆ Set breakpoints that stop the program at a specific line of code
- ◆ Step through the code line by line

When you start gdb, you can specify a number of options on the command line. You will probably run gdb most often with this command:

```
gdb filename
```

When you invoke gdb in this way, you are specifying the executable file that you want to debug. You can also tell gdb to inspect a core file that was created by the executable file being examined or attach gdb to a currently running process. To get a listing and brief description of each of these other options, refer to the gdb man page or type gdb -h at the command line.

To get gdb to work properly, you must compile your programs so that the compiler generates debugging information. The debugging information that is generated contains the types for each of the variables in your program as well as the mapping between the addresses in the executable program and the line numbers in the source code. The gdb debugging program uses this information to relate the executable code to the source code. To compile a program with the debugging information turned on, use the -g compiler option.

SUMMARY

Recompiling the kernel source and adding new features to the kernel proceeds smoothly as long as you know what you are doing. Don't let the process scare you, but always keep boot disks on hand. Follow instructions wherever available as most new software has special requirements for linking into the kernel or replacing existing systems.

- Creating and Running
  Shell Programs

- Using Variables

- Using Quotation
  Marks

- Using the test
  Command

- Using Conditional
  Statements

- Using Iteration
  Statements

- Using Functions

CHAPTER 26

Shell Programming

Shell programming is one of the most useful tools a system administrator has. The ability to write a short program to complete an otherwise time-consuming task is much more powerful than knowing every Linux administration tool in detail. Shell programming can make a system administrator's life so much easier that it should be a mandatory skill.

If these statements sound a little too good to be true, consider the many tasks that system administrators face every day involving multiple files or directories. Whenever you deal with a number of files, shell programming can make your job easier. This chapter can't show you much more than the basics, but they should help you in your daily work. Many excellent books on shell programming are available, so be sure to keep one handy.

Creating and Running Shell Programs

At the simplest level, shell programs are just files that contain one or more shell or Linux commands. You can use these programs to simplify repetitive tasks, to replace two or more commands that are always executed together with a single command, to automate the installation of other programs, and to write simple interactive applications.

To create a shell program, you must create a file using a text editor and put the shell or Linux commands that you want to be executed into that file. Suppose that you have a CD-ROM drive mounted on your Linux system. This CD-ROM device is mounted when the system is first started. If you change the CD that is in the drive at a later time, you must force Linux to read the new directory contents. One way of achieving this task is to put the new CD into the drive, unmount the CD-ROM drive using the umount command, and then remount the drive using the mount command. The following commands show this sequence of steps:

```
umount /dev/cdrom
mount /dev/cdrom /cdrom
```

Instead of typing both of these commands each time you change the CD, you can create a shell program that executes both of these commands for you. To create this shell program, put the two commands into a file and call the file remount (or any other name you want).

There are several ways of executing the commands in the remount file. One way is to make the file executable by entering the following command:

```
chmod +x remount
```

This command changes the permissions of the file so that it is executable. To run your new shell program, type remount on the command line.

Note

The `remount` shell program must be in a directory that is in your search path or the shell will not be able to find the program to execute. If you can't run the command because it isn't found, specify the path.

Also, if you are using `tcsh` to write programs, the first line of the shell program must start with a # in order for `tcsh` to recognize it as a `tcsh` program file. In fact, it is safest to make sure that the first line of every shell program is `#!/bin/sh` in order to make sure the shell program is executed as a Bourne shell process. This prevents many problems with the C shell trying to interpret Bourne shell syntax.

26

Another way that you can execute the shell program is to run the shell that the program was written for and pass the program as a parameter to the shell. In the case of a `tcsh` program, you enter the following command:

```
tcsh remount
```

This command starts up a new shell and tells it to execute the commands in the remount file.

A third way of executing the commands that are in a shell program file is to use the . (dot) command (with both the `pdksh` and `bash` shells) or the `source` command in the `tcsh` shell. These commands tell the shell to execute the file that is passed as an argument. For example, you can use the following command to tell `bash` or `pdksh` to execute the commands in the remount file:

```
. remount
```

To do the same thing in `tcsh`, use the following command:

```
source remount
```

The following example shows another situation in which a simple shell program can save a lot of time. Suppose that you were working on three different files in a directory every day, and you wanted to back up those three files onto a floppy disk at the end of each day. To do this task, you type in a series of commands:

```
mount -t msdos /dev/fd0 /a
cp file1 /dev/fd0
cp file2 /dev/fd0
cp file3 /dev/fd0
```

One way of backing up the files is to mount the floppy disk and then type three `copy` commands, one for each file that you want to copy. A simpler way is to put the four commands into a file called backup and then execute the `backup` command when you want to copy the three files onto the floppy disk drive.

Note

> You still have to ensure the backup shell program is executable and is in a directory that is in your path before you run the command. Also, be careful about using a filename that corresponds to a command name. If there is a program called backup, for example, in the shell's search path before it reads the current directory, that command would execute instead of the shell command file. For this reason, try to use filenames for your shell scripts that are not close to Linux commands.

USING VARIABLES

As is the case with almost any language, the use of variables is very important in shell programs. You have seen several types of variables before, of course. Some examples of commonly used variables are the PATH variable and the TERM variable. These variables are examples of built-in shell variables, which are variables defined by the shell program that you are using. This section describes how you can create your own variables and use them in simple shell programs.

ASSIGNING A VALUE TO A VARIABLE

In all three of the shells supplied with Linux (Bourne, Korn, and C shell variants), you can assign a value to a variable by typing the variable name followed by an equal sign and then typing the value that you want to assign to the variable. For example, to assign a value of five to the variable named count, enter the following command in bash or pdksh:

```
count=5
```

With tcsh, enter the following command to achieve the same results:

```
set count = 5
```

Note

> When setting a variable for the bash and pdksh shells, make sure that there are no spaces on either side of the equal sign. With tcsh, spaces do not matter.

Because the shell language is a non-typed interpretive language, you do not have to declare the variable as you would if you were programming in C or Pascal. You can use the same variable to store character strings or integers.

You store a character string into a variable in the same way you store an integer into a variable, as shown in the following example:

```
name=Garry (for pdksh and bash)
set name = Garry (for tcsh)
```

After you store a value into a variable, how do you get the value back out? You precede the variable name with a dollar sign ($).To print the value that stored in the count variable to the screen, enter the following command:

```
echo $count
```

If you omit the $ from the preceding command, the echo command displays the word count on-screen.

UNDERSTANDING POSITIONAL PARAMETERS AND OTHER BUILT-IN SHELL VARIABLES

When you run a shell program that requires or supports a number of command line options, each of these options is stored into a positional parameter. The first parameter is stored into a variable named 1, the second parameter is stored into a variable named 2, and so on. The shell reserves these variable names so you cannot use them as variables that you define. To access the values that are stored in these variables, you must precede the variable name with a dollar sign ($) just as you do with variables that you define.

The following shell program expects to be invoked with two parameters. The program takes the two parameters and prints the second parameter that was typed on the command line first and the first parameter that was typed on the command line second:

```
#program reverse, prints the command line parameters out in reverse #order
echo "$2"
echo "$1"
```

If you invoked this program by entering the command

```
reverse hello there
```

the program would return the output

```
there hello
```

A number of other built-in shell variables are important to know about when you are doing a lot of shell programming. Table 26.1 lists these variables and gives a brief description of what each is used for.

26

SHELL PROGRAMMING

TABLE 26.1. BUILT-IN SHELL VARIABLES.

Variable	Use
$#	Stores the number of command line arguments that were passed to the shell program
$?	Stores the exit value of the last executed command
$0	Stores the first word of the entered command, which is the name of the shell program
$*	Stores all the arguments that were entered on the command line ("$1 $2 ...")
"$@"	Stores all arguments that were entered on the command line, individually quoted ("$1" "$2" ...)

USING QUOTATION MARKS

The use of the different types of quotation marks is very important in shell programming. The shell uses both kinds of quotation marks and the backslash character to perform different functions. The double quotation marks (""), the single quotation marks ('), and the backslash (\) are all used to hide special characters from the shell. The back quotes have a special meaning for the shell and should not be used to enclose strings. Each of these methods hide varying degrees of special characters from the shell.

The double quotation marks are the least powerful of the three methods. When you surround characters with double quotes, all the whitespace characters are hidden from the shell, but all other special characters are still interpreted. This type of quoting is most useful when you are assigning strings that contain more than one word to a variable. For example, to assign the string hello there to the variable called greeting, enter the following commands:

```
greeting="hello there" (in bash and pdksh)
set greeting = "hello there" (in tcsh)
```

This command stores the whole hello there string into the greeting variable as one word. If you typed in this command without using the quotes, bash and pdksh wouldn't understand the command and would return an error message, and tcsh would assign the value hello to the greeting variable and ignore the rest of the command line.

Single quotes are the most powerful form of quoting. They hide all special characters from the shell. This type of quoting is useful if the command you enter is intended for a program other than the shell. You can, for example, use single quotes to write the `hello there` variable assignment, but you can't use this method in some instances. If the string being assigned to the `greeting` variable contains another variable, for example, you have to use double quotes. Suppose you wanted to include the name of the user in your greeting. You would type the following commands:

```
greeting="hello there $LOGNAME" (for bash and pdksh)
set greeting="hello there $LOGNAME" (for tcsh)
```

Note

The `LOGNAME` variable is a shell variable that contains the Linux username of the person that is logged on to the system.

These commands stores the value `hello there root` into the `greeting` variable if you are logged into Linux as root. If you try to write this command using single quotes, the single quotes hide the dollar sign from the shell, and the shell doesn't know that it is supposed to perform a variable substitution. As a result, the `greeting` variable is assigned the value of `hello there $LOGNAME`.

Using the backslash is the third way of hiding special characters from the shell. Like the single quotation mark method, the backslash hides all special characters from the shell, but it can hide only one character at a time, as opposed to groups of characters. You can rewrite the greeting example using the backslash instead of double quotation marks by using the following commands:

```
greeting=hello\ there (for bash and pdksh)
set greeting=hello\ there (for tcsh)
```

In this command, the backslash hides the space character from the shell and the string `hello there` is assigned to the `greeting` variable.

Backslash quoting is used most often when you want to hide only a single character from the shell. This situation occurs when you want to include a special character in a string. For example, to store the price of a box of computer disks into a variable named `disk_price`, use the following command:

```
disk_price=\$5.00 (for bash and pdksh)
set disk_price = \$5.00 (tcsh)
```

The backslash in this example hides the dollar sign from the shell. If the backslash were not there, the shell would try to find a variable named 5 and perform a variable substitution on that variable. If there were no variables named 5 defined, the shell would assign a value of .00 to the `disk_price` variable. (This shell would substitute a value of null for the $5 variable.) You could also use single quotes in the `disk_price` example to hide the dollar sign from the shell.

The back quote marks (") perform a different function. You use them when you want to use the results of a command in another command. For example, to set the value of the contents variable to be equal to the list of files that are in the current directory, type the following command:

```
contents='ls' (for bash and pdksh)
set contents = 'ls' (for tcsh)
```

This command executes the ls command and stores the results of the command into the contents variable. As shown later in the iteration statements section, this feature can be very useful when you want to write a shell program that performs some action on the results of a another command.

USING THE *TEST* COMMAND

In bash and pdksh, the test command is used to evaluate conditional expressions. You typically use the test command to evaluate a condition in a conditional statement or to evaluate the entrance or exit criteria for an iteration statement. The test command has the following syntax:

```
test expression
```

or

```
[ expression ]
```

You can use several built-in operators with the test command. These operators are classified into four different groups: string operators, integer operators, file operators, and logical operators.

You use the string operators to evaluate string expressions. Table 26.2 lists the string operators that the three shell programming languages support.

TABLE 26.2. STRING OPERATORS FOR THE test COMMAND.

Operator	Meaning
str1 = str2	Returns true if str1 is identical to str2
str1 != str2	Returns true if str1 is not identical to str2
str	Returns true if str is not null
-n str	Returns true if the length of str is greater than zero
-z str	Returns true if the length of str is equal to zero

The shell integer operators perform similar functions to the string operators except that they act on integer arguments. Table 26.3 lists the test command's integer operators.

TABLE 26.3. INTEGER OPERATORS FOR THE test COMMAND.

Operator	Meaning
int1 -eq int2	Returns true if int1 is equal to int2
int1 -ge int2	Returns true if int1 is greater than or equal to int2
int1 -gt int2	Returns true if int1 is greater than int2
int1 -le int2	Returns true if int1 is less than or equal to int2
int1 -lt int2	Returns true if int1 is less than int2
int1 -ne int2	Returns true if int1 is not equal to int2

You use the test command's file operators to perform functions such as checking to see whether a file exists and checking to see what kind of file the file passed as an argument to the test command is. Table 26.4 lists the test command's file operators.

TABLE 26.4. FILE OPERATORS FOR THE test COMMAND.

Operator	Meaning
-d file	Returns true if the specified file is a directory
-f file	Returns true if the specified file is an ordinary file
-r file	Returns true if the specified file is readable by the process
-s file	Returns true if the specified file has a non-zero length
-w file	Returns true if the file is writable by the process
-x file	Returns true if the specified file is executable

You use the test command's logical operators to combine integer, string, or file operators or to negate a single integer, string, or file operator. Table 26.5 lists the test command's logical operators.

TABLE 26.5. LOGICAL OPERATORS FOR THE test COMMAND.

Command	Meaning
! expr	Returns true if expr is not true
expr1 -a expr2	Returns true if expr1 and expr2 are true
expr1 -o expr2	Returns true if expr1 or expr2 are true

The tcsh shell does not have a test command, but tsch expressions perform the same function. The expression operators that tcsh supports are almost identical to those supported by the C language. You use these expressions mostly in if and while commands. Later in this chapter, the sections "Using Conditional Statements" and "Using Iteration Statements" cover these commands. Like the bash and pdksh test command, tcsh expressions support integer, string, file, and logical operators. Table 26.6 lists the integer operators supported by tcsh expressions.

TABLE 26.6. INTEGER OPERATORS FOR tcsh EXPRESSIONS.

Operator	Meaning
int1 <= int2	Returns true if int1 is less than or equal to int2
int1 >= int2	Returns true if int1 is greater than or equal to int2
int1 < int2	Returns true if int1 is less than int2
int1 > int2	Returns true if int1 is greater than int2

Table 26.7 lists the string operators that tcsh expressions support.

TABLE 26.7. STRING OPERATORS FOR tcsh EXPRESSIONS.

Operator	Meaning
str1 == str2	Returns true if str1 is equal to str2
str1 != str2	Returns true if str1 is not equal to str2

Table 26.8 lists the file operators that tcsh expressions support.

TABLE 26.8. FILE OPERATORS FOR tcsh EXPRESSIONS.

Operator	Meaning
-r file	Returns true if file is readable
-w file	Returns true if file is writable
-x file	Returns true if file is executable
-e file	Returns true if file exists
-o file	Returns true if file is owned by the current user
-z file	Returns true if file has a size of zero
-f file	Returns true if file is a regular file
-d file	Returns true if file is a directory file

Table 26.9 lists the logical operators that tcsh expressions support.

TABLE 26.9. LOGICAL OPERATORS FOR tcsh EXPRESSIONS.

Operator	Meaning
exp1 ¦¦ exp2	Returns true if exp1 is true or if exp2 is true
exp1 && exp2	Returns true if both exp1 and exp2 are true
! exp	Returns true if exp is not true

USING CONDITIONAL STATEMENTS

The bash, pdksh, and tcsh shells each have two different forms of conditional statements, the if statement and the case statement. You use these statements to execute different parts of your shell program depending on whether certain conditions are true. As with most statements, the syntax for these statements is slightly different between the different shells.

THE *IF* STATEMENT

All three shells support nested if...then...else statements. These statements provide you with a way of performing complicated conditional tests in your shell programs. The syntax of the if statement in bash and pdksh is the same:

```
if [ expression ]
then
    commands
elif [ expression2 ]
    commands
else
    commands
fi
```

Note that bash and pdksh use the reverse of the statement name in most of their complex statements to signal the end of the statement. In the preceding statement, the fi keyword is used to signal the end of the if statement.

The elif and else clauses are both optional parts of the if statement. The elif statement is an abbreviation for else if. This statement is executed only if none of the expressions associated with the if statement or any elif statements before it were true. The commands associated with the else statement are executed only if none of the expressions associated with the if statement or any of the elif statements were true.

In `tcsh`, the `if` statement has two different forms. The first form provides the same function as the `bash` and `pdksh` `if` statement. This form of `if` statement has the following syntax:

```
if (expression1) then
    commands
else if (expression2) then
    commands
else
    commands
endif
```

Once again the `else if` and `else` parts of the `if` statement are optional. This statement could have been written with an `elif`, as well. If the preceding code shown is the entire `tcsh` program, it should begin with the following line to make sure it runs properly:

```
#!/bin/sh
```

The second form of `if` statement that `tcsh` provides is a simple version of the first `if` statement. This form of `if` statement only evaluates a single expression. If the expression is true, it executes a single command. If the expression is false, nothing happens. The syntax for this form of `if` statement is the following.

```
if (expression) command
```

The following is an example of a `bash` or `pdksh` `if` statement. This statement checks to see whether there is a .profile file in the current directory:

```
if [ -f .profile ]
then
    echo "There is a .profile file in the current directory."
else
    echo "Could not find the .profile file."
fi
```

The same statement written using the `tcsh` syntax looks like the following:

```
#
if ( { -f .profile } ) then
    echo "There is a .profile file in the current directory."
else
    echo "Could not find the .profile file."
endif
```

Notice that in the `tcsh` example the first line starts with a #. This sign is required in order for `tcsh` to recognize the file containing the commands as a `tcsh` script file.

THE *CASE* STATEMENT

The case statement enables you to compare a pattern with a number of other patterns and execute a block of code if a match is found. The shell case statement is quite a bit more powerful than the case statement in Pascal or the switch statement in C. In the shell case statement, you can compare strings with wildcards in them; you can only compare enumerated types or integer values with the Pascal and C equivalents.

The syntax for the case statement in bash and pdksh is the following:

```
case string1 in
    str1)
        commands;;
    str2)
        commands;;
    *)
        commands;;
esac
```

String1 is compared to str1 and str2. If one of these strings matches string1, the commands up until the double semi-colon (;;) are executed. If neither str1 or str2 match string1, the commands that are associated with the asterisk are executed. These commands are the default case condition because the asterisk matches all strings.

The tcsh equivalent of the bash and pdksh case statement is called the switch statement. This statement closely follows the C switch statement syntax. The syntax for the switch statement is the following:

```
switch (string1)
    case    str1:
        statements
    breaksw
    case str2:
        statements
    breaksw
    default:
        statements
    breaksw
endsw
```

This statement behaves in the same manner as the bash and pdksh case statement. Each string following the case keyword is compared with string1. If any of these strings matches string1, the code following it up until the breaksw keyword is executed. If none of the strings match, the code following the default keyword up until the breaksw keyword is executed.

The following code is an example of a bash or pdksh case statement. This code checks to see whether the first command line option is an -i or an -e. If it is an -i, the program counts the number of lines in the file specified by the second command line option that begins with the letter i. If the first option is an -e, the program counts the number of lines in the file specified by the second command line option that begins with the letter e. If the first command line option is not an -i or an -e, the program prints a brief error message to the screen.

```
case $1 in
  -i)
   count='grep ^i $2 ¦ wc -l'
   echo "The number of lines in $2 that start with an i is $count"
   ;;
  -e)
   count='grep ^e $2 ¦ wc -l'
   echo "The number of lines in $2 that start with an e is $count"
   ;;
  * )
   echo "That option is not recognized"
   ;;
esac
```

The following is the same example written in tcsh syntax:

```
# remember that the first line must start with a # when using tcsh
switch ( $1 )
   case -i ¦ i:
    set count = 'grep ^i $2 ¦ wc -l'
    echo "The number of lines in $2 that begin with i is $count"
   breaksw
   case -e ¦ e:
    set count = 'grep ^e $2 ¦ wc -l'
    echo "The number of lines in $2 that begin with e is $count"
   breaksw
   default:
    echo "That option is not recognized"
   breaksw
endsw
```

USING ITERATION STATEMENTS

The shell languages also provide several iteration or looping statements. The most commonly used is the for loop statement. These iterative statements are handy when you need to perform an action repeatedly, such as when you are processing lists of files.

THE *FOR* STATEMENT

The for statement executes the commands that are contained within it a set number of times. The for statement has two different variations in bash and pdksh. The first form of for statement that bash and pdksh support has the following syntax:

```
for var1 in list
do
    commands
done
```

In this form, the for statement executes once for each item that is in the list. This list can be a variable that contains several words separated by spaces, or it can be a list of values that is typed directly into the statement. Each time through the loop, the variable var1 is assigned to the current item in the list until the last one is reached.

The second form of for statement has the following syntax:

```
for var1
do
    statements
done
```

In this form, the for statement executes once for each item that is in the variable var1. When you use this syntax of the for statement, the shell program assumes that the var1 variable contains all of the positional parameters that are passed into the shell program on the command line. Typically, this form of for statement is the equivalent of writing the following for statement:

```
for var1 in "$@"
do
    statements
done
```

The equivalent of the for statement in tcsh is called the foreach statement. It behaves in the same manner as the bash and pdksh for statements. The syntax of the foreach statement is the following:

```
foreach name (list)
    commands
end
```

Again, if this code were the complete program, it should start with a pound sign (and preferably #!/bin/sh to force execution in the Bourne shell). The following is an example of the bash or pdksh style of for statement. This example takes as command line options any number of text files. The program reads in each of these files, converts all of the letters to uppercase, and then stores the results in a file of the same name but with a .caps extension.

```
for file
do
tr a-z A-Z < $file >$file.caps
done
```

The following is same example written in tcsh shell language:

```
#
foreach file ($*)
    tr a-z A-Z < $file >$file.caps
end
```

THE *WHILE* STATEMENT

Another iteration statement that is offered by the shell programming language is the while statement. This statement causes a block of code to be executed while a provided conditional expression is true. The syntax for the while statement in bash and pdksh is the following:

```
while expression
do
    statements
done
```

The syntax for the while statement in tcsh is the following:

```
while (expression)
    statements
end
```

The following is an example of the bash or pdksh style of while statement. This program lists the parameters that are passed to the program along with the parameter number.

```
count=1
while [ -n "$*" ]
do
    echo "This is parameter number $count $1"
    shift
    count='expr $count + 1'
done
```

The shift command moves the command line parameters over one to the left (see the following section, "The shift Command," for more information). The following is the same program written in the tcsh language:

```
#
set count = 1
while ( "$*" != "" )
    echo "This is parameter number $count $1"
    shift
    set count = 'expr $count + 1'
end
```

THE *UNTIL* STATEMENT

The until statement is very similar in syntax and function to the while statement. The only real difference between the two is that the until statement executes its code block while its conditional expression is false and the while statement executes its code block while its conditional expression is true. The syntax for the until statement in bash and pdksh is the following:

```
until expression
do
    commands
done
```

To make the example that was used for the while statement work with the until statement, all you have to do is negate the condition, as shown in the following code:

```
count=1
until [ -z "$*" ]
do
    echo "This is parameter number $count $1"
    shift
    count='expr $count + 1'
done
```

The only difference between this example and the while statement example is that the -n test command option, which means that the string has non-zero length, was replaced by the -z test option, which means that the string has a length of zero. In practice, the until statement is not very useful because any until statement that you write can also be written as a while statement. The until command is not supported by tcsh.

THE *SHIFT* COMMAND

The bash, pdksh, and tcsh shells all support a command called shift. The shift command moves the current values stored in the positional parameters one position to the left. For example, if the values of the current positional parameters are

```
$1 = -r    $2 = file1    $3 = file2
```

and you executed the shift command

```
shift
```

the resulting positional parameters would be the following:

```
$1 = file1    $2 = file2
```

You also can shift the positional parameters over more than one place by specifying a number with the shift command. The following command shifts the positional parameters two places:

```
shift 2
```

This command is very useful when you have a shell program that needs to parse command line options. Options are typically preceded by a hyphen and a letter that indicates what the option is to be used for. Because options are usually processed in a loop of some kind, you will often want to skip to the next positional parameter once you have identified which option should be coming next. For example, the following shell program expects two command line options, one that specifies an input file and one that specifies an output file. The program reads the input file, translates all of the characters in the input file into uppercase, and then stores the results in the specified output file:

```
while [ "$1" ]
do
    if [ "$1" = "-i" ] then
        infile="$2"
        shift 2
    else if [ "$1" = "-o" ] then
        outfile="$2"
        shift 2
    else
        echo "Program $0 does not recognize option $1"
    fi
done

tr a-z A-Z <$infile >$outfile
```

THE *SELECT* STATEMENT

The pdksh shell offers one iteration statement that neither bash nor tcsh provides. This statement is the very useful select. statement. It is quite a bit different from the other iteration statements because it does not execute a block of shell code repeatedly while a condition is true or false. What the select statement does is enable you to automatically generate simple text menus. The syntax for the select statement is as follows:

```
select menuitem [in list_of_items]
do
    commands
done
```

When you execute a select statement, pdksh creates a numbered menu item for each element that is in the list_of_items. This list_of_items can be a variable that contains more that one item such as choice1 choice2 or it can be a list of choices typed in the command, as in the following example:

```
select menuitem in choice1 choice2 choice3
```

If the list_of_items is not provided, the select statement uses the positional parameters just as the for statement does.

When the user of the program that contains a `select` statement picks one of the menu items by typing in the number associated with it, the `select` statement stores the value of the selected item in the `menuitem` variable. The statements in the `do` block can then perform actions on this menu item.

The following is an example of how you can use the `select` statement. This example displays three menu items. When the user chooses an item, the program asks whether that item is the intended selection. If the user enters anything other than `y` or `Y`, the program redisplays the menu.

```
select menuitem in pick1 pick2 pick3
do
    echo "Are you sure you want to pick $menuitem"
    read res
    if [ $res = "y" -o $res = "Y" ]
    then
        break
    fi
done
```

This example introduces a few new commands. The `read` command is used to get input from the user. It stores anything that the user types into the specified variable. The `break` command is used to exit a `while`, `select`, or `for` statement.

THE *REPEAT* STATEMENT

The `tcsh` shell has an iteration statement that has no equivalent in the `pdksh` or `bash` shells. This statement is the `repeat` statement. The `repeat` statement executes a single command a specified number of times. The syntax for the `repeat` statement is the following:

```
repeat count command
```

The following example of the `repeat` statement takes a set of numbers as command line options and prints out that number of periods onto the screen. This program acts as a very primitive graphing program.

```
#
foreach num ($*)
    repeat $num echo -n "."
    echo ""
end
```

Tip

You can rewrite any `repeat` statement as a `while` or `for` statement; the repeat syntax is just more convenient.

26

SHELL PROGRAMMING

USING FUNCTIONS

The shell languages enable you to define your own functions. These functions behave in much the same way as functions that you define in C or other programming languages. The main advantage of using functions as opposed to writing all of your shell code in line is for organization. Code written using functions tends to be much easier to read and maintain and also tends to be smaller because you can group common code into functions instead of putting it everywhere that it is needed.

The syntax for creating a function in bash and pdksh is the following:

```
fname () {
    shell commands
}
```

In addition to the preceding syntax, pdksh allows the following syntax:

```
function fname {
    shell commands
}
```

Both of these forms behave in the same way.

After you have defined your function using one of the preceding forms, you can invoke it by entering the following command:

```
fname [parm1 parm2 parm3 ...]
```

Notice that you can pass any number of parameters to your function. When you do pass parameters to a function, it sees those parameters as positional parameters just as a shell program does when you pass it parameters on the command line. For example, the following shell program contains several functions each of which is performing a task that is associated with one of the command line options. This example illustrates many of the concepts covered in this chapter. It reads all the files that are passed in on the command line and, depending on the option that was used, writes the files out in all uppercase letters, writes the files out in all lowercase letters, or prints the files.

```
upper () {
    shift
    for i
    do
        tr a-z A-Z <$1 >$1.out
        rm  $1
        mv $1.out $1
        shift
    done; }
```

```
lower () {
    shift
    for i
    do
        tr A-Z a-z <$1 >$1.out
        rm $1
        mv $1.out $1
        shift
    done; }

print () {
    shift
    for i
    do
        lpr $1
        shift
    done; }

usage_error () {
    echo "$1 syntax is $1 <option> <input files>"
    echo ""
    echo "where option is one of the following"
    echo "p  — to print frame files"
    echo "u  — to save as uppercase"
    echo "l  — to save as lowercase"; }

case $1
in
    p ¦ -p)      print $@;;
    u ¦ -u)      upper $@;;
    l ¦ -l)      lower $@;;
    *)           usage_error $0;;
esac
```

The tcsh program does not support functions.

SUMMARY

In this chapter, you have seen many of the features of the bash, pdksh and tcsh programming languages. As you become used to using Linux, you will find that you use shell programming languages more and more often. Even though the shell languages are very powerful and quite easy to learn, you may run into some situations where shell programs are not suited to the problem you are solving. In these cases, you may want to investigate the possibility of using one of the other languages that is available under Linux.

- UUCP

- TCP/IP and Networks

- Configuring Hardware
  and the Kernel for
  Networking

- Configuring TCP/IP

- Configuring SLIP and
  PPP

- TCP/IP Utilities

- NFS and NIS

P A R T   IV

Networking

- Configuring UUCP

- Configuring Taylor
  UUCP

- Configuring HDB
  UUCP

- Understanding UUCP
  Connections

- UUCP Security

- Using UUCP

CHAPTER 27

UUCP

UUCP (UNIX to UNIX CoPy) was developed to provide a simple dialup networking protocol for UNIX systems. It is most often used today as an e-mail transfer system, allowing non-networked machines to transfer e-mail easily over a modem connection. You also can use it for USENET news and access to similar services that do not require a dedicated connection. UUCP is a two-machine connection between your Linux machine and another machine running UUCP. You cannot use UUCP as a remote system access system (like FTP or Telnet), nor can you use it as a standard login because the protocols do not support this type of interactive behavior. Chapter 24, "Security," looked briefly at some of the security problems inherent with UUCP. You should read that section of the chapter when setting up your UUCP system if you are susceptible to unauthorized access.

Linux can run any of several different versions of UUCP, most of which are compatible with each other to a reasonable extent except when it comes to configuration and installation procedures. Many Linux versions offer you a choice between the Taylor UUCP version and the HDB (HoneyDanBer) UUCP. You can use whichever single version came with your Linux software, or, if you have both, you can choose between the two (or use both versions as the mood strikes you).

Many Linux users prefer the Taylor UUCP implementation. Users who have worked on other UNIX systems prefer HDB because it is more recent and a little more logical in its file handling and configuration. If you have a choice, you should probably use HDB. This chapter looks at both of these versions. (Although even more UUCP versions exist, they are seldom used under Linux.) The first part of the chapter deals with configuring UUCP, and the rest of the chapter explains how to use it.

CONFIGURING UUCP

Most of the configuration required for UUCP takes place in the /usr/lib/uucp directory. UUCP uses several files, most of which need direct administrator modification to be set up properly. Although the configuration process can seem complex to someone who has never done it before, only a few files need changing, and each file has only one or two entries.

Because the configuration processes for Taylor UUCP and HDB UUCP are completely different, this section looks at them separately. You don't have to worry about which version of UUCP is being run at the remote end of the connection, however, because both versions can talk to each other (at least that's usually the case) as long as the configuration files are set up properly.

Some versions of Linux have semi-automated UUCP configuration scripts. These scripts are more common with HDB UUCP than Taylor UUCP, but a few helpful scripts are available for the latter. If you have one of these scripts, use it, but do check the files manually afterwards.

In the following examples of configuration processes, the host machine's name is merlin, and it is being connected through UUCP to another Linux system called arthur. As you go through the process, take care to enter the information in the same format as the examples, but don't mix Taylor and HDB UUCP information.

Configuring Taylor UUCP

The following list contains the filenames and the primary purposes of the configuration files for the Taylor UUCP system:

/usr/lib/uucp/config	This file defines the local machine name.
/usr/lib/uucp/sys	This file defines the remote systems and how to call them.
/usr/lib/uucp/port	This file describes each port for calling out and its parameters.
/usr/lib/uucp/dial	This file describes the dialers for calling out.
/usr/lib/uucp/dialcodes	This file contains expansions for symbolic dialcodes, but it is rarely used when a straight-out telephone connection exists.
/usr/lib/uucp/call	This file contains the login name and password for remote systems, but it is rarely used now.
/usr/lib/uucp/passwd	This file contains the login names and passwords used when remote systems connect to your local machine. This file is used only when uucico is password checking instead of using the login process.

To make the configuration process easier, this section proceeds with a sample configuration. You need only modify the entries to suit your own names, telephone numbers, device files, and so on. You can then repeat the process for as many systems as you want to connect to.

Specifying Your System's Name

The first file you need to modify holds your system name and other general parameters. The file /usr/lib/uucp/config needs a single line entry for your system name, such as this one:

```
hostname        merlin
```

The keyword hostname must be first on the line, followed by whitespace (spaces or tabs) and your machine name. The information in this file may have been completed when you installed Linux, but you should check the contents to make sure. If your system's name isn't set correctly, the connection to the remote system won't work properly.

> ### Note
>
> To use UUCP, you must have a system name. For compatibility with most versions of UUCP, keep the name to seven characters or less. Ideally, the UUCP name is the same name you assigned to your host during configuration. The name doesn't have to follow a convention (like the system name used by TCP/IP for Internet access), but if you use other network protocols, keep a consistent name. If you have a domain name (for TCP/IP access), use the first component of the machine's full TCP/IP name as the UUCP name. For example, if your full domain name is merlin.wizards.com, use the UUCP name merlin.

Setting Up Remote Systems

You also need to provide information about the remote system you want to connect to. The /usr/lib/uucp/sys file holds all the information about remote systems. This file usually has a few sample entries in it that you can copy or modify. Don't leave comment marks (pound or hash marks) in the first column or the entries will be ignored. A /usr/lib/uucp/sys entry for the remote machine arthur looks like the following:

```
# system: arthur (Bill Smallwood's Linux system)
system    arthur
time      Any
phone      555-1212
port      com1
speed       9600
chat       login: merlin password: secret1
```

The first line in the preceding extract is a comment line. Most system administrators like to put in a comment line to identify each system. The next lines identify the different aspects of the remote system, including its name (arthur), times at which it can be called (Any in this case, meaning no restrictions), the telephone number (including any area code or special digits that have to be dialed), the serial port to be used for the connection (in this case, com1), the speed at which to connect (9600 baud), and the chat script or login process. In this case, the chat script tells UUCP to wait until it sees the string login: and then send merlin. Then UUCP waits for the prompt password: and sends secret1.

Most login scripts require a login and password, and you must place these items in the configuration file because UUCP doesn't allow interactive sessions. This requirement can be a bit of a problem because it allows other users on your system to see the login password for the remote machine. But because only UUCP can use this password, this problem is not a major concern. Also, you can set the file permissions on the UUCP configuration files to prevent any system users (other than root) looking into the file.

Note

> Not all remote sites need a password for entry through UUCP. For example, some public archives let you log in and retrieve files using the uucp login with no password. Other sites use readily available passwords, such as uucp.

PORTS AND MODEMS

The port name used in the /usr/lib/uucp/sys entry does not have to match a device name on the Linux system because the file /usr/lib/uucp/port is used to match the entry to a physical device. This file requires an entry similar to the following for a 9600 baud modem:

```
# com1 device port
port        com1
type        modem
device      /dev/cua0
speed       9600
dialer      Hayes
```

In the /usr/lib/uucp/port file, the name of the port used in the /usr/lib/uucp/sys file is identified on the first line. The type of connection to be used (usually modem) is on the next. The Linux device that corresponds to the port name is specified as a device driver (for many Linux systems this driver can be /dev/modem, which is linked to the serial port device driver).

The modem connection speed comes next, and it shows the maximum speed of the modem. Finally, the name of a dialer is entered. This parameter is a throwback to the days when modems couldn't dial themselves and used another device (called a dialer) to make the connection. The dialer entry in the /usr/lib/uucp/port file is then matched to an entry in the file /usr/lib/uucp/dial, which tells the modem how to dial the phone. Here's a sample entry:

```
# Hayes modem
dialer      Hayes
chat        "" ATZ OK ATDT\T CONNECT
```

27

UUCP

This entry shows the script that the system uses to communicate to the Hayes modem. In this case, the \T in the command line is replaced with the telephone number to be called. Some Linux system combine the /usr/lib/uucp/port and /usr/lib/uucp/dial files into a single entry in the /usr/lib/uucp/sys file that names the modem file directly.

The remote end of the connection (in this case, the system arthur) must have corresponding entries for merlin. The files are similar with only name, telephone number, device name (possibly), and chat script changed. Until both ends are configured properly, you can't get a connection between the two machines. Some Linux systems with Taylor UUCP have a utility called uuchk that verifies the syntax in the UUCP configuration files and prints out summary information. If you don't have the uuchk utility, you can download it from many FTP and BBS sites.

ACCESS PERMISSIONS

By default, Taylor UUCP allows a remote system to execute only a limited number of commands when it logs into your system. Typically, the remote is only allowed to execute rmail and rnews to transfer mail and news respectively. If you want to allow extra programs to be executed, add a line to the /usr/lib/uucp/sys file that includes all the commands the remote system can execute. For example, the entry

```
system      chatton
....
commands      rmail rnews rstmp rdataupdate
```

specifies that the system chatton can execute any of the four commands given after the commands keyword. Note that all four commands must be in the usual search path used by the UUCP utilities (actually by uuxqt).

If you intend to transfer files between two machines, you must also modify the configuration files. When a remote system sends a file to your machine, the files usually should be stored in the directory /usr/spool/uucppublic (some systems use /var/spool/uucppublic) as a safety precaution. You don't want to allow a remote system to write files anywhere on your filesystem, or it could overwrite critical system files. The convention for most UUCP systems is to always use /usr/spool/uucppublic as the transfer directory.

You can specify transfer and receive directories in the /usr/lib/uucp/sys file. For example, the following entry for the remote system chatton has been modified to include specific directories for file transfers:

```
system        chatton
...
local-send    ~/send
local-receive    ~/receive
```

In this configuration, the users on your local machine can send any file that is in the /send directory under the UUCP directory (~/send, which means that any file to be sent to a remote system must be transferred there first), and any file incoming from a remote system is stored in the receive directory under the UUCP directory. If you want to allow transfers from a user's home directory, you can specify the /usr directory as a starting point. Multiple entries are separated by spaces, so the entry

```
local-send    ~/send /usr
```

allows transfers from the /send directory under the UUCP directory or from any directory under /usr.

The preceding two lines deal only with file transfers requested or sent from your machine. If you want to enable requests for transfers from the remote machine, you need to add two more lines:

```
remote-send     /usr/lib/uucppublic
remote-request    /usr/lib/uucppublic
```

These lines force the remote machine to request files and send them only to the /usr/lib/uucppublic directory. Again, you can offer several choices if you want, as long as they are separated by spaces.

Finally, UUCP allows machines to forward data through other machines, a process called *hopping*. In other words, if you want to send mail to the system warlock but can only get there through the system wizard, you have to instruct UUCP that your local system can get to warlock through wizard by adding a forward command to the /usr/lib/uucp/sys file:

```
system    wizard
...
forward    warlock
```

You should then add an entry for the warlock system that tells UUCP that any mail for you will be coming back through wizard:

```
system    warlock
...
forward-to    merlin
```

The forward-to command ensures that any files returned by warlock are passed to merlin, the local host machine. Otherwise, UUCP would discard these files for not being routable. By default, Taylor UUCP does not allow forwarding, and most system administrators should think carefully about allowing forwarding, as the potential for abuse is high.

27

UUCP

CONFIGURING HDB UUCP

HDB UUCP is a more recent version of UUCP and its configuration files are different from Taylor UUCP. In many ways, the HDB configuration is easier than the Taylor UUCP configuration, although neither is difficult once you know the basic process. Instead of setting the name of the local system in the UUCP configuration files, you use the `hostname` command (see Chapter 17, "System Names and Access Permissions").

SPECIFYING REMOTE SYSTEMS

The names of the remote systems are stored in the file /usr/lib/uucp/Systems (some older versions used the name /usr/lib/uucp/L.sys). Each remote system that will be connected to the local system has a single line. The format of each line is

```
sitename  schedule  device_type  speed  phone  login_script
```

where `sitename` is the name of the remote machine, `schedule` is when the machine can be connected to the local system, `device_type` is the type of device used to call the remote system, `speed` is the speed (or range of speeds) that you can use to connect to the remote system, `phone` is the telephone number of the remote system, and `login_script` is the script used when a connection is made (like the `chat` script in Taylor UUCP). For example, to call the remote system arthur, the /usr/lib/uucp/Systems file has a line like the following:

```
arthur Any ACU 9600 555-1212 login: uucp password: secret1
```

The `Any` entry in the `schedule` field tells UUCP that it can call at any time. The `ACU` entry in the `device_type` field tells UUCP to use the ACU (automatic calling unit) defined in the /usr/lib/uucp/Devices file.

SETTING THE MODEM DEVICE

The /usr/lib/uucp/Devices file (or /usr/lib/uucp/L-devices file in some older versions) contains information about the devices (usually modems) that you can use to call the remote systems. The Devices file follows this syntax

```
devicetype  ttyline  dialerline  speed  dialer  [token Dialer  ...]
```

where `devicetype` is the name of the device (which should match the device name in the /usr/lib/uucp/Systems file), `ttyline` is the device driver to be used for the connecting port (usually a serial line, such as /dev/tty2a or /dev/modem), `dialerline` is an obsolete field left as a hyphen, `speed` is the speed range of the device, and `dialer` is the name of the file that tells UUCP how to use the device. A sample line for a Hayes 9600 baud modem used to connect on the second serial port of the system might have an entry in the /usr/lib/uucp/Devices file like the following:

```
ACU tty2A - 9600 dialHA96
```

This entry identifies the ACU entry as a 9600 baud connection through /dev/tty2A (the /dev portion of the name is not needed with HDB UUCP), and it uses a program called dialHA96 to handle the setup and dialing of the modem. Most popular modems usually have programs available that set the modem configuration parameters automatically, leaving Linux out of that process. If a program is not available to handle the modem, you can use an entry in the file /usr/lib/uucp/Dialers. The format of the Dialers entries is

```
dialer  translation  expect  send  ...
```

where dialer is the name of the dialer (matching the Devices file), translation is the translation table to use for the phone number (converting characters where needed to pauses, beeps, and so on), and the expect and send entries are the chat script to set up the modem. A sample line in the Dialers file looks like the following:

```
hayes1200 =,-,    "" AT\r\c OK\r \EATDT\T\r\c CONNECT
```

This entry is for a Hayes 1200 Smartmodem, identified by the name hayes1200, with translations for the = and - characters, followed by the AT commands used to set up the modem. These entries are usually supplied in the Dialers file for most popular modems.

SETTING ACCESS PERMISSIONS

Permissions for file transfers are a little more convoluted with HDB UUCP than Taylor UUCP, as HDB UUCP adds many features for special handling. This section gives you the fundamentals you need to set up properly. For more detailed information, consult a specialty book on UUCP; the subject can easily consume 100 pages by itself!

The file /usr/lib/uucp/Permissions handles permissions for remote system access and file transfers. The general format of the entries in this file is

```
MACHINE=remotename LOGNAME=uucp \
    COMMANDS=rmail:rnews:uucp \
    READ=/usr/spool/uucppublic:/usr/tmp \
    WRITE=/usr/spool/uucppublic:/usr/tmp \
    SENDFILES=yes REQUEST=no
```

where MACHINE identifies the remote machine's name, LOGNAME is the name the users of the remote machine use to log in (or you use to log into their system), COMMANDS are the commands they can execute on your local system, READ is the list of directories from which they can read files, WRITE is the list of directories where they can write files, SENDFILES means that they can send files (yes or no), and REQUEST means that they can request files from your system (yes or no). Notice the slashes at the end of the first four lines. These slashes are a typical UUCP convention to indicate that this code is a single long line broken up for readability.

27

UUCP

A complete entry for the remote system wizard shows that it is allowed to both send and receive files, but only from the /usr/spool/uucppublic directory, and it can only execute `mail` and `uucp` commands (the later transfers files):

```
MACHINE=wizard LOGNAME=uucp1 \
    COMMANDS=rmail: uucp \
    READ=/usr/spool/uucppublic: \
    WRITE=/usr/spool/uucppublic: \
    SENDFILES=yes REQUEST=yes
```

To prevent the remote system from sending files, change `SENDFILES` to `no`. To prevent the remote system from requesting files, change `REQUEST` to `no`.

UNDERSTANDING UUCP CONNECTIONS

When UUCP connects to a remote machine, it follows a particular series of steps. You can better understand the configuration files UUCP uses and the processes that are involved by following through a typical session. UUCP uses `uucico` (UUCP Call In/Call Out) to handle the process of connecting and sending information. You can start a UUCP connection with the `uucico` command followed by the remote system name:

```
uucico -s arthur
```

When `uucico` starts, it examines the /usr/lib/uucp/sys file (Taylor UUCP) or the /usr/lib/uucp/Systems file (HDB UUCP) to see whether the remote system name exists there. When it finds the proper remote system name, `uucico` reads the rest of the entries for that system, including the port to be used. From there, `uucico` uses /usr/lib/uucp/port and /usr/lib/uucp/dial (Taylor UUCP) or /usr/lib/uucp/Devices and /usr/lib/uucp/Dialers (HDB UUCP) to start the modem connection (assuming it is a modem used to establish the session, of course). When the modem is in use, `uucico` creates a lock on it so that no other application can use it (the lock is a file starting with LCK.. and followed by the device name, such as LCK..cua0).

After the `chat` scripts for setting up and dialing the modem have been executed and the remote system is connected, `uucico` uses the `chat` script in the /usr/lib/uucp/sys file or the /usr/lib/uucp/Systems file to log in to the remote system. After the the local system is logged into the remote system, the remote machine starts up its copy of `uucico`, and the two `uucico` processes establish handshaking. After the handshaking has been established, `uucico` goes ahead and handles any transfers that are queued. When finished with the session, the local machine checks that the remote has nothing further to send, and then breaks the connection. Finally, `uucico` terminates.

DIRECT CONNECTIONS

If your two machines are directly connected (no modems involved in the connection), through a serial port for example, you can use UUCP as a simple network protocol for file transfer. The only changes to the configuration files mentioned earlier are in the port specification. Instead of using a modem device, you specify a direct connection. For example, in the /usr/lib/uucp/sys file (Taylor UUCP), you would have an entry like the following:

```
port        direct1
```

A matching entry in the /usr/lib/uucp/port file would look like the following:

```
port        direct1
type        direct
speed       38400
device       /dev/cua1
```

These entries specify the the port that uses the direct connection and the speed of the connection. The entries in the HDB UUCP version are similar, using the /usr/lib/uucp/Systems and /usr/lib/uucp/Devices files.

LOGIN SCRIPTS

The login scripts that form part of the /usr/lib/uucp/sys or /usr/lib/uucp/Systems file can be the most difficult part of a UUCP connection to get correct. If the machine you are logging into is a typical UNIX system, you usually only have to worry about the login and password prompts. Other systems may require some special handling to gain access. For this reason, the login script is worth a quick look.

Generally, the layout of the login script is in a pattern-action pair, with the pattern coming from the remote machine and the action from the local machine. The simple login scripts shown earlier serve as an example:

```
login: merlin password: secret1
```

In this case, the local system waits until it sees the string login: coming from the remote system, sends merlin, waits for password:, and then sends secret1. You can simplify the script a little by cutting out extra letters from the remote system, because all you really need are the last couple of characters and the colon. You could write the script as follows:

```
gin: merlin word: secret1
```

This type of script has a good use. If the remote system sends Login: instead of login:, the shortened script works and the longer script doesn't.

One useful feature of the uucicio login script is its capability to wait for the remote machine to reset itself (or start a getty process, more likely). To implement this feature, you use a hyphen and the word BREAK in the script to tell uucico to send a break sequence if the remote site doesn't respond in a timely manner. Look at the following sample script:

```
ogin:-BREAK-ogin: merlin sword: secret1
```

In this case, if the remote machine doesn't respond with a ogin: prompt after a short period of time, the local machine sends a break sequence and waits for the prompt again.

You can use a few special characters in the login script. The most important ones for most UUCP purposes are the following:

\c	Suppress sending carriage return (send only)
\d	Delay one second (send only)
\p	Pause for a fraction of a second (send only)
\t	Send a tab (send and receive)
\r	Send a carriage return (send and receive)
\s	Send a space (send and receive)
\n	Send a newline (send and receive)
\\	Send a backslash (send and receive)

Sometimes you need to use one or more of the characters to get the remote machine to respond to a modem login. For example, the script

```
\n\r\p ogin: merlin word: secret1
```

sends a carriage return–line feed pair before starting to match characters. This action is usually enough to get the remote machine to start a getty on the port.

ACCESS TIMES

Both Taylor and HDB UUCP versions let you specify a time to call the remote systems. Although the previous examples show Any (meaning the system can be called at any time, day or night), you may want to restrict calls to certain times or to certain days of the week. The reason for limiting calls may be at your end (costs, for example) or at the remote (limited access times during the day, for example).

To specify particular days of the week to allow calls, use a two-character abbreviation of the day (Mo, Tu, We, Th, Fr, Sa, Su), Wk for weekdays (Monday through Friday), Any (for any time), or Never (for not allowed to connect). You can use any combination of the days. The times for connecting are specified as a range in 24-hour format when a time span is required. If no time is given, the systems assume that anytime during the day is allowed.

Dates and times are run together without spaces; commas separate subsequent entries. Examples of restricted access times are as follows:

```
Wk1800-0730
MoWeFi
Wk2300-2400, SaSu
```

The first example allows connection only on weekdays between 6:00 pm and 7:30 am. The second example allows connection any time on Monday, Wednesday, and Friday. The last example allows connections only between 11:00 pm and midnight on weekdays and any time on weekends. You can build up any time and date specifications you want. These guidelines apply to both Taylor and HDB UUCP versions.

UUCP Security

The permissions of the UUCP configuration files must be properly set to enable UUCP to function properly, as well as to provide better security for the system. The files should all be owned by uucp, and uucp should be the group on most systems that have that group in the /etc/group file. You can set the ownerships either by making all the file changes explained previously while logged in as uucp or by setting the changes as root and then issuing the commands

```
chown uucp *
chgrp uucp *
```

when you are in the /usr/lib/uucp directory. As a security precaution, set a strong password for the uucp login if one exists on your system. Some versions of Linux do not supply a password by default, leaving the system wide open for anyone who can type uucp at the login prompt!

Set the file permissions very tightly, preferably to read-write-execute only for the owner (uucp). Blank the group and other permissions—a read access can give valuable login information, as well as passwords, to someone. When UUCP logs into a remote system, it requires a password and login. The /usr/lib/uucp/sys and /usr/lib/uucp/Systems files contain this information. To protect them from unauthorized snooping, set file ownerships and permissions as mentioned.

If you have several systems connecting into yours, they can all use the same uucp login and password, or you can assign new logins and passwords as you need them. All you need to do is create a new /etc/passwd entry for each login (with a different login name from uucp, such as uucp1, uucp_arthur, and so on) and a unique

27

UUCP

password. The remote system can then use that login to access your system. When you create the new UUCP user in the /etc/passwd directory, force the user to use uucico only to prevent access to other areas of your system. For example, the following uucp1 login forces uucico as the startup command:

```
uucp1::100:1:UUCP Login for Arthur:/usr/spool/uucppublic:/usr/lib/uucp/uucico
```

The home directory is set to the uucppublic directory, and uucico is the only startup program that can be run. Using different logins for remote machines also allows you to grant different access permissions for each system, preventing unwanted access.

Carefully control the commands that remote systems can execute on your local machine through the permissions fields of the local access file. Monitor these fields carefully to prevent abuse and unauthorized access. In a similar manner, if you are allowing forwarding of files through your system, control who is allowed to forward files and where the files are forwarded to.

Most important of all is to ensure that whoever accesses your system on a regular basis is someone you want to have access. If you leave your system wide open for anyone to enter, you are inviting disaster. Carefully watch logins, and make sure file permissions and ownerships are properly set at all times.

USING UUCP

Once you have configured UUCP, you can use it to transfer files and e-mail. In order to use UUCP, you have to know the addressing syntax, which is different from the Internet addressing syntax. The UUCP address syntax is

```
machine!target
```

where machine is the remote machine name and target is the name of the user or file that you are trying to get to. For example, to send mail to the user yvonne on machine arthur, you would use the mail command with a username destination:

```
mail arthur!yvonne
```

UUCP lets you move through several machines to get to a target. This feature can help save money on telephone bills or make a much wider network available to you from a small number of connections. Suppose you want to send mail to a user called bill on a system called warlock, which isn't in your configuration files but can be connected to through arthur. If you have permission to send mail through the system arthur (called a *hop*), you can send the mail with this command:

```
mail arthur!warlock!bill
```

When UUCP decodes this address, it reads the first system name (arthur) and sends it to that system. UUCP processes on arthur, and then examines the rest of the address and realizes that the mail is to be sent on to warlock. If you have permission to forward through arthur, UUCP on arthur sends the mail through to warlock for you. You can have many hops in an address, as long as each system you are connecting to allows the pass-through and can connect to the next machine on the list. For example, the address

```
arthur!warlock!chatton!vader!alex
```

sends data through arthur, warlock, chatton, and vader in order, and then to the user alex. You must specify the addresses in the proper hop order or the address will fail. This multihop addressing can be very useful if a number of friends have local connections to other machines, allowing you to easily set up a complex network. The hard part is usually tracking the names of the systems involved.

Note

The exclamation mark in the address is called a *bang*, so the preceding address is spoken or written as "arthur-bang-warlock-bang-chatton-bang-vader-bang-alex." Shells like the C shell use the exclamation mark to recall previous commands, so you must escape the bang character with a slash to prevent the shell's interpretation. Addresses then become `arthur\!chatton\!yvonne`. This looks funny, but you get used to it.

Depending on how you have set your UUCP system, it may call out to the other systems in an address whenever something is submitted to it, or if callout times are limited, the data may be spooled until a call is allowed. You have already seen how to set callout times in the /usr/lib/uucp/sys and /usr/lib/uucp/Systems files.

A quick caution about relying on UUCP for delivery of information. If the systems that are being used are not set to call immediately when something is queued, your data can take a long time to get to its destination. For example, if one of the hops in your address only calls the next machine in the address once a day, you may have a 24-hour delay in delivery. This delay can be exacerbated by each machine in the network.

Also, don't rely on the contents of your data sent through UUCP to be kept confidential. Once your data is on a remote system, any user with access privileges to the queue could snoop into your data. Ideally, the file permissions will prevent anyone but the superuser accessing the data, but not all systems keep tight security. If you must send sensitive data, encrypt it and let the recipient know the decryption key through another format (not in a mail message).

27

UUCP

UUCP deals with all transfers as *jobs*, a term you'll encounter often when working with UUCP and its documentation. A *job* is a command that is to be executed on the remote system, a file that is to be transferred to or from the remote system, or any other task that you want performed between the two systems.

SENDING E-MAIL WITH UUCP

Because most utilities, like mail packages, understand the UUCP addresses, you don't have to worry about e-mail not reaching the proper destination. You usually don't have to make any changes at all to applications running under Linux to get them to understand the UUCP address format. In the last section, you saw how you can use the mail package with UUCP addresses.

You can use any of the usual `mail` command options to modify the behavior of the package. For example, to send the contents of the file data_1 to yvonne on system chatton through the system arthur and tag the mail with a subject heading, issue the command:

```
mail -s "Data file" arthur!chatton!yvonne < data_1
```

Most mail packages available for Linux, including X-based mailers, work perfectly well with UUCP addresses as well as the more common Internet addresses, but you may want to check before adopting a new mail package.

TRANSFERRING FILES WITH UUCP

UUCP's most common use is to transfer files from one machine to another. To transfer files using UUCP, you use the `uucp` command. The syntax of this command is as follows:

```
uucp [options] source destination
```

The options supported by `uucp` vary a little depending on the version and type of UUCP implementation, but most versions support the following useful options:

`-c`	This option tells the program not to copy the file to a spool directory before sending. The default action is to copy to a spool directory. You can use the `-c` option to explicitly specify this action.
`-f`	This option tells the program not to create directories on the remote system if needed. The default action is to create directories as needed. You can use the `-d` option to explicitly specify this action.
`-m`	This option tells the program to send mail to the person who issued the `uucp` command when the copy is complete.
`-nuser`	This option tells the program to send mail to the user on the remote system when the copy is complete.

The default behaviors are usually sufficient for most users, although you may want the mail options when you need confirmation of an action.

Both source and destination are the names of files or directories as appropriate, much like the cp command. However, when you are dealing with a remote system for the source or destination, you need to format the file or directory in valid UUCP address format. For example, to send the data_1 file from your local machine's current directory to the directory /usr/spool/uucppublic on the machine arthur, use the command:

```
uucp data_1 arthur!/usr/spool/uucppublic
```

Notice that the remote machine name was prepended to the full target directory name. In most cases, when transferring files to remote systems, you should use the uucppublic directories as you likely will not have permission to transfer files anywhere else in the filesystem. Once the file is on the remote system in the /usr/spool/uucppublic directory, it is up to the remote system's users to find the file and copy it to its intended destination directory.

If you want to send the same file to the user bill on the remote machine, store it in a subdirectory called /usr/spool/uucppublic/bill, and send mail to both yourself and bill when the copy is completed, issue the command:

```
uucp -m -nbill data_1 arthur!/usr/spool/uucppublic/bill/
```

To copy a file from a remote machine to yours, you need to specify the location of the remote machine. Remember you must have access to the directory that the files reside in (as well as read permission on the file) or have the sender copy them to uucppublic. The command

```
uucp chatton!/usr/tmp/bigfile /usr/tparker/
```

transfers the bigfile file from the directory /usr/tmp on the machine chatton to your /usr/tparker directory.

UUCP allows you to use wildcards, although you must escape them in quotation marks to prevent the shell misinterpreting them. For example, to copy all the files starting with chap on the remote machine warlock's /usr/bill/book directory (assuming you have permissions) to your own /usr/bigbook directory, issue the command:

```
uucp "warlock!/usr/bill/book/chap*" /usr/bigbook/
```

You can specify hops in the machine transfers by adding the extra machine names to the command. This task requires permissions to be set on all the machines that the hop will pass through and is seldom done. You can transfer files from one remote system to another by specifying their names on the command line, as in the following example:

```
uucp arthur!/usr/lib/uucppublic/bigfile warlock!/usr/lib/uucppublic/
```

27

UUCP

This command sends the file from the arthur system to the warlock system. In most cases, the users on either of the two remote systems would issue the commands, relieving some of the file permission problems.

CHECKING TRANSFERS

You can check on the status of transfers that are scheduled but haven't taken place yet by using the uustat command. When you issue the uustat command, all the UUCP transfers that are queued are listed. The format of the list is

```
jobID system user date command size
```

where jobID is the identification number of the UUCP job, system is the name of the system to transfer to (the first system in an address when multiple hops are taking place), user is the username who queued the job, date is when the job was queued, command is the exact command to be executed, and size is the size of the transfer in bytes.

If you issue the command as a user (not superuser), only your jobs are listed. The superuser lists all jobs that are queued. If you are logged in as a regular user and want to see all jobs, use the -a option:

```
uustat -a
```

To cancel a queued job, use the -k option of the uustat command along with the jobID. For example, to cancel jobID 17, issue the command:

```
uustat -k 17
```

You can only cancel your own jobs, unless you are logged in as superuser, in which case you can cancel any jobs.

SUMMARY

UUCP is quite easy to set up as long as you follow the rules. Once the configuration files are properly set, UUCP can transfer e-mail, news, and files to other systems. Using UUCP to transfer mail and files is as easy as using the usual mail and cp commands. Although UUCP is less popular nowadays because of the LAN craze, it does provide a simple, very low-cost network for those who need to connect only a couple of machines. It's also great for connecting your machine to your friends' machines, allowing e-mail back and forth, and making your Linux system seem like a well-connected workstation.

- Network Terminology

- What Is TCP/IP?

- IP Addresses

- The Domain Name System

- Network Basics

CHAPTER 28

TCP/IP and Networks

Whenever you deal with networking for Linux or any UNIX product, you inevitably deal with TCP/IP. The term TCP/IP has become a catch-all phrase for many things, most of which don't really apply to the network protocol. Understanding what TCP/IP is isn't strictly necessary to install TCP/IP networking on your Linux machine, but it does help. This chapter begins with a look at network terminology. Then it defines what TCP/IP is and does and what IP addressees and Domain Names are. It ends with a look at the basics of networking.

NETWORK TERMINOLOGY

Unfortunately, it's difficult to talk about networking unless the terms used are well understood, because a lot of terms in common usage can mean different things depending on the context. To avoid confusion, it's better to begin with the basic definitions. Each term has a formal, rigorous definition, usually in some standard document. Standards are not written in easily understood language usually, so we've tried to simplify the terms a little and use generalizations where possible.

SERVERS

A server is any machine that can provide files, resources, or services for you. Any machine that you request a file from is a server. In fact, that's the essence of client/server systems, where one machine (the client) requests something from another (the server). One machine may be both client and server many times.

The more common definition for server is directly related to local area networks, where the server is a powerful machine that holds all the files and large applications. The other machines on the network connect to the server to access their files. In this type of network, a single machine usually acts as the server (and all the others are clients).

Large server-based networks may have special servers for specific purposes. For example, one server may handle files for the network (the file server), another may handle all print requests (the print server), yet another may handle connections to the outside world through modems (the communications server), and so on. One or more of these functions may be on any individual machine on the network, or you may have several machines on a large network acting as a specific kind of server. You may have two file servers, for example.

For our purposes in this section, we will need to use both the central and client/server definitions of server, depending on the type of LAN and network services we are dealing with. Simply put, the server is the machine that your machine requests something from.

CLIENTS

As you may have figured out from the definition of server, a client is any machine that requests something from a server. In the more common definition of a client, the server supplies files and sometimes processing power to the smaller machines connected to it. Each machine is a client. Thus, a typical ten-PC local area network may have one large server with all the major files and databases on it, and all the other machines connect as clients.

In the client/server sense of the word, a client is the machine that initiates a request to the server. This type of terminology is common with TCP/IP networks, where no single machine is necessarily the central repository.

NODES

Small networks that comprise a server and a number of PC or Macintosh machines connected to the server are common. Each PC or Macintosh on the network is called a node. A *node* essentially means any device that is attached to the network (regardless of the size of the network). Since each machine has a unique name or number (so the rest of the network can identify it), you will hear the term node name or node number quite often. It is more proper to describe each machine as a client, although the term node is in common use. On larger networks involving thousands of workstations and printers, each device is still called a node. If the device has an address on the network, it is a node.

LOCAL AND REMOTE RESOURCES

A local resource is any device that is attached to your machine, such as a printer, modem, scanner, or hard disk. Since the machine doesn't have to go out to the network to get to the device, it is called a local device or local resource.

Following the same logic, any device that must be reached through the network is a remote resource. Any devices attached to a server, for example, are remote resources. A high-speed color laser printer that may be part of the network is also a remote resource.

NETWORK OPERATING SYSTEM

A network operating system—often called a NOS—controls the interactions between all the machines on the network. The NOS is responsible for controlling the way information is sent over the network medium (a coaxial or twisted-pair cable, for example). It handles the way in which data from a machine is packaged and sent to others, as well as what happens when two or more machines try to send information at the same time. The NOS can also handle shared peripherals, such as a laser printer, scanner, or CD-ROM drive that is on one machine but is accessible by other machines on the network.

With local area networks that have a single server and many clients hanging off it, the NOS resides on the server. This is the way Novell's NetWare works. The main part of the NOS sits on the server, while smaller client software packages are loaded onto each client.

With larger networks that don't use a single server, such as a Linux network running TCP/IP, the NOS may be part of each machine's software. Linux, for example, has the networking code for TCP/IP built into the operating system kernel so it is always available. A PC that wants to connect to the TCP/IP network must have a software package installed that handles the TCP/IP protocol.

Networks such as Microsoft Windows for Workgroups and Artisoft's LANtastic do not use a single primary server (although they can). Instead, each machine acts as its own server, containing all the NOS that is needed to talk to any other machine on the network.

NETWORK PROTOCOLS

The network protocol is the name of the communications system by which machines on the network interact. On a UNIX system, for example, TCP/IP (Transmission Control Protocol/Internet Protocol) is the most common. TCP/IP is the network protocol. (Actually, TCP/IP is a whole family of protocols, but we'll deal with that later.) Novell NetWare usually uses a network protocol called IPX (InterPacket Exchange).

The different protocols mostly use the same approach to communications: they assemble information into blocks of data called a packet, and send that across the network. However, the way the packet is made up, and the type of information attached to control its routing, differs with each NOS.

NETWORK INTERFACE CARD

The network interface card (NIC) is an adapter that usually sits in a slot inside your PC. Some NICs now plug into parallel or SCSI ports on the back of your system. These are very useful for portable machines, although they are still rare for desktops.

The network interface card handles the connection to the network itself through one or more connectors on the backplane of the card. The most common network connectors are similar to telephone jacks, with coaxial cable (like cable TV) a close second. You must make sure that the network interface card you are using in your machine works with the network operating system.

BRIDGES, ROUTERS, AND BROUTERS

You may hear the terms bridge and router often. They are simply machines that connect two or more networks together. The difference between a bridge and a router is that a bridge simply connects two local area networks running the same network operating system (it acts as a bridge between two LANs primarily to reduce traffic on the larger network), while a router connects LANs that may be running different operating systems. The router can have special software that converts one NOS' packets to the other's.

A router is more complicated than a bridge, in that it can make decisions about where and how to send packets of information (routing it, hence the name) to its destination. A brouter is a relatively new device that combines the capabilities of both bridges and routers (hence its name).

GATEWAYS

In common usage terms, a gateway is a machine that acts as an interface between a small network and a much larger one, such as a local area network connecting to the Internet. Gateways are also used in large corporations, for example, to connect small, office-based LANs to the larger corporate mainframe network. Usually, the gateway connects to a high-speed network cable or medium called the backbone. More formally, a gateway can perform protocol translations between two networks.

WHAT IS TCP/IP?

Put in simple terms, TCP/IP is the name of a networking protocol family. Protocols are sets of rules that all companies and software products must adhere to in order to make their products compatible with each other. A protocol defines how software will communicate with each other. A protocol also defines how each part of the overall package manages the transfer of information.

In essence, a protocol is a written set of guidelines that defines how two applications or machines can communicate with each other, each conforming to the same standards. TCP/IP is not restricted to the Internet. It is the most widely used networking software protocol in the world, used for large, multi-site, corporate local area networks as well as small, three- or four-PC LANs.

TCP/IP stands for Transmission Control Protocol/Internet Protocol, which are really two separate protocols. Despite what many people think, the term TCP/IP refers to a whole family of related protocols, all designed to transfer information across a network. TCP/IP is designed to be the software component of a network. The parts of the TCP/IP protocol family all have dedicated tasks, such as sending electronic mail, transferring files, providing remote logon services, routing messages, or handling network crashes.

28

The different services involved with TCP/IP and their functions can be grouped according to purpose. Transport protocols control the movement of data between two machines and include the following:

◆ **TCP (Transmission Control Protocol)**   A connection-based service, meaning that the sending and receiving machines are connected and communicating with each other at all times.

◆ **UDP (User Datagram Protocol)**   A connectionless service, meaning that the data is sent without the sending and receiving machines being in contact with each other. It's like sending snail-mail (regular postal service) with an address but with no way of knowing whether the mail will ever be delivered.

Routing protocols handle the addressing of the data and determine the best means of getting to the destination. They can also handle the way large messages are broken up and reassembled at the destination:

◆ **IP (Internet Protocol)**   Handles the actual transmission of data.

◆ **ICMP (Internet Control Message Protocol)**   Handles status messages for IP, such as error and changes in network hardware that affect routing.

◆ **RIP (Routing Information Protocol)**   One of several protocols that determine the best routing method to deliver a message.

◆ **OSPF (Open Shortest Path First)**   An alternate protocol for determining routing.

Network Address protocols handle the way machines are addressed, both by a unique number and a name:

◆ **ARP (Address Resolution Protocol)**   Determines the unique numeric addresses of machines on the network.

◆ **DNS (Domain Name System)**   Determines numeric addresses from machine names.

◆ **RARP (Reverse Address Resolution Protocol)**   Determines addresses of machines on the network, but in a backwards manner from ARP.

User Services are applications a user (or a machine) can use:

◆ **BOOTP (Boot Protocol)**   Starts up a network machine by reading the boot information from a server.

◆ **FTP (File Transfer Protocol)**   Transfers files from one machine to another.

◆ **TELNET**   Allows remote logins, which means a user on one machine can connect to another and behave as through he or she were sitting at the remote machine's keyboard.

Gateway protocols help the network communicate routing and status information, as well as handle data for local networks:

- **EGP (Exterior Gateway Protocol)**   Transfers routing information for external networks.

- **GGP (Gateway-to-Gateway Protocol)**   Transfers routing information between gateways.

- **IGP (Interior Gateway Protocol)**   Transfers routing information for internal networks.

The following protocols don't fall into the categories mentioned previously, but they provide important services over a network:

- **NFS (Network File System)**   Allows directories on one machine to be mounted on another and accessed by a user as though they were on the local machine.

- **NIS (Network Information Service)**   Maintains user accounts across networks, simplifying logins and password maintenance.

- **RPC (Remote Procedure Call)**   Enables remote applications to communicate with each other in a simple, efficient manner.

- **SMTP (Simple Mail Transfer Protocol)**   A dedicated protocol that transfers electronic mail between machines.

- **SNMP (Simple Network Management Protocol)**   An administrator's service that sends status messages about the network and devices attached to it.

The different protocols within TCP/IP are maintained by a governing standards body that is part of the Internet organization. Changes to the protocols occur when new features or better methods of performing older ones are developed, but this is a rare occurrence and usually results in backward compatibility.

TCP/IP, THE INTERNET, AND LAYERED ARCHITECTURE

The Internet is not a single network but rather a collection of many networks communicating through TCP/IP. TCP/IP and the Internet are so closely interwoven that TCP/IP's architecture is often called the Internet architecture. Almost from the start of the Internet as the ARPAnet, it became obvious that existing protocols couldn't handle the sheer volume of traffic that the network had to carry, so a project was undertaken to develop new communications protocols.

The TCP/IP protocols were first proposed in 1973 and led to a standardized version in 1982. One of the research sites for networking software was the University of

28

TCP/IP AND NETWORKS

California at Berkeley. UCB was the center of development for the UNIX operating system for many years; the research done there also helped refine TCP/IP. In 1983, UCB released a version of UNIX that incorporated TCP/IP as an integral part of the operating system. TCP/IP became very popular because UNIX was widely used, especially as more sites connected to the growing ARPAnet.

When TCP/IP was designed, all of the services that had to be provided were considered. The best approach to implement all the services was to divide the different services into categories, such as end-user services (file transfer and remote logon), transport services (the way data is sent back and forth, invisible to the user), and network (how the data is packaged for transfer). A layered architecture was developed that isolates each set of services from the other.

A layered approach to designing the software requires more work initially, but has several important benefits. First, since each layer is independent of the others, changes to one service won't cause problems with other services. As new services are developed, they can be added without changing any other parts of the software system. Most importantly, layering makes it possible for a set of small, efficient programs to be developed for specific tasks, each of which can be independent of the others.

One condition needed to allow layered architecture to work properly is that each layer must know what is coming from the layer above or below. The layer may not care about the actual contents of the message, but it must know what to do with it. For example, if you are sending an e-mail message, you write the message and instruct the application layer to transmit it to the destination. The application layer sends the message down the layers until another layer sends it out across the network cable. Each layer handles the e-mail message but has no interest in the actual contents of the message.

To simplify this task, each layer adds a block of data at the front and the back of the message that indicates which layer is involved as well as all the other bits of information the other layers and the receiving machine needs to handle the message properly. The data within the message is ignored. This is called "encapsulation," as each layer adds a capsule of information around the original data. Each layer performs its own encapsulation, adding header and trailer blocks to the message from the layer above. This results in several sets of headers and trailers by the time a message makes it to the network.

IP ADDRESSES

Every machine that is connected to a TCP/IP-based network has to be uniquely identified somehow. Without a unique identifier, the network wouldn't know how to get messages to your machine. If there were more than one machine with the same identifier, the network wouldn't know to which one to send the message. To understand IP addresses, which uniquely identify each machine, it is useful to relate to the Internet's problem of identifying not only each machine on the huge Internet, but also each organization.

The Internet identifies networks by assigning an Internet address or, more properly, an IP address to each company or organization on the Net. IP addresses are all 32 bits in length, and are broken into four 8-bit parts. This allows each part to have numbers ranging from 0 to 255. The four parts are combined in a notation called *dotted quad*, which means each 8-bit value is separated by a period. For example, 255.255.255.255 and 147.120.3.28 are both dotted-quad IP addresses. When someone asks you for your network address, they usually mean your IP address.

Assigning IP addresses is not a simple matter of starting with the number 1 and counting upwards. Each machine (called a host) that can be attached to the Internet needs to be numbered. Even the dotted-quad 32-bit numbering scheme couldn't handle all the machines just by counting them. Instead, IP addresses work by identifying a network, then a machine on that network.

The IP address really consists of two parts: the network number and the host number within that network. By using two parts to the IP address, machines on different networks can have the same host number, but because the network number is different, the machines are uniquely identified. Without this type of scheme, the numbering would become unwieldy very quickly.

IP addresses are assigned on the basis of the size of the company or organization. If the company is small, there is no need for many machine identifiers within the network. On the other hand, a large corporation may have thousands of hosts. To provide for the maximum flexibility, IP addresses are assigned according to the size of the user, referred to as Class A, Class B, or Class C. Class D and Class E have special purposes and are not used as part of the IP address numbering.

The three classes allow the IP address numbers to be assigned on the basis of company size. Since 32 bits is the total size allowable, the classes break the four 8-bit parts into the network and host identifiers depending on the class. One or more bits is reserved at the start of the 32-bit IP address to identify the type of class (hence, how other machines that analyze the IP address should decode the numbers). The three classes have the following breakdowns:

◆ Class A: network 7 bits; host 24 bits
◆ Class B: network 14 bits; host 16 bits
◆ Class C: network 21 bits; host 8 bits

A Class A address has only a 7-bit address for the network address but 24 bits for the host address. This allows over 16 million different host addresses, enough for the very largest organization. Of course, there can only be 128 of these Class A addresses, maximum.

Class B networks have 14 bits for the network and 16 bits for the host, allowing more Class B networks but fewer hosts. Still, 16 bits allow over 65,000 hosts. Finally, Class C IP addresses can have a maximum of 254 hosts (because the numbers 0 and 255 are reserved for each of the parts of the IP address) but have a lot of network IDs. The majority of networks are Class B and Class C.

It is possible to tell the type of class a company belongs to by the first number of the IP address. The rules for the first 8-bit number are:

- ◆ Class A addresses are between 0 and 127
- ◆ Class B addresses are between 128 and 191
- ◆ Class C addresses are between 192 and 223

So, if your host machine's IP address is 147.14.87.23, you know that your machine is on a Class B network, the network identifier is 147.14, and your host's unique number in that network is 87.23. If the IP address is 221.132.3.123, the machine is on a Class C network with a network identifier of 221.132.3, and a host number of 123.

Whenever a message is sent to a host anywhere on the Internet, the IP address is used to indicate its destination and the host that sent it. Luckily, because of another TCP/IP service called the Domain Name System, you don't have to keep track of all these IP addresses yourself.

THE DOMAIN NAME SYSTEM

When a company or organization wants to use the Internet, they must decide whether they want to do it by directly attaching to the Internet system or whether they will use another company to supply the connection. Many companies choose to use another company, called a service provider, because it reduces the amount of equipment, administration, and costs involved.

If the company or organization wants to directly connect (and sometimes when they are using a service provider), they may want to have a unique identification for themselves. For example, ABC Corporation may want to have electronic mail through the Internet addressed to them as abc.com. The name helps identify the company or organization to the sender.

To obtain one of these unique identifiers called a domain name, the company or organization sends a request to the body that controls access to the Internet: the Network Information Center, or NIC. If the NIC approves the company's name, it is added to the Internet database. Domain names must be unique, to prevent confusion.

The part of the name that comes last (such as .com) is the domain identifier. These are the seven domain names established by the NIC:

.arpa	an ARPAnet-Internet identification
.com	commercial company
.edu	educational institution
.gov	any governmental body
.mil	military
.net	network service providers
.org	anything that doesn't fall into one of the other categories

The NIC also allows special letters to identify the country of the company or organization. Designators exist for all countries in the world, such as .ca for Canada and .uk for the United Kingdom.

Not all companies that are outside the U.S. have country identifiers. To some extent, the date of registration may affect the use of the country identifier, as companies that joined the Internet when it was still relatively uncrowded would have been given a standard identifier. Also, some non-U.S. corporations use a U.S.-based company to register for them, giving them a choice of using a country designator or not.

The Domain Name System (DNS) is a service provided by the TCP/IP family of protocols that helps in the addressing of messages. When you address mail to bozo@clowns_r_us.com, the DNS system translates this symbolic name into an IP address by looking up the domain name in a database. DNS lets you forget about those IP addresses, allowing much simpler names: the domain name. The usual syntax for sending a message to a user on the Internet is username@domain_name, as the "bozo" example shows. (DNS doesn't have to run on top of TCP/IP, but it usually will on Linux systems.)

If a company decides not to get their own domain name but will use an on-line service (such as CompuServe or America Online), a unique domain name is not needed. Instead, the domain name of the service provider is part of the address. A user is then identified by a name or number of the service provider, such as 12345.123@compuserve.com.

In practice, when you send a symbolic name to DNS, it doesn't check the user's actual host, otherwise there would be millions of IP addresses in the database. Instead, DNS is concerned with only the network part of the address, which it translates to the network IP address and sends out over the network. When the receiving network's Internet machine receives the message, it uses an internal database of its own to look up the user's host and takes care of that part of the trip.

NETWORK BASICS

A network topology is the way the cabling is laid out. This doesn't mean the physical layout (how it loops through walls and floors) but rather how the logical layout looks when viewed in a simplified diagram. You may hear many different names for the type of network you have: ring, bus, star, and so on. They all refer to the shape of the network schematic.

NETWORK TOPOLOGIES

One of the most widely used network topologies (and the one most often used in medium to large LAN) is the bus network. A bus network uses a cable to which are attached all the network devices, either directly or through a junction box of some sort. Each device uses a transceiver to connect to the backbone. The manner of attachment depends on the type of bus network, the protocol in use, and the speed of the network. The main cable that is used to connect all the devices is called the backbone. Each end of the backbone (also called a bus) is terminated with a block of resistors or similar electrical device. Most large TCP/IP networks used by Linux are bus topologies.

A popular variation of the bus network topology is found in many small LANs. This consists of a length of cable that snakes from machine to machine. Unlike with the bus network, there are no transceivers along the network. Instead, each device is connected into the bus directly using a T-shaped connector on the network interface card, often using a connector called a BNC. The connector connects the machine to the two neighbors through two cables, one to each neighbor. At the ends of the network, a simple resistor is added to one side of the T-connector to terminate the network electrically.

This machine-to-machine network is not capable of sustaining the higher speeds of the backbone-based bus network, primarily because of the medium of the network cable. A backbone network can use fiber optics, for example, with small coaxial or twisted-pair cables from a junction box to the device. A machine-to-machine network is usually built using twisted pair or coaxial cable. (With Ethernet, these cables are called 10Base-T and 10Base-2 respectively.) Until recently, these networks were limited to a throughput of about 10 megabits per second (Mbps). A recent development of two slightly different protocols called 100VG AnyLAN and Fast Ethernet allows 100Mbps on this type of network, though. Most small Linux networks use this topology, because it is inexpensive, easy to wire and control, and relatively simple to administer.

The problem with the type of bus network that involves T-shaped connectors between the backbone cable and the PC is that if one connector is taken off the network cable or the network interface card malfunctions, the backbone is broken and must be tied together again with a jumper of some sort. This can cause erratic behavior of the network or a complete failure of all network traffic. To help avoid this problem, an alternate method of connection to the network can be used. This method employs boxes with a number of connectors (usually similar to telephone jacks, but wider) that connect between the box and the PC network card. Disconnecting a cord from a PC to the box doesn't compromise the integrity of the network as the box is still handling the backbone properly. The 10Base-T Ethernet system uses this approach.

Another network topology is the ring network. Although most people think the network cable is made into a physical loop joining into a large circle, that's not the case in the most common form of ring network called Token Ring. The ring name comes from the design of the central network device, which has a loop inside it to which are attached juntions for cables of all the devices on the network.

With a Token Ring network, the central control unit is called a Media Access Unit, or MAU. Inside the MAU is the cable ring to which all devices are attached, and which is similar to the backbone in a bus network. IBM's Token-Ring is the most commonly encountered network system that uses a ring topology. Linux networks can be set up to use Token Ring, but few are.

A star network is arranged in a structure that looks like a central star with branches radiating from it. As you will see shortly, this is a common layout with twisted-pair peer-to-peer networks. The central point of the star structure is called a concentrator, into which plug all the cables from individual machines. One machine on the network usually acts as the central controller or network server. A star network has one major advantage over the bus and ring networks: when a machine is disconnected from the concentrator, the rest of the network continues functioning unaffected. True star networks are very seldom used for Linux, although a single Linux server in the center of a number of terminals or PC clients is, in a sense, a star network. In some networks, such as 10Base-T (twisted pair), that use a box with cables snaking off to each device, the box and cables make up a small star network, albeit in a larger bus topology.

The last type of topology that concerns us is called the hub network. It is similar to the bus network in that it uses a backbone cable that has a set of connectors on it. The cable is called a backplane in a hub network. Each connector leads to a hub device, which leads off to network devices. This allows a very high speed backplane to be used, which can be as long and complex as needed. Hub networks are commonly found in large organizations that must support many network devices and need high speeds.

The hubs that lead off the backplane can support many devices, depending on the type of connector. They can, for example, support hundreds of PC or Macintosh machines each, so a hub network can be used for very large (tens of thousands of network devices) networks. The cost of a hub network is high, though.

NETWORK MEDIA

The type of cabling used in a network is called the network medium. Today, networks use many types of cables, although only a few types are in common usage. Some of the more exotic types of cables are very expensive. The type of cabling can have an influence on the speed of the network, although for most small- to medium-sized local area networks this is not a major issue.

Twisted-pair cabling is one of the most commonly used network mediums because it is cheap and easy to work with. Unshielded twisted-pair cables—often called UTP—look just like the cable that attaches your household telephone to the wall jack. Twisted-pair cables have, as its name suggests, a pair of wires twisted around each other to reduce interference. There can be two, four, or even more sets of twisted pairs in a network cable.

Twisted-pair cables usually attach to network devices with a jack that looks like a telephone modular jack but is a little wider (supporting up to eight wires). The most commonly used jacks are called RJ-11 and RJ-45, depending on the size of the connector (and the number of wires inside). The RJ-11 connector is the same as the modular jack on household telephones, holding four wires. The RJ-45 jack is wider than an RJ-11 and holds eight wires.

A variation on unshielded twisted-pair cables is shielded twisted pair, often called STP. The shielded twisted-pair cable has the same basic construction as its unshielded cousin, but the entire cable is wrapped with a layer of insulation for protection from interference, much like a cable for connecting speakers to your stereo system. The same types of connectors are used with both forms of twisted-pair cables.

Twisted-pair cables have one major limitation. They only support one channel of data. This is called baseband or single channel cabling. Other types of cables can support many channels of data, although sometimes only one channel is used. This is called broadband or multiple channel cabling. You can use twisted-pair cabling for a small Linux network without any problem, but a much easier and more economical (in the long run) system is to use coaxial cable.

Coax cable is designed with two conductors, one (usually a number of strands intertwined) in the center surrounded by a layer of inner insulation, and the second a mesh or foil conductor surrounding the insulation. Outside the mesh is a layer of outer insulation. Because of its reduced electrical impedance, coaxial is capable of faster transmissions than twisted pair cables. Coax is also broadband, supporting several network channels on the same cable.

Coaxial cables come in two varieties: thick and thin. Thick coax is a heavy, usually yellow, cable that is used as a network backbone for bus networks. This cable is formally known as Ethernet PVC coax, but is usually called 10Base5. Because thick coax is so heavy and stiff, it is difficult to work with and is quite expensive. Linux systems that are attaching to a large commercial network may have to use thick coax, but this is very seldom encountered.

Thin coax is the most common type used in Ethernet networks used by Linux. It goes by several names, including thin Ethernet, thinnet, 10Base2, and somewhat derogatorily as cheapernet. Formally, thin coax is called RG-58. Thin coax is the same as your television cable. The inner connector can be made of a single, solid copper wire or fashioned out of thin strands of wire braided together. Thin coax is also used in other networks like ARCnet, although the specification is known as RG-62.

Thin coax is quite flexible and has a low impedance so it is capable of fast throughput rates. It is not difficult to lay out, because it is quite flexible, and it is easy to construct cables with the proper connectors at each end. Thin coax is broadband, although most networks use only a single channel.

NETWORKING HARDWARE

Establishing a Linux TCP/IP network requires two components of hardware: the network interface card (NIC) and the network medium. As with most things in life, you can opt to go for an inexpensive card and medium or spend lots more money for full-featured items. As the amount you spend increases, you get more functionality and benefits, although usually with diminishing returns for your dollar.

Before deciding on the type of network interface cards to use (unless you already have some), you should decide on the type of cabling the network will use so the connectors on the network interface card can match. 10Base2 and 10Base-T are really the only two cables that you'll want to consider. The alternatives are much more expensive or require special hardware.

The most common choice is 10Base2 (Thin Ethernet). A 10Base2 network interface card has a male plug jutting out from the back to which is attached a T-shaped connector. Both ends of the T are attached to coaxial cables running to the two neighboring machines. If the machine happens to be at the end of the chain, a terminating resistor plug is attached instead (to electrically terminate the cable).

Once you've decided on the type of cabling, you can choose network interface cards with the proper connectors. (You can use RJ-45 connectors with a 10Base2 network, and vice versa, although you have to purchase special adapters which cost more than a new network interface card.) Don't forget to check the bus architecture (local machine, not network architecture) the card is designed for, because the same manufacturer may have ISA, EISA, and MCA versions in the same packaging. It is a good idea to check the hardware compatibility lists provided with each release of Linux to make sure that the network cards you are considering purchasing have been tested and found to work properly with Linux.

Many network interface cards provide more than one connector on the back plane of the card. It is not unusual to have both a 10Base2 BNC and 10Base5 AUI (thick Ethernet, used for much larger networks) connector on a single card, with either available for use. The same applies to RJ-45 and 10Base5 AUI connectors. A few cards provide 10Base2 BNC and 10Base-T RJ-45 connectors in addition to the 10Base5 AUI connector. These provide the ultimate in flexibility for the user and allow you to change your network from one format to the other as your network grows or shrinks.

You can find network interface cards on the market from many different manufacturers, including brand name vendors such as Novell, Artisoft, Intel, SMC, and Hewlett-Packard; original equipment manufacturers (OEM); and some lesser-known brands, which are usually cheaper. Most network interface cards are clearly labeled with the type of connector (RJ-45 or BNC) and the network systems it supports.

Some network interface cards require you to manually select the card's parameters, such as interrupt (IRQ) and interface address, by changing jumpers on the card. This can be daunting for novices, as well as difficult if you are not sure whether a setting will conflict with another card in your system. Watch the boot messages from Linux to see what the potential conflicts might be, use a DOS-based utility, or simply experiment! It doesn't hurt Linux to change settings, although you may end up with a frozen machine that requires rebooting and cleaning.

More recently, auto-configuring cards have been appearing (such as the Intel EtherExpress series) which use DOS- or Windows-based software to set the parameters. You can use these features on a Linux system by booting into DOS (from a DOS boot disk or a DOS partition) to set the parameters, and then moving back to Linux and use the set parameters. Linux will recognize the card at those settings, as the hardware responds to its requests.

SUMMARY

This chapter has covered a lot of ground, ranging from TCP/IP to network cabling. However, now that the basics are out of the way, the next few chapters can focus on networking with Linux and connecting to the Internet.

- Configuring the Kernel

- Setting Up PLIP

- Setting Up SLIP and PPP Serial Ports

## CHAPTER 29

Configuring Hardware and the Kernel for Networking

To network your Linux machine, you need to connect it to others. The last chapter showed you the basics of networking, as well as the different network topologies you can use for local area networks. The next step is to configure the hardware and Linux kernel for networking.

This chapter looks at the configuration settings you need to worry about on your Ethernet board (if you are using one) and the changes you need to make to the Linux kernel to invoke networking. Depending on the type of network and version of Linux you are using, the exact steps you need to take may differ slightly from the ones explained in this chapter, but the basic procedures are the same.

CONFIGURING THE KERNEL

Practically all Linux versions have a number of default configurations built into the boot disks. When you selected a boot kernel, you could have chosen one with the Linux networking drivers already installed and configured. If you knew in advance that you were going to use networking and you chose one of these boot kernels, you have little work to do to complete the configuration.

You probably didn't choose a networking kernel when you first installed Linux because you didn't know you would need the drivers for networking or you didn't have the proper configurations available. Luckily, you don't have to go back and reinstall your entire system. Instead, you can link in the networking drivers and rebuild the kernel. (If you have not added any peripherals or saved any files you want to keep, however, reinstalling may be the fastest approach.)

In order to configure network hardware (an Ethernet board, most likely), you need to install the board in your machine with known IRQ, DMA, and I/O address values. These addresses are usually set on the network board with DIP switches or jumpers or with software (which usually works only under DOS) in more recent boards. Choose values for the IRQ, DMA, and I/O address that do not conflict with other boards or devices in your system.

Note

If you are unsure of what settings are available, watch the boot messages from Linux or use a utility under DOS like MSD or Norton Utilities to examine the hardware. If these methods don't help you determine available settings, make a good guess and use trial and error. Be warned that some network boards use the same DMA channel as popular SCSI controllers. If your network board is one of these and you don't change its DMA, the network board's instructions may overwrite data on your hard disk.

Many network boards have default values that work unless your system has a lot of additional cards installed. For example, many Ethernet boards default to values such as 15 for the IRQ and 300H for the I/O address. These values are not commonly used by sound cards, video capture boards, CD-ROM drivers, or SCSI cards. The IRQ setting is usually the easiest to select because a typical PC has only a few IRQ values preassigned, most of which are in the lower values from 1 to 7. The usual IRQ assignments for a basic AT-class machine (as opposed to the older XT class) are as follows:

IRQ 3	COM2 (second serial port)
IRQ 4	COM1 (first serial port)
IRQ 5	LPT2 (second parallel port)
IRQ 6	Floppy controller
IRQ 7	LPT1 (first parallel port)

Because most machines have two serial ports and at least one parallel port, these IRQ values are not available for you to use. IRQ 5 is often used by bus mouse controller boards if a second parallel port is not installed on your system. SCSI controller boards often default to IRQ 11, and 16-bit sound cards frequently use IRQ 10 as a default value. The most commonly available IRQ for a network board is IRQ 15, which is often the board's default value.

I/O addresses for network boards are usually restricted to a few settings, and you have to choose one that doesn't conflict with other devices. The most common setting is 300-31FH (300 to 31F hexadecimal), although this setting is often used by default settings on sound cards. The only commonly reserved I/O address on PC machines is 360-37FH, which is used by LPT2, the second parallel port. If you have a sound card installed at 300H, switch your network card to use an alternate address such as 320-33FH or 340-35FH. Both address blocks are usually available on a PC unless you have installed special hardware.

Many recent network boards allow you to select between 8-bit and 16-bit modes. The 16-bit mode is the fastest and most versatile and is therefore the default for most network boards. If you have only an 8-bit slot available for the network board, set your board to use 8-bits only (many boards detect this change automatically).

Many Linux kernel network drivers use an autoprobe routine that can detect the network board and its settings at boot time. The autoprobe routine uses a set of checks for network board addresses. If this routine succeeds in finding your network card, you see messages about the driver during the boot stage. You can redisplay the boot messages at any time with the dmesg command. Sometimes the autoprobe routine doesn't work or causes problems. In that case, be ready to enter the IRQ, DMA, and I/O address in the configuration files manually.(See the section "Forcing a Network Card Recognition" for more information.)

UNDERSTANDING NETWORK DRIVERS

The Linux kernel accesses network connections (whether an Ethernet board or a modem) through a device driver, which acts as an interface to the network service. Because the kernel can have many of these interfaces defined, including more than one per device driver, talking in terms of interfaces instead of device drivers helps to keep the concepts clear.

Each interface corresponds to a device driver file in the /dev directory. (The exception is SLIP device drivers, which are assigned dynamically and don't have a dedicated device driver file.) The Ethernet device drivers are usually called /dev/eth0, /dev/eth1, and so on. Each device driver can correspond to a different kind of device, so /dev/eth0 may be a device driver for an Intel Ethernet board, /dev/eth1 may be a device driver for a Novell Ethernet board, and so on. Alternatively, two or more boards can share the same device driver if they are the same kind of board. Usually, of course, a typical system has only one Ethernet board, and the device driver is designed for that board.

You may run into several different device driver names when using Linux. Knowing what the names mean helps you understand how they relate to the network protocols. The device driver names commonly encountered with Linux are as follows:

dl	D-Link DE-600 pocket adapters (an Ethernet device connecting to the parallel port)
eth	Ethernet boards
lo	A loopback driver (used primarily for testing and to maintain the network daemons when the network isn't active)
ipx	IPX interfaces (for Novell NetWare compatibility)
plip	PLIP interfaces (a parallel-port version of SLIP)
ppp	PPP interfaces
sl	SLIP interfaces

All these device driver names are followed by a number, such as /dev/ppp0 /dev/ppp1, and so on to indicate whether it is the first, second, or higher device driver of that type. A few other device drivers are appearing for ISDN, X.25, and similar high-speed protocols, although they are not a part of most Linux distributions yet. You can usually obtain the latest device drivers from FTP or BBS sites.

ADDING NETWORK SUPPORT TO THE KERNEL

If you need to add or configure network drivers because the kernel doesn't have them or the autoprobe routine didn't work, run the kernel build routines again. (If you are not familiar with the kernel build process, check the documentation that came with your Linux system.) Change to the directory used to store your Linux source files, which usually is /usr/src/Linux, and then start the kernel build process with the command

```
make config
```

During the build routine (on all Linux kernels from version 1.0 and later), you are asked whether you want to include TCP/IP network support. Answer y to this question or the kernel will not be built with networking support.

Following the TCP/IP question, Linux's configuration routine asks more questions. The exact questions differ depending on the version of Linux you have. Usually, you are asked whether you want support for several different types of networking, including whether you want network board TCP/IP network support (if you use a network card, such as an Ethernet board, answer y), SLIP and CSLIP support (if you plan on using SLIP, answer y), PPP support (again, if you plan to use PPP, answer y), and PLIP. (PLIP is a parallel-port version of SLIP/PPP, which is seldom used. Answer n unless you are only connecting two machines. See "Setting Up PLIP.") For most installations, answer y to all prompts for support except PLIP to configure your network any way you want. You will probably use SLIP and PPP at some time.

Versions of Linux later than 1.1.14 add more specific questions about network support, such as whether you want IP forwarding and gatewaying (answer n for this question unless your system acts as a gateway to another network). Your Linux version may ask about PC/TCP compatibility modes. Answer this question with n; it refers to an old incompatibility with ftp Software's PC/TCP PC client software product.

Some versions of Linux ask whether you want to enable RARP (Reverse Address Resolution Protocol), which allows remote terminals to obtain their IP addresses when they boot. In most cases, answer n to this question. The exception is if you have X terminals or diskless workstations attached directly to your Linux system. Another question asked with later versions of Linux relates to IPX protocol support. The IPX protocol is used with Novell NetWare; you can ignore it unless your Linux system is part of a NetWare network that doesn't use TCP/IP.

Other questions that may get asked relate to network masks, algorithms used, and dummy driver support, which is a loopback mechanism. In almost all cases, you are safe using the default answers provided by the configuration routine unless you specifically want to override a setting. If you indicated that your system is using a network adapter board, you are asked more questions about the type of support you need for the board. Most versions of Linux go through a series of popular network cards and ask which one you want support for. Choose the network card that matches yours, or choose one that is supported by emulation.

After you have specified all the protocols you want to support, the kernel rebuilds. The rebuilt kernel doesn't enable all the protocols, but it does add the drivers to the kernel. You still have to activate the protocols in the configuration routines and startup process.

FORCING A NETWORK CARD RECOGNITION

If the autoprobe routine in the Linux kernel doesn't recognize your network card, you must specifically tell it the network card's configuration. You can do this task by adding information to the boot process or by embedding configuration information within the startup information the kernel uses.

To add network card information to the boot process, use LILO. The routine lilo.conf (see Chapter 4, "LILO") enables you to issue an append instruction, after which you can enter a line that provides the device parameters. The format for the instruction to add an Ethernet card is as follows:

```
ether=IRQ,ADDRESS,PARM1,PARM2,NAME
```

In this code, IRQ is the IRQ setting, Address is the base I/O address of the network board, PARM1 and PARM2 are optional parameters that some boards use, and NAME is the name of the device. Usually boards use the optional parameters to set starting and ending addresses of shared memory boards (if they are supported), although some boards use them to set a debug level. For more information on the values to use for these parameters, see the list of network cards supported by Linux that is included with your Linux distribution, or check BBSs, FTP sites, or the Linux newsgroups on USENET.

This command format is quite easy to use. For example, after issuing the append instruction in lilo.conf, you can specify the following line:

```
ether=5,0x220,0,0,eth0
```

This line sets the device /dev/eth0 with IRQ 5 and base address 220H. The zeros for the parameters mean no value for most boards. If you want LILO to invoke the kernel's autoprobe routine, leave the values for IRQ and the I/O address set to zero.

To embed configuration information within the startup information the kernel uses, edit the file drivers/net/Space.c in the kernel source code directory. (Some Linux versions use a different path, but the file Space.c should exist). Use this approach only if you are familiar with network boards and their settings. The LILO approach is preferable.

When you have the Linux kernel configured to handle the network board, reset the machine and watch the startup messages. These messages should include a message indicating the network board has been successfully found. (If the messages scroll by too quickly for you to read, use the dmesg command to recall them from the shell prompt.) For example, the following prompts are displayed during system boot to indicate recognition of a Novell NE2000 Ethernet card:

```
NE*000 ethercard probe at 0x300: 00 00 6e 24 1e 3e
eth0: NE2000 found at 0x300, using IRQ 15.
```

This message shows that the NE2000 card was found to have an IRQ of 15 and an I/O address of 300H.

SETTING UP PLIP

PLIP (Parallel Line IP) is a method of networking two machines together using their parallel ports. PLIP uses a special cable that allows sustained transfer speeds up to 20kbps. The cable required is a null printer cable that crosses some pins. The cables from parallel port versions of some PC-to-PC software packages like LapLink also work.

If you want to make your own PLIP cable, use the following pin-out settings at each end:

connector 1 pin	connector 2 pin
2	15
3	13
4	12
5	10
6	11
1	5
1	6
12	4
13	3
15	2
25	25

All other pins are unconnected. Disconnect the shielding at one end as well.

If you select the PLIP option in the kernel configuration, the device drivers for PLIP are set up as /dev/plip0 (IRQ 7, I/O 3BC), /dev/plip1 (IRQ 7, I/O 378), and /dev/plip2 (IRQ 5, I/O 278). The IRQ and base I/O address settings are those of the normal parallel port IRQs and addresses on a PC and shouldn't be changed unless you modified the parallel port settings in the Linux kernel. When you connect your machine to another machine, your machine's /dev/plip0 connects to /dev/plip1 on the other machine, and the other machine's /dev/plip0 connects to your machine's /dev/plip1.

SETTING UP SLIP AND PPP SERIAL PORTS

Both SLIP and PPP use a serial port that is already configured on the Linux system, so no hardware configuration is required. Before running SLIP or PPP, however, you should check that the serial ports are configured properly. The serial ports on the PC are recognized as /dev/cua when used to drive modems, so you can perform a quick directory check to see whether they are already configured for you. Use the command

```
ls -l /dev/cua*
```

to display all the serial modem devices. You should see four devices configured; the output is similar to the following listing:

```
crw-rw-rw-   1    root    root      5, 64   Mar 14 12:26 /dev/cua0
crw-rw-rw-   1    root    root      5, 65   Mar 14 12:26 /dev/cua1
crw-rw-rw-   1    root    root      5, 66   Mar 14 12:26 /dev/cua2
crw-rw-rw-   1    root    root      5, 67   Mar 14 12:26 /dev/cua3
```

The dates and creation times may be different, but the device major and minor numbers, as well as the device names, should be the same. If these devices do not show up in your /dev directory, create them with the mknod command (see Chapter 6, "Devices and Device Drivers"). For example, to set up the four devices shown in the preceding code, issue the following commands:

```
mknod -m 666 /dev/cua0 c 5 64
mknod -m 666 /dev/cua1 c 5 65
mknod -m 666 /dev/cua2 c 5 66
mknod -m 666 /dev/cua3 c 5 67
chown root.root /dev/cua*
```

The last command changes the ownerships of the device drivers. You can also set up a link to the device name /dev/modem with the following command:

```
ln /dev/cua0 /dev/modem
```

Substitute whichever device is your default modem device, such as /dev/cua1, if you haven't created a link between the device and /dev/modem. If you have a link between the modem device and the device called /dev/modem, don't use both /dev/modem and the actual device names intermingled in your software or device conflicts can occur. When you start one software application that uses /dev/modem, it creates a set of lock files for /dev/modem. If you then start another application using the device's real name, such as /dev/cua1, the second application creates lock files for /dev/cua1, not realizing the device is already in use under the name /dev/modem.

When Linux restarts, you should see messages during the system boot that show the PPP, PLIP, or SLIP device drivers (whichever were linked into the kernel) being loaded. You can replay the boot messages with the dmesg command. The following startup messages show the PPP and SLIP drivers:

```
PPP: version 0.2.7 (4 channels) NEW_TTY_DRIVERS OPTIMIZE_FLAGS
PPP line discipline registered.
SLIP: version 0.8.3-NET3.019-NEWTTY (4 channels) (6 bit encapsulation enabled)
```

Copyright messages and other status information may also be displayed, depending on the version of drivers your system is using.

SUMMARY

This chapter examined the changes that you must make to the kernel to provide networking support and create the hardware and device driver files necessary to run networks. After you reconfigure and reboot the kernel, and the kernel properly recognizes the new devices, you can go on to configure the network software.

- Getting Ready to Configure TCP/IP

- Setting Up the Basics

- Configuring PLIP

- Gateways

- Name Service and Name Resolver

CHAPTER 30

Configuring TCP/IP

Despite what you may have heard, configuring TCP/IP is an easy process requiring usually only a little preparation work and a couple of commands to install the network IP addresses and names. This chapter looks at the process, setting up the support files, TCP/IP route files, and a PLIP interface. It also looks at how to set up your system to act as a gateway between networks, or use another machine as a gateway. Most of the steps you have to go through in this chapter are required only when you initially set up the system or when you make a network configuration change.

The last section of this chapter deals with name service, which you may need to install and configure if your machine is connected to a lot of other networks and machines. The name service and name resolver that goes with it are optional and are not necessary for your configuration unless you feel they will add to the usefulness of the network. You'll find a short discussion about name service in the preamble to the configuration steps.

GETTING READY TO CONFIGURE TCP/IP

You must conduct a few housekeeping steps before you can configure your system's TCP/IP files. These are easy to accomplish and need only be done once. Some of the steps may have been done for you automatically when the system was installed, and others have been taken care of in earlier chapters of this book.

Some versions of Linux networking reply on the /proc filesystem (any Linux kernel that uses the Net-2 or later releases usually has this dependency). Most Linux kernels that support networking automatically create the /proc filesystem when the system is installed, so you shouldn't have to do anything more than make sure it is properly mounted by the kernel. The /proc filesystem is essentially a quick interface point for the kernel to obtain network information easily, as well as maintain important tables (which are usually kept in the subdirectory /proc/net, created by the network installation routine).

You should make sure the /proc filesystem is mounted automatically on your Linux system by examining the startup code for the kernel. To force the /proc filesystem to be mounted automatically, modify the /etc/fstab file and add the mount command there. (The /etc/fstab file was covered in more detail in Chapter 18, "Filesystems and Disks.") Check the entries in /etc/fstab for a line like this:

```
none    /proc    proc    defaults
```

If no such line exists, you should add it to the contents of the /etc/fstab file using an ASCII editor.

If the /proc filesystem is not created by your Linux kernel, you will have to rebuild the kernel and select the /proc option. Change to the source directory (such as /usr/src/Linux) and run the configuration routine with the following command:

```
make config
```

When you are asked whether you want the procfs (the /proc filesystem) support, answer y. If you do not get asked about the /proc filesystem support, and the /proc directory is not created on your filesystem, then you need to upgrade your kernel in order to support networking.

Another step you must take before configuring TCP/IP is to set the hostname. We examined this process in Chapter 17, "System Names and Access Permissions." To set the hostname, use the command

```
hostname name
```

where name is the system name you want for your local machine. If you have a full domain name assigned to your network and your machine, you can use that name for your system. For example, if your Linux machine is attached to the domain star.com and your machine's name is dark, you can set the full domain name using the command:

```
hostname dark.star.com
```

If you don't have a fully qualified domain name (one approved by the Internet Network Information Center), you can make up your own domain name as long as you are not connected to the Internet in any way. Such a domain name will not have any meaning outside your local area network. Alternatively, you do not have to assign a domain at all for your machine, but simply enter the short name:

```
hostname dark
```

When you set the local machine's name with the hostname command, an entry is usually made in the /etc/hosts file. You should verify that your machine name appears in that file.

You should also know the IP address assigned to your machine. Chapter 28, "TCP/IP and Networks," looked at IP addresses. You should have a unique IP address ready for your local machine.

One file that may be handy for you if you plan to direct information across many networks is the /etc/networks file. This file contains a list of network names and their IP addresses. Applications on your machine can use this file to determine target networks based on their name. The file consists of two columns, one for the symbolic name of the remote network and the second for the IP address of the network (minus any host identifiers).

Most /etc/networks files have at least one entry for the loopback driver. The following is an extract from an /etc/networks file:

```
loopback        127.0.0.0
merlin-net      147.154.12.0
BNR              47.0.0.0
```

This file has two networks entered in it with their network IP addresses. The entries are used primarily when the network boots, but can be used for other purposes including establishing routing.

SETTING UP THE BASICS

The first step in setting up TCP/IP on your Linux machine is to make the network interface accessible. This is done with the ifconfig command. When run, ifconfig essentially makes the network layer of the kernel work with the network interface by giving it an IP address, and then issuing the command to make the interface active. When the interface is active, the kernel can send and receive data through the interface.

You need to set up several interfaces for your machine, including the loopback driver and the Ethernet interface (or whatever other network interface you are using). The ifconfig command is used for each interface in turn. The general format of the ifconfig command is

```
ifconfig interface_type IP_Address
```

where interface_type is the interface's device driver name, such as lo for loopback, ppp for PPP, and eth for Ethernet. (See Chapter 29, "Configuring Hardware and the Kernel for Networking," for interface names.) The IP_Address is the IP address used by that interface.

Once the ifconfig command has been run and the interface is active, you must use the route command to add or remove routes in the kernel's routing table. This command is needed to allow the local machine to find other machines. The general format of the route command is:

```
route add¦del IP_Address
```

where either add or del is specified to add or remove the route from the kernel's routing table, and IP_Address is the remote route being affected.

You can display the current contents of the kernel's routing table at any time by entering the command route all by itself on the command line. For example, if your system is set up only with the loopback driver, you will see an output like this:

```
$ route
Kernel Routing Table
```

```
Destination     Gateway   Genmask    Flags  MSS  Window  Use Iface
loopback        *         255.0.0.0  U      1936 0        16 lo
```

The important columns are the destination name, which shows the name of the configured target (in this case only loopback), the mask to be used (Genmask), and the interface (Iface, in this case /dev/lo). You can force route to display the IP addresses instead of symbolic names by using the -n option:

```
$ route -n
Kernel Routing Table
Destination     Gateway   Genmask    Flags  MSS  Window  Use Iface
127.0.0.1       *         255.0.0.0  U      1936 0        16 lo
```

A typical Linux network configuration will include a couple of interfaces. The loopback interface should exist on every machine. The network interface, whether Ethernet or other device, is also present (unless you only want a loopback driver). This chapter assumes you want to set up your system for a loopback and an Ethernet card, both of which need to be done separately.

Setting Up the Loopback Interface

The loopback interface should exist on every networked machine (as well as machines that are stand-alone, for that matter). The loopback interface always has the IP address 127.0.0.1, so the /etc/hosts file should have an entry for this interface. The loopback driver may have been created by the kernel during software installation, so check the /etc/hosts file for a line similar to this:

```
127.0.0.1    localhost
```

If the line exists, the loopback driver is in place. Make sure the line doesn't have a pound sign ahead of it to comment it out. If the line doesn't exist in the /etc/hosts file, add it using an ASCII editor.

If the loopback interface was not in the /etc/hosts file, you will need to create the interface as well using the ifconfig command. Issue the following command to complete the addition of the loopback driver:

```
ifconfig lo 127.0.0.1
```

If you are not sure about the configuration, you can use the ifconfig command to display all the information it knows about the loopback driver. Use the following command:

```
ifconfig lo
```

You should see several lines of information like the following:

```
merlin:~# ifconfig lo
lo        Link encap:Local Loopback
          inet addr:127.0.0.1  Bcast:127.255.255.255  Mask:255.0.0.0
```

```
UP BROADCAST LOOPBACK RUNNING  MTU:2000  Metric:1
RX packets:0 errors:0 dropped:0 overruns:0
TX packets:12 errors:0 dropped:0 overruns:0
```

If you get an error message such as unknown interface, the loopback driver does not exist and must be added.

Once the ifconfig routine has been checked, add the loopback driver to the kernel routing tables with one of these two commands:

```
route add 127.0.0.1
route add localhost
```

It doesn't matter which command you use because they both refer to the same thing. The command essentially tells the kernel that it can use the route for address 127.0.0.1 or the name localhost.

As a quick check that all is correct with the loopback driver, you can use the ping command to check the routing (see Chapter 32, "TCP/IP Utilities," for more information on ping). For example, if you issue either of these two commands

```
ping localhost
ping 127.0.0.1
```

you should see output like this:

```
PING localhost: 56 data bytes
64 bytes from 127.0.0.1: icmp_seq=0. ttl=255 time=1 ms
64 bytes from 127.0.0.1: icmp_seq=1. ttl=255 time=1 ms
64 bytes from 127.0.0.1: icmp_seq=2. ttl=255 time=1 ms
64 bytes from 127.0.0.1: icmp_seq=3. ttl=255 time=1 ms
64 bytes from 127.0.0.1: icmp_seq=4. ttl=255 time=1 ms
64 bytes from 127.0.0.1: icmp_seq=5. ttl=255 time=1 ms
64 bytes from 127.0.0.1: icmp_seq=6. ttl=255 time=1 ms
64 bytes from 127.0.0.1: icmp_seq=7. ttl=255 time=1 ms
^C
--- localhost PING Statistics ---
7 packets transmitted, 7 packets received, 0% packet loss
round-trip (ms) min/avg/max = 1/1/1
```

The ping command's progress was interrupted by the user issuing a Ctrl+C after seven transmissions. You can let as many transmissions as you want go by. If you get a no replies message from the ping command, then the address 127.0.0.1 or the name localhost wasn't recognized and you should check the configuration files and route entry again.

If the configuration files look correct and the route command was accepted properly, but the ping command still doesn't produce the proper results, then you have a serious problem. In some cases, the network kernel is not properly configured and the entire process must be conducted again. Sometimes a mismatch in versions of kernel drivers and network utilities can cause hang-ups with the ping routine as well.

SETTING UP AN ETHERNET INTERFACE

Now that the loopback driver is installed and operational, you can do the same configuration process with the Ethernet driver (or whatever driver you are using). The process is exactly the same: use `ifconfig` to tell the kernel about the interface, and then add the routes to the remote machines on the network. If the network is attached, you can then test the connections with `ping`.

To begin, set up the Ethernet interface using `ifconfig`. To make the interface active, use the `ifconfig` command with the Ethernet device name and your local IP address. For example, use the command

```
ifconfig eth0 147.123.20.1
```

to set up the local machine with the IP Address `147.123.20.1`. The interface is to the Ethernet device /dev/eth0. You don't have to specify the network mask with the `ifconfig` command because it will deduce the proper value from the IP address entered. If you want to explicitly provide the network mask value, append it to the command line with the keyword `netmask`:

```
ifconfig eth0 147.123.20.1 netmask 255.255.255.0
```

This command explicitly sets the network mask to `255.255.255.0`. You can then check the interface with the `ifconfig` command using the interface name:

```
$ ifconfig eth0
eth0        Link encap 10Mps: Ethernet Hwaddr
            inet addr 147.123.20.1 Bcast 147.123.1.255 Mask 255.255.255.0
            UP BROADCAST RUNNING   MTU 1500 Metric 1
            RX packets:0 errors:0 dropped:0 overruns:0
            TX packets:0 errors:0 dropped:0 overruns:0
```

You may have noticed in the output from the command that the broadcast address was set based on the local machine's IP address. This address is used by TCP/IP to access all machines on the local area network at once. The Message Transfer Unit (MTU) size is usually set to the maximum value of 1500 (for Ethernet networks).

Next, you need to add an entry to the kernel routing tables that lets the kernel know about the local machine's network address. That entry lets it send data to other machines on the same network. The IP address that is used with the `route` command to do this is not your local machine's IP address, but that of the network as a whole without the local identifier. To set the entire local area network at once, the `-net` option of the `route` command is used. In the case of the IP addresses shown previously, the command would be:

```
route add -net 147.123.20.0
```

This command adds all the machines on the network identified by the network address 147.123.20 to the kernel's list of accessible machines. If you didn't do it this way, you would have to manually enter the IP address of each machine on the network. An alternative method is to use the /etc/networks file, which can contain a list of network names and their IP addresses. If you have an entry in the /etc/networks file for a network called foobar_net, you could add the entire network to the routing table with the command:

```
route add foobar_net
```

Once the route has been added to the kernel routing tables, you can try out the Ethernet interface. This step assumes, of course, that you are connected to other machines and that you know the IP address of one of them. If your network isn't installed yet or you are not connected to another machine that is running TCP/IP, you can't try this step now. To ping another machine, you need either its IP address or its local name. Suppose you know the IP address and want to ping the machine 142.12.130.12. The command and output looks like the following:

```
tpci_sco1-45> ping 142.12.130.12
PING 142.12.130.12: 64 data bytes
64 bytes from 142.12.130.12: icmp_seq=0. time=20. ms
64 bytes from 142.12.130.12: icmp_seq=1. time=10. ms
64 bytes from 142.12.130.12: icmp_seq=2. time=10. ms
64 bytes from 142.12.130.12: icmp_seq=3. time=20. ms
64 bytes from 142.12.130.12: icmp_seq=4. time=10. ms
64 bytes from 142.12.130.12: icmp_seq=5. time=10. ms
64 bytes from 142.12.130.12: icmp_seq=6. time=10. ms
^C
--- 142.12.130.12 PING Statistics ---
7 packets transmitted, 7 packets received, 0% packet loss
round-trip (ms) min/avg/max = 10/12/20
```

Again, the ping routine was interrupted after seven attempts. You can see the diagnostic messages and summaries as ping sends a request to the remote machine and waits for a reply.

If you don't get anything back from the remote machine, verify that the remote is connected and you are using the proper IP address. If all is well there, check the configuration and route commands. If that checks out, try using the ping command with another machine. If that fails, you can resort to the netstat utility, discussed in more detail in Chapter 32, "TCP/IP Utilities."

Configuring PLIP

The PLIP (parallel port IP) interface is used to connect only two machines through their parallel ports. (Chapter 29 looked briefly at PLIP.) Configuring PLIP is different from configuring TCP/IP, especially since the interface is not a standard TCP/IP interface and only two machines are involved.

Suppose that there is a simple PLIP interface between your local Linux machine called Darkstar and a sibling's machine called x-wing. The two are connected by a null-parallel cable (see the previous chapter for wiring specifications). Both machines have only one parallel port used for PLIP. When PLIP is configured as shown in Chapter 29, "Configuring Hardware and the Kernel for Networking," the devices are set up as /dev/plip1 on both machines.

To configure the PLIP interface between the two machines, use the `ifconfig` command again with the keyword `pointopoint` (a condensed and confusing form of point-to-point, which describes the network type). The `ifconfig` command needed for the connection is as follows:

```
ifconfig plip1 x-wing pointopoint Darkstar
```

Note that the device is `/dev/plip1`, the remote machine is `x-wing`, and your local machine is `Darkstar`. The order of arguments must be exact for the command to work properly.

Once the `ifconfig` command has been issued, you can follow it with an update of the kernel routing table with the `route` command:

```
route add x-wing gw Darkstar
```

The `gw` keyword indicates that `Darkstar` is a gateway to the `x-wing` machine. The next section covers gateways in more detail.

The same sort of entries must be made on the other machine to enable two-way communications. In this case, the remote machine would have entries like this:

```
ifconfig plip1 Darkstar pointopoint x-wing
route add Darkstar gw x-wing
```

Once both configurations are complete, you should be able to use the PLIP interface to send data between the two machines.

GATEWAYS

Local area networks are connected by a gateway. The gateway is one machine that acts as the connection between the two networks, routing data between the two based on the IP address of the destination machine. The simplest use of a gateway is to connect to the rest of the world through the Internet. A machine that connects into the Internet can then connect to any other network on the Internet.

You have to make some changes to the network configuration files whenever your local machine is going to use a gateway, as well as if your machine is going to act as a gateway. To use the services of another machine as a gateway, you have to tell the routing tables about the gateway and the networks it connects to by using the `route` command

```
route add default gw net_gate
```

where `net_gate` is the name of the machine on your local area network that acts as the gateway out. The gateway machine follows the keyword `gw` in the `route` command. The use of the word `default` in the command indicates that the kernel's routing table should assume all networks can be reached through that gateway. (Physically, the default network setting translates to an IP address of 0.0.0.0.)

If you want to configure a gateway to another network, the name of that network should be in the /etc/networks file (see earlier in this chapter for details of the /etc/networks file). For example, if you have a gateway machine called gate_serv that leads from your own local area network to a neighboring network called big_corp (and an entry exists in the /etc/networks file for big_corp with their network IP address), you could configure the routing tables on your local machine to use gate_serv to access big_corp machines with this command:

```
route add big_corp gw gate_serv
```

An entry should be made on the remote network's routing table to reflect your network's address, otherwise you would only be able to send data and not receive it.

If you want to set up your local machine to act as a gateway itself, you need to configure the two network connections that your machine is joining. This usually requires two network boards, PPP connections, or SLIP connections in some combination. Assume your machine is going to act as a simple gateway between two networks called small_net and big_net, and you have two Ethernet cards installed in your machine. You configure both Ethernet interfaces separately with their respective network IP addresses, as you saw in Chapter 29, "Configuring Hardware and the Kernel for Networking." (For example, your machine may have an IP address on big_net of 163.12.34.36 and have the IP address 147.123.12.1 on small_net.)

Add the two IP addresses to your /etc/hosts file to simplify resolution. For the networks and IP addresses mentioned previously, you will have the following two entries in the /etc/hosts file:

```
163.12.34.36        merlin.big_net.com merlin-iface1
147.123.12.1        merlin.small_net.com merlin-iface
```

In this case, the fully qualified domain names have been added to the /etc/hosts file (this example assumes the machine has the name `merlin` on both networks, which is perfectly legal). You can also add shorter forms of the name, as well (such as `merlin`, `merlin.big_net`, and so on). Finally, the interface names have been included for convenience (so `merlin-iface1` is the first interface on merlin, while `merlin-iface2` is the second).

You then use the ifconfig commands to set up the connections between the interface and the names used in the /etc/hosts file:

```
ifconfig eth0 merlin-iface1
ifconfig eth1 merlin-iface2
```

These commands assume that the Ethernet device /dev/eth0 is for the interface to big_net, and /dev/eth1 is for small_net. Of course, you could have used the IP addresses of the networks instead of the interface name, as you saw earlier in this chapter.

Finally, the kernel routing table must be updated to reflect the two network names. The commands for this example are:

```
route add big_net
route add small_net
```

When these steps are completed, you must make sure that IP Forwarding has been enabled in the kernel. You can enable IP Forwarding by rebuilding the kernel. Once the kernel supports IP Forwarding, you can use your machine as a gateway between the two networks. Other machines on either network can also use your machine as a gateway between the two networks.

Although the examples shown here are for Ethernet connections to two networks, you could have any kind of interface. You could, for example, use an Ethernet card for your local area network, and then use a SLIP or PPP connection to another network (including the Internet).

NAME SERVICE AND NAME RESOLVER

TCP/IP uses the /etc/hosts file to resolve symbolic names into IP addresses. For example, when you specify the name Darkstar for a target machine, TCP/IP will examine the /etc/hosts file for a machine of that name, and then read off the IP address. If the name isn't in the file, you can't send data to it. Suppose you connect to a lot of different machines, though. Your local area network may have dozens of machines on it, and your friend's network may have more. Adding all those entries to the /etc/hosts file can be tiresome and difficult, and maintaining the file as changes occur in the networks can be even more bothersome. To solve this problem, a couple of services were developed.

BIND (Berkeley Internet Name Domain service) was developed to help resolve the IP addresses of remote machines. BIND was later developed into DNS (Domain Name Service). Most Linux network systems implement the BIND version, although a few DNS-specific versions of software are appearing. Both BIND and DNS are complex subjects and involve many details that simply are not of interest to most Linux users. This section looks at the basics to get your Linux machine using BIND or DNS.

Configuring BIND or DNS can be a bothersome process and should only be done if your /etc/hosts file can't handle your requirements. For example, if you only connect to about a dozen machines, maintaining the /etc/hosts file is much easier than configuring BIND. For larger systems, or if you want to run the full Internet services available to your Linux machine, you need to configure BIND properly. Luckily, BIND usually has to be configured only once, and then it can be ignored. (If you do go through the process of configuring BIND, make sure you have backups!)

You will need the BIND software, which is usually included in the distribution software of most Linux recent releases. The BIND package includes all the files and executables, as well as a copy of the BOG (BIND Operator's Guide). Without the BIND software you can't configure your Linux system to use BIND or DNS.

THE NAMED DAEMON AND NAME SERVERS

BIND and DNS are implemented through a daemon called named. The named daemon always runs on a machine called a name server, which is the machine on your network that handles the resolution of symbolic names to IP addresses. There can be several name servers on your network, or your machine can be the name server if you are running stand-alone.

Part of the name server system is a library of functions that are used by applications to set up queries for the name server, and to obtain answers from the name server. These functions are called the resolver or name resolver. The library of functions does not really have to be on the same machine as the name server.

The named daemon is usually started as part of the normal networking startup of Linux, although if you installed networking after your Linux system was installed, you may have to manually add the startup command to the rc files. The named daemon uses a file called /etc/named.boot that lists the master files used by other name servers. The /etc/named.boot file is covered later in this section.

Grossly simplified, BIND and DNS can be thought of as working like a set of telephone operators. If you are living in New York and want the number of a friend in London, England, you call your long distance operator to get the country code for England. That operator may connect to the English operator to give you the area code for London. Finally, that operator may connect to the London area operator to get your directory assistance number. BIND and DNS work in much the same way. When a name server can't figure out a name, it communicates with another name server that appears to be on the route to the target and waits for a reply to a directory query. That name server may contact others down the network, until some machine resolves the name and passes the message back to you.

Each name server manages a distinct area of a network (or an entire domain, if the network is small). The set of machines managed by the name server is called a zone. One name server may manage several zones. Within each zone, there is almost always a designated secondary or backup name server, with the two (primary and secondary) name servers holding duplicate information. The name servers within a zone communicate using a zone transfer protocol.

DNS operates by having a set of nested zones. Each name server communicates with the one above it (and the one below it, if one exists). Each zone has at least one name server responsible for knowing the address information for each machine within that zone. Each name server also knows the address of at least one other name server.

When an application needs to resolve a symbolic name into a network address, the application sends a query to the resolver process, which then communicates the query to the name server. The name server checks its own tables and returns the network address corresponding to the symbolic name. If the name server doesn't have the information it requires, it can send a request to another name server. Both the name servers and the resolvers use database tables and caches to maintain information about the machines in the local zone, as well as recently requested information from outside the zone.

When a name server receives a query from a resolver, the name server can perform several types of operations. Name resolver operations fall into two categories called non-recursive and recursive. A recursive operation is one in which the name server must access another name server for information. Non-recursive operations performed by the name server include a full answer to the resolver's request, a referral to another name server (which the resolver must address a query to itself), or an error message. When a recursive operation is necessary, the name server contacts another name server with the resolver's request. The remote name server will reply to the request with either a network address or a negative message indicating failure. Rules prohibit a remote name server from sending a referral on to yet another name server.

The resolver is intended to replace existing name resolution systems such as the /etc/hosts file. The replacement of these common mechanisms is transparent to users, although the administrator must know whether the native name resolution system or BIND/DNS is to be used on each machine so the correct tables can be maintained.

When the resolver acquires information from a name server, it stores the entries in its own cache to reduce the need for more network traffic if the same symbolic name is used again (as is often the case with applications that work across networks).

Under Linux, several different implementations of the name resolver are in use. The original resolver supplied with the BSD-based versions of Linux is somewhat limited, offering neither a cache nor iterative query capabilities. To solve these limitations, the Berkeley Internet Name Domain (BIND) server was added. BIND provides both caching and iterative query capabilities in three different modes: primary server, secondary server, or caching-only server (which doesn't have a database of its own, only a cache). The use of BIND on BSD systems allows another process to take over the workload of name resolution, a process that may be on another machine entirely.

THE HOSTS.CONF FILE AND RESOLVER VARIABLES

The file /etc/hosts.conf is used as the central reference for the resolver. The /etc/hosts.conf file is used to tell the resolver which services it can use to resolve a name, and in what order they should be used. A sample /etc/hosts.conf file looks like this:

```
# /etc/host.conf
order    bind hosts         # named running
multi    on                 # allow multiple addresses
nospoof  on                 # protect from spoofing
trim     merlin.com         # local domain trim
```

Several options are possible in a /etc/hosts.conf file, each of which must be on a separate line of its own. The following are valid options:

alert   If this option is active, any spoof attempt (see nospoof) logs a
          message in the syslog facility. This option is active if argument
          is on.

multi   This option determines whether a host in /etc/hosts is allowed to
          have several IP addresses. Valid values for this option are on
          and off.

nospoof   This option checks IP addresses to make sure the request is a
          valid one and not an attempt to break into the network. This
          check is not very secure, but it is a good first measure. If this
          option is specified with the argument on, nospoof is active.

order   This option specifies the order in which resolving services
          should be tried. Valid options are bind (query the name server),
          hosts (use the /etc/hosts file), and nis (use NIS lookups).

trim   This option takes a domain name as an argument. It removes
          that domain name from hostnames before a lookup. You can use
          it to allow /etc/hosts to take precedence over name resolver for
          local networks, for example.

The settings in the /etc/hosts.conf file can be overridden by some special resolver environment variables. Valid environment variables (which may be set for the session or by an application) are the following:

- RESOLV_ADD_TRIM_DOMAINS specifies a list of trim domains to add to those given in /etc/hosts.conf.

- When followed by a filename, RESOLV_HOST_CONF specifies the file to use instead of /etc/hosts.conf.

- RESOLV_MULTI overrides multi argument in /etc/hosts.conf. Valid values are on and off.

- RESOLV_OVERRIDE_TRIM_DOMAINS specifies a list of trim domains to override those given in /etc/hosts.conf.

- RESOLV_SERV_ORDER overrides the order option in the /etc/hosts.conf file.

- RESOLV_SPOOF_CHECK turns spoof checks on or off. Also allowed is the warn argument, which checks for spoofing and logs results, and warn off, which checks but doesn't log results. This variable also allows an asterisk argument, which turns on spoof checks but leaves logging as set in /etc/hosts.conf.

NAME SERVER LOOKUPS: THE RESOLV.CONF FILE

The file /etc/resolv.conf is used to tell the resolver which name servers to use. At least one name server must be specified for the resolver to be able to communicate with the server. If the /etc/resolv.conf file doesn't exist or is empty, the resolver will assume that your local machine is the name server and try to send resolution requests to it.

A sample /etc/resolv.conf file shows the general format and the entries most systems will need. For a machine that uses a name server elsewhere on the network, this format is usually sufficient:

```
# /etc/resolv.conf
domain          merlin.com      # the local domain
nameserver      147.23.1.23     # the name server
```

The important keyword is the second one in the file, called nameserver. As you can guess, this keyword gives the IP address of the name server your local machine should use to resolve addresses.

You can specify more than one name server by using extra lines with the keyword (do not put the IP addresses on a single line). For example, the entries

```
nameserver      147.23.1.23     # primary name server
nameserver      147.23.1.46     # secondary name server
nameserver      147.23.2.1      # extra name sever
```

use the name servers in the order they are encountered in the file. The most reliable name server should always be listed first. Most Linux versions allow only three name servers to be specified.

The domain and search keywords are used to allow shortcuts to identify addresses. The domain keyword is used to append a full address to a name instead of forcing you to specify it. For example, if you are on a local area network and want to FTP files from another system, you can use the name wizard instead of specifying the full domain names (such as wizard@foobar.com), as long as the domain line in the /etc/resolv.conf file contains the line:

```
domain      foobar.com
```

This feature makes addressing machines on the local area network much easier.

The search option does much the same thing as the domain keyword, except it can apply to other networks instead of just your own. Both search and domain keywords can only appear once in the /etc/resolv.conf file.

THE /ETC/NAMED.BOOT FILE

The /etc/named.boot file is used to specify the master files that contain zone information and name servers. The /etc/named.boot file is often set up by the software installation routine, but you should know the format of the file. One important difference between the named.boot file and most other files is the use of semi-colons for comments instead of the pound sign. A sample /etc/named.boot file looks like this:

```
; /etc/named.boot
; this is a comment line
directory              /var/named
; now the domains and files they use
cache                  named.ca
primary      merlin    named.hosts
```

The directory keyword shows the directory in which the zone files are found. For most Linux installations, this directory should be /var/named. The cache line indicates that the cache for BIND is to be enabled and load some basic information from the file named.ca. The primary keyword indicates the primary server is merlin and the zone information file is named.hosts.

The options (and their arguments) of the most commonly used values allowed in the named.boot file are:

cache	Indicates the domain name and filename of the "root server hints" file and the cache
directory	Lists the directory in which zone files are found

	forwarders	Indicates the IP addresses of a list of name severs that the named daemon can query
	primary	Indicates the domain name and filename of the primary name server
	secondary	Indicates the domain name and filename of the secondary name server
	slave	Sets the name server as a slave

RESOURCE RECORDS

The name server maintains the information required to resolve symbolic names to their IP addresses in a set of resource records, which are entries in a database. Resource records (often abbreviated to RR) contain information in ASCII format. Because ASCII is used, it is easy to update the records. Each RR has a specific format:

```
domain_name, type, class, TTL, Routing_Data
```

The domain name field is the machine the record refers to. If no name is specified, the name in the previous RR is used. The Type field identifies the type of resource record. The different types of resource records have different purposes, such as mapping names to addresses and defining zones. A mnemonic code or a number identifies the type of resource record. These codes and their meanings are listed in Table 30.1.

TABLE 30.1. CODES AND NUMBERS FOR RESOURCE RECORD TYPES.

Number	Code	Description
1	A	Network address
2	NS	Authoritative name server
3	MD	Mail destination. Now replaced by MX.
4	MF	Mail forwarder. Now replaced by MX.
5	CNAME	Canonical alias name
6	SOA	Start of zone authority
7	MB	Mailbox domain name
8	MG	Mailbox member
9	MR	Mail rename domain
10	NULL	Null resource record
11	WKS	Well-known service

continues

30

Configuring TCP/IP

TABLE 30.1. CONTINUED

Number	Code	Description
12	PTR	Pointer to a domain name
13	HINFO	Host information
14	MINFO	Mailbox information
15	MX	Mail exchange
16	TXT	Text strings
17	RP	Responsible person
18	AFSDB	AFS-type services
19	X.25	X.25 address
20	ISDN	ISDN address
21	RT	Route through

Some of the resource record types are now obsolete (numbers 3 and 4), and others are considered experimental at this time (numbers 13 and 17 through 21). In most resource records, you find only types A, NS, SOA, and PTR.

The Class field in the resource record format contains a value for the class of record. If no value is specified, the class of the previous RR is substituted. Internet name servers usually have the code IN in this field.

The Time-to-Live (TTL) field specifies the amount of time in seconds that the resource record is valid in the cache. If a value of zero is used, the record should not be added to the cache. If the Time-to-Live field is omitted, a default value is used. Usually this field tells the name server how long the entry is valid before it has to ask for an update.

The data section of the resource record contains two parts: the length of the current record and the data itself. The Data Length field specifies the length of the data section. The data is a variable length field (hence the need for a length value) that describes the entry. The use of this field differs with the different types of resource records.

Some resource record types have a single piece of information in the data area, such as an address, or at most three pieces of information. The only exception is the Start of Authority (SOA) resource record. The contents of the resource record data areas (except SOA's) are:

RR Type	Field Name	Description
A	Address	A network address
NS	NSDNAME	Domain name of host
MG	MGNAME	Domain name of mailbox
CNAME	CNAME	Alias for the machine
HINFO	CPU	String identifying CPU type
	OS	String identifying operating system
MINFO	RMAILBX	Mailbox responsible for mailing lists
	EMAILBOX	Mailbox for error messages
MB	MADNAME	Now obsolete
MR	NEWNAME	Rename address of a specific mailbox
MX	PREFERENCE	The precedence for delivery
	EXCHANGE	Domain name of host that will act as mail exchange
	NULL	Anything can be placed in the data field
PTR	PTRDNAME	Domain name that acts as a pointer to a location
TXT	TXTDATA	Any kind of descriptive text
WKS	Address	A network address
	Protocol	Protocol used
	Bitmap	Ports and protocols

The Start of Authority (SOA) resource record format is used to identify the machines that are within a zone. There is only one SOA record in each zone. The fields in the SOA resource record are mostly used for administration and maintenance of the name server. The order of fields in the SOA RR is:

```
MNAME, RNAME, Serial, Refresh, Retry, Expiry, Minimim
```

The MNAME field is the domain name of the source of data for the zone. The RNAME field is the domain name of the mailbox of the administrator of the zone (the responsible person name). The Serial field contains a version number for the zone. It is incremented when the zone is changed; otherwise, it is maintained as the same value for all such messages.

30

CONFIGURING TCP/IP

The Refresh Time is the number of seconds between data refreshes for the zone. The Retry Time is the number of seconds to wait between unsuccessful refresh requests. The Expiry Time is the number of seconds after which the zone information is no longer valid. Finally, the Minimum Time is the number of seconds to be used in the Time-to-Live field of resource records within the zone.

Some sample resource records will show the formats used. Address resource records consist of the machine name, the type of resource record indicator ("A" for address RRs, for example), and the network address. A sample address resource record would look like this:

```
merlin _4      IN     A     143.23.25.7
```

The IN tags the resource record as an Internet class. This format makes it easy to locate a name and derive its address. (The reverse, going from address to name, is not as easy and requires a special format called IN-ADDR-ARPA.)

For Well-Known Service resource records (WKS or Type 11), the data field of the record contains three fields used to describe the services supported at the address the record refers to. A sample WKS resource record might look like this:

```
wizard.merlin.com.    IN    WKS    143.23.1.34.
                                   FTP  TCP  SMTP  TELNET
```

If you want to specify the full domain name in the resource record, you must provide a trailing period. If you don't, the domain name will be added again, resulting in wizard.merlin.com.merlin.com in the preceding example. Alternatively, you can let the domain name get appended and just leave the machine name wizard in the resource record. The full domain name and Internet address are shown in the preceding example, as is the IN to show the Internet class of resource records. The type of record is indicated with the WKS. The protocols supported by the machine at that address are listed after the address. In reality, these protocols are a bitmap that corresponds to ports. When the port bit is set to a value of one, the service is supported. The list of ports and services are defined by an Internet RFC.

RESOURCE RECORD FILES

The main file that resource records reside in is usually called /var/named/named.ca on Linux systems. This file consists of hints to the resolver, which help it decide where to find information about name servers. A sample extract from the /var/named/named.ca file looks like this (comments are preceded by semi-colons):

```
; /var/named/named.ca - the cache file name
; this points to the primary name server
.                         99999999   IN  NS big_boy.big_net.com
big_boy.big_net.com       99999999   IN  A   156.23.14.2
```

The /var/named/named.hosts file lists the local hosts and maps the hostname to an IP address. The file includes alias names, as well. A sample /var/named/named.hosts file looks like this:

```
; /var/named/named.hosts
@                     IN     SOA      merlin.tpci.com merlin. (
                                      16  ; serial
                                      86400 ; refresh
                                      3600 ; retry
                                      36000 ; expiry
                                      604800 ; expiry
                                      )
                      IN     NS       merlin.tpci.com
; the local machine
localhost.            IN     A        127.0.0.1
merlin                IN     A        176.23.1.34
merlin.if1            IN     CNAME    merlin
```

The file /var/named/named.local helps with reverse mapping of locally-accessible addresses using the IN-ADDR-ARPA format (discussed in a section later in this chapter). A sample named.local file looks like this:

```
; /var/named/named.local
@                     IN     SOA      merlin.tpci.com merlin (
                                      16  ; serial
                                      86400 ; refresh
                                      3600 ; retry
                                      36000 ; expiry
                                      604800 ; expiry
                                      )
                      IN     NS       merlin.tpci.com.
1                     IN     PTR      localhost.
```

Finally, the file /var/named/named.rev is used for reverse mapping of other machines using IN-ADDR-ARPA. A sample named.rev file looks like this:

```
; /var/named/named.rev
@                     IN     SOA      merlin.tpci.com merlin (
                                      16  ; serial
                                      86400 ; refresh
                                      3600 ; retry
                                      36000 ; expiry
                                      604800 ; expiry
                                      )
                      IN     NS       merlin.tpci.com.
1.1                   IN     PTR      wizard.tpci.com.
2.1                   IN     PTR      chatton.tpci.com.
3.1                   IN     PTR      walter.tpci.com
```

All these files are created for you with default information when you install BIND. The process to update them to contain your information isn't as bad as you may think. First, edit the /var/named/named.hosts file. For each machine to be added to the file, you need the machine's symbolic name, its IP address, any host information you want to include, and any aliases that should be recognized. For example, to add the machine artemis (which is also called the_ark) to the named.hosts file, add these lines:

```
ARTEMIS         IN    A       146.12.23.1
                IN    HINFO   PC UNIX
THE_ARK         IN    CNAME   ARTEMIS
```

Next, edit the /var/named/hosts.rev file to provide reverse IN-ADDR-ARPA mapping for each newly added machine. For the machine used in the preceding example, this line would be added:

```
1.23            IN    PTR     ARTEMIS.TPCI.COM.
```

Note that the address portion of the IP address is reversed, as it should be (i.e. 1.23 instead of 23.1). Also the trailing period needs to be put in place.

IN-ADDR-ARPA

The address fields, such as in the Address resource record type, use a special format called IN-ADDR-ARPA. This format allows reverse mapping from the address to the host name as well as from the host to the address mapping. To understand IN-ADDR-ARPA, it is useful to begin with a standard-format resource record. One of the simplest types of resource record is for the address (type A). The following is an extract from an address file:

```
TPCI_HPWS1     IN    A     143.12.2.50
TPCI_HPWS2     IN    A     143.12.2.51
TPCI_HPWS3     IN    A     143.12.2.52
TPCI_GATEWAY   IN    A     143.12.2.100
               IN    A     144.23.56.2
MERLIN         IN    A     145.23.24.1
SMALLWOOD      IN    A     134.2.12.75
```

Each line of the file represents one resource record. In this case, they are all simple entries that have the machine's symbolic name, the class of machine (IN for Internet), A to show it is an address resource record, and the Internet address. The entry for the machine TPCI_GATEWAY has two corresponding addresses because it is a gateway between two networks. The gateway has a different address on each of the networks, which results in two resource records in the same file.

This type of file makes name-to-address mapping easy. The name server simply searches for a line that has the symbolic name requested by the application and returns the Internet address at the end of that line. The databases are indexed on the name, so these searches proceed very quickly.

Searching from the address to the name is not quite as easy. If the resource record files were small, time delays for a manual search would not be appreciable, but with large zones there can be thousands or tens of thousands of entries. The index is on the name, so searching for an address would be a slow process. To solve this "reverse mapping" problem, IN-ADDR-ARPA was developed. IN-ADDR-ARPA uses the host address as an index to the host's resource record information. When the proper resource record is located, the symbolic name can be extracted.

IN-ADDR-ARPA uses the PTR resource record type (see Table 30.1) to point from the address to the name. There may be one of these pointer indexes maintained on each name server. An example of a "number-to-name" file is shown below:

```
23.1.45.143.IN-ADDR-ARPA.    PTR     TPCI_HPWS_4.TPCI.COM
1.23.64.147.IN-ADDR-ARPA.    PTR     TPCI_SERVER.MERLIN.COM
3.12.6.123.IN-ADDR-ARPA.     PTR     BEAST.BEAST.COM
143.23.IN-ADDR-ARPA          PTR     MERLINGATEWAY.MERLIN.COM
```

The Internet addresses are reversed in the IN-ADDR-ARPA file for ease of use. As shown in the sample file above, it is not necessary to specify the complete address for a gateway, because the domain name will provide enough routing information.

SUMMARY

Once you've followed the steps in this chapter, your TCP/IP connection is properly configured (except for PPP and SLIP, which are discussed in Chapter 31, "Configuring SLIP and PPP.") The process for configuring TCP/IP is simple: run ifconfig, and then run route. As long as the arguments are in the proper order, and the support files (such as /etc/hosts and /etc/networks) are correct, TCP/IP will be fully accessible by your applications.

30

CONFIGURING TCP/IP

- Setting Up the Dummy Interface

- Setting Up SLIP

- Setting Up PPP

- Using DNS for SLIP and PPP

CHAPTER 31

Configuring SLIP and PPP

This chapter looks at the configuration and setup required to use either SLIP (Serial Line Internet Protocol) or PPP (Point to Point Protocol) on your Linux system. This follows the general TCP/IP configuration performed in the previous chapter. Both SLIP and PPP work over a dialup modem, essentially establishing a normal modem link with a remote system, then invoking either the SLIP or PPP protocols. In many ways, SLIP and PPP are like PLIP interfaces; even though SLIP and PPP use a serial modem port, they are really point-to-point interfaces involving two machines. Unfortunately, SLIP and PPP are more complicated to configure than PLIP.

You can do the SLIP and PPP configuration when you are configuring the general TCP/IP files, or you can wait until you need to set them up for SLIP or PPP access. Since not all installations will require SLIP or PPP, you can quite easily wait. However, most Internet service providers prefer SLIP or PPP access from small systems because they provide fast, efficient transfers.

SETTING UP THE DUMMY INTERFACE

What's a dummy interface? It's a bit of a trick to give your machine an IP address to work with when it uses only SLIP and PPP interfaces. A dummy interface solves the problem of a stand-alone machine (no network cards connecting it to other machines) whose only valid IP address to which data can be sent is the loopback driver (127.0.0.1). Although SLIP and PPP may be used for connecting your machine to the outside world, you have no internal IP address that applications can use when the interface is not active.

This problem arises with some applications that require a valid IP address to work. Some word processors and desktop layout tools, for example, require the TCP/IP system to be operational with an IP address for the target machine. The dummy interface essentially sets an IP address for your local machine that is valid as far as TCP/IP is concerned, but doesn't really get used except to fool applications.

Creating a dummy interface using the loopback driver is very simple. If your machine has an IP address already assigned for it in the /etc/hosts file, all you need to do is set up the interface and create a route. The following two commands are required:

```
ifconfig lo 127.0.0.1
route add 127.0.0.1
```

The lo portion of the ifconfig command indicates that the line refers to the loopback driver. This line creates a link to the IP address 127.0.0.1. If you do not have an IP address for the localhost already in the /etc/hosts file, add one before you create the dummy interface. To create the loopback interface, edit the /etc/hosts file so it includes a line like the following:

```
127.0.0.1        localhost
```

This line sets up your local machine to use the IP address 127.0.0.1 as the localhost interface. You can verify that the loopback interface is working properly after you have used the `ifconfig` command by using the `ifconfig` command with the interface name to show statistics:

```
merlin $ ifconfig lo
lo        Link encap:Local Loopback
          inet addr:127.0.0.1  Bcast:127.255.255.255  Mask:255.0.0.0
          UP BROADCAST LOOPBACK RUNNING  MTU:2000  Metric:1
          RX packets:0 errors:0 dropped:0 overruns:0
          TX packets:12 errors:0 dropped:0 overruns:0
```

The statistics show that the loopback interface is running, has been assigned the IP address 127.0.0.1, and has the broadcast mask of 255.0.0.0.

After you add the loopback driver to the routing table using the `route` command, you can use the `ping` command to check that the interface is responding properly:

```
merlin $ ping localhost
PING localhost (127.0.0.1): 56 data bytes
64 bytes from 127.0.0.1: icmp_seq=0 ttl=255 time=0.8 ms
64 bytes from 127.0.0.1: icmp_seq=1 ttl=255 time=0.7 ms
64 bytes from 127.0.0.1: icmp_seq=2 ttl=255 time=0.7 ms
64 bytes from 127.0.0.1: icmp_seq=3 ttl=255 time=0.7 ms
64 bytes from 127.0.0.1: icmp_seq=4 ttl=255 time=0.7 ms

--- localhost ping statistics ---
5 packets transmitted, 5 packets received, 0% packet loss
round-trip min/avg/max = 0.7/0.7/0.8 ms
```

You must interrupt the `ping` command with a Ctrl+C to stop it. The output above shows that the packets destined for the localhost machine were properly delivered and replies were almost immediate. If you receive output anything like this output, your interface is properly set up. If you receive an `unknown host` message, your localhost name is not recognized. Check the /etc/hosts file and use `ifconfig` to verify that the loopback driver is installed properly.

Setting Up SLIP

SLIP can be used with many dialup Internet service providers, as well as for networking with other machines. When a modem connection is established, you don't get to see a shell prompt, but SLIP takes over and maintains the session for you. The SLIP driver is usually configured as part of the Linux kernel. The Linux SLIP driver also handles CSLIP, a compressed SLIP version that is available with some implementations.

For most Linux systems that use SLIP, a serial port has to be dedicated to the device. This means that a serial port must be specifically configured to use SLIP and cannot be used for any other purpose. The kernel uses a special program called SLIPDISC (SLIP discipline) to control the serial port and blocks other non-SLIP applications from using it.

The Linux SLIP driver is installed into the kernel usually by default, but some versions of Linux require you to rebuild the kernel and answer y to a question about SLIP and CSLIP usage. Once you have the kernel SLIP drivers in place, you can configure the serial port to be used for SLIP.

Configuring SLIP

The easiest way to dedicate a serial port for SLIP is to use the slattach program. This program takes the device name of the serial port as an argument. For example, to dedicate the second serial port (/dev/cua1) to SLIP, you would issue the command:

```
slattach /dev/cua1 &
```

The command is set to background mode by the ampersand. Failure to send to background means the terminal or console the command was issued from is not usable until the process is terminated. You can embed the slattach command in a startup file if you want.

Once the attachment has succeeded, the port is set to the first SLIP device /dev/sl0. If you are using more than one serial port for SLIP lines, you need to issue the command for each line. Subsequent SLIP devices (/dev/sl1, /dev/sl2, and so on) will be assigned by slattach. Most versions of Linux will support up to eight SLIP lines.

By default, most Linux systems set the SLIP port to use CSLIP. If you want to override this default, use the -p option and the slip name:

```
slattach -p slip /dev/cua1 &
```

You can use modes other than slip and cslip to follow the -p option: slip6 (a six-bit version of SLIP) and adaptive (for adaptive SLIP, which adjusts to whatever is at the other end of the connection).

You must make sure that both ends of the connection use the same form of SLIP. For example, you cannot set your device for CSLIP and communicate with another machine running SLIP. If the versions of SLIP don't match, commands such as ping will fail.

Once the serial port has been set for SLIP usage, you can configure the network interface using the same procedure used for normal network connections (including the dummy interface set up earlier). The commands used are ifconfig and route. For example, if your machine is called merlin and you are calling arthur, issue the commands:

```
ifconfig sl0 merlin-slip pointopoint arthur
route add arthur
```

The `ifconfig` command configures the interface `merlin-slip` (the local address of the SLIP interface) to be a point-to-point connection to `arthur`. The `route` command adds the remote machine called `arthur` to the routing tables. You can also issue another `route` command to set the default route to `arthur` as a gateway:

```
route add default gw arthur
```

If you want to use the SLIP port for access to the Internet, it has to have an IP address and an entry in the /etc/hosts file. That gives the SLIP system a valid entry on the Internet. A better approach is to use DNS, but the configuration is more complex (see "Using DNS for SLIP and PPP").

Once the `ifconfig` and `route` commands have been executed, you can test and use your SLIP network. If you decide to remove the SLIP interface in the future, you must remove the routing entry, use `ifconfig` to take down the SLIP interface, and then kill the `slattach` process. The first two steps are done with these commands:

```
route del arthur
ifconfig sl0 down
```

To terminate the `slattach` process, find the process ID (PID) of `slattach` (with the `ps` command), and then issue a `kill` command. See Chapter 20, "Managing Processes," for more information on the `ps` and `kill` commands.

USING DIP

Many Linux versions include a utility program called `dip` (Dial-up IP), which helps to automate the preceding steps, as well as provide an interpretive language for the SLIP line. Many versions of `dip` are currently available, some of which have different capabilities. This section doesn't go into exhaustive detail about `dip`, primarily because most of its functionality is not used by most users. This section looks at a typical setup file and leaves the rest to the documentation supplied with `dip`.

The `dip` system uses scripts to control its behavior. The following is a sample `dip` script to connect to a remote machine with comments (prefaced by a pound sign) to explain each action:

```
# dip script to connect to remote darkstar
# begin by setting local interface name and address
get $local merlin-slip
# now set the remote end name and address
get $remote darkstar
# now set parameters
port cua1                # serial port /dev/cua1 used for SLIP
speed 38400              # use 38,400 as the modem speed
modem HAYES              # set the command set type for the modem
# initialize modem
reset                    # reset the modem and port
flush                    # remove any modem responses
# dial darkstar and log in
dial 5551234             # dial the remote
```

```
wait CONNECT              # wait for the CONNECT message
send \r\n\r\n             # send a couple of CR/LFs
wait ogin:                # wait for login prompt
send $merlin\n
wait word:                # wait for password prompt
send secret1\n
print Connected to the remote
# now clean up
default                   # set this link to default
mode SLIP                 # go to SLIP mode
```

The script would be called and executed with a command like this

```
dip script_file
```

where `script_file` is the name of the file containing the script. You can put lots of extra steps in the script, including multiple levels of error checking; however, since most people find SLIP fairly easy to work with anyway, the `dip` utility is really for the person who wants to perform extra automated steps.

SETTING UP PPP

PPP is a more talented protocol than SLIP and is preferable for most uses. However, the configuration is a little more complex than SLIP's. Linux divides the PPP functions into two parts, one for the High-Level Data Link Control (HLDC) protocol, which helps define the rules for sending PPP datagrams between the two machines, and one for the PPP daemon, called `pppd`, which handles the protocol once the HLDC system has established communications parameters. In addition, Linux uses a program called `chat`, which calls the remote system.

As with SLIP, PPP establishes a modem link between the two machines, and then hands over the control of the line to PPP. You, as the user, never get to see a shell prompt or login because PPP handles it all for you. Both `HLDC` and `pppd` are complex utilities with many options available to fine-tune their behavior. This section covers the most important aspects necessary to get a PPP connection up and running properly.

Prior to establishing a PPP link, you must have a loopback driver established (see Chapter 30, "Configuring TCP/IP"). You should also have a name resolution system in operation, even if it's the /etc/hosts file or a simple DNS cache-only name server (see "Using DNS for SLIP and PPP").

SETTING UP A PPP ACCOUNT

If you are worried about compromising your system's security, it is best to use PPP with a special user account (for example, one called ppp) for optimum protection and behavior. If you use a standard user login, there is a chance that people calling your system can exploit file permission weaknesses to access parts of the system you don't want them to touch. The use of a dedicated login for PPP is not strictly necessary, and you can easily use PPP from any user account, but for more secure operation, you should consider creating a ppp user. The process is simple. First, you need to add a new user to the /etc/passwd file. You can use whatever script your system normally uses to add new users, or edit the /etc/passwd file yourself. (See Chapter 16, "Users and Logins," for more information about users and /etc/passwd.)

A sample /etc/passwd entry for the ppp account (with UID set to 201 and GID set to 51) looks like this:

```
ppp:*:201:51:PPP account:/tmp:/etc/ppp/pppscript
```

In this case, the account is set with no password (so no one can log in to the account) and a home directory of /tmp (since no files are created). The startup program is set to /etc/ppp/pppscript, a file you create with the configuration information in it (you can use any filename, of course). A sample contents for the pppscript file looks like this:

```
#!/bin/sh
mesg n
stty -echo
exec pppd -detach silent modem crtscts
```

The first line forces execution of the script into the Bourne shell. The second command turns off all attempts to write to the ppp account's tty. The stty command is necessary to stop everything the remote sends from being echoed again. Finally, the exec command runs the pppd daemon (which handles all PPP traffic). You will see the pppd daemon and the options later in this section.

DIALING OUT: CHAT

PPP requires you to establish a modem connection to the remote machine before it can take over and handle the communications. The chat program is the most commonly used of the utilities available to do this. The chat program is popular because it uses a scripting style similar to that used by UUCP (see Chapter 27, "UUCP").

To use chat, you have to assemble a command line that looks almost the same as a UUCP /etc/Systems file entry. For example, to call a remote machine with a Hayes-compatible modem (using the AT command set) at the number 555-1234, use the following command. It is all formatted as a chat script, UUCP style:

```
chat "" ATZ OK ATDT5551234 CONNECT "" ogin: ppp word: secret1
```

If you read the UUCP chapter, this code may look familiar. If not, all the entries are in a send-expect format, with what you send to the remote specified after what you receive from it. The chat script always starts with an expect string, which you must set to be empty because the modem won't talk to you without any signal to it. After the empty string, send the ATZ (reset) command, wait for an OK back from the modem, and then send the dial command. Once a CONNECT message is received back from the modem, the login script for the remote machine is executed. Send a blank character, wait for the ogin: (login) prompt, send the login name ppp, wait for word: (password) prompt, and then send your password. After the login is complete, chat terminates but leaves the line open.

If you want to see all the activity that goes on with the chat program, you can force all messages to the syslog daemon for future study. The -v option forces the messages to syslog, so the command would be:

```
chat -v "" ATZ OK ATDT5551234 CONNECT "" ogin: ppp word: secret1
```

If the other end of the connection doesn't answer with a login script as soon as its modem answers, you may have to force a Break command down the line to jog the remote end. This is done the same way as with UUCP:

```
chat -v "" ATZ OK ATDT5551234 CONNECT "" ogin:-BREAK-ogin: ppp word: secret1
```

Because any user doing a ps -ef command sees the entire command line (with its passwords), this type of chat entry has a security problem. If you are the only user of your system, this isn't a concern, but to save yourself any problems, you can embed the script portion of the command in a file and read the file in to chat. Then the script will not appear on a ps output. To call a file for use with chat, use the -f option:

```
chat -f chat_file
```

The chat_file will contain the string:

```
"" ATZ OK ATDT5551234 CONNECT "" ogin: ppp word: secret1
```

The chat script can help you detect common error conditions, such as a line busy or no connection established. The messages from your modem (Hayes uses BUSY and NO CARRIER respectively) are embedded in the chat script with the ABORT option, which enables you to exit from the chat script gracefully if one of these error conditions occurs.

To handle these abort conditions, embed the chat keyword ABORT, followed by the message that should trigger an abort, prior to your normal chat script. For example, to modify the chat script above to abort on a BUSY or NO CARRIER message from the modem, the script should look like this:

```
ABORT BUSY ABORT 'NO CARRIER' "" ATZ OK ATDT5551234 CONNECT "" ogin: ppp word:
    secret1
```

You need two ABORT commands because each takes only one argument. The rest of the chat script is as usual. Note the need to put quotation marks around the NO CARRIER message: the space in the middle would confuse the script otherwise.

Running pppd

To set up a PPP connection, you need to invoke the pppd daemon. If you have a PPP connection already established and your machine is logged into a remote using the ppp account, you can start the pppd daemon. Assuming that your local machine is using the device /dev/cua1 for its PPP connection at 38,400 baud, you would start up the pppd daemon with this command:

```
pppd /dev/cua1 38400 crtscts defaultroute
```

This command tells the Linux kernel to switch the interface on /dev/cua1 to PPP and to establish an IP link to the remote machine. The crtscts option, which is usually used on any PPP connection of about 9,600 baud, switches on hardware handshaking. The IP address the local system will use is taken from the local hostname, unless one is specified on the pppd command line (which you will seldom need to do, since the localhost IP address should be correct for the PPP line).

If you want to force the local or remote IP addresses to be something other than the machine's default values, you can add the addresses with an option to pppd. The general format is to specify the local IP address, a colon, and then the remote IP address. For example, the option

```
147.23.43.1:36.23.1.34
```

when added to the pppd command line, sets the local IP address as 147.23.43.1 and the remote IP address to 36.23.1.34, regardless of what the local values are. If you only want to modify one IP address, leave the other portion blank. The command

```
147.23.43.1:
```

just sets the local IP address and accepts the remote IP address as whatever the machine sends.

Because you need chat to establish the connection in the first place, you can embed the chat command as part of the pppd command if you want. This is best done when reading the contents of the chat script from a file (using the -f option). For example, you could issue the pppd command:

```
pppd connect "chat -f chat_file" /dev/cua1 38400 -detach crtscts modem defaultroute
```

You will notice a few modifications to the pppd command other than the addition of the chat command in quotation marks. The connect command specifies the dialup script that pppd should start with, while the -detach command tells pppd not to detach from the console and not to move to the background. The modem keyword tells pppd to monitor the modem port (in case the line drops prematurely) and hang up the line when the call is finished.

The pppd daemon begins setting up the connection parameters with the remote by exchanging IP addresses, and then sets communications values based on transferred information. Once that is done, pppd will set the network layer on your Linux kernel to use the PPP link by setting the interface to /dev/ppp0 (if it's the first PPP link active on the machine). Finally, pppd establishes a kernel routing table entry to point to the machine on the other end of the PPP link.

If you want to change the default behavior of the pppd daemon, you can do it through command line options or a control file. The file is a better approach if you want to change the parameters for every connection established using PPP.

Before completing the command line, pppd scans a number of possible options files. The more common file is /etc/ppp/options, which usually is used to set global defaults. An example of a /etc/ppp/options file looks like this:

```
# /etc/ppp/options: globabl definitions
domain merlin.com
auth                    # force authentication
usehostname             # use local hostname for authentication
lock                    # use file locking UUCP-style
```

The domain is established with the domain keyname followed by the full domain name (minus the machine name). The next two lines above (auth and usehostname) deal with authentication of the PPP line, preventing unwanted usage and access. The lock keyword tells pppd to use UUCP-style file locking to prevent device clashes. Locking should be used on all PPP systems to prevent problems.

CHECKING PROBLEMS

The pppd daemon echoes all warnings and error messages to the syslog facility. If you used the -v option with the chat script, chat's messages are also sent to syslog. If you are having trouble with your PPP connections, you can check the syslog for details and try to isolate the problem.

Syslog discards incoming error and warning messages, unless an entry in the /etc/syslog.conf file redirects them to another file. To save the messages from pppd and chat, add this line to the /etc/syslog.conf file:

```
daemon.*        /tmp/ppp-log
```

This entry tells syslog to save any incoming messages from a daemon to the /tmp/ppp-log file. You can use any filename you want instead of /tmp/ppp-log. Many Linux versions of the syslog.conf file insist on tabs to separate the columns instead of spaces. Once your script is working, remember to remove this line or the log file will grow quite large!

If you really want to watch what is going on with pppd, you can invoke a debugging option with the kdebug command followed by a number. The three values for debugging are:

1	Displays general debug messages
2	Displays incoming HLDC data
4	Displays outgoing HLDC data

The numbers are added together to give the debug level you want. For example, the command kdebug 5 will display all general debug messages and all outgoing HLDC data. A value of 7 displays everything (this display gets very long). You can send the output to a file or the console.

PPP AUTHENTICATION

PPP is a wonderful protocol for modem-based communications, but it has one major problem: it has security holes large enough to drive a bus through. If incorrectly configured even slightly, anyone can use the PPP line to get into your machine, or use the PPP line to get out to other systems. To help prevent this, authentication is often used. Authentication essentially makes sure that each end of the connection is who they say they are and is allowed to use the link.

PPP uses two authentication schemes: the Password Authentication Protocol (PAP) and the Challenge Handshake Authentication Protocol (CHAP). PAP is much like a login procedure. When one machine sends the login name and password to the other, the receiving machine verifies the information with a database on its end. While simple, PAP has the problem that anyone can tap into the line and monitor the passwords being sent.

CHAP solves this problem, and hence is the most favored form of authentication for PPP links. CHAP enables one machine to send a random string to the other, along with its hostname. The other end uses the hostname to look up the proper reply, combine it with the first string, encrypt it, and then resend it to the first machine along with its hostname. The first machine performs the same sort of manipulation on the random string it first sent, and if the two replies match, the authentication is complete. CHAP doesn't authenticate only at start time, but at random intervals throughout the connection, which adds to its power.

When two machines connect, they don't use authentication unless explicitly instructed to do so (see the auth entry in the /etc/ppp/options file, discussed earlier). When authentication is active, one end will try to use CHAP first; then, if that fails because the other end doesn't support CHAP, it will use PAP. If neither authentication scheme is supported by the other end, the connection is terminated. If you are going to use authentication for all your PPP connections, put the auth entry in the

/etc/ppp/options file. If not all your connections support authentication, then those connections will fail if `auth` is specified.

The information needed for both CHAP and PPP is kept in two files called /etc/ppp/chap-secrets and /etc/ppp/pap-secrets respectively. When authentication is active, one end checks the other for these files, trying CHAP first. If you are going to use authentication for all your connections (which is a very good idea), you can build up the chap-secrets and pap-secrets files. If you configure both chap-secrets and pap-secrets and specify the `auth` option in /etc/ppp/options, no unauthenticated host can connect to your machine.

The /etc/ppp/chap-secrets file consists of four columns for the client name, the server name, the secret password string, and an optional list of IP addresses. The behavior of the system is different depending on whether the local machine is being challenged to authenticate itself or is issuing a challenge to the remote. When the local machine has to authenticate itself, `pppd` examines the /etc/ppp/chap-secrets file for an entry in the client field that matches the local host name and the server field equal to the remote hostname, and then uses the string to build the authentication message. Such an entry in the /etc/ppp/chap-secrets file looks like this:

```
#   client                 server             string         addresses
merlin.tpci.com            big_guy.big_net.com "I hate DOS"
```

This entry will use the string `"I hate DOS"` to build an authentication message back to `big_guy.big_net.com`. The quotations are necessary to surround the string in the file. (The addresses column is discussed below.) If you are setting up your system to connect to three different PPP remotes, you will want an entry for each server, so your file may look like this:

```
#   client                 server             string         addresses
merlin.tpci.com            big_guy.big_net.com "I hate DOS"
merlin.tpci.com            chatton.cats.com    "Meow, Meow, Meow"
merlin.tpci.com            roy.sailing.ca      "Hoist the spinnaker"
```

When your machine is sending the challenge, the process is reversed. The `pppd` daemon looks for the remote hostname in the client field, the local hostname in the server field, and uses the string to compare the encryption results with the string sent back by the remote. Entries in the /etc/ppp/chap-secrets file for this purpose look like this:

```
#   client                 server             string         addresses
big_guy.big_net.com        merlin.tpci.com     "Size isn't everything"
```

Again, you will have an entry for each remote machine you may need to authenticate. You can see that you will end up having mirror image entries for the client and server fields for each machine you connect to (as either end may require authentication at any time). A simple /etc/ppp/chap-secrets file looks like this:

```
#   client                  server              string              addresses
merlin.tpci.com             big_guy.big_net.com "I hate DOS"
big_guy.big_net.com merlin.tpci.com             "Size isn't everything"
merlin.tpci.com             chatton.cats.com    "Meow, Meow, Meow"
chatton.cats.com merlin.tpci.com                "Here, Kitty, Kitty"
merlin.tpci.com             roy.sailing.ca      "Hoist the spinnaker"
roy.sailing.ca              merlin.tpci.com     "Man overboard"
```

The size of the file could get quite large, so CHAP enables you to use a wildcard match, usually only for your local machine. For example, in this /etc/ppp/chap-secrets file:

```
#   client                  server              string              addresses
merlin.tpci.com             big_guy.big_net.com "I hate DOS"
big_guy.big_net.com merlin.tpci.com             "Size isn't everything"
merlin.tpci.com             chatton.cats.com    "Meow, Meow, Meow"
chatton.cats.com            merlin.tpci.com     "Here, Kitty, Kitty"
merlin.tpci.com             roy.sailing.ca      "Hoist the spinnaker"
*                           merlin.tpci.com     "Man overboard"
```

the last entry enables any other machine connecting to the localhost and requiring authentication to use the same string. Of course, the remote must have the same string in its chap-secrets file. This method is a little less secure than a dedicated string for each remote, but can be a handy time-saver when using a number of machines only rarely.

The addresses field, which wasn't used in the samples above, enables you to list either symbolic names or IP addresses for the clients. This field is necessary if the remote wants to use an IP address other than its normal one, which would cause the authentication to fail normally. If the address field is empty (as they all are in the samples), any IP address is allowed. A hyphen in the field disallows all IP addresses with that client.

The /etc/ppp/pap-secrets file is much the same as the chap-secrets file. The fields in the pap-secrets file are the client (called a user in the pap-secrets format) and server names, a secret string, and valid address aliases. However, the look of the file is different because the client and server names are not full domain names and the secret string is a single block of text. A sample pap-secrets file looks like this:

```
# /etc/ppp/pap-secrets
#   user        server          string          addresses
merlin          darkstar        yG55Sj29        darkstar.big_net.com
darkstar        merlin          5Srg7S          merlin.tpci.com
merlin          chatton         MeowMeow        chatton.cats.com
chatton         merlin          73wrh6s         merlin.tpci.com
```

In this example, the first two lines show a connection to the machine darkstar. The first line is how you authenticate a request from darkstar, and the second how you authenticate a request from you to them. The username in the first column is the name you send to the remote, and the server field is their identification to you. This poses a problem: the pppd daemon has no way of knowing the remote host's name, because all it gets is an IP address. You can put the IP address in the `addresses` column of the file, or you can specify the remote host name at the end of the `pppd` command line like this:

```
pppd ..... remotename chatton user merlin
```

This line shows that the remote is called `chatton` and the local host is `merlin`. The last portion giving the local host name overrides the default values, if specified.

USING DNS FOR SLIP AND PPP

If you are using SLIP or PPP to connect to the Internet for more than simple tasks (such as downloading e-mail and news), you will probably want to use DNS. The basic configuration for DNS and BIND were discussed in Chapter 30, "Configuring TCP/IP."

The easiest method of using DNS for your SLIP and PPP connections is to put the IP address of a name server you can access in the /etc/resolv.conf file. For example, if you can access a name server with an IP address of 45.2.12.1, you would make the following addition to your /etc/resolv.conf file:

```
# /etc/resolv.conf
domain          merlin.com       # the local domain
nameserver      145.2.12.1       # the Internet name server
```

Once this entry has been established, SLIP or PPP will send requests for address resolution to the name server and wait for replies. The more accessible the name server is, the better the performance will be. For this reason, choose a name server that is relatively close (in network terms).

Using this approach has a problem, though: all address resolution attempts must go out over the SLIP or PPP line. This can slow down applications, as well as increase the amount of network traffic over your SLIP or PPP line, sometimes to the detriment of other applications. A way around this problem is to set up a cache-only name server on your machine. As you may recall from Chapter 30, a name server uses a cache to retain the most commonly used addresses. Since most SLIP and PPP connections are to a few machines only, the cache can dramatically reduce the amount of resolution traffic on the SLIP or PPP link.

To set up a cache-only name server, you need to modify the /etc/named.boot file. To set your local machine up as a cache-only name server, your named.boot file would look like this:

```
; /etc/named.boot
directory      /var/named
cache                                    db.cache    ; cache-only
primary        0.0.147.in-addr-arpa      db.cache ; loopback
```

This file uses the local network name in IN-ADDR-ARPA format to specify the loopback driver, and the cache points to the file db.cache, which contains a list of root name servers.

SUMMARY

Once you have performed all the configuration steps and startup instructions mentioned above for SLIP and PPP, you can use the interfaces to connect to the outside world. The applications that make use of SLIP and PPP usually expect only to be told where the interface is and then to work without any interference from you. SLIP is much easier to configure than PPP, but PPP has faster throughput and more security features that make it attractive if you are using a modem connection a lot.

- Configuration Files

- The Loopback Driver

- The ifconfig Command

- The inetd Daemon

- The netstat Command

- The ping Command

- The arp Command

- The traceroute Command

- The rpcinfo Command

CHAPTER 32

TCP/IP Utilities

Linux's version of TCP/IP has several utility programs that provide status information and statistics on network performance. Several debugging utilities are available that enable a developer or knowledgeable user to trace a network problem. This chapter examines the basic set of these tools. It begins with a look at the primary configuration files involved in TCP/IP. Although these files have been discussed in earlier chapters, it is worth examining them again in closer detail.

Not all of these tools and configuration files will be supplied with every version of Linux, especially because two variants (BSD and System V) of these utilities are in general distribution. Check your software package to see which utilities you are supplied with. If you need a utility that wasn't included, download it from a BBS or FTP site and hope for no incompatibility problems! Most of the commands and utilities mentioned in this chapter are not made available to all users, although the superuser can access them all.

Configuration Files

Several files are involved in the complete specification of network addresses and configuration for TCP/IP. Linux allows comments on every line of these configuration files, as long as they are prefaced by a pound sign (#). Many Linux systems will have default, empty configuration files with many default entries commented out until the system administrator removes the comment symbols.

Symbolic Machine Names: /etc/hosts

A symbolic name is an alternative to using an IP address. For example, it is much easier to call a neighboring machine darkstar than 147.23.13.32. Whenever a symbolic name is used as an address by an application, the TCP/IP software must be able to resolve that name into a network address (as TCP/IP only uses IP addresses). The ASCII file /etc/hosts is usually employed, with the symbolic names matched to network addresses. (Note that the /etc/hosts file does not apply when Yellow Pages (YP), Network Information Services (NIS), or Domain Name Server (DNS) systems are used. These services use their own configuration files.)

Linux uses the file /etc/hosts to hold the network addresses and symbolic names, as well as a connection called the loopback (which is examined later in this chapter in the section, "Loopback Drivers"). The loopback connection address is usually listed as the machine name loopback or localhost.

The /etc/hosts file consists of the network address in one column and the symbolic name in another. Although the network addresses can be specified in decimal, octal, or hexadecimal format, decimal is the most commonly used form (and use of the others can be downright confusing). You can specify more than one symbolic name on a line by separating the names with white space characters (spaces or tabs). The following is a sample Linux /etc/hosts file:

```
# network host addresses
127.0.0.1               localhost local merlin_server
157.40.40.12            artemis
157.40.40.2             darkstar
143.10.12.62            big_bob
153.21.63.1             tpci_server tpci_main tpci
191.13.123.4            kitty_cat
```

Whenever a user or an application specifies a symbolic name, Linux searches the /etc/hosts file for a matching name and then reads the proper address from the same line. You can change the contents of the /etc/hosts file at any time, and the changes are essentially in effect immediately.

NETWORK NAMES: /ETC/NETWORKS

Chapter 30, "Configuring TCP/IP," mentioned the /etc/networks file. This file allows networks to be addressed by a symbolic name, just as machines are, instead of by their IP address. To resolve the network names, the file /etc/networks is used to specify symbolic network names. The format of the file provides a network symbolic name, its network address, and any alias that might be used. A sample /etc/networks file is shown below:

```
# local network names
tpci        146.1           tpci_network   tpci_local
bnr         47.80           BNR bnr.ca
big_net     123.2.21
unique      89.12323        UNIQUE
loopback    127             localhost
```

The last entry in the file gives the loopback name. The first entry specifies the local machine name, its network address, and its name variants that may be used by applications.

NETWORK PROTOCOLS: /ETC/PROTOCOLS

TCP/IP uses a special number, called a protocol number, to identify the specific transport protocol a Linux system receives. This allows the TCP/IP software to properly decode the information coming in. A configuration file called /etc/protocols identifies all the transport protocols available on the Linux and gives their respective protocol numbers. All systems have this file, although some entries may be commented out to prevent unwanted intrusion or abuse.

Usually the /etc/protocols file is not modified by the administrator. Instead, the file is maintained by the networking software and updated automatically as part of the installation procedure. The file contains the protocol name, its number, and any alias that may be used for that protocol. A sample /etc/protocols file is shown below:

```
# protocols

ip     0    IP     # internet protocol, pseudo protocol number
icmp   1    ICMP   # internet control message protocol
igmp   2    IGMP   # internet group multicast protocol
ggp    3    GGP    # gateway-gateway protocol
tcp    6    TCP    # transmission control protocol
pup    12   PUP    # PARC universal packet protocol
udp    17   UDP    # user datagram protocol
idp    22   IDP    # WhatsThis?
raw    255  RAW    # RAW IP interface
```

The exact contents of the /etc/protocols file on your system may differ a little from the file shown above, but the protocol numbers and names are probably very similar. There may be additional protocols listed, depending on the version of Linux and networking software.

NETWORK SERVICES: /ETC/SERVICES

The last TCP/IP configuration file used on most Linux systems identifies existing network services. This file is called /etc/services. As with the /etc/protocols file, this file is not usually modified by an administrator, but is maintained by software when installed or configured. The exception is when the /etc/services file has services missing that the application software did not add automatically. In addition, a system administrator can trim the /etc/services file in order to enhance security, such as when setting up a firewall to the local area network.

The /etc/services file is in ASCII format, and consists of the service name, a port number, and the protocol type. The port number and protocol type are separated by a slash. Any optional service alias names follow. The following is a short extract from a sample /etc/services file (the file is usually quite lengthy):

```
# network services
echo      7/tcp
echo      7/udp
discard   9/tcp     sink  null
discard   9/udp     sink  null
ftp       21/tcp
telnet    23/tcp
smtp      25/tcp    mail mailx
tftp      69/udp
# specific services
login     513/tcp
who       513/udp   whod
```

Most /etc/services files will have many more lines, because a wide number of TCP/IP services are supported by most versions of Linux. Most Linux systems are not used as firewalls to the Internet or between LANs, so administrators of most Linux machines will never have to worry about the contents of this file. On the other hand, if your machine is going to act as a firewall or you are very worried about security, you may want to manually modify the /etc/services file.

The Loopback Driver

The loopback driver is one of the most fundamental and oft-used diagnostic tools available to a system administrator. The loopback driver acts like a virtual circuit out of and back into the host machine. All outgoing information is immediately rerouted back to an input. You can use the loopback driver to test your machine's circuits by eliminating any external influences (including the network card, the network itself, gateways, or remote machines). With the loopback driver, you can ensure that the local machine is working properly and that any problems are from further out on the network. Loopback drivers are embedded as part of the Linux operating system kernel.

Because TCP/IP requires a destination IP address in order to send data, a loopback driver is set up as a special network address with the IP address 127.0.0.1. The loopback driver entries are always made in the /etc/hosts file, as shown below:

```
loopback    127            localhost
```

The loopback driver is also known as the localhost, and you can use either name. If the loopback driver doesn't already exist on your machine, you must create it with the `ifconfig` command. For more information, see Chapter 30, "Configuring TCP/IP."

The *ifconfig* Command

With the `ifconfig` program, you can activate and deactivate network interfaces, as well as configure them. Access to the `ifconfig` program is generally restricted to the superuser. Many options are available with `ifconfig`, most of which system administrators never use. Most of the time, you will use `ifconfig` only to enable an interface, as shown in Chapter 30, "Configuring TCP/IP."

The format of `ifconfig` commands always follow the same syntax. The syntax is

```
ifconfig interface [address [parms]]
```

where `interface` is the name of the interface, `address` is the (optional) IP address or symbolic name to be assigned to the interface (which is verified in /etc/hosts or /etc/networks), and `parameters` is one of a list of optional arguments for the address.

When used with only the name of an interface, `ifconfig` returns information about the current state of the interface, as shown in the following code. In this example, a query of both an Ethernet card and the loopback driver is performed. The status

32

TCP/IP Utilities

flags of the interface are followed by the Internet address, broadcast address, and optionally provides a network mask which defines the Internet address used for address comparison when routing. Your output may be different, but ifconfig should always display information about the interface (unless one has not been defined).

```
$ ifconfig eth0
eth0          Link encap 10Mps: Ethernet Hwaddr
              inet addr 147.123.20.1 Bcast 147.123.1.255 Mask 255.255.255.0
              UP BROADCAST RUNNING   MTU 1500 Metric 1
              RX packets:0 errors:0 dropped:0 overruns:0
              TX packets:0 errors:0 dropped:0 overruns:0
$ ifconfig lo
lo            Link encap: Local Loopback
              inet addr 127.0.0.1 Bcast {NONE SET] Mask 255.0.0.0
              UP BROADCAST LOOPBACK RUNNING   MTU 2000 Metric 1
              RX packets:0 errors:0 dropped:0 overruns:0
              TX packets:0 errors:0 dropped:0 overruns:0
```

The output from the ifconfig command shows the interface, any characteristics it has assigned to it, broadcast addresses, and network masks. MTU stands for maximum transfer unit. The Maximum Transfer Unit size is usually set to the maximum value the interface type will support (1,500 for Ethernet networks). Some operating systems use the Metric field to compute the cost of any particular route, although Linux doesn't use this field.

The RX and TX lines show how many packets of data have been received and transmitted respectively, both in total and those with errors, since the interface started in the current session.

As mentioned earlier, ifconfig accepts a long list of optional arguments to tailor the behavior of the interfaces. The following arguments are available with most versions of Linux:

allmulti	This argument sets multicast mode. It is not currently supported by Linux.
-allmulti	This argument turns off multicast mode.
arp	Use this argument to enable Address Resolution Protocol to detect physical address on network machines. This argument is set to on by default.
-arp	This argument disables ARP. It sets characteristic flag NOARP.
broadcast	Followed by the broadcast address of the network, this argument sets the address used to address all machines on the network. This argument is used if the broadcast address is different than the normal address calculated by TCP/IP based on the Class type of the network.

down	This argument makes the interface unusable by the IP software until taken up again.
metric	This argument sets the metric value for the interface. Although Linux doesn't use this argument, it is included for compatibility with older TCP/IP implementations.
mtu	Followed by a value in bytes, this argument sets the Maximum Transmission Unit size (the number of octets the interface can handle in one datagram). System defaults are usually accurate. (Ethernet defaults to 1500, SLIP to 296.)
netmask	Followed by a mask value, this argument sets the subnet mask.
pointopoint	This argument is used for point-to-point IP (PLIP) interfaces connecting two machines through the parallel port
promisc	This argument sets the interface to promiscuous mode (receives all packets, whether they're for that machine's IP address or not). Used for analyzing network traffic, this argument sets the characteristic flag PROMISC.
-promisc	This argument turns off promiscuous mode.
up	Implied when an address is given, the up argument makes the interface available to the IP software. When active, the interface has the characteristics of UP and RUNNING.

You can use most of these arguments when you use the ifconfig command, although most are not necessary for a well-configured network.

THE *INETD* DAEMON

When a networked Linux machine is started, it activates TCP/IP and immediately accepts connections at its ports, spawning a process for each. To control the processes better, the inetd program was developed to handle the port connections itself, offloading that task from the server. The primary difference is that inetd creates a process for each connection that is established, whereas the server would create a process for each port (which leads to many unused processes). On many systems, some of the test programs and status information utilities are run through inetd.

The inetd program uses the configuration file /etc/inetd.conf. The following code is an extract of a sample /etc/inetd.conf file. The first column shows the service name (which corresponds to an entry in the services file such as /etc/services), the socket type (stream, raw, or datagram), protocol name, whether inetd can accept further connections at the same port immediately (nowait) or must wait for the server to finish (wait), the login that owns the service, the server program name, and any optional parameters needed for the server program.

```
#inetd.conf
ftp     stream   tcp    nowait    NOLUID    /etc/ftpd      ftpd
telnet  stream   tcp    nowait    NOLUID    /etc/telnetd   telnetd
shell   stream   tcp    nowait    NOLUID    /etc/rshd      rshd
login   stream   tcp    nowait    NOLUID    /etc/rlogind   rlogind
exec    stream   tcp    nowait    NOLUID    /etc/rexecd    rexecd
finger  stream   tcp    nowait    nouser    /etc/fingerd   fingerd
comsat  dgram    udp    wait      root      /etc/comsat    comsat
ntalk   dgram    udp    wait      root      /etc/talkd     talkd
echo    stream   tcp    nowait    root      internal
discard stream   tcp    nowait    root      internal
chargen stream   tcp    nowait    root      internal
daytime stream   tcp    nowait    root      internal
time    stream   tcp    nowait    root      internal
echo    dgram    udp    wait      root      internal
discard dgram    udp    wait      root      internal
chargen dgram    udp    wait      root      internal
daytime dgram    udp    wait      root      internal
time    dgram    udp    wait      root      internal
```

The actual /etc/inetd.conf file may be much longer, but the extract above shows the general format of the file. The /etc/inetd.conf file is read when the server is booted and every time a hangup signal is received from an application. This allows dynamic changes to the file, as any modifications would be read and registered on the next file read.

THE *NETSTAT* COMMAND

The netstat program provides comprehensive information about the local system and its TCP/IP system. Administrators commonly use this program to quickly diagnose a problem with TCP/IP. Although netstat's format and specific information differ with the version of Linux, netstat usually supplies the following important summaries, each of which is covered in more detail later:

◆ Communications end points

◆ Network interface statistics

◆ Routing table information

◆ Protocol statistics

With some later versions, information about the interprocess communications and other protocol stacks may be appended as well. The information to be displayed can usually be toggled with a command line option. The following are valid options for most versions of netstat are:

-a   Displayd information about all interfaces

-c   Displays continuously, updating every few seconds

-i	Displays information about the interfaces
-n	Displays IP addresses instead of symbolic names
-o	Displays additional information about timer states, expiration times, and backoff times
-r	Displays information about the kernel routing table
-t	Displays information about TCP sockets only
-u	Displays information about UDP sockets only
-v	Displays version information
-w	Displays information about raw sockets only
-x	Displays information about sockets

The output from a typical Linux installation that uses the netstat command is shown in the next few sections, which discuss netstat and its output in more detail. As already mentioned, the output and meaning may be different with other versions, but the general purpose of the diagnostic tool remains the same.

COMMUNICATIONS END POINTS

The netstat command with no options provides information on all active communications end points. To display information about a particular type of end point, use the letter of the type from the following list:

-a	All connections
-t	TCP connections only
-u	UDP connections only
-w	RAW connections only
-x	Socket connections only

To display all end points that are waiting for a connection (in addition to the sockets specified by one of the above flags), netstat uses the -a option. The -a option by itself will display all sockets.

The output is formatted into columns showing the protocol (Proto), the amount of data in the receive and send queues (Recv-Q and Send-Q), the local and remote addresses, and the current state of the connection. The following is a truncated sample output:

```
$ netstat -ta
Active Internet connections (including servers)
Proto Recv-Q Send-Q  Local Address          Foreign Address      (state)
ip         0      0   *.*                    *.*
tcp        0   2124   tpci.login             merlin.1034          ESTABL.
tcp        0      0   tpci.1034              prudie.login         ESTABL.
```

32

TCP/IP UTILITIES

```
tcp     11212     0   tpci.1035         treijs.1036       ESTABL.
tcp         0     0   tpci.1021         reboc.1024        TIME_WAIT
tcp         0     0   *.1028            *.*               LISTEN
tcp         0     0   *.*               *.*               CLOSED
tcp         0     0   *.6000            *.*               LISTEN
tcp         0     0   *.listen          *.*               LISTEN
tcp         0     0   *.1024            *.*               LISTEN
tcp         0     0   *.sunrpc          *.*               LISTEN
tcp         0     0   *.smtp            *.*               LISTEN
tcp         0     0   *.time            *.*               LISTEN
tcp         0     0   *.echo            *.*               LISTEN
tcp         0     0   *.finger          *.*               LISTEN
tcp         0     0   *.exec            *.*               LISTEN
tcp         0     0   *.telnet          *.*               LISTEN
tcp         0     0   *.ftp             *.*               LISTEN
tcp         0     0   *.*               *.*               CLOSED
```

In the preceding sample extract, three TCP connections are active, as identified by the state ESTABL. One has data being sent (as shown in the Send-Q column), while another has incoming data in the queue. The network names and port numbers of the connection ends is shown whenever possible. An asterisk means no end point has yet been associated with that address.

One connection is waiting to be hung up, identified by TIME_WAIT in the state column. After thirty seconds, these sessions are terminated and the connection freed. Any row with LISTEN as the state has no connection at the moment, and is waiting.

You can use the -a option by itself to display a complete list of all connections. The output, which is quite lengthy, looks the same, but includes all connections (active and passive):

```
$ netstat -a
Active Internet connections (including servers)
Proto Recv-Q Send-Q  Local Address     Foreign Address   (state)
ip         0     0    *.*               *.*
tcp        0  2124    tpci.login        merlin.1034       ESTABL.
tcp        0     0    tpci.1034         prudie.login      ESTABL.
tcp    11212     0    tpci.1035         treijs.1036       ESTABL.
tcp        0     0    tpci.1021         reboc.1024        TIME_WAIT
tcp        0     0    *.1028            *.*               LISTEN
tcp        0     0    *.*               *.*               CLOSED
tcp        0     0    *.6000            *.*               LISTEN
tcp        0     0    *.listen          *.*               LISTEN
tcp        0     0    *.1024            *.*               LISTEN
tcp        0     0    *.sunrpc          *.*               LISTEN
tcp        0     0    *.smtp            *.*               LISTEN
tcp        0     0    *.time            *.*               LISTEN
tcp        0     0    *.echo            *.*               LISTEN
tcp        0     0    *.finger          *.*               LISTEN
tcp        0     0    *.exec            *.*               LISTEN
tcp        0     0    *.telnet          *.*               LISTEN
tcp        0     0    *.ftp             *.*               LISTEN
tcp        0     0    *.*               *.*               CLOSED
udp        0     0    *.60000           *.*
udp        0     0    *.177             *.*
udp        0     0    *.1039            *.*
udp        0     0    *.1038            *.*
```

```
udp        0       0    localhost.1036       localhost.syslog
udp        0       0    *.1034               *.*
udp        0       0    *.*                  *.*
udp        0       0    *.1027               *.*
udp        0       0    *.1026               *.*
udp        0       0    *.sunrpc             *.*
udp        0       0    *.1025               *.*
udp        0       0    *.time               *.*
udp        0       0    *.daytime            *.*
udp        0       0    *.chargen            *.*
udp        0       0    *.route              *.*
udp        0       0    *.*                  *.*
```

The output is similar to that for the -ta options shown previously, except the UDP (User Datagram Protocol) connections have been added. UDP sessions have no state column because they do not have an end-to-end connection.

NETWORK INTERFACE STATISTICS

The behavior of the network interface (such as the network interface card) can be shown by using the -i option to the netstat command. This information quickly shows you whether major problems exist with the network connection.

The netstat -i command displays the name of the interface (Iface), the maximum number of characters a packet can contain (MTU), the metric value (not used with Linux), and a set of columns for the number of packets received without problem (RX-OK), received with errors (RX-ERR), received but dropped (RX-DRP), and received but lost due to overrun (RX-OVR). The transmitted packets have similar columns. The last column contains a list of flags set for the interface. The following is a sample output from a netstat -i command:

```
$ netstat -i
Kernel Interface table
Iface   MTU Met  RX-OK RX-ERR RX-DRP RX-OVR  TX-OK TX-ERR TX-DRP TX-OVR Flags
lo     2000   0    231      0      0      0    231      0      0      0 BLRU
eth0   1500   0   1230      2      9     12   1421      3      2      1 BRU
```

This extract shows two interfaces in use: an Ethernet device (/dev/eth0) and the loopback driver (lo0). In this case, you can see the Ethernet interface has had a few bad packet receptions. This is normal because of the nature of the Ethernet system, although if the numbers become too high a percentage of the total packets sent, you should start diagnostic methods to find out why.

You can obtain more specific information about one interface by using the -i option with a device name and a time interval, specified in seconds, such as netstat -i eth0 30, to obtain specific information about the behavior of the "eth0" (Ethernet) interface over the last thirty seconds. For example, the output below shows the activity of the Ethernet interface for the last 30 seconds:

```
$ netstat -i eth0 30
Kernel Interface table
```

32

```
Iface   MTU Met  RX-OK RX-ERR RX-DRP RX-OVR  TX-OK TX-ERR TX-DRP TX-OVR Flags
eth0    1500  0   2341     3      5     112   2111     5      8      8 BRU
```

The flags column in the `netstat` output matches the types of flags you saw with the `ifconfig` command. The meaning of the flags is shown in the following list:

B	Broadcast address has been set
L	Loopback driver
M	Promiscuous mode
N	Trailers are avoided
O	ARP turned off
P	Point-to-point connection
R	Running
U	Interface is up

As you can see in the extracts from the previous commands above, several of the flags can be combined into one block.

DATA BUFFERS

Versions of `netstat` that are based on System V UNIX (instead of BSD UNIX) allow displays of data buffer statistics. Information about the TCP/IP data buffers can be obtained with the `netstat` command's `-m` option. Monitoring the behavior of the buffers is important, because they directly impact the performance of TCP/IP. The output of the `netstat -m` command differs depending on the version of Linux networking software in use, reflecting the different implementations of the TCP/IP code.

The `netstat -m` command output is shown below. In this version, entries are provided for the streamhead, queue, message descriptor table (mblks), data descriptor table (dblks), and the different classes of data descriptor tables. The columns show the number of blocks currently allocated (alloc), the number of columns free (free), the total number of blocks in use (total), the maximum number of blocks that were in use at one time (max), and the number of times a block was not available (fail).

```
$ netstat -m
streams allocation:
                      config   alloc    free   total     max    fail
streams                  292      79     213     233      80       0
queues                  1424     362    1062     516     368       0
mblks                   5067     196    4871    3957     206       0
dblks                   4054     196    3858    3957     206       0
class 0,    4 bytes      652      50     602     489      53       0
class 1,   16 bytes      652       2     650     408       4       0
class 2,   64 bytes      768       6     762    2720      14       0
class 3,  128 bytes      872     105     767     226     107       0
```

```
class 4,   256 bytes      548      21     527     36     22      0
class 5,   512 bytes      324      12     312     32     13      0
class 6, 1024 bytes       107       0     107      1      1      0
class 7, 2048 bytes        90       0      90      7      1      0
class 8, 4096 bytes        41       0      41     38      1      0
total configured streams memory: 1166.73KB
streams memory in use: 44.78KB
maximum streams memory used: 58.57KB
```

The `failure` column is important, and tt should always show zeros. If a larger number appears there, it means that the particular resource in question has been overtaxed and the number of blocks assigned to that resource should be increased (followed by a kernel rebuild and a reboot of the system to effect the changes).

ROUTING TABLE INFORMATION

Routing tables are continually updated to reflect connections to other machines. To obtain information about the routing tables, the `netstat -r` and `-rs` options are used (the latter generates statistics about the routing tables).

The output from `netstat -r` and `netstat -rs` commands are shown below. The columns show the destination machine, the address of the gateway to be used (an asterisk means no gateway to be used), the Genmask which specifies the generality of the route (which IP addresses can be matched to it), a set of flags, a metric value (not used), a reference counter (Refs) that specifies how many active connections may use that route simultaneously, the number of packets that have been sent over the route (Use), and the interface name.

```
$ netstat -r
Kernel routing table
Destination    Gateway       Genmask        Flags Metric Ref Use    Iface
loopback       *             255.0.0.0      U     0      0   21 lo
big_system     *             123.23.1.0     UGN   1      0      321 eth0
small_system   *             165.213.14.0   UN    1      0     1213 eth0
```

The flags are used to show different characteristics of the route. The following are valid flags:

D   Generated by ICMP

G   Uses a Gateway

H   Only a single host can be reached this way (such as loopback)

M   Modified by ICMP

U   Interface is up

You can combine the `-s` and `-rs` options with the `-n` option to display the IP addresses of the entries in the routing table, instead of the symbolic name (as shown above). The layout and information displayed by the `netstat` command will vary depending on the Linux implementations, as in the following example:

```
$ netstat -nr
Kernel routing table
Destination     Gateway        Genmask         Flags Metric Ref Use   Iface
127.0.0.1       *              255.0.0.0       U     0      0   21 lo
123.23.1.2      *              123.23.1.0      UGN   1      0      321 eth0
165.213.14.1m   *              165.213.14.0    UN    1      0     1213 eth0
```

This flag saves you from having to figure out the symbolic to IP address translations
yourself.

PROTOCOL STATISTICS

System V-based versions of `netstat` (as opposed to most Linux BSD-based versions)
enable you to display protocol statistics. Statistics about the overall behavior of
network protocols can be obtained with the `netstat -s` command. This usually
provides summaries for IP (Internet Protocol), ICMP (Internet Control Message
Protocol), TCP (Transmission Control Protocol), and UDP (User Datagram Protocol). The output from this command is useful for determining where an error in a
received packet was located, and then leading the user to try to isolate whether that
error was due to a software or network problem.

Issuing the `netstat -s` command provides a verbose output, as shown in the following
example:

```
$ netstat -s
ip:
    183309 total packets received
    0 bad header checksums
    0 with size smaller than minimum
    0 with data size < data length
    0 with header length < data size
    0 with data length < header length
    0 with unknown protocol
    13477 fragments received
    0 fragments dropped (dup or out of space)
    0 fragments dropped after timeout
    0 packets reassembled
    0 packets forwarded
    0 packets not forwardable
    75 no routes
    0 redirects sent
    0 system errors during input
    309 packets delivered
    309 total packets sent
    0 system errors during output
    0 packets fragmented
    0 packets not fragmentable
    0 fragments created
icmp:
    1768 calls to icmp_error
    0 errors not generated because old message was icmp
    Output histogram:
        destination unreachable: 136
```

```
        0 messages with bad code fields
        0 messages < minimum length
        0 bad checksums
        0 messages with bad length
        Input histogram:
                destination unreachable: 68
        0 message responses generated
        68 messages received
        68 messages sent
        0 system errors during output
tcp:
        9019 packets sent
                6464 data packets (1137192 bytes)
                4 data packets (4218 bytes) retransmitted
                1670 ack-only packets (918 delayed)
                0 URG only packets
                0 window probe packets
                163 window update packets
                718 control packets
                        24 resets
        9693 packets received
                4927 acks (for 74637 bytes)
                37 duplicate acks
                0 acks for unsent data
                5333 packets (1405271 bytes) received in-sequence
                23 completely duplicate packets (28534 bytes)
                0 packets with some dup. data (0 bytes duped)
                38 out-of-order packets (5876 bytes)
                0 packets (0 bytes) of data after window
                0 window probes
                134 window update packets
                0 packets received after close
                0 discarded for bad checksums
                0 discarded for bad header offset fields
                0 discarded because packet too short
                0 system errors encountered during processing
        224 connection requests
        130 connection accepts
        687 connections established (including accepts)
        655 connections closed (including 0 drops)
        24 embryonic connections dropped
        0 failed connect and accept requests
        0 resets received while established
        5519 segments updated rtt (of 5624 attempts)
        5 retransmit timeouts
                0 connections dropped by rexmit timeout
        0 persist timeouts
        0 keepalive timeouts
                0 keepalive probes sent
                0 connections dropped by keepalive
        0 connections lingered
                0 linger timers expired
                0 linger timers cancelled
                0 linger timers aborted by signal
udp:
        0 incomplete headers
        0 bad data length fields
        0 bad checksums
```

32

TCP/IP UTILITIES

```
68 bad ports
125 input packets delivered
0 system errors during input
268 packets sent
```

Again, the exact layout of the output changes depending on the version of the networking code. However, you can use the basic information with all formats.

THE *PING* COMMAND

Chapter 30, "Configuring TCP/IP," showed you how to use the ping command to check whether interfaces were functioning correctly. You use the ping (Packet Internet Groper) utility to query another system to ensure a connection is still active.

The ping program operates by sending out an Internet Control Message Protocol (ICMP) echo request. If the destination machine's IP software receives the ICMP request, it will issue an echo-reply back immediately. The sending machine will continue to send an echo request until the ping program is terminated with a break sequence (Ctrl-c or DEL in UNIX). After termination, ping displays a set of statistics. The following is a sample ping session:

```
$ ping merlin
PING merlin: 64 data bytes
64 bytes from 142.12.130.12: icmp_seq=0. time=20. ms
64 bytes from 142.12.130.12: icmp_seq=1. time=10. ms
64 bytes from 142.12.130.12: icmp_seq=2. time=10. ms
64 bytes from 142.12.130.12: icmp_seq=3. time=20. ms
64 bytes from 142.12.130.12: icmp_seq=4. time=10. ms
64 bytes from 142.12.130.12: icmp_seq=5. time=10. ms
64 bytes from 142.12.130.12: icmp_seq=6. time=10. ms
--- merling PING Statistics ---
7 packets transmitted, 7 packets received, 0% packet loss
round-trip (ms) min/avg/max = 10/12/20
```

An alternate method to invoke ping is to provide the number of times you want it to query the remote. Also, you could provide a packet length as a test. The following command instructs ping to use 256 data byte packets and to try five times:

```
$ ping merlin 256 5
PING merlin: 256 data bytes
256 bytes from 142.12.130.12: icmp_seq=0. time=20. ms
256 bytes from 142.12.130.12: icmp_seq=1. time=10. ms
256 bytes from 142.12.130.12: icmp_seq=2. time=10. ms
256 bytes from 142.12.130.12: icmp_seq=3. time=20. ms
256 bytes from 142.12.130.12: icmp_seq=4. time=10. ms
--- merling PING Statistics ---
5 packets transmitted, 5 packets received, 0% packet loss
round-trip (ms) min/avg/max = 10/13/20
```

Using ping to send large packets is one method of determining the network's behavior with large packet sizes, especially when fragmentation must occur. The ping program is also useful for monitoring response times of the network, by observing the reply time on packets sent as the network load (or the machine load) changes. This information can be very useful in optimization of TCP/IP. Some older implementations of ping simply reply with a message that the system at the other end is active (the message is of the form "X is alive"). To obtain the verbose messages shown previously, you must use the -s option.

The ping program is useful for diagnostics because it tells you whether the TCP/IP software is functioning correctly, whether a local network device can be addressed (validating its address), and whether a remote machine can be accessed (again validating the address and testing the routing). It also verifies the software on the remote machine.

THE *ARP* COMMAND

The arp program manages entries in the system's Address Resolution Protocol (ARP) tables. ARP provides the link between the IP address and the underlying physical address. With arp, you can create, modify, or delete entries in the ARP table. Typically, this will have to be performed whenever a machine's network address changes (either because of a change in the network hardware or because of a physical move).

To use the arp program, you need to follow one of the following formats:

```
arp [-v] [-t type] -a [hostname]
arp [-v] [-t type] -s hostname hwaddress
arp [-v] -d hostname [hostname ...]
```

When specifying a hostname you can use either a symbolic name or the IP address.

To display the entry for a host or IP address, use the first format shown above. If you do not give a hostname, all hosts are shown. For example, to check the ARP entry for the remote machine darkstar, issue the following command:

```
$ arp -a darkstar
IP address      HW type         HW address
147.12.32.1     10Mbps Ethernet  00:00:C0:5A:3F:C2
```

This command shows that the machine darkstar has the IP address 147.12.32.1, and is reached through a 10Mbps Ethernet connection. You can slightly alter the output by using the -t option with a specific type of interface. Valid values are ax25 (AMPR AX.25 networks), ether (10Mbps Ethernet), and pronet (IEEE 802.5 Token Ring). For example, to show all the Ethernet connections only, use the following command:

```
arp -t ether -a
```

To add an entry to the ARP tables, use the second format of the command shown earlier, using the -s option. When adding an entry, the hwaddress refers to the

32

hardware address of the adapter (usually six sets of hexadecimal digits separated by colons). For example, to add an entry for the remote system big_cat, you would issue the command

```
arp -s big_cat 00:00:c0:10:A1
```

where the hardware address of the network card is as shown.

Finally, the last format of the arp command shown above is used to delete entries from the ARP table. This format may be necessary when you have incorrectly added an entry to the table or the network has changed. To delete the entry for the machine x-wing, issue this command:

```
arp -d x-wing
```

Several other options are valid with many versions of arp, but you will probably never have to use the arp command at all (let alone these more obscure options). If you need more information, the man pages include a list of all valid options and their functions.

THE *TRACEROUTE* COMMAND

Most Linux systems have a utility called traceroute available that sends a series of UDP (User Datagram Protocol) datagrams to a target machine. The datagrams are constructed slightly differently depending on their location in the stream sent to the remote machine. The first three datagrams have a field called Time to Live (TTL) set to a value of one, meaning that the first time a router encounters the message it is returned with an expiry message (the datagram has been discarded). The next three messages have the TTL field set to two, three, four, and so on so that each router the messages pass through will return an expiry message until the destination machine is successfully reached.

The traceroute output shows the round trip time of each message (which is useful for identifying bottlenecks in the network) and the efficiency of the routing algorithms (through a number of routers which may not be the best route). The following is sample output from a traceroute command:

```
$ traceroute black.cat.com
1  TPCI.COM (127.01.13.12)   51ms   3ms   4ms
2  BEAST.COM (143.23.1.23)   60ms   5ms   7ms
3  bills_machine.com (121.22.56.1)   121ms   12ms   12ms
4  SuperGateway.com (130.12.14.2)   75ms   13ms   10ms
5  black.cat.com  (122.13.2.12)   45ms   4ms   6ms
```

This output shows each router the messages were received by until the destination machine was reached. The traceroute command has many options to tailor its behavior, which are all explained in the man page. The traceroute command is usually used by system or network administrators when there are delivery problems with messages or network behavior seems very slow. Because most Linux systems are on small local area networks or are stand-alone, you may never have to use traceroute.

THE *RPCINFO* COMMAND

For RPC (Remote Procedure Call) services, a utility called rpcinfo can determine which RPC services are currently active on the local machine or any remote system that supports RPC. The options supported by rpcinfo vary with the implementation, but all implementations allow flags to decide which type of service to check.

For example, the -p option displays the local portmapper. The following example shows the options supported by the Slackware Linux version of rpcinfo, as well as the output for the portmapper:

```
merlin:~# rpcinfo
Usage: rpcinfo [ -n portnum ] -u host prognum [ versnum ]
       rpcinfo [ -n portnum ] -t host prognum [ versnum ]
       rpcinfo -p [ host ]
       rpcinfo -b prognum versnum
       rpcinfo -d prognum versnum
merlin:~# rpcinfo -p
   program vers proto   port
    100000    2   tcp    111  portmapper
    100000    2   udp    111  portmapper
    100005    1   udp    650  mountd
    100005    1   tcp    652  mountd
    100003    2   udp   2049  nfs
    100003    2   tcp   2049  nfs
```

As with the traceroute command, most system administrators will never need to use rpcinfo. If you are a network programmer or a network administrator, they may be handy utilities to know about, though.

SUMMARY

This chapter has shown you the basic administration programs used with TCP/IP, as well as the configuration files that are necessary to use TCP/IP properly. Knowing the tools available and the type of diagnostics that can be produced is useful to better understanding TCP/IP and especially handy when you are having a problem.

- What Is NFS?

- NFS Administration

- What Are NIS
  and YP?

- Installing NIS

CHAPTER 33

NFS and NIS

Network File System (NFS) has a reputation for being difficult to set up and install. The truth is that NFS is quite easy to implement on Linux systems, and if your machine is one of a few Linux systems on a local area network (LAN), NFS can give you enormous flexibility.

This chapter explains the benefits of NFS, and how you can set up your system to act as both a client and server for other machines on your LAN. If you are running as a stand-alone Linux machine, NFS will be of no value (other than academic) to you, but if you are part of a LAN (whether composed of PC, Mac, UNIX, or Linux machines doesn't matter), you should at least find out what NFS has to offer.

The second part of this chapter looks at the Network Information Service (NIS), an early version of which was previously called Yellow Pages, and how it works over a network. Although you probably will not need NIS unless you are part of a very large network, you can see how the system works. The chapter also looks at some system administration tools for managing NFS (Network File System), NIS (Network Information Service), and RPC (Remote Procedure Call).

WHAT IS NFS?

NFS was developed to help solve a common problem on UNIX-based networks. With the trend to distributed processing and client-server networks, many users end up with small, powerful machines that communicate with a server. The applications users need are often located in places other than on their desktop, so some method of accessing remote files is needed. Although utilities such as Telnet enable users to use remote machines, they don't take advantage of the desktop machine's CPU, transferring the load to the remote. Another important aspect of the shift to distributed computing was peripheral sharing and the need to provide access for many users to some devices. To help integrate workstations into local area networks, as well as to simplify remote file access and peripheral sharing, Sun Microsystems introduced the Network File System (NFS). NFS uses a system called RPC (Remote Procedure Calls).

Sun designed NFS to enable machines from different manufacturers to work together independent of their operating systems. By publishing the NFS specifications, Sun allowed other vendors to modify their systems to work with NFS, resulting in a completely homogeneous network. NFS is now a de facto standard among UNIX environments, with strong support in other operating systems.

NFS actually refers to two different things: a product and a protocol. The NFS product is a set of protocols for different tasks. The NFS protocol is the single protocol of the NFS product that deals with file access. NFS is now intimately tied with UNIX and TCP/IP. For other operating systems (such as Novell NetWare), NFS is an extension that is added by the system administrator. Linux (and most UNIX versions) uses the process nfsd to manage NFS access.

NFS allows an application to read and write files that reside on NFS servers. Access to the NFS server is transparent to the application and the user. Transparent access to another machine's file structure is achieved by logically mounting the NFS server to the client. You can mount the NFS server's filesystem in whole or in part. The mount is handled in the same way as any other filesystem mount (see Chapter 18, "Filesystems and Disks," for information on the mount command), although a special keyword is added to the command to show that NFS is being used. For example, to mount the directory /usr/database/data on the remote machine wizard onto your directory /usr/data, you would issue the following command:

```
mount -t nfs wizard:/usr/database/data /usr/data
```

When the command is issued, the local machine checks with the remote machine for permission to access the directory. If all is well, the remote machine sends a file handle that is used to redirect all requests for that directory from the local machine. Whenever the user of an NFS-mounted directory issues a request, a daemon called nfsd handles the transfers.

NFS uses the term *client* to represent any machine that requests a file from another machine, which is the server. Multitasking operating systems can act as both client and server simultaneously. Usually, restrictions are imposed on the files or portions of a filesystem that can be shared, both for security and speed considerations.

A typical NFS installation uses personal computers or diskless workstations as clients accessing a powerful server system. (Since personal computer operating systems such as MS-DOS are single-tasking, PCs usually act as clients only, unless they run a multitasking operating system such as Windows NT, Windows 95, or OS/2.) For Linux-based networks, you can have several Linux systems sharing their drives with other machines on the network. It is possible to have an entire network of multitasking computers sharing their drives with each other, although in practice this works well only with small networks.

Due to the requirement transferring files quickly with NFS, network speed becomes important. When it was designed, the original goal for an NFS-mounted filesystem was to provide performance equivalent to 80 percent of the performance expected from a locally mounted hard disk. This goal puts the performance emphasis on both the NFS disk drive and the network. Typically, NFS disk drives on a dedicated server are amongst the fastest available in order to reduce bottlenecks at the drive end. In practice for most networks, the NFS systems use standard equipment, which isn't a problem for sharing a few directories among a small network.

Typically, for a small Linux network, NFS offers a few useful benefits. Primarily, it allows data and large applications to be kept on a single drive on the network that all other machines have access to (hence saving the disk space independent copies would require). For a system administrator, NFS offers the option of keeping applications in one location (or even placing all user directories on one machine) for ease of updating, backups, and management.

The Linux version of FTP differs slightly from the standard UNIX versions, in that many of the features of the NFS system are embedded in the code for the Virtual File System (VFS) kernel layer. Early versions of Linux have a problem with Linux FTP because of the maximum size of TCP datagrams, which must be reduced in size to function properly. This had the effect of slowing performance dramatically.

Because NFS is UNIX-based, the security offered is rudimentary. For this reason, Sun has introduced Secure NFS, which implements an encrypted messaging protocol for added protection against unauthorized access to NFS-mounted file systems. This version is not available in a Linux implementation yet.

INSTALLING NFS

The first step to installing NFS on your Linux system is to ensure that the NFS support is compiled into the kernel. Most later Linux versions have this by default, but if you are running an early version you should verify the NFS code. Versions of Linux after 1.1 can confirm support for NFS by examining the /proc/filesystems file. An entry in this file should show nfs with the command nodev. An extract from the /proc/filesystems file looks like this:

```
    minix
    ext2
    umsdos
    msods
nodev   proc
nodev   nfs
    iso9660
```

The second line from the bottom shows that the NFS code is included in the kernel. If the NFS code is not included, you will have to rebuild the kernel including the NFS drivers.

Versions of Linux before 1.1 are more difficult to easily check for NFS code. The best way to perform the check is to try to mount an NFS directory. If it fails, it is likely the NFS code is missing (assuming the mount commands are correct, of course). As a fast check, you can mount a local directory onto your own machine (which is perfectly legal with all versions of NFS, although it can be confusing at times). To perform this check, create a new subdirectory and issue the mount command with an existing directory. For example, these commands try to mount /usr on the empty directory /tmp/nfstest:

```
mkdir /tmp/nfstest
mount localhost:/usr /tmp/nfstest
```

If the mount command is successful (you can go into the /tmp/nfstest directory and examine the same file listing as in /usr), your kernel has the NFS code embedded in it. If you get an error message similar to this:

```
fs type nfs not supported
```

then the NFS code is missing and you should rebuild a new kernel with the NFS drivers added.

Note

When you perform this NFS code check you may see many error messages. The only message that matters is nfs not supported. The rest of the messages have to do with the lack of NFS configuration.

The NFS daemons need to be set up on your system. If you are going to act as an NFS server (allow your directories to be mounted by others), you must install both the nfsd and mountd daemons. These daemons start when your machine boots, reading the rc files. Both daemons need the program rpc.portmap to function because they both register themselves with the portmapper utility.

The startup commands for the daemons usually are placed in the /etc/rc.d/rc.inet2 file (or wherever you have installed the rc files). Most newer versions of Linux will have the proper section already in the /etc/rc.d/rc.inet2 file. For example, the section dealing with NFS will look much like this:

```
# # Start the various SUN RPC servers.
if [ -f ${NET}/rpc.portmap ]; then
  # Start the NFS server daemons.
  if [ -f ${NET}/rpc.mountd ]; then
    echo -n " mountd"
    ${NET}/rpc.mountd
  fi
  if [ -f ${NET}/rpc.nfsd ]; then
    echo -n " nfsd"
    ${NET}/rpc.nfsd
  fi
#  # Fire up the PC-NFS daemon(s).
#  if [ -f ${NET}/rpc.pcnfsd ]; then
#    echo -n " pcnfsd"
#    ${NET}/rpc.pcnfsd ${LPSPOOL}
#  fi
#  if [ -f ${NET}/rpc.bwnfsd ]; then
#    echo -n " bwnfsd"
#    ${NET}/rpc.bwnfsd ${LPSPOOL}
#  fi
fi # Done starting various SUN RPC servers.
```

If your inet2 file doesn't have any lines similar to these, find a location below the rpc.portmapper startup command. The portmapper startup section will look similar to this:

```
# Start the SUN RPC Portmapper.
if [ -f ${NET}/rpc.portmap ]; then
   echo -n " portmap"
   ${NET}/rpc.portmap
fi
```

Below these lines, enter the following commands to start the rpcd and mountd daemons:

```
  if [ -x /usr/sbin/rpc.mountd ]; then
    echo -n " mountd"
    /usr/sbin/rpc.mountd
  fi
  if [ -x /usr/sbin/rpc.nfsd ]; then
    echo -n " nfsd"
    /usr/sbin/rpc.nfsd
  fi
```

If the rpc.nfsd and rpc.mountd daemons are not in /usr/sbin, enter the proper pathnames. These lines don't make use of a prior defined path. The paths to the deamons should be explicitly specified.

The next step in configuring your system for NFS server duty is to set up a file listing all the clients who can attach to your system and mount directories. This is done through the /etc/exports file. The /etc/exports file is read every time the mountd daemon receives a request to mount a directory. The file contains a list of directories that you want to allow to be mounted, and the remote systems that can mount them followed by a permission indication.

The best way to explain the /etc/exports file is to examine a sample. The following file shows several systems allowed to mount directories on the local machine:

```
# /etc/exports for merlin
/usr/database/data    chatton(rw)  big_roy (rw)  wizard (rw)
/usr/book         chatton(rw)  wizard (ro)
/usr/bin/bigapp       big_roy(rw)  wizard (ro)
/usr/ftp          (ro)
```

This file shows that the three machines chatton, big_roy, and wizard can all mount the local directory /usr/database/data in read-write mode (meaning they can modify the contents). The directory /usr/book can be mounted read-write by remote machine chatton, and read-only (no writing allowed) by wizard. The /usr/ftp directory can be mounted read-only by any machine that wants to.

When you are specifying machine names in the /etc/exports file, you can use explicit names, or a combination of asterisk and question mark wildcards to match multiple machines. For example, the entry

```
/usr/tim/book        big_*(rw)
```

allows any machine starting with `big_` to mount the directory as read-write. When no hostname is provided (as with the /usr/ftp directory in the previous example), any machine can mount the directory.

The /etc/exports file allows a long list of possible permissions for a remote machine to mount a local directory. Although most systems use only `rw` and `ro` (for read-write and read-only respectively), you may need more permissions occasionally. The following are valid permissions:

`insecure`	Allows non-authenticated access for the specified machine (overrides authentication requirements)
`kerberos`	Forces Kerberos authentication from the remote (not implemented for Linux NFS)
`link_absolute`	Leaves symbolic links as they are
`link_relative`	Converts absolute symbolic links to relative links by prepending ../ as necessary
`root_squash`	Denies root users on remote machines root access on local machine
`secure-rpc`	Forces RPC authentication from the remote (on by default, although not implemented in most Linux NFS versions)

How does NFS handle file and user permissions across mountings? When the NFS daemon transfers files or requests, it passes the user and group ID numbers. If the client and the server have the same user and group ID numbers (called sharing the same uid/gid space), there is no problem with permissions. When the UID and GID numbers do not match, the daemon can handle translations between them.

MOUNTING NFS DIRECTORIES

Once NFS is configured, you can use it to mount remote directories on your local filesystem. This is done with the `mount` command. The general format of the `mount` command when dealing with NFS is

```
mount -t nfs remote_dir        local_dir    [-o options]
```

where `remote_dir` is the name of the remote machine and directory to be NFS mounted, `local_dir` is where you want to mount the remote directory, and `options` can be any of the permissible flags used by NFS. The `remote_dir` is always specified by the format

```
remote_name:remote_dir
```

such as wizard:/usr/lib. Many administrators leave off the `-t nfs` component of the `mount` command since this format is unique to NFS. Others feel it is good practice to leave the `-t` option in as it is a constant reminder that the remote is NFS mounted.

Although many options are possible for the `mount` command in NFS mode, only a few are ever used in real situations. You can select valid options from the following list:

hard	This option explicitly tags the directory as hard-mounted. This is a default action.
intr	This option allows interrupts to the NFS call.
rsize	This option specifies the datagram size used for read requests (default is 1,024 bytes).
soft	This option soft-mounts the directory (instead of hard mounting).
timeo	This option specifies the timeout in tenths of a second for completion of an NFS request (default is 7/10ths).
wsize	This option specifies the datagram size used for write requests (default is 1,024 bytes).

The `rsize`, `timeo`, and `wsize` options are followed by an equal sign and the value they are to be assigned. The `rsize` and `wsize` options are used primarily to switch the remote machine to another datagram size (in case it uses a larger size than Linux can handle). All NFS options must follow the `-o` switch on the command line, if the options are set there. For example, to set the timeout to 2 seconds on the remote `mount` of a directory and allow interrupts, you could issue the command:

```
mount -t nfs wizard:/usr/data  /usr/data    -o timeo=20,intr
```

Alternatively, if you don't want to specify the options on the command line for frequently mounted volumes, you can use the /etc/fstab file to provide them. The same command line as above can be placed in the /etc/fstab file like this:

```
wizard:/usr/data        /usr/data    nfs    timeo=20,intr
```

When you use the /etc/fstab file to specify options and mount points, you can mount the remote volume much more easily by issuing the command:

```
mount wizard:/usr/data
```

33

The mount command examines the /etc/fstab file for the mount point and options to use, as well as recognizes the command as an NFS mount. For remote directories you will need often, this command is much easier than typing the entire command line every time.

Two of the NFS mount options deal with hard and soft mounting. The default with NFS is to hard mount a directory. What this means is that if NFS is unable to mount a requested volume, it times out, generates an error message, and tries again with double the timeout value. This goes on forever until the remote directory is mounted (generating error messages each time a timeout occurs). Any remote directory that is repeatedly tried until successfully mounted is called a hard mount. A soft mount is one that acts the same way but generates error messages only after a major timeout, which is every 60 seconds. The error messages are not displayed, since they are in the I/O queue, but you can usually gain control of the system more easily with a soft mount after a major timeout.

NFS ADMINISTRATION

NFS (and RPC, which NFS depends on) has two primary administration tools available for providing status updates and indications of trouble within the system. Running any single tool is usually not sufficient to isolate a problem. It often happens that one tool reports a problem with a port, but, upon closer examination, you find out that the port is functioning and the process at the other end has died. Therefore, these tools are designed to be used as a complement to each other until an accurate diagnosis can be produced.

RPCINFO

The rpcinfo program monitors the port mapper of the machine on which it is running and, through the network, the port mappers of servers. Because the port mapper is the program that controls access to RPCs, this type of information is important in tracking problems. The rpcinfo program can display the contents of the mapping tables, showing the port and program numbers for each connection, and is able to activate remote servers for testing a connection.

Typically, rpcinfo is called with the -p option to show the list of RPC programs that are currently tracked by the port mapper. An optional machine name can be added to display only connections with one machine. A typical output from the rpcinfo program is shown below:

```
$ rpcinfo -p
   program vers proto   port
    100000    2   tcp    111  portmapper
    100000    2   udp    111  portmapper
    100008    1   udp   1026  walld
```

```
150001   1   udp   1027   pcnfsd
150001   2   udp   1027   pcnfsd
100002   1   udp   1028   rusersd
100002   2   udp   1028   rusersd
100024   1   udp   1029   status
100024   1   tcp   1024   status
100020   1   udp   1034   llockmgr
100020   1   tcp   1025   llockmgr
100021   2   tcp   1026   nlockmgr
100021   1   tcp   1027   nlockmgr
100021   1   udp   1038   nlockmgr
100021   3   tcp   1028   nlockmgr
100021   3   udp   1039   nlockmgr
```

In case of a problem contacting the port mapper, rpcinfo returns an error message. In such a case, the port mapper is not functioning correctly and there may be no contact with other machines. A check using ping will verify this. An example of this kind of fatal error message is:

```
$ rpcinfo -p
rpcinfo: can't contact port mapper:
RFC: Remote system error -125
```

Specific connections can be tested with rpcinfo by using the machine and process name, as the following example shows:

```
$ rpcinfo -u merlin walld
program 100008 version 1 is ready and waiting
```

Note that the -u option is used for UDP connections, while -t must be used with TCP connections. In this example, the client rpcinfo sent a request to the program specified and waited for a reply. A successful reply results in the message shown above. If a reply is not received before a timer expires, an error message is displayed.

In the sample output above, there is a process called pcnfsd, which is an RPC server developed for use with DOS-based machines. It handles access rights and spooling services for the DOS side, while simplifying the DOS machine's access to NFS services.

NFSSTAT

The nfsstat program, as its name suggests, provides statistics about the number and type of RPC requests that are made. Although this command is usually called without an option, several options exist (depending on the implementation and version) to show specific statistics or sample only certain parts of the connection. The nfsstat program is not part of most Linux distributions, but you can find it on some Linux FTP and BBS sites and as part of some system administration utility packages. The output from nfsstat is shown below for a typical small network:

```
Server rpc:
calls      badcalls   nullrecv   badlen    xdrcall
10465      0          0          0         0
```

33

```
Server nfs:
calls       badcalls
10432       0
null        getattr     setattr     root        lookup      readlink    read
1 0%        24 0%        1 0%        0 0%        10123 0%    0 0%        5 0%
wrcache     write       create      remove      rename      link        symlink
0 0%        2 0%        0 0%        1 0%        0 0%        1 0%        0 0%

Client rpc:
calls       badcalls    retrans     badxid      timeout     wait        newcred
8273        2           0           0           0           0           0

Client nfs:
calls       badcalls
8263        0
null        getattr     setattr     root        lookup      readlink    read
1 0%        24 0%        1 0%        0 0%        10123 0%    0 0%        5 0%
wrcache     write       create      remove      rename      link        symlink
0 0%        2 0%        0 0%        1 0%        0 0%        1 0%        0 0%
```

The output from nfsstat is useful for diagnosing connection problems. The number shown as badcalls shows the number of defective RPC messages processed by the system. The numbers for nullrecv and badlen show the number of empty or incomplete messages. The number for xdrcall shows the number of errors in understanding messages.

For the client side, badxid shows the number of received messages that did not match with a sent request (based on the identification numbers). The timeout and retrans numbers show the number of times a message had to be resent. If these numbers are high it usually means the connection is too slow or there is a fault with UDP. The wait number shows the number of times a process had to be delayed due to a lack of available ports.

These types of statistics are useful for configuring RPC properly. System administrators can adjust (tweak) values for the NFS system and monitor their effect on performance over time.

WHAT ARE NIS AND YP?

The Yellow Pages (YP) protocol is an RPC application service (like NFS) that provides a directory service. Due to copyright requirements, Yellow Pages was renamed to Network Information Service (NIS), although both terms are in common use and mean much the same thing. YP was developed for several reasons, but the one that affects users the most is access permissions.

If you are a user on a large network and you connect to other machines (through Telnet or FTP, for example), you must maintain accounts on each machine you connect to. You therefore would need user accounts on every machine you could conceivably want to access. Maintaining the passwords on a large number of machines is awkward, because you must log in to each one to perform password changes. Yellow Pages was developed to allow one central password file to be shared over the network.

NIS is a distributed access system in that each machine on the network that uses NIS accesses a central server, called the NIS master or ypmaster, for access permission. On larger networks, a number of other machines can be designated as slaves or ypslaves, maintaining up-to-date access information. In case of a failure of the master server, a slave takes up the validation functions.

Note

> Two versions of YP or NIS are in general use. The first release (Version 1) had serious problems under certain circumstances, so Version 2 was quickly released. However, some systems use the older version.

The YP or NIS protocol (both names are valid, although NIS should be used if you have a choice) has a set of procedures that allow a search for master servers, access to the user files, and system management functions. Another procedure is used to transfer copies of master access files. With NIS, a number of machines are grouped together into one NIS subnetwork called a "domain" (not to be confused with the Internet domain). Each domain has master and slave machines of their own.

NIS keeps access information in a set of "maps," each map corresponding to a particular area or domain of a network. This allows several groups to use the same NIS master but have different access permissions. The NIS maps do not have to correspond to DNS domains, which allows more versatility in configuration. Maps consist of a set of records in ASCII format, each with an index for fast lookup (the index is usually the user name). The records have the same structure as a normal /etc/passwd file), for compatibility and simplicity.

Note

> The use of NIS does not negate the need for a complete set of access files on each machine, since NIS or YP is loaded after the machine has been booted. The stand-alone files should have access for a system administrator at least, although it is good practice to also include the most frequent users in case of a network crash preventing access to the NIS directories.

NIS is not restricted to just users. Any file can be set up to use NIS, such as the list of machines on a network (/etc/hosts file). Thus, only one change needs to be made to these files on any network. A set of aliases can also be managed by NIS or YP.

Several YP/NIS-specific commands are involved with the protocol, although most system administrators set up aliases to minimize the impact on users. For most users, only one command is necessary on a regular basis: yppasswd to change a password. This is usually aliased to passwd, the normal password change command.

Some implementations of NIS for Linux are better than others. A new release is appearing, called NYS, that offers the most flexibility. NYS (or an earlier version of one of the Linux NIS versions) is included with most CD-ROM distributions of Linux.

INSTALLING NIS

NIS has two components: the server and the client. If an NIS server is already on your network, you need only to install the client portions. However, to set up a Linux server system, you need both.

You can choose between two NIS server products currently in general distribution for Linux: ypserv and yps. The choice of which server to use is not important, since both provide complete services. If anything, though, the ypserv system has a slightly better security system than yps. You can obtain the NIS software from Linux FTP and BBS sites.

To install either server program, copy it to /usr/sbin (or some other commonly accessed binary file location). Next, create a directory specifically to hold the map files for your domain (remember, that's an NIS domain, not an Internet domain). Usually, the map files go in a directory such as /var/yp/tpci (the last component of the pathname is the name of your domain).

Your NIS server can support several map files. In general, the files are mirrors of standard Linux files, but named to reflect whether they are accessed by name or by some other criteria (such as IP address or user name). For example, there are two copies of the /etc/passwd file maintained by NIS: passwd.byname and passwd.byuid. The following files are handled by NIS and their corresponding maps:

/etc/group	group.byname, group.bygid
/etc/hosts	hosts.byname, hosts.byaddr
/etc/networks	networks.byname, networks.byaddr
/etc/passwd	passwd.byname, passwd.byuid
/etc/protocols	protocols.byname, protocols.bynumber
/etc/rpc	rpc.byname, rpc.bynumber
/etc/services	service.byname, services.bynumber

All these map files are stored in a format called DBM (a simple database program). Linux systems often include a GNU version of DBM called gdbm.

If you are using `ypserv`, use the `ypMakefile` utility to build the database files for NIS. Copy the file to the directory containing the map files, rename it to Makefile, and edit it to show the maps you want on your domain. This is handled by one of the first few lines, which looks like this:

```
all: hosts networks protocols rpc services passwd group
```

Remove the entries you don't want map files for. If you choose to use the `yps` server, you have to use the `makedbm` program to build the indexes from the map files.

To set up the client software on your Linux system (allowing it to connect through a `ypmaster` on another server), you have to instruct your kernel to use the NIS system. Begin by setting up the name of the `ypmaster` in the /etc/yp.conf file. This file will have a line that looks like this:

```
ypserver        wizard.tpci.com
```

This line tells the local machine where to reach the `ypserver`. (Some versions of Linux use the word server interchangeably with `ypserver` in the yp.conf file.) Some older Linux systems use a two-line /etc/yp.conf file that lists the domain name and the server on separate lines, like this:

```
domainname      tpci.com
server          wizard
```

Set the yp.conf file to readable by user, group, and other. Then test the NIS installation by using the `ypcat` command:

```
ypcat passwd.byname
```

This command should list the master server's passwd.byname map. If you get error messages, it is probably because the local machine has not contacted the remote server properly. If you see the message:

```
Can't bind to server which serves domain
```

you either have a faulty server or the wrong name in the /etc/yp.conf file. To check the server, use the `ping` command to verify that the network connection is intact.

Once you are sure the NIS connection is functioning properly, you can decide which files you want to retrieve from the `ypmaster` and which are to be kept local. In most cases, you want to get the passwd and group files from the server, but the rest of the files can be kept locally. The order in which the local and NIS server machines are checked for each type of map file is controlled by the file /etc/nsswitch.conf. This file looks like this:

```
hosts:    nis files
networks: nis files
services: files
rpc: files
protocols: files
```

33

Each line starts with the name of a file, followed by keywords that control where the Linux system looks for the file. The following are valid values in the list (which are read and processed in order):

dbm	Use a file in the DBM files under /var/dbm
dns	Use the domain name server
files	Use local files
nis	Use NIS server

Many more options are available with some feature-laden versions of NIS, but these are the primary choices (and should be sufficient for most Linux systems).

SUMMARY

As you have seen, NFS is quite easy to implement on a local area network. It is especially handy for sharing files between machines if you have two or more networked together. In most cases, there is no reason not to use NFS with a LAN, especially since the code is linked into the server anyway. NFS does provide a flexible way of transferring files across operating systems, too, if you can find a TCP/IP NFS implementation for the other operating systems (such as DOS or Windows).

NIS is often useful on large networks, but is seldom necessary for small Linux-based systems, except when you move around your LAN a lot. However, NIS is quite easy to install and use, so it remains an option for those with larger networks.

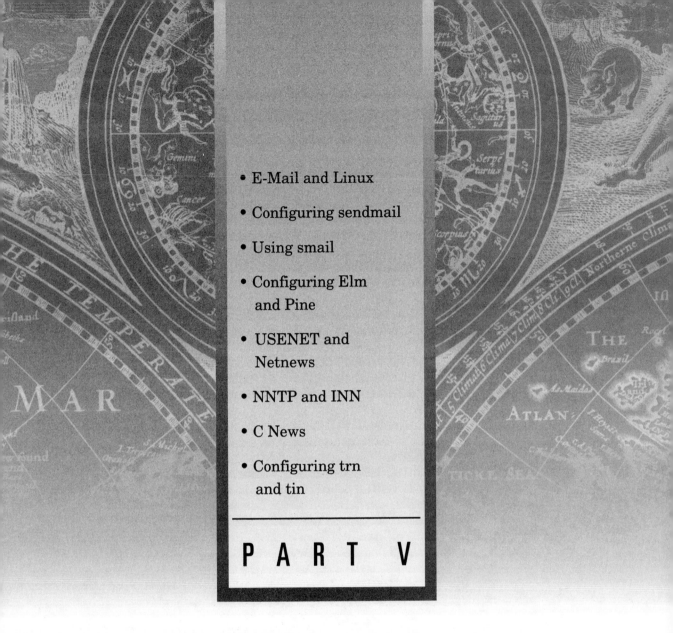

- E-Mail and Linux
- Configuring sendmail
- Using smail
- Configuring Elm and Pine
- USENET and Netnews
- NNTP and INN
- C News
- Configuring trn and tin

PART V

E-Mail and News

- Linux Mail Software

- E-Mail Structure

CHAPTER 34

E-Mail and Linux

Almost everyone who has a Linux system wants to expand its use to allow e-mail. Local area network users especially want to implement e-mail because it is one of the primary attractions of LANs. Linux offers its users several different e-mail systems. The next few chapters look at the most popular and useful of these systems. This chapter explains the background information that's necessary to know in order to use e-mail as well as the basic configuration steps for all e-mail packages.

LINUX MAIL SOFTWARE

An e-mail system on Linux has two components: the mail user agent (called an MUA), which is your interface to the mail package that you use to write and read mail, and the underlying mail transport agent (called an MTA), which handles the sending and receiving of mail. There are two MTAs in common use with Linux and dozens of MUAs available.

There are probably more versions of e-mail MTAs and MUAs available for Linux than any other software application (with the possible exception of editors). The most widely used e-mail MTA system for Linux is sendmail, which is based on an e-mail system developed at the University of California at Berkeley. Several versions of sendmail are available for Linux; each version has slightly different capabilities. Another commonly used e-mail system for Linux is smail, developed by Curt Noll and Ronald Karr. Again, several versions of smail are currently available for Linux.

Because both sendmail and smail are supplied with most CD-ROM distributions of Linux, you may be wondering which mail system you should use. For small installations, either system works fine. In some ways, smail is slightly easier to configure and use, primarily because it is a more modern product. For larger systems or those with special configuration requirements, sendmail is more flexible and offers more configuration capabilities.

Both sendmail and smail require you to customize the packages through configuration files, although the processes are different for each package. For basic e-mail requirements, such as a connection to a mail server or other machines in a network, the process is quite simple. The exception is sendmail, which has a very complex configuration file. Its configuration file is so complex that sendmail is usually used with a utility called IDA (the set is called sendmail+IDA), which makes configuring the package much easier.

When you write a mail message using one of the mail user agent (MUA) user interface programs (such as Elm, Pine, or mail) on your Linux system, the application passes the message to the mail transfer agent (MTA), such as sendmail or smail. (Actually, the MUAs pass the message to a generic delivery transport called rmail, which is usually aliased to the specific MTA you want to use.) You can have several

MTAs running at once (such as one package for LAN-based e-mail delivery and another for UUCP delivery), although most systems only use one for convenience.

If the mail message is for someone on the local area network (or even the same machine), the MTA should be able to figure out this information from the address. MTAs must be able to understand aliasing as well, in case you call machines, networks, or users by different names. If the message is for a remote system user, the MTA must be able to establish a connection to a mail machine somewhere along the route to the destination and transfer the mail. The connection can be either UUCP or TCP based. If the latter is used, a transfer protocol called Simple Mail Transfer Protocol (SMTP) is often employed. The MTA must also be able to handle problems with the delivery of mail, such as when the destination machine is unavailable or the user doesn't exist. In this case, the mail is returned to the sender with an error message.

An e-mail system must be able to handle addresses for the sender and recipient in several formats. Commonly used formats are the UUCP-style bang addresses, such as merlin!brutus!tpci.com!tparker (which means transfer the mail to merlin, then brutus, and then tpci.com to the user tparker), and domain names, such as tparker@tpci.com. The UUCP style usually shows the complete path to the target machine, and domain names use an address resolution system to work out the path. Other address systems are also used (such as DECnet and % addressing), although UUCP and domain names are the most often used.

The routing of the mail messages to the destination is an important aspect of the MTA software and differs depending on whether UUCP (in which case the complete path is usually specified) or domain name (in which case the route must be deduced) addressing is used. For TCP-based addressing (usually using domain names), the default action is for an MTA to deliver messages to the destination machine based on the IP address and ignore the routing, leaving that to the IP software in the TCP/IP drivers.

To simplify mail delivery for larger networks or systems where a single machine acts as the interface to the Internet, a local area network can publish an MX (Mail Exchanger) record that is interpreted by the domain name system (DNS) as an instruction to route all mail for that domain to the single machine (which further distributes it through the LAN). The MX record allows machines that are not connected to the Internet all the time to have mail received by a host, which UUCP or TCP can then connect to occasionally. An MX record looks like the following:

```
merlin.tpci.com    IN    MX    3    bigserver.tpci.com
```

This line tells the DNS system that any mail for merlin.tpci.com should be sent to the system bigserver.tpci.com. The IN entry identifies the type of resource record involved (important to TCP/IP), and MX shows that this record is an MX record. The

34

E-MAIL AND LINUX

number 3 in this example is a preference number. A network can have several mail servers, each of which has a preference number. The lower numbers are used by transfer software first; the software moves to the higher numbers only when the lower numbered machines aren't responding.

A UUCP network handles mail differently. In the early days of UUCP usage, the entire path to the destination machine had to be specified, with each hop along the way explicitly laid out. The increasing size of networks made this specification impractical for all but small local area networks, so a mapping system was developed. The UUCP Mapping Project maintains a list of all official UUCP site names and their neighbors, allowing a UUCP-based transport to find the route to a destination machine by querying the map. The maps are called USENET Maps and are sent out over the Internet regularly to update hosts.

E-MAIL STRUCTURE

To understand how mail systems work, you should know what a mail message looks like. A mail message consists of the text of the message (called the body) and a chunk of information at the beginning of the message that contains information about who sent the message, where it is going, and so on (called the header). Usually the header and body of the mail message are separated by a blank line. Many messages also include a chunk of data at the end of the message that is called the signature. The signature is a bit of ASCII data written by the sender to be included in every message; it usually gives information about the sender and may contain a pithy saying.

The header is made up of two parts. The first part contains information about the sender and recipient and includes their addresses. This portion is often called the envelope. The second part of the header has information specific to the handling of the mail message, including the subject, the transport used to send the message, recipients on a copy list, the date, and similar information.

The header of a mail message consists of a number of lines separated by newline characters. Each line has a field name followed by a colon and the contents of the field. The following is an extract from a header file:

```
From brutus!bignet.com Thu Sep 21 17:40:32 1995
Received: from bignet.com by tpci.tpci.com id aa00184; 21 Sep 95 17:39 EDT
Received: from mailserv.biggernet.com ([147.77.1.1]) by bignet.com with
    SMTP id <250079-4>; Thu, 21 Sep 1995 20:48:04 -0400
Received: by biggernet.com (4.1/SMI-4.1)
    id AA00266; Thu, 21 Sep 95 17:39:03 PDT
Date: Thu, 21 Sep 1995 20:39:03 -0400
From: Yvonne <yvonne@chatton.bignet.com>
Message-Id: <9509220039.AA00266@yvonne@chatton.bignet.com>
To: tparker@tpci.com
Subject: Important stuff
Cc: prudie@bignet.com
```

The first few lines of the header show who sent the message and how it got to its destination. The rest of the header shows the date, message ID (each message has a unique identification number), the subject line, and any users copied on the message. Each line has the field:value format, although the exact layout of each line changes depending on the field. The following fields are normally found in a mail message:

- There are two From fields. The first shows which machine last transferred the mail to your system, and the second (further down the header) is the sender's e-mail address (and sometimes the sender's name from the /etc/passwd file). This field can have many different formats, including UUCP-style bang addressing and full domain name formats.

- Each machine that the message passes through adds a line to the Received field to show where the message was received from and when it was received. This information enables you to trace the message back to its source.

- The Date field shows the date that the e-mail was sent (based on local machine time and date).

- The Message-Id field lists a unique identifying number for the message.

- The To field shows who the e-mail is for.

- The sender provides the information in the Subject field to describe what the mail is about.

- The Cc field gives the ID of anyone else who was copied on the message.

Depending on the mail system in use, some mail message headers include the following fields as well:

- The Reply-To field shows the address that the sender wants any reply sent to. This field is usually used when you have more than one user account and want the replies sent to an account other than the sending one.

- The Organization field provides the name of the company that owns the machine you are using. This optional field is often left blank or set to private for non-corporate machines.

- The letter x followed by identifying tags is used to add features to the basic message format. Both ends of the connection must be able to handle this feature.

Almost all mail systems used with Linux have a common layout based on a formal specification called RFC 822. RFC 822 is only a base set, however, and many products have built on it to include extensions for multimedia, special character sets, encryption, and so on. For messages to be read properly, both ends of the mail path (sender and receiver) have to be able to handle the extensions in the same manner.

Summary

E-mail has its own sophisticated format and transport systems, but most of the details are hidden from users and system administrators. Once a system has been configured with local site information, an administrator's involvement is finished except for checking for proper functioning and cleaning up log files.

Now that you've seen the basics of an e-mail system, you can move in to specific MTAs. The two most often found in Linux are smail and sendmail+IDA, which are covered in their own chapters. After that, you can look at configuring a typical mail reader (MUA).

- Configuring sendmail
- Using sendmail
  Version 8

CHAPTER 35

Configuring sendmail

The most commonly used e-mail program is sendmail, which is supplied with most Linux versions. The sendmail system is extremely powerful and flexible, but it can at times be annoying and difficult to configure and administer because of these very attributes. Setting up sendmail and managing its use for most common e-mail tasks, however, is quite easy, as this chapter will show you. If you are planning to use sendmail as your mail system, you will find that this chapter provides enough information for all but the most complex networked system.

Before getting started, note that this chapter shows you how to set up more than sendmail. Because sendmail is complex (the best reference manual to the mailer approaches 800 pages), it is often teamed with a utility called IDA, for a combined product often known as sendmail+IDA. IDA makes sendmail much easier to use and is the most common method of using sendmail with Linux. Indeed, with IDA in tow, sendmail becomes the easiest mail transport package available for Linux.

If your system offers only a sendmail version prior to release 8, consider getting sendmail+IDA from an FTP or BBS site. The convenience sendmail+IDA offers far outweighs any hassles in obtaining the files. Some current Linux releases are offering sendmail version 8, which is usually not supplied with IDA. Version 8 of sendmail is considerably easier to set up than previous versions, and because this version is now supplied with most Slackware Linux CD-ROMs (including the one supplied with this book), this chapter also covers sendmail version 8 (without IDA). Check the FTP or BBS sites for more information about sendmail+IDA for this (and later) releases.

Configuring *SENDMAIL*

The sendmail system by itself (without IDA) is configured primarily though a file usually stored as /etc/sendmail.cf (although some systems place the file in /usr/lib/sendmail.cf or other locations). The language used in the sendmail.cf file is completely different than other configuration files and is very complex. To see for yourself, examine the sendmail.cf file and try to make sense of it.

The sendmail.cf file handles the default actions of the sendmail system. Several other files are involved in the configuration, too:

decnetxtable	Converts generic addresses to DECnet addresses
genericfrom	Converts internal addresses into generic ones
mailertable	Defines any special treatment for remote hosts and domains
pathtable	Defines the UUCP paths to remote machines and domains
uucpxtable	Forces the delivery of UUCP mail from DNS addresses

| uucprelays | Allows shortcuts to remote hosts |
| xaliases | Converts generic addresses to internal ones |

These tables are detailed later in this chapter. As mentioned, all the sendmail configuration files are difficult to edit manually. Using sendmail+IDA makes configuration much easier, as IDA handles configuration through table-driven options. Each table has a much simpler syntax than the sendmail.cf file.

The sendmail+IDA system uses a preprocessor such as m4 or dbm to generate the proper configuration files after you have specified values for many parameters. After using the preprocessor, the system uses a Makefile to create the final configuration files.

THE SENDMAIL.CF FILE

When you use sendmail+IDA, the sendmail.cf file is not edited directly. Instead, a configuration process generates the changes. The configuration routine is driven by a file called sendmail.m4, which provides basic information about your system's name, the pathnames used on your system, and the default mailer used. Although the sendmail.m4 file can get pretty long, it needs only basic information for most Linux installations that use UUCP or SMTP for mail transfers.

Note

Many system administrators like to rename sendmail.m4 to match their system name (such as tpci.m4) in order to prevent the file from being overwritten by accident and to make it obvious which machine the file refers to. If you choose to rename your file, alter all references to sendmail.m4 in this chapter to reflect your new filename.

One of the most important sections of the sendmail.m4 file is the area that defines directories. This area usually starts with a line defining LIBDIR:

```
dnl #define(LIBDIR, /usr/local/lib/mail)
```

The LIBDIR directory is where sendmail+IDA looks for configuration files and routing tables. Usually this line is left alone, as the default path is the general location for all Linux mail systems. If the path shown in the sendmail.m4 file is correct, don't modify the file. This path is usually hardcoded into the sendmail binary, and doesn't need to be overwritten by the sendmail.m4 file (or its generated sendmail.cf file). If you need to change this path, you have to remove the dnl from the beginning of the line (which essentially makes the line a comment), add the correct path, and then rebuild sendmail.cf.

35

CONFIGURING SENDMAIL

The local mailer used by sendmail is defined in the line that contains the variable LOCAL_MAILER_DEF:

```
define(LOCAL_MAILER_DEF, mailers.linux)dnl
```

This line is necessary because sendmail doesn't handle mail delivery. Another program takes care of this step instead. By default, the value used for the local mailer (which is almost always deliver) is contained in a file called mailers.linux. This file is referenced in the LOCAL_MAILER_DEF entry in the sendmail.m4 file, which means you need to check the mailers.linux file in the same subdirectory (usually /usr/local/lib/mail/mailers.linux) to ensure the deliver program (or whatever delivery agent you use) is properly entered. A typical mailers.linux file looks like the following:

```
# mailers.linux
Mlocal, P=/usr/bin/deliver, F=SlsmFDMP, S=10, R=25/10, A=deliver $u
Mprog, P=/bin/sh, F=lsDFMeuP, S=10, A=sh -c $u
```

The deliver mail delivery agent is also specified in the file Sendmail.mc, which is used to build sendmail.cf. If the name of your delivery agent is not deliver, check the Sendmail.mc file to make sure your mail delivery agent is properly specified. (If you are using deliver, don't worry about this file.) The Sendmail.mc file is important and must be read in when sendmail.m4 is processed. There is usually a line in sendmail.m4 that makes sure this action occurs. The line, which usually occurs at the top of the sendmail.m4 file, looks like the following:

```
include(Sendmail.mc)dnl
```

You may need to specify some entries in the PSEUDODOMAINS variable. This variable is used to handle systems that can't expand into domain names properly, usually UUCP networks. The entries in the PSEUDODOMAINS field tells sendmail+IDA not to use DNS for these networks (which would always fail). Typically, the PSEUDODOMAINS variable is set to the following values:

```
define(PSEUDODOMAINS, BITNET UUCP)dnl
```

You can use the PSEUDONYMS variable to hide your machine names from the outside world. For example, a mail recipient on another network sees only the address tpci.com regardless of whether mail was sent from merlin.tpci.com or chatton.tpci.com. When you use the PSEUDONYMS variable, sendmail accepts mail from all machines identified in the PSEUDONYMS field. The PSEUDONYMS field is usually used as shown in the following line:

```
define(PSEUDONYMS, tpci.com)dnl
```

This entry lets any machine with the network type tpci.com send mail through sendmail.

To define the name of your local machine, you use the DEFAULT_HOST variable. This variable is usually defined as the same name as your mail server (or your basic machine's name if you are not on a network). For example, you can use the following entry to set the default mail server's name:

```
define(DEFAULT_HOST, merlin.tpci.com)dnl
```

If you do not set a valid name for the DEFAULT_HOST variable, no mail will be returned properly to your system.

If your system is not a mail gateway to the Internet (or other networks that are accessible from your LAN), you can set your Linux system to send mail on to another machine for processing by setting the RELAY_HOST and RELAY_MAILER variables in sendmail.c4. These variables set the name of the mail server that all mail should be passed on to. For example, to set your local system to route all outbound mail to a machine called wizard, you set the following two lines as shown:

```
define(RELAY_HOST, wizard)dnl
define(RELAY_MAILER, UUCP=A)dnl
```

The RELAY_MAILER line specifies the mailer to use to send messages on to the RELAY_HOST.

UUCP-Specific Modifications

If you are working with a UUCP-based mail system, you should modify a few more entries in the sendmail.m4 file. These modifications are necessary because a UUCP mail system is often addressed differently than a DNS-based system. The UUCP-specific entries in the sendmail.m4 file usually look like the following:

```
define(UUCPNAME, tpci)dnl
define(UUCPNODES, ¦uuname¦sort¦uniq)dnl
define(BANGIMPLIESUUCP)dnl
define(BANGONLYUUCP)dnl
```

The first line defining UUCPNAMES specifies the name of the local system in UUCP terms. This name can be different than the name used in DNS, although usually these names will be similar. The UUCPNODES variable defines the commands that are used to produce a list of hostnames for systems you connect to via UUCP.

The BANGIMPLIESUUCP variable tells sendmail to assume that any address containing an exclamation mark (called a bang) is UUCP style. The BANGONLYUUCP variable does the same thing. Both variables are usually set to on (not commented out) because few DNS users use the bang addressing method.

Configuration Table Locations

Several lines in the sendmail.m4 file define configuration tables. For the most part, these configuration tables are under the directory defined by LIBDIR. This section of the sendmail.m4 file has several lines that look like the following:

```
define(ALIASES, LIBDIR/aliases)dnl
define(DOMAINTABLE, LIBDIR/domaintable)dnl
```

There are about seven configuration file definitions in total. You can change any of these values if you want, but be sure to move the files themselves to the specified location. On the whole, it is best to leave the files in their default locations.

Configuring decnetxtable

The file decnetxtable is used to translate domain names into DECnet style names. This file is a holdover from earlier versions of sendmail and will probably never be necessary for Linux users (unless your Linux machine is on a DECnet system).

Configuring domaintable

The domaintable file forces sendmail to perform specific instructions after using DNS. The file, which is almost never used on Linux systems, allows you to provide expansion of short-form names. Suppose you often send mail to the host reallylongname.reallybignet.com, but you don't want to type that entry each time. You could place the following entry in the domaintable file

```
reallylongname.reallybignet.com        big.com
```

so that whenever you send mail to bill@big.com sendmail expands the address to bill@reallylongname.reallybignet.com. You also can use the domaintable file to correct common typographic mistakes. For example, if many users accidently send mail to abcdef.com instead of abcdfe.com, you could add a line to the domaintable file that corrects the domain name:

```
abcdfe.com        abcdef.com
```

The format of the domaintable file is always the correct domain name followed by the incorrect (or shortened) domain name.

Configuring genericfrom

The genericfrom table hides local usernames and machine addresses by converting local usernames to a generic ID that has no obvious connection to the username. Linux systems seldom use this table because the general convention is to use real names on e-mail and similar data. The companion file, xaliases, performs the generic to real conversion when mail comes back from the outside world.

Configuring mailertable

The mailertable table defines any special handling for hosts or domains. Most often, mailertable specifies how certain domains or hosts are accessed and which protocol to use for these domains and hosts. You don't have to modify this file if your system only uses UUCP, but you should verify its contents if you use SMTP or DNS.

The mailertable file is read from the first line down, and `sendmail` processes mail based on each line in the file. For this reason, place the most specific rules at the top of the file, followed by more general rules. Rules give the method of connection first and then list the remote system or domain:

```
mailer delimiter relayname     remote
```

In this syntax, `mailer` is the transport to use, `delimiter` is a special character, `relayname` is the name of the system to pass the mail to, and `remote` is the remote host or domain name. The mailer can be one of the following values:

TCP-A	TCP with Internet-style addresses
TCP-U	TCP with UUCP-style addresses
UUCP-A	UUCP with Internet-style addresses

The delimiter has a special meaning and must be one of the following characters:

!	Strips the hostname from the address before forwarding
,	Doesn't modify the address at all
:	Removes the hostname only if intermediate hosts are specified

You can build the mailertable rules quite easily when you are forwarding mail to a remote mail server. For example, to force `sendmail` to use UUCP through a remote mail server called `wizard` to connect to the remote system `roy.sailing.org`, add a rule like the following to the mailertable file:

```
UUCP-A,wizard    roy.sailing.org
```

On a more general level, a rule like this one

```
TCP-A,wizard     chatton.com
```

forwards any mail destined for the remote network `chatton.com` to the local mail server `wizard` via TCP.

CONFIGURING PATHTABLE

The pathtable table defines explicit routing to remote hosts and networks. The format of each line in the pathtable file uses a syntax similar to a UUCP path alias, with entries appearing alphabetically in the file. The pathtable file is rarely used because most Linux systems can handle the routing without explicit instructions.

CONFIGURING UUCPRELAYS

The uucprelays file short-circuits the UUCP path to a remote site when a better path exists. For example, if your users often use the path wizard!bignet!merlin!tpci and you create a direct link to tpci, you could use the uucprelays file to redirect the mail.

CONFIGURING UUCPXTABLE

The uucpxtable file is used when a UUCP style address has to be used for mail delivery. The file provides the instructions for converting a DNS format address to a UUCP format address. If you are using a mail server other than your current machine or want to use UUCP to connect to specific machines because of reliability factors, this table is necessary.

This file contains entries that lists the UUCP style name followed by the domain name, as follows:

```
chatton        chatton.com
```

This entry tells sendmail that any mail for chatton.com should be rerouted via UUCP to chatton (UUCP style addressing). This entry forces mail addresses to yvonne@chatton.com to be rewritten as chatton!yvonne, an address that UUCP can handle.

BUILDING SENDMAIL.CF FROM SENDMAIL.M4

Now that you have configured the sendmail.m4 file and its dependent files, you can use the m4 processor to generate the sendmail.cf file. When the sendmail.m4 file is ready to be processed, issue the command

```
make sendmail.cf
```

or substitute your site name if you renamed your sendmail.m4 file to reflect your site name. (In other words, if you created a file called tpci.m4, specify tpci.cf in the command).

Once the file has been processed, copy it to the /etc directory (which is where the file normally resides) and start up sendmail with the command

```
/usr/lib/sendmail -bd -q1h
```

or reboot your machine (as sendmail usually starts from the rc startup files).

USING *SENDMAIL* VERSION 8

The latest version of sendmail supplied for most Linux systems is version 8. If you didn't see versions 6 or 7, don't worry; they didn't exist. The sendmail system jumped from release 5.X to 8. As of the date of publication, sendmail8+IDA wasn't in general distribution, but it should be available by the time you read this. There are several releases of sendmail version 8, just to make life more complicated. They are all pretty much the same as far as installation and configuration are concerned.

Most Linux CD-ROMs have the source code for sendmail version 8 already compiled into a binary. If you do not have the binary, change to the source directory and use the make command. The Slackware CD-ROM includes the precompiled binaries.

Note

Each release of sendmail version 8 has an installation guide included. To format and display this file properly on the screen, use the following command:

```
nroff -me op.me ¦ more
```

If you want to send the output to the printer instead, replace the more command with lp, or save the output to a file and print that file directly.

For the most part, sendmail version 8 is similar in configuration details to the other releases of sendmail. One change is the inclusion of four different UUCP mail routines. Choose one of the four UUCP versions based on the following features:

◆ uucp-old (same as uucp) is classic UUCP that uses a bang-style address and can send to only one address at a time (duplicate messages are sent when multiple recipients are specified). Use this version only if you need compatibility with old-style UUCP systems.

◆ uucp-new (previously known as suucp) is the same as UUCP except it provides the rmail command to allow several recipients. This version is not much of an improvement over uucp-old.

◆ uucp-dom allows domain name-style addressing. This version may not be compatible with some systems you have to connect to.

◆ uucp-uudom is a combination of uucp-new and uucp-dom to provide the best features of both. It allows bang- and DNS-style addresses with proper handling of headers.

Whichever version of UUCP you choose, copy or link it to the normal UUCP binary on your Linux system.

CONFIGURING SENDMAIL

As mentioned earlier in this chapter, the sendmail configuration files are daunting to say the least. To make matters easier for administrators, a number of templates

35

are supplied with version 8 that cover most of the common installation configurations. You have to copy one of these templates over the sendmail configuration file and change a few parameters relating to your specific system, but you can leave the majority of the file. Using these templates greatly shortens and simplifies the installation process. (If none of these templates suits your installation, you must manually adjust the configuration file. This process is beyond the scope of this book, so check the supplied documentation for more information.)

The sendmail system uses a number of directories to hold the files it needs, including the configuration file templates. Most of these files are processed by the macro language processor m4. The directories and their contents are as follows:

cf	This directory provides descriptions of hosts used by sendmail. The raw data files end in .mc (for master configuration) and are used as input; the output produces a file ending with .cf.
hack	This directory is a list of hacks used by the m4 macros to provide fixes or extra specifications. These should be avoided as much as possible. The information they supply is properly provided in the main configuration files.
m4	This directory contains files with information applicable to all configuration files (site-independent information).
mailer	This directory contains files defining the mailers that are used by m4. The files generally provide information for local, UUCP, USENET, fax software, and similar types of mailers.
ostype	This directory contains files describing the operating system and its environment.
sh	This directory contains shell files used by m4.
siteconfig	This directory contains local site information.

A number of files are important to the sendmail installation and configuration process. These files, their ownership and permission settings (where appropriate), and their purposes are as follows:

◆ The /usr/sbin/sendmail file is the sendmail binary (the location can change, for example to /usr/lib/sendmail, depending on your installation setup). The file should be owned by root and have permissions set to 553.

◆ The /etc/sendmail.cf file is the configuration file used by sendmail. This file is sometimes installed as /usr/lib/sendmail.cf.

- The /usr/bin/newaliases file is a symbolic link to the sendmail binary. Create it with the command ln -s /usr/sbin/sendmail /usr/bin/newaliases if the link isn't already installed.

- The /var/spool/mqueue directory is used to hold the mail queue. Create this directory with root as the owner and permissions set to 700. Some installations may prefer the directory /usr/spool/mqueue.

- The /etc/aliases file contains system aliases. This file should include the aliases provided in the lib/aliases file under the sendmail distribution directory.

In order to start sendmail automatically when your Linux system boots, modify the /etc/rc files to include these lines (if they don't already exist):

```
if [ -f /usr/sbin/sendmail -a -f /etc/sendmail.cf ]; then
        (cd /var/spool/mqueue; rm -f [lnx]f*)
        /usr/sbin/sendmail -bd -q30m &
        echo -n ' sendmail' >/dev/console
fi
```

The directory paths should reflect the paths used on your system, of course. The rm command used in this script removes any lock files that are left over from the system after the last shutdown.

USING THE SENDMAIL TEMPLATES

The Slackware Linux distribution that accompanies this book, and most other releases of Linux that provide sendmail version 8, have a few templates provided that set most of the needed parameters. When the sendmail package is installed from the accompanying CD-ROM, the following templates are in the directory /usr/src/sendmail/cf/cf:

- The linux.smtp.mc template is for systems directly connected to the Internet (the default configuration).

- The linux.nodns-smtp.mc template is similar to the above configuration but it's for systems with no nameserver (such as most small LANs).

- The linux.uucp.mc template is for for UUCP-based connections.

If you choose to use one of the template files, examine it carefully to make sure the directories and system names are correct for your system. Make any changes directly into the file. To install one of these configuration files (or any other that you may find that suits your needs), issue the command

```
m4 config_file.mc > /etc/sendmail.cf
```

where `config_file.mc` is the configuration file you want to install. This command executes the macro language processor and copies the resulting file over the standard `sendmail` configuration file.

SUMMARY

This chapter examined the configuration process for `sendmail+IDA`, the most common form of `sendmail` used with Linux. If you plan on using `smail` instead, read Chapter 36.

- How smail
  Handles Mail

- Setting Up smail

- Modifying smail's
  Behavior

CHAPTER 36

Using smail

The smail mail system is similar to the sendmail system in most of its actions, although the configuration process is different. In some ways, smail is easier to work with than sendmail, and it can be a good choice for smaller systems. If you choose to use smail as your mailer, you will have to make some manual modifications to configuration files because there are few automated or scripted routines available.

The smail system has many options and configuration details, most of which are never used. This chapter looks at the primary controlling parameters that most Linux users may need and essentially ignores those that are very seldom (if ever) used in real situations. For more information on the options and configuration controls not covered in this chapter, see the man pages or smail documentation. Essentially, this chapter shows you how to get smail up and running quickly to handle the situations most Linux systems will find themselves working with.

HOW *SMAIL* HANDLES MAIL

The smail system is governed by a daemon that is usually started when the system enters multiuser run mode. From then on, smail watches for incoming connections (TCP or UUCP, usually), and it processes any incoming mail when it is received. Because smail runs as a daemon, this allows fast processing and delivery of incoming mail without having to physically start a mail program at intervals. When mail is received through a UUCP connection, the rmail program is often called to handle the delivery of the mail.

The smail system was designed to process incoming mail immediately, routing it to the receiver. You can override this in the main configuration file, usually called /usr/lib/smail/config, which may be necessary in high-traffic situations or when a machine is heavily loaded. When desired, the inetd daemon can handle incoming mail traffic and spawn smail to handle the delivery at specific intervals. However, using smail as a daemon generally involves less overhead and system resources than spawning it every time mail has to be handled, so the daemon approach is recommended.

The smail system handles outgoing mail through the use of a connection to a user's mailer. For example, if you send a message from one of the Linux mailer agents such as Elm or mail, that application sends the mail and recipient names to the rmail (usually /usr/bin/rmail) program for delivery. Some mail agents send outgoing mail to the sendmail program instead of rmail, which also has to be accounted for. As you will see in the next section, both incoming and outgoing mail is usually handled by creating links between smail, rmail, and sendmail.

The smail mail-handling routine is broken into three distinct and separate parts: the router, the director, and the transport. The router handles address resolution and the way in which messages are sent between machines. The director handles forwarding and aliases that may be used in messages. The transport handles the actual transfer of messages. Each of the three components can be configured separately within smail using separate files called routers, directors, and transports (which usually reside in the /usr/lib/smail directory with the smail configuration files). You will look at modifying the default behavior of each component later in this chapter.

Most Linux systems have the smail program reside in the directory /usr/local/bin, although a few other locations are popular as well. You need to know the exact directory path to smail in order to properly configure the system, so find the executable. You can locate its path with the following command:

```
find / -name smail -print
```

Note the output.

SETTING UP *SMAIL*

The smail system requires several links to exist so smail can execute properly. The two most important links are to the files /usr/bin/rmail and /usr/lib/sendmail (sometimes located as /usr/sbin/sendmail, depending on the version of Linux). These links are necessary because most user mail applications send outgoing mail to either rmail or sendmail (depending on the mail software), and this has to be redirected to smail. Links allow this redirection to occur transparently without altering the user mail applications.

Verify that the rmail and sendmail files are linked to smail, and if not, establish the links. Usually, the links established are symbolic, and they will show in a directory listing with an entry like this:

```
lrwxrwxrwx  1  root   root    6 Sep 16:35   file1 -> file2
```

The arrow (->) shows that a symbolic link exists. (For more information on links and symbolic links, see Chapter 18, "Filesystems and Disks.") Check both the rmail and sendmail binaries for these symbolic links. If the symbolic links do not exist already, create them with the following commands:

```
ln -s /usr/local/bin/smail /usr/bin/rmail
ln -s /usr/local/bin/smail /usr/lib/sendmail
```

Of course, you should substitute whatever directory pathnames are valid on your system for smail, sendmail, and rmail. Once you have created the links, verify that they exist by displaying the directories and looking for the symbolic link notation shown earlier.

If mail may enter or leave your system through an SMTP channel, you should also establish a link between the smail program and the smtp system. Use the following command to set up the link (substituting proper paths for your system):

```
ln -s /usr/local/bin/smail /usr/sbin/smtpd
```

Next, the SMTP service has to be enabled through the TCP configuration files. You do this by setting the /etc/services file to specifically enable SMTP connections. There is a line in the /etc/services file that looks like this:

```
smtp    25/tcp    # Simple Mail Transfer Protocol
```

Verify that this line is not commented out (has a pound sign as the first character). This line allows the SMTP link to be established as TCP port number 25 (the default value).

If you are going to leave smail as a daemon (started automatically with the system boot), ensure that the smail daemon is started in the rc files (such as rc.inet2). The usual command line for the smail daemon looks like this:

```
/usr/local/bin/smail -bd -q15m
```

The -bd option turns the daemon operation of smail on, and the -q15m tells smail to process messages every 15 minutes. If you want more frequent mail delivery, change the value in the rc file. Alternatively, if you want mail processing less often to relieve a heavily loaded system, increase the value.

If you decide not to run smail as a daemon and want it spawned by inetd whenever mail arrives, comment out the daemon lines in the rc files (usually rc.inet2). You cannot run smail in both daemon and spawned mode. Next, modify the /etc/inetd.conf file to contain an entry like the following:

```
smtp    stream    tcp    nowait    root    /usr/sbin/smtpd    smtpd
```

You must have the symbolic link between smtpd and the smail program for this command to function properly.

The configuration file changes necessary for smail depend on which connection system you use for obtaining mail. In other words, the configurations change if you are using UUCP (which is the easiest to set up) or a TCP connection on a network. This chapter looks at each of the configuration processes separately. You can follow both discussions, if you enable mail through both methods.

Configuring smail for UUCP

Configuring the smail system for use with UUCP incoming and outgoing mail messages is very simple. You need to edit the default smail configuration file, usually stored as /usr/lib/smail/config. Some versions of smail include a sample configuration file as config.sample in the same directory. You can use either as a template for the UUCP modifications.

Use any ASCII editor to edit /usr/lib/smail/config. You need to make four changes. The changes are for these variables:

visible_domain	The domain name your site belongs to
visible_name	Your site's full domain name
uucp_name	Your site's UUCP-based name (usually the same as visible_name)
smart_host	The name of the UUCP host

Each parameter in the /usr/lib/smail/config file uses the same format of variable=value. There should be no spaces on either side of the equal sign on any line. A pound sign precedes comments in the file.

SETTING THE LOCAL DOMAIN NAME

Begin by setting the domain name of the local machine. Locate the line in the /usr/lib/smail/config file that defines the variable visible_domain, which will usually look similar to this:

```
# Our domain name
visible_domain=tpci
```

The visible_domain variable sets the domain name your site belongs to, and it will usually be the fully qualified domain name and any aliases that may be in effect. This field is used by smail to find out whether the recipient of a message is local. The smail system takes the message and extracts the recipient's address, comparing it against the local machine name (from the hostname command) and all values specified on the visible_domain variable. If there is a match to any of these names, the message is for a local recipient. If no match occurs, the message is routed externally.

If there is more than one valid value for a local domain name, the values are separated by colons, as shown in this example:

```
visible_domain=tpci:tpci.com:tpci.UUCP
```

If your site is properly registered on UUCP maps, add the domain uucp to the list of valid values, as well. In this example, you belong to the domain tpci (from the full domain name tpci.com) and uucp:

```
visible_domain=tpci:tpci.com:uucp
```

36

SETTING THE LOCAL DOMAIN NAME FOR OUTGOING MAIL

When a message is to be routed out of the local machine, the smail system appends the local machine's full domain name as part of the routing information. The full local machine name is defined in the /usr/lib/smail/config line that deals with the visible_name variable. The line looks something like this:

```
# Our domain name for outgoing mail
visible_name=tpci.com
```

As a general rule, the visible_name value must be a combination of the hostname and one of the domains given in the visible_domain variable. Otherwise, the smail system may bounce incoming mail issued as a reply to mail sent from your site as being unrecognizable. The visible_name value is usually your fully qualified domain name (if you have one) or a domain name that exists in other routing tables.

ALTERNATE UUCP NAMES

The /usr/lib/smail/config file sometimes contains an entry for a variable called uucp_name. This variable is usually optional, as long as the variables visible_domain and visible_name are properly filled in. The uucp_name variable is used when the name of the system returned by the hostname command is not the name that is registered with the UUCP mapping tables. For example, your UUCP mapping name may be darkstar, but you may have changed your machine's name to vader for any number of reasons. You can use the uucp_name variable to correct this change, without requiring updates to the UUCP mapping tables.

To set a value for the uucp_name variable, look for (or create, if one doesn't exist) the lines that define the variable. Usually, the lines look like this:

```
# UUCP mapping name
uucp_name=tpci.com
```

If your name is properly registered as set in the visible_name variable, you can simply repeat the value in the uucp_name variable with no ill effects. If your site name has changed, enter the proper value instead.

SETTING A UUCP SMART HOST

Some systems use another machine as a smart host that handles the routing of messages to and from other networks. If you are using a smart host, you should put its name in the /usr/lib/smail/config file next to the variable smart_host. Look for entries in the file that resemble these lines:

```
# Smart host
smart_host=merlin
```

In this case, any mail for other networks is forwarded by smail to the machine merlin (in the fully resolved domain name merlin.tpci.com, based on the smart_host and visible_name variables). That machine can then take care of the routing out of the network. Any machine name given in the smart_host field must be reachable by UUCP, which means having a corresponding UUCP configuration entry. (See Chapter 27, "UUCP," for more information.)

CONFIGURING SMAIL FOR TCP USE

If you are going to use a network connection to transfer mail, you need to make modifications to the /usr/lib/smail/config file that specify the types of connections and host names. There are several different methods of configuring mail systems for a network. These methods include using NFS (Network File System) to allow a single configuration file shared by all machines, using POP (Post Office Protocol) or IMAP (Interactive Mail Access Protocol) to handle mail on a central site, and setting up each machine as an independent mail handler. The configuration process for all these methods is much the same. The difference is whether the configuration files reside on each machine in the network, or on a single machine that is then accessed by NFS or SMTP by other machines.

Start the configuration process by establishing the local domain name using the variables visible_domain and visible_name. These variables were discussed in detail in the section on configuring smail for UUCP. An example of these variable definitions looks like this:

```
# Our domain name
visible_domain=tpci.com
# Our domain name for outgoing mail
visible_name=tpci.com
```

This code sets the local domain name and domain resolution names. The entry for visible_domain is attached by smail to all outgoing mail packages (instead of whatever name is generated by the hostname command). Both visible_domain and visible_name are often the same.

The next configuration step is to set the name of a smart host that handles out-of-network messages. If you are not using a smart host, or your machine handles the network connections itself, you won't need to enter these values. The variables involved in setting up a smart host are smart_path and smart_transport. The smart_path sets the machine name of the smart host (which must be resolvable with the domain name given in visible_domain). The smart_transport variable specifies the type of protocol to be used to connect to the smart host. Because most smart hosts communicate (for mail purposes, at least), with SMTP, that is the most often used value, as shown in this extract from a /usr/lib/smail/config file:

```
# smart host routing
# smart host name
smart_host=merlin
# communications protocol to smart host
smart_transport=smtp
```

The smart_transport value of smtp (lowercase letters only) is used to identify the SMTP connection protocol.

USING OTHER OPTIONS

As mentioned at the start of this chapter, smail can use many configuration options and command line options, although most are of little interest to most Linux system users. A few of the options may be of interest if you want to modify the basic behavior of smail. This section examines these options.

SETTING AN AUTHORITATIVE DOMAIN NAME

Both UUCP and TCP-based smail systems can add an entry to the /usr/lib/smail/ config file that prevents misrouted mail from bouncing around the network until it dies from excess hops. This is controlled by the auth_domains variable, which is used by smail to validate any incoming mail package. When smail receives a message for the local network machine, it checks to see whether the local machine's name is known. If not, the message is returned to the sender.

To set an authoritative name validation in the /usr/lib/smail/config file, check for (or add) these lines:

```
# auth domain name
auth_domains=tpci.com
```

This code limits the mail messages bouncing around the local network to any valid host name in the domain tpci.com. If the name is not recognized in the local network, it doesn't get circulated. This sometimes can help prevent congestion on a network when large files are misrouted.

SETTING THE DELIVERY MODE

You can set the smail system to process incoming mail in different ways (other than the daemon or spawned process startup options discussed earlier). You can set smail to store incoming and outgoing messages in a queue and process them at later times, or to process mail immediately. This process is controlled with the queue_only and delivery_mode variables.

The queue_only variable is a Boolean value that, if set, enables the delivery_mode variable, which can be set to one of three values:

foreground   Processes incoming messages immediately

background   The message is delivered by a child process

queued   Holds the message for later processing

When queuing is enabled, messages are held in a smail queue (usually in /var/spool/smail/messages) until the queue is processed. The processing is controlled by the -q option on the smail command line (if smail is started as a daemon) or by issuing the command runq from a crontab file (if smail is run from inetd). (For the latter to work properly, runq must be linked to smail.)

Recall the startup command line from the rc file shown earlier:

```
/usr/local/bin/smail -bd -q15m
```

You remember that the queue is processed every 15 minutes in this example. The queue process command can be set to any value, but it should not be left for too long as the queue files can get very large.

You can display the current contents of the smail queue by issuing the smail command with the -bp option or with the command mailq, which should be linked to smail.

SETTING THE POSTMASTER

Every network should have a postmaster, which is a user who receives all the status messages from the mail systems as well as queries from other networks about the local area network and its users. By default, the postmaster ID is set to root, although you can override it with the command like this in the /usr/lib/smail/config file:

```
postmaster=tparker
```

This command routes all messages for the postmaster to the user tparker. You only need to specify this option in the /usr/lib/smail/config file if you want to change the default setting of root.

You can configure the postmaster to receive all error messages that are generated because of configuration errors. Add the Boolean variable to the /usr/lib/smail/config file:

```
+error_copy_postmaster
```

If this entry doesn't exist with a plus sign ahead of it, messages are not copied to the postmaster.

DEBUGGING SMAIL

In normal operation, smail uses two log files to record actions. Most transactions are recorded in the file /var/spool/smail/log/logfile (your path may differ, depending on the version of Linux). Each entry in the log reflects a complete smail transaction and includes the identification number of the message, sender, recipient, times, size, and routing information. You can use the contents of the log file to check for proper behavior of the smail system.

Errors and other problems are recorded in the file paniclog (usually /var/spool/smail/log/paniclog). An entry in this file tends to show the basic information about a message as well as the reason the message couldn't be sent. For example, the most common error is a failure to route a message through SMTP, which produces the log summary:

```
(ERR_148) transport smtp: connect: Connection refused
```

If you see these error messages in the paniclog file, it usually means SMTP has failed, the connection is not responding because the remote host is down, or the TCP service is not enabled (check /etc/services).

If the entries in the paniclog file don't help you isolate a problem, you can enable a debugging mode on smail by adding the option -d followed by a number to the startup command. The number reflects the amount of debugging information to be generated and displayed on the screen. It is best to kill the smail daemon (if one is being used) and restart it at a shell prompt with this option active, instead of embedding the debug option in the rc file.

If you are not getting any mail forwarded to your mailbox, check the pathnames of the mailbox files. Usually, mailboxes are stored in /usr/spool/mail/username where username is each user's mailbox. Some versions of Linux use /var/spool/mail instead, and some mail applications may be expecting a specific address for the mailbox. If you are not sure whether the mailbox location is correct, try creating links between /usr/spool/mail/username and /var/spool/mail/username.

MODIFYING *SMAIL*'S BEHAVIOR

The configuration files and processes mentioned earlier apply for most Linux systems, and many systems will require no further actions than those already covered. However, as mentioned earlier in this chapter, smail's three components (router, director, and transport) can each be further configured to modify their behavior. This capability can help you fine-tune or modify your smail installation to meet particular network needs. The only component you really need to examine in detail is the router, as the director and transport seldom need customization for a typical Linux installation.

In most cases, the behavior of each smail component is handled by a file (or several files) based in the smail configuration directory (usually /usr/lib/smail). Many sample configuration files are available from Linux distribution CD-ROMs and FTP sites that show different configurations. Obtaining one of these sample files, and then modifying it for your host-specific details, is easier than building the files from scratch. The number of options and details change with the release of smail, so check to see whether you have a complete version.

The router component of smail handles the resolution of destination addresses, routing to the next mail host for further forwarding, and determination of which transport should be used to send the message on. The router component performs a number of tasks, first determining if the message is for a local or remote machine (using the variable values defined in /usr/lib/smail/config). If the message is for a local machine, the message is handed off to the director.

If the message is for a remote machine, the message's address is given to router drivers to determine which host the message should be forwarded to. The router drivers are specified in the file routers (usually /usr/lib/smail/routers). The file contains the names of the router drivers, each of which (in the order presented in the routers file) is given the message destination address to see if they have information about the specific route required to send the message.

You don't need to specify any other routers than the default configuration in most cases. The default setup uses the following router steps, in order:

◆ Resolution directly by dotted quad IP address using gethostbyaddr library call

◆ Resolution by symbolic name using gethostbyname library calls

◆ Resolution using the pathalias database (given in the file /usr/lib/smail/paths—see below)

◆ For UUCP addresses, resolution to see whether the destination is a UUCP neighbor

◆ Routing to a smart host, if one exists, when other methods to resolve the name have failed

These default routings work for most systems, although you should comment out the UUCP router if your system is not properly configured to handle UUCP. Otherwise, you will get tons of error messages. If you do not plan to use UUCP for mail, you should also comment out this router line to simplify the entire smail system.

A couple of other common situations need to be dealt with. If you are connected to the Internet, there is a problem in that smail's router doesn't recognize the MX record format. In order to properly support Internet mail, comment out the default router and enable the BIND router instead. (If your version of Linux doesn't support BIND, you can obtain and link a more recent version from FTP and BBS sites.)

If you are using both SLIP/PPP and UUCP connections, you may encounter problems with smail waiting too long for a connection. To simplify this type of installation, rearrange the order the routers are checked so that the paths file is checked before the resolver router. In many cases, because UUCP is more efficient and faster than SMTP over a SLIP/PPP line, you can disable the resolver-based router entirely.

When a router identifies the best route to the destination machine, it also gives the transport required to communicate with that machine's mail router. The actual path to the destination may be modified at this point. For example, if the remote machine chatton@bigcat.com can best be reached through a UUCP link instead of SMTP, the destination address may be modified by the router to bigcat!chatton (UUCP-style addressing). Alternatively, a destination address may become more specific. For example, the address chatton@bigcat.com may be resolved to a specific machine such as chatton@whiskers.bigcat.com, if that address will get the message delivered more efficiently.

Some UUCP routers use the /usr/lib/smail/paths file to determine a path alias. The paths file is ASCII only and contains a sorted list of entries with two columns separated by a tab: the destination site name and its UUCP bang path. No comments are allowed in the file.

SUMMARY

This chapter has looked at the configuration of the smail mail system for UUCP and TCP-based mail connections. In either case, the configuration process is usually a matter of modifying a single file, unless you have several different connections to the outside world. It is the simplicity of configuration that makes smail popular with Linux users.

- Configuring Elm
- Configuring Pine

CHAPTER 37

Configuring Elm and Pine

Now that you've gone to all the trouble of setting up either sendmail+IDA or smail, it's time to send and receive mail. That's where the user agents come in, otherwise known as mail readers. The mail reader displays your mail, enables you to manage your mailbox, and sends out new mail to others. Dozens of mail readers are available for UNIX and Linux, but the most popular of them all is Elm.

Elm and Pine are included with practically every distribution of Linux, although Elm is the most widely used at the moment so it's the mail reader this chapter examines first. If you decide to use another reader, check the documentation that accompanies the reader for configuration details. If you want to get going quickly with a very good reader, configure Elm or Pine on your system based on this chapter. You can have as many mail readers configured at a time as you want, so start with Elm or Pine and move on if it doesn't meet your needs.

CONFIGURING ELM

Elm (ELectronic Mail) is a full-screen user interface to the Linux mail system, as shown in Figure 37.1. It is quite powerful and offers a very good help system for times when you get stuck. Elm will run on most systems without any special configuration, as long as the mail system is working properly. A few options help the system run better, though.

Figure 37.1.
Elm offers a full-screen
interface to mail that is
very easy to configure
and use.

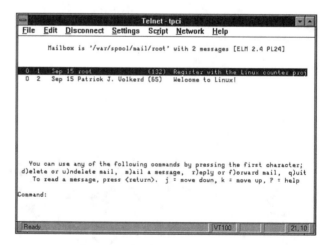

Elm's configuration information is stored in a file called /usr/lib/elm/elm.rc (sometimes just /usr/lib/elm.rc) and in each user's home directory in a file called .elm/elm.rc, both of which are created automatically by Elm the first time it is started. The file in each user's home directory is not editable by users, but it is modified when a user issues a save configuration command.

The primary changes to be made to the /usr/lib/elm/elm.rc file have to do with your machine's name and domain. You need to fill in a set of entries in the /usr/lib/elm/ elm.rc file. Edit the file and update the hostname and domain name options so that they look like this:

```
# Local hostname
hostname = merlin
#
# Domain name
hostdomain = .tpci.com
#
# fully qualified domain name
hostfullname = merlin.tpci.com
```

Each setting has the keyword, a space, an equal sign, a space, then the value. Note that the domain name needs a preceding period to allow it to be tacked on to machine names properly. Elm doesn't use these settings much, but they are occasionally useful.

If you need to change the default character set used by the system (the normal character set is called ISO-8859-1), you will need to make changes in Elm's configuration file, too. This change affects only the way Elm shows information, and it should correspond to the character set used by Linux on your system. By default, Elm uses an ASCII character set unless it recognizes some codes it can't handle with that set, in which case it switches to an alternate system called metamail to display the codes.

To make sure that Elm can process the standard character set used by Linux (and avoid calling the metamail system, which slows down mail reader processing), add this line to the /usr/lib/elm/elm.rc file (if it isn't already there):

```
displaycharset = iso-8859-1
```

There are some special characters in the ISO 8859-1 character set that Elm still can't quite handle properly, so you can add the following two lines to the file, as well:

```
charset = iso-8859-1
textencoding = 8bit
```

The latter command sets the system to 8 bits, instead of stripping off the last bit (the default action) to produce a 7-bit character.

CONFIGURING PINE

Most mail readers will have a configuration file similar to Elm's that controls the access and behavior of the mail reader. The most commonly available is Pine (Pine Is No longer Elm), also a full-screen mail reader, as shown in Figure 37.2. Pine can use system variables to a large extent, but it can also be customized by users.

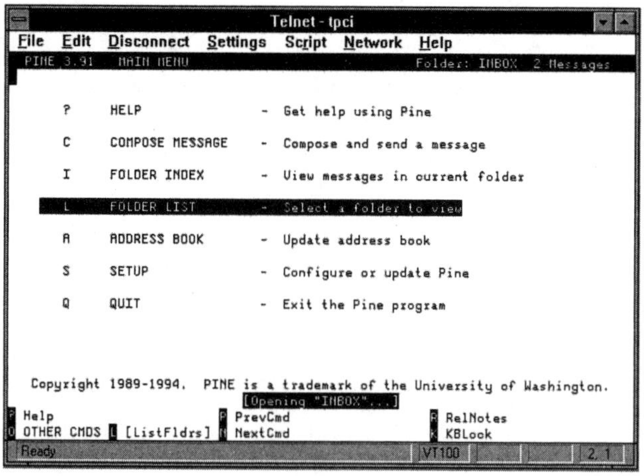

Figure 37.2.
Pine is an alternate to
Elm, offering a differ-
ent look and several
different functions.

Pine stores its configuration file at .pinerc in the user's home directory. This is a large ASCII file, with lots of comments to explain what is going on. The areas that you need to examine to configure Pine involve the system names and user identification. At the top of the .pinerc file is the user information:

```
personal-name=
```

If you want to override the default setting gathered from the login name, you can enter a name here. For most users, you will want to leave it blank. (If a .pinerc file doesn't exist, run Pine and it will create the file automatically.)

The domain name and address has to be set with lines like these:

```
# Sets domain part of From: and local addresses in outgoing mail.
user-domain=
# List of SMTP servers for sending mail. If blank: Unix Pine uses sendmail.
smtp-server=
# NNTP server for posting news. Also sets news-collections for news reading.
nntp-server=
# Path of (local or remote) INBOX, e.g. ={mail.somewhere.edu}inbox
# Normal Unix default is the local INBOX (usually /usr/spool/mail/$USER).
inbox-path=
```

Again, blank entries are used to indicate that Pine should use the system default values. If you want to customize any of the entries, add the values after the equal sign. As you can see in the code, the comments are descriptive enough to let you figure out what each variable does.

A large chunk of the .pinerc file is devoted to providing information about the mailboxes used by Pine. Leave the defaults alone for most systems, unless you want to alter the behavior of the mail system. The variables that fall into this area are:

```
# List of incoming msg folders besides INBOX, e.g. ={host2}inbox, {host3}inbox
# Syntax: optnl-label {optnl-imap-host-name}folder-path
incoming-folders=
```

```
# List of directories where saved-message folders may be. First one is
# the default for Saves. Example: Main {host1}mail/[], Desktop mail\[]
# Syntax: optnl-label {optnl-imap-hostname}optnl-directory-path[]
folder-collections=

# List, only needed if nntp-server not set, or news is on a different host
# than used for NNTP posting. Examples: News *[] or News *{host3/nntp}[]
# Syntax: optnl-label *{news-host/protocol}[]
news-collections=

# Over-rides default path for sent-mail folder, e.g. =old-mail (using first
# folder collection dir) or ={host2}sent-mail or ="" (to suppress saving).
# Default: sent-mail (Unix) or SENTMAIL.MTX (PC) in default folder collection.
default-fcc=

# Over-rides default path for postponed messages folder, e.g. =pm (which uses
# first folder collection dir) or ={host4}pm (using home dir on host4).
# Default: postponed-mail (Unix) or POSTPONE.MTX (PC) in default fldr coltn.
postponed-folder=
# If set, specifies where already-read messages will be moved upon quitting.
read-message-folder=

# Over-rides default path for signature file. Default is ~/.signature
signature-file=

# List of file or path names for global/shared addressbook(s).
# Default: none
# Syntax: optnl-label path-name
global-address-book=

# List of file or path names for personal addressbook(s).
# Default: ~/.addressbook (Unix) or \PINE\ADDRBOOK (PC)
# Syntax: optnl-label path-name
address-book=
```

The final section of the .pinerc file that you may want to examine deals with personal preferences for the reader:

```
# List of features; see Pine's Setup/options menu for the current set.
# e.g. feature-list= select-without-confirm, signature-at-bottom
# Default condition for all of the features is no-.
feature-list=

# Pine executes these keys upon startup (e.g. to view msg 13: i,j,1,3,CR,v)
initial-keystroke-list=

# Only show these headers (by default) when composing messages
default-composer-hdrs=

# Add these customized headers (and possible default values) when composing
customized-hdrs=

# Determines default folder name for Saves...
# Choices: default-folder, by-sender, by-from, by-recipient, last-folder-used.
# Default: "default-folder", i.e. "saved-messages" (Unix) or "SAVEMAIL" (PC).
saved-msg-name-rule=
```

```
# Determines default name for Fcc...
# Choices: default-fcc, by-recipient, last-fcc-used.
# Default: "default-fcc" (see also "default-fcc=" variable.)
fcc-name-rule=
# Sets presentation order of messages in Index. Choices:
# subject, from, arrival, date, size. Default: "arrival".
sort-key=

# Sets presentation order of address book entries. Choices: dont-sort,
# fullname-with-lists-last, fullname, nickname-with-lists-last, nickname
# Default: "fullname-with-lists-last".
addrbook-sort-rule=

# Reflects capabilities of the display you have. Default: US-ASCII.
# Typical alternatives include ISO-8859-x, (x is a number between 1 and 9).
character-set=

# Specifies the program invoked by ^_ in the Composer,
# or the "enable-alternate-editor-implicitly" feature.
editor=

# Program to view images (e.g. GIF or TIFF attachments).
image-viewer=

# If "user-domain" not set, strips hostname in FROM address. (Unix only)
use-only-domain-name=
```

As with all the other sections of the .pinerc file, most of these entries can be left in their default blank state unless you specifically need to override an entry. The final section of the .pinerc file is updated by Pine itself, and it should not be modified by users (as all these settings are lost when Pine runs, so if users do make changes to this section they are not retained). This final section or /pinerc deals with printers and the version of Pine.

SUMMARY

Setting up any of the mail readers is usually a matter of editing the configuration file for the reader. In almost all cases, the configuration files have a lot of comments to explain what is going on. You only need to read these files to understand the configuration steps you must take. In general, you don't need to do anything with most mail readers, assuming that you have a typical Linux system using sendmail.

- What Is USENET?

- A Brief History of
  USENET

- How USENET News
  Is Handled

CHAPTER 38

USENET and Netnews

If you have an Internet connection, eventually you are going to want to access USENET and its newsgroups. USENET is one of the most dynamic (and often controversial) aspects of the Internet. With access to the Internet, you can set up, access, and work with all kinds of newsgroups, but most Linux users will be interested in using USENET specifically. This chapter looks at the background of USENET and news services for UNIX in particular, as well as how the Linux news programs handle the news.

WHAT IS USENET?

USENET is one of the most misunderstood aspects of the Internet. At the same time, it is one of the most popular and frequently used aspects of the Internet (with the possible exception of e-mail). To many users, especially those who don't use Internet's mail facilities, USENET is Internet, and vice-versa.

USENET was originally developed to facilitate discussion groups (called newsgroups in USENET jargon). A newsgroup lets any user with access to the system participate in a public dialogue with everyone else. By the end of 1995, USENET carried over 9,000 different newsgroups totaling well over 100M of information every day. USENET is supported in millions of networks in hundreds of countries and reaches hundreds of millions of users.

Despite what most people think, USENET is not a formal network or entity. Instead, it is a number of networked machines that exchange electronic mail (articles) tagged with predetermined subject headers for specific areas of interest (newsgroups). The articles are handled as electronic mail messages by most network machines; articles are processed as news information only by the applications called newsreaders that send and receive the messages.

Any machine that can attach itself to the Internet either directly, through a gateway, or through a forwarding service (such as an online service provider) can become part of USENET. All that is required to use USENET is the software that downloads and uploads the newsgroup mail and a reader package that lets users read and write articles.

The software that implements the passing of USENET messages over local area networks from one machine to another is the Network News Transfer Protocol (NNTP). Using NNTP, your Linux machine can interact with any other machines that handle the news. NNTP software is an integral part of most Linux versions, so you don't need to purchase or look for additional software. Indeed, many people establish Linux machines just to access Internet services like USENET, e-mail, and the World Wide Web.

A BRIEF HISTORY OF USENET

USENET was developed out of a UNIX release known as UNIX V7, which implemented UUCP (UNIX to UNIX CoPy) for the first time. As UUCP became popular for communications between machines, it was expanded with program extensions and supplementary programs. USENET began at the University of North Carolina, where Steve Bellovin used shell scripts to write the first version of news software. UNC and Duke used this software to pass messages and commentary between the two universities. Interest in the news software spread when the UNC system was described at a Usenix conference in 1980. Steve Daniel was the first to implement the news software in the C programming language. This version eventually became the first general release of the news software, which was called release A.

To cope with the increasing volume of messages as new news sites were added to the expanding informal network, two University of California students, Mark Horton and Matt Glickman, rewrote the software and added new functionality. After a further revision of their release B, the news software was generally released in 1982 as version 2.1. From there, the Center for Seismic Studies' Rick Adams took over maintenance of the software in 1984, at which point it was up to release 2.10.2. One of Rick's first additions was the capability for moderated newsgroups, resulting in release 3.11 in 1986.

Since then, several contributors have added features to the software, the most important of which was a complete rewrite of the software undertaken in 1987 by the University of Toronto's Geoff Collyer and Henry Spencer. Their rewrite greatly increased the speed with which message mail could be processed and was generally released under the name C News (from Release C). Over the next few years, the basic news package went through some minor revisions but has remained true to Collyer and Spencer's version. Important changes were made to the way machines transferred news messages, and a daemon was added to process incoming and outgoing postings.

All the versions of news software developed to this point had used UUCP as the transport. To allow transfer of messages over a network, a protocol called the Network News Transfer Protocol (NNTP) was developed in 1986. NNTP-based software began to be refined, and a widely used version was implemented in software written by Brian Barber and Phil Lapsley, called nntpd. An alternative NNTP system that is widely available is INN (Internet News), which provides a complete news package (user interface and underlying software).

Apart from the underlying mechanics for transferring messages for newsgroups, developments also were continuing in the user interface area, where the newsreader exists. Newsreader software lets you read articles in newsgroups as they arrive. The original reader was called readnews, and it remains one of the most widely used newsreader packages, primarily because it is easy to use and is available on practically every UNIX system.

Several alternate newsreaders were developed, expanding on the features offered by readnews. Software such as rn (a more flexible version of readnews), trn (threaded readnews), and vnews (visual newsreader) are freely distributed now. All are character-based systems originally developed for UNIX and ported to many other operating systems. With the popularity of graphical user interfaces, newsreaders were also ported to these environments, resulting in software such as xrn (X Windows-based readnews). Most of the readnews variants share a basic command set, although each adds features that may appeal to some users.

How USENET News Is Handled

Two types of software are involved in making a news service work on a Linux machine. The transport software (usually C News for UUCP connections or NNTP for TCP connections) gets the newsgroups to your machine. The newsreader then assembles and presents the articles to the user. Newsreaders are only involved in the actual user interface; they simply pass and receive news articles from the underlying software. For that reason, you don't need to look at the mechanics of a newsreader to understand how Linux processes news. The original news system relied completely on UUCP, so much of the news software was designed for UUCP and then modified later to accommodate alternate methods.

To transfer news from one machine to another, a technique called flooding is used. One machine calls another and transfers all the news articles. The machine that just received the news calls another and transfers the articles again. The news articles flow across the networks by moving from machine to machine instead of all the machines polling a single main news source. Each machine maintains a list of other sites it can contact to transfer mail. Each connection to another machine is called a newsfeed.

Each machine can generate new articles as the system's users interact with newsgroups. When new articles are created, the machine checks its list of newsfeeds and calls them to transfer the new mail. Because each article generated by a newsreader has a list of the machines that it has passed through (called the Path), the local machine knows whether the remote sites on its newsfeed list have already seen the article. As articles move from machine to machine, each machine adds its own identifier to the article's Path field, using the UUCP bang-style notation.

An entry in the Distribution field of the header may place a restriction on the machines that can be sent an article. For example, if you write an article that you want to stay within your local area network, you can specify this in the Distribution field of the message when you write it. Then when a newsfeed to a machine outside the local area network is created, the Distribution field prevents the article from being sent.

To help prevent duplicates of articles moving around USENET, each article has a unique identifying number called a message ID (which sits in the Message-Id field in the article header). The message ID is a combination of a unique number and the name of the machine that the article was originally posted on. Machines use these message ID numbers when a connection to a newsfeed is established. A history file on each system contains a list of all message ID numbers that the local system has. When the two machines communicate with each other, they can check the history file to find out whether the message should be sent. This process is part of a news transfer protocol called ihave/sendme.

With the ihave/sendme protocol, one machine sends a list of all the message ID numbers it currently has and waits for the other machine to identify the ones it wants. These numbers are transferred one at a time in response to sendme messages. Then the process can be reversed to update the other machine. This type of protocol works well, but it does involve a lot of overhead in the communications process. For that reason (coupled with the generally slow lines used by UUCP modem links), ihave/sendme protocols are not often used when a very large newsgroup transfer has to take place at regular intervals. You wouldn't want to use ihave/sendme to transfer 100M of articles every day, for example.

An alternative method used for large transfers is batching of articles. In this method, one machine sends everything it has to another machine. The receiving machine then performs a check of the newly arrived articles to see whether it already has them. By looking at the message ID number, the machine can discard duplicates. This method tends to be faster for transferring, although it does have more processing overhead for the receiving machine when the machine deals with the newly arrived batch of articles.

For network-based news access, there are three ways to get articles from another machine. Using NNTP, your machine can download articles you want using a technique called pushing the news, which is similar to the ihave/sendme protocol. Your machine can also request specific newsgroups or articles from the remote based on the date of arrival, which is called pulling the news. Alternatively, you can interact on an article-by-article basis with the remote, never downloading the articles to your local machine. This process is called interactive newsreading, and it works only when you have a newsfeed you can log in to (which is common these days).

SUMMARY

This chapter looked at the basics of USENET and news. This information provides a foundation for the next two chapters, which look at NNTP (for network-based access to news) and C News (for UUCP and network access to news). Entire books are written on the subject of USENET and the protocols it uses. Check out one of them if you need more information on this subject.

- How NNTP Handles News

- Installing the NNTP Server Program

- Configuring nntpd

- Using INN

CHAPTER 39

NNTP and INN

Network News Transfer Protocol (NNTP) is often used for TCP-based newsfeeds. In other words, if you are using a network to connect to a newsfeed, you can use NNTP to download your newsgroups instead of UUCP. Although UUCP users can use NNTP, the C News package is more popular and easier to work with (see Chapter 40, "C News") for UUCP transfers as it leaves off the complexities NNTP adds. The primary advantage of NNTP-based network newsfeeds is the much higher throughput that can be achieved. UUCP is limited to modem speeds, but NNTP can function over fast local area networks at many megabits per second. This capability allows for larger downloads in the same timespan, which can be important if you receive a lot of newsgroups. NNTP is not a stand-alone package; it requires another news server system to be running. NNTP works with both the older B News (which is seldom available for Linux now) and the better C News (discussed in the next chapter).

This chapter looks at how you can implement NNTP for a local area network news system. Although this chapter doesn't cover every NNTP option and feature, the information presented here should be sufficient to get an NNTP feed working properly. The end of this chapter looks at INN (Internet News), an alternate package for handling news. INN is a complex package capable of supporting very complex networks and news requirements, but it is often overkill for small Linux systems.

HOW NNTP HANDLES NEWS

NNTP operates in two modes: active and passive. The active mode, often called pushing, is much the same as C News' ihave/sendme protocol in which the sender (server) offers a particular article and waits for the receiver (client) to accept or refuse the article. Pushing has a disadvantage for the server in that it has a high overhead because each article must be checked in turn.

In the passive mode, called pulling, the receiving machine requests a list of all articles in a particular newsgroup that have arrived since a specified date. This request is sent through a newnews command. When the receiving machine has all the articles, it then discards any that are duplicated or not wanted using the article command. This mode is much easier for the sending machine because it simply sends a mass of articles, but the server does have to make sure it sends information that is allowed to pass to the receiver for security's sake.

NNTP is implemented on a Linux system with the NNTP daemon developed by Stan Barber and Phil Lapsley. This daemon is known almost universally as the reference implementation. Usually, you will only have the source code for the NNTP daemon, which is called nntpd, supplied with a Linux distribution because several site-specific details must be linked into the binary. The nntpd system consists of a server program and two different client programs (one for pushing and one for pulling). In addition, most Linux nntpd systems include a replacement for the inews program.

An alternative to nntpd is the INN (InterNet News) package developed by Rich Salz. This package is supplied with many Linux distribution packages. INN allows both UUCP and network-based newsfeeds, but it is really designed for large machines. If you anticipate a lot of newsgroup access, INN may be a better choice than nntpd, although nntpd can handle full newsfeeds almost as well.

When NNTP receives an article from a remote machine, it passes it on to one of the news subsystems that must be in place. Usually, this subsystem is rnews or inews. (You can also use NNTP for batching of articles, as explained in Chapter 40 "C News." In this case, the relaynews program handles the batch of articles.) NNTP uses the /usr/lib/news/history file to properly perform some protocol transfers, so this file must be configured correctly (Chapter 40 explains how to configure this file).

Installing the NNTP Server Program

The NNTP server, which is called nntpd or in.nntpd, is usually supplied as source code only, as was previously mentioned. In most cases, you must compile it on your machine to include machine-specific information. To configure nntpd, you use a program usually stored as /usr/lib/news/common/conf.h. You can search for the source files with the command:

```
find / -name conf.h -print
```

Run this program (which is a number of macros) and answer all the questions about your system.

Begin the NNTP installation process by creating a directory for nntpd to store incoming articles. You should create this directory as /usr/spool/news/.tmp (or /var/spool/news/.tmp). Set the ownership of the directory to news. The two commands to perform these steps are as follows:

```
mkdir /usr/spool/news/.tmp
chown news.news /usr/spool/news/tmp
```

You can configure the NNTP server in one of two different modes. The first mode is as a stand-alone daemon, which starts itself from the rc startup files (usually rc.inet2) when the Linux system is booted. Alternatively, you can configure nntpd to be managed through inetd instead of running all the time.

If you are configuring nntpd to run as a stand-alone daemon, make sure that no line in the /etc/inetd.conf file calls the daemon. Alternatively, check the /etc/inetd.conf file for potential conflicts if you start the nntpd daemon in the rc files.

To configure nntpd to run through inetd, which can reduce the overall load on your system except when news must be processed, you need to add an entry to the inetd configuration file. This file is usually stored as /etc/inetd.conf. Add the following line to this file with an ASCII editor:

```
nntp    stream    tcp    nowait    news    /usr/etc/in.nntpd    nntpd
```

The inetd.conf file may already have a line like this one commented out. In this case, verify that the line reads the same as the preceding one and remove the comment symbol.

Whether you are configuring nntpd to run as a stand-alone daemon or to be started by inetd, you need to verify that there is a line for the nntp service in the TCP /etc/ services file that looks like the following:

```
nntp    119/tcp        readnews       untp
```

This line is commented out when you install most versions of Linux, so remove the comment symbol.

CONFIGURING *NNTPD*

Once the nntpd binaries have been created by running the conf.h file, you can configure the file /usr/lib/news/nntp_access to control which remote machines can use NNTP on your system. The file is organized in a set of lines, one for each remote, using the format

```
sitename        read¦xfer¦both¦no    post¦no        except
```

where sitename is the name of the remote machine, which can be identified by its sitename, a fully qualified domain name, or the IP address. NNTP allows for partial matches of the domain name and IP address, which are useful for providing multiple lines of information about newsgroups. If the remote machine's name or IP address matches the sitename exactly, only that one line is read (the rest of the file is ignored). If the match is only partial, that line is read, and then the rest of the file is examined to find further matches. If you want to match all remote machines, you can use the sitename default.

The access permissions for the site are defined in the second field. There are four legal values, which have these meanings:

read	The remote can retrieve articles (pulling).
xfer	The remote can send articles (pushing).
both	The remote can send and receive articles.
no	The remote has no access to articles.

The third field indicates whether the remote site can post articles. If the keyword post is used, the remote can send articles and the local NNTP system completes the header information. If the keyword no appears in the second or third field, the remote cannot post articles.

The last field identifies any newsgroups that the remote is denied access to. The newsgroups are separated by commas, and an exclamation mark precedes the field (you will see this format frequently in C News). For example, the entry

```
chatton.bignet.com    both    post    !alt,local
```

allows the remote machine chatton.bignet.com to send and receive all articles except those in the alt and local newsgroup hierarchies. The remote may also post articles.

Usually, you set up the /usr/lib/news/nntp_access so that there is a default value for all machines, and then add specific entries for machines you want to work with. Look at the following sample /usr/lib/news/nntp_access file:

```
# default entry
default         xfer    no
# allow chatton full access
chatton.bignet.com    both    post
# allow brutus to read but not post
brutus.bignet.com    read    no
```

This file lets any machine other than those explicitly specified transfer articles to your machine but not post articles. The machine called chatton can read and post articles, but brutus can only read articles.

Some versions of NNTP have implemented authorization systems to ensure that your machine does not get fooled into thinking another machine is at the other end of a connection. The authorization system has not been working well for most versions of nntpd and is best left alone at this point. Check future releases of nntpd for more information about the authorization process.

USING INN

The Internet News (NNT) package is an alternative to NNTP. INN is designed to handle much larger and more complex news systems than NNTP and is therefore not used as much with Linux. However, there is no reason why you can't employ INN instead of NNTP on your Linux system. An INN version is included with most Linux distributions. If you have to support complex mail systems, the INN configuration process can get convoluted. For simpler LAN and stand-alone systems, though, you can easily configure INN for typical usage.

INN's behavior revolves around the server daemon called innd. The innd daemon does more than the nntpd daemon because it allows multiple streams to be handled at once. A different daemon, called nnrpd, handles the newsreader service, and a dedicated copy is spawned for each newsreader client application.

INSTALLING THE INN SOFTWARE

Most Linux distributions (including the Slackware CD-ROM accompanying this book) include the precompiled binaries for INN, so you needn't bother generating the binaries from the source code. If you have to generate the binaries, use the Makefile that builds the application. Check the Makefile and accompanying source file documentation for compilation instructions if you have to compile the code.

Once you have the INN binaries ready, you can follow a straightforward procedure to install the software in the proper locations and with the correct permissions and ownerships. Follow these steps:

1. If one doesn't already exist in /etc/passwd, create a user called news. Also create a group called news if one doesn't already exist in the /etc/group file. The news user should belong to the news group by default.

2. If one doesn't already exist, create a mail alias in the alias file (usually /usr/lib/aliases) for the username usenet to the root, postmaster, or other username that is used at regular intervals. (This alias must exist because some INN scripts send mail to the user usenet, which can be redirected by the alias entry.) If you have to add the alias, you must rebuild the alias database using the `newaliases` command.

3. Check the system startup files for an entry for the INN daemons. These daemons will probably not appear by default, so add the following lines to the startup file (such as rc.local) to call the INN `rc startup` script:

   ```
   # start the INN daemon
   /usr/lib/news/etc/rc.news
   ```

4. Create a symbolic link to the new INN news directory with the following command (substitute your directory path):

   ```
   ln -s /usr/lib/news /usr/local/lib/news
   ```

   You may have to remove the directory /usr/local/lib/news if it already exists before creating the symbolic link. (This step is necessary because most newsreaders expect the news configuration files to be in /usr/lib/news.)

5. Because you will want INN to be running all the time, you should use `cron`. Edit the file crontab-news to include the name of your newsfeed and local site, and then copy it into the cron spool directory (usually /usr/spool/cron/crontabs) as the news file.

6. Modify the news configuration file /usr/lib/news to include specifics about your newsfeed and local site.

7. Create an empty log file and history database. You can do both tasks with the script `makedirs.sh` provided with most INN distributions.

After all these steps, INN is ready to start. You can either reboot your machine and let the daemons start from the rc startup files, or execute the daemon directly from the command line.

CONFIGURING INN

When the INN software is installed and the directories are ready, you can configure the software. This section assumes you are working with a fairly straightforward installation where you use one or more newsfeeds and handle the news on the downloading machine. More complex installations are certainly possible with INN, but you should read all the documentation to understand the process.

Begin by editing the hosts.nntp file, which lists the newsfeed locations for your system. When a machine connects to the INN daemon, it examines the hosts.nntp file for a match to the connecting machine's IP address or name. If a match is found, INN assumes the machine is feeding news. Otherwise, INN assumes a newsreader wants access and spawns a process (nnrpd) for this function. For this reason, INN must know the IP address or resolvable symbolic name for the newsfeed servers in the hosts.nntp file.

To configure the hosts.nntp file, enter the names of the newsfeed machine or machines. The file contains only the name or IP address, one newsfeed on a line. If you have only a single newsfeed called big_boy, the nntp.hosts file looks like the following:

```
big_boy:
```

Note that a colon must follow the name of the newsfeed. Alternatively, you could specify the IP address of big_boy. If you have several newsfeeds, each gets a line of its own. Some systems use a password to log in for newsfeeds. If you need to specify a password, it is included after the colon.

Machines that are connecting to act as newsreaders are listed in the file nnrp.access, which is checked by nnrpd when it is spawned. The machine names that are included in nnrp.access must match what the NNTP system thinks the machine name is, not necessarily what you think it is symbolically (or even by IP address). The best way to verify the machine name is to use the finger command. Whatever name finger displays is the name that must be used in nnrp.access. (Usually, this name matches the symbolic name, but some systems have two different names in use.) The syntax of the nnrp.access file is

```
hostname:permission:user:password:groups
```

where the hostname is the machine name of IP address (wildcards are allowed), permission is Read for read access, Post for post authorization, or RP for both, user is a username used for authentication before posting is allowed, password is a password for authentication, and groups are a pattern of newsgroup names that can be read or not read. If you want to prevent a client from posting, put a space in the user and password field (as they can't be matched). The default settings, if not specified, are no access, no authentication, and no groups, which is written as follows:

```
*:: -no- : -no- :!*
```

To add a machine to the nnrp.access file, use the following syntax and set the permissions:

```
*.tpci.com:Read Post:::*
```

This line lets any machine from the domain tpci.com read and post news in all newsgroups with no authentication process necessary. To create a wide-open system, use the following line:

```
*:Read Post:::*
```

This line lets anyone read and post. Don't use this line unless you know who can connect to your news system! For a client system to post news to INN, it must use the program inews.

Many things can go wrong with INN, but the error messages tend to be useful in isolating the problem. There are usually three files called faq-inn-1, faq-inn-2, and faq-inn3 that describe most aspects of the INN system, including installation, configuration, debugging, and special setups. Consult these files if you have any problems with your INN system.

SUMMARY

Once you have completed the compilation and configuration of the NNTP system, you can continue to configure the underlying news subsystem (usually C News). Once that is done, you should be able to use NNTP to transfer articles from your newsfeed.

- How C News Handles News

- Configuring C News

- C News Utilities

CHAPTER 40

C News

Probably the most widely used and most popular method of distributing news on Linux systems is C News, designed for UUCP connections (although you can use C News with NNTP, too). Configuring C News to transfer newsgroups between your machine and others is not too difficult, although it can be time-consuming. This chapter walks through the steps necessary to configure C News and explains most of the files that C News uses.

HOW C NEWS HANDLES NEWS

When news is transferred in from a remote newsfeed, the rnews program accepts it and stores it in a spooling directory (usually /usr/spool/news/in.coming or /var/spool/news/in.coming). From the spool directory, the news messages are picked up and processed by the newsrun program. Outgoing news (such as from a local user) is usually sent from the users' newsreader to the inews program, which completes all the header details and stores it ready for transfer in the directory /usr/spool/news/out.going (or /var/spool/news/out.going).

Both incoming and outgoing messages pass through the relaynews program, which is responsible for checking whether the message has already been seen on the local site. To do this, relaynews checks the message ID against the history file (which contains a list of all processed messages). If the message has already been accepted at the local site, it is discarded.

If the message is new, relaynews checks the Newsgroups heading of the message to verify that the local site accepts articles for that newsgroup. If the newsgroup is not supported, relaynews discards the message. If the newsgroup exists in the active file, relaynews moves the message into the proper newsgroup spool directory. If the newsgroup is not listed in the active file, the article is moved to a miscellaneous group (often called junk).

The relaynews program also checks the header information of messages to verify that they are not stale. If a stale article is found, it is discarded. If a message is not processed for any other reason (such as incomplete header, improper date, and so on), it is moved to the directory /usr/spool/news/in.coming/bad or /var/spool/news/in.coming.bad) and an error message logged. After all these checks, the message ID is logged to the history file.

Messages that are to be sent further on through a news network are checked against the Path field in the header to make sure they haven't already received the article. If they haven't, the message can be forwarded on using UUCP (or in rarer cases, NNTP).

If batching of news articles is in effect, incoming and new articles are not forwarded on to other news machines in the UUCP network immediately but are held until the batch is transferred as a whole. This is usually controlled through a crontab entry.

Configuring C News

Configuring the C News system is a matter of verifying that necessary directories are accessible by C News, and that configuration files have valid values in them. Finally, all the file ownerships and permissions have to be checked. The configuration is best done in steps.

C News Configuration Files

To begin the configuration process for C News, obtain copies of the *active* and *newsgroup* files from your newsfeed. You can usually obtain the files with a UUCP command or an e-mail message to the postmaster at that site. Place the active and newsgroup files in the news directory (usually /usr/lib/news), and change the ownership to the user news. Next, change the file permissions to mode 644. You can do both these steps with the following commands:

```
chown news /usr/lib/news/active /usr/lib/news/newsgroup
chmod 644 /usr/lib/news/active /usr/lib/news/newsgroup
```

Edit the active file with any ASCII editor. Remove any line from the file that has the line "to.*". Add two lines that add your machine name and newsfeed site names, so that you have lines like this:

```
to.merlin
to.brutus
```

These lines assume that your local site is called merlin and your feed site is called brutus. The order of the entries doesn't matter. These entries are used with the news ihave/sendme message system, and they should exist in the active file even if you are not using the ihave/sendme system.

Next, add the following lines to the /usr/lib/news/active file:

```
junk
control
```

These lines are used for handling unidentified newsgroup articles and other functions. Not all versions of C News let you access this file directly. Instead, two utilities called addgroup and rmgroup perform the same function. In this case, use the function addgroup to add the two lines.

40

C News

Note

Whenever you or C News create a new entry in the active file, an entry is made in the file /usr/lib/news/active.times that indicates the name of the newsgroup, when it was created, who created it, and how it was done. Newsreaders often use this file to detect new newsgroups, but it can also serve as a handy log of newsgroup creation for system administrators.

The /usr/lib/news/active file lists all groups that are known to exist (and are wanted) at your site, as well as the article numbers that are currently on the system. The format of each line in the active file is as follows:

```
newsgroup high low permission
```

In this format, newsgroup is the name of the newsgroup, high and low are the highest and lowest article numbers that are on your system, although C News doesn't update this field automatically. To update this field (which many newsreaders require to properly track article threads), you need to run the updatemin program that accompanies most recent versions of C News (older versions of C News have a program called upact instead). When the numbers are incorrect (high lower than low, or high missing), the default is to set high to low+1.

The permission field gives the access system users have for the group. The permission is one of the following values:

=	This value marks the newsgroup as having an alias, followed by the name of the local alias. For example, the entry =naughty_stuff would post any articles sent to the newsgroup to a local newsgroup alias named naughty_stuff.
m	This value indicates a moderated newsgroup. Articles posted to a moderated newsgroup are e-mailed to the moderator. The moderator's address is in the file /usr/lib/news/moderators.
n	With this value, users are not allowed to post to the group, but they can read articles.
x	The value means that the group is disabled (no reading allowed), although articles can still be forwarded to other machines.
y	This value means that users can post to the newsgroup.

Finally, you have to renumber all the article numbers in the second and third fields of the new /usr/lib/news/active files to 0 (starting article number) and 1 (ending article number), so that you will receive all the articles properly. This process requires a lot of manual editing, or you can perform the entire process with one sed command (which is best performed on a copy of the original active file):

```
cp active active.original
sed 's/ [0-9]* [0-9]* / 0000000000 00001 /' active.original > active
```

Manually check the new active file to make sure that the format of the file is correct. The entire second column should be a set of zeros, and the third column should be the number one.

The newsgroups file is a list of all newsgroups with a one-line description of its purpose. The descriptions are used by many newsreader applications to display groups users subscribe to. You may have to update this file occasionally to ensure that it is accurate, because newsgroups change frequently. For an initial configuration, you can leave the file as it was sent from your news feed.

A number of configuration files are usually maintained in the C News directory, usually /usr/lib/news. Each file shown in the following list needs to be checked for the proper entries that work with your site. You can edit each file with any ASCII editor.

Check and modify the following C News configuration files:

explist	This file specifies expiration times of some newsgroups.
mailname	This file is your machine's name as it should appear on outgoing mail, usually as your full domain name (such as tpci.com).
organization	This file is your organization's name used to identify the originating site on outgoing articles.
sys	For most installations, modify the ME line to contain all/all. The sys file is discussed in more detail in the section "The sys File" later in this chapter.
whoami	This file is your machine's name in UUCP format (such as tpci).

C News Directories

After you have made these configuration changes, you should check that the necessary C News directories exist, or create them if they do not. The in.coming and out.going directories should exist below the spool directory, which may be /usr/spool or /var/spool depending on your directory structure. To create these two directories, issue the command (assuming /usr/spool is the spool directory):

```
mkdir /usr/spool/news/in.coming /usr/spool/news/out.going
```

If the /usr/spool/news directory doesn't already exist when you issue these commands, you may have to create it first. More recent versions of C News also require a directory called /usr/spool/news/out.master (or the /var equivalent). You don't need to create separate spool directories for each of the newsgroups you intend to receive because C News will create directories when necessary.

Once these directories have been created, or you have checked for their existence, you should also check their ownerships. For security reasons, the directories should all be owned by the user news in the group news. The file permissions should be set to mode 755. You can set the ownerships and permissions with the commands:

```
cd /usr/spool
chown -R news.news news
chmod -R 755 news
```

40

C News

These commands assume that your versions of chown and chmod accept the recursive -R option (which most Linux versions do). If not, issue the chown and chmod commands for each directory mentioned above.

THE SYS FILE

As mentioned earlier, the /usr/lib/news/sys file is one of the configuration files that needs to be tailored for your system. Because the sys file has several important aspects, this section looks at the file in more detail. The sys file controls the hierarchies of newsgroups that are downloaded to your site and forwarded on to other sites, depending on the configuration.

The sys file is composed of a set of entries for each site that you forward news to. It also lists the newsgroups that you will accept from other sites. The sys file uses a particular format for each entry, which follows this general syntax:

```
site/exclusions:groups/distribution_list:flags:cmds
```

All of the parameters of the entry are optional except the sitename, although the colons must be left in place. The parameters have the following meaning:

- ◆ The site parameter is the name of the site the entry refers to (usually its UUCP name). You need an entry for each remote site you connect to, as well as for your site (designated by the special sitename ME).

- ◆ The exclusions parameter defines newsgroups that are not returned to the remote site (because you probably downloaded them from that site). This field is optional. If you are a leaf site (only downloading and uploading to a news server), this entry can be all.

- ◆ The groups parameter is a list of newsgroups and hierarchies that are downloaded or uploaded. Multiple entries are separated by commas.

- ◆ The distribution_list parameter specifies newsgroups to be forwarded. This optional addendum to the groups entry is set apart with a slash. You can use this field to prevent some newsgroups from being sent on to another site.

- ◆ The flags parameter sets optional flags to control transfer parameters. Valid values of the flags are listed later in this section.

- ◆ The cmds parameter is a command to be executed for each article if batching is not enabled with a flag or command line parameter. See later in this section for a description of the use of this field.

When specifying remote machine names in the site field of a sys entry, make sure you account for possible variations in the Path header of articles. This usually means providing both the UUCP and full domain name formats for the site, as well as any aliases that may be used. Separate multiple entries in the site specification with a slash. For example, your entry for a machine called brutus may look like this:

```
brutus/brutus.bignet.com
```

The sys file entry for your own machine is important. Any newsgroups next to the ME name are handled as newsgroups you specifically want to keep track of, while all others are sent to the junk newsgroup.

You have to add a line for each site that connects to your machine for its newsfeed (if there are any). If you are at the end of a newsfeed, you can enter the name of your newsfeed (as all locally generated articles are sent back to that machine only).

The newsgroups that are to be transferred to and from the remote site are specified in the groups field. You can set this to transfer several specific newsgroups by separating them with commas. For example, the following entry transfers only the three newsgroups specified:

```
rec.audio.high-end,rec.video.laserdisk,rec.bicyles.tech
```

If you want to transfer all the newsgroups that are available, use the keyword all.

To specify a specific hierarchy to be transferred in the group field, use the prefix that you want followed by the keyword all (such as rec.audio.all to transfer all newsgroups starting with rec.audio).

To prevent a hierarchy from being transferred, precede the name with an exclamation mark. For example, !sci.biology rejects any newsgroups with the sci.biology prefix. You can use the formats interchangeably in the list, such as this entry:

```
!rec.audio,rec.audio.high-end,!sci,sci.biology.all,comp.os.all
```

This entry does not transfer any newsgroups starting with rec.audio except rec.audio.high-end. It also prevents all sci. newsgroups except those starting with sci.biology. In addition, all comp.os newsgroups are transferred.

You can use this field as a handy filter to suppress major hierarchies. For example, if you want to accept or transfer all newsgroups except those starting with alt (which can be the most amusing and controversial newsgroups on USENET), you would enter the following in the field:

```
all,!alt
```

This field is often used by sites to suppress not only the alt groups, but also all sex-oriented groups.

If you are forwarding newsgroups on to other machines, you can specify the newsgroups that are to be sent with the optional distribution list entry, which is separated from the groups list by a slash. Again, this is a command-separated list

40

that uses the same format as the groups field. For example, this entry forwards all newsgroups to the remote machine except those starting with alt and those starting with tpci (which are local newsgroups specific to the tpci network):

```
all,!alt,!tpci
```

The flags that are allowed in the flag field of the sys file can be any combination of the following (or none at all):

F   Enables batching

f   Enables batching (functions almost the same as the F flag)

I   Forces C News to produce an article list for use by ihave/sendme

L   Transmits only articles posted in your machine (or when followed by a number, limits transfers to articles posted within that number of hops of your machine, based on the Path field in the article header)

m   Batches only articles from moderated newsgroups

n   Creates batch files for NNTP transfer clients

u   Batches only articles from unmoderated newsgroups

The flags F, f, I, and n are mutually exclusive, meaning that you can only use one of them in a single entry.

The cmds field is usually used to force the transfer of the article to other machines in the news chain. The default value (if none other is specified) on non-batching news systems is as follows:

```
uux - -r -z remote_name!rnews
```

In this example, remote_name is the name of the machine the article is to be transferred to. The article is fed to rnews through standard input by this command. Several alternate commands are supplied with some C News versions in the directory /usr/lib/news/bin/batch, mostly starting with the filename via.

If batching is enabled (the flags field has one of F, f, I, or n), this field should specify a filename. The default value if none is specified is /usr/spool/news/out.going/ remote_name/togo where remote_name is the name of the remote system. Any entry in this field that does not start with a slash is assumed to be relative to the directory /usr/spool/news/out.going (or the /var equivalent, depending on the Linux directory structure).

A few simple examples of sys files show their usage. If your machine is downloading only from a newssite, and uploading only articles generated at your site (you are a leaf node), then your sys file needs entries only for your machine and the news feed. For example, the following sys file sets up your site to receive all newsgroups from brutus and to send back to brutus all the newsgroups you get and new articles you generate:

```
# our site, accepting all newsgroups
ME:all/all::
# newsfeed machine called brutus
brutus/brutus.com:all/all::
```

This configuration does not impose batching, so connections are performed as required.

Suppose you have another machine on your news route to which you send the sci.biology newsgroups, using a batch routine. If the remote machine's name is chatton, you may have an entry like this in the sys file:

```
# send chatton the sci.biology groups by batch
chatton:sci.biology/all:f:
```

Depending on how many machines you connect to, you may have many suc entries in your sys file.

IMPLEMENTING BATCHING

If you want to use batching on your news system, you have to make some more changes to configuration files other than the batch indicators in the sys file. Each article in a news batch has a line that identifies the size of the file, such as:

```
#! rnews 3634
```

When compression is used, another line precedes this line to reflect the type of compression used to extract the article. The two schemes most often found use the UNIX compress utility and the GNU gzip utility (which is not supported by most versions of C News). The header lines look like this for each, respectively:

```
#!cunbatch
#!zunbatch
```

Occasionally an article has a heading like the following to indicate that the batch uses c7 encoding, which removes the eighth bit from data:

```
#!c7unbatch
```

C News processes batches by executing the program /usr/lib/news/bin/batch/ sendbatches. This uses the list of articles that are to be sent from /usr/lib/news/site/ togo and packages them into one or more newsbatches. The size of the batches is determined by a variable in the file /usr/lib/news/batchparms. This file also gives the compression program to be used if the default is not desired, as well as the type of transport to use to connect to the remote site.

The format of each line in the batchparms file is as follows:

```
sitename size max batch_program muncher transport
```

In this format, sitename is the name of the remote site, size is the maximum size of a batch before compression (except when a single article is larger, in which case the article is processed as a batch by itself), and max is the maximum number of batches to be stored before this site is ignored (to prevent batches accumulating when a remote site doesn't connect). Also, batch_program is the command used for generating the batches (usually the default value of batcher is best), muncher is the compression system (the default value of compcun uses compress), and transport is the connection method (for UUCP it is often viauux). A sample entry in the batchparms file looks like this:

```
brutus   10000   20   batcher   compcun   viauux
```

You can have a default value for all sites except those specifically mentioned by embedding the word default in slashes:

```
/default/   100000   20   batcher   compcun   viauux
```

This default line should come before the other site lines. Substitute whatever values you want for the sizes.

Usually, C News should use crontab to start the batch file transfers at regular intervals (depending on the frequency of posting to the newsgroups). You can instruct C News to process a batch at any time with the command:

```
news /usr/lib/news/bin/batch/sendbatches sitename
```

In this command, sitename is the name of the remote site you want to connect to. If you don't specify a remote site name, all sites are processed. Issue this command as root, or use su with the command.

FINAL STEPS

Once all you have dealt with these configuration issues, you are ready to receive news. You should have your system poll your news site and wait for the results. The most common problem that occurs is a mistake in the configuration file information, which can usually be spotted by verifying each file in turn.

By default, C News sends error messages to the user "usenet," which may or may not exist on your system. It is useful to create an alias in the mail system that redirects C News error messages to a real system administrator's mailbox when a problem occurs. (An alternative to setting up a mail alias is to modify the C News; NEWSMASTER variable, but this must be done with every new session. The alias route is much easier.)

If a newsreader doesn't find any articles after you know a download has taken place, chances are that the newsreader is following the wrong path. Linux systems use /var/spool/news and /usr/spool/news, so your newsreader may be looking in the wrong place. Establish a symbolic link between the two directories with the following command:

```
ln -s /usr/spool/news /var/spool/news
```

See whether that corrects the problem.

The newsgroups' spool directories tend to get very large, especially newsgroups that appear even though you have not explicitly subscribed to them, as well as the junk newsgroup (or equivalent). On a regular basis, you should go into the spool directories and clean out unwanted newsgroup entries. You can erase the entire directory and contents with the -r option to rm (although you should be careful of this rather dangerous command!).

C NEWS UTILITIES

The C News system as found on most Linux distributions has a number of utility programs stored in the directory /usr/lib/news/bin/maint. The superuser can use these programs to control the behavior of the C News system. Some of these utilities and the files they operate on have already been mentioned. The usual utilities found with C News are the following:

◆ The addgroup utility adds a newsgroup to the active file and uses the same format. For example, to add a new group called local.stuff that all users can read, issue the following command:

```
addgroup local.stuff y
```

◆ The delgroup utility deletes a newsgroup from the active file. Issue the command followed by the newsgroup name.

◆ The newsboot utility removes lock files created by improperly terminated news programs.

◆ Run the newsdaily utility to to clean up logs, check expiries and batches, and so on. Any generated messages are mailed to the newsmaster.

◆ The newsrunning utility takes either on or off as an argument and controls the unbatching of incoming newsaccordingly.

◆ The newswatch utility checks the news files for inconsistencies and errors. Generated messages are mailed to the newsmaster.

Most of the utilities are for use occasionally, except the newsdaily, which you can place in a crontab file. For extra safety regarding the news files, add the newswatch program to the crontab file , too.

SUMMARY

This chapter has shown you how to get C News up and running for most installations. You should be able to use this information to start sending and receiving newsgroups from your newsfeed. This chapter didn't look at all the special files involved with C News in detail because most are seldom used. If you want more information on C News, check the documentation and help files that accompany most distributions.

- Configuring `trn`

- Configuring `tin`

CHAPTER 41

Configuring trn and tin

A newsreader is a user interface to the newsgroups stored by a news download program such as NNTP or C News. Newsreaders let users read, print, save, and perform many other actions on newsgroups, including replying to an article. At the newsgroup level, newsreaders let users examine newsgroup lists and subjects, subscribe or unsubscribe to newsgroups, and generally manage their news access.

Newsreaders vary considerably from the simple to the very complex, from character-based to graphic, and from useful to atrocious. Many newsreaders are currently available with Linux distributions, and more newsreaders are appearing as programmers convert their favorite UNIX- or DOS-based newsreaders to work under Linux.

Although this chapter can't look at every newsreader currently available, it can show you the basic configuration requirements for the most commonly used newsreaders. This information, coupled with the documentation that accompanies new newsreaders, should help you set up your Linux system for optimum behavior of the news system. Because most Linux systems are supplied with trn and tin (both threaded newsreaders), they are the primary packages that this short chapter examines.

CONFIGURING *TRN*

The trn newsreader is widely used by UNIX users. It is based on the classic newsreader rn (read news). The primary advantage to trn over rn is its capability to follow threads (articles that are related by subject). Most systems can run trn without any modifications to the files, unless they want to use threads.

To enable threads to be followed, trn needs to be able to construct a thread database that shows the interrelationships between articles. The trn newsreader relies on a program called mthreads (usually stored as /usr/local/bin/rn/mthreads) to help it create this database. The mthreads utility is best run in a crontab file at regular intervals (usually as often as you download full newsfeeds)., You can use trn without mthreads, but you cannot then follow threads.

Without any arguments, mthreads generates index files for the thread databases only for newly arriving articles in all newsgroups. To index all the newsgroups from scratch, issue the command:

```
mthreads all
```

This command examines the /usr/lib/news/active file and reindexes every newsgroup in that file.

If you want to index only a few newsgroups, you can supply the newsgroup names as arguments either in the crontab file or at the shell prompt. For example, the command

```
mthreads rec.auto.antique
```

reindexes the rec.auto.antique thread database. You can reindex more than one newsgroup at a time by separating the names with a comma. You can also force entire hierarchies to be reindexed by specifying only the hierarchical name. For example, the command

```
mthreads alt
```

reindexes all the alt newsgroups. To exclude certain newsgroups, preface them with an exclamation mark. For example, this command:

```
mthreads rec.auto,rec.audio,!rec.audio.tech
```

reindexes all the rec.auto newsgroups, as well as all the rec.audio newsgroups except rec.audio.tech.

If your site has very heavy news traffic, you can run mthreads in daemon mode. In daemon mode, mthreads doesn't have to be started at regular intervals and immediately processes arriving articles. However, it does take system resources away. To set mthreads in daemon mode, use the -d option. By default, mthreads checks the newsgroups every 10 minutes. You can place this command in the rc startup files, if you want.

CONFIGURING *TIN*

Unlike trn, the tin newsreader doesn't need to be told to reindex the thread databases at intervals. The tin newsreader generates the thread indexes every time a user enters a newsgroup. The reindexing is quite fast, unless the newsgroup has more than 500 articles or so.

When tin reindexes a newsgroup, it stores the index file under the user's home directory as .tin/index/newsgroup_name. The total size of all these index files can become quite large if a user reads a lot of newsgroups or if there are many users on the system. The easy way to prevent the growth of index files is to force tin to keep a single master index in one location that all users can access. To set up a single index, set the owner of tin to news with the following command (when you are in the tin directory, of course):

```
chown news.news tin
```

This way, `tin` stores the index files under /usr/spool/news/.index (or /var/spool/news/.index).

You can install a daemon called `tind` that keeps the index files constantly updated. Some versions of Linux supply the `tind` daemon source code, but few have a compiled version. You need a compiler and the `make` utility to build a version for your system.

SUMMARY

Most newer newsreaders have simple configuration requirements that are explained in accompanying README files, although not all distributions of Linux offer any other newsreaders than `tin` and `trn`. A few add `nn`, which is also a threaded newsreader. X-based newsreaders vary in their quality and requirements, although a few distributions are offering a version of `xrn` (an X-based `tn` newsreader). For the most part, newsreaders require little interaction from a system administrator other than watching for excessive bloat in log files.

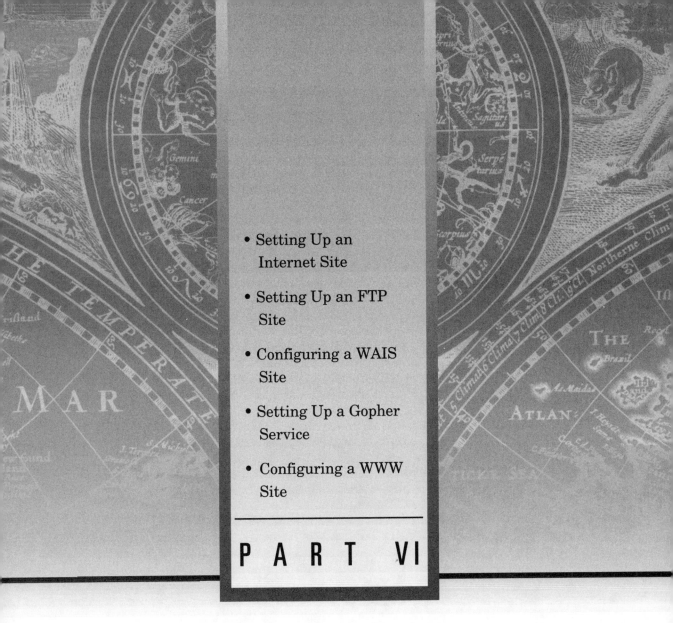

- Setting Up an Internet Site

- Setting Up an FTP Site

- Configuring a WAIS Site

- Setting Up a Gopher Service

- Configuring a WWW Site

PART VI

The Internet

- Choosing a
  Connection Method

- Deciding What
  Services You Need

- Directly Connecting
  through a Gateway

- Connecting through
  Another Gateway

- Using a Service
  Provider

CHAPTER 42

Setting Up an
Internet Site

Linux is well suited for connecting to the Internet and using many of the Internet services. Earlier chapters looked at e-mail and USENET news; this chapter focuses on setting up your Linux machine as a server for FTP, Gopher, WAIS, and the World Wide Web. This chapter looks at the ways you can connect to the Internet. The following chapters then show you how to set up your Linux system as a server for four popular services.

If you only want to use your Linux system to access other servers, you don't have to worry about any of the material in the next four chapters (although you might want to read this chapter to find out how to connect to the Internet). On the other hand, sharing your system's resources with others, whether in a local area network, a small circle of friends, or the worldwide Internet community can be most of the fun.

If your Linux system is to offer services such as FTP, WWW, or Gopher to your local area network or to friends connecting by modem, but you don't want to provide Internet-wide access, you don't need to worry about connecting to the Internet. You still have to set up the server software, though.

CHOOSING A CONNECTION METHOD

There are many different ways to connect to the Internet. Your choice of method depends primarily on your usage habits and the services you want access to. Although it may seem as though there is an overwhelming number of companies offering Internet access or services, there are really only four ways to connect to the Internet:

◆ **A direct connection to the Internet**   This method uses a dedicated machine (a gateway) to connect into the Internet backbone. This method gives you full access to all services, but it is expensive to set up and maintain.

◆ **Connecting through someone else's gateway**—This method usually involves getting permission to use someone else's machine for full access to all Internet services.

◆ **Using a direct service provider**   This method uses a specialty company's gateway that your machine can access to provide limited or full access to Internet services. All these companies do is act as a gateway to the Internet; they are not the same as on-line services. Usually, this type of service provider uses modem or dedicated telephone connections with high-speed lines to provide fast service.

◆ **Using an indirect service provider**   This method involves using an on-line company (such as Delphi or CompuServe) to access some or all of the Internet's services. This method is usually suitable only for low-volume usage and doesn't take advantage of Linux at all.

It is rare to find a gateway that you can borrow for access of your own, unless you are willing to share the costs of the gateway. Most companies that have a gateway are reluctant to allow outsiders to use their system.

If you are part of a company or sharing the costs with a number of friends, on-line service providers seldom are able to offer the level of performance you need for support of e-mail, FTP, and other Internet services. In addition, most on-line services do not allow you to have your own domain name.

That leaves only a direct gateway to the Internet of your own or the use of a service provider. The choice between these two options usually comes down to an issue of the costs to connect both ways. Setting up your own gateway is expensive, but it may be cheaper than arranging accounts with a service provider if the volume of traffic is high. If you just want access for yourself or for a very small company, having your own dedicated gateway is probably too expensive. Setting up an account with a service provider is possible for individuals, but sometimes the costs and machine overhead are too high. Service providers are typically used by small companies, but you may want to use a service provider if you anticipate a high Internet usage.

DECIDING WHAT SERVICES YOU NEED

When deciding which method to use to access the Internet, one of the important items to consider is the type of services you want from the Internet. If all you need is e-mail, any kind of access will provide it, but some may be ridiculously expensive for what you get. As a starting point, decide which of the following services are necessary and which are less important:

e-mail	Sending mail to and from other Internet users
Telnet	Remote logins to other machines on the Internet
FTP	File transfers between machines
World Wide Web (WWW) access	A graphic information service
USENET newsgroups	A set of bulletin boards for conversations on many different subjects
Gopher	An information search and retrieval system
WAIS	A graphic document search and retrieval system
Archie	A method for finding files to transfer
Internet Relay Chat (IRC)	A conversation system much like a CB

Any system that is directly connected to the Internet through a gateway (yours, a borrowed gateway, or most direct service providers) provides complete access to all the services listed. Some direct service providers support all the services but at a slower speed than a gateway. Slower speeds may be a limitation for World Wide Web, which is heavily dependent on graphics. Some service providers limit their access to e-mail and newsgroups, so a little research is necessary.

DIRECTLY CONNECTING THROUGH A GATEWAY

A direct connection, often called a dedicated connection, is one in which you attach into the Internet backbone through a dedicated machine called a gateway or IP router. The connection is over a dedicated telephone line capable of high-speed transfers (usually at 1.44mbps or faster, although ISDN lines at 65kbps are also available). The gateway becomes part of the Internet architecture and must remain on-line at all times. You can then use any other computer on the gateway's network to access the Internet services.

Typically, dedicated connections mean high volumes of traffic and require systems with an absolute minimum line speed of 9,600 baud, although high-speed fiber-optic lines with speed capabilities of 45mbps are not unusual. An individual or small company is unlikely to have direct gateway access, primarily because of the high cost of installation and maintenance requirements.

To create a direct access system, you must work with the Internet Network Information Center (NIC) to set up the proper gateways on the Internet backbone for your domain. The capital expense of such a system is high, both for the initial hardware and software and for continuing support. High costs may also be involved with a dedicated telephone line capable of supporting high-speed data transfer.

CONNECTING THROUGH ANOTHER GATEWAY

An alternative method of connecting to the Internet through a gateway relies on using a friendly machine or network. In such a system, a corporation or educational institution that has an Internet gateway may allow you to access the Internet through their system. Because this type of access gives you freedom on their networks, many organizations now refuse this type of piggy-back access.

If you are lucky enough to find a company or school that will let you use their network, you simply call into a communications port on the network or gateway, and then route through the gateway to the Internet. In many ways, it is as though you are a machine on the provider's network. Typically, you have unlimited access to the Internet's services, although some companies do set restrictions.

USING A SERVICE PROVIDER

Service providers are companies that have an Internet gateway that they share, although the gateway is often transparent to the users. This type of connection is often called dialup and uses SLIP (serial line interface protocol) or PPP (point-to-point protocol). Some service providers offer UUCP connections for e-mail. Service providers usually offer dedicated connection lines to their Internet gateways, although the dedicated lines can be expensive.

Service providers usually charge a flat fee for membership with an additional charge based on the amount of time or the number of characters transferred. Joining one of these services is quite easy, although some insist that you maintain a minimum amount of usage a month. You can register domain names through many service providers, too, which enables you to use your own domain even though you use a provider.

The primary advantage of direct service providers is that you are effectively directly connected to the Internet. The communication between your machine and the service provider's gateway is hidden inside your operating system's setup. A disadvantage to this method is that you cannot always arrange full access to the Internet. Some services do not allow you to FTP through their gateway to another Internet site, for example.

If you are considering using a direct service provider, ask the providers in your area about the services they offer, whether special hardware or software is needed, what the fees are and whether they are based on a flat monthly rate or based on usage, and the kind of technical support available in case you have trouble.

An alternative to using a commercial service provider is to rely on one of the command-line access systems that are springing up in major cities. Such systems provide Internet access through their own gateways as a free service (subsidized by a corporation or government) or at a minimal cost. One popular access provider of this type is FreeNet, an international organization that gives users a unique username through the FreeNet domain. FreeNet is currently only available in some cities, but it does provide an extremely inexpensive and easy access method to the Internet. All you need is an account (which is usually just a telephone call away), a modem, and communications software.

SUMMARY

Choosing the method with which you connect to the Internet is up to you, but most individuals find a direct service provider the best balance between cost and features. Once you have a connection to the Internet, you can set up your server, as explained in the next four chapters.

- What Is FTP?

- Using FTP

- Configuring FTP

- Securing FTP

CHAPTER 43

Setting Up an FTP Site

What is the most widely used TCP/IP and Internet service? If you answered FTP, you're right. (If you didn't choose FTP, this answer may come as a bit of a surprise, but FTP remains the most widely used service, although the World Wide Web is quickly catching up.) FTP's popularity is easy to understand. The FTP software is supplied with every version of UNIX and Linux; it's easy to install, configure, and use; and it gives users access to a wealth of information with very little effort.

Earlier chapters of this book have mentioned FTP, and most user-oriented books deal with using FTP in some detail. If all you want to use FTP for is connecting to another machine and transferring files, then you don't have to do much more than enable the FTP service on your system. Much more interesting to many is turning your Linux machine into an FTP site, where others can call in and obtain files you make available. That's the primary focus of this chapter: setting up an FTP site on your Linux machine. The chapter begins, though, with a quick look at using FTP and the way FTP runs on TCP. This information should help you understand how FTP works and what it does with TCP/IP.

WHAT IS FTP?

The File Transfer Protocol (FTP) is one protocol in the TCP/IP family used to transfer files between machines running TCP/IP (FTP-like programs are also available for some other protocols). The File Transfer Protocol enables you to transfer files back and forth and manage directories. FTP is not designed to give you access to another machine to execute programs, but it is the best utility for file manipulation. To use FTP, both ends of a connection must be running a program that provides FTP services. The end that starts the connection (the client) calls the other end (the server) and establishes the FTP protocol through a set of handshaking instructions.

Usually, when you connect to a remote system via FTP, you must log in. In order to log in, you must be a valid user with a username and password for that remote machine. Because it is impossible to provide logins for everyone who wants to access a machine that allows anyone to gain access, many systems use anonymous FTP instead. Anonymous FTP allows anyone to log in to the system with the login name of ftp, guest, or anonymous and either no password or a login name for their local system.

USING FTP

Using FTP to connect to a remote site is easy. You have access to the remote machine either through the Internet (directly or through a service provider) or through a wide or local area network if the remote machine is directly reachable. To use FTP, you start the FTP client software and provide the name of the remote system to which you want to connect. For example, assuming you can get to the remote machine through a LAN or the Internet (which knows about the remote machine thanks to DNS), you issue the following command:

```
ftp chatton.com
```

This command instructs your FTP software to try to connect to the remote machine `chatton.com` and establish an FTP session.

When the connection is completed (and assuming that the remote system allows FTP logins), the remote prompts for a userID. If anonymous FTP is supported on the system, a message usually tells you exactly that. The login following is shown for the Linux FTP archive site sunsite.unc.edu:

```
ftp sunsite.unc.edu
331 Guest login ok, send your complete e-mail address as password.
Enter username (default: anonymous): anonymous
Enter password [tparker@tpci.com]:
¦FTP¦ Open
230-                WELCOME to UNC and SUN's anonymous ftp server
230-                       University of North Carolina
230-                     Office FOR Information Technology
230-                           SunSITE.unc.edu
230 Guest login ok, access restrictions apply.
FTP>
```

After the login process is completed, you see the prompt `FTP>` indicating that the remote system is ready to accept commands.

When you log on to some systems, you may see a short message that may contain instructions for downloading files, any restrictions that are placed on you as an anonymous FTP user, or information about the location of useful files. For example, you may see messages like the following (taken from the Linux FTP site):

```
To get a binary file, type:  BINARY and then: GET "File.Name" newfilename
To get a text file, type:    ASCII  and then: GET "File.Name" newfilename
Names MUST match upper, lower case exactly. Use the "quotes" as shown.
To get a directory, type: DIR. To change directory, type: CD "Dir.Name"
To read a short text file, type: GET "File.Name" TT
For more, type HELP or see FAQ in gopher.
To quit, type EXIT or Control-Z.

230-  If you email to info@sunsite.unc.edu you will be sent help information
230-  about how to use the different services sunsite provides.
230-  We use the Wuarchive experimental ftpd. if you "get" <directory>.tar.Z
230-  or <file>.Z it will compress and/or tar it on the fly. Using ".gz"  instead
230-  of ".Z" will use the GNU zip (/pub/gnu/gzip*) instead, a superior
230-  compression method.
```

Once you are on the remote system, you can use familiar Linux commands to display file contents and move around directories. To display the contents of a directory, for example, use the command `ls` (some systems support the DOS equivalent `DIR`). To

43

change to a subdirectory, use the `cd` command. To return to the parent directory (the one above the current directory), use the command `cd ..`. As you can see, these commands are the same ones you would use on your local machine, except that you are now navigating on the remote system. To change directories on your local machine, you can use the `lcd` command.

> **Note**
>
> FTP has no keyboard shortcuts (such as pressing the Tab key to fill in names that match). You have to type in the name of files or directories in their entirety (and do so correctly). If you misspell a file or directory name, you will get error messages and have to try again. If you are performing the FTP session through an X window, you can cut and paste lines from earlier in your session. Users of `gpm` can cut and paste from character-based screens.

TRANSFERRING FILES

Transferring files is the whole point of FTP, so you need to know how to retrieve a file from the remote system, as well as how to put a new file there. When you have moved through the remote system's directories and found a file you want to move back to your local system, use the `get` command. Place the filename after the command, for example:

```
get "soundcard_driver"
```

This command transfers the file `soundcard_driver` from the remote machine to the current directory on your local machine. When you issue a `get` command, the remote system transfers data to your local machine and displays a status message when it is completed. There is no indication of progress when a large file is being transferred, so be patient. Many versions of FTP support a command called `hash` that displays a pound sign after every 1024 bytes has been transferred. This command gives you a visual indication of the progress of the transfer.

```
FTP> get "file1.txt"
200 PORT command successful.
150 BINARY data connection for FILE1.TXT (27534 bytes)
226 BINARY Transfer complete.
27534 bytes received in 2.35 seconds (12 Kbytes/s).
```

If you want to transfer a file the other way (from your machine to the remote, assuming you are allowed to write to the remote machine's filesystem), use the `put` command in the same way. The following command transfers the file comments from your current directory on the local machine (you can specify full pathnames) to the current directory on the remote machine (unless you change the path).

```
put "comments"
```

The commands get (download) and put (upload) are always relative to your home machine. You are telling your system to get a file from the remote and put it on your local machine, or to put a file from your local machine onto the remote machine. (This process is the exact opposite of Telnet, which has everything relative to the remote machine. It is important to remember which command moves in which direction, or you could overwrite files accidentally.)

The quotation marks around the filenames in the preceding examples are optional for most versions of FTP, but they do prevent shell expansion of characters, so they can be recommended. For most files, the quotation marks are not needed, but using them is a good habit to get into.

Some FTP versions provide a wildcard capability using the commands mget and mput. Both the FTP get and put commands usually transfer only one file at a time, which must be specified completely (no wildcards). The mget and mput commands enable you to use wildcards. For example, to transfer all the files with a .doc extension, you could issue the following command:

```
mget *.doc
```

You have to try the mget and mput commands to see if they work on your FTP version. (Some FTP get and put commands allow wildcards, too, so you can try wildcards in a command line to see if they work.)

Different File Formats

FTP allows file transfers in several formats, which are usually system-dependent. The majority of systems (including Linux systems) have only two modes: ASCII and binary. Some mainframe installations add support for EBCDIC, while many sites have a local type that is designed for fast transfers between local network machines (the local type may use 32- or 64-bit words).

The difference between the binary and ASCII modes is simple. Text transfers use ASCII characters separated by carriage return and newline characters. Binary mode allows transfer of characters with no conversion or formatting. Binary mode is faster than text and also allows for the transfer of all ASCII values (necessary for non-text files). FTP cannot transfer file permissions, as these are not specified as part of the protocol.

Linux's FTP provides two modes of file transfer: ASCII and binary. Some systems automatically switch between the two when they recognize that a file is in binary format, but you shouldn't count on the switching unless you've tested it before and know it works. To be certain, it is a good idea to set the mode manually. By default, most FTP versions start up in ASCII mode, although a few start in binary.

To set FTP in binary transfer mode (for any executable file or file with special characters embedded for spreadsheets, word processors, graphics, and so on), type the following command:

```
binary
```

You can toggle back to ASCII mode with the command `ascii`. Because you will most likely be checking remote sites for new binaries or libraries of source code, it is a good idea to use binary mode for most transfers. If you transfer a binary file in ASCII mode, it will not be executable on your system.

ASCII mode includes only the valid ASCII characters and not the Ctrl-key sequences used within binaries. Transferring an ASCII file in binary mode does not affect the contents except in very rare instances. When transferring files between two Linux (or any UNIX) systems, using binary mode will handle all file types properly, but transfers between a Linux and non-UNIX machine can cause problems with some types of files. ASCII mode is only suitable for transferring straight text files.

QUITTING FTP

To quit FTP, type the command `quit` or `exit`. Both will close your session on the remote machine, and then terminate FTP on your local machine. Users have a number of commands available within most versions of FTP, the most frequently used of which are the following:

ascii	Switches to ASCII transfer mode
binary	Switches to binary transfer mode
cd	Changes directory on the server
close	Terminates the connection
del	Deletes a file on the server
dir	Displays the server directory
get	Fetches a file from the server
hash	Displays a pound character for each block transmitted
help	Displays help
lcd	Changes directory on the client
mget	Fetches several files from the server
mput	Sends several files to the server
open	Connects to a server
put	Sends a file to the server
pwd	Displays the current server directory

quote	Supplies an FTP command directly
quit	Terminates the FTP session

For most versions, FTP commands are case-sensitive. If you type commands in uppercase, FTP will display error messages. Some versions perform a translation for you, so it doesn't matter which case you use. Because Linux uses lowercase as its primary character set for everything else, you should probably use lowercase with all versions of FTP, too.

How FTP Uses TCP

The File Transfer Protocol uses two TCP channels: TCP port 20 is used for data, and port 21 is for commands. Both these channels must be enabled on your Linux system for FTP to function. The use of two channels makes FTP different from most other file transfer programs. By using two channels, TCP allows simultaneous transfer of FTP commands and data. FTP works in the foreground and does not use spoolers or queues.

FTP uses a server daemon that runs continuously and a separate program that is executed on the client. On Linux systems, the server daemon is called ftpd. The client program is ftp.

During the establishment of a connection between a client and server, and whenever a user issues a command to FTP, the two machines transfer a series of commands. These commands are exclusive to FTP, and are known as the internal protocol. FTP's internal protocol commands are four-character ASCII sequences terminated by a newline character, some of which require parameters. One primary advantage of using ASCII characters for commands is that users can observe the command flow and understand it easily, which helps in a debugging process. Also, a knowledgeable user can use the ASCII commands directly to communicate with the FTP server component without invoking the client portion (in other words, communicating with ftpd without using ftp on a local machine). This procedure is seldom done, however, except when debugging (or showing off).

After logging in to a remote machine using FTP, you are not actually on the remote machine. You are still logically on the client, so all instructions for file transfers and directory movement must be with respect to your local machine and not the remote one. The process followed by FTP when a connection is established is as follows:

1. **Log in.** This step verifies user ID and password.
2. **Define directory.** This step identifies the starting directory.
3. **Define file transfer mode.** This step defines the type of transfer.
4. **Start data transfer.** User commands are followed.
5. **Stop data transfer.** This step closes the connection.

43

A debugging option is available from the FTP command line by adding -d to the command. This option displays the command channel instructions. Instructions from the client are shown with an arrow as the first character; instructions from the server have three digits in front of them. A PORT in the command line indicates the address of the data channel on which the client is waiting for the server's reply. If no PORT is specified, channel 20 (the default value) is used. Unfortunately, the progress of data transfers cannot be followed in the debugging mode. The following is a sample session with the debug option enabled:

```
$ ftp -d tpci_hpws4
Connected to tpci_hpws4.
220 tpci_hpws4 FTP server (Version 1.7.109.2 Tue Jul 28 23:32:34 GMT 1992) ready.
Name (tpci_hpws4:tparker):
---> USER tparker
331 Password required for tparker.
Password:
---> PASS qwerty5
230 User tparker logged in.
---> SYST
215 UNIX Type: L8
Remote system type is UNIX.
---> Type I
200 Type set to I.
Using binary mode to transfer files.
ftp> ls
---> PORT 47,80,10,28,4,175
200 PORT command successful.
---> TYPE A
200 Type set to A.
---> LIST
150 Opening ASCII mode data connection for /bin/ls.
total 4
-rw-r-----  1 tparker   tpci    2803  Apr 29 10:46 file1
-rw-rw-r--  1 tparker   tpci    1286  Apr 14 10:46 file5_draft
-rwxr-----  2 tparker   tpci   15635  Mar 14 23:23 test_comp_1
-rw-r-----  1 tparker   tpci      52  Apr 22 12:19 xyzzy
Transfer complete.
---> TYPE I
200 Type set to I.
ftp> <Ctrl-d>
$
```

You may have noticed in the preceding code how the mode changed from binary to ASCII to send the directory listing, and then back to binary (the system default value).

CONFIGURING FTP

Whether you decide to provide an anonymous FTP site or a user-login FTP system, you need to perform some basic configuration steps to get the FTP daemon active and get the directory system and file permissions properly set to prevent users from destroying files or accessing files they shouldn't. The process can start with choosing an FTP site name. You don't really need a site name, although it can be easier for others to access your machine (especially anonymously) if you have one. The FTP site name is in the following format:

```
ftp.domain_name.domain_type
```

In this syntax, domain_name is the domain name (or an alias) of the FTP server's domain, and domain_type is the usual DNS extension. For example, you could have an FTP site name like the following example:

```
ftp.tpci.com
```

This name shows that this is the anonymous FTP access for anyone accessing the tpci.com domain. It is usually a bad idea to name your FTP site with a specific machine name, such as the following:

```
ftp.merlin.tpci.com
```

This name makes it difficult to move the FTP server to another machine in the future. Instead, use an alias to point to the actual machine on which the FTP server sits. This is not a problem if you are a single machine connected to the Internet through a service provider, for example, but is often necessary with a larger network. The alias is easy to set up if you use DNS. Set the alias in the DNS databases with a line like the following:

```
ftp.tpci.com.    IN    CNAME    merlin.tpci.com.
```

This line points anyone accessing the machine ftp.tpci.com to the real machine merlin.tpci.com. If the machine merlin has to be taken out of its FTP server role for any reason, a change in the machine name on this line points the ftp.tpci.com access to the new server. (A change in the alias performed over DNS can take a while to become active, as the change must be propagated through all the DNS databases.) The period following the domain name is very important because it prevents expansion of the name to include the domain again (which would result in merlin.tpci.com.tpci.com).

SETTING UP FTPD

The FTP daemon, ftpd, must be started on the FTP server (some Linux versions use the daemon wu.ftpd as the server). The daemon is usually handled by inetd instead of the rc startup files, so ftpd is only active when someone needs it. This approach is best for all but the most heavily laden FTP sites. When ftpd is started using inetd, the inetd daemon watches the TCP command port (channel 21) for an arriving data packet requesting a connection, and then spawns ftpd.

Make sure that inetd can start the ftpd daemon by checking the inetd configuration file (usually /etc/inetd.config) for a line that looks like the following:

```
ftp    stream   tcp    nowait    root    /usr/etc/ftpd    ftpd -1
```

If the line doesn't exist, add it to the file. With most Linux systems, the line is already in the file although it may be commented out. Remove the comment symbol if this is the case. The FTP entry essentially specifies to inetd that FTP is to use TCP and that it should spawn ftpd every time a new connection is made to the FTP port. In the preceding example, the ftpd daemon is started with the -1 option, which enables logging. You can ignore this option if you want.

There are several ftpd daemon options that you can add to the /etc/inetd.config line to control ftpd's behavior. The most commonly used options are as follows:

-d   This option adds debugging information to the syslog.

-1   This option activates logging of sessions (only failed and successful logins, not debug information). If the -1 option is specified twice, all commands are logged, too. If specified three times, the size of all get and put file transfers are added, as well.

-t   This option sets the timeout period before ftpd terminates after a session is concluded (default is 15 minutes). The value is specified in seconds after the -t option.

-T   This option sets the maximum timeout period (in seconds) that a client can request. The default is two hours. This enables a client to alter the normal default timeout for some reason.

-u   This option sets the umask value for files uploaded to the local system. The default umask is 022. Clients can request a different umask value.

FTP LOGINS

If you are going to set up a user-based FTP service, where each person accessing your system has a valid login name and password, then you must create an account for each user in the /etc/passwd file. If you are not allowing anonymous FTP access, do not create a generic login that anyone can use.

To set up an anonymous FTP server, you must create a login for the anonymous user ID. This is done in the normal process of adding a user to the /etc/passwd file. The login name is whatever you want people to use when they access your system, such as "anonymous" or "ftp." You need to select a login directory for the anonymous users that can be protected from the rest of the filesystem. A typical /etc/passwd entry looks like the following:

```
ftp:*:400:51:Anonymous FTP access:/usr/ftp:/bin/false
```

This entry sets up the anonymous user with a login of ftp. The asterisk password prevents anyone gaining access to the account. The user ID number (400) is, of course, unique to the entire system. For better security, it is a good idea to create a separate group just for the anonymous FTP access (edit the /etc/group file to add a new group), then set the ftp user to that group. Only the anonymous FTP user should belong to that group, as it can be used to set file permissions to restrict access and make your system more secure. The login directory in the example above is /usr/ftp, although you could choose any directory as long as it belongs to the anonymous FTP user (for security reasons, again). The startup program shown in the preceding example is /bin/false, which helps protect your system from access to accounts and utilities that do not have a strong password protection.

SETTING UP THE DIRECTORIES

As you will see in the next section, "Setting Permissions," you can try to make the entire anonymous FTP subdirectory structure a filesystem unto itself, with no allowance for the anonymous user to get anywhere other than /usr/ftp (or whatever directory you use for anonymous access). For this reason, you need to create a mini-filesystem just for the anonymous FTP access, which holds the usual directory names and basic files anyone logging in needs. Part of the procedure is summarized in a checklist at the end of this chapter.

The process for setting up the directories your anonymous FTP login needs is simple, requiring you to create a number of directories and copy files into them. Here are the basic procedures:

♦ Create the bin directory (/usr/ftp/bin, for example) and copy the directory listing commands (ls, l, and so on) that users need to view directory and file details. You can also copy some utilities like more and less, if you want.

♦ Create the etc directory (usr/ftp/etc, for example) and copy your passwd file (/etc/passwd) and group file (/etc/group) into it. You'll edit these files in a moment.

♦ Create the lib directory (/usr/ftp/lib, for example) and copy the files /lib/rld and /lib/libc.so.1 into it. These files are used by ls. Do this step only if your ls command requires these files: not all versions of Linux have this dependency, so check first to prevent unnecessary work.

♦ Create the pub directory (/usr/ftp/pub, for example) to hold your accessible files. You'll look at this directory in more detail in a moment.

♦ Create the dev directory (/usr/ftp/dev, for example) and use the mknod command to copy the /dev/zero file. You need to retain the same major and minor device numbers as the /dev/zero file in /dev. This device driver is used by rld (and hence ls). Do this step only if ls requires the /lib directory files mentioned earlier.

The copies of the /etc/passwd and /etc/group files are copied into the ~ftp/etc directory to bypass the actual files in /etc. Edit these files to remove all passwords and replace them with an asterisk, preventing access to those accounts through anonymous FTP. Remove all entries in both /etc/passwd and /etc/group that are used names or groups (in other words, used by a valid user or group on your system), as well as most other entries except those used by the anonymous FTP login (usually just anonymous and bin).

You can use the ~ftp/pub directory structure to store the files you want to allow anonymous users to access. Copy them into this directory. You can create subdirectories as you need them for organizational purposes. It may be useful to create an upload directory somewhere in the ~ftp/pub directory structure that has write permission, so that users can upload files to you only into this upload area.

SETTING PERMISSIONS

You can use the chroot command to help protect your system. The chroot command makes the root directory appear to be something other than / on a filesystem. For example, when chroot has been set for the anonymous FTP login, any time the anonymous user types a cd command, it can always be relative to their home directory. In other words, when they type cd /bin, they will really be changing to /usr/ftp/bin if the root has been set to /usr/ftp. This helps prevent access to any other areas of the filesystem than the FTP directory structure. The changes are effective only for the user ID the chroot command was run for.

If you do create an upload area, you may want to set the permissions to allow execute and write, but not read (to prevent another user downloading the files someone else has uploaded).

To set the permissions for files and directories used by your anonymous FTP users, follow the following procedure. If the directories or files do not already exist, copy or create them as necessary:

1. Set the ~ftp directory to have root as owner and access permissions of 555.
2. Set the ~ftp/bin directory to have root as owner and access permissions of 555.
3. Set the file ~ftp/bin/ls to have root as owner and access permissions of 111.
4. Set the ~ftp/etc directory to have root as owner and access permissions of 555.
5. Set the ~ftp/etc/passwd and ~ftp/etc/group files to have root as owner and access permissions of 444.
6. If used, set the ~ftp/lib directory to have root as owner and access permissions of 555.

7. If used, set the files ~ftp/lib/rld and ~ftp/lib/libc.so.1 to have root as owner and access permissions of 444.

8. If used, set the ~ftp/dev directory to have root as owner and access permissions of 555.

9. If required, use the `mknod` command to create ~ftp/dev/zero with the same major and minor node numbers as /dev/zero.

In general, you should have your FTP directories set so that all permissions for directories under ~ftp prevent write access by user, group, and other. Make sure the directories and files under ~ftp are set to allow the anonymous login to read them. (The directories need execute permission to allow the anonymous users to enter them and obtain directory listings.) This set of permissions provides pretty good security.

You can set the ownership of files and directories with the `chown` command. This command

```
chown root ~ftp/dev
```

sets the owner of ~ftp/dev to root, for example. All directories in the ~ftp directory structure should have the permissions set with the `chmod` command. This command

```
chmod 555 dir_name
```

sets read-execute permission only for the directory, for example. The exception to this rule is the upload directory, which can have write permission, as noted earlier.

Testing the System

Before you let anyone else onto your Linux FTP system, log in to it yourself and try to access files you shouldn't be able to, try to move into directories that are outside of the ~ftp structure, and try to write files where you shouldn't be able to. This provides a useful test of the permissions and directory structure. Spend an hour or so trying to read, write, copy, and move files, then try some `su` commands to try and log in as someone else (such as root or a valid system user). Make sure your system is buttoned up: if you don't, someone else will find the holes and exploit them.

It is a useful idea to set up a mailbox for the FTP administrator so that users on other systems who need help or information can send mail to you. Create a user and mailbox for a login such as `ftp-admin` and alias the mailbox to yourself or another person (or just log in as ftp-admin occasionally to check the mail).

Because this book covers system administration, it won't go into much detail about how to organize your directory structure, but a few useful tips may help you. To begin, decide what you want to store on your FTP directories and organize the structure logically. For example, if you are making available programs you have written, set up separate directories for each. A README file in each directory will help show browsers what is contained therein. A master README or INSTRUCTIONS file in the ~ftp directory can help explain how your site is set up and its contents (the uppercase letters draw a user's attention to the files immediately).

SECURING FTP

The FTP system discussed earlier, supplied with practically every Linux distribution, requires a bit of work to make it secure. Even then, it is still vulnerable to very experienced hackers. A better alternative is available if you are paranoid about your system's security: WU FTP. Developed at Washington University, WU FTP adds some extra features to the standard FTP system:

◆ Better control of user and group ID

◆ Better tracking of uploads and downloads

◆ Automatic shutdown

◆ Automatic compression and decompression of files

If these features sound useful, you can obtain a copy of the source code of WU FTP from several sites, although the primary site is wuarchive.wustl.edu. Check for the file /packages/wuarchive-ftpd/wu-ftpd-X.X.tar.Z (where X.X is the latest version number). You will get the source code, which needs to be compiled on your Linux system.

WU FTP uses a number of environment variables to control the service, and the accompanying documentation helps you set it up properly. Setting up WU FTP is much more complex than standard FTP, and the extra security, which is useful, may be unnecessary for many FTP site machines you may set up at home or work (unless you have sensitive information).

SUMMARY

The information in this chapter enables you to set your system up as a full anonymous FTP site, or just for users you want to gain access. The process is simple, although you have to take care to ensure that the file permissions are properly set. Once your FTP site is up, you can let others on the Internet or your local area network know you are running, and the type of material you store on your system. Then sit back and share!

CHECKLIST

Protecting an Anonymous FTP System

☐   Create a user account called ftp. Edit the /etc/passwd file manually and replace the password with an asterisk in the second field. This prevents anyone gaining access through the ftp account.

☐   If a home directory wasn't created for the ftp user when you created the account, set up a home directory for the ftp user's sole use (such as /usr/ftp or /u/ftp)

☐   Set the ftp home directory so that the ftp user is the owner:

```
chown ftp /usr/ftp
```

☐   Make the ftp home directory unwritable to anyone with the command:

```
chmod ugo-w /usr/ftp
```

☐   Create a bin directory under the ftp home directory:

```
mkdir ~ftp/bin
```

☐   Make the ~ftp/bin directory owned by root and unwritable to anyone else:

```
chown root ~ftp/bin
chmod ugo-w ~ftp/bin
```

☐   Place a copy of the listing commands (and any others that you want anonymous FTP users to use) in the bin directory:

```
cp /bin/l ~ftp/bin
cp /bin/lc ~ftp/bin
cp /bin/ls ~ftp/bin
```

☐   Create an etc directory under the ftp home directory and make it owned by root and unwritable:

```
mkdir ~ftp/etc
chown root ~ftp/etc
chmod ugo-w ~ftp/etc
```

☐   Copy the /etc/passwd and /etc/group files into the ~ftp/etc directory. Edit both files to remove all user accounts except ftp (and ftp's group). (At the very least, remove all passwords for other accounts by placing asterisks in the password field.)

continues

CHECKLIST
PROTECTING AN ANONYMOUS FTP SYSTEM

☐ Create the directory ~ftp/pub, and make it owned by ftp. Then, make the directory writable by anyone:

```
mkdir ~ftp/pub
chown ftp ~ftp/pub
chmod ugo+w ~ftp/pub
```

☐ Place any files you want accessible by anonymous FTP into the ~ftp/pub directory. Users logging in through anonymous FTP can transfer the files out. Allowing users to write files into the directory may not be desirable, so change the permissions or check the files frequently.

☐ Edit the ftp login's startup file (.profile, .cshrc, or .kshrc as appropriate) to have the path include only the ~/ftp/bin directory and perhaps ~ftp/pub.

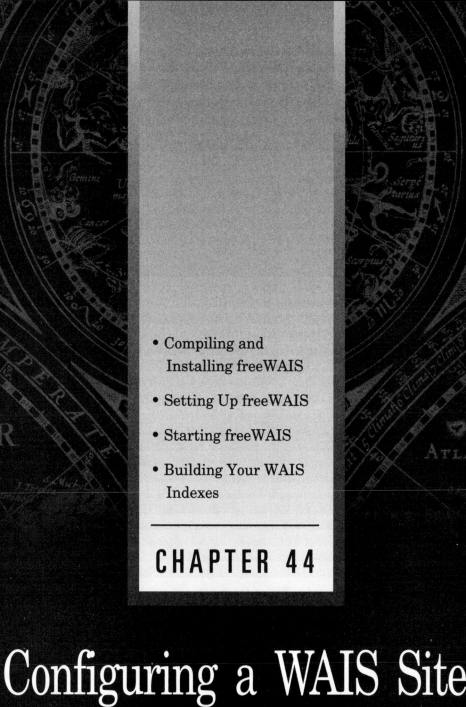

- Compiling and
  Installing freeWAIS

- Setting Up freeWAIS

- Starting freeWAIS

- Building Your WAIS
  Indexes

CHAPTER 44

Configuring a WAIS Site

WAIS (Wide Area Information Service) is a tool that enables users to search for keywords in a database of documents available on your system and show the results. WAIS was developed by Thinking Machines but spun off to a separate company called WAIS Inc. when it became immensely popular. A free version of WAIS was made available to the Clearinghouse for Networking Information Discovery and Retrieval (CNIDR) as freeWAIS, which is the version most often found on Linux systems.

WAIS lets a user enter some keywords or phrases, and then searches a database for those terms. A typical WAIS search screen is shown in Figure 44.1. (This screen is a Windows-based Web browser accessing the primary WAIS server at http://www.wais.com. This server is a good place to look for examples of how you can use WAIS.) This example shows a search for the keyword "hubble" (WAIS usually ignores case). You can enter long and complex or relatively simple search criteria on a WAIS search line. After searching all the database indexes it knows about, WAIS shows its results, as shown in Figure 44.2. This screen shows the search results based on the keywords "hubble" and "magnitude."

Figure 44.1.
A search screen from a
WAIS site.

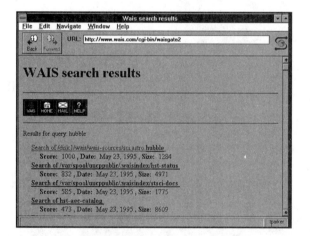

The display generated by WAIS, often displayed in a WWW browser or a WAIS browser as in these figures, gives each match with a score from 0 to 1000 indicating the manner in which the keywords match the index (the higher numbers are better matches). Users can then refine the list, expand it, or examine documents listed. In Figure 44.3, one of the documents listed in the search results is displayed in the WWW browser window. WAIS can handle many file formats, including text and documents, audio, JPEG and GIF files, and binaries.

Figure 44.2.
After a search has been
conducted, WAIS
displays the results
with a score showing
how well each docu-
ment on the system
matches the search
criteria.

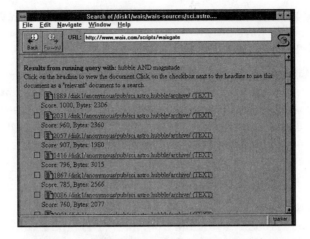

Figure 44.3.
Selecting any entry on
the WAIS search results
screen lets you see the
document, video, or
graphics file, or listen
to audio (assuming
your system can handle
multimedia output).

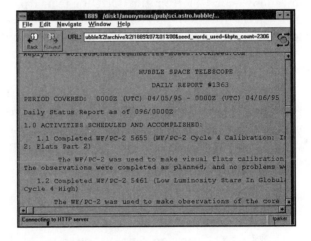

The Linux version of WAIS is called freeWAIS. This chapter looks at how you can
set up a freeWAIS server on your Linux machine. WAIS is a useful tool to provide
if you deal with a considerable amount of information you want to make generally
available. This information could be product information, details about a hobby, or
practically any other type of data. All you have to want to do is make it available to
others, either on your local area network or to the Internet as a whole.

The freeWAIS package has three parts to it: an indexer, a WAIS service, and a client.
The indexer handles database information and generates an index that contains
keywords and a table indicating the word's occurrences. The service component does
the matching between a user's requests and the indexed files. The client is the user's

44

vehicle to access WAIS and is usually a WAIS or WWW browser. WWW browsers usually have an advantage over WAIS browsers in that the latter cannot display HTML documents.

A follow-up backward-compatible WAIS system is currently available in a beta version called ZDIST. ZDIST's behavior will be much like freeWAIS, with any changes noted in the documentation. ZDIST adds some new features and is a little smaller and faster than freeWAIS. Because of the unstable beta nature of ZDIST, this chapter concentrates on freeWAIS.

COMPILING AND INSTALLING FREEWAIS

The freeWAIS software is often included in a complete Linux distribution CD-ROM and is readily available from many FTP and BBS sites. Alternatively, you can get it by anonymous FTP from the CNIDR site as ftp.chidr.org. The freeWAIS system resides in the directory /pub/NDIR.tools/freewais/freeWAIS-X.X.tar.Z where X.X is the latest version number. The CNIDR site has many binaries available for different machines, as well as generic source code that can be tailored to many different systems.

One of the files in the distribution software, which should be placed in the destination directory, is the Makefile used to create the program. If you are compiling the freeWAIS source yourself, examine the Makefile to ensure that the variables are set correctly. Most are fine by default, pointing to standard Linux utilities. The exceptions that you may have to tweak yourself are as follows:

CC	This variable is the name of the C compiler you use (usually cc or gcc).
CURSELIB	This variable should be set to the current version of the curses library on your system.
RESOLVER	Leave this variable blank unless you are using a namespace resolver, in which case set it to -lresolc.
TOP	This variable specifies the full path to the freeWAIS source directory.

The CFLAGS options enable you to specify compiler flags when the freeWAIS source is compiled. Many options are supported, all of which are explained in the documentation files that accompany the source. Most of the flag settings can be left as their default values in Linux systems. A few of the specific flags you may want to alter are worth mentioning, though. The most useful are the indexer flags, of which two are potentially useful:

-DBIO	This flag is used to allow indexing on biological symbols and terms. Use it only if your site will deal with biological documents.
-DBOOLEANS	This flag enables you to use Booleans such as AND and NOT. This flag can be handy for extending the power of searches.

The -DBOOLEANS flag handles logical searches. For example, if you are looking for the keywords green leaf, WAIS by default searches for the words green and leaf separately and judges matches on the two words independently. With the -DBOOLEANS flag set, you can join the two words with AND so that a match has to be with green leaf.

A couple of other flags that may be useful for freeWAIS sites deal with the behavior of the system as a whole:

-DBIGINDER	Set this flag when there are many (thousands) of documents to index.
-DLITERAL	This flag allows a literal search for a string, as opposed to using partial hits on the string's component words.
-DPARTIALWORD	This flag allows searches with asterisks as wildcards (such as "auto*").
-DRELEVANCE_FEEDBACK	When this flag is set to ON, it allows clients to use previous search results as search criteria for a new search.

A number of directories are included in the distribution software, most of which are of obvious intent (bin for binaries, man for man pages, and so on). The directories used by freeWAIS in its default configuration are:

bin	Binaries
config.c	C source code for configuration
doc	Doc files, help files, and FAQs
include	Header files used by the compiler
lib	Library files
man	Man pages
src	freeWAIS source code
wais-sources	Directory of Internet servers
wais-test	Sample indexer and service scripts

Once you have fine-tuned the configuration file information, you can compile the freeWAIS source with the `make` command:

```
make default
```

By default, the `make` utility compiles two clients called `swais` and `waisq`. If you want to compile an X version of WAIS called `xwais` (useful if you want to allow access from X terminals or consoles), uncomment the line in the Makefile that ends with `makex`.

Setting Up freeWAIS

When you have the compiled freeWAIS components installed and configured properly, you can begin setting up the WAIS index files to documents available on your system. Start by creating an index directory whose default name is wsindex. The directory usually resides just under the root of the filesystem (/wsindex), but many administrators like to keep it in a reserved area for the WAIS software (such as /usr/wais/wsindex). If the index files are difficult to locate, problems can result when users try to find them.

The wais-test directory created when you installed freeWAIS contains a script called test.waisindex that creates four WAIS index files for you automatically. You use these files to test the WAIS installation for proper functionality. They can also show you how to use the different search and index capabilities of freeWAIS. The following are the four index files:

◆ The test-BOOL file is an index of three example documents that use the Boolean capabilities and synonyms.

◆ The test-Comp file is an index that demonstrates compressed source file handling.

◆ The test-Docs file is an index of files in the /doc directory that shows a recursive directory search.

◆ The test-Multi file is an index of GIF images and demonstrates multidocument capabilities.

Only graphically based browsers (usually X-based) can handle the multidocument formats, although any type of browser should be able to handle the other three index formats.

Once you have verified that the indexing system works properly and all the components of freeWAIS are properly installed, you need to build an index file for the documents available on your system. You can do this with the `waisindex` command. The `waisindex` command enables you to index files two ways by using the `-t` option followed by one of these keywords:

◆ The `one_line` keyword indexes each line of a document so a match can show the exact line the match occurred in.

◆ The `text` keyword indexes whole documents so a match shows the entire document with no indication of the exact line the match occurred in. This option is the default.

The `waisindex` command takes arguments for the name of the destination index file (`-d` followed by the filename), and the directory or files to be indexed. For example, to index a directory called /usr/sales/sales_lit into a destination index file called sales using the one_line indexing approach, you would issue the following command:

```
waisindex -d sales -t one_line /usr/sales/sales_lit
```

Because no path is provided for the sales index file in this example, it would be stored in the current directory.

Once you have started the WAIS server software (see "Starting freeWAIS" below), you can test newly created indexes. To test the indexes, use the `waissearch` command. For example, to look for the word "WAIS" in the index files, issue the following command:

```
waissearch -p 210 -d index_file WAIS
```

In this example, `-p` gives the port number (default value is 210), and `-d` is the path to the index file. If the search was successful (and you have something that matches), you will see messages about the number of records returned, and the scores of each match. If you see error messages or nothing, check the configuration information and the index files.

A final step you can take if you want Internet users to be able to access your freeWAIS system is to issue the following command:

```
waisindex -export -register Filenames
```

In this example, `Filenames` is the name of the index. This name is registered with the Directory of Servers at cnidr.org and quake.think.com. These addresses are reached automatically with the `-register` option. Do this step only if you want all Internet users to be accessing your WAIS service. (See the section "The `waisindex` Command" for more information on the `waisindex` command.)

If you want to allow clients to connect to your freeWAIS system with a WWW browser (such as Mosaic or Netscape) and access HTML sources on your system through WAIS, you must issue the following command:

```
waisindex -d WWW -T HTML -contents -export /usr/resources/*html
```

This line enables WAIS clients to perform keyword searches on HTML documents as well.

If you want, you can set WAIS to allow only certain domains to connect to it. You can do this in the ir.h file, which has a line like the following:

```
define SERVSECURITYFILE    "SERV_SEC"
```

This line is commented out by default. Remove the comment symbol. You have to place a copy of an existing SERV_SEC file or one you create yourself in the same directory as the WAIS index files. If there is no SERV_SEC file accessible to WAIS, all domains are allowed access. (You can change the name of the file, of course, as long as the entry in ir.h matches the filename with quotation marks around it.)

Each ASCII entry in the SERV_SEC file follows a strict format for defining the domains that are granted access to WAIS. The format of each line is as follows:

```
domain    [IP address}
```

Each line has the domain name of the host to which you want to grant access, with its IP address an optional add-on to the line. If the domain name and IP address do not match, it doesn't matter because WAIS allows access to a match of either name or address. A sample SERV_SEC file looks likes this:

```
chatton.com
roy.sailing.org
bighost.bignet.com
```

Each of these three domain names can access WAIS, but any connection from a host without these domain names is refused.

The SERV_SEC file should be owned and accessible by the login name and group the freeWAIS system is run under (it should not be run as root to avoid security problems), and the file should be modifiable only by root. In other words, if you are letting freeWAIS run under the login waismgr, all the files should be owned by the user waismgr and that login's group (which ideally would be unique for extra security). The files should not have write access for user, group, or other (making root the only login that can write these files).

Similar to the SERVSECURITYFILE variable is DATASECURITYFILE, which controls access to the databases. Again, there is a line in the ir.h file that you should uncomment to look like the following:

```
#define DATASECURITYFILE    "DATA_SEC"
```

DATA_SEC is a file listing each database file and the domains that have access to it. The file should reside in the same directory as the index files. The format of the DATA_SEC file is as follows:

```
database       domain       [IP address]
```

In this example, database is the name of the database the permissions refer to, and domain and optional IP address are the same as the SERV_SEC file. A sample DATA_SEC file looks like the following:

```
primary         chatton.com
primary         bignet.org
primary         roy.sailing.org
sailing         roy.sailing.org
```

In this example, three domains are granted access to a database called primary (note that primary is just a filename and has no special meaning), and one domain has access to the database called sailing. If you want to allow all hosts with access to the system (controlled by SERV_SEC) to access a particular database, you can use asterisks in the domain name and IP address fields. For example, the following entries allow anyone with access to WAIS to use the primary database, with one domain only allowed access to the sailing database:

```
primary                  *
sailing         roy.sailing.org
```

In both the SERV_SEC and DATA_SEC files, you have to be careful with the IP addresses to avoid inadvertently granting access to hosts not wanted on your system. For example, if you specify the IP address 150.12 in your file, then any IP address from 150.12 through 150.120, 151.121, and so on are also granted access as they match the IP components. Specify IP addresses explicitly to avoid this problem.

STARTING FREEWAIS

As with the FTP services, you can set freeWAIS to start up when the system boots by using the rc files from the command line at any time, or you can have inetd start the processes when a service request arrives. If you want to start freeWAIS from the command line, you need to specify a number of options. A sample startup command line looks like this:

```
waisserver -u username -p 210 -l 10 -d /usr/wais/wais_index
```

The -u option tells waisserver to run as the user *username* (which has to be a valid user in /etc/passwd, of course). The -p option tells waisserver what port to use (the default is 210, as shown in the /etc/services file). The -d option shows the default location of WAIS indexes. If you want to invoke logging of sessions to a file, use the -e option followed by the name of the logfile.

You should run waisserver as another user instead of root to prevent holes in the WAIS system being exploited by a hacker. If the service is run as a standard user (such as wais), only the files that the user would have access to are in jeopardy.

If the port for waisserver is set to 210, the service corresponds to the Internet standards for access. If you set the value to another port, you can configure the system for local area access only. If the port number is less than 1023, root must start and manage the WAIS service, but any port over 1023 can be handled by a normal user. If you intend to use port 210, you don't have to specify the number in the command line, although you must still use the -p option.

If you want to let inetd handle the waisserver startup, you need to ensure that the file /etc/services has an entry for WAIS. The line in the /etc/services file will look like this:

```
z3950        210/tcp        #WAIS
```

In this example, 210 is the port number WAIS uses, and tcp is the protocol. After modifying or verifying the entry in /etc/services, you need to add a WAIS entry to the inetd.conf file to start up waisserver whenever a request is received on port 210 (or whatever other port you are using). The entry looks like this:

```
z3950    stream    tcp    nowait    root
    /usr/local/bin/waisserver/waisserver.d -u username -d /usr/wais/wais_index
```

The options are the same as for the command line startup mentioned earlier. The daemon waisserver.d is used when starting up in that mode, instead of waisserver. Again, you can use the -e option to log activity to a file.

BUILDING YOUR WAIS INDEXES

Once you have the freeWAIS server ready to run and everything seems to be working, it's time to provide some content for your WAIS system. Usually, documents are the primary source of information for WAIS, although you can index any type of file. The key step to providing WAIS service is to build the WAIS index using the waisindex command. The waisindex command can be a bit obtuse at times, but a little practice and some trial and error will help you master its somewhat awkward behavior.

The waisindex program works by examining all the data in the files for which you want to create an index. From its examination, waisindex usually generates seven different index files (depending on the content and your commands). Each file holds a list of unique words in the documents. The different index files are then combined into one large database, often called the source (or WAIS source). Whenever a client WAIS package submits a search, the search strings are compared to the source and the results displayed with accuracy analysis.

> ## Note
>
> The use of `waisindex` allows a client search to proceed much faster because the keywords in the data files have already been extracted. However, the mass of data in the index files can be sizable, so allow lots of disk space for a WAIS server to work with.

WAIS Index Files

A system user usually cannot read the freeWAIS index files (although one or two files can be read with some success). Usually, `waisindex` creates seven index files, although the number may vary depending on requirements. The index files all have a specific file extension to show their purpose, based on a root name (specified on the `waisindex` command line, or defaulting to "index"). The index files and their purposes are described in the following list:

- The index.doc document file contains a table with the filename, a headline (title) from the file, the location of the first and last characters of an entry, the length of the document, the number of lines in the document, and the time and date the document was created.

- The index.dct dictionary file contains a list of every unique word in the files cross-indexed to the inverted file.

- The index.fn filename file contains a table with a list of the filenames, the date they were created in the index, and the type of file.

- The index.hl headline file contains a table of all headlines (titles). The headline is displayed in the search output when a match occurs.

- The index.inv inverted file contains a table associating every unique word in all the files with a pointer to the files themselves and the word's importance (determined based on how close the word is to the start of the file, the number of times the word occurs in the document, and the percentage of times the word appears in the document).

- The index.src source description file contains descriptions of the information indexed, including the host name and IP address, the port watched by WAIS, the source filename, any cost information for the service, the headline of the service, a description of the source, and the e-mail address of the administrator. ASCII editors can edit the source description file. You will look at this file in a little more detail shortly.

- The index.status status file contains user-defined information.

The source description file is a standard ASCII file that is read by waisindex at intervals to see if information has changed. If the changes are significant, waisindex updates its internal information. A type source file looks like this:

```
(:source
    :version 2
    :ip-address "147.120.0.10"
    :ip-name: "wizard.tpci.com"
    :tcp-port 210
    :database-name "Linux stuff"
    :cost 0.00
    :cost-unit: free
    :maintainer "wais_help@tpci.com"
    :subjects "Everything you need to know about Linux"
    :description "If you need to know something about Linux, it's here."
```

You'll want to edit this file when you set up freeWAIS because the default descriptions are rather spare and useless.

THE WAISINDEX COMMAND

The waisindex command provides a number of options, some of which you have seen earlier in this chapter. The primary waisindex options of interest to most users are the following:

◆ The -a option appends data to an existing index file (used to update index files instead of regenerating them each time a new document is added).

◆ The -contents—option indexes the file contents (default action).

◆ The -d option gives the filename root for index files (for example, -d /usr/ wais/foo names all index files as /usr/wais/foo.xxx).

◆ The -e option gives the name of the log file for error information (default is stderr, which is usually the console, although you can specify -s for /dev/ null).

◆ The -export option adds the host name and TCP port to descriptions for easier Internet access.

◆ The -l option gives the level of log messages. Valid values are 0 = no log; 1 = log only high priority errors and warnings; 5 = log medium priority errors and warnings as well as index filename information; and 10 = log every event.

◆ The -M option links multiple types of files.

◆ The -mem option limits memory usage during indexing (the higher the number specified, the faster the indexing process and the more memory used).

◆ The -nocontents option prevents a file from being indexed (indexes only the document header and filename).

- The -nopairs option instructs waisindex to ignore adjacent capitalized words from being indexed together.
- The -nopos— option ignores the location of keywords in a document when determining scores.
- The -pairs option indexes adjacent capitalized words as a single entry.
- The -pos option determines scores based on locations of keywords (proximity of keywords increases scores).
- The -r option activates recursive subdirectory indexing.
- The -register option registers your indexes with the WAIS Directory of Services.
- The -stdin option uses a filename from the keyboard instead of a filename on the command line.
- The -stop option indicates a file containing stopwords (words too common to be indexed), usually defined in src/ir/stoplist.c.
- The -t option indicates the data file type.
- The -T option sets the type of data to whatever follows, such as HTML, text, or ps.

You must tell the waisindex program what type of information is in a file, or it may not be able to generate an index properly. Many filetypes are currently defined with freeWAIS, which you can display by entering the command with no argument:

```
waisindex
```

Although many different types are supported by freeWAIS, only a few are really in common use. The most common file types supported by freeWAIS are the following:

- The filename type is the same as text except that the filename is used as the headline.
- The first_line type is the same as text except that the first line in the file is used as the headline.
- The ftp type contains FTP code that users can use to retrieve information from another machine.
- The GIF type is for GIF images, one image per file. The filename is used as the headline.
- The HTML type is for HTML source code (usually used for WWW browsers). The headline is taken from the HTML code.
- The mail_or_rmail type indexes the mbox mailbox contents as individual items.
- The mail_digest type indexes standard e-mail as individual messages. The subject field is the headline.

◆ The netnews type is standard USENET news, each article a separate item. The subject field is the headline.

◆ The one_line type indexes each sentence in a document separately.

◆ The PICT type is for a PICT image, one image per file. The filename is used as the headline.

◆ The ps type is a PostScript file with one document per file.

◆ The text type indexes the file as one document. The pathname is used as the headline.

◆ The TIFF type is for TIFF images, one image per file. The filename is used as the headline.

To tell `waisindex` the type of file to be examined, use the `-t` option followed by the proper type. For example, to index standard ASCII text, you could use the command:

```
waisindex -t text -r /usr/waisdata/*
```

This command indexes all the files in /usr/waisdata recursively, assuming they are all ASCII files.

> **Note**
>
> When a document has been indexed, any changes in the document will not be reflected in the WAIS index unless a complete reindex is performed. Using the `-a` option does not update existing index entries. Instead, start the index process again. You should do this at periodic intervals as a matter of course.

Getting Fancy

You can provide some extra features for users of your freeWAIS service in a number of ways. Although this section is not exhaustive by any means, it will show you two of the easily implementable features that make a WAIS site more attractive.

To begin, suppose you want to make video, graphics, or audio available on a particular subject. As an example, imagine that your site deals with musical instruments and you have lots of documents on violins. You may want to provide an audio clip of a violin being played, a video of the making of a violin body, or a graphic image of a Stradivarius violin. To make these extra files available, you should have all the files with the same filename but different extensions. For example, if your primary document on violins is called violins.txt, you may have the following files in the WAIS directories:

violins.TEXT	Document describing violins
violins.TIFF	Image of a Stradivarius
violins.MPEG	Video of the making of a violin body
violins.MIDI	MIDI file of a violin being played

All these files should have the same root name (violins) but different types (recognized by waisindex). Then you have to associate the multimedia files with the document file. You can do this with the following command:

```
waisindex -d violin -M TEXT,TIFF,MPEG,MIDI -export /usr/waisdata/violin/*
```

This tells waisindex that all four types of files are to be handled. When a user searches for the keyword violin, all four types of files will be matched, and options on the browser may let them play, view, or hear the non-text components.

Another common feature is the use of synonyms to account for different methods of specifying a subject. For example, a scientist may use the keyword feline, but a non-scientist may use cat. You want to be able to match these two words to the same thing. You can do this through a file called SOURCE.syn, which is automatically read by the search engine when it is working. The SOURCE.syn file has the following format:

```
word    synonym [synonym ...]
```

Here, word is the word to be used to search the databases, and synonym is the word(s) that should match it. For example, if you are dealing with domestic pets in your WAIS site, you may have the following entries in the SOURCE.syn file:

```
cat     feline
dog     canine hound pooch
bord    parrot budgie
```

The synonym file can be very useful when people use different terms to refer to the same thing. An easy way to check for the need for synonyms is to set the logging option for waisindex to 10 for a while, and see what words people are using on your site. Don't keep it on too long, as the logfiles can become enormous with a little traffic.

Summary

Now that WAIS is up and running on your server, you can go about the process of building your index files and letting others access your server. WAIS is quite easy to manage, and offers a good way of letting other users access your system's documents. The alternative approach, for text-based systems, is Gopher, which you examine in the next chapter.

44

- Gopher and Linux

- Configuring Gopher

- Setting Up Your
  Gopher Directories

- Starting Gopher

- Letting the World
  Know

CHAPTER 45

Setting Up a Gopher Service

Gopher is one of the most useful Internet services available, and it is widely used by beginner and veteran alike. Gopher is a menu-based file location system, which leads you through a series of hierarchical menus to find specific files you want. Setting up a Gopher site is really just a matter of configuring the Gopher server software and creating a number of logical directory structures with files indexed in a Gopher format.

Gopher works by having a client program started by a user connect to a Gopher server and retrieve information about files available on the Internet (or local area network, if the Gopher server is limited to that area). By the end of 1995, there were more than 6,000 Gopher servers on the Internet, all accessible by anyone with a Gopher client. Those servers contain information about more than 10 million items, ranging from text files to movies, sounds, images, and many types of application binaries. Gopher enables you to display and manipulate lists of files, looking for items of interest to you.

If you or the users of your Linux system want to connect to another Gopher server, you need a Gopher client. There are several clients available with Linux distributions, on FTP and BBS sites, and through several other sources. If you don't want to allow users (or yourself) to start a Gopher client, you can use Telnet to connect to sites known as public Gopher clients. These sites allow you to log in as an anonymous user and access the Gopher system. Most Gopher client packages offer more than just Gopher, as well. Typical Gopher clients enable you to access WAIS indexes, use FTP, and to some extent, work with the World Wide Web.

This chapter looks at how you can set up a Gopher server, allowing others to access your machine's Gopher listings. Although the chapter won't go into detail about how you should structure your Gopher service, you will see how to configure your software.

GOPHER AND LINUX

Currently, two versions of Gopher are available for Linux systems: Gopher and Gopher+ (Gopher Plus). Gopher is freely available, but Gopher+ is a commercial product. The difference between the two is functionality. If Gopher+'s additional capabilities are important to you and your Gopher site, you may want to consider purchasing the product. Essentially, Gopher+ adds the following features:

◆ Extended file information

◆ File descriptions offered

◆ Recovery of multiple versions of a file at one time (such as ASCII and PostScript simultaneously)

◆ File retrieval based on search criteria determined by the user

Gopher+ works with Gopher, but Gopher cannot use the advanced features of Gopher+. Gopher+ also works with WWW browsers, while Gopher doesn't always function well in a graphical browser. Gopher+ licenses tend to cost about $100 or $500, depending on the site's conditions.

The versions of Gopher usually offered with Linux come from one of two sources: the University of Minnesota Gopher and Gopher+, or GN Public License Gopher. The last public version of UM Gopher was version 1.3 (version 2.13 is free only to educational institutions), but the University is no longer working on the freeware Gopher product, concentrating instead on the commercial Gopher+ product. The GN Public License Gopher includes a WWW service, but it does not provide full functionality at present.

Gopher uses a TCP/IP family protocol known, surprisingly enough, as the Gopher protocol. This is a fairly simple request-answer protocol that is implemented for speed. When Gopher transfers information about a file it knows about (called a Gopher menu file), it follows a set format. The format used by Gopher is:

```
<type><display_name><selector string><hostname><port>
```

The fields in the Gopher menu file have the following meanings:

type	This field is a a one-character description of the item (see the next list for valid codes).
display_name	This field is the the menu or display name, followed by a tab character.
selector_string	This field is a unique identifier for a document on each server (usually based on the filename). The selector string is followed by a tab character.
hostname	This field is the host where the file resides, followed by a tab character.
port	This field is the port to access the host, followed by a carriage return/line feed pair (usually port 70).

The Gopher+ version of the system adds a few new attributes to each line, including the name of the system administrator responsible for the service, a simple description of the document type (text, for example), the language the file was written in, the last date the file was updated, and the size in bytes.

When a file is to be retrieved through the Gopher system, the hostname and port are used to create the connection to the remote, while the selector string can be used to identify the file to be downloaded.

Several types of files are supported by Gopher, all given a unique one-character type code. Valid codes are:

0	Plain text file
1	Gopher directory
2	CSO phonebook server (the hostname is the machine to connect to, the selector string is blank)
3	Error
4	BinHex Macintosh file
5	Binary DOS archive file
6	UNIX Uuencoded file
7	Index-search server
8	Pointer to text-based Telnet session (hostname is the machine name to connect to and selector string is the name to log in as)
9	Binary file
g	GIF file
h	HTML document
I	Graphic image
i	Unselectable inline text
M	MIME encapsulated mail document
P	Adobe PDF file
s	Sound
T	Pointer to 3270 Telnet session (hostname is machine to connect to and selector string is login name)

You must have the following files on your Linux system for Gopher to work:

◆ The tn3270 or similar 3270 emulator is used for Telnet 3270 connections.

◆ You need the kermit or zmodem communications programs to download files. The binaries are usually called kermit, sz, sb, and sx.

◆ If you allow the display of graphics, you need a graphics utility such as xv.

You can modify these requirements if you have a private site (such as for your local area network). If you are offering open access, you should have all the components.

CONFIGURING GOPHER

Installing and configuring Gopher (and Gopher+) is a matter of setting a number of configuration options prior to compiling the system software (it is usually not precompiled for you) and configuring some standard files. Gopher+ installation is done in the same manner, although with some extra parameters. Because Gopher is more likely to be on a Linux site than Gopher+, this chapter concentrates on Gopher.

This section uses filenames without full path extensions because it really doesn't matter where you install the Gopher software, as long as the directory paths are set correctly. There is no defined standard configuration for directory locations, so feel free to choose whatever works best for you.

The gopherd.conf File

The configuration parameters for Gopher (and Gopher+) are in a file called gopherd.conf, which is read by the Gopher daemon gopherd. The default settings generally need a little modification, although many changes are simply changing commented lines to uncommented, and vice versa.

The first step is to create an alias for the Gopher service on your machine. You can do this with the line that defines the host alias. There should be a line in the file that looks like this:

```
hostalias: tpci
```

The alias is used to find the Gopher server on your system, and it should not be directly tied to a real machine to allow you to make changes whenever you want. The best approach is to create an alias and tie it to a physical machine with DNS. If you are running a stand-alone machine, you can either use an alias tied to your machine name, or use your machine name directory.

You can control the number of Gopher connections permitted at one time. This is sometimes necessary to prevent a system from bogging down due to excessive user load. The maximum number of connections Gopher permits is given in a file, usually in the directory PIDS_Directory. A line in the gopherd.conf file usually has this variable commented out because early versions didn't implement it properly, or it was unstable. If you want to enable this feature, remove the comment symbol and make sure that the directory pointed to has the necessary files for your version of Gopher. The line usually looks like this:

```
#PIDS_Directory: /pids
```

A better way to handle the load on your system is to use the MaxConnections keyword, which sets the number of clients you support concurrently. You have to experiment to determine the best balance between system load and user service. A good starting point for a fast Linux system (80486 or Pentium CPU) is 15 to 25 users. This variable is set like this:

```
MaxConnections: 15
```

You can set a number of file decoders for your system. This setting is used when a user requests a file from Gopher and adds an extension (such as .Z, .gz, or .zip) for a compression or archive utility. The decoders recognize the extension the user supplies and invoke the proper utility to send the file in that format. Most gopherd.conf files have the following decoder lines already in the setup:

```
decoder: .Z /usr/ucb/zcat
decoder: .gz /usr/gnu/bin/zcat
#decoder: .adpcm /usr/openwin/bin/adpcm_dec
#decoder: .z /usr/gnu/bin/zcat
```

The last two decoders are commented out and can be uncommented if you want to offer the programs through Gopher. You can also add other extensions, such as .zip, .tar, and so on by adding new lines with the binary name (and its full path).

The amount of time a cache file stays valid should be set. This is controlled by the line using the keyword Cachetime. Set this value to a reasonable value, such as 180 seconds. You should have a line that looks like this in the gopherd.conf file:

```
Cachetime: 180
```

You can use the gopherd.conf file to restrict access to some files on your system by using the ignore keyword. Usually the gopherd.conf file has a number of defined ignores, such as these:

```
ignore: lib
ignore: bin
ignore: etc
ignore: dev
```

Any file with this type of extension is ignored. If you have a particular file extension you want to protect, add it to the list. For example, if your accounting system uses the extension .acct, you could have the Gopher clients ignore all these files by adding this line:

```
ignore: acct
```

Note that these `ignore` statements work only with file extensions. To create a broader search, you can use wildcards and the keyword ignore_patt (for ignore pattern). For example, the following line will ignore any file with the letters usr anywhere in the name:

```
ignore_patt: ^usr$
```

THE GOPHERDLOCAL.CONF FILE

In the file gopherdlocal.conf, you have to make two small changes to identify the system administrator. Otherwise, your system will generate lots of annoying notes. The lines in the gopherdlocal.conf file look like this by default:

```
Admin: blank
AdminEmail: blank
```

If you do not change these entries to actual values, Gopher can generate all kinds of weird error messages. The Admin field usually has the administrator's name and sometimes a telephone number. For example, the file could be filled out as follows:

```
Admin: Yvonne Chow, 555-1212
AdminEmail: ychow@chatton.com
```

Another setting you should provide in the gopherdlocal.conf file is the Abstract, which is a short description of what your particular Gopher service provides. If you don't change the default setting, users get a message prompting them to get you to set the Abstract, so you may as well do it right away. Multiple lines in an abstract value are followed by a backslash to show the continuation. A sample Abstract setting looks like this:

```
Abstract: This server provides sound and graphics files \
collected by the administrator on a recent trip to Outer \
Mongolia.
```

General information about your site is provided with a number of general settings for the site name, the organization that runs the site, your machine's geographic location, the latitude and longitude of your site, and a timezone setting. You can leave these blank if you want, but providing the information leads to a more complete Gopher site. The settings in a sample gopherdlocal.conf file look like this:

```
Site: Explore_Mongolia
Org: Mongolia Tourist Bureau
Loc: North Bay, Ontario, Canada
Geog: blank
TZ: EDT
```

The setting of blank for Geog will leave the setting with no value. Obviously, the system administrator didn't know the latitude and longitude settings.

You can set a language option used by Gopher clients to show what language most of the documents available on your site are written in. For American English, for example, you set the option like this:

```
Language: En_US
```

The setting BummerMsg is used to display a brief text string to a user who exceeds your maximum number of concurrent users or causes an error when accessing the system. The default value is the following:

```
BummerMsg: We're sorry, we6 don't allow off-site access to this server
```

You can change this to whatever message you want. Try not to be rude or obnoxious, because you never know who will get this message.

The last step in modifying the gopherdlocal.conf file is to set access procedures for users who log in to your Gopher server. By using entries with the keyword access, you can limit the users who can get to your server. The general format of the access line is:

```
access: hostname permissions num_users
```

In this example, `hostname` is either the name or IP address of the host that is connecting to your server, `permissions` is the permission set for those users, and `num_users` is the maximum number of users that can be connected to the service concurrently.

The permissions are set using any combination of the following four words, either as they are or preceded by an exclamation mark to mean "not allowed." The permission keywords are as follows:

◆ The `browse` keyword means that the user can examine directory contents. If you forbid this permission, users can access entries, but they can't get directory contents.

◆ The `ftp` keyword enables the server to act as gateway to FTP services.

◆ The `read` keyword means that users can access a file. If you don't give this permission, users get the `BummerMsg` when they ask for the file.

◆ The `search` keyword means that users can access indexes (type seven items). This keyword is used primarily with Gopher+.

For example, to set access permissions to allow up to 10 users from the network chatton.com to access your Gopher server with full rights, you add a line like the following:

```
access: chatton.com   browse ftp read search 10
```

There is at least one space between each entry, even between permissions. Take a look at this access entry:

```
access: bignet.org !browse !ftp read search 3
```

This entry allows three concurrent users from bignet.org to access the Gopher server and read and search, but not use FTP gateways or browse the directory listings.

If you are using IP addresses, you can use a subset of the IP address to indicate the entire network. For example, if bignet.com's network address is 147.12, you can indicate the entire network with a line like this:

```
access: 147.12. !browse !ftp read search 3
```

You must follow the last quad of numbers specified in the IP address with a period, otherwise 147.120 through 147.129 will also have the same permissions (because they match the digits specified).

If you want to enable access from a particular machine, you can do that, too. For example, to allow your friend's darkstar machine to access your Gopher server with full permissions, you would add a line like this:

```
access: darkstar.domain.name browse ftp read search 1
```

Most general Gopher servers tend to allow anyone to connect, so they use a default entry to refer to anyone not explicitly defined by another access entry. The default setting is usually like this:

```
access: default !browse !ftp read search 15
```

This setting allows anyone to read and search Gopher directories, but not move through them or use your machine as an FTP gateway.

SETTING UP THE MAKEFILE

You need to modify two files for the compilation process to proceed properly. These two files are Makefile.config and conf.h. With many versions of Gopher available on Linux systems, the configuration parameters these files need have already been set, but you should check the values carefully to prevent problems.

The Makefile.config file (used by Makefile to build the executable) is a lengthy file, so you should be careful moving through it to avoid accidental changes. The important areas to examine are the directory definitions and server and client settings. These are dealt with individually later in this section.

One setting you may want to alter is the debugging utility, which is enabled by default in most systems. This can help you get the system running properly. When the operation is correct, however, you should recompile the source with the debugging features removed to make the process faster and smaller, as well as reduce debug information overhead. To remove debugging features, comment out the DEBUGGING line so it looks like this:

```
#DEBUGGING = -DDEBUGGING
```

By default, this line is probably not commented out.

The directory definitions are usually in a block with five to seven entries, depending on the number of entries for the man pages. A typical directory definition block looks like this:

```
PREFIX = /usr/local
CLIENTDIR = $(PREFIX)/bin
CLIENTLIB = $(PREFIX)/lib
SERVERDIR = $(PREFIX)/etc

MAN1DIR = $(PREFIX)/man/man1
MAN5DIR = $(PREFIX)/man/man5
MAN8DIR = $(PREFIX)/man/man8
```

The primary change to most Makefile.config files will be the PREFIX, which is used to set the basic directory for Gopher. The default value is usually /usr/local, although you can change it to anything you want (such as /usr/gopher). The rest of the variables define subdirectories under the primary Gopher directory, and they are usually acceptable as they are. You can leave all of the subdirectories the way they are, or you can change them to suit your own needs. You can place all the files in one directory, if you want. The meaning of each variable is as follows:

CLIENTDIR	Gopher client software
CLIENTLIB	client help file (gopher.hlp)
MAN1DIR	man pages for gopher client
MAN8DIR	man pages for gopherd
SERVERDIR	Gopher server (gopherd) and configuration file (gopherd.conf)

For a Gopher client to run properly on your system, you must modify the CLIENTOPTS line in the Makefile.config file. The two options for controlling the behavior of the CLIENTOPTS line are as follows :

◆ The -DNOMAIL option forbids remote users from mailing files.

◆ The -DAUTOEXITONU option allows the Gopher client to be exited with the u command as well as q command.

To use either or both of these options, add them to the CLIENTOPS line, like this:

```
CLIENTOPTS = -DNOMAIL -DAUTOEXITONU
```

You need to set four variables relating to the Gopher server. These variables specify the host domain name, the port Gopher should use to listen for connections, the location of the data files, and option flags.

The domain name is set with the DOMAIN variable. It should have a leading period in the name, such as:

```
DOMAIN = .tpci.com
```

You do not need to set this variable if the hostname command returns the fully qualified domain name of the server. In this case, leave the value blank.

The SERVERPORT variable defines the port Gopher uses to wait for services, and it is usually set for TCP port 70. This line usually looks like this:

```
SERVERPORT = 70
```

If you are not allowing general access to your Gopher site by Internet users, you can change this value. However, if you want to allow Internet users (even a very small subset) to gain access, you should leave this as port 70. If you are setting up your

45

Gopher site for a small network only, then choose any port number you want (between 1024 and 9999) and make sure all the Gopher clients use that number, too.

The SERVERDATA variable defines the location of the data your Gopher server offers. Its default setting is usually like this:

```
SERVERDATA = /gopher-data
```

Set the variable to point to the file location you use for your Gopher items.

The SERVEROPTS variable accepts a number of keywords that change the behavior of the Gopher service. A typical entry looks like this:

```
SERVEROPTS = -DSETPROCTITLE -DCAPFILES # -DBIO -DDL
```

Any keywords after the pound sign are ignored when Makefile runs, so you can adjust its location to set the options you want if the order of the variables allows such a simple approach. The meanings of the different keywords allowed in the SERVEROPTS entry are as follows:

- The -DADD_DATE_AND_TIME keyword adds dates and times to titles.
- The -DBIO keyword is used only with the WAIS versions developed by Don Gilbert (wais8b5).
- The -DDL keyword provides support for the dl database utility. (This keyword requires the dl system in a directory variable called DLPATH and the DLOBJS line commented out to show the files getdesc.o and enddesc.o locations.)
- The -DCAPFILES keyword offers backwards compatibility with the cap directory.
- The -DLOADRESTRICT keyword restricts user access based on the number of concurrent users (see following details).
- The -DSETPROCTITLE keyword sets the name displayed by the ps command (BSD UNIX-based systems only).

You can use the DLOADRESTRICT keyword instead of other mechanisms in the configuration files for setting the maximum number of concurrent users. If you want to use DLOADRESTRICT, you should also modify the conf.h file (see the next few paragraphs) and make sure that the Makefile.config file has this entry:

```
LOADLIBS = -lkvm
```

Most Makefile.config versions have this line commented out. Remove the comment symbol.

The conf.h file is used during the compilation to set other parameters about the Gopher service. The important settings, at least as far as setting up a Gopher service, are those that relate to the number of queries and timeout variables. These tend to occur at the end of the conf.h file.

The WAISMAXHITS variable defines the maximum number of hits a query to a WAIS database can offer, usually set to around 40. This variable is defined like this:

```
#define WAISMAXHITS 40
```

Note that the pound sign is not a comment symbol, because this is written in C. The pound sign is an important part of the processor directive and should be left in place. There is no equal sign in the definition, either.

The MAXLOAD variable is used if the -DLOADRESTRICT keyword was used in the SERVEROPTS variable of Makefile.config. The MAXLOAD variable defines the maximum load the Gopher service can handle before refusing service (you can override this value on the command line). The usual definition is like this:

```
#define MAXLOAD 10.0
```

The READTIMEOUT and WRITETIMEOUT variables set the amount of time a service waits for a network read or write operation before timing out. The default settings are usually adequate. These lines look like this:

```
#define READTIMEOUT (1*60)
#define WRITETIMEOUT (3*60)
```

The Gopher client configuration is straightforward. Begin by defining the Gopher servers the local machine is to connect to with the CLIENT1_HOST and CLIENT2_HOST entries. The Gopher client will choose one of the two (if both are defined) when it is started. The entries look like this:

```
#define CLIENT1_HOST "gopher_serv.tpci.com"
#define CLIENT2_HOST "other_gopher_serv.tpci.com"
```

The ports to be used to connect to the hosts are defined with these options:

```
#define CLIENT1_PORT 70
#define CLIENT2_PORT 70
```

If you have a local service and don't want to use port 70 (to prevent access from the Internet, for example), set the proper port values. If only one Gopher server is used, set the second value to 0.

The language the Gopher client is to use is defined by choosing one value out of a number of options. The default is American English, set by this command:

```
#define DEFAULT_LANG "En_US"
```

There are other language definintions commented out below this one. If you want to change the default language, comment the American English setting and uncomment the one you want.

When all the configuration changes have been made, you can invoke the compilation process for the client and server with these commands:

```
make client
make server
```

Or you can do both client and server systems at once by using the make command with no argument. The installation procedure must be compiled, too, using the following command:

```
make install
```

After that, run the installation script and follow the prompts to install Gopher.

WAIS AND GOPHER

Gopher clients have the ability to use WAIS indexes to search for a document, but the system must be configured to allow this. You looked at WAIS in the last chapter, so for the sake of providing WAIS index access to Gopher, this section assumes that you have installed WAIS properly and have WAIS indexes ready for Gopher.

To provide WAIS services through Gopher, you may have to make a change in the WAIS source code. Examine the WAIS source code for a line that looks like this:

```
if (gLastAnd) printf("search_word: boolean 'and' scored/n:);
```

This line should be commented out to provide Gopher services. If it is not, add C comment symbols before and after the line, like this:

```
/* if (gLastAnd) printf("search_word: boolean 'and' scored/n:); */
```

If the line was already commented out (or didn't exist), then you need not make any change. If you changed the line, though, you have to recompile WAIS by changing into the WAIS top directory and running the makefile (type the command make).

Next, examine the Gopher Makefile.config file and look for the WAISTYPE variable. It should be defined on a line like this:

```
WAISTYPE = #-DFREREWAUS_0_4
```

Then you have to link the Gopher and WAIS services. Suppose your Gopher source directory is /usr/gopher/source and the WAIS source directory is /usr/wais/source. You can link these services by entering the following commands:

```
cd /usr/gopher/source
ln -s /usr/wais/source/include ./ir
ln -s /usr/wais/source/client/ui .
ln -s /usr/wais/source/bin .
```

When Gopher is recompiled, it will make the links between Gopher and freeWAIS and allow the two services to interwork.

SETTING UP YOUR GOPHER DIRECTORIES

Gopher directories and files are quite simple to set up, and they follow standard naming conventions for the most part. Before you begin, though, you should know which documents and files are to be provided through Gopher to others, and you should be able to write a short description of each. (If you don't know the contents of a file, either read it or get the author to summarize the file for you.) To begin, assume that you are using only a single directory for all your Gopher documents.

Begin by changing to the top directory you use for your Gopher directories (which you may have to create if you haven't already done so). For convenience, this directory should not be where the Gopher source and configuration files are located. Simply choose a useful name and create the directory. For example, to create the Gopher home directory /usr/gopher/data, you issue a standard `mkdir` command:

```
mkdir /usr/gopher/data
```

Change into your Gopher directory and copy the files you want to make available into it. When you have done that, you can create a descriptive filename for each file, instead of the more obtuse filenames usually used, up to 80 characters long. For example, if you have a file called q1.sales, you may want to rename it to Company_Sales_1887_Q1 to help users identify the contents a little more easily. If you don't like this type of entry (using underscores and other fillers because the shell doesn't allow spaces in a filename), you can get even more elegant by using a .cap directory.

SETTING GOPHER FILENAMES

The process for providing better filenames is to first create a .cap directory under your Gopher main directory (such as /usr/gopher/data/.cap). For each file in the main directory, you want to create a file in the .cap directory with the same name, but with a name and number. For example, suppose you have a file called q1.sales in /usr/gopher/data. In /usr/gopher/data/.cap, you would create a file with the same name, q1.sales, which has the following contents:

```
Name=Company Sales for the First Quarter, 1887
Numb=1
```

The Name entry can have spaces or other special symbols in it, as it is echoed as a complete string. The Numb entry is for the location of the entry on your Gopher menu. Suppose you had the entry just shown and two other files, shown by using `cat` to display their contents:

```
$ cat q1.sales
Name=Company Sales for the First Quarter, 1887
Numb=1
```

```
$ cat q2.sales
Name=Company Sales for the Second Quarter, 1887
Numb=2

$cat q3.sales
Name=Company Sales for the Third Quarter, 1887
Numb=3
```

When these entries are displayed in a Gopher menu, they look like this:

```
1. Company Sales for the First Quarter, 1887
2. Company Sales for the Second Quarter, 1887
3. Company Sales for the Third Quarter, 1887
```

The order of filenames in the .cap directory doesn't matter, but you shouldn't have the same Numb entry more than once.

USING A MASTER FILE

An alternative to using the .cap directory approach (which allows for easy addition of new files) is to use a single master file for each document you are making available. This file goes in your Gopher top directory and is called .names. Here's the .names file for the same three files just mentioned:

```
$ cd /usr/gopher/data
$ cat .names
#  My Gopher main .names file

Path=./q1.sales
Name=Company Sales for the First Quarter, 1887
Numb=1

Path=./q2.sales
Name=Company Sales for the Second Quarter, 1887
Numb=2

Path=./q3.sales
Name=Company Sales for the Third Quarter, 1887
Numb=3
```

As you can see, this format contains the same information but adds the filenames (which were not needed in .cap because the filenames were the same). One advantage to using a .names file is that you can reorder your menu entries much more easily because you only have one file to work with instead of several. Also, the .names file enables you to add an abstract describing the file. For example, you could have the following entry in a .names file:

```
Path=./gopher
Name=How to Set up A Gopher Service
Numb=16
Abstract=This document shows the steps you need to take to set up a Gopher service.
```

USING LINKS

You can get a little fancier with Gopher and have a menu item lead to another menu, or to another machine entirely. You can do this with links, controlled by a link file, which ends with .link. A .link file has five pieces of information in it, in the same format as this example:

```
Name=More Sales Info
Type=1
Port=70
Path=/usr/gopher/data/more_sales
Host=wizard.tpci.com
```

The Name entry is what a user sees on the Gopher menu, and it can be any type of description you want regardless of what else is in the link file. The Type field has a number showing the type of document the file links to. Valid numbers are as follows:

0	Text
1	Directory
2	CSO name server
7	Full text index
8	Telnet session
9	Binary
h	HTML file
I	Image file
M	MIME file
s	Sound file

These types are the same as the list shown earlier in this chapter for the types of files Gopher supports, although a little shorter.

The Port field is the port for a connection to a remote system (if that's where the link leads), and the Path field is where the file is on the local or remote server. The Host field, not surprisingly, is the name of the host the file resides on. If you are setting up a link to another machine via FTP or WAIS, you need to specify the path to include the service name and any arguments. For example, if your Gopher menu leads users to a file on another machine through FTP, your link file may look like this:

```
Name=More Sales Info
Type=1
Port=+
Path=ftp:chatton@bigcat.com/usr/gopher/cats
Host=+
```

The plus sign used in the Port and Host fields instruct the FTP service on the remote machine to return results to this machine using default ports (such as TCP port 21 for FTP). For a link to a WAIS directory, the format is:

```
Name=More Sales Info
Type=7
Port=+
Path=waisrc:/usr/wais/data
Host=+
```

Finally, you may want to have a menu item execute a program. You can do this by having the Path field use the exec command:

```
Path=exec: "args" : do_this
```

In this example, do_this is the program you want to execute and "args" are any arguments to be passed to do_this. If you have no arguments to pass, leave the quotation marks empty. This format is a little awkward, but it does work.

STARTING GOPHER

A Gopher server can be started either from the rc startup files, from the command line, or from the inetd daemon. From the command line or the rc files, you will have a command line similar to this:

```
/usr/local/etc/gopherd /usr/gopher/gopher-data 70
```

This line starts the daemon with the directory the startup Gopher menus reside in and the port number for connections.

The gopherd command line accepts a number of optional flags to control its behavior, although most flags mirror entries in the configuration files. The following are valid flags:

-C	Disables directory caching
-c	Runs without chroot restrictions
-D	Enables debugging
-I	Uses inetd to invoke gopherd
-L	Specifies the maximum load average when followed by a value
-l	Specifies log file to record connections (filename follows the option)
-o	Specifies an alternate configuration files from gopherd.conf (filename follows the option)
-u	Sets the name of the owner running gopherd (valid username must follow the option)

To help secure your system, use chroot to create a separate filesystem structure for the gopher area (as you did with FTP: see Chapter 43, "Setting Up an FTP Site"). The -c option is not as secure as running gopherd with chroot active. Also, the -u option should be used to make `gopherd` run as a standard user's process, instead of as root. This helps protect against holes in the daemon that a hacker could exploit.

If you want to run Gopher under inetd (started whenever a request for the service arrives), modify the /etc/services and /etc/inetd.conf file to include a line for Gopher. Normally, the entry in /etc/services looks like this:

```
gopher    70/tcp
```

The entry in /etc/inetd.conf looks like this:

```
gopher    stream    tcp    nowait    root    /usr/local/etc/gopherd gopherd -I -u
username
```

In this entry, username is the name of the user to run gopherd as (you can set up a specific account for gopher in /etc/passwd with standard permissions).

Once the Gopher server process is up and running, you can test your Gopher installation. You will need a Gopher client. Use the Gopher client to connect to your Gopher server (using your host name) and you should see the top directory of your Gopher resources. Another way to test your Gopher system is to use Telnet. Use Telnet to connect to the gopher port, using a command like this:

```
telnet gopher 70
```

If the connection is properly made, you will see your Gopher system on the screen.

Yet another alternative to test your system is to use the program `gopherls`, which requires the name of the directory your Gopher source resides in. To start `gopherls`, you issue a command like this:

```
gopherls /usr/wais/gopher/data
```

This command specifies your Gopher data directory. You can use this technique to test new Gopher directories as you develop them.

Letting the World Know

Because you have spent a lot of time setting up your Gopher service, you can let everyone else on the Internet know about it. (Of course, you should only do this when your Gopher service is ready, and if you want to allow general access. Don't follow these steps if you are granting access only to a few people or to your local area network.)

To have your Gopher service listed in the main Gopher service directories, send an e-mail message to the address:

```
gopher@boombox.micro.umn.edu
```

Include the Gopher service's full name as it appears on your main menu, your host's name and IP address, the port number Gopher uses (which should be TCP port 70 for general Internet access), the e-mail account of the Gopher administrator, and a short paragraph describing your service. You can also provide a string that gives the path to the data directory, if you want. Because most Gopher systems start in the root directory, however, this string isn't needed unless you have sub-menus for different purposes.

Summary

After you have done all that, your Gopher service should be ready to use. You need to set up the Gopher file entries, but that is beyond the scope of this chapter. Consult a good Internet or Gopher book for more information on Gopher directories, files, and entries. Gopher is a handy utility if you have lots of information you want to share. Although the configuration process can take a while, the Gopher system tends to work very well once it is completed.

- Web Server Software

- Setting Up Your
  Web Site

CHAPTER 46

Configuring a WWW Site

Just about everyone on the planet knows about the World Wide Web. It's the most talked-about aspect of the Internet. With the WWW's popularity, more system users are getting into the game by setting up their own WWW servers and home pages. Sophisticated packages now act as Web servers for many operating systems, although UNIX users have always done it from scratch. Linux, based on UNIX, has the software necessary to provide a Web server readily available.

You don't need fancy software to set up a Web site, only a little time and the correct configuration information. That's what this chapter is about. The chapter looks at how you can set up a World Wide Web server on your Linux system, whether for friends, your LAN, or the Internet as a whole.

The major aspect of the Web that attracts users and makes it so powerful, aside from its multimedia capabilities, is the use of *hyperlinks*. A hyperlink lets you move with only one mouse click from document to document, site to site, graphic to movie, and so on. All the instructions of the move are built into the Web code.

There are two aspects to the World Wide Web: server and client. Client software is the best known, such as Mosaic and Netscape. However, there are many different Web client packages available other than these two, some specifically for X or Linux.

WEB SERVER SOFTWARE

There are three primary versions of Web server software that will run under Linux. They are from NCSA, CERN, and Plexus. The most readily available system is from NCSA, which also provides Mosaic. NCSA's Web system is fast and quite small, can run under inetd or as a stand-alone daemon, and provides pretty good security. This chapter uses NCSA's Web software, although you can easily use any of the other two packages instead (some of the configuration information will be different, of course).

Note

The Web server software is available via anonymous FTP or WWW from one of the three following sites, depending on the type of server software you want:

CERN: ftp//info.cern.ch.pub/www.bin (FTP)

NCSA: ftp.ncsa.edu (FTP) http://boohoo.ncsa.uiuc.edu (WWW)

Plexus: ftp://autsin.bsdi.com/plexus/2.2.1/dist/Plexus.html (WWW)

The NCSA Web software is available for Linux in both compiled and source code forms. Using the compiled version is much easier because you don't have to configure and compile the source code for the PC and Linux platforms. The binaries are often provided compressed and tarred, so you will have to uncompress and then extract the tar library. Alternatively, many CD-ROMs provide the software ready-to-go. If you do obtain the compressed form of the Web server software, follow the installation or README files to place the Web software in the proper location.

Unpacking the Web Files

If you have obtained a library of source code or binaries from an FTP or BBS site, you will probably have to untar and uncompress them first. (Check with any README files before you do this, if there are any; otherwise, you may be doing this step for nothing.) Usually, you proceed by creating a directory for the Web software, then changing into it and expanding the library with a command like this:

```
zcat httpd_X.X_XXX.tar.Z | tar xvf -
```

The software is often named by the release and target platform, such as httpd_1.5_linux.tar.Z. Use whatever name your tar file has in the above line. Installation instructions are sometimes in a separate tar file, such as Install.tar.z, which you will have to obtain and uncompress with the following command:

```
zcat Install.txt.z
```

Make sure you are in the target directory when you issue the commands above, though, or you will have to move a lot of files. You can place the files anywhere, although it is often a good idea to create a special area for the Web software that can have its permissions controlled, such as /usr/web, /var/web, or similar name.

Once you have extracted the contents of the Web server distribution and the library files are in their proper directories, you can look at what has been created automatically. You should have the following subdirectories:

cgi-bin	Common gateway interface binaries and scripts
conf	Configuration files
icons	Icons for home pages
src	Source code and (sometimes) executables
support	Support applications

Compiling the Web Software

If you don't have to modify the source code and recompile it under Linux, you can skip the configuration details mentioned in the rest of this section. On the other hand, you may want to know what is happening in the source code anyway, because you can better understand how Linux works with the Web server code. If you obtained a generic, untailored version of the NCSA Web server, you will have to configure the software.

Begin by editing the src/Makefile file to specify your platform. You have to check several variables for proper information:

AUX_CFLAGS	Uncomment the entry for Linux (identified by comment lines and symbols, usually)
CC	Specify the name of the C compiler (usually cc or gcc)
EXTRA_LIBS	Add any extra libraries that need to be linked in (none are required for Linux)
LFLAGS	Add any flags you need for linking (none are required for most Linux linkers)

Finally, look for the CFLAGS variable. Some of the values for CFLAGS may be set already. Valid values for CFLAGS are as follows:

DESCURE_LOGS	Prevents CGI scripts from interfering with any log files written by the server software
DMAXIMUM_DNS	Provides a more secure resolution system at the cost of performance
DMINIMAL_DNS	Doesn't allow reverse name resolution, but speeds up performance
DNO_PASS	Prevents multiple children from being spawned
DPEM_AUTH	Enables PEM/PGP authentication schemes
DXBITHACK	Provides a service check on the execute bit of an HTML file
O2	Is an optimizing flag

It is unlikely that you will need to change any of the flags in the CFLAGS section, but at least you now know what they do. Once you have checked the src/Makefile for its contents, you can compile the server software. Change into the src directory and issue the command:

```
make
```

If you see error messages, check the configuration file carefully. The most common problem is the wrong platform (or multiple platforms) selected in the file.

Once the Web server software has been compiled, you have to compile the support applications, too. Change into the support directory and check the Makefile there. Once it is correct, issue the make command again. Then, change to the cgi-src directory and repeat the process.

Note

Some versions of NCSA Web server software (notably releases 1.4 or later) enable you to compile all three sets of source code with the command `make sgi` from the Web directory.

CONFIGURING THE WEB SOFTWARE

Once the software is in the proper directories and compiled for your platform, it's time to configure the system. Begin with the httpd.conf-dist file. This file handles the `httpd` server daemon. Before you edit the file, you have to decide whether you will install the Web server software to run as a daemon, or whether it will be started by `inetd`. If you anticipate a lot of use, run the software as a daemon. For occasional use, either is acceptable.

Several variables in httpd.conf-dist need to be checked or have values entered for them. All the variables in the configuration file follow the following syntax:

```
variable value
```

Note that there is no equal sign or special symbol between the variable name and the value assigned to it. For example, a few lines would look like this:

```
FancyIndexing on
HeaderName Header
ReadmeName README
```

Where pathnames or filenames are supplied, they are usually relative to the Web server directory, unless explicitly declared as a full pathname. The variables you need to supply in httpd.conf-dist are as follows:

- The `AccessConfig` variable is the location of the access.conf configuration file. The default value is conf/access.conf. You can use either absolute or relative pathnames.
- The `AgentLog` variable is the log file to record details of transactions. The default value is logs/agent_log.
- The `ErrorLog` variable is the name of the file to record errors in. The default is /logs/error_log.
- The `Group` variable is the Group ID the server should run as (used only when server is running as a daemon). It can be either a group name or group ID number. If it is a number, it must be preceded by #. The default is #-1.

◆ The `IdentityCheck` variable is used to verify that a remote user has logged in as himself/herself. Not many systems support this variable. The default is Off.

◆ The `MaxServers` variable is the maximum number of children allowed.

◆ The `PidFile` variable is the file in which you want to record the process ID of each httpd copy. The default is /logs/httpd.pid. Used only when the server is in daemon mode.

◆ The `Port` variable is the port number httpd should listen to for clients. The default port is 80. If you don't want the Web server to be generally available, choose another number.

◆ The `ResourceConfig` variable is the path to the srm.conf file, usually conf/srm.conf.

◆ The `ServerAdmin` variable is the e-mail address of the administrator.

◆ The `ServerName` variable is the domain name of the server.

◆ The `ServerRoot` variable is the path above which users cannot move (usually the Web server top directory or usr/local/etc/httpd).

◆ The `ServerType` variable is either stand-alone (daemon) or `inetd`.

◆ The `StartServers` variable is the number of server processes that can run concurrently (that is, the number of clients allowed).

◆ The `TimeOut` variable is the amount of time in seconds to wait for a client request, after which it is disconnected (default is 1800, which should be reduced).

◆ The `TransferLog` variable is the path to the location of the logs. The default is logs/access_log.

◆ The `TypesConfig` variable is the path to the location of the MIME configuration file. The default is conf/mime.conf.

◆ The `User` variable defines the user ID the server should run as (only valid if running as daemon). It can be a name or number, but it must be preceded by # if it is a number. The default is #-1.

The next configuration file to check is srm.conf, which is used to handle the server resources. The variables that have to be checked or set in the srm.conf file are as follows:

◆ The `AccessFileName` variable is the file that gives access permissions (default is .htaccess).

◆ The `AddDescription` variable provides a description of a type of file. For example, an entry could be `AddDescription "PostScript file" *.ps`. Multiple entries are allowed.

◆ The AddEncoding variable indicates that filenames with a specified extension are encoded somehow, such as AddEncoding compress Z. Multiple entries are allowed.

◆ The AddIcon variable gives the name of the icon to display for each type of file.

◆ The AddIconbyEncoding variable is the same as AddIcon, but it adds encoding information.

◆ The AddIconType variable uses MIME type to determine the icon to use.

◆ The AddType variable overrides MIME definitions for extensions.

◆ The Alias variable substitutes one pathname for another, such as Alias data /usr/www/data.

◆ The DefaultType variable is the default MIME type, usually text/html.

◆ The DefaultIcon variable is the default icon to use when FancyIndexing is on (default is /icons/unknown.xbm).

◆ The DirectoryIndex variable is the filename to return when the URL is for your service only. The default value is index.html.

◆ The DocumentRoot variable is the absolute path to the httpd document directory. The default is /usr/local/etc/httpd/htdocs.

◆ The FancyIndexing variable adds icons and filename information to the file list for indexing. The default is on. (This option is for backward compatibility with the first release of HTTP.)

◆ The HeaderName variable is the filename used at the top of a list of files being indexed. The default is HEADER.

◆ The IndexOptions variable specifies the indexing parameters (including FancyIndexing, IconsAreLinks, ScanHTMLTitles, SuppressLastModified, SuppressSize, and SuppressDescription).

◆ The OldScriptAlias variable is the same as Alias. It is included for backward compatibility with HTPP 1.0.

◆ The ReadmeName variable is the footer file attached to directory indexes. The default is README.

◆ The Redirect variable maps a path to a new URL.

◆ The ScriptAlias variable is similar to Alias, but it's for scripts. The default is /usr/local/etc/httpd/cgi-bin.

◆ The UserDir variable is the directory users can use for httpd access. The default is public_html. This variable is usually set to a user's home page directory, or you can set it to DISABLED.

The third file to examine and modify is access.conf-dist, which defines the services available to WWW browsers. Usually, everything is accessible to a browser, but you may want to modify the file to tighten security or disable some services not supported on your Web site. The format of the conf-dist file is different from the two configuration files you saw above. It uses a set of sectioning directives delineated by angle brackets. The general format of an entry is:

```
<Directory>
...
</Directory>
```

Any items between the beginning and ending delimiters (<Directory> and </Directory> respectively) are directives. It's not quite that easy because several variations can exist in the file. The best way to customize the access.conf-dist file is to follow these steps for a typical Web server installation:

1. Locate the Options directive and remove the Indexes option. This step prevents users from browsing the httpd directory. Valid Options entries are discussed shortly.

2. Locate the first Directory directive and check the path to the cgi-bin directory. The default path is /usr/local/etc/httpd/cgi-bin.

3. Locate the second Directory directive for the sym.conf file and verify the path. The default is /usr/local/etc/httpd/htdocs.

4. Find the AllowOverride variable and set it to None (this setting prevents others from changing the settings). The default is All. Valid values for the AllowOverride variable are discussed shortly.

5. Find the Limit directive and set to whichever value you want (see the next list).

The Limit directive controls access to your server. The valid values for the Limit directive are:

allow	Permits specific hostnames following the allow keyword to access the service
deny	Denies specific hostnames following the deny keyword from accessing the service
order	Specifies the order in which allow and deny directives are evaluated (usually set to deny,allow but can also be allow,deny)
require	Requires authentication through a user file specified in the AuthUserFile entry

The Options directive can have several entries, all of which have a different purpose. The default entry for Options is:

```
Options Indexes FollowSymLinks
```

The authors removed the Indexes entry from the Options directive in the first step of the customization procedure. These entries all apply to the directory the Options field appears in. The valid entries for the Options directive are as follows:

All	Enables all features
ExecCGI	Specifies that CGI scripts can be executed in this directory
FollowSymLinks	Enables httpd to follow symbolic links
Includes	Enables include files for the server
IncludesNoExec	Enables include files for the server but disables the exec option
Indexes	Enables users to retrieve indexes (doesn't affect precompiled indexes)
None	No features are enabled
SymLinksIfOwnerMatch	Follows symbolic links only if the user ID matches

The AllowOverride variable is set to All by default, and you should change this setting. There are several valid values for AllowOverride, but the recommended setting for most Linux systems is None. The valid values for AllowOverride are as follows:

◆ A value of All means unrestricted access.

◆ The AuthConfig value enables some authentication routines. Valid values are AuthName (sets authorization name of directory), AuthType (set authorization type of the directory, although there is only one legal value: Basic), AuthUserFile (specifies a file containing user names and passwords), and AuthGroupFile (specifies a file containing group names).

◆ The FileInfo value enables AddType and AddEncoding directives.

◆ The Limit value enables the Limit directive.

◆ A value of None means that no access files are allowed.

◆ The Options value enables the Options directive.

After you have done all that, your configuration files should be properly set. Although the syntax is a little confusing, reading the default values will show you the proper format to use when changing entries. Next, you can start the Web server software.

STARTING THE WEB SOFTWARE

Begin by copying all your *.conf-dist files (modified in the previous section) to *.conf (a change in the extension only). Copy the files instead of renaming them so that you have the original .conf-dist file for future modifications. The server looks for files with the .conf extension and will ignore .conf-dist files.

When your configuration is complete, it's time to try out the Web server software. In the configuration files, you made a decision as to whether the Web software will run as a daemon (stand-alone) or be started from inetd. The startup procedure is a little different for each method (as you would expect), but both startup procedures can use one of the following three options on the command line:

◆ The -d option specifies the absolute path to the httpd binary (used only if the default location is not valid).

◆ The -f option lists the configuration file to read if it is different from the default value of httpd.conf.

◆ The -v option displays the version number.

If you are using inetd to start your Web server software, you need to make a change to the /etc/services file to enable the Web software. Add a line like this to the /etc/services file:

```
http     port/tcp
```

In this line, port is the port number used by your Web server software (usually 80).

Next, modify the /etc/inetd.conf file to include the startup commands for the Web server:

```
httpd stream tcp nowait nobody /usr/web/httpd
```

The last entry is the path to the httpd binary. Once this is done, restart inetd by killing the inetd process or by rebooting your system, and the service should be available through whatever port you specified in /etc/services.

If you are running the Web server software as a daemon, you can start it at any time from the command line with the following command:

```
httpd
```

Even better, add the startup commands to the proper rc startup files. The entry usually looks like this:

```
# start httpd
if [ -x /usr/web/httpd ]
then
  /usr/web/httpd
fi
```

You should substitute the proper paths for the httpd binary, of course. Rebooting your machine should start the Web server software on the default port number.

To test the Web server software, use any Web browser and issue a command in the URL field like this:

```
http://machinename
```

Replace `machinename` with the name of your Web server. If you see the contents of the root Web directory or the index.html file, all is well. Otherwise, check the log files and configuration files for clues as to the problem.

If you haven't loaded a Web browser yet, you can still check whether the Web server is running by using Telnet. Issue a command like this:

```
telnet www.wizard.tpci.com 80
```

Substitute the name of your server (and your Web port number if different than 80). You should get a message similar to this if the Web server is responding properly:

```
Connected to wizard.tpci.com
Escape character is '^]'.
HEAD/HTTP/1.0
HTTP/1.0 200 OK
```

You should also get some more lines showing details about the date and content. You may not be able to access anything, but this shows that the Web software is responding properly.

SETTING UP YOUR WEB SITE

Having a server with nothing for content is useless, so you need to set up the information you will share through your Web system. This begins with Uniform Resource Locators (URLs), which are search paths for data files. Anyone using your service only has to know the URL. You don't need to have anything fancy. If you don't have a special home page, anyone connecting to your system will get the contents of the Web root directory's index.html file, or failing that, a directory listing of the Web root directory. That's pretty boring, though, and most users want fancy home pages. To write a home page, you need to use HTML (HyperText Markup Language).

A home page is like a main menu. Many users may not ever see it because they can enter any of the subdirectories on your system or obtain files from another Web system through a hyperlink, without ever seeing your home page. Many users, however, want to start at the top, and that's where your home page comes in. A home page file is usually called index.html (or home.html if an index file exists). It usually is at the top of your Web source directories.

Writing an HTML document is not too difficult. The language uses a set of tags to indicate how the text is to be treated (such as headlines, body text, figures, and so on). The tricky part of HTML is getting the tags in the right place, without extra material on a line. HTML is rather strict about its syntax, so errors must be avoided to prevent problems.

In the early days of the Web, all documents were written with simple text editors. As the Web expanded, dedicated Web editors that understand HTML and the use of tags began to appear. Their popularity has driven developers to produce dozens of editors, filters, and utilities, all aimed at making a Web documenter's life easier (and ensure that the HTML language is properly used). HTML editors are available for many operating systems.

HTML AUTHORING TOOLS

You can write HTML documents in many ways: you can use an ASCII editor, a word processor, or a dedicated HTML tool. The choice of which you use depends on personal preference and your confidence in HTML coding, as well as which tools you can obtain easily. Because many HTML-specific tools have checking routines or filters to verify that your documents are correctly laid out and formatted, they can be appealing. They also tend to be more friendly than non-HTML editors. On the other hand, if you are a veteran programmer or writer, you may want to stick with your favorite editor and use a filter or syntax checker afterwards.

One of the best sites to look for new editors and filters is CERN. Connect to http://info.cern.ch/WWW/Tools and check the document Overview.html. Also check the NCSA site, accessible at http://www.ncsa.uiuc.edu/SDG/Software/Mosaic/Docs where the document faq-software.html contains an up-to-date list of offerings.

You can use any ASCII editor to write HTML pages, including simple line-oriented editors based on vi or emacs. They all enable you to enter tags into a page of text, but the tags are treated as words with no special meaning. There is no validity checking performed by simple editors, as they simply don't understand HTML. There are some extensions for emacs and similar full-screen editors that provide a simple template check, but they are not rigorous in enforcing HTML styles.

If you want to use a plain editor, you should carefully check your document for valid use of tags. One of the easiest methods of checking a document is to import it into an HTML editor that has strong type checking. Another easy method is to simply call up the document on your Web browser and carefully study its appearance.

You can obtain a dedicated HTML authoring package from some sites, although they are not as common for Linux as for DOS and Windows. If you are running both operating systems, you can always develop your HTML documents in Windows, then import them to Linux. Several popular HTML tools for Windows are available, such as HTML Assistant, HTMLed, and HoTMetaL. A few of the WYSIWYG editors, such as HoTMetaL are also available for X, and hence run under Linux. Some HTML authoring tools are fully WYSIWYG, and others are character-based. Most offer strong verification systems for generated HTML code.

For the latest Linux or Windows version of HoTMetaL, try the Web site: ftp://ftp.ncsa.uiuc.edu/Web/html/hotmetal.

An alternative to using a dedicated editor for HTML documents is to enhance an existing WYSIWYG word processor to handle HTML properly. The most commonly targeted word processors for these extensions are Word for Windows, WordPerfect, and Word for DOS. Several extension products are available, of varying degrees of complexity. Most run under Windows, although a few have been ported to Linux.

The advantage to using one of these extensions is that you retain a familiar editor and make use of the near-WYSIWYG features it can provide for HTML documents. Although it can't show you the final document in Web format, it can be close enough to prevent all but the most minor problems.

CU_HTML is a template for Microsoft's Word for Windows that gives an almost WYSIWYG view of HTML documents. CU_HTML is a template, meaning that it adds its own DLLs to Word to enhance the system. Graphically, it looks much the same as Word, but with a new toolbar and pull-down menu item. CU_HTML provides a number of different styles and a toolbar of often-used tasks. Tasks like linking documents are easy, as are most tasks that tend to worry new HTML document writers. Dialog boxes are used for many tasks, simplifying the interface considerably.

The only major disadvantage to CU_HTML is that it can't be used to edit existing HTML documents because they are not in Word format. When CU_HTML creates an HTML document, two versions are produced, one in HTML and the other as a Word .DOC file. Without both, the document can't be edited. An existing document can be imported, but it loses all the tags.

Like CU_HTML, ANT_HTML is an extension to Word. ANT_HTML has some advantages and disadvantages over CU_HTML. The documentation and help are better with ANT_HTML, and the toolbar is much better. There's also automatic insertion of opening and closing tags as needed.

However, ANT_HTML requires that any inline GIF images be inserted instead of using a DLL. This means that you may have to hunt for a suitable filter. Also, like CU_HTML, ANT_HTML can't handle documents that were not produced with ANT_HTML.

One system that has gained popularity among Linux users is tkWWW. A tool for the Tcl language and its Tk extension for X, tkWWW is a combination of a Web browser and a near-WYSIWYG HTML editor. Although originally UNIX-based, tkWWW has been ported to several other platforms, including Windows and Macintosh.

Note

tkWWW can be obtained through anonymous ftp to ftp.aud.alcatel.com in the directory /pub/tcl/extensions. Copies of Tcl and Tk can be found in several sites depending on the platform required, although most versions of Linux have Tcl and Tk included in the distribution set. As a starting point, try anonymous FTP to ftp.cs.berkeley.edu in the directory /ucb/tcl.

When you create a Web page with tkwww in editor mode, you can then flip modes to browser to see the same page properly formatted. In editor mode, most of the formatting is correct, but the tags are left visible. This makes for fast development of a Web page.

Unfortunately, tkwww must rely on Tk for its windowing, which tends to slow things down a bit on average processors. Also, the browser aspect of tkwww is not impressive, using standard Tk frames. However, as a prototyping tool, tkwww is very attractive, especially if you know the Tcl language.

Another option is to use an HTML filter. An HTML filter is a tool that lets you take a document produced with any kind of editor (including ASCII text editors) and convert the document to HTML. Filters are useful when you work in an editor that has its own proprietary format, such as Word or nroff.

HTML filters are attractive if you want to continue working in your favorite editor and simply want a utility to convert your document with tags to HTML. Filters tend to be fast and easy to work with because they take a filename as input and generate an HTML output file. The degree of error checking and reporting varies with the tool.

Filters are available for most types of documents, many of which are available directly for Linux, or as source code that can be recompiled without modification under Linux. Word for Windows and Word for DOS documents can be converted to HTML with the CU_HTML and ANT_HTML extensions mentioned earlier. A few stand-alone conversion utilities have also begun to appear. The utility WPTOHTML converts WordPerfect documents to HTML. WPTOHTML is a set of macros for WordPerfect versions 5.1, 5.2, and 6.0. The WordPerfect filter can also be used with other word processor formats that WordPerfect can import.

FrameMaker and FrameBuilder documents can be converted to HTML format with the tool FM2HTML. FM2HTML is a set of scripts that converts Frame documents to HTML while preserving hypertext links and tables. It also handles GIF files without a problem. Because Frame documents are platform-independent, Frame documents developed on a PC or Macintosh could be moved to a Linux platform and FM2HTML executed there.

> *Note*
>
> A copy of FM2HTML is available by anonymous FTP from bang.nta.no in the directory /pub. The UNIX set is called fm2-html.tar.v.0.n.m.Z.

LaTex and TeX files can be converted to HTML with several different utilities. Quite a few Linux-based utilities are available, including LATEXTOHTML, which can even handle in-line LaTeX equations and links. For simpler documents, the utility VULCANIZE is faster but can't handle mathematical equations. Both LATEXTOHTML and VULCANIZE are Perl scripts.

> *Note*
>
> LATEXTOHTML is available through anonymous FTP from ftp.tex.ac.uk in the directory pub/archive/support as the file latextohtml. VULCANIZE can be obtained from the Web site http://www/cis.upenn.edu in the directory mjd as the file vulcanize.html.

RTFTOHTML is a common utility for converting RTF format documents to HTML. Many word processors handle RTF formats, so you can save an RTF document from your favorite word processor and then run RTFTOHTML against it.

> *Note*
>
> RTFTOHTML is available through anonymous FTP from ftp.cray.com in the directory src/WWWstuff/RTF. Through the Web, try http://info.cern.ch/hypertext/WWW/Tools and look for the file rtftoftml-2.6.html (or a later version).

MAINTAINING HTML

Once you have written a Web document and it is available to the world, your job doesn't end. Unless your document is a simple text file, you will have links to other documents or Web servers embedded. You must verify these links at regular intervals. Also, the integrity of your Web pages should be checked at intervals, to ensure that the flow of the document from your home page is correct.

Several utilities are available to help you check links and to scan the Web for other sites or documents you may want to provide a hyperlink to. These utilities tend to go by a number of names, such as robot, spider, or wanderer. They are all programs that moves across the Web automatically, creating a list of Web links that you can access. (Spiders are similar to the Archie and Veronica tools for the Internet, although neither of these cover the Web.)

Although they are often thought of as utilities for users only (to get a list of sites to try), spiders and their kin are useful for document authors, too, as they show potentially useful and interesting links. One of the best known spiders is the World Wide Web Worm, or WWWW. WWWW enables you to search for keywords or create a Boolean search, and it can cover titles, documents, and several other search types (including a search of all known HTML pages).

A similarly useful spider is WebCrawler, which is similar to WWWW, except that it can scan entire documents for matches of any keywords and display the result in an ordered list from closest match to least match.

Note

A copy of World Wide Web Worm can be obtained from http:
/www.cs.colorado.edu/home/mcbryan/WWWW.html. WebCrawler is
available from http://www.biotech.washington.edu/WebCrawler/
WebCrawler.html.

A common problem with HTML documents as they age is that links that point to files or servers may no longer exist (either because the locations or documents have changed). Therefore, it is good practice to validate the hyperlinks in a document on a regular basis. A popular hyperlink analyzer is HTML_ANALYZER. It examines each hyperlink and the contents of the hyperlink to ensure that they are consistent. HTML_ANALYZER functions by examining a document to all links, then creating a text file that has a list of the links in it. HTML_ANALYZER uses the text files to compare the actual link content to what it should be.

HTML_ANALYZER actually does three tests: it validates the availability of the documents pointed to by hyperlinks (called validation); it looks for hyperlink contents that occur in the database but are not themselves hyperlinks (called completeness); and it looks for a one-to-one relation between hyperlinks and the contents of the hyperlink (called consistency). Any deviations are listed for the user.

HTML_ANALYZER users should have a good familiarity with HTML, their operating system, and the use of command-line driven analyzers. The tool must be compiled using the "make" utility prior to execution. There are several directories that must be created prior to running HTML_ANALYZER, and it creates several temporary files when it runs that are not cleaned up, so this is not a good utility for a novice.

Summary

Setting up your home page requires you to either use an HTML authoring tool or write HTML code directly into an editor. The HTML language is beyond the scope of this book, but you should find several good guides to HTML at your bookstore. HTML is rather easy to learn. With the information in this chapter, you should be able to set up your Web site to enable anyone on the Internet to connect to you. Enjoy the Web!

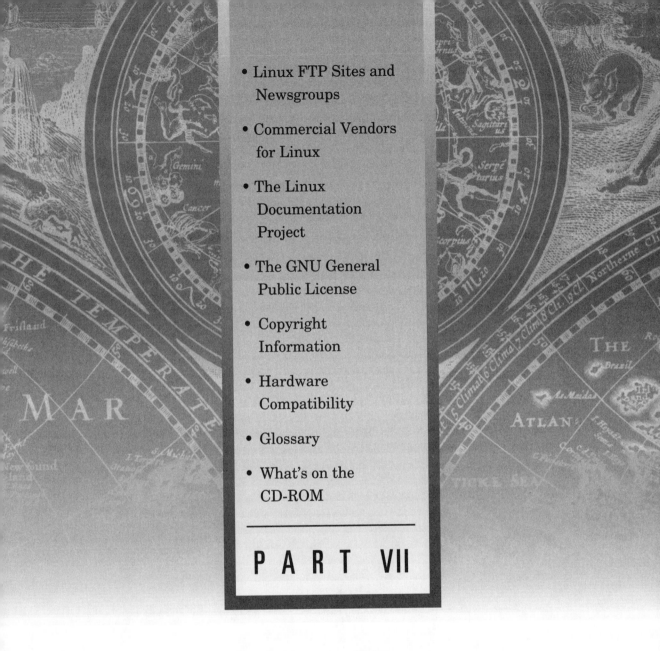

- Linux FTP Sites and Newsgroups

- Commercial Vendors for Linux

- The Linux Documentation Project

- The GNU General Public License

- Copyright Information

- Hardware Compatibility

- Glossary

- What's on the CD-ROM

PART VII

Appendixes

- FTP Sites
- Bulletin Boards
- USENET Newsgroups

APPENDIX A

Linux FTP Sites
and Newsgroups

If you have access to the Internet, either directly or through an online service provider such as CompuServe, Delphi, or America Online, you can access additional sources of Linux software and information. Two popular sources of Linux software and help are available, one through FTP and the other through Linux-specific USENET newsgroups.

If you don't have access to the Internet, you may still be able to get some of the information available through other sources, such as Bulletin Board Systems (BBSs) and CD-ROMs published by companies specializing in redistributing public domain material.

FTP SITES

FTP is a method of accessing remote systems and downloading files. It is quite easy to use and provides users who have Internet access with a fast method for updating their list of binaries.

For those without FTP access but who can use electronic mail through the Internet, the utility `ftpmail` can provide access to these FTP sites.

WHAT IS FTP?

File Transfer Protocol (FTP) is one protocol in the TCP/IP family of protocols. TCP/IP is used extensively as the communications protocol of the Internet, as well as in many Local Area Networks (LANs). UNIX systems almost always use TCP/IP as their protocol.

FTP is used to transfer files between machines running TCP/IP. FTP-like programs are also available for some other protocols.

To use FTP, both ends of a connection must be running a program that provides FTP services. To download a file from a remote system, you must start your FTP software and instruct it to connect to the FTP software running on the remote machine.

The Internet has many FTP *archive sites*. These are machines that are set up to allow anyone to connect to them and download software. In some cases, there are FTP archive sites that mirror each other. A *mirror site* is one that maintains exactly the same software as another site, so you simply connect to the one that is easiest for you to access, and you have the same software available for downloading as if you had connected to the other site.

Usually, when you connect to a remote system, you must log in. This means that you must be a valid user, with a username and password for that remote machine. Because it is impossible to provide logins for everyone who wants to access a public archive, many systems use anonymous FTP. *Anonymous FTP* enables anyone to log into the system with the login name of guest or anonymous and either no password or the user's login name or e-mail address (used for auditing purposes only).

Connecting and Downloading Files with FTP

Using FTP to connect to a remote site is quite easy. Assuming that you have access to the Internet either directly or through a service provider, you must start FTP and provide the name of the remote system to which you want to connect. If you are directly connected to the Internet, the process is simple: you enter the ftp command with the name of the remote site:

```
ftp sunsite.unc.edu
```

If you are using an online service, such as Delphi, you must access its Internet services menus and invoke FTP from that. Some online services enable you to enter the name of any FTP site at a prompt, whereas others have some menus that list all available sites. You may have to hunt through the online documentation for your service provider to find the correct procedure.

After you issue the ftp command, your system will attempt to connect to the remote machine. When it does (if the remote system allows FTP logins), the remote will prompt you for a user ID. If anonymous FTP is supported on the system, a message will usually tell you that. The following login is shown for the Linux FTP archive site sunsite.unc.edu:

```
ftp sunsite.unc.edu
331 Guest login ok, send your complete e-mail address as password.
Enter username (default: anonymous): anonymous
Enter password [tparker@tpci.com]:
¦FTP¦ Open
230-              WELCOME to UNC and SUN's anonymous ftp server
230-                        University of North Carolina
230-                      Office FOR Information Technology
230-                             SunSITE.unc.edu
230 Guest login ok, access restrictions apply.
FTP>
```

After the login process is completed, you will see the prompt FTP>, indicating that the system is ready to accept commands. When you log in to some systems, you see a short message that might contain instructions for downloading files, any restrictions that are placed on you as an anonymous FTP user, or information about the location of useful files. For example, you might see messages like this one:

```
To get a binary file, type:  BINARY and then: GET "File.Name" newfilename
To get a text file, type:    ASCII  and then: GET "File.Name" newfilename
Names MUST match upper, lower case exactly. Use the "quotes" as shown.
To get a directory, type: DIR. To change directory, type: CD "Dir.Name"
To read a short text file, type: GET "File.Name" TT
For more, type HELP or see FAQ in gopher.
To quit, type EXIT or Control-Z.
```

```
230-   If you email to info@sunsite.unc.edu you will be sent help information
230-   about how to use the different services sunsite provides.
230-   We use the Wuarchive experimental ftpd. if you "get" <directory>.tar.Z
230-   or <file>.Z it will compress and/or tar it on the fly. Using ".gz"  instead
230-   of ".Z" will use the GNU zip (/pub/gnu/gzip*) instead, a superior
230-   compression method.
```

After you are connected to the remote system, you can use familiar Linux commands to display file contents and move around the directories. To display the contents of a directory, for example, use the command ls or the DOS equivalent DIR. To change to a subdirectory, use the cd command. To return to the parent directory (the one above the current directory), use the command cdup or cd ... FTP has no keyboard shortcuts, so you have to type in the name of files or directories in their entirety.

When you have moved through the directories and have found a file you want to move back to your home system, use the get command:

```
get "file1.txt"
```

The commands get (download) and put (upload) are relative to your home machine. You are telling your system to get a file from the remote location and put it on your local machine, or to put a file from your local machine onto the remote machine. This is the exact opposite of another commonly used TCP/IP protocol, telnet, which has everything relative to the remote machine. It is important to remember which command moves in which direction, or you could overwrite files accidentally.

The quotation marks around the filename are optional for most versions of FTP, but they do provide specific characters to the remote version (preventing shell expansion), so you should use the quotation marks to avoid mistakes. FTP provides two modes of file transfer: ASCII and binary. Some systems will automatically switch between the two, but it is a good idea to set the mode manually to ensure that you don't waste time. To set FTP in binary transfer mode (for any executable file), type the following command:

```
binary
```

You can toggle back to ASCII mode with the command ASCII. Because you will most likely be checking remote sites for new binaries or libraries of source code, it is a good idea to use binary mode for most transfers. If you transfer a binary file in ASCII mode, it will not be executable (or understandable) on your system. ASCII mode includes only the valid ASCII characters and not the Ctrl-key sequences used within binaries. Transferring an ASCII file in binary mode does not affect the contents, although spurious noise may cause a problem in rare instances.

When you issue a get command, the remote system will transfer data to your local machine and display a status message when it is finished. There is no indication of progress when a large file is being transferred, so be patient.

```
FTP> get "file1.txt"
200 PORT command successful.
150 BINARY data connection for FILE1.TXT (27534 bytes)
226 BINARY Transfer complete.
27534 bytes received in 2.35 seconds (12 Kbytes/s).
```

To quit FTP, type the command quit or exit. Either will close your session on the remote machine, then terminate FTP on your local machine.

USING FTPMAIL

If you don't have access to a remote site through FTP, all is not lost. If you have electronic mail, you can still get files transferred to you. Some online systems allow Internet mail to be sent and received but do not allow direct access to FTP. Similarly, some Internet service providers offer UUCP accounts that do not allow direct connection but do provide e-mail. To get to FTP sites and transfer files, you use the ftpmail utility.

The site mentioned earlier, sunsite.unc.edu, is a major Linux archive site that supports ftpmail. All of the sites listed in this Appendix as Linux FTP sites also support ftpmail. To find out how to use ftpmail, send an e-mail message to the login ftpmail at one of the sites, such as ftpmail@sunsite.unc.edu, and have the body of the message contain only one word: help.

By return mail, the ftpmail utility will send instructions for using the service. Essentially, you send the body of the ftp commands you want executed in a mail message, so you could get back a directory listing of the Linux directory in a mail message with this text:

```
open sunsite.unc.edu
cd /pub/Linux
ls
quit
```

You could transfer a file back through e-mail with a similar mail message:

```
open sunsite.unc.edu
cd /pub/Linux
binary
get README
quit
```

The ftpmail system is relatively slow, as you must wait for the e-mail to make its way to the target machine and be processed by the remote, then for the return message to make its way back to you. It does provide a useful access method for those without FTP connections, though, and a relatively easy way to check the contents of the Linux directories on several machines.

Linux FTP Archive Sites

The list of Linux FTP archive sites changes slowly, but the sites listed in Table A.1 were all valid and reachable when this book was written. Many of these sites are mirror sites, providing exactly the same contents.

To find the site nearest you, use the country identifier at the end of the site name (uk=United Kingdom, fr=France, and so on). Most versions of FTP allow either the machine name or the IP address to be used, but if the name cannot be resolved by the local Internet gateway, the IP address is the best addressing method.

Table A.1. Linux FTP archive sites.

Site name	IP Address	Directory
tsx-11.mit.edu	18.172.1.2	/pub/linux
sunsite.unc.edu	152.2.22.81	/pub/Linux
nic.funet.fi	128.214.6.100	/pub/OS/Linux
ftp.mcc.ac.uk	130.88.200.7	/pub/linux
ftp.dfv.rwth-aachen.de	137.226.4.111	/pub/linux
ftp.informatik.rwth-aachen.de	137.226.255.3	/pub/Linux
ftp.ibp.fr	132.227.60.2	/pub/linux
ftp.uu.net	192.48.96.9	/systems/unix/linux
wuarchive.wustl.edu	128.252.135.4	/systems/linux
ftp.win.tue.nl	131.155.70.19	/pub/linux
ftp.stack.urc.tue.nl	131.155.140.128	/pub/linux
ftp.ibr.cs.tu-bs.de	134.169.34.15	/pub/ linux
ftp.denet.dk	130.255.250.7	/pub/OS/Llinux

The primary home sites for the Linux archives are tsx-11.mit.edu, sunsite.unc.edu, and nic.funet.fi. *Home* sites are where most of the new software loads begin. The majority of sites in Table A.1 mirror one of these three sites.

Bulletin Boards

There are literally hundreds of Bulletin Board Systems (BBSs) across the world that offer Linux software. Some download new releases on a regular basis from the FTP home sites, whereas others rely on the users of the BBS to update the software.

A complete list of BBSs with Linux software available would be too lengthy (as well as out-of-date almost immediately) to include here. Zane Healy maintains a complete list of BBSs offering Linux material. To obtain the list, send e-mail requesting the Linux list to healyzh@holonet.net.

If you don't have access to e-mail, try posting messages on a few local bulletin board systems asking for local sites that offer Linux software, or ask someone with Internet access to post e-mail for you.

LINUX-RELATED BBSs

Zane Healy (healyzh@holonet.net) maintains this list. If you know of or run a BBS that provides Linux software but isn't on this list, you should get in touch with him.

You can also get an up-to-date list on BBSs from tsx-11.mit.edu in the /pub/linux/docs/bbs.list file. The following lists were up-to-date at the time this book went to print.

UNITED STATES BBSs

Here is a list of some of the BBSs in the United States that carry Linux or information about Linux:

1 Zero Cybernet BBS, 301-589-4064. MD.

AVSync, 404-320-6202. Atlanta, GA.

Allentown Technical, 215-432-5699. 9600 v.32/v.42bis Allentown, PA. WWIVNet 2578

Aquired Knowledge, 305-720-3669. 14.4k v.32bis Ft. Lauderdale, FL. Internet, UUCP

Atlanta Radio Club, 404-850-0546. 9600 Atlanta, GA.

Brodmann's Place, 301-843-5732. 14.4k Waldorf, MD. RIME ->BRODMANN, Fidonet

Centre Programmers Unit, 814-353-0566. 14.4k V.32bis/HST Bellefonte, PA.

Channel One, 617-354-8873. Boston, MA. RIME ->CHANNEL

Citrus Grove Public Access, 916-381-5822. ZyXEL 16.8/14.4 Sacramento, CA.

CyberVille, 817-249-6261. 9600 TX. FidoNet 1:130/78

Digital Designs, 919-423-4216. 14.4k, 2400 Hope Mills, NC.

Digital Underground, 812-941-9427. 14.4k v.32bis IN. USENET

Dwight-Englewood BBS, 201-569-3543. 9600 v.42 Englewood, NJ. USENET

EchoMania, 618-233-1659. 14.4k HST Belleville, IL. Fidonet 1:2250/1

Enlightend, 703-370-9528. 14.4k Alexandria, VA. Fidonet 1:109/615

Flite Line, 402-421-2434. Lincoln, NE. RIME ->FLITE, DS modem

Georgia Peach BBS, 804-727-0399. 14.4k Newport News, VA.

Harbor Heights BBS, 207-663-0391. 14.4k Boothbay Harbor, ME.

Horizon Systems, 216-899-1293. 2400 Westlake, OH.

Information Overload, 404-471-1549. 19.2k ZyXEL Atlanta, GA. Fidonet 1:133/308

Intermittent Connection, 503-344-9838. 14.4k HST v.32bis Eugene, OR. 1:152/35

Horizon Systems, 216-899-1086. USR v.32 Westlake, OH.

Legend, 402-438-2433. Lincoln, NE. DS modem

Lost City Atlantis, 904-727-9334. 14.4k Jacksonville, FL. FidoNet

MAC's Place, 919-891-1111. 16.8k, DS modem Dunn, NC. RIME ->MAC

MBT, 703-953-0640. Blacksburg, VA.

Main Frame, 301-654-2554. 9600 Gaithersburg, MD. RIME ->MAIN-FRAME

MegaByte Mansion, 402-551-8681. 14.4 V,32bis Omaha, NE.

Micro Oasis, 510-895-5985. 14.4k San Leandro, CA.

My UnKnown BBS, 703-690-0669. 14.4k V.32bis VA. Fidonet 1:109/370

Mycroft QNX, 201-858-3429. 14.4k NJ.

NOVA, 703-323-3321. 9600 Annandale, VA. Fidonet 1:109/305

North Shore BBS, 713-251-9757. Houston, TX.

PBS BBS, 309-663-7675. 2400 Bloomington, IL.

Part-Time BBS, 612-544-5552. 14.4k v.32bis Plymouth, MN.

Programmer's Center, 301-596-1180. 9600 Columbia, MD. RIME

Programmer's Exchange, 818-444-3507. El Monte, CA. Fidonet

Programmer's Exchange, 818-579-9711. El Monte, CA.

Rebel BBS, 208-887-3937. 9600 Boise, ID.

Rem-Jem, 703-503-9410. 9600 Fairfax, VA.

Rocky Mountain HUB, 208-232-3405. 38.4k Pocatello, ID. Fidonet, SLNet, CinemaNet

Ronin BBS, 214-938-2840. 14.4 HST/DS Waxahachie (Dallas), TX.

S'Qually Holler, 206-235-0270. 14.4k USR D/S Renton, WA.

Slut Club, 813-975-2603. USR/DS 16.8k HST/14.4K Tampa, FL. Fidonet 1:377/42

Steve Leon's, 201-886-8041. 14.4k Cliffside Park, NJ.

Tactical-Operations, 814-861-7637. 14.4k V32bis/V42bis State College, PA. Fidonet 1:129/226, tac_ops.UUCP

Test Engineering, 916-928-0504. Sacramento, CA.

The Annex, 512-575-0667. 2400 TX. Fidonet 1:3802/216

The Annex, 512-575-1188. 9600 HST TX. Fidonet 1:3802/217

The Computer Mechanic, 813-544-9345. 14.4k v.32bis

The Laboratory, 212-927-4980. 16.8k HST, 14.4k v.32bis NY. FidoNet 1:278/707

The Mothership Connection, 908-940-1012. 38.4k Franklin Park, NJ.

The OA Southern Star, 504-885-5928. New Orleans, LA. Fidonet 1:396/1

The Outer Rim, 805-252-6342. Santa Clarita, CA.

The Sole Survivor, 314-846-2702. 14.4k v.32bis St. Louis, MO. WWIVnet, WWIVlink, etc.

Third World, 217-356-9512. 9600 v.32 IL.

Top Hat BBS, 206-244-9661. 14.4k WA. Fidonet 1:343/40

UNIX USER, 708-879-8633. 14.4k Batavia, IL. USENET, Internet mail

Unix Online, 707-765-4631. 9600 Petaluma, CA. USENET access

VTBBS, 703-231-7498. Blacksburg, VA.

VWIS Linux Support BBS, 508-793-1570. 9600 Worcester, MA.

Valhalla, 516-321-6819. 14.4k HST v.32 Babylon, NY. Fidonet (1:107/25 5), USENET

Walt Fairs, 713-947-9866. Houston, TX. FidoNet 1:106/18

WaterDeep BBS, 410-614-2190. 9600 v.32 Baltimore, MD.

WayStar BBS, 508-480-8371. 9600 V.32bis or 14.4k USR/HST Marlborough, MA. Fidonet 1:333/16

WayStar BBS, 508-481-7147. 14.4k V.32bis USR/HST Marlborough, MA. Fidonet 1:333 /14

WayStar BBS, 508-481-7293. 14.4k V.32bis USR/HST Marlborough, MA. Fidonet 1:333 /15

alaree, 512-575-5554. 14.4k Victoria, TX.

hip-hop, 408-773-0768. 19.2k Sunnyvale, CA. USENET access

hip-hop, 408-773-0768. 38.4k Sunnyvale, CA.

splat-ooh, 512-578-2720. 14.4k Victoria, TX.

splat-ooh, 512-578-5436. 14.4k Victoria, TX.

victrola.sea.wa.us, 206-838-7456. 19.2k Federal Way, WA. USENET

OUTSIDE OF THE UNITED STATES

If you live outside the US, you can get information about Linux from these BBSs:

500cc Formula 1 BBS, +61-2-550-4317. V.32bis Sydney, NSW, Australia.

A6 BBS, +44-582-460273. 14.4k Herts, UK. Fidonet 2:440/111

Advanced Systems, +64-9-379-3365. ZyXEL 16.8k Auckland, New Zealand.

BOX/2, +49.89.601-96-77. 16.8 ZYX Muenchen, BAY, Germany.

Baboon BBS, +41-62-511726. 19.2k Switzerland.

Basil, +33-1-44670844. v.32bis Paris, Laurent Chemla, France.

BigBrother / R. Gmelch, +49.30.335-63-28. 16.8 Z16 Berlin, BLN, Germany.

Bit-Company / J. Bartz, +49.5323.2539. 16.8 ZYX MO Clausthal-Zfd., NDS, Germany.

CRYSTAL BBS, +49.7152.240-86. 14.4 HST Leonberg, BW, Germany.

CS-Port / C. Schmidt, +49.30.491-34-18. 19.2 Z19 Berlin, BLN, Germany.

Cafard Naum, +33-51701632. v.32bis Nantes, Yann Dupont, France.

DUBBS, +353-1-6789000. 19.2 ZyXEL Dublin, Ireland. Fidonet 2:263/167

DataComm1, +49.531.132-16. 14.4 HST Braunschweig, NDS, Germany. Fidonet 2:240/55

DataComm2, +49.531.132-17. 14.4 HST Braunschweig, NDS, Germany. Fidonet 2:240/55

Die Box Passau 2+1, +49.851.555-96. 14.4 V32b Passau, BAY, Germany.

Die Box Passau ISDN, +49.851.950-464. 38.4/64k V.110/X.75 Passau, BAY, Germany.

Die Box Passau Line 1, +49.851.753-789. 16.8 ZYX Passau, BAY, Germany.

Die Box Passau Line 3, +49.851.732-73. 14.4 HST Passau, BAY, Germany.

DownTown BBS Lelystad, +31-3200-48852. 14.4k Lelystad, Netherlands.

Echoblaster BBS #1, +49.7142.213-92. HST/V32b Bietigheim, BW, Germany.

Echoblaster BBS #2, +49.7142.212-35. V32b Bietigheim, BW, Germany.

FORMEL-Box, +49.4191.2846. 16.8 ZYX Kaltenkirchen, SHL, Germany.

Fiffis Inn BBS, +49-89-5701353. 14.4-19.2 Munich, Germany.

Fractal Zone BBS /Maass, +49.721.863-066. 16.8 ZYX Karlsruhe, BW, Germany.

Galaktische Archive, 0043-2228303804. 16.8 ZYX Wien, Austria. Fidonet 2:310/77 (19:00-7:00)

Galway Online, +353-91-27454. 14.4k v32b Galway, Ireland.

Gunship BBS, +46-31-693306. 14.4k HST DS Gothenburg, Sweden.

Hipposoft /M. Junius, +49.241.875-090. 14.4 HST Aachen, NRW, Germany.

Le Lien, +33-72089879. HST 14.4/V32bis Lyon, Pascal Valette, France.

Linux Server /Braukmann, +49.441.592-963. 16.8 ZYX Oldenburg, NDS, Germany.

Linux-Support-Oz, +61-2-418-8750. v.32bis 14.4k Sydney, NSW, Australia.

LinuxServer / P. Berger, +49.711.756-275. 16.8 HST Stuttgart, BW, Germany.

Logical Solutions, 403 299-9900 through 9911. 2400 AB, Canada.

Logical Solutions, 403 299-9912, 299-9913. 14.4k AB, Canada.

Logical Solutions, 403 299-9914 through 9917. 16.8k v.32bis AB, Canada.

MM's Spielebox, +49.5323.3515. 14.4 ZYX Clausthal-Zfd., NDS, Germany.

MM's Spielebox, +49.5323.3516. 16.8 ZYX Clausthal-Zfd., NDS, Germany.

MM's Spielebox, +49.5323.3540. 9600 Clausthal-Zfd., NDS, Germany.

MUGNET Intl-Cistron BBS, +31-1720-42580. 38.4k Alphen a/d Rijn, Netherlands.

Magic BBS, 403-569-2882. 14.4k HST/Telebit/MNP Calgary, AB, Canada. Internet/Usenet

Modula BBS, +33-1 4043 0124. HST 14.4 v.32bis Paris, France.

Modula BBS, +33-1 4530 1248. HST 14.4 V.32bis Paris, France.

Nemesis' Dungeon, +353-1-324755 or 326900. 14.4k v32bis Dublin, Ireland.

On the Beach, +444-273-600996. 14.4k/16.8k Brighton, UK. Fidonet 2:441/122

Pats System, +27-12-333-2049. 14.4k v.32bis/HST Pretoria, South Africa.

Public Domain Kiste, +49.30.686-62-50. 16.8 ZYX BLN, Germany. Fidonet 2:2403/17

Radio Free Nyongwa, 514-524-0829. v.32bis ZyXEL Montreal, QC, Canada. USENET, Fidonet

Rising Sun BBS, +49.7147.3845. 16.8 ZYX Sachsenheim, BW, Germany. Fidonet 2:2407/4

STDIN BBS, +33-72375139. v.32bis Lyon, Laurent Cas, France.

Synapse, 819-246-2344. 819-561-5268 Gatineau, QC, Canada. RIME->SYNAPSE

The Controversy, (65)560-6040. 14.4k V.32bis/HST Singapore.

The Field of Inverse Chaos, +358 0 506 1836. 14.4k v32bis/HST Helsinki, Finland.

The Purple Tentacle, +44-734-590990. HST/V32bis Reading, UK. Fidonet 2:252/305

The Windsor Download, (519)-973-9330. v32bis 14.4 ON, Canada.

Thunderball Cave, 472567018. Norway.

UB-HOFF /A. Hoffmann, +49.203.584-155. 19.2 ZYX+ Duisburg, Germany.

V.A.L.I.S., 403-478-1281. 14.4k v.32bis Edmonton, AB, Canada. USENET

bakunin.north.de, +49.421.870-532. 14.4 D 2800 Bremen, HB, Germany.

nonsolosoftware, +39 51 432904. ZyXEL 19.2k Italy. Fidonet 2:332/417

nonsolosoftware, +39 51 6140772. v.32bis, v.42bis Italy. Fidonet 2:332/407

r-node, 416-249-5366. 2400 Toronto, ON, Canada. USENET

USENET NEWSGROUPS

USENET is a collection of discussion groups (called *newsgroups*) that is available to Internet users. There are over 9,000 newsgroups with over 100MB of traffic posted every single day. Of all of these newsgroups (which cover every conceivable topic), several are dedicated to Linux.

You can access USENET newsgroups through special software called a *newsreader* if you have access to a site that downloads the newsgroups on a regular basis. Alternatively, most online services such as CompuServe, America Online, and Delphi also offer access to USENET. Some BBSs also provide limited access to newsgroups.

USENET newsgroups fall into three categories: primary newsgroups, which are readily available to all USENET users; local newsgroups with a limited distribution; and alternate newsgroups that may not be handled by all news servers. The primary newsgroups of interest to Linux users are

comp.os.linux.admin	Installing and administering Linux systems
comp.os.linux.advocacy	Proponents of the Linux system
comp.os.linux.announce	Announcements important to the Linux community (moderated)
comp.os.linux.answers	Questions and answers to problems
comp.os.linux.development	Ongoing work on Linux
comp.os.linux.development.apps	Ongoing work on Linux applications
comp.os.linux.development.system	Ongoing work on the Linux operating system

comp.os.linux.hardware	Issues with Linux and hardware
comp.os.linux.help	Questions and advice about Linux
comp.os.linux.misc	Linux-specific topics not covered by other groups
comp.os.linux.networking	Making the Linux system network properly
comp.os.linux.setup	Setup and installation problems with Linux

These newsgroups should be available at all USENET sites unless the system administrator filters them out for some reason.

The other newsgroups tend to change frequently, primarily because they are either regional or populated with highly opinionated users who may lose interest after a while. The .alt (alternate) newsgroups are particularly bad for this. Only one .alt newsgroups was in operation when this book was written:

```
alt.uu.comp.os.linux.questions
```

There are also regional newsgroups that usually are not widely distributed, or that have specific issues which may be in a language other than English. Some sample regional newsgroups carried by USENET are:

- u dc.org.linux-users
- u de.comp.os.linux
- u fr.comp.os.linux
- u tn.linux

If you do have access to USENET newsgroups, it is advisable to regularly scan the newsgroup additions and deletions to check for new Linux newsgroups or existing groups that have folded. Most online services that provide access to USENET maintain lists of all active newsgroups that can be searched quickly.

The traffic on most of these Linux newsgroups deals with problems and issues people have when installing, configuring, or using the operating system. Usually, a lot of valuable information is passing through the newsgroups, so check them regularly. The most interesting messages that deal with a specific subject (called *threads*) are collected and stored for access through an FTP site.

Commercial Vendors
for Linux

This appendix lists all the commercial vendors that sell Linux distributions. See Appendix A for a list of FTP sites that have Linux for free. The advantage of getting Linux from a commercial vendor is that you get a lot of software bundled in one package instead of having to do it for yourself. You can also get a list of these vendors from the *Linux Journal,* a monthly periodical:

> *Linux Journal*
> P.O. Box 85867
> Seattle, WA 98145-1867
> Phone: (206) 527-3385
> Fax: (206) 527-2806

The `Linux Distribution-HOWTO` file contains up-to-date information on Linux vendors that bundle packages together for sale. This list is maintained by Matt Welsh, `mdw@sunsite.unc.edu`. You can find the `HOWTO` file in `/pub/linux/docs/HOWTO/Distribution-howto` at `tsx-11.mit.edu`.

Debian Linux Distribution

> The Debian Linux Association
> Station 11
> P.O. Box 3121
> West Lafayette, IN 47906

Beta releases are available to the general public at `sunsite.unc.edu` in the directory `/pub/Linux/distributions/debian`.

Fintronic Linux Systems

> Fintronic USA, Inc.
> 1360 Willow Rd., Suite 205
> Menlo Park, CA 94025
> Phone: (415) 325-4474
> Fax: (415) 325-4908
> E-mail: `linux@fintronic.com`
> `http://www.fintronic.com/linux/catalog.html`

InfoMagic Developer's Resource CD-ROM Kit

> InfoMagic, Inc.
> P.O. Box 30370
> Flagstaff, AZ 86003-0370
> Toll-free: (800) 800-6613
> Phone: (602) 526-9565
> Fax: (602) 526-9573
> E-mail: `Orders@InfoMagic.com`

Linux from Nascent CD-ROM

Nascent Technology
Linux from Nascent CD-ROM
P.O. Box 60669
Sunnyvale, CA 94088-0669
Phone: (408) 737-9500
Fax: (408) 241-9390
E-mail: nascent@netcom.com

Linux Quarterly CD-ROM

Morse Telecommunication, Inc.
26 East Park Ave., Suite 240
Long Beach, NY 11561
Orders: (800) 60-MORSE
Tech Support: (516) 889-8610
Fax: (516) 889-8665
E-mail: Linux@morse.net

Linux Systems Labs

Linux Systems Labs
18300 Tara Dr.
Clinton Twp, MI 48036
Toll-free: (800) 432-0556
E-mail: dirvin@vela.acs.oakland.edu

Sequoia International Motif Development Package

Sequoia International, Inc.
600 West Hillsboro Blvd., Suite 300
Deerfield Beach, FL 33441
Phone: (305) 480-6118

Takelap Systems Ltd.

The Reddings
Court Robin Lane, Llangwm
Usk, Gwent, United Kingdom NP5 1ET
Phone: +44 (0)291 650357
E-mail: info@ddrive.demon.co.uk

Trans-Ameritech Linux Plus BSD CD-ROM

Trans-Ameritech Enterprises, Inc.
2342A Walsh Ave.
Santa Clara, CA 95051
Phone: (408) 727-3883
E-mail: roman@trans-ameritech.com

The Linux
Documentation Project

The Linux Documentation Project is a loose team of writers, proofreaders, and editors who are working on a set of definitive Linux manuals. The overall coordinator of the project is Matt Welsh, aided by Lars Wirzenius and Michael K. Johnson.

Matt Welsh maintains a Linux home page on the World Wide Web at `http://sunsite.unc.edu/mdw/linux.html`.

They encourage anyone who wants to help to join them in developing any Linux documentation. If you have Internet e-mail access, you can join the DOC channel of the Linux-Activists mailing list by sending mail to `linux-activists-request@niksula.hut.fi` with the following line as the first line of the message body:

```
X-Mn-Admin: join DOC
```

Feel free to get in touch with the author and coordinator of these manuals if you have questions, postcards, money, or ideas. You can reach Matt Welsh through Internet e-mail at `mdw@sunsite.unc.edu` or at the following address:

205 Gray St.
Wilson, NC 27893

The GNU General
Public License

Linux is licensed under the GNU General Public License (the GPL or copyleft), which is reproduced here to clear up some of the confusion about Linux's copyright status. Linux is not shareware, nor is it in the public domain. The bulk of the Linux kernel has been copyrighted since 1993 by Linus Torvalds, and other software and parts of the kernel are copyrighted by their authors. Thus, Linux is copyrighted. Everyone is permitted to copy and distribute verbatim copies of this license document, but changing it is not allowed. However, you may redistribute it under the terms of the GPL, which follows.

GNU GENERAL PUBLIC LICENSE, VERSION 2, JUNE 1991

Copyright 1989, 1991
Free Software Foundation, Inc.
675 Mass Ave.
Cambridge, MA 02139
USA

Everyone is permitted to copy and distribute verbatim copies of this license document, but changing it is not allowed.

E.1 Preamble

The licenses for most software are designed to take away your freedom to share and change it. By contrast, the GNU General Public License is intended to guarantee your freedom to share and change free software to make sure the software is free for all its users. This General Public License applies to most of the Free Software Foundation's software and to any other program whose authors commit to using it. (Some other Free Software Foundation software is covered by the GNU Library General Public License instead.)

You can apply it to your programs, too.

When we speak of free software, we are referring to freedom, not price. Our General Public Licenses are designed to make sure that you have the freedom to distribute copies of free software (and charge for this service if you wish), that you receive source code or can get it if you want it, that you can change the software or use pieces of it in new free programs; and that you know you can do these things.

To protect your rights, we need to make restrictions that forbid anyone to deny you these rights or to ask you to surrender the rights.

These restrictions translate to certain responsibilities for you if you distribute copies of the software or if you modify it.

For example, if you distribute copies of such a program, whether gratis or for a fee, you must give the recipients all the rights that you have. You must make sure that they, too, receive or can get the source code. And you must show them these terms so they know their rights.

We protect your rights with two steps:

1. *We copyright the software.*
2. *We offer you this license, which gives you legal permission to copy, distribute, and/or modify the software.*

Also, for each author's protection and ours, we want to make certain that everyone understands that there is no warranty for this free software. If the software is modified by someone else and passed on, we want its recipients to know that what they have is not the original so that any problems introduced by others will not reflect on the original authors' reputations.

Finally, any free program is threatened constantly by software patents. We wish to avoid the danger that redistributors of a free program will individually obtain patent licenses, in effect making the program proprietary. To prevent this, we have made it clear that any patent must be licensed for everyone's free use or not licensed at all.

The precise terms and conditions for copying, distribution and modification follow.

E.2. GNU General Public License: Terms and Conditions for Copying, Distribution, and Modification

0. This License applies to any program or other work which contains a notice placed by the copyright holder saying it may be distributed under the terms of this General Public License. The "Program," below, refers to any such program or work, and "a work based on the Program" means either the Program or any derivative work under copyright law: that is to say, a work containing the Program or a portion of it, either verbatim or with modifications and/or translated into another language. (Hereinafter, translation is included without limitation in the term "modification.") Each licensee is addressed as "you."

Activities other than copying, distribution, and modification are not covered by this License; they are outside its scope. The act of running the Program is not restricted, and the output from the Program is covered only if its contents constitute a work based on the Program (independent of having been made by running the Program).

Whether that is true depends on what the Program does.

1. *You may copy and distribute verbatim copies of the Program's source code as you receive it, in any medium, provided that you conspicuously and appropriately publish on each copy an appropriate copyright notice and disclaimer of warranty; keep intact all the notices that refer to this License and to the absence of any warranty; and give any other recipients of the Program a copy of this License along with the Program.*

   You may charge a fee for the physical act of transferring a copy, and you may at your option offer warranty protection in exchange for a fee.

2. *You may modify your copy or copies of the Program or any portion of it, thus forming a work based on the Program, and copy and distribute such modifications or work under the terms of Section 1 above, provided that you also meet all of these conditions:*

   a. *You must cause the modified files to carry prominent notices stating that you changed the files and the date of any change.*

   b. *You must cause any work that you distribute or publish, that in whole or in part contains or is derived from the Program or any part thereof, to be licensed as a whole at no charge to all third parties under the terms of this License.*

   c. *If the modified program normally reads commands interactively when run, you must cause it, when started running for such interactive use in the most ordinary way, to print or display an announcement including an appropriate copyright notice and a notice that there is no warranty (or else, saying that you provide a warranty) and that users may redistribute the program under these conditions and telling the user how to view a copy of this License. (Exception: if the Program itself is interactive but does not normally print such an announcement, your work based on the Program is not required to print an announcement.)*

   These requirements apply to the modified work as a whole. If identifiable sections of that work are not derived from the Program and can be reasonably considered independent and separate works in themselves, then this License and its terms do not apply to those sections when you distribute them as separate works. But when you distribute the same sections as part of a whole which is a work based on the Program, the distribution of the whole must be on the terms of this License, whose permissions for other licensees extend to the entire whole and thus to each and every part regardless of who wrote it.

   Thus, it is not the intent of this section to claim rights or contest your rights to work written entirely by you; rather, the intent is to exercise the right to control the distribution of derivative or collective works based on the Program.

In addition, mere aggregation of another work not based on the Program with the Program (or with a work based on the Program) on a volume of a storage or distribution medium does not bring the other work under the scope of this License.

3. *You may copy and distribute the Program (or a work based on it, under Section 2) in object code or executable form under the terms of Sections 1 and 2 above provided that you also do one of the following:*

   a. *Accompany it with the complete corresponding machine-readable source code, which must be distributed under the terms of Sections 1 and 2 above on a medium customarily used for software interchange, or*

   b. *Accompany it with a written offer, valid for at least three years, to give any third party, for a charge no more than your cost of physically performing source distribution, a complete machine-readable copy of the corresponding source code to be distributed under the terms of Sections 1 and 2 above on a medium customarily used for software interchange, or*

   c. *Accompany it with the information you received as to the offer to distribute corresponding source code. (This alternative is allowed only for noncommercial distribution and only if you received the program in object code or executable form with such an offer, in accord with Subsection b above.)*

   The source code for a work means the preferred form of the work for making modifications to it. For an executable work, complete source code means all the source code for all modules it contains, plus any associated interface definition files, plus the scripts used to control compilation and installation of the executable. However, as a special exception, the source code distributed need not include anything that is normally distributed (in either source or binary form) with the major components (compiler, kernel, and so on) of the operating system on which the executable runs, unless that component itself accompanies the executable.

   If distribution of executable or object code is made by offering access to copy from a designated place, then offering equivalent access to copy the source code from the same place counts as distribution of the source code, even though third parties are not compelled to copy the source along with the object code.

4. *You may not copy, modify, sublicense, or distribute the Program except as expressly provided under this License. Any attempt otherwise to copy, modify, sublicense, or distribute the Program is void and will automatically*

terminate your rights under this License. However, parties who have received copies or rights from you under this License will not have their licenses terminated so long as such parties remain in full compliance.

5. *You are not required to accept this License, since you have not signed it. However, nothing else grants you permission to modify or distribute the Program or its derivative works. These actions are prohibited by law if you do not accept this License. Therefore, by modifying or distributing the Program (or any work based on the Program), you indicate your acceptance of this License to do so and all its terms and conditions for copying, distributing, or modifying the Program or works based on it.*

6. *Each time you redistribute the Program (or any work based on the Program), the recipient automatically receives a license from the original licensor to copy, distribute, or modify the Program subject to these terms and conditions. You may not impose any further restrictions on the recipients' exercise of the rights granted herein. You are not responsible for enforcing compliance by third parties to this License.*

7. *If, as a consequence of a court judgment or allegation of patent infringement or for any other reason (not limited to patent issues), conditions are imposed on you (whether by court order, agreement, or otherwise) that contradict the conditions of this License, they do not excuse you from the conditions of this License. If you cannot distribute so as to satisfy simultaneously your obligations under this License and any other pertinent obligations, then as a consequence you may not distribute the Program at all. For example, if a patent license would not permit royalty-free redistribution of the Program by all those who receive copies directly or indirectly through you, then the only way you could satisfy both it and this License would be to refrain entirely from distribution of the Program.*

If any portion of this section is held invalid or unenforceable under any particular circumstance, the balance of the section is intended to apply and the section as a whole is intended to apply in other circumstances.

It is not the purpose of this section to induce you to infringe any patents or other property right claims or to contest validity of any such claims; this section has the sole purpose of protecting the integrity of the free software distribution system, which is implemented by public license practices. Many people have made generous contributions to the wide range of software distributed through that system in reliance on consistent application of that system; it is up to the author/donor to decide if he or she is willing to distribute software through any other system and a licensee cannot impose that choice.

This section is intended to make thoroughly clear what is believed to be a consequence of the rest of this License.

8. *If the distribution and / or use of the Program is restricted in certain countries either by patents or by copyrighted interfaces, the original copyright holder who places the Program under this License may add an explicit geographical distribution limitation excluding those countries so that distribution is permitted only in or among countries not thus excluded. In such case, this License incorporates the limitation as if written in the body of this License.*

9. *The Free Software Foundation may publish revised and / or new versions of the General Public License from time to time. Such new versions will be similar in spirit to the present version, but may differ in detail to address new problems or concerns.*

    Each version is given a distinguishing version number. If the Program specifies a version number of this License which applies to it and "any later version," you have the option of following the terms and conditions either of that version or of any later version published by the Free Software Foundation. If the Program does not specify a version number of this License, you may choose any version ever published by the Free Software Foundation.

10. *If you wish to incorporate parts of the Program into other free programs whose distribution conditions are different, write to the author to ask for permission. For software which is copyrighted by the Free Software Foundation, write to the Free Software Foundation; we sometimes make exceptions for this. Our decision will be guided by the two goals of preserving the free status of all derivatives of our free software and of promoting the sharing and reuse of software generally.*

No warranty

11. *Because the program is licensed free of charge, there is no warranty for the program to the extent permitted by applicable law. Except when otherwise stated in writing, the copyright holders and / or other parties provide the program "as is" without warranty of any kind, either expressed or implied, including, but not limited to, the implied warranties of merchantability and fitness for a particular purpose. The entire risk as to the quality and performance of the program is with you. Should the program prove defective, you assume the cost of all necessary servicing, repair, or correction.*

12. *In no event, unless required by applicable law or agreed to in writing, will any copyright holder, or any other party who may modify and / or redistribute the program as permitted above, be liable to you for damages, including any general, special, incidental, or consequential damages arising out of the*

use or inability to use the program (including but not limited to loss of data or data being rendered inaccurate or losses sustained by you or third parties or a failure of the program to operate with any other programs), even if such holder or other party has been advised of the possibility of such damages.

End of terms and conditions

HOW TO APPLY THESE TERMS TO YOUR NEW PROGRAMS

If you develop a new program and you want it to be of the greatest possible use to the public, the best way to achieve this goal is to make it free software that everyone can redistribute and change under these terms.

To do so, attach the following notices to the program. It is safest to attach them to the start of each source file to most effectively convey the exclusion of warranty. Each file should have at least the copyright line and a pointer to where the full notice is found:

```
<one line to give the program's name and a brief idea of what it does.>
    Copyright (C) 19yy  <name of author>
This program is free software; you can redistribute it and/or modify it under
the terms of the GNU General Public License as published by the Free Software
Foundation; either version 2 of the License, or (at your option) any later
version.
This program is distributed in the hope that it will be useful, but WITHOUT ANY
WARRANTY; without even the implied warranty of MERCHANTABILITY or FITNESS FOR
A PARTICULAR PURPOSE. See the GNU General Public License for more details.
You should have received a copy of the GNU General Public License along with
this program; if not, write to the Free Software Foundation, Inc., 675 Mass
Ave, Cambridge, MA 02139, USA.
```

Also add information on how to contact you by electronic and paper mail.

If the program is interactive, make it output a short notice like the following when it starts in an interactive mode:

```
Gnomovision version 69, Copyright (C) 19yy name of author Gnomovision comes
with ABSOLUTELY NO WARRANTY; for details type 'show w'. This is free software,
and you are welcome to redistribute it under certain conditions; type 'show c'
for details.
```

The hypothetical commands 'show w' and 'show c' should show the appropriate parts of the General Public License. Of course, the commands you use may be called something other than 'show w' and 'show c'; they could even be mouse clicks or menu items—whatever suits your program.

You should also get your employer (if you work as a programmer) or your school, if any, to sign a copyright disclaimer for the program, if necessary. Here is a sample; alter the names:

> *Yoyodyne, Inc., hereby disclaims all copyright interest in the program 'Gnomovision' (which makes passes at compilers) written by James Hacker.*
>
> *<signature of Ty Coon>, 1 April 1989*
>
> *Ty Coon, President of V.*

This General Public License does not permit incorporating your program into proprietary programs. If your program is a subroutine library, you may consider it more useful to permit linking proprietary applications with the library. If this is what you want to do, use the GNU Library General Public License instead of this License.

Copyright Information

The Slackware distribution contains Info-ZIP's compression utilities. Info-ZIP's software (Zip, UnZip, and related utilities) is free and can be obtained as source code or executables from various anonymous FTP sites, including `ftp.uu.net:/pub/archiving/zip/*`. This software is provided free—there are no extra or hidden charges resulting from the use of this compression code. Thanks Info-ZIP! :^)

You can also find Zip/Unzip source code in the `slackware_source/a/base` directory.

The Slackware Installation scripts are Copyright 1993, 1994, Patrick Volkerding, Moorhead, Minnesota, USA. All rights reserved.

Redistribution and use of this software, with or without modification, is permitted provided that the following conditions are met:

1. Redistributions of this software must retain the above copyright notice, this list of conditions, and the following disclaimer.

THIS SOFTWARE IS PROVIDED BY THE AUTHOR "AS IS" AND ANY EXPRESS OR IMPLIED WARRANTIES, INCLUDING, BUT NOT LIMITED TO, THE IMPLIED WARRANTIES OF MERCHANTABILITY AND FITNESS FOR A PARTICULAR PURPOSE ARE DISCLAIMED. IN NO EVENT SHALL THE AUTHOR BE LIABLE FOR ANY DIRECT, INDIRECT, INCIDENTAL, SPECIAL, EXEMPLARY, OR CONSEQUENTIAL DAMAGES (INCLUDING, BUT NOT LIMITED TO, PROCUREMENT OF SUBSTITUTE GOODS OR SERVICES; LOSS OF USE, DATA, OR PROFITS; OR BUSINESS INTERRUPTION) HOWEVER CAUSED AND ON ANY THEORY OF LIABILITY, WHETHER IN CONTRACT, STRICT LIABILITY, OR TORT (INCLUDING NEGLIGENCE OR OTHERWISE) ARISING IN ANY WAY OUT OF THE USE OF THIS SOFTWARE, EVEN IF ADVISED OF THE POSSIBILITY OF SUCH DAMAGE.

Slackware is a trademark of Patrick Volkerding. Permission to use the Slackware trademark to refer to the Slackware distribution of Linux is hereby granted if the following conditions are met:

1. In order to be called Slackware, the distribution may not be altered from the way it appears on the central FTP site (`ftp.cdrom.com`). This is to protect the integrity, reliability, and reputation of the Slackware distribution. Anyone wishing to distribute an altered version must have the changes approved by `volkerdi@ftp.cdrom.com` (i.e. certified to be reasonably bug-free). If the changed distribution meets the required standards for quality, then written permission to use the Slackware trademark will be provided.

2. All related source code must be included. (This is also required by the GNU General Public License.)

3. Except by written permission, the Slackware trademark may not be used as (or as part of) a product name or company name. Note that you can still redistribute a distribution that doesn't meet these criteria; you just can't call it Slackware. Personally, I hate restricting things in any way, but these restrictions are not designed to make life difficult for anyone. I just want to make sure that bugs are not added to commercial redistributions of Slackware. They have been in the past, and the resulting requests for help have flooded my mailbox! I'm just trying to make sure that I have some recourse when something like that happens.

Any questions about this policy should be directed to Patrick Volkerding `<volkerdi@ftp.cdrom.com>`.

Copyright notice for XView3.2-X11R6:

©Copyright 1989, 1990, 1991 Sun Microsystems, Inc. Sun design patents pending in the U.S. and foreign countries. OPEN LOOK is a trademark of USL. Used by written permission of the owners.©

©Copyright Bigelow & Holmes 1986, 1985. Lucida is a registered trademark of Bigelow & Holmes. Permission to use the Lucida trademark is hereby granted only in association with the images and fonts described in this file.

SUN MICROSYSTEMS, INC., USL, AND BIGELOW & HOLMES MAKE NO REPRESENTATIONS ABOUT THE SUITABILITY OF THIS SOURCE CODE FOR ANY PURPOSE. IT IS PROVIDED "AS IS" WITHOUT EXPRESS OR IMPLIED WARRANTY OF ANY KIND. SUN MICROSYSTEMS, INC., USL, AND BIGELOW & HOLMES, SEVERALLY AND INDIVIDUALLY, DISCLAIM ALL WARRANTIES WITH REGARD TO THIS SOURCE CODE, INCLUDING ALL IMPLIED WARRANTIES OF MERCHANTABILITY AND FITNESS FOR A PARTICULAR PURPOSE. IN NO EVENT SHALL SUN MICROSYSTEMS, INC., USL, OR BIGELOW & HOLMES BE LIABLE FOR ANY SPECIAL, INDIRECT, INCIDENTAL, OR CONSEQUENTIAL DAMAGES, OR ANY DAMAGES WHATSOEVER RESULTING FROM LOSS OF USE, DATA, OR PROFITS, WHETHER IN AN ACTION OF CONTRACT, NEGLIGENCE, OR OTHER TORTIOUS ACTION, ARISING OUT OF OR IN CONNECTION WITH THE USE OR PERFORMANCE OF THIS SOURCE CODE.

Various other copyrights apply. See the documentation accompanying the software packages for full details.

Although every effort has been made to provide a complete source tree for this project, it's possible that something may have been forgotten. If you discover anything is missing, we will provide copies—just ask!

Note

We are required to provide any missing source code to GPLed software for three years, per the following section of the GNU General Public License:

"b. Accompany it with a written offer, valid for at least three years, to give any third party, for a charge no more than your cost of physically performing source distribution, a complete machine-readable copy of the corresponding source code, to be distributed under the terms of Sections 1 and 2 above on a medium customarily used for software interchange,..."

If you find something is missing (even if you don't need a copy), please point it out to `volkerdi@ftp.cdrom.com` so it can be fixed.

- CPUs and FPUs

- Video Cards

- Hard Disk Controllers

- Hard Drives

- Multiport Cards

- Sound Cards

- CD-ROM Drives

- Tape Drives

- Network Adapters

- ISDN Cards

- Printers/Plotters

- Scanners

- Video Capture Boards

APPENDIX F

Hardware Compatibility

In most of the chapters dealing with hardware in this book, you've been referred to compatibility files supplied on many versions of the Linux distribution. For convenience, this appendix summarizes the main contents of the Hardware How-To file. This version of the compatibility list is current with the Linux version supplied on the CD-ROM that accompanies this book.

SYSTEM ARCHITECTURES

This appendix deals with only Linux for Intel platforms. For other platforms, check the following:

Linux/68k	<http://www-users.informatik.rwth-aachen.de/~hn/linux68k.html>
Linux/MIPS	<http://www.waldorf-gmbh.de/linux-mips-faq.html>
Linux/PowerPC	<ftp://sunsite.unc.edu/pub/Linux/docs/ports/Linux-PowerPC-FAQ.gz>
Linux for Acorn	<http://www.ph.kcl.ac.uk/~amb/linux.html>
MacLinux	<http://www.ibg.uu.se/maclinux/>

COMPUTERS/MOTHERBOARDS/BIOS

ISA, VLB, EISA, and PCI buses are all supported. PS/2 and Microchannel (MCA) are not supported in the standard kernel. Alpha test PS/2 MCA kernels are available but are not yet recommended for serious use.

Some laptops have unusual video adapters or power management; it is not uncommon to be unable to use the power management features.

PCMCIA drivers currently support all common PCMCIA controllers, including Databook TCIC/2, Intel i82365SL, Cirrus PD67xx, and Vadem VG-468 chipsets. The Motorola 6AHC05GA controller used in some Hyundai laptops is not supported.

CPUs AND FPUs

Basically all 386 or better processors will work, including Intel/AMD/Cyrix 386SX/DX/SL/DXL/SLC, 486SX/DX/SL/SX2/DX2/DX4, and Pentium. Linux has built-in FPU emulation if you don't have a math coprocessor.

Linux does not support SMP yet. Multiprocessor systems will run Linux, but only the first processor will be used. Some work on this area is being done right now; check the Linux Project Map for details.

A few very early AMD 486DX processors may hang in some special situations. All current chips should be OK, and getting a chip swap for old CPUs should not be a problem.

ULSI Math*Co series has a bug in the FSAVE and FRSTOR instructions that causes problems with all protected mode operating systems. Some older IIT and Cyrix chips may also have this problem.

There are problems with TLB flushing in UMC U5S chips. Newer kernels have fixed these problems.

VIDEO CARDS

Linux works with all video cards in text mode. VGA cards not listed in the hardware compatibility list probably will still work with mono VGA and/or standard VGA drivers. If you're looking into buying a cheap video card to run X, keep in mind that accelerated cards (ATI Mach, ET4000/W32p, S3) are much faster than unaccelerated or partially accelerated (Cirrus, WD) cards. S3 801 (ISA), S3 805 (VLB), ET4000/W32p, and ATI Graphics Wonder (Mach32) are good low-end accelerated cards.

Cards advertised as 32 bpp are actually 24-bit color aligned on 32-bit boundaries. It does not mean the cards are capable of 32-bit color; 32 bpp is still 24-bit color (16,777,216 colors). XFree86 does not support 24-bit packed pixels modes, so cards that can display 24-bit color modes in other operating systems may not able to do this in X. These cards include Mach32, Cirrus 542x, S3 801/805, ET4000, and others.

The current release of XFree86 supports most recent Diamond cards. Early Diamond cards are not supported by XFree86, but there are ways of getting them to work. Diamond support for XFree86 is available at <http://www.diamondmm.com/linux.html>.

HARD DISK CONTROLLERS

Linux works with standard IDE, MFM, and RLL controllers. When using MFM/RLL controllers, use ext2fs and the bad block checking options when formatting the disk. Enhanced IDE (EIDE) interfaces with up to two IDE interfaces and up to four hard drives and/or CD-ROM drives are also supported. ESDI controllers that emulate the ST-506 (that is MFM/RLL/IDE) interface also work with Linux. The bad block checking comment also applies to these controllers. Generic 8-bit XT controllers also work with Linux.

Be careful when picking a SCSI controller. Parallel-port SCSI controllers are not supported. Many cheap ISA SCSI controllers are designed to drive CD-ROMs only. Such low-end SCSI controllers are no better than IDE. See the SCSI HOWTO file and look at performance figures before buying a SCSI card. The following SCSI controllers are supported:

- AMD AM53C974, AM79C974 (PCI) (Compaq, Zeos on-board SCSI) (requires patch)
- AMI Fast Disk VLB/EISA (BusLogic compatible)
- Acculogic ISApport / MV Premium 3D SCSI (NCR 53c406a) (requires patch)
- Adaptec ACB-40xx SCSI-MFM/RLL bridgeboard Adaptec AVA-1505/1515 (ISA) (Adaptec 152x compatible) (requires patch)
- Adaptec AHA-1510/152x (ISA) (AIC-6260/6360)
- Adaptec AHA-154x (ISA) (all models)
- Adaptec AHA-174x (EISA) (in enhanced mode)
- Adaptec AHA-274x (EISA) / 284x (VLB) (AIC-7770)
- Adaptec AHA-294x (PCI) (AIC-7870)
- Adaptec APA-1460 SlimSCSI (PCMCIA) (requires patch)
- Always AL-500 (requires patch)
- Always IN2000
- BusLogic (ISA/EISA/VLB/PCI) (all models)
- DPT PM2001, PM2012A (EATA-PIO)
- DPT Smartcache (EATA-DMA) (ISA/EISA/PCI) (all models)
- DTC 329x (EISA) (Adaptec 154x compatible)
- Future Domain TMC-16x0, TMC-3260 (PCI)
- Future Domain TMC-8xx, TMC-950
- Iomega PC2/2B (requires patch)
- NCR 53c7x0, 53c8x0 (PCI)
- Pro Audio Spectrum 16 SCSI (ISA)
- Qlogic / Control Concepts SCSI/IDE (FAS408) (ISA/VLB/PCMCIA)
- PCMCIA cards must boot DOS to init card
- Seagate ST-01/ST-02 (ISA)
- Sound Blaster 16 SCSI-2 (Adaptec 152x compatible) (ISA)
- Trantor T128/T128F/T228 (ISA)
- UltraStor 14F (ISA), 24F (EISA), 34F (VLB)
- Western Digital WD7000 SCSI

HARD DRIVES

Large IDE (EIDE) drives work fine with newer kernels. The boot partition must lie in the first 1024 cylinders due to PC BIOS limitations.

Some Conner CFP1060S drives may have problems with Linux and `ext2fs`. The symptoms are i-node errors during `e2fsck` and corrupt filesystems. Conner has released a firmware upgrade to fix this problem; contact Conner at 1-800-4CONNER (US) or +44-1294-315333 (Europe). Have the microcode version number (found on the drive label, 9WA1.6x) handy when you call.

Certain Micropolis drives have problems with Adaptec and BusLogic cards; contact the drive manufacturers for firmware upgrades if you suspect problems.

REMOVABLE DRIVES

All SCSI drives should work if the controller is supported, including optical drives, WORM, CD-R, floptical, and others. Iomega Bernoulli and Zip drives and SyQuest drives all work fine. Linux supports both 512 and 1024 bytes/sector disks.

MOUSES

The following pointing devices are supported:

- ◆ Microsoft serial mouse
- ◆ Mouse Systems serial mouse
- ◆ Logitech Mouseman serial mouse
- ◆ Logitech serial mouse
- ◆ ATI XL Inport bus mouse
- ◆ C&T 82C710 (QuickPort) (Toshiba, TI Travelmate)
- ◆ Microsoft bus mouse
- ◆ Logitech bus mouse
- ◆ PS/2 (auxiliary device) mouse
- ◆ Sejin J-mouse
- ◆ MultiMouse (use multiple mouse devices as single mouse)

Pad devices like Glidepoint also work, as long they're compatible with another mouse protocol. Newer Logitech mice (except the Mouseman) use the Microsoft protocol and all three buttons do work. Even though Microsoft's mouses have only two buttons, the protocol allows three buttons.

The mouse port on the ATI Graphics Ultra and Ultra Pro uses the Logitech bus mouse protocol.

I/O CONTROLLERS

Linux supports any standard serial/parallel/joystick/IDE combo cards. Linux also supports 8250, 16450, 16550, and 16550A UARTs. For more information on UARTs, see National Semiconductor's Application Note AN-493 by Martin S.Michael. Section 5.0 describes in detail the differences between the NS16550 and NS16550A. Briefly, the NS16550 had bugs in the FIFO circuits, but the NS16550A (and later) chips fixed those bugs. National produced very few NS16550s, however, so these chips should be very rare. Many of the 16550 parts in modern boards are from the many manufacturers of compatible parts, which may not use the National A suffix. Also, some multiport boards use 16552 or 16554 or various other multiport or multifunction chips from National or other suppliers (generally in a dense package soldered to the board, not a 40-pin DIP). Mostly, don't worry about it unless you encounter a very old 40-pin DIP National NS16550 (no A) chip loose or in an old board; in this case, treat it as a 16450 (no FIFO) rather than a 16550A.

MULTIPORT CARDS

The following multiport cards are supported by Linux (some require drivers from the manufacturers):

- ◆ AST FourPort and clones
- ◆ Accent Async-4
- ◆ Bell Technologies HUB6
- ◆ Boca BB-1004, 1008 (4, 8 port) (no DTR, DSR, and CD)
- ◆ Boca BB-2016 (16 port)
- ◆ Boca IO/AT66 (6 port)
- ◆ Boca IO 2by4 (4S/2P) (works with modems, but uses 5 IRQ's)
- ◆ Comtrol RocketPort (8/16/32 port)
- ◆ Cyclades Cyclom-8Y/16Y (8, 16 port)
- ◆ DigiBoard COM/Xi
- ◆ DigiBoard PC/Xe (ISA) and PC/Xi (EISA)
- ◆ PC-COMM 4-port
- ◆ Specialix SIO/XIO (modular, 4 to 32 ports)
- ◆ Stallion EasyIO (ISA) / EasyConnection 8/32 (ISA/MCA)
- ◆ Stallion EasyConnection 8/64 / ONboard (ISA/EISA/MCA) / Brumby /

◆ Stallion (ISA)STB 4-COM

◆ Twincom ACI/550

◆ Usenet Serial Board II

SOUND CARDS

Linux supports the following sound cards (although not all will have full functionality):

◆ 6850 UART MIDI

◆ Adlib (OPL2)

◆ Audio Excell DSP16

◆ Aztech Sound Galaxy NX Pro

◆ ECHO-PSS cards (Orchid SoundWave32, Cardinal DSP16)

◆ Ensoniq SoundScape

◆ Gravis Ultrasound

◆ Gravis Ultrasound 16-bit sampling daughterboard

◆ Gravis Ultrasound MAX

◆ Logitech SoundMan Games (SBPro, 44kHz stereo support)

◆ Logitech SoundMan Wave (Jazz16/OPL4)

◆ Logitech SoundMan 16 (PAS-16 compatible)

◆ MPU-401 MIDI

◆ MediaTriX AudioTriX Pro

◆ Media Vision Premium 3D (Jazz16)

◆ Media Vision Pro Sonic 16 (Jazz)

◆ Media Vision Pro Audio Spectrum 16

◆ Microsoft Sound System (AD1848)

◆ OAK OTI-601D cards (Mozart)

◆ OPTi 82C928/82C929 cards (MAD16/MAD16 Pro)

◆ Sound Blaster

◆ Sound Blaster Pro

◆ Sound Blaster 16 family

◆ Wave Blaster (and other SB16 daughterboards)

The ASP chip on Sound Blaster 16 series and AWE32 is not supported. AWE32's on-board MIDI synthesizer is not supported. These two things will probably never be supported. Sound Blaster 16s with DSP 4.11 and 4.12 have a hardware bug that causes hung/stuck notes when playing MIDI and digital audio at the same time. The problem happens with either Wave Blaster daughterboards or MIDI devices attached to the MIDI port. There is no known fix for this problem.

CD-ROM DRIVES

Linux supports the following types of CD-ROM drives:

- ◆ SCSI CD-ROM drives (Any SCSI CD-ROM drive with a block size of 512 or 2048 bytes should work under Linux, which includes the vast majority of CD-ROM drives on the market.)
- ◆ EIDE (ATAPI) CD-ROM drives
- ◆ Aztech CDA268, Orchid CDS-3110, Okano/Wearnes CDD-110
- ◆ GoldStar R420
- ◆ LMS Philips CM 206
- ◆ Matsushita/Panasonic, Kotobuki (SBPCD)
- ◆ Mitsumi
- ◆ Optics Storage Dolphin 8000AT
- ◆ Sanyo H94A
- ◆ Sony CDU31A/CDU33A
- ◆ Sony CDU-535/CDU-531
- ◆ Teac CD-55A SuperQuad

PhotoCD (XA) is also supported. All CD-ROM drives should work similarly for reading data. Various compatibility problems exist with utilities that play audio CDs. Early (single-speed) NEC CD-ROM drives may have trouble with currently available SCSI controllers.

TAPE DRIVES

Linux supports the following types of tape drives:

- ◆ SCSI tape drives (Drives using both fixed and variable length blocks smaller than the driver buffer length, which are set to 32K in the distribution sources, are supported. Virtually all drives should work.)
- ◆ QIC-02
- ◆ QIC-117, QIC-40/80 drives

Most tape drives using the floppy controller should work. Various dedicated QIC-80 controllers (Colorado FC-10, Iomega Tape Controller II) are also supported.

Drives that connect to the parallel port (such as the Colorado Trakker) are not supported. Also, some high-speed tape controllers (Colorado TC-15 / FC-20, Irwin AX250L/Accutrak 250, IBM Internal Tape Backup Unit, and COREtape Light) are not supported.

MODEMS

All internal modems or external modems connected to the serial port are supported. A small number of modems come with DOS software that downloads the control program at runtime. You can normally use these modems by loading the program under DOS and doing a warm boot. Such modems are probably best avoided because you won't be able to use them with non-PC hardware in the future. PCMCIA modems should work with the PCMCIA drivers. Fax modems need appropriate fax software to operate.

NETWORK ADAPTERS

Ethernet adapters vary greatly in performance. In general, the newer designs work better. The only advantage to using some very old cards like the 3C501 is that you can find them in junk heaps for $5. Be careful with clones; not all clones are good clones, and bad clones often cause erratic lockups under Linux. Read the Ethernet HOWTO file for full detailed descriptions of various cards. Linux supports the following Ethernet cards:

- 3Com 3C503, 3C505, 3C507, 3C509/3C509B (ISA) / 3C579 (EISA)
- AMD LANCE (79C960) / PCnet-ISA/PCI (AT1500, HP J2405A, NE1500/NE2100)
- AT&T GIS WaveLAN
- Allied Telesis AT1700
- Ansel Communications AC3200 EISA
- Apricot Xen-II
- Cabletron E21xx
- DEC DE425 (EISA) / DE434/DE435 (PCI)
- DEC DEPCA and EtherWORKS
- HP PCLAN (27245 and 27xxx series)
- HP PCLAN PLUS (27247B and 27252A)
- Intel EtherExpress
- Intel EtherExpress Pro
- NE2000/NE1000 (be careful with clones)

- ◆ New Media Ethernet
- ◆ Racal-Interlan NI5210 (i82586 Ethernet chip)
- ◆ Racal-Interlan NI6510 (am7990 lance chip) (Doesn't work with more than 16M of RAM.)
- ◆ PureData PDUC8028, PDI8023
- ◆ SEEQ 8005
- ◆ SMC Ultra
- ◆ Schneider & Koch G16
- ◆ Western Digital WD80x3
- ◆ Zenith Z-Note / IBM ThinkPad 300 built-in adapter

The following pocket and portable adapters work with Linux:

- ◆ AT-Lan-Tec/RealTek parallel port adapter
- ◆ D-Link DE600/DE620 parallel port adapter

Linux works with all ARCnet cards and the IBM Tropic Token Ring cards.

ISDN Cards

The following cards are known to work with Linux:

- ◆ Diehl SCOM card
- ◆ ICN ISDN card
- ◆ Teles ISDN card

Printers/Plotters

All printers and plotters connected to the parallel or serial port should work.

Many Linux programs output PostScript files. Non-PostScript printers can emulate PostScript Level 2 using Ghostscript. Ghostscript supported printers include the following:

- ◆ Apple Imagewriter
- ◆ C. Itoh M8510
- ◆ Canon BubbleJet BJ10e, BJ200
- ◆ Canon BJC600 and Epson ESC/P color printers
- ◆ Canon LBP-8II, LIPS III
- ◆ DEC LA50/70/75/75plus
- ◆ DEC LN03, LJ250

- Epson 9 pin, 24 pin, LQ series, Stylus, AP3250
- HP 2563B
- HP DesignJet 650C
- HP DeskJet/Plus/500
- HP DeskJet 500C/520C/550C/1200C color
- HP LaserJet/Plus/II/III/4
- HP PaintJet/XL/XL300 color
- IBM Jetprinter color
- IBM Proprinter
- Imagen ImPress
- Mitsubishi CP50 color
- NEC P6/P6+/P60
- Okidata MicroLine 182
- Ricoh 4081
- SPARCprinter
- StarJet 48 inkjet printer
- Tektronix 4693d color 2/4/8 bit
- Tektronix 4695/4696 inkjet plotter
- Xerox XES printers (2700, 3700, 4045, etc.)

SCANNERS

The following scanners have been known to work well with Linux, although most non-SCSI models need a driver available from the manufacturer:

- A4 Tech AC 4096
- Fujitsu SCSI-2 scanners
- Genius GS-B105G
- Genius GeniScan GS4500 handheld scanner
- HP ScanJet, ScanJet Plus
- HP ScanJet II series SCSI
- Logitech Scanman 32 / 256
- Mustek M105 handheld scanner with GI1904 interface
- UMAX SCSI scanners

Video Capture Boards

These video capture boards will work with Linux-based applications (some require drivers from the manufacturer):

- ◆ FAST Screen Machine II
- ◆ ProMovie Studio
- ◆ VideoBlaster, Rombo Media Pro+
- ◆ WinVision video capture card

UPS

Practically any UPS on the market will provide protection for the system, but the APC SmartUPS system provides software drivers.

Glossary

10Base2   An Ethernet term meaning a maximum transfer rate of 10 Megabits per second, which uses baseband signaling, with a contiguous cable segment length of 100 meters and a maximum of two segments.

10Base5   An Ethernet term meaning a maximum transfer rate of 10 Megabits per second, which uses baseband signaling, with five continuous segments not exceeding 100 meters per segment.

10Base-T   An Ethernet term meaning a maximum transfer rate of 10 Megabits per second, which uses baseband signaling and twisted-pair cabling.

Acknowledgment   A positive response returned from a receiver to the sender indicating success. TCP uses acknowledgments to indicate the successful reception of a packet.

Address   A memory location in a particular machine's RAM; a numeric identifier or symbolic name that specifies the location of a particular machine or device on a network; and a means of identifying a complete network, subnetwork, or a node within a network.

Address Mask (also called the subnet mask)   A set of rules for omitting parts of a complete IP address in order to reach the target destination without using a broadcast message. The mask can, for example, indicate a subnetwork portion of a larger network. In TCP/IP, the address mask uses the 32-bit IP address.

Address Resolution   Mapping of an IP address to a machine's physical address. TCP/IP uses the Address Resolution Protocol (ARP) for this function.

Address Resolution Protocol (ARP)   See Address Resolution.

Address Space   A range of memory addresses available to an application program.

Agent   In TCP/IP, an agent is an SNMP process that responds to get and set requests. Agents can also send trap messages.

American National Standards Institute (ANSI)   The body responsible for setting standards in the U.S.

Application Programming Interface (API)   A set of routines that are available to developers and applications to provide specific services used by the system, usually specific to the application's purpose. They act as access methods into the application.

Application Layer   The highest layer in the OSF model. It establishes communications rights and can initiate a connection between two applications.

ASCII (American National Standard Code for Information Interchange)   An 8-bit character set defining alphanumeric characters.

Asynchronous   Communications without a regular time basis allowing transmission at unequal rates.

Bandwidth   The range of frequencies transmitted on a channel, or the difference between the highest and lowest frequencies transmitted across a channel.

Baseband   A type of channel in which data transmission is carried across only one communications channel, supporting only one signal transmission at a time. Ethernet is a baseband system.

Baud   The number of times a signal changes state in one second.

Berkeley Software Distribution (BSD)   A version of the UNIX operating system that first included TCP/IP support. The UNIX operating systems that included TCP/IP are referred to as 4.2BSD or 4.3BSD.

Bit rate   The rate that bits are transmitted, usually expressed in seconds.

Block Mode   A string of data recorded or transmitted as a unit. Block mode transmission is usually used for high-speed transmissions and in large, high-speed networks.

Broadcast   The simultaneous transmission of the same data to all nodes connected to the network.

Buffer   A memory area used for handling input and output.

Cache   A memory location that keeps frequently requested material ready. Usually a cache is faster than a storage device. It is used to speed data and instruction transfer.

Client   A program that tries to connect to another program (usually on another machine) called a server. The client calls the server. The server listens for calls.

Client-Server Architecture   A catchall term used to refer to a distributed environment in which one program can initiate a session and another program answers its requests. The origin of client-server designs is closely allied with the TCP/IP protocol suite.

Connection   A link between two or more processes, applications, machines, networks, and so on. Connections may be logical, physical, or both.

Connectionless   A type of network service that does not send acknowledgments upon receipt of data to the sender. UDP is a connectionless protocol.

Connection-Oriented   A type of network service in which the transport layer protocol sends acknowledgments to the sender regarding incoming data. This type of service usually provides for retransmission of corrupted or lost data.

Cyclic Redundancy Check (CRC)   A mathematical function performed on the contents of an entity that is then included to allow a receiving system to recalculate the value and compare to the original. If the values are different, corruption of the contents has occurred.

Daemon   A UNIX process that operates continuously and unattended to perform a service. TCP/IP uses several daemons to establish communications processes and provide server facilities.

DARPA (Defense Advanced Research Project Agency)   The governmental body that created the DARPANET for widespread communications. DARPANET eventually became the Internet.

Datagram   A basic unit of data used with TCP/IP.

Data Circuit-Terminating Equipment (DCE)   Required equipment to attach Data Terminal Equipment (DTE) to a network or serial line. A modem is a DCE device. Also called Data Communications Equipment and Data Circuit Equipment.

Data Encryption Standard (DES)   An encryption standard officially sanctioned in the U.S.

Data Link   The part of a node controlled by a data link protocol. It is the logical connection between two nodes.

Data Link Protocol   A method of handling the establishment, maintenance, and termination of a logical link between nodes. Ethernet is a DLP.

Data Terminal Equipment (DTE)   The source or destination of data, usually attached to a network by DEC devices. A terminal or computer acting as a node on a network is usually a DTE device.

Defense Communications Agency (DCA)   The governmental agency responsible for the Defense Data Network (DDN).

Defense Data Network (DDN)   Refers to military networks such as MILNET, ARPANET, and the communications protocols (including TCP/IP) that they employ.

Destination Address   The destination device's address.

Distributed Processing   When a process is spread over two or more devices, it is distributed. It is usually used to spread CPU loads among a network of machines.

Domain Name System (DNS)   A service that converts symbolic node names to IP addresses. DNS is frequently used with TCP/IP. DNS uses a distributed database.

Dotted Decimal Notation   A representation of IP addresses. Also called dotted-quad notation because it uses four sets of numbers separated by decimals (such as 255.255.255.255).

Double-Byte Character Set   A character set in which alphanumeric characters are represented by two bytes, instead of one byte as with ASCII. Double-byte characters are often necessary for oriental languages that have more than 255 symbols.

Dumb Terminal   A terminal with no significant processing capability of its own, usually with no graphics capabilities beyond the ASCII set.

Emulation   A program that simulates another device. For example, a 3270 emulator emulates an IBM 3270 terminal, sending the same codes as the real device would.

Ethernet   A data link level protocol comprising the OSI model's bottom two layers. It is a broadcast networking technology that can use several different physical media, including twisted pair cable and coaxial cable. TCP/IP is commonly used with Ethernet networks.

Ethernet Address   A 48-bit address commonly referred to as a "physical" or "hard" address, which uniquely identifies the Ethernet Network Interface Card (NIC) and hence the device the card resides in.

Ethernet Meltdown   A slang term for a situation in which an Ethernet network becomes saturated. The condition usually persists only for a short time and is usually caused by a misrouted or invalid packet.

Extended Binary Coded Decimal Interchange Code (EBCDIC)   An alternative to ASCII used extensively in IBM machinery. Some other vendors use it for mainframes. EBCDIC and ASCII are not compatible but are easy to convert between.

File Server   A process that provides access to a file from remote devices.

File Transfer Protocol (FTP)   A TCP/IP application used for transferring files from one system to another.

Frame Relay   A network switching mechanism for routing frames as quickly as possible.

Gateway   In Internet terms, a gateway is a device that routes datagrams. More recently, the term "gateway" has been used to refer to any networking device that translates protocols of one type network into those of another network.

Gigabyte   One billion bytes corresponding to decimal 1,073,741,824 (as a "kilobyte" is 1,024 decimal).

Hardware Address   The low-level address associated with each device on a network, usually corresponding to the unique identifier of the network interface card (NIC). Ethernet addresses are 48 bits.

Institute of Electrical and Electronic Engineers (IEEE)   A professional organization for engineers that also proposes and approves standards.

Integrated Service Digital Network (ISDN)   A set of standards for integrating multiple services (voice, data, video, and so on).

International Organization for Standardization (ISO)   An international body composed of individual country's standards groups that focuses upon international standards.

Internet   A collection of networks connected together that span the world, which uses the NFSNET as its backbone. The Internet is the specific term for a more general internetwork or collection of networks.

Internet Address   A 32-bit address used to identify hosts and networks on the Internet.

Internet Control Message Protocol (ICMP)   A control and error message protocol that works in conjunction with the Internet Protocol (IP).

Internet Protocol (IP)   The part of TCP/IP that handles routing.

IP Address   A 32-bit identifier that is unique to each network device.

IP Datagram   The basic unit of information passed through a TCP/IP network. The datagram header contains source and destination IP addresses.

Kerberos   An authentication scheme developed at MIT used to prevent unauthorized monitoring of logins and passwords.

LAN (Local Area Network)   A collection of devices connected to enable communications between themselves on a single physical medium.

Leased Line   A dedicated communication line between two points. Usually used by organizations to connect computers over a dedicated telephone circuit.

Mail Exchanger   A system used to relay mail into a network.

Management Information Base (MIB)   A database used by SNMP containing configuration and statistical information about devices on a network.

Media Access Control (MAC)   The lower half of the data link sublayer that is responsible for framing data and controlling the physical link between two end points.

Medium Access Unit (MAU)   A device for the central connection of devices operating on a network.

Modem (Modulator-Demodulator)   A device that converts digital signals into analog signals and vice versa. Used for conversion of signals for transmission over telephone lines.

Modem Eliminator   A device that functions as two modems to provide service for data terminal equipment (DTE) and data communication equipment (DCE).

Multihomed Host   A device attached to two or more networks.

Multiplex   Simultaneously transmitting multiple signals over one channel.

Name Resolution   The process of mapping aliases to an address. The Domain Name System (DNS) is one system that does this.

NetBIOS (Network Basic Input/Output Operating System)   A network programming interface typically used to connect PCs together.

Network   A number of devices connected to enable the device to communicate with any other device over a physical medium.

Network Address   For TCP/IP, the 32-bit IP address of a device.

Network File System (NFS)   A protocol developed by Sun Microsystems that enables clients to mount remote directories onto their own local filesystem.

Network Information Center (NIC)   The Internet administration facility that controls the naming of networks accessible over the Internet.

Network Information Service (NIS)   A set of protocols developed by Sun Microsystems, which provides directory services for network information.

Network Interface Card (NIC)   A generic term for a networking interface board used to connect a device to the network. The NIC is where the physical connection to the network occurs.

Network Virtual Terminal (NVT)   Protocols that govern virtual terminal emulation.

Node   A generic term used to refer to network devices.

Open Software Foundation (OSF)   A consortium of hardware and software vendors collaborating to produce technologies for device-independent operation.

Packet   In TCP/IP, a term referring to the data passing between the Internet layer and the data link layer. Also a generic term used to refer to data transferred through a network.

PING (Packet Internet Groper)   A utility program used to test a system's TCP/IP software by sending an ICMP echo request and then wait for a response.

Point-to-Point Protocol (PPP)   A TCP/IP protocol that provides host-to-network and router-to-router connections. Can be used to provide a serial line connection between two machines.

Port   A number used to identify TCP/IP applications. Generally a port is an entry or exit point.

Protocol   Rules governing the behavior or method of operation of something.

Protocol Conversion   The process of changing one protocol to another.

RARP   See Reverse Address Resolution Protocol.

Remote Procedure Call (RPC)   A TCP/IP protocol that provides a routine to call a server, which returns output and status (return) codes to the client.

Resolver   Software that enables clients to access the Domain Name System (DNS) database and acquire an address.

Reverse Address Resolution Protocol (RARP)   A TCP/IP protocol that enables a device to acquire its IP address by performing a broadcast on the network.

rlogin   Remote login service that enables a user on one machine to log in as a user on another. It is similar to Telnet.

Router   A device that connects LANs into an internetwork and routes traffic between them.

Routing   The process of determining a path to use to send data to its destination.

Routing Information Protocol (RIP)   A protocol used to exchange information between routers.

Routing table   A list of valid paths through which data can be transmitted.

RS232C   A physical layer specification for connecting devices. Commonly used for serial lines.

Serial   A sequence of events occurring one after another.

Serial Line Internet Protocol (SLIP)   A protocol used to utilize TCP/IP over serial lines.

Server   An application that answers requests from other devices (clients). Also used as a generic term for any device that provides services to the rest of the network, such as printing, high-capacity storage, network access, and so on.

Simple Mail Transfer Protocol (SMTP)   In TCP/IP, an application providing electronic mail services.

Socket   In TCP/IP, an addressable point that consists of an IP address and a TCP or UDP port number that provides applications with access to TCP/IP protocols.

Socket Address   The complete designation of a TCP/IP node consisting of a 32-bit IP address and a 16-bit port number.

Socket Descriptor   An integer used by an application to identify the connection.

Subnet   In TCP/IP, part of a TCP/IP network identified by a portion of the Internet address.

Subnet Address   The part of the IP address that identifies the subnetwork.

Subnet Mask   A set of bits that excludes networks from having a system-wide broadcast, instead of restricting the broadcast to a subnetwork.

Synchronous Data Transfer   The transfer of data between two nodes at a timed rate (as opposed to asynchronously).

Telnet   A TCP/IP application that enables a user to log in to a remote device.

TCP/IP   Transmission Control Protocol/Internet Protocol.

Terminator   A resistor that must be on both ends of a thick-and-thin Ethernet network.

Throughput   The amount of data that can be transferred through a medium within a certain time period.

Token Ring   A lower layer connection-based networking protocol using a token passing method to control data traffic.

Traffic   A general term used to describe the amount of data on a network backbone.

Transceiver   A network device required in baseband networks that takes a digital signal and puts it on the analog baseband medium. Transceivers can sense collisions.

Transmission Control Protocol (TCP)   A transport layer protocol that is part of the TCP/IP protocol suite and provides a connection-based, reliable data stream.

Trivial File Transfer Protocol (TFTP)   A mechanism for remote logins similar to Telnet but which uses UDP as a transport layer protocol instead of TCP.

UDP (User Datagram Protocol)   A connectionless transport layer protocol. It does not perform retransmission of data.

User Agent   An electronic mail program that helps end users manage messages.

User Service   A service provided by TCP permitting an application to specify that data being transmitted is urgent and should be processed as soon as possible.

Wide Area Network (WAN)   Usually used to refer to a network spanning large geographic distances.

X.400   A protocol defining standards for electronic mail in an open network.

G

GLOSSARY

X.500   A protocol defining standards for directory services in an open network.

X Series   A collection of widely accepted standards, including data communications.

XNS (Xerox Networking Standard)   Networking protocols developed by Xerox, similar to TCP/IP.

X Window   A software protocol developed at MIT for a distributed windowing system. X uses TCP for a transport protocol.

- Sams Publishing Support

- InfoMagic Support

APPENDIX H

What's on the CD-ROM

The CD-ROM accompanying this book contains the latest SlackWare Linux 3.0 distribution from InfoMagic. This includes the latest versions of the kernel (1.3.18), XFree86 3.1.2, and most utilities, as well as some collections from the Linux archives.

The CD-ROM is readable directly by DOS, Windows, and Linux. The root directory contains a number of text files that relate to the disc's contents and installation instructions. Beneath the root directory are a number of directories used to install Linux for the first time. If you are installing Linux, use the bootdsks.12 and bootdsks.133 directories to locate the proper boot disk kernel; the rootdsks directory holds the root filesystem images. The RAWRITE utility needed to copy the boot and root images to a disk are in the /install directory. Follow the instructions in the early chapters of this book for details on how to use these files.

The directories on the CD-ROM have the following contents:

◆ bootdsks.12   1.2MB floppy kernel images

◆ bootdsks.144   1.44MB floppy kernel images

◆ contents   Lists of files comprising each installable software package used during the installation routines. You don't need to use this directory.

◆ contrib   Software packages not part of the basic Linux distribution. These packages include the Andrew User Interface System, GNU Fortran 77, GNU Common LISP, GNU gnat (Ada), GNU Pascal, NCSA httpd, ircII, Lucid Emacs, SLiRP, and more.

◆ docs   Subdirectories contain the full set of Linux HOWTO files, man pages, FAQs, and some Linux Documentation Project documents.

◆ kernels   Many precompiled Linux kernels (used during installation)

◆ install   Installation utilities, including RAWRITE, GZIP, and FIPS. FIPS lets you shrink the size of an existing MS-DOS partition to make room for a Linux partition without damaging existing files. (But make backups!)

◆ rootdsks   Root filesystem images for initial floppy installation

◆ slaktest   Files used to let you run Linux from a CD-ROM using the least amount of hard drive space.

◆ slakware   The SlackWare Linux distribution that is installed to your hard drive. This includes other software such as Xfree86, X applications, development tools, networking tools, and more.

◆ source   Source code for much of SlackWare 3.0 and utilities

The CD-ROM can be used as an installation source with most of the needed files copied to your hard drive, or you can run your Linux system with the CD-ROM as part of the filesystem. The latter approach reduces the amount of hard disk space you need for Linux, but the speed of the system is slower as a CD-ROM is inherently much slower than a hard drive. Also, you must keep the CD-ROM in the drive at all times with this approach.

If you are looking for a specific file or utility, you can use the `find` command to search the CD-ROM.

SAMS PUBLISHING SUPPORT

We can help you if you have a question about the book, or if you have a defective CD-ROM.

E-mail:	support@mcp.com
Mail:	Macmillan Computer Publishing Support Department 201 West 103rd Street Indianapolis, IN 46290
Phone:	(317) 581-3833
Fax:	(317) 581-4773

VISIT US ON-LINE

World-Wide Web: http://www.mcp.com/sams

Internet FTP: ftp.mcp.com/pub/sams

CompuServe: "GO SAMS"

INFOMAGIC SUPPORT

Support for installing running Linux is available through InfoMagic. Limited support for configuring X-Windows is available only through e-mail, due to the overwhelming number of combinations of video cards and monitors. If you need support for specific Linux utilities and programs, you need to contact the author of the program. Support is available only for purchasers of this book and CD-ROM.

BY E-MAIL

Send Internet e-mail to support @infomagic.com for free technical support. There is no charge for e-mail support, but you may not get an immediate response. Response-time guarantees are not made for support via e-mail.

Please include the following information in your e-mail message:

◆ Model and manufacturer of your computer

◆ Number, type, capacity, and "geometry" of your hard drives

◆ Manufacturer, model, I/O port, and IRQ information on all installed cards (especially sound cards and SCSI interfaces)

◆ Complete text of any error messages

◆ Model and manufacturer of your CD-ROM drive and interface details (dedicated card, sound card, IDE, SCSI, etc.)

BY PHONE

Call 1-900-786-5555 for immediate technical support. You will be charged $2.00 per minute for calls to this number. When contacting InfoMagic tech support by phone, have the following information available:

◆ Model and manufacturer of your computer

◆ Number, type, capacity and "geometry" of your hard drives

◆ Model, manufacturer, I/O port, and IRQ information on all installed cards (especially sound cards and SCSI interfaces)

◆ Complete text of any error messages

◆ Model and manufacturer of your CD-ROM drive and interface details (dedicated card, sound card, IDE, SCSI, etc.)

It will also be helpful if you can be near your system when you call, as we will often ask you to check configuration details or manually adjust system startup files.

SYMBOLS

" " (double quotation marks), shell programs, 382
' ' (single quotation marks), shell programs, 382
- (hyphen), access permissions, 281
? (question mark) command, 317
\ (backslash), shell programs, 382
10Base2 network medium, 433
80386 CPU, 5
80386SX processors, minimum requirements, 18
80486DX processors, 18

A

-a option
    df command, 300
    du command, 302
    fsck utility, 298
    ps command, 325
    quotacheck command, 335
A resource record, 465
abort printer_name | all command, 316

Index

access permissions, 281-282
  default, 282-283
  editing, 283-286
  execute, 281
  HDB UUCP, 409-410
  hyphens (-), 281
  links, 304
  read, 281
  SGID, 296
  SUID, 296
  Taylor UUCP, 406-407
  write, 281
accessing
  directories
    permission blocks, 279-287
    read permissions, 281
    write permissions, 281
  files
    execute permissions, 281
    hyphens (-), 281
    permission blocks, 279-287
    read permissions, 281
    write permissions, 281
  utilities, default system groups, 272
accounts
  PPP, 476-477
  root, 260
  superuser, 260-261
  user
    comments, 265
    configurations, 268
    creating, 261-262
    deleting, 269-270
    disabling, 269-270
    /etc/passwd file, 261-262
    group IDs, 264-265
    home directories, 265
    login command, 266
    passwords, 263-264, 269
    user IDs, 264
    usernames, 262-263

acquiring Linux, 24-25
  BBSs, 31-32
  CD-ROMs, 25
  e-mail, 30-31
  FTP sites, 26
    downloading files, 26-28
    finding FTP archive sites, 28-29
  World Wide Web sites, 29-30
active partitions, changing, 78
Ada compiler, 6
addgroup utility (C News), 585
addresses, 720
  DMA, 66
  e-mail, 528
  hardware addresses, 723
  I/O, 66
  Internet addresses, 724
  IP addresses, 278, 426-428
    address masks, 720
    address resolution, 720
    dotted decimal notation, 722
    resolving, 457-469
  IRQ, 66
  network names, 489
  symbolic machine names, 488-489
  UUCP, 414-416
adm login, 266
af parameter (/etc/printcap file), 314-315
agents (TCP/IP), 720
alias=name option (map installer), 89
-all option
  df command, 300
  du command, 302
American National Standard Code for Information Interchange, *see* ASCII

American National Standards Institute (ANSI), 720
anonymous FTP, 600-601
  logins, 608
  permissions, 610
ANSI (American National Standards Institute), 720
API (Application Programming Interface), 720
append=string (map installer), 89
application layer (OSF model), 720
Application Programming Interface (API), 720
applications
  DOS, portability, 7
  sound, 191-192
  Windows, portability, 7
Archie, 595
archive FTP sites, locating Linux files, 28-29
archives, *see* backups
ARP (Address Resolution Protocol), 424, 503-504, 720
arp command, 503-504
.arpa domain name, 429
.arpa extension, 277
articles
  batching, 565
    C News, 583-584
  compression, 583
  interactive newsreading, 565
  receiving, 584-585
  threads, 588
ASCII (American National Standard Code for Information Interchange), 720
  resource records, 463
ascii command (FTP), 604
ASCII transfer mode (FTP), 603

assigning values to variables, 380-381
at program, 355-357
-au option (ps command), 325
audio CDs, *see* music CDs
authentication (PPP), 481-484
auto-configuring NICs, 434
automatic mounts, 293-295
automating
    startup functions, 218
    tasks
        at program, 355-357
        cron utility, 350-354
aztech images, hardware compatibility, 38

B

-b dev option (map installer), 87
-b option (du command), 302
backslash (\), shell programs, 382
backup=file option (map installer), 89
backups
    blocking factors, 345
    frequency, 342-343
    full, 341-342
    incremental, 341
    listing, 345
    logs, 343-344
    media types, 339-340
    memory management, 303
    necessity, 338-339
    scheduling, 340-343
    tape drives, 227-228
    tar utility, 344-346
    UPSs, 238-239
bad geometry error messages, 71

bad geometry message, 92
bandwidth, 721
    horizontal, 124
bare images, hardware compatibility, 38
bash shell
    case statement, 389
    for, 390
    test command, 384-387
    until statement, 393
    while statement, 392
Basic compiler, 6
batch processes, 322
batching articles, 565
    C News, 583-584
BBSs (Bulletin Board Systems), 676-682
    Linux files, 31-32
Berkeley Internet Name Domain (BIND) service, 457
Berkeley Software Distribution (BSD), 721
bin login, 266
binary command (FTP), 604
binary transfer mode (FTP), 604
BIND (Berkeley Internet Name Domain service), 457
-bios option (SuperProbe), 108
BIOS compatibility, 708
block mode devices, 138-139
    file types, 280
    printers, 308
block permissions
    SGID, 296
    SUID, 296
blocking factors (backups), 345
blocks (tape drives), 223
book floppy disks, starting Linux with, 247-249

boot disks
    creating, 36-37, 40-41, 58
    installation, 37-39
boot flopy disk, creating, 247-248
boot images, viewing, 85
boot kernels
    names, 37
    selecting, 37-39
    see also kernel images
boot parameters, 85-86
boot process, configurations, 76-79
    boot parameters, 85-86
    BOOTACTV utility, 77-78
    BOOTLIN, 79-80
    dedicated Linux hard disk, 76-77
    LILO utility, 80-85
boot sectors, 74-75
    MBR, 74
    saving, 75
    updating, map installer utility, 86-91
boot=dev option (map installer), 89
BOOTACTV utility, 77-78
bootdsks, 37
BOOTLIN, boot process configurations, 79-80
BOOTP (Boot Protocol), 424
boots
    first-stage boot loader, 246
    init daemon, 252-256
        /etc/inittab file, 253-256
        run levels, 252-253
    kernel images, 91
    LILO utility, 62, 246-247
        disabling, 93
        disk parameter tables, 92-93
    logging in, 202-203
    maintenance disks, 249
    troubleshooting, 77
        Linux, 68

bridges, 423
brouters, 423
BSD (Berkeley Software Distribution), 721
BSD UNIX, 9
buffers, 721
  block mode devices, 138
  character mode devices, 138
Bulletin Board Systems, *see* BBSs
bus mouse, 61
bus networks, 430, 431
-bytes option (du command), 302

C

C compiler, 6, 373
  compiler options, 374-375
  debugging options, 375-376
-C file option (map installer), 87
.c files, sound card configurations, 188
C News
  batching articles, 583-584
  configuration files, 577-579
  directories, 579-580
  receiving articles, 584-585
  sys file, 580-583
  utilities, 585
-c option
  du command, 302
  map installer, 87
  term utility, 215
C++ compiler, 6
cabling, 432-433
  DCE cables, 201
  DTE cables, 201-202
  serial cables, wiring, 200-202
caches, 721

callback modems, 362
Can't put the boot sector on logical partition X message, 94
.cap directory (Gopher), 644
case sensitivity (usernames), 262-263
case statement, 389-390
cat command, 190
cd command (FTP), 604
CD-ROM drives, 167
CD-ROM drive compatibility, 714
CD-ROM drive not recognized message, 68
CD-ROMs
  CD-ROM drives, 167
  changer drives, 162-163
  drive bays, 162
  drive installation, 167-168
    device files, creating, 171-174
    kernel configurations, 168-170
    mounting, 174-176
    physical, 168
    testing, 176
  drives
    backups, 340
    mounting automatically, 177
    power supply, 163
    troubleshooting, 179-181
    unmounting, 176
  external drives, 162-163
  filesystems
    mounting, 292
  formatting, 164
  IDE CD-ROM drives, 166
  interfaces, 165-167
  internal drives, 162-163
  Linux distributions, 25
  Linux requirements, 22-23

  memory, 162
  music CDs, playing, 164, 176-178
  PhotoCD, 164, 179
  primary boot images, 38
  primary root images, 39
  propietary CD-ROM drives, 166-167
  RAM, 167
  recordable, 167
  SCSI device drivers, 147-149
    mounting, 148-149
  setup utility, 54
  speed, 164-167
  XFree86, 100
cdu31a images, hardware compatibility, 38
cdu535 images, hardware compatibility, 38
cf files, 312
Challenge Handshake Authentication Protocol (CHAP), 481-484
changer CD-ROM drives, 162-163
CHAP (Challenge Handshake Authentication Protocol), 481-484
character mode devices, 138-139
  file types, 280
  printers, 308
chat program (PPP), 477-478
chgrp command, 287
chown command, 286-287, 611
chroot command (FTP), 610
clean printer_name | all command, 316
client-server architecture, 721
clients, 421, 721

close command (FTP), 604
CNAME resource record, 465
coaxial cabling, 432
coherent filesystem, 295
color image, 39
color planes (video cards), 128
.com domain name, 277, 429
command-line options
  df command, 300-301
  du command, 302
  edquota command, 333-334
  map installer utility, 87-88
  ps command, 324-326
  quota command, 334
  quotacheck command, 335
  SuperProbe, 108-109
  tar command, 344-345
  top command, 328-330
commands
  arp, 503-504
  at, 355-357
  chown (FTP), 611
  chroot (FTP), 610
  configuring term utility environment variables, 211-212
  connect, 479
  cron utility, 354
  executing as another user, 274
  exit (FTP), 604
  fdisk utility, 47
  get (FTP), 603, 674
  ifconfig, 450, 491-493
  lpc utility, 316-317
  ls, 384
  mount, 509
  netstat, 494-502
  ping, 452, 502-503
  put (FTP), 603, 674
  quit (FTP), 604

  route, 450
  shift, 393-394
  slattach, 474-475
  test, 384-387
  traceroute, 504-505
  UUCP
    uucico, 410
    uucp, 416
    uustat, 418
  waisindex, 620, 626-628
  see also utilities
comments, 265
communications
  bandwidths, 721
  leased lines, 724
  modems, 724
communications parameters, configurations, 204-206
Compact Disk-Recordable drive, *see* CD-ROM drives
compact option (map installer), 89
compatibility
  CD-ROM drives, 162-163
  filesystems, 295
  SCSI devices, 146
  sound cards, 185
compilers, 6
compiling
  C compiler, 373-376
  freeWAIS, 618-620
  kernel source code, 370-372
  sound card drivers, 188-189
  Web software, 653-655
compressed kernels, 248
conditional statements
  case, 389-390
  if, 387-388
configuration files
  /etc/hosts, 488-489
  /etc/networks, 489
  /etc/protocols, 489-490
  /etc/services, 490-491

configuration utility, modem configurations, 233
configuring
  boot process, 76-79
    BOOTACTV utility, 77-78
    BOOTLIN, 79-80
    dedicated Linux hard disk, 76-77
    LILO utility, 80-85
    parameters, 85-86
  C News, 577-579
  CD-ROM drives, 181
  communications parameters, 204-206
  ConfigXF86 utility, 109-120
    keyboard settings, 121-122
    monitor settings, 124-126
    mouse definitions, 122-123
    pathnames, 120
    server, 127-129
    testing, 129-131
    video cards, 126-127
  device conflicts, 65-67
  Elm, 556-557
  Ethernet drivers, 453
  FTP, 606-612
  Gopher, 634-635
    gopherd.conf file, 635-636
    gopherdlocal. conf file, 636-639
    Makefile, 639-643
    WAIS, 643
  INN, 573-574
  installation, 59-62
  kernel
    CD-ROM drive installation, 168-170
    kernel images, 91-92

map installer utility, 86-91
modems, 233-235
  *handshaking proto-
    cols, 234*
  Linux installation, 60
  manual, 233
  speeds, 235
  symbolic links, 234
monitors
  *horizontal band-
    width, 124*
  vertical refresh rate, 125
  video modes, 125
networks
  gateways, 455-457
  kernel, 438
  network drivers, 440
  serial ports, 444-445
nntpd, 570-571
Pine, 557-560
PLIP, 454-455
printer devices, 310
printers, 314
  parallel, 308-309
SCSI devices, 145
  tape drives, 223
  troubleshooting, 66
sendmail program,
  532-541
  decnetxtable file, 536
  domaintable file, 536
  genericfrom table, 536
  *mailertable table,
    536-537*
  pathtable table, 537
  sendmail.cf file, 533-535
  *UUCP-based mail
    systems, 535*
  uucprelays file, 538
  uucpxtable file, 538
SLIP, 474-475
smail
  for TCP, 549-550
  for UUCP, 546-549
sound cards, 186-190
  device files, 187
  DMA values, 194

IRQ values, 194
  *linking sound files,
    187-189*
  *mknod command,
    188-189*
  parameters, 189
  *troubleshooting,
    192-193*
TCP/IP, 448-450
  ifconfig command, 450
term utility configura-
  tions, 215-220
terminals
  reconfiguring, 210
  stty command, 208-209
  tset command, 209
  viewing, 209
tin newsreader, 589-590
trn newsreader, 588-589
user accounts, 268
UUCP, 402-403
  HDB UUCP, 408-410
  Taylor UUCP, 403-407
Web software, 655-659
xf86config utility, 109-120
  *keyboard settings,
    121-122*
  *monitor settings,
    124-126*
  *mouse definitions,
    122-123*
  pathnames, 120
  server, 127-129
  testing, 129-131
  video cards, 126-127
XFree86, 104-119
  *directory location,
    106-107*
  *SuperProbe utility,
    107-109*
  testing, 129
**ConfigXF86 utility, 104,
109-119**
  keyboard settings, 121-122
  monitor settings, 124-126
  mouse definitions, 122-123

pathnames, 120
server, 127-129
testing, 129-131
video cards, 126-127
connect command, 479
**connecting to Internet,
594-595**
  borrowing gateways, 596
  command-line access
    systems, 597
  dedicated connections, 596
  FreeNet, 597
  service providers, 597
connections
  SCSI devices, 144
  term utility, 215
  terminals, 198
    adding, 207-208
    detecting, 203
    logging in, 202-207
    *multiport cards,
      198-200*
    reconfiguring, 210
    *serial cables, wiring,
      200-202*
    serial ports, 200
connectors
  multiport cards, 199
  serial cables, 200-202
**controller compatibility,
709-710**
**controller systems (hard
disks), 20-21**
controllers
  ESDI, 156
  IDE controllers, 156
  interfaces, 156-157
**converting sound
files, 192**
copy-on-write pages, 5
copying quotas, 333
**copyright information,
702-705**
copyrights to Linux, 9
corrupted floppy disks, 65
**countries, system
names, 277**

CPUs
80386, 5
CPU compatibility, 708-709
requirements for Linux, 18
CRC (Cyclic Redundancy Check), 722
cron utility, 350-351
commands, 354
crontab file
creating, 351-352
managing, 353-354
submitting, 353-354
CSLIP, 473
customizing
freeWAIS, 628-629
smail, 552-554
XFree86, 129
Cyclic Redundancy Check (CRC), 722
Cylinder number is too big message, 94
Cylinders Beyond 1024 message, 68

D

d command, 47
-d option (quotacheck command), 335
d option (top command), 328
-d secs option (map installer), 87
daemon group, 272
daemon login, 266
daemon processes, 322
daemons, 722
ftpd, 607-608
inetd, 493-494
init, 252-256
/etc/inittab file, 253-256
multiuser mode, 252
run levels, 252-253
lpd, 310-315

named, 458-460
NFS (Network File System), 511
nntpd, 568
pppd, 479-480
smail, 546
DARPA (Defense Advanced Research Project Agency), 722
data buffers, netstat command, 498-499
Data Circuit-Terminating Equipment (DCE), 722
data compression (term utility), 215
Data Encryption Standard (DES), 722
Data Terminal Equipment (DTE), 722
datagrams, 722
DCE (Data Circuit-Terminating Equipment), 722
DCE cables, 201
DDN (Defense Data Network), 722
Debian Linux Distribution, 686
debugging
options for kernel software, 375-376
smail, 552
decnetxtable file, configuring sendmail, 536
dedicated hard disks, installation, 76-77
default groups (users), 270-272
default permissions, 282-283
Defense Advanced Research Project Agency (DARPA), 722
Defense Data Network (DDN), 722
del command (FTP), 604

delay=secs (map installer), 89
deleting
partitions, 47
print jobs, 318
queued, 316-319
user accounts, 269-270
user groups, 273
delgroup utility (C News), 585
DES (Data Encryption Standard), 722
detecting terminal connections, 203
/dev/sndstate file, troubleshooting sound cards, 193
development of Linux, 8-9
device busy errors (CD-ROM drives), 181
device busy message, 194
device drivers, 136-137
block mode devices, 138-139
character mode devices, 138-139
identification, 139-141
linking, 136
to kernel software, 372
major numbers, 139-141
minor numbers, 139-141
mknod command, 140-141
mounting, 177-178
names, 139
optical readers, 241
permissions, 137-141
porting files, 241
removable cartridge drives, 240
scanners, 241
SCSI, 146-150
CD-ROMs, 147-149, 165
hard disks, 146-147
major device numbers, 146-150

minor device numbers, 147-150
miscellaneous, 150
partitions, 147
tape drives, 149-150
troubleshooting, 150-153
serial ports, 233-234
software device, 200
sound cards, 187
device files, 137
CD-ROM drive installation, 171-174
location, 137
sound card configurations, 187
device full message, 64
df command, 299, 300
command-line options, 300-301
df file, 312
diagnostic utilities, troubleshooting device conflicts, 66
dial-in modems, 233-234
dial-out modems, 233-234
Dial-up IP (dip), 475-476
dialing out, chat program (PPP), 477-478
dip (Dial-up IP), 475-476
dir command (FTP), 604
director (smail program), 545
directories
accessing, permission blocks, 279-287
C News, 579-580
displaying by size, 302
FTP, 609-610
Gopher, 644
filenames, 644-645
master files, 645
home, 265
mounting NFS remote directories, 513-515

owners, changing, 286-287
print spoolers, 311-312
read permissions, 281
root
bootdsks, 37
mounting as read-only, 257
sound card drivers, 186
write permissions, 281
XFree86, 100-101
directory files, 280
disable printer_name I all parameter (/etc/printca, 316
disabling
LILO utility, 93
printers, 316
user accounts, 269-270
disk controllers, troubleshooting, 65
disk errors (LILO utility installation), 71
disk parameter tables, 92-93
disk sets, viewing, 63
disk sets (Linux), 32-33
disks
backups, *see* backups
book floppy disks, starting Linux with, 247-249
boot floppy disks, creating, 36-37, 40-41, 58, 247-248
emergency boot, 249-250
hard
dedicated, 76-77
filesystem partitions, 53
layouts, 72-74
partitions, 157-159
platters, 73
SCSI device drivers, 146-147
single-purpose, 73
troubleshooting, 65
upgrading, 156-157
hard disks, partitions, 42-46

maintenance, 249-250
memory management, 296-297
filesystem checks, 297-298
optimizing disk space, 302-304
quotas, 332-333
creating, 333-334
displaying, 334
hard limits, 332
necessity of, 333
quotacheck command, 335
soft limits, 332
turning on, 334
RAM sizes, 257
root, creating, 36-37, 40-41
see also drives
disks sets, installation, 55-57
disktab=file option (map installer), 89
displaying
directories by size, 302
filesystem statistics, 299-302
filesystem types, 49
partitions, 50
current, 47
permission blocks, 279
print queues, 318
quotas, 334
root partitions, 257
distributed processing, 722
DMA addresses, 66
DMA values (sound card configurations), 194
dmesg command, 169, 175, 189
dmesg1 command, 175
DNS (Domain Name Service), 424, 428-430, 457, 722
name resolution, 725
nested zones, 459

PPP, 484-485
SLIP, 484-485
documentation for Linux, 690
Domain Name System, *see* **DNS**
domain names (smail), 550
configuring, 547-548
domaintable file, configuring sendmail, 536
DOS
boot sector, 74-75
MBR, 74
creat boot and root disks from, 40-41
Linux interface, 7
dotted decimal notation, 722
double quotation marks (" "), shell programs, 382
double-speed CD-ROM drives, 164
down printer_name message command, 316
downloading
articles, 565
FTP, 603, 673-675
Linux FTP site files, 26-28
drive bays, 162
drivers
device drivers, 136-137
block mode devices, 138-139
character mode devices, 138-139
/etc/fstab file, 177-178
identification, 139-141
linking, 136
major numbers, 139-141
minor numbers, 139-141
mknod command, 140-141
names, 139
optical readers, 241
permissions, 137-141

porting files, 241
removable cartridge drives, 240
scanners, 241
SCSI, 146-150
sound card, 187
linking to kernel software, 372
sound cards
compiling, 188-189
directories, 186
testing, 189-190
drives
CD-ROM
CD-R, 167
changer, 162-163
drive bays, 162
external, 162-163
IDE CD-ROM drives, 166
installation, 167-176
interfaces, 165-167
internal, 162-163
mounting automatically, 177
music CDs, playing, 176-178
power supply, 163
proprietary, 166-167
RAM, 167
speed, 164-167
troubleshooting, 179-181
unmounting, 176
magneto-optical, 339
removable cartridge, 240
SCSI tape drives, 222-223
major device numbers, 222
minor device numbers, 222
system requirements, 18
tape drives
backups, 227-228
file restoration, 228
installation, 222
see also disks

DTE (Data Terminal Equipment), 722
cables, 201-202
du command, 301-302
dumb terminals, 723
dummy interfaces, 472-473
duplicating quotas, 333
dynamically shared libraries, 5

E

e-mail
Elm, configuring, 556-557
ftpmail, 675
Internet use, 595
Linux files, 30-31
Pine, configuring, 557-560
rmail program, 544
sending (UUCP), 414-416
sendmail program
configuring, 532-538
decnetxtable file, 536
domaintable file, 536
generating sendmail.cf file, 538
genericfrom table, 536
IDA, 532
mailertable table, 536-537
pathtable table, 537
sendmail.cf file, 533-535
templates, 541-542
UUCP-based mail systems, 535
uucprelays file, 538
uucpxtable file, 538
version 8, 538-539
smail program, 544-545
customizing, 552-554
debugging, 552
delivery mode, 550-551
director, 545
domain names, 550
postmaster, 551
router, 545

setup, 545-546
smail daemon, 546
TCP, configuring for, 549-550
transport, 545
UUCP, configuring for, 546-549
software, 526-528
structure of messages, 528-530
EBCDIC (Extended Binary Coded Decimal Interchage Code), 723
echo command, 216
editing
access permissions, 283-286
group quotas, 333
partition type codes, 47
run levels, 253
user quotas, 334
edquota command, 333-334
.edu domain name, 429
.edu extension, 277
EGP (Exterior Gateway Protocol), 425
EIDE (Extended Integrated Drive Electronics) contr, 20-21
EISA (Extended Industry Standard Architecture), 18
eject command, 176
Elm, configuring, 556-557
emergency boot disks, 249-250
emulation, 723
enable printer_name | all command, 317
environment variables
PATH, 103-104
term utility, 211
error messages
bad geometry, 71, 92
device busy errors, 181
device full, 64

file not found, 65
LILO utility, 94-95
mount command, 175
read error, 65
SCSI devices, 67-68
sound cards, 193-194
swap partitions, 52
tar: read error, 65
term utility, 215
ESDI (Enhanced Small Device Interface) controllers, 20-21, 156
/etc/fstab file, 177-178
/etc/hosts file, 488-489
/etc/networks file, 489
/etc/protocols file, 489-490
/etc/services file, 490-491
/etc/fstab file options, 296
/etc/group file, 272-273
/etc/hosts file, 278-279
/etc/init daemon, 202-203
/etc/inittab, logging in, 203-204
/etc/inittab daemon, 202-203
/etc/inittab file, 253-256
/etc/passwd file, 261-262
/etc/printcap file, 313
parameters, 314-315
/etc/rc initialization file, 293-295
/etc/termcap, 206-207
/etc/ttys, logging in, 203-204
Ethernet, 720, 723
10Base2, 433
cabling, 433
network interface cards, 24
setting up interfaces, 453-454
execute permissions, 281
executing commands as another users, 274
exit command, 317
FTP, 604

ext filesystem, 295
ext2 filesystem, 295
ext2fs filesystem, 6
Extended Binary Coded Decimal Interchange Code (EBCDIC), 723
Extended filesystem, 53
extended filesystem, 295
extended partitions, 49
extensions
kernal images, 39
system names, 277-278
external CD-ROM drives, 162-163
external modems, installation, 232-233

F

-f file option (map installer), 87
FAQ (Frequently Asked Questions) files, 11
FATs (File Allocation Tables), 73
fdisk utility, 43-45, 157-159
commands, 47
Linux, 47-48
fdiskutility, 48
fet utility, 218
File Allocation Tables, *see* **FATs**
file not found error, 65
file security, 361
file servers, 723
File Transfer Protocol, *see* **FTP**
files
accessing, permission blocks, 279-287
backups
frequency, 342-343
logs, 343-344
media types, 339-340
necessity, 338-339

scheduling, 340-343
tape drives, 227-228
tar utility, 344-346
block mode devices, 280
booting kernel images
  from, 91
.c, sound card configura-
  tions, 188
cf, 312
character mode devices,
  280
/dev/sndstate, trouble-
  shooting sound cards,
  193
device, 137
  CD-ROM drive installa-
    tion, 171-174
  location, 137
  sound card configura-
    tions, 187
df, 312
directory, 280
/etc/fstab, 177-178
  options, 296
/etc/group file, 272-273
/etc/hosts, 278-279
/etc/inittab, 253-256
/etc/passwd, 261-262
/etc/printcap, 313
/etc/rc initialization,
  293-295
execute permissions, 281
Gopher directories,
  644-645
.h, sound card configura-
  tions, 188
linking, 304-305
  hard links, 304-305
  i-node tables, 304-305
  symbolic links, 305
MIDI, 191
ordinary, 280
owners, changing, 286-287
permission blocks, 279-280
porting, 241
read permissions, 281

restoring, 228
software, viewing, 63
sound
  converting, 192
  mixing, 191
  only part of file
    plays, 194
  sounds stop and start
    when playing, 194-195
sound cards, linking,
  187-189
startup (quotacheck
  command), 335
transferring
  FTP, 602-604
  UUCP, 416-418
write permissions, 281
.xinitrc, 129-131
filesystem partitions, 42
creating, 50, 53
Extended, 53
Minix, 53
Second Extended
  filesystem, 53
Xia, 53
filesystems
backups, 227
  frequency, 342-343
  logs, 343-344
  media types, 339-340
  necessity, 338-339
  scheduling, 340-343
  tar utility, 344-346
CD-ROMs, mounting, 292
compatibility, 295
cylinder limitations, 49
ext2fs, 6
extended, 295
High Performance, 295
ISO 9660, 295
memory management,
  297-298
  backups, 303
  optimizing disk space,
    302-304
  statistics, 299-302

Minix, 295
mounting, 290-293
  as read-only, 292
  automatically, 293-295
  /etc/rc initialization,
    293-295
  options, 296
  types, 295
restoring, 345
second extended, 295
types, displaying, 49
UMS-DOS, 295
unmounting, 290-293
Xia, 295
Fintronic Linux Sys-
  tems, 686
FIPS utility, 43
First sector doesn't have a
  valid boot signature
  message, 94
first-stage boot loader, 246
fix-table option (map
  installer), 89
floating-point units
  (FPUs), requirements for
  Linux, 18
flooding (transferring
  news articles), 564
floppy disks
  backups, 340
  corrupted, 65
  tar utility, 346
FM2HTML, 664
fonts, Linux instal-
  lation, 62
for statement, 390-392
force-backup=file option
  (map installer), 89
formatting CD-ROMs, 164
Fortran compiler, 6
FPU compatibility,
  708-709
FPUs (floating-point
  units), requirements for
  Linux, 18

FreeNet, 597
freeWAIS, 616-618
    customizing, 628-629
    installing, 618-620
    setup, 620-623
    starting, 623-624
Frequently Asked Questions (FAQ) files, 11
front-panel information (UPSs), 239
fsck utility, 297-298
ftape utility, 223-226
FTP (File Transfer Protocol), 26, 424, 510, 595, 600-602, 672, 723
    anonymous FTP, 601
    archive sites, 676
    ASCII transfer mode, 603
    BBSs, 676-682
    binary transfer mode, 604
    configuring, 606-612
    connecting to, 673-675
    directories, 609-610
    downloading files, 673-675
    ftpd (FTP daemon), 607-608
    ftpmail, 675
    logins, 608-609
    permissions, 610-611
    quitting, 604-605
    security, 612
    TCP, 605-606
    testing system, 611-612
    transferring files, 602-604
    WU FTP, 612
FTP sites
    Linux distributions, 26
        downloading files, 26-28
        finding FTP archive sites, 28-29
    primary boot images, 38
    primary root images, 39
ftpd (FTP daemon), 607-608
full backups, 341-342
functions, shell programming, 396-397

G

-g option
    edquota command, 333
    quota command, 334
    quotacheck command, 335
Gateway protocols, 425
gateways, 423-435, 455-457, 723
    connecting to Internet, 594
        borrowing gateways, 596
        dedicated connections, 596
gcc (GNU C compiler), 373-376
gdb (gcc debugging program), 375-376
genericfrom table, configuring sendmail, 536
get command (FTP), 603-604, 674
GGP (Gateway-to-Gateway Protocol), 425
GID, see group ID
GNU C compiler (gcc), 373-376
GNU General Public License (GPL), 9, 692-699
GNU software, 6
Gopher, 595, 632-634
    configuring, 634-635
        gopherd.conf file, 635-636
        gopherdlocal. conf file, 636-639
        Makefile, 639-643
        WAIS, 643
    directories, 644
        filenames, 644-645
        master files, 645
    links, 646-647
    listing Gopher services, 648
    starting, 647-648
Got bad geometry message, 94

.gov domain name, 429
.gov extension, 277
group IDs, 264-265, 271
group quotas, 333
    displaying, 334
    editing, 333
groups (users), 270-271
    creating, 272-273
    daemon, 272
    default, 270-272
    deleting, 273
    IDs, 271
    kmem, 272
    names, 271
    passwords, 271
    root/wheel/system, 272
    su command, 274
    sys, 272
    tty, 272
GUIs (graphical user interface), 6
    XFree86, 98-99
        directories, 100-101
        hardware requirements, 99
        installation, 100-104
gzip command, 102

H

-h option (rdev utility), 257
.h files, sound card configurations, 188
handshaking protocols, 234
hard disk requirements, 20-21
hard disks
    backups, 339
    boot sectors, saving, 75
    dedicated, 76-77
    layouts, 72-74
    partitions, 42-46, 157-159
        active, 78
        assigning types, 49
        bad blocks, 51

creating, 44-45
cylinder limitations, 49
displaying, 50
extended, 49
fdisk utility, 44-45
filesystem, 50, 53
installation, 46-47
multiple, 73-74
primary, 49
root, 257
sizes, 53
swap, 48-52
swap partitions, 43-44
UMSDOS utility, 46
platters, 73
removable hard disks,
  backups, 339
SCSI device drivers,
  146-147
single-purpose, 73
troubleshooting, 65
upgrading, 156-157
**hard drive compatibil-
ity, 711**
hard limits (quotas), 332
hard links, 304-305
hardware
device drivers, 136-137
Linux requirements
  CD-ROMs, 22-23
  Ethernet network
    cards, 24
  hard disks, 20-21
  modems, 23-24
  motherboards, 18-20
  mouses, 22
  multiport cards, 24
  printers, 23
  removable media, 23
  tape drives, 22
  terminals, 24
  video systems, 21
optical readers, 241
removable cartridge
  drives, 240

requirements
  boot images, 38
  root images, 39
  XFree86, 99
scanners, 241
UPSs, 238-240
hardware addresses, 723
hash command (FTP), 604
HDB UUCP
access times, 412-413
configuring
  access permissions,
    409-410
  modems, 408-409
remote systems, 408
headers (e-mail), 528
help (fdisk utility), 48
help command, 317
  FTP, 604
**--help option (mknod
command), 141**
**-help option (df com-
mand), 300**
help resources, 10
documentation, 10-11
Linux Journal, 15
USENET newsgroups,
  11-13
  FAQ files, 11
World Wide Web sites,
  13-15
**High Performance
filesystem, 295**
**HINFO resource record,
465**
**home directories, user
accounts, 265**
home pages, 661
horizontal bandwidth, 124
hostname command, 276
hostnames, 449
  saving, 278-279
hosts.conf file, 460-461
hpfs filesystem, 295
**HTML (HyperText
Markup Language),
662-665**

hub networks, 431
hung processes, 326
**hyphens (-), access per-
missions, 281**

I-J

**-I name option (map
installer), 88**
**-i option (df com-
mand), 300**
**i option (top com-
mand), 328**
**-i sector option (map
installer), 87**
**i-node tables, effects of
file links on, 304-305**
I/O addresses, 66
**I/O controller compatibil-
ity, 712**
**ICMP (Internet Control
Message Protocol), 424,
502, 724**
IDA (sendmail utility), 532
**IDE (Integrated Drive
Electronics) control-
lers, 20**
IDE CD-ROM drives, 166
  installation, 170
IDE controllers, 156
idecd images
  hardware compatibility, 38
identification
  device drivers, 139-141
  SCSI devices, 144
IDs, 271
**IEEE (Institute of Electri-
cal and Electronic
Engineers), 724**
if statement, 387-388
**ifconfig command, 450,
491-493**
**IGNORECASE parameter
(Makefile), 72**
**IGP (Interior Gateway
Protocol), 425**

ihave/sendme protocol, 565
images
aztech, 38
bare, 38
boot
names, 37
selecting, 37-39
viewing, 85
cdu31a, 38
cdu535, 38
color, 39
idecd, 38
kernel
booting from files, 91
booting from other
devices, 91
configurations, 91-92
names, 39
SCSI device configura-
tions, 66
searches, 248
mitsumi, 38
net, 38
root
Linux software installa-
tion, 54
selecting, 37-39
sbpcd, 38
scsi, 38
scsinet1, 38
scsinet2, 38
tape, 39
tty, 39
umsdos, 39
xt, 38
IN-ADDR-ARPA, 468-469
incoming mail (smail),
550-551
incremental backups, 341
indexes (WAIS), 620,
624-629
inetd daemon, 493-494
-info option (SuperProbe),
108
INFO-SHEET, 10

InfoMagic, technical
support, 731
InfoMagic Developer's
Resource CD-ROM
Kit, 686
init daemon, 252-256
/etc/inittab file, 253-256
run levels, 252-253
init daemons
multiuser mode, 252
run levels, editing, 253
INN (InterNet News), 569
configuring, 573-574
installing, 572-573
-inode option (df com-
mand), 300
install=sector option (map
installer), 89
installation
boot disks, 58
boot kernels, 37-39
creating, 36-37, 40-41
BOOTACTV utility, 77-78
BOOTLIN, 79-80
CD-ROM drives, 167-168
device files, creating,
171-174
kernel configurations,
168-170
mounting, 174-176
physical instal-
lation, 168
testing, 176
configurations, 59-62
dedicated hard disks,
76-77
disk sets, 55-57
freeWAIS, 618-620
INN, 572-573
kernel software, 368-369
LILO utility, 70-71
disk errors, 71
Makefile, 72
Linux, 36, 54-62
boot device, 62
modems, 60
mouse setup, 60

screen fonts, 62
source, 55
swap partitions, 51-52
target, 55
modems, 232-233
multiport cards, 200
NFS (Network File
System), 510-513
NIS (Network Information
Service), 519-521
NNTP server program,
569-570
partitions, 46-47
root disks, creating, 36-37,
40-41
SCSI drives, 222
term utility, 211-212
troubleshooting
device conflicts, 65-67
disk controllers, 65
hard disks, 65
software, 64-65
XFree86, 100-104
manual, 102-103
PATH environment
variable, 103-104
server selection, 101-102
setup script, 103
Institute of Electrical and
Electronic Engineers
(IEEE), 724
Integrated Service Digital
Network (ISDN), 724
Intel 80386 CPU, 5
intelligent controller, 199
interactive processes, 322
interfaces
CD-ROM drives, 165-167
controllers, 156-157
tape drives (ftape pro-
gram), 223-226
internal CD-ROM drives,
162-163
internal modems
advantages, 232
installation, 232-233

**International Organiza-
tion for Standardization
(ISO), 724**
Internet, 724
  access, SLIP ports, 475
  addresses, 724
  connecting to, 594-595
    *borrowing gateways,
    596*
    *command-line access
    systems, 597*
    *dedicated connections,
    596*
    FreeNet, 597
    service providers, 597
  DARPA (Defense Ad-
  vanced Research Project
  Agency), 722
  FTP, 600-602, 672-673
    anonymous FTP, 601
    archive sites, 676
    *ASCII transfer
    mode, 603*
    BBSs, 676-682
    *binary transfer mode,
    604*
    configuring, 606-612
    connecting to, 673-675
    directories, 609-610
    *downloading files,
    673-675*
    *ftpd (FTP daemon),
    607-608*
    ftpmail, 675
    logins, 608-609
    permissions, 610-611
    quitting, 604-605
    security, 612
    TCP, 605-606
    testing system, 611-612
    *transferring files,
    602-604*
    WU FTP, 612
  Gopher, 632-634
    configuring, 634-643
    links, 646-647

    *listing Gopher ser-
    vices, 648*
    starting, 647-648
  NIC (Network Information
  Service), 725
  services, 595-596
  WAIS, 616-618
    *customizing freeWAIS,
    628-629*
    indexes, 624-629
    *installing freeWAIS,
    618-620*
    *setting up freeWAIS,
    620-623*
    *starting freeWAIS,
    623-624*
    *waisindex command,
    626-628*
  WWW (World Wide Web)
    home pages, 661
    HTML, 662-665
    server software, 652-661
    site setup, 661-666
    URLs, 661
**Internet architecture,
425-426**
InterNet News, *see* INN
**Internet Relay Chat
(IRC), 595**
**Invalid partition table,
entry X message, 94**
IP addresses, 278, 426-428
  address masks, 720
  address resolution, 720
  ARP (Address Resolution
  Protocol), 503-504
  dotted decimal nota-
  tion, 722
  dummy interfaces,
  472-473
  network names, 489
  resolving, 457-458
    hosts.conf file, 460-461
    *IN-ADDR-ARPA,
    468-469*
    named daemon, 458-460

    named.boot file, 462-463
    resolv.conf file, 461-462
    *resource records,
    463-468*
IP Forwarding, 457
**IRC (Internet Relay
Chat), 595**
IRQ addresses, 66
**IRQ values, sound card
configurations, 194**
**ISA (Industry Standard
Architecture)
motherboards, 18**
**ISDN (Integrated Service
Digital Network), 724**
  compatibility, 716
**ISO (International Orga-
nization for Standardiza-
tion), 724**
ISO 9660 disk format, 164
iso9660 filesystem, 295
iteration statements
  for, 390-392
  repeat, 395
  select, 394-395
  shift command, 393-394
  until, 392-393
  while, 392

K

-k option
  df command, 300
  du command, 302
Kerberos, 724
kernel, 5-6
  C compiler, 373
    *compiler options,
    374-375*
    *debugging options,
    375-376*
  CD-ROM drives
    installation, 168-170
    *troubleshooting,
    179-180*

compiling source code, 370-372
compressed, 248
configuring for networks, 438-442
  network card recognition, 442-443
  network drivers, 440
installing, 368-369
IP Forwarding, 457
libraries, upgrading, 372-373
linking device drivers, 372
locating new release sources, 369-370
SCSI tape drives, 223
searches, 248
upgrading, 368-369
kernel images
booting from files, 91
booting from other devices, 91
configurations, 91-92
extensions, 39
names, 39
SCSI device configurations, 66
see also boot kernels
Kernel XXX is too big messge, 95
keyboard
ConfigXF86 utility configurations, 121-122
xf86config utility configurations, 121-122
kill command, 326-328
-kilobyte option (df command), 300
kmem group, 272

L

l command, 47
l file types, 280
-l option
du command, 302
map installer, 88

ps command, 326
term utility, 215
label=name option (map installer), 89
language compilers, 6
LANs (local area networks), 724
Linux TCP/IP implementation, 7
security, 364-365
see also networks
LATEXTOHTML, 665
layouts
DOS boot sector, 74
hard disks, 72-74
lcd command (FTP), 604
leased lines, 724
lf parameter (/etc/printcap file), 314-315
libraries
dynamically shared, 5
statically linked, 5
upgrading, 372-373
LILO utility, 62, 80-85
booting Linux with, 246-247
disabling, 93
disk parameter tables, 92-93
installation, 70-71
  disk errors, 71
  Makefile, 72
troubleshooting, 94-95
updating, 70, 72
line printer daemon, see lpd
linear option (map installer), 90
linecheck utility, 213-214
linked libraries, 5
linking
device drivers, 136
files, 304-305
  hard links, 304-305
  i-node tables, 304-305

sound card files, 187-189
symbolic links
  modem configurations, 234
  SCSI tape drives, 225
links
Gopher, 646-647
symbolic, 305
Linux, 4
acquiring, 24-25
  BBSs, 31-32
  CD-ROMs, 25
  e-mail, 30-31
  FTP sites, 26-29
  World Wide Web sites, 29-30
copyright information, 9, 702-705
development of, 8-9
distributions, 686-688
DOS interface, 7
fdisk utility, 47-48
GNU software, 6
help sources, 10
  documentation, 10-11
  Linux Journal, 15
  USENET newsgroups, 11-13
  World Wide Web sites, 13-15
installation, 36
  boot device, 62
  boot disks, 58
  configurations, 59-62
  device conflicts, 65-67
  disk sets, 55-57
  modems, 60
  mouse setup, 60
  screen fonts, 62
  software, 54-62
  swap partitions, 51-52
  troubleshooting, 64-68
kernel (operating system), 5-6

logging in
  boots, 202-203
  communications
    parameters configurations, 204-206
  detecting terminal
    connections, 202-203
  /etc/getty, 204-206
  /etc/gettydefs, 204-206
  /etc/inittab, 203-204
  /etc/termcap, 206-207
  /etc/ttys, 203-204
  terminal configurations, 203-204
pronunciation, 4
quitting, 250-251
releases, 32-33
starting, 246
  booting with LILO, 246-247
  with boot floppy disks, 247-249
system requirements
  (minimum), 18
  CD-ROMs, 22-23
  Ethernet network cards, 24
  hard disks, 20-21
  modems, 23-24
  motherboard, 18-20
  mouses, 22
  multiport cards, 24
  printers, 23
  removable media, 23
  tape drives, 22
  terminals, 24
  video cards, 21
TCP/IP, 7
Unix compared to, 4-5
versions, recent, 16
X GUI, 6
Linux Documentation Project, 10-11, 690
Linux Journal, 15, 686
Linux Loader, *see* **LILO**

Linux Software Map (LSM), 11
  Web site, 14
Linux Systems Labs, 11, 687
LISP compiler, 6
listing
  backups, 345
  partitions, 47
literal=string option (map installer), 90
loading operating systems, 247
local area networks, *see* **LANs; networks**
local resources (networks), 421
localhosts, 491
logging in
  boots, 202-203
  communications
    paramters configurations, 204-206
  detecting terminal connections, 202-203
  /etc/getty, 204-206
  /etc/gettydefs, 204-206
  /etc/inittab, 203-204
  /etc/termcap, 206-207
  /etc/ttys, 203-204
  root logins, 260
  superuser accounts, 260-261
  terminal configurations, 203-204
  user accounts
    comments, 265
    creating, 261-262
    /etc/passwd file, 261-262
    group IDs, 264-265
    home directories, 265
    login command, 266
    passwords, 263-264

  system-dependent usernames, 266
  user IDs, 264
  usernames, 262-263
login command, 266
login scripts (UUCP), 411-412
logins (FTP), 608-609
logs, backups, 343-344
loopback drivers, 491
  dummy interfaces, 472
loopback interfaces, setup, 451-452
lpc utility, 315-317
lpd daemon, 310-315
lpq command, 318
lprm command, 318-319
ls command, 384

M

m command, 48
-m option
  map installer, 88
  mknod command, 141
magneto-optical drives, backups, 339
mail
  Elm, configuring, 556-557
  ftpmail, 675
  Pine, configuring, 557-560
  rmail program, 544
  sendmail program
    configuring, 532-538
    decnetxtable file, 536
    domaintable file, 536
    generating sendmail.cf file, 538
    genericfrom table, 536
    IDA, 532
    mailertable table, 536-537
    pathtable table, 537
    sendmail.cf file, 533-535
    templates, 541-542

*UUCP-based mail
systems, 535*
uucprelays file, 538
uucpxtable file, 538
version 8, 538-539
smail program, 544-545
customizing, 552-554
debugging, 552
delivery mode, 550-551
director, 545
domain names, 550
postmaster, 551
router, 545
setup, 545-546
smail daemon, 546
*TCP, configuring for,
549-550*
transport, 545
*UUCP, configuring for,
546-549*
software, 526-528
structure of messages,
528-530
**mailertable table, config-
uring sendmail, 536-537**
**maintenance disks,
249-250**
boots, 249
major device numbers
device drivers, 139-141
modems, 233, 234
SCSI device drivers,
146-150
SCSI tape drives, 222
Makefile (LILO utility), 72
Gopher, configuring,
639-643
parameters, 72
map installer utility
command-line options,
87-88
configurations, 86-91
**map=file option (map
installer), 90**
Master Boot Record, 74

master files (Gopher), 645
math co-processors
requirements for Linux, 18
**MAUs (Medium Access
Units), 724**
**Maximum Transfer Unit
(MTU), 492**
MB resource record, 465
**MBR (Master Boot
Record), 74**
memory
buffers, 721
caches, 721
CD-ROMs, 162
Linux requirements, 19-20
management, 296-297
*filesystem checks,
297-298*
*filesystem statistics,
299-302*
*optimizing disk space,
302-305*
see also quotas
RAM (CD-ROM
drives), 167
sharing, 5
system requirements, 18
**memory management,
backups, 303**
**message=file option (map
installer), 90**
MG resource record, 465
**mget command (FTP),
603-604**
MIDI files, playing, 191
**.mil domain name,
277, 429**
**MINFO resource rec-
ord, 465**
Minix filesystem, 53, 295
minor device numbers
device drivers, 139-141
modems, 233-234
SCSI device drivers,
147-150
SCSI tape drives, 222

**mitsumi, hardware com-
patibility, 38**
mixing sound files, 191
mke2fs command, 53
mkefs command, 53
mkfs command, 53
**mknod command, 140-141,
171-173, 208**
sound card configurations,
188-189
mkswap command, 51-52
mkxfs command, 53
**mode names (video
cards), 128**
modem compatibility, 715
modems, 724
configurations, 233-235
Linux installation, 60
manual, 233
symbolic links, 234
dial-in, 233-234
dial-out, 233-234
establishing connections,
chat program (PPP),
477-478
handshaking proto-
cols, 234
HDB UUCP, 408-409
installation, 232-233
internal modems, 232
Linux support, 23-24
purchasing, 230-232
security, 361-363
callback modems, 362
dialup passwords, 363
speeds, 231, 235
Taylor UUCP, configuring,
405-406
V.FC, 230
Modula-2 compiler, 6
monitoring ports, 218
monitors
ConfigXF86 utility con-
figurations, 124-126
horizontal bandwidth, 124

vertical refresh rate, 125
xf86config utility configurations, 124-126
Morse Telecommunication, Inc. (Linux distributor), 687
motherboards
compatibility, 708
system requirements, 18-20
mount command, 148-149, 175, 291-293, 509
mountd daemon, 512
mounting
CD-ROM drives, 174-176
automatically, 177
SCSI device drivers, 148-149
device drivers (/etc/fstab file), 177-178
filesystems, 290-293
as read-only, 292
automatically, 293-295
/etc/rc initialization, 293-295
options, 296
types, 295
NFS remote directories, 513-515
root directories as read-only, 257
mouse
bus, 61
compatibility, 711-712
ConfigXF86 utility configurations, 122-123
Linux requirements, 22
serial, 61
setup, 60
xf86config utility configurations, 122-123
moving root partitions, 257
mput command (FTP), 603-604

MR resource record, 465
MS-DOS, Linux interface, 7
msdos filesystem, 295
MTAs (mail transport agents), 526-528
mthreads utility (trn newsreader), 588
MTU (Maximum Transfer Unit), 492
MUAs (mail user agents), 526-528
multihomed hosts, 725
multiple partitions, 73-74
multiplexing serial lines (term utility), 210-220
multiport cards, 198-200
compatibility, 712-713
connectors, 199
installation, 200
Linux support, 24
serial ports, 199
multitasking, 5
multiuser mode
init daemons, 252
music CDs, playing, 176-178
mx parameter (/etc/printcap file), 314-315
MX resource record, 465

N

n command, 47-65
NAME column column (ps command output), 323
name resolution, 725
named daemon, 458-460
named.boot file, 462-463
names
boot kernel images, 37
compressed kernels, 248
device drivers, 139
groups, 271
kernel images, 39

processes, 323
system names, 276
countries, 277
creating, 277-278
extensions, 277-278
hostname command, 276
saving hostnames, 278-279
unique, 277
Nascent Technology (Linux distributor), 687
NCSA, Web server software, 652
.net domain name, 277, 429
NetBIOS, 725
netstat command, 494-495
communications end points, 495-497
data buffers, 498-499
network information, 497-498
protocol statistics, 500-502
routing table information, 499-500
NetWare, 422
network adapter compatibility, 715-716
Network Address protocols, 424
network cards
conflicts, 66
forcing recognition, 442-443
Linux support, 24
Network File System, *see* NFS
Network Information Center, *see* NIC
Network Information Service, *see* NIS
network interfaces, ifconfig command, 491-493

network names, 489
Network News Transfer Protocol, *see* **NNTP**
networks, 725
bridges, 423
brouters, 423
cabling, 432-433
clients, 421
configuring
kernel, 438
network drivers, 440
DNS (Domain Name System), 428-430
gateways, 423-435, 455-457, 723
hardware, 433-434
IP Forwarding, 457
local resources, 421
multihomed hosts, 725
network services, 490-491
NFS (Network File System), 508-510, 725
daemons, setup, 511
installing, 510-513
mounting NFS server, 509
nfsstat program, 516-517
port mappers, monitoring, 515-516
remote directories, mounting, 513-515
RPC requests, 516-517
rpcinfo program, 515-516
NICs (network interface cards), 422, 433, 725
nodes, 421, 725
NOS (network operating system), 421
PLIP, 443
PPP ports, 444-445
protocols, 422
remote resources, 421
routers, 423, 726
security, 364-365

servers, 420
SLIP ports, 444-445
system names, 276-279
TCP/IP, 423-425
accessing network interface, 450-451
configuring, 448-450
Ethernet interfaces, setup, 453-454
hostnames, 449
IP addresses, 426-428
loopback interfaces, setup, 451-452
UDP, 424
topologies, 430-432
Token Ring, 727
WANs, 727
newsboot utility (C News), 585
newsdaily utility (C News), 585
newsgroups, 595
articles
batching, 565
compression, 583
downloading, 565
message ids, 565
threads, 588
C News
batching articles, 583-584
configuration files, 577-579
directories, 579-580
receiving articles, 584-585
sys file, 580-583
utilities, 585
ihave/sendme protocol, 565
INN, installing, 572-573
interactive news-reading, 565
newsreaders
tin, 589-590
trn, 588-589

NNTP, 568-569
configuring nntpd, 570-571
INN, 569
installing server program, 569-570
relaynews program, 576
USENET
definition, 562
history, 563-564
newsreaders, 564-565
NNTP (Network News Transfer Protocol), 562-563
transport software, 564-565
see also e-mail
newsreaders, 564-565
tin, 589-590
trn, 588-589
newsrunning utility (C News), 585
newswatch utility (C News), 585
NFS (Network File System), 425, 508-510, 725
daemons, setup, 511
installing, 510-513
mouting NFS server, 509
nfsstat program, 516-517
port mappers, monitoring, 515-516
remote directories, mounting, 513-515
RPC requests, 516-517
rpcinfo program, 515-516
nfsstat program, 516-517
NIC (Network Information Center), 428, 725
decidated connections to Internet, 596
NICs (network interface cards), 422, 725

NIS (Network Information Service), 425, 517-519, 725
   installing, 519-521
NNTP (Network News Transfer Protocol), 562-563, 568-569
   configuring nntpd, 570-571
   INN, 569
   installing server program, 569-570
nntpd daemon, 568
No such device message, 194
No such file or directory message, 193
-no_16 option (SuperProbe), 108
-no_bios option (SuperProbe), 108
-no_dac option (SuperProbe), 108
-no_mem option (SuperProbe), 108
NO1STDIAG parameter (Makefile), 72
no387 parameter, 85
nodes, 421, 725
NOINSTDEF parameter (Makefile), 72
NOS (network operating system), 421
Novell NetWare, 422
NS resource record, 465

O

of parameter (/etc/ printcap file), 314-315
offsets (rdev command), 257
on-line services, 594
ONE_SHOT parameter (Makefile), 72
open command (FTP), 604

opening X windows on remote terminals, 219-220
operating systems
   kernel, 5-6
   loading, 247
optical readers, 241
optimizing
   disk space, 302-304
   performance, quotas, 332-333
optional option (map installer), 90
-order option (SuperProbe), 108
ordinary files, 280
.org domain name, 277, 429
OSF model, application layer, 720
OSPF (Open Shortest Path First), 424
owners
   files, 286-287
   groups, 286-287

P

p command, 47, 50
-P fix option (map installer), 88
-P ignore option (map installer), 88
-p option
   df command, 300
   edquota command, 333-334
   mknod command, 141
Packet Internet Groper, *see* **ping command**
packets, 725
PAP (Protocol Authentication Protocol), 481
Parallel Line IP, *see* **PLIP**
parallel printers, 308-309

parameters
   boot, 85-86
   communications, configurations, 204-206
   /etc/printcap file, 314-315
   Makefile (LILO utility), 72
   sound cards, 189
   tape drives, 223
partition check messages, 65
Partition entry not found message, 95
partitions
   active, changing, 78
   bad blocks, 51
   creating, 44-50
   cylinder limitations, 49
   deleting, 47
   displaying, 47, 50
   extended, 49
   fdisk utility, 44-45
      Linux, 47-48
   filesystem, 42
      creating, 50, 53
      Extended, 53
      Minix, 53
      Second Extended filesystem, 53
      Xia, 53
   hard disks, 42-46, 157-159
   installation, 46-47
   listing, 47
   multiple, 73-74
   primary, 49
   quota checking, 334
   root
      current, 257
      moving, 257
   saving, 47, 50
   SCSI disks, 147
   sizes, 53
   swap, 42, 51-52
      creating, 48-50
      size, 43-44
      starting, 52
      troubleshooting, 52

type code, editing, 47
types, assigning, 49
UMSDOS utility, 46
Pascal compiler, 6
password=password option (map installer), 90
passwords, 263-264, 269, 360-361
dialup passwords for modems, 363
user groups, 271
UUCP, 363
PATH environment variable, 103-104
pathnames (ConfigXF86 utility), 120
pathtable table, configuring sendmail, 537
PC Speaker, 191
see also sound cards
pdksh shell
case statement, 389
for, 390
select statement, 394-395
test command, 384-387
until statement, 393
while statement, 392
permission blocks, 279
access permissions, 281-282
default, 282-283
editing, 283-286
execute, 281
hyphens (-), 281
links, 304
read, 281
write, 281
displaying, 279
file types, 279-280
permissions
device drivers, 137-141
FTP, 610-611
PhotoCD, 164, 179
PID column (ps command output), 323
Pine, configuring, 557-560

PING (Packet Internet Groper), 725
ping command, 452, 502-503
pkgtool utility, 63
platters (hard disks), 73
playing
MIDI files, 191
music CDs, 164, 176-178
sound files
only part of file plays, 194
sounds stop/start when playing, 194-195
PLIP (Parallel Line IP), 443
configuring, 454-455
plotter compatibility, 716-717
port mappers, monitoring, 515-516
porting files, 241
ports, 726
monitoring, 218
Taylor UUCP, configuring, 405
serial, *see* serial ports
positional parameters, 381-382
postmaster (smail), 551
power supply
CD-ROM drives, 163
failure of, 255-256
PPP, 725
account setup, 476-477
authentication, 481-484
CHAP, 481-484
chat program, 477-478
DNS, 484-485
dummy interfaces, 472-473
error messages, 480-481
PAP, 481
pppd daemon, 479-480
setup, 476

PPP ports, 444-445
pppd daemon, 479-480
primary partitions, 49
print jobs
deleting, 316-319
terminating, 316
print queues, displaying, 318
print requests, 312-313
printer compatibility, 716-717
printers, 308
configurations, 310, 314
destination, 312-313
disabling, 316
Linux support, 23
lockups, troubleshooting, 319
parallel, 308-309
printing
/etc/printcap file, 313
lpc utility, 315-317
lpd, 310-315
spoolers, 311-312
proc filesystem, 295
processes, 322
hung, 326
identification numbers, 323
kill command, 326-328
names, 323
origin, determining, 323-325
ps command, 322-326
status, 322-326
viewing
individual, 324
top command, 328-330
processors, requirements for Linux, 18
programming software (GNU), 6
prompt option (map installer), 90
proprietary CD-ROM drives, 166-167
installation, 170

protocols, 726
ARP (Address Resolution
Protocol), 503-504, 720
Ethernet, 723
FTP, 510, 600, 672, 723
archive sites, 676
connecting to, 673-675
downloading files,
673-675
ftpmail, 675
Gopher protocol, 633
handshaking, 234
ICMP, 724
ihave/sendme protocol, 565
IP (Internet Protocol), 724
network protocols, 422
gateway protocols, 425
Network Address
protocols, 424
routing protocols, 424
TCP/IP, 423-426
User Services, 424
NFS, 508
NIS (Network Information
Service), 517-519, 725
installing, 519-521
NNTP, 562-563, 568-569
configuring nntpd,
570-571
INN, 572-574
installing server
program, 569-570
PPP, 725
account setup, 476-477
authentication, 481-484
CHAP, 481-484
DNS, 484-485
error messages, 480-481
PAP, 481
pppd daemon, 479-480
protocol numbers, 489-490
RARP, 726
RIP, 726
SLIP, 726
configuring, 474-475
dip, 475-476
DNS, 484-485

SMTP, 527
TCP/IP, 7, 727
agents, 720
datagrams, 722
DNS, 722
netstat command,
500-502
packets, 725
PING (Packet Internet
Groper), 725
RPC, 726
SMTP, 726
TFTP, 727
UDP, 727
XNS, 728
ps command, 322-326
PTR resource record, 465
purchasing modems,
230-232
put command (FTP),
603-604, 674
pwd command (FTP), 604

Q

q command, 47
-q option
map installer, 88
quota command, 334
q option (top com-
mand), 328
quad-speed CD-ROM
drives, 164
question mark (?) com-
mand, 317
quit command, 317
FTP, 604-605
quitting
FTP, 604-605
Linux, 250-251
quota command, 334
quotacheck command, 335
quotaoff command, 334
quotaon command, 334
quotas, 332
creating, 333-334
displaying, 334

duplicating, 333
hard limits, 332
necessity of, 333
soft limits, 332
turning on, 334
quotation marks ("), shell
programs, 382-384
quote command
(FTP), 605

R

-R option (rdev util-
ity), 257
-r dur option (map in-
staller), 88
-r option
fsck utility, 298
mount command, 292
rdev utility, 257
term utility, 216
-R words option (map
installer), 88
RAM
CD-ROM drives, 167
disk sizes, 257
Linux requirements, 19-20
sharing, 5
ramdisk=size (map in-
staller), 90
ramsize command, 257
RARP (Reverse Address
Resolution Protocol),
424, 441, 726
rdev command, off-
sets, 257
rdev utilities, 256-258
read error message, 65
read permissions, 281
read-only
directories, 257
map installer option, 90
mounting filesystems
as, 292
read-write option (map
installer), 90

READONLY parameter (Makefile), 72

receiving news articles, 584-585

reconfiguring terminals, 210

recordable CD-ROMs, 167

recording sound, 190-192

relaynews program, 576

releases (Linux), 32-33

remote resources, 421

remote systems
  connecting UUCP, 410
  HDB UUCP, 408
  Taylor UUCP, configuring, 404-407

remote terminals, opening X windows on, 219-220

removable cartridge drives, 240

removable hard disks, backups, 339

removable media, 23

repeat statement, 395

resolv.conf file, 461-462

resolving IP addresses, 457-458
  hosts.conf file, 460-461
  named daemon, 458-460
  named.boot file, 462-463
  resolv.conf file, 461-462
  resource records, 463-466
    files, 466-468
    IN-ADDR-ARPA, 468-469

resource records, resolving IP addresses, 463-466

restart printer_name | all command, 317

restoring
  files, 228
  filesystems, 345

restricted option (map installer), 90

ring networks, 431

RIP (Routing Information Protocol), 424, 726

RLL (Run Length Limited) controllers, 20-21

rlogin, 726

rmail, 544

rn newsreader, 564

ro parameter, 85

root accounts, 260

root directories
  bootdsks, 37
  mounting as read-only, 257

root disks
  creating, 36-37, 40-41
  installation, 37-39

root images
  Linux software installation, 54
  selecting, 37-39

root login, 266

root logins, 260

root parameter, 85

root partitions
  current, 257
  moving, 257

root/wheel/system group, 272

root=dev option (map installer), 90

rootdsks, 37

rootflags command, 257

route command, 450

routers, 423, 726
  smail program, 545

Routing protocols, 424

routing tables (netstat command), 499-500

RPC (Remote Procedure Call), 425, 726
  nfsstat program, 516-517
  rpcinfo command, 505

rpcd daemon, 512

rpcinfo command, 505

rpcinfo program, 515-516

RR (resource records), resolving IP addresses, 463-466

RTFTOHTML, 665

run levels
  editing, 253
  init daemons, 252-253

running shell programs, 378-380

rw parameter, 85

S

-s option
  du command, 302
  map installer, 88
  rdev utility, 257
  term utility, 215
  top command, 330

-S option
  hostname command, 276
  map installer, 88

S option (top command), 328

s option (top command), 328

saving
  boot sectors, 75
  partitions, 47, 50

sbpcd images (hardware compatibility), 38

scanner compatibility, 717

scanners, 241

scheduling backups, 340-343

screen fonts, 62

scripts
  cron utility, 352
  soundinstall, 188

SCSI (Small Computer System Interface) controllers, 20-21

SCSI adapter not detected message, 67

SCSI chains, 144-145

SCSI device at all possible IDs message, 67

SCSI device drivers, 146-150
- CD-ROMs, 147-149, 165
  - *drives, installation, 170*
  - *mounting, 148-149*
- hard disks, 146-147
- major device numbers, 146-150
- minor device numbers, 147-150
- miscellaneous, 150
- partitions, 147
- tape drives, 149-150
- troubleshooting, 150-153

SCSI devices, 144-145
- compatibility, 146
- configurations, 145
- connections, 144
- error messages, 67-68
- identification, 144
- troubleshooting, 66, 67-68

SCSI drives, installation, 222

scsi images, hardware compatibility, 38

SCSI tape drives, 222-223
- block sizes, 223
- ftape program, 223-226
- kernels, 223
- major device numbers, 222
- minor device numbers, 222
- parameters, 223
- symbolic links, 225

SCSI terminators, 145

SCSI-based cartridge drives, 240

scsinet1 images, hardware compatibility, 38

scsinet2 images, hardware compatibility, 38

sd parameter (/etc/ printcap file), 314

searches
- kernels, 248
- sound card drivers, 186

Second Extended filesystem, 53

second extended filesystem, 295

security
- auditing system connections, 365
- file security, 361
- FTP, 612
- modems, 361-363
  - *callback modems, 362*
  - *dialup passwords, 363*
- networks, 364-365
- passwords, 263-264, 269, 360-361
- PPP, 481-484
- UUCP, 363-364, 413-414

select statement, 394-395

selecting
- boot kernels, 37-39
- root images, 37-39
- servers, XFree86 installation, 101-102
- video mode, 257, 258

sending mail (UUCP), 414-416

sendmail, 526
- configuring, 532-538
- decnetxtable file, 536
- domaintable file, 536
- generating sendmail.cf file, 538
- genericfrom table, 536
- IDA, 532
- mailertable table, 536-537
- pathtable table, 537
- sendmail.cf file, 533-535
- templates, 541-542
- UUCP-based mail systems, 535
- uucprelays file, 538
- uucpxtable file, 538
- version 8, 538-539

Sense errors message, 67

Sequoia International Motif Development Package, 687

serial cables, wiring, 200-202

serial lines, multiplexing (term utility), 210-220

serial mouse, 61

serial ports
- device drivers, 233-234
- multiport cards, 199
- networking, 444-445
- terminal connections, 200
- *see also* multiport cards

serial=parms option (map installer), 90

servers, 420, 726
- ConfigXF86 utility configurations, 127-129
- selecting, XFree86 installation, 101-102
- serial port, 199
- xf86config utility configurations, 127-129

service providers, connecting to Internet, 594, 597

Set Group ID (SGID), 296

Set User ID (SUID), 296

setserial command, 235

setup utility, 54
- modem configurations, 233

SGID (Set Group ID), 296

shell programs
- conditional statements
  - *case, 389-390*
  - *if, 387-388*
- creating, 378-380
- functions, 396-397
- iteration statements
  - *for, 390-392*
  - *repeat, 395*
  - *select, 394-395*
  - *shift command, 393-394*
  - *until, 392-393*
  - *while, 392*
- quotation marks, 382-384
- running, 378-380

test command, 384-387
variables
   assigning values to,
      380-381
   built-in shell variables,
      381
   positional parameters,
      381-382
shielded twisted-pair
   cabling, 432
shift command, 393-394
shutdown command, 251
signatures (e-mail), 528
single parameter, 85
single quotation marks
   (' '), shell programs, 382
single-purpose hard
   disk, 73
single-speed CD-ROM
   drives, 164
six-speed CD-ROM
   drives, 164
sizes
   displaying directories
      by, 302
   partitions, 53
   RAM disks, 257
Slackware, copyright
   information, 702-705
slattach command,
   474-475
SLIP (Serial Line Internet
   Protocol), 726
   configuring, 474-475
   CSLIP, 473
   dip, 475-476
   DNS, 484-485
   dummy interfaces,
      472-473
   setup, 473-474
SLIP ports, 444-445
smail, 526, 544-545
   customizing, 552-554
   debugging, 552
   delivery mode, 550-551

director, 545
domain names, 550
postmaster, 551
router, 545
setup, 545-546
smail daemon, 546
TCP, configuring for,
   549-550
transport, 545
UUCP, configuring for,
   546-547
   domain names, 547-548
   smart hosts, 548-549
   UUCP names, 548
Small Computer Systems
   Interface, *see* **SCSI**
Smalltalk compiler, 6
smart hosts, configuring
   smail for UUCP, 548-549
SMTP (Simple Mail Trans-
   fer Protocol), 425,
   527, 726
SNMP (Simple Network
   Management Proto-
   col), 425
SOA (State of Authority)
   resource record, 464
sockets, 726
soft limits, 332
   editing, 334
software
   disk sets, viewing, 63
   files, viewing, 63
   Linux installation, 54-62
      troubleshooting, 64-65
   UPSs, 239
software device drivers
   multiport cards, 200
Sorry, don't know how to
   handle device XXX
   message, 95
sound, 191-192
Sound Blaster, 185
sound card compatibility,
   713-714

sound cards
   compatibility, 185
   configurations, 186-190
      device files, 187
      linking sound files,
         187-189
      mknod command,
         188-189
      parameters, 189
      sounds stop/start when
         playing, 194-195
      troubleshooting,
         192-193
   /dev/sndstate file, 193
   DMA values, 194
   drivers, 187
      compiling, 188-189
      directories, 186
      testing, 189-190
   error messages, 193-194
   IRQ values, 194
   recording, 190
   recording with, 192
   sound files
      linking, 187-189
   troubleshooting
      configurations, 192-193
      /dev/sndstate file, 193
      error messages, 193-194
      only part of file
         plays, 194
      sounds start/stop when
         playing, 194-195
   see also PC Speaker
sound files
   converting, 192
   mixing, 191
soundinstall script, 188
Sox, 192
speed
   CD-ROM drives, 164-167
   modems, 231, 235
spike filters, 238
spoolers, print, 311-312
star networks, 431

start printer_name command, 317

starting
  freeWAIS, 623-624
  Gopher, 647-648
  Linux, 246
    booting with LILO,
    246-247
    with boot floppy disks,
    247-249
  swap partitions, 52
  Web software, 659-661

startup files
  quotacheck command, 335
  .xinitrc, 129-131

startup functions, automating, 218

STAT column column (ps command output), 323

State of Authority (SOA) resource record, 464

statically linked libraries, 5

status printer_name command, 317

stop printer_name command, 317

stty command, 208-209

su command, 274

subnet masks, 720, 727

subnets, 727

SUID (Set User ID), 296

SuperProbe utility, 107-109
  command-line options, 108-109

superuser accounts, 260-261, 266

swap devices
  identifying, 257

swap partitions, 42, 51-52
  creating, 48-50
  size, 43-44
  starting, 52
  troubleshooting, 52

swapdev, 257

swapon command, 52

symbolic links, 305
  modem configurations, 234
  SCSI tape drives, 225

symbolic machine names, 488-489

symbolic mode, access permissions, 284

sys file, configuring C News, 580-583

sys group, 272

sys login, 266

system connections, 365

system names, 276
  countries, 277
  creating, 277-278
  extensions, 277-278
  hostname command, 276
  hostnames, saving, 278
  unique, 277

system requirements for Linux, 18
  CD-ROMs, 22-23
  Ethernet network cards, 24
  hard disks, 20-21
  modems, 23-24
  motherboard, 18-20
  mouses, 22
  multiport cards, 24
  printers, 23
  removable media, 23
  tape drives, 22
  terminals, 24
  video cards, 21

System V. BSD UNIX, 9

system-dependent usernames, 266

sysv filesystem, 295

T

t command, 47

-T option (df command), 301

-t option
  df command, 301
  edquota command, 334
  fsck utility, 298
  map installer, 88
  term utility, 215

tables
  disk parameter, 92-93
  i-nodes, effects of file links on, 304-305

Takelap Systems Ltd., 687

tape backups, 339

tape drive compatibility, 714-715

tape drive requirements, 22

tape drives
  backups, 227-228
  file restoration, 228
  SCSI, 222-223
    block sizes, 223
    ftape program, 223-226
    installation, 222
    kernels, 223
    parameters, 223
  SCSI device drivers, 149-150
  symbolic links, 225

tape image, 39

tar command, 227

tar utility, 344-346
  flags, 103

tar: read error, 65

Taylor UUCP
  access times, 412-413
  configuring, 403
    access permissions,
    406-407
    modems, 405-406
    ports, 405
    remote systems, 404-407
    system name, 403-404

TCP/IP (Transmission Control Protocol/ Internet Protocol). 7, 422-425, 727
accessing network interface, 450-451
agents, 720
arp command, 503-504
BIND (Berkeley Internet Name Domain service), 457
configuring, 448-450
ifconfig command, 450
PLIP, 454-455
datagrams, 722
DNS (Domain Name Service), 428-430, 457, 722
nested zones, 459
Ethernet interfaces, setup, 453-454
FTP, 600-602, 723
anonymous FTP, 601
ASCII transfer mode, 603
binary transfer mode, 604
configuring, 606-612
directories, 609-610
ftpd (FTP daemon), 607-608
logins, 608-609
permissions, 610-611
quitting, 604-605
security, 612
TCP, 605-606
testing system, 611-612
transferring files, 602-604
WU FTP, 612
Gateway protocols, 425
hostnames, 449
ifconfig command, 491-493
inetd daemon, 493-494
Internet architecture, 425-426

IP (Internet Protocol), 724
IP addresses, 426-428
dummy interfaces, 472-473
resolving, 457-469
loopback drivers, 491
loopback interfaces, setup, 451-452
named daemon, 458-460
netstat command, 494-495
communications end points, 495-497
data buffers, 498-499
network information, 497-498
protocol statistics, 500-502
routing table information, 499-500
Network Address protocols, 424
network names, 489
network services, 490-491
NIC (Network Information Center), 428
packets, 725
PING (Packet Internet Groper), 725
ping command, 502-503
ports, 726
PPP, 725
account setup, 476-477
authentication, 481-484
CHAP, 481-484
chat program, 477-478
DNS, 484-485
error messages, 480-481
pppd daemon, 479-480
setup, 476
protocol numbers, 489-490
RARP, 726
routing protocols, 424
RPC, 726
rpcinfo command, 505

SLIP, 726
configuring, 474-475
CSLIP, 473
dip, 475-476
DNS, 484-485
setup, 473-474
SMTP, 726
sockets, 726
symbolic machine names, 488-489
Telnet, 727
tracerout command, 504-505
UDP, 424
User Services, 424
tcsh shell
case statement, 389
for statement, 391
if statement, 388
repeat statement, 395
while statement, 392
technical support, 731
telinit command, 253
TELNET, 424
Telnet, 595, 727
term utility, 210-220
commands, 218-220
configurations, 215-220
connection speeds, 215
data compression, 215
environment variables, 211
installation, 211-212
terminating, 216
testing configurations, 213-214
X windows, 216-217
XFree86, 216-217
TERMDIR variable, 211
terminals
adding, 207-208
configurations
stty command, 208-209
tset command, 209
viewing, 209

connections, 198
  detecting, 203
  logging in, 202-207
  multiport cards,
    198-200
  reconfiguring, 210
  serial cables, wiring,
    200-202
  serial ports, 200
  definition, 198
  dumb terminals, 723
  hung processes, 326
  Linux support, 24
  remote
    opening X windows on,
    219-220
terminating
  hung processes, 326-328
  print jobs, 316
  resistors, 145
  SCSI devices, 145
  term utility, 216
TERMMODE variable, 211
TERMSHARE vari-
  able, 211
test command, 384-387
testing
  CD-ROM drives, 176
  ConfigXF86 utility con-
    figurations, 129
  sound card device drivers,
    189-190
  term utility configura-
    tions, 213-214
  xf86config utility configu-
    rations, 129
  XFree86 configura-
    tions, 129
TFTP (Trivial File Trans-
  fer Protocol), 727
The system is halted
  message, 251
thinnet network medium,
  433

threads (newsgroup
  articles), 588
TIME column column (ps
  command output), 323
Timeout errors mes-
  sage, 67
timeout=secs (map in-
  staller), 90
tin newsreader, 589-590
tkWWW, 663
tmon utility, 218
Token Ring networks,
  431, 727
top command, 328-330
topologies, 430-432
  Token Ring networks, 727
topq printer_name
  print_ID command, 317
topq printer_name
  username command, 317
-total option (du com-
  mand), 302
tracerout command,
  504-505
Trans-Ameritch Enter-
  prises, Inc. (Linux
  distributor), 688
transferring files
  FTP, 602-604
  UUCP, 416-418
trdate utility, 218
trdated utility, 218
tredir utility, 218-220
Trivial File Transfer
  Protocol (TFTP), 727
trn newsreader, 564,
  588-589
troubleshooting
  boots, 77
    Linux, 68
  CD-ROM drives
    checking for drive
      activity, 180
    configurations, 181
    device busy errors, 181
    kernels, 179-180

corrupted floppy disks, 65
device conflicts, 65-67
disk controllers, 65
emergency boot disks,
  249-250
error messages
  bad geometry, 71, 92
  device busy errors, 181
  device full, 64
  file not found, 65
  LILO utility, 94-95
  mount command, 175
  read error, 65
  sound cards, 193-194
  swap partitions, 52
  tar: read error, 65
  term utility, 215
file restoration, 228
hard disks, 65
hung processes, 326
LILO utility, 94-95
maintenance disks,
  249-250
network cards, 66
partition check mes-
  sages, 65
power supply
  failure of, 255-256
printer lockups, 319
SCSI device drivers,
  150-153
SCSI devices, 66, 67-68
software installation,
  64-65
sound cards
  configurations, 192-193
  /dev/sndstate file, 193
  error messages, 193-194
  only part of file
    plays, 194
  sounds stop/start when
    playing, 194-195
terminal connections,
  reconfiguring, 210
UPSs, 238-240

trsh utility, 218
tset command, 209
TTL (Time to Live) field, traceroute command, 504
TTY column (ps command output), 323
tty group, 272
tty image, 39
tupload utility, 218
twisted-pair cabling, 432
TXT resource record, 465
type codes (partitions), editing, 47

U

-U dev option (map installer), 88
-u dev option (map installer), 88
-u option
    edquota command, 334
    ps command, 324
    quota command, 334
    quotacheck command, 335
UDP (User Datagram Protocol), 424, 727
    traceroute command, 504-505
UID, 264
umask, 361
umount command, 176
umsdos filesystem, 295
umsdos image, 39
UMSDOS utility, 46
Uniform Resource Locators (URLs), 661
Uninterruptible Power Supply, see UPS
UNIX
    compared to Linux, 4-5
    Linux development from, 8-9
UNIX to UNIX CoPy, see UUCP

unmount command, 292-293
unmounting
    CD-ROM drives, 176
    filesystems, 290-293
unpacking Web files, 653
unshielded twisted-pair cabling, 432
until statement, 392-393
up printer_name command, 317
updating
    boot sectors (map installer utility), 86-91
    LILO utility, 70, 72
upgrading
    hard disks, 156-157
       partitions, 157-159
    kernel software, 368-369
uploading files (FTP), 603
UPS (Uninterruptible Power Supply), 238-240
    battery backups, 238-239
    front-panel information, 239
    software, 239
    spike filters, 238
URLs (Uniform Resource Locators), 661
USENET, 595
    articles
       batching, 565
       downloading, 565
       message ids, 565
    definition, 562
    history, 563-564
    ihave/sendme protocol, 565
    INN, installing, 572-573
    interactive newsreading, 565
    newsreaders, 564-565
       tin, 589-590
       trn, 588-589

NNTP, 562-563, 568-569
    configuring nntpd, 570-571
    INN, 569
    installing server program, 569-570
    transport software, 564-565
    see also newsgroups
user accounts
    comments, 265
    configurations, 268
    creating, 261-262, 267-269
    deleting, 269-270
    disabling, 269-270
    /etc/passwd file, 261-262
    group IDs, 264-265
    home directories, 265
    login command, 266
    passwords, 263-264, 269
    superuser, 266
    system-dependent usernames, 266
    user IDs, 264
    usernames, 262-263
USER column (ps command output), 324
user IDs, 264
user quotas
    creating, 333-334
    editing, 334
User Services (TCP/IP), 424
usernames, 262-263
    case sensitivity, 262-263
    system-dependent, 266
users
    groups, 270-271
       creating, 272-273
       creating users, 273
       daemon, 272
       default, 270-272
       deleting, 273
       IDs, 271
       kmem, 272

names, 271
passwords, 271
root / wheel / system, 272
su command, 274
sys, 272
tty, 272
root accounts, 260
superuser accounts,
260-261
utilities
BOOTACTV, 77-78
C News, 585
ConfigXF86, 104, 109-119
data compression, 215
default system groups, 272
fdisk, 43-45, 157-159
commands, 47
help, 48
Linux, 47-48
fet, 218
FIPS, 43
fsck, 297-298
ftape, 223-226
GNU, 6
LILO, 62
boot process configura-
tions, 80-85
disabling, 93
disk parameter tables,
92-93
installation, 70-72
Makefile, 72
troubleshooting, 94-95
updating, 70, 72
linecheck, 213-214
lpc, 315-317
map installer
command-line options,
87-88
configurations, 86-91
pkgtool, 63
redev, 256-258
setup, 54
SuperProbe, 107-109
command-line options,
108-109

tar, 344-346
term, 210-220
configurations, 215-220
connection speeds, 215
environment vari-
ables, 211
installation, 211-212
terminating, 216
testing configurations,
213-214
utility commands,
218-220
X windows, 216-217
tmon, 218
trdate, 218
trdated, 218
tredir, 218-220
troubleshooting device
conflicts, 66
trsh, 218
tupload, 218
UMSDOS, 46
xconn, 216
xf86config, 104, 109-119
XFree86, 216-217
see also commands
**uucico command
(UUCP), 410**
**UUCP (UNIX to UNIX
CoPy), 402**
addressing syntax,
414-416
commands
uucico, 410
uucp, 416
uustat, 418
configuring, 402-403
HDB UUCP, 408-410
connections, 410
access times, 412-413
direct connections, 411
login scripts, 411-412
HDB UUCP, 408
security, 363-364, 413-414
sending mail, 414-416, 416

sendmail, configuring, 535
smail, configuring,
546-547
domain names, 547, 548
smart hosts, 548-549
UUCP names, 548
Taylor UUCP
configuring, 403-407
remote systems, 404-405
transferring files, 416-418
verifying transfers, 418
uucp command, 416
uucp login, 266
**uucprelays file, configur-
ing sendmail, 538**
**uucpxtable file, configur-
ing sendmail, 538**
**uustat command
(UUCP), 418**

V

**-v option (rdev util-
ity), 257**
v command, 47
**-V level option (map
installer), 88**
**-v level option (map
installer), 88**
-v option
df command, 301
du command, 302
fsck utility, 298
quota command, 334
quotacheck command, 335
V.FC (modems), 230
variables
assigning values to,
380-381
built-in shell vari-
ables, 381
environment
PATH, 103-104
term utility, 211
positional parameters,
381-382

vendors, 686-688
-verbose option
(SuperProbe), 109
verbose=level option (map
installer), 90
--version option (mknod
command), 141
versions of Linux, 16
vertical refresh rate
(monitors), 125
VESA local bus
motherboards, 19
vga=mode option (map
installer), 91
video capture board
compatibility, 718
video cards
color planes, 128
compatibility, 709
ConfigXF86 utility con-
figurations, 126-127
mode names, 128
SuperProbe utility,
107-109
system requirements, 21
virtual desktop size, 128
xf86config utility configurations, 126-127
XFree86 installation, 102
XFree86 support, 6
video mode
configurations, 125
selecting, 257-258
vidmode, 257-258
viewing
boot images, 85
disk sets, 63
files, 63
processes
individual, 324
top command, 328-330
terminal configurations,
209
virtual desktop size (video
cards), 128
vnews newsreader, 564

W

w, 50
w command, 47
-w option (term util-
ity), 215
WAIS, 595, 616-618
freeWAIS
customizing, 628-629
installing, 618-620
setup, 620-623
starting, 623-624
Gopher, 643
indexes, 624-629
waisindex command,
626-628
waisindex command, 620,
626-628
WANs (wide area net-
works), 727
Web, see WWW
while statement, 392
Windows, Linux compat-
ibility, 7
WINE (WINdows Emula-
tor), 7
wiring serial cables,
200-202
WKS resource record, 465,
466
World Wide Web, see
WWW
WORM drives, back-
ups, 340
write permissions, 281
WU FTP, 612
WWW (World Wide
Web), 595
FM2HTML, 664
home pages, 661
HTML, 662-665
LATEXTOHTML, 665
Linux sites, 13-15, 29-30
maintaining documents,
665-666

RTFTOHTML, 665
server software, 652-653
compiling, 653-655
configuring, 655-659
starting, 659-661
unpacking files, 653
site setup, 661-662
tkWWW, 663
URLs (Uniform Resource
Locators), 661

X-Y-Z

X (graphical user inter-
face), 6
hard disk require-
ments, 21
video card require-
ments, 21
-x option (df com-
mand), 301
-x option (du com-
mand), 302
X windows, 728
opening
on remote terminals,
219-220
term utility, 216-217
xconn utility, 216
xenix filesystem, 295
xf86config utility, 104,
109-119
configurations, 109-120
keyboard settings,
121-122
monitor settings,
124-126
mouse definitions,
122-123
pathnames, 120
server, 127-129
testing, 129-131
video cards, 126-127

XFree86, 6, 98-99
    configurations, 104-119
        directory location,
          106-107
        SuperProbe utility,
          107-109
        testing, 129
    customizing, 129
    directories, 100-101
    hardware require-
      ments, 99
    installation, 100-104
        manual, 102-103
        PATH environment
          variable, 103-104
        server selection, 101-102
        setup script, 103
    term utility, 216-217
    .xinitrc startup file,
      129-131
    see also ConfigXF86
      utility;
xia filesystem, 53, 295
.xinitrc file, 129-131
XNS (Xerox Networking
Standard), 728
xt images, hardware
compatibility, 38
XXX doesn't have a valid
LILO signature mes-
sage, 94
XXX has an invalid stage
code message, 95

YP (Yellow Pages) proto-
col, 517-519

Add to Your Sams Library Today with the Best Books for Programming, Operating Systems, and New Technologies

The easiest way to order is to pick up the phone and call

1-800-428-5331

between 9:00 a.m. and 5:00 p.m. EST.
For faster service, please have your credit card available.

ISBN	Quantity	Description of Item	Unit Cost	Total Cost
0-672-30908-4		Linux Unleashed, 2E (Book/CD-ROM)	$49.99	
0-672-30840-1		Understanding Local Area Networks, 5E	$29.99	
0-672-30537-2		The Waite Group's UNIX Communications and the Internet, 3E	$35.00	
0-672-30584-4		Networking UNIX	$35.00	
0-672-30542-9		X Window System Programming, 2E (Book/Disk)	$39.99	
0-672-30540-2		Teach Yourself the UNIX C Shell in 14 Days	$29.99	
0-672-30586-0		Teach Yourself Perl in 21 Days	$29.99	
0-672-30402-3		UNIX Unleashed, 2E (Book/CD-ROM)	$49.95	
0-672-30714-6		The Internet Unleashed, 2E	$35.00	
0-672-30737-5		The World Wide Web Unleashed, 2E	$39.99	
1-57521-014-2		Teach Yourself Web Publishing with HTML in 14 Days	$39.99	
1-57521-005-3		Teach Yourself More Web Publishing with HTML in a Week	$29.99	
0-672-30745-6		HTML & CGI Unleashed	$49.99	

❏ 3 ½" Disk

❏ 5 ¼" Disk

Shipping and Handling: See information below		
TOTAL		

Shipping and Handling: $4.00 for the first book, and $1.75 for each additional book. Floppy disk: add $1.75 for shipping and handling. If you need to have it NOW, we can ship product to you in 24 hours for an additional charge of approximately $18.00, and you will receive your item overnight or in two days. Overseas shipping and handling adds $2.00 per book and $8.00 for up to three disks. Prices subject to change. Call for availability and pricing information on latest editions.

201 W. 103rd Street, Indianapolis, Indiana 46290

1-800-428-5331 — Orders   1-800-835-3202 — FAX   1-800-858-7674 — Customer Service

Book ISBN 0-672-30850-9